Left, Odeon Glasgow, circa May 1951. (Courtesy of Bruce Peter.) Above, J. Arthur Rank in leopard skin seat at the Odeon Leicester Square. (CTA Archive.) Below left, the new Odeon Southend multiplex in 1996. (Courtesy of Northern Building Design Associates.)

ODEON CINEMAS

2: From J. Arthur Rank To The Multiplex

Odeon Muswell Hill in August 1980 and in October 2002. Opposite, Odeon Exeter in July 2003. (Photographs by Allen Eyles.)

ODEON CINEMAS

2: From J. Arthur Rank To The Multiplex

ALLEN EYLES

CINEMA THEATRE ASSOCIATION
DISTRIBUTED BY BFI PUBLISHING

 Publishing

First published
in 2005 by the
Cinema Theatre Association
34 Pelham Road
London N22 6LN

Distributed by
bfi Publishing
British Film Institute
21 Stephen Street
London W1T 1LN

The CINEMA THEATRE ASSOCIATION
was formed in 1967 to promote serious
interest in all aspects of cinema buildings.
It publishes a newsletter and the journal
Picture House, maintains an Archive, and
organises visits and lectures.

For further details, contact
Membership Secretary – CTA
Flat One, 128 Gloucester Terrace
London W2 6HP
or visit: www.cinema-theatre.org.uk

The BRITISH FILM INSTITUTE exists
to promote greater understanding and
appreciation of, and access to, film
and moving-image culture in the UK.

For details of *bfi* services and current
activities, please call the 24-hour *bfi*
events line: 0870 240 40 50 (national
call rate) or visit: www.bfi.org.uk

ISBN 1-84457-048-7

Design consultant
Malcolm Johnson

Printed in Great Britain by
Biddles Limited
Oxford and King's Lynn

CONTENTS

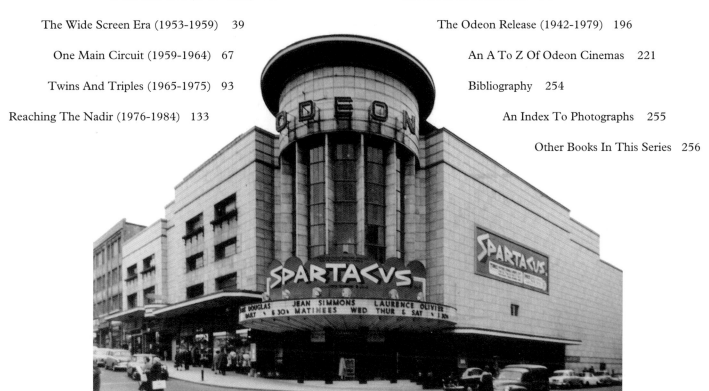

Odeon Bristol, 1961. (Courtesy of Bruce Peter.)

ACKNOWLEDGEMENTS

In writing this second volume, I have often been reminded of the help provided and the interest shown by the late Chris Moore in the 1970s when, as Rank's Information Services Controller, he provided me with a letter of introduction to managers of Rank's cinemas and bingo clubs and tipped me off on forthcoming closures and disposals, enabling me to visit many Odeons in the nick of time. Chris also put me in touch with two retired Rank executives, Dickie Dewes and Sidney Swingler, who provided substantial insights into Odeon's modus operandi, particularly for the first volume.

On several research trips to Rank's offices at Whyteleafe, Surrey, for an earlier history of Odeon in the magazine *Focus On Film* and for the book *Gaumont British Cinemas*, I was given generous access to information and photographic records.

In writing this present volume, which rather skimpily covers fifty-eight years of Odeon history, I am well aware of how much more I might have done, especially in interviewing more Odeon executives, managers and staff – but there simply hasn't been the time, the financial resources, or the space.

Nevertheless, I am particularly grateful to former Rank executives Stan Fishman, Jim Whittell and Tony Williams who kindly answered specific questions and offered general comments on my rough draft of the periods they knew best – in particular, Jim and Stan greatly clarified my thinking with regard to the multiplex era. Through the ever-helpful Brian Gauntlett, I was able to borrow the records of attendance figures kept by James E. Tilmouth for the Odeons he managed, and am grateful for the opportunity to quote extensively from them in the book; and, through the thoughtfulness of Richard Jones, I was introduced to former Rank film booker Michael Fisher whose meticulous records of circuit releases enabled me to crosscheck my own work to 1959 and provided the basis for extending it another twenty years. In various conversations, James Bettley kept coming up with more and more clear-cut memories of working for Odeon and kindly wrote them down at my request.

Space limitations have also prevented me from illustrating as many Odeons as I would have liked. But Carl Chesworth, besides being a fund of information, was a source of many photographs of northern Odeons. Bruce Peter sent me a stack of historic Odeon pictures to pick and choose – to the great benefit of this book. Derek Knights' collection of photographs was another valuable resource. John D. Sharp readily consented to my use of two of his photographs found in the CTA Archive. And Glyn Mellor of Northern Building Design Associates kindly came up with some elusive images from the earlier multiplex era (as well as more recent work by the company).

I am most appreciative of the patient support provided by the committee of the Cinema Theatre Association over five volumes of chronicling the history of Britain's leading cinema circuits and I am indebted to Carol Gibbons, whose donation to the CTA provided the revolving fund which has made their publication possible. I would particularly like to thank Giles Woodforde for his liaison work with the printers of this as well as the previous Odeon book; Jeremy Buck who, as CTA Sales Officer, will be undertaking the huge task of distributing the book to members; Kevin Gooding, for his technical help with some of the illustrations; and Neville Taylor, the CTA's Treasurer, for so efficiently handing the financial aspects. Rachel Marks and Brian Oakaby were of great assistance at the CTA Archive. David Simpson was most generous in supplying prints of Odeon multiplexes for my consideration. Adam Unger kindly located the original slide of the front cover image taken by the late John Squires. Many other committee members assisted with queries on specific site usage and are credited elsewhere. Richard Norman was most helpful with regard to possible use of The Tony Moss Collection.

Once again, it has been a pleasure to work with Malcolm Johnson, the graphic designer who has transferred and finessed my layout concept into the current technology of printing, and who continues to remember the Astoria Streatham in the 1950s as clearly as I do.

John Fernee has kindly commented on the text and allowed me to reproduce some of his rare Odeon colour images. Uncredited illustrations are from the author's collection.

BFI Publishing has again been a patient and helpful partner in the trade distribution of the book and of great assistance with promotion and publicity (Claire Milburn).

In updating the present use of former Odeon cinemas or their sites, I received a huge amount of assistance from CTA members whose names appear at the start of the A to Z of Odeons (some former Rank projectionists provided further elaboration, adopted for the main text). Beyond that, I am most grateful to Ray Dolling, Spencer P. Hobbs and Clifford Shaw for supplying me with copies of their local research; and David F. Cheshire, Alan Davis, David Daykin, Barry Fishman, Ken George, Brian Hall, Jim Leworthy, Keith Parkinson, Stephen Peart, CTA committee member Ken Roe, Bernard Tonks and many others for pieces of assistance.

Now let the story continue...

ENTER J. ARTHUR (1941-1945)

In December 1941, J. Arthur Rank was chairman of both the Odeon cinema chain and the Gaumont-British Picture Corporation with its circuit of Gaumont cinemas. His only substantial rival was Associated British with its interests in production, distribution and exhibition (ABC cinemas).

Rank had fulfilled the ambition of Odeon founder Oscar Deutsch to control these two major exhibition concerns and their merger seemed inevitable – although it would take nearly twenty years to complete. Oscar Deutsch's declining health and death from cancer at the age of 48 had given Rank his opportunity and he seized it boldly. Rank had huge financial resources and was keen to expand even further at a time when others, with World War Two raging, were hesitant and willing to sell.

Although he was a millionaire (who liked to jangle small change in his trouser pockets), as a devout Methodist and teetotaller Joseph Arthur Rank was a highly unlikely candidate for the position of the most powerful individual in the British film industry. But he turned it into a mission and that gave him the drive and strength of purpose.

Born in Hull on 23 December 1888, he was the youngest of the three sons of flour magnate Joseph Rank (who also had four daughters). Instead of attending university, he started work at age 17 in his father's flour mill, learning the business from the ground up, and served in World War One, becoming a sergeant in charge of ambulances at the front line. By 1933 he was the managing director of the family business, Joseph Rank Ltd.

He worked in London and lived on a 300-acre estate near Reigate in Surrey where he could indulge his passion for blood sports and country life. He taught Sunday school at his local church, became treasurer of the Religious Film Society and was behind a scheme started in 1933 to provide projection equipment for Methodist churches, including the one at Reigate. While excited by the potential of cinema as a means of enlivening Christian education, he was unhappy with the quality of religious films that were available and commissioned producer John Corfield to provide two short films: *St. Francis Of Assisi* and *Let There Be Love*. This was followed by *Mastership*, a dramatised Christian tract produced in 1934.

At this time, an immensely rich widow, Lady Yule, had decided to make films about the British character and way of life. She appointed John Corfield as her producer, and Corfield introduced her to J. Arthur Rank in 1934. Together they started British National Films in October 1934 and John Corfield produced the feature film *Turn Of The Tide*, based on a novel about Yorkshire fishermen and partly filmed at Whitby with a professional cast. It was assigned to Gaumont-British for distribution, trade shown in October 1935 and generally released on 20 April 1936 (the gap was quite normal). It was well received by the critics but little shown (this writer checked several months of press advertising for seven Gaumont halls in south London and could not see any sign of it). This can be attributed to the limited mass market appeal of the film and the large number of pictures then available to the Gaumont circuit's bookers, plus the fact that Gaumont did not have the same incentive to push a production which it hadn't financed.

Rank determined from the poor showing of *Turn Of The Tide* that it was necessary to control the release of a film and therefore become a distributor. Through John Corfield, he met one of the most important figures in the British film industry, C. M. Woolf, at just the right moment.

Woolf had begun his career in the fur business, entered films through forming the W&F distribution company in 1919, making a small fortune out of distributing Harold Lloyd comedies but also backing British productions as chairman of Gainsborough Pictures which released through W&F. He became joint managing director of the huge Gaumont-British company in 1929, leaving it after a row in 1935. It was from J. Arthur Rank and Lord Portal, a wealthy paper manufacturer, that he received the backing to set up a new distribution company, General Film Distributors (GFD), in May 1935. The logo was originally to feature a wolf but in the end it was decided to have a man striking a gong.[*]

In 1936, Rank helped to create the General Cinema Finance

---

[*] John Fernee suggests that someone may have remembered the striking credit titles of Paramount's *Shanghai Express* (1932).

Corporation (GCF), registered in March with £1,225,000 in capital for film production and distribution. His fellow directors were C. M. Woolf, Paul Lindenberg (representing Japhets, an investment bank), Lord Luke (chairman of Bovril) and L.(Leslie) W. Farrow, an accountant. GCF acquired GFD (leaving C. M. Woolf in command), backed GFD's British productions (Woolf was managing director of British & Dominions and of Herbert Wilcox Productions), and contributed $2 million towards the refinancing of the ailing American company Universal Pictures in exchange for a quarter share in the concern, the right to distribute its output in Britain through GFD (Universal's own renting subsidiary was merged into it from May 1936), and the acquisition of Universal News, the company's British newsreel. Universal made losses for the next two years until, helped by hugely successful films starring the young Deanna Durbin, it bounded back and became increasingly profitable during the war years. Woolf also resumed a link with Gaumont, with GFD investing in its productions in exchange for distribution rights.

Rank further teamed up with Lady Yule to build Pinewood Studios, which opened in September 1936 (the company was registered in August 1935). But in 1937 the two fell out and ended their partnerships with J. Arthur Rank taking Pinewood and Lady Yule keeping British National.

Rank's first cinemas

The big money was to be made in film exhibition and Rank realised that the possession of cinemas would ensure screening time for films in which he had a financial interest through his investments in production and distribution. Consulting C. M. Woolf, J. Arthur Rank made his first moves into exhibition. The earliest press mention of this seems to occur in the *Kine Weekly* dated Thursday 3 September 1936:

Plans for the building up of a new kinema group which eventually will comprise a hundred theatres are stated to be practically consummated. The name of J. Arthur Rank is mentioned in connection with the deal. The proposed circuit is negotiating for the acquisition of some of the best independent properties available in London and the provinces. It is understood that two important London circuits possessing recently built and up-to-date kinemas will form the nucleus of the group, and a further purchase of four or five theatres in the Midlands is stated also to be contemplated.

The unnamed "new kinema group" proved to be GCF expanding beyond its distribution and production interests and the two London-area circuits were those of D. J. James and Kay Bros. (Kessex). No cinemas were acquired in the Midlands.

In fact, another deal, in advanced negotiations by October

1936, was the first to be fully revealed in December. A newly formed Cinema Theatres (GCF) Ltd. acquired half the capital of several companies owning fifteen cinemas in Wales and the west of England that were valued at £500,000. These companies and their cinemas were:

Aberaman Cinemas: Aberaman Grand
AOC Picture Corporation: Barry Royal and Savoy
Avenue Cinema Company: Bristol (Clifton) Embassy
Avon Cinema Company: Bath Forum
Barry Docks Kinemas: Barry Palace
Belle Cinema: Codoxton Palace
Elton Cinema Company: Gloucester Plaza
Empire Mountain Ash: Mountain Ash Empire and Palace
Fairbanks Cinema Company: Llanelly Regal
Glaudwr Cinema Company: Llanelly Hippodrome
Picton Cinemas: Swansea Plaza and Rialto
Regent Cinemas: Morriston Gem

There were links between some of the companies: AOC owned Belle Cinema (it went on to plan two south London cinemas, selling one site and building the Regal Kennington on the other).

The fifteen cinemas never became part of Odeon and remained independently run. But in some cases – Plaza Swansea, Forum Bath – Rank retained a financial interest well into the 1950s.

Another GCF subsidiary, Eastern Cinemas (GCF) Ltd., was registered in February 1937 with capital of £250,000 and in early April completed the purchase of most of D. J. James's circuit. The properties involved were in south and east London, Essex and Hertfordshire:

Bethnal Green Museum
Greenwich Trafalgar
Hatfield Regent
Hornchurch Towers
Romford Havana and Plaza
St. Albans Capitol and Grand Palace
Stepney Mayfair
Upminster Capitol
Whalebone Lane Mayfair

These eleven cinemas were absorbed into the Odeon circuit in 1943. (James held onto the Studio One and Two at Oxford Circus as well as the Park at Hither Green, south London. He also retained and opened the uncompleted Mayfair Caledonian Road but sold his Florida Camberwell scheme to ABC.)

Around this same time, Kessex Cinemas was acquired by GCF and continued under the same name. It had these cinemas:

Interior views of two cinemas taken over by General Cinema Finance in 1937 and absorbed into the Odeon circuit in 1943. Above, the Savoy, Gants Hill, Ilford, 1934. Below, the Mayfair Stepney, 1936. Both were renamed Odeon in 1949-50.

Barking Rio
Becontree Regent
Dagenham Grange
Dagenham Heathway
Ilford (Gants Hill) Savoy

All five properties also joined the Odeon circuit in 1943. Kay Bros., which owned Kessex, applied the proceeds of the sale to building further cinemas, including the Rio Sheerness (sold to Gaumont before opening) and the State Barkingside.

Later in 1937, GCF acquired the Leicester Square Theatre as a launching pad for GFD releases in London's West End. Opened in 1930 as a joint venture by performer Jack Buchanan and Walter Gibbons, it had a troubled early start before settling down in 1933 as a showcase for United Artists pictures. But the American distributor pulled out in July 1937 as its interest in the Odeon circuit ensured that the new Odeon shortly to open across the square would become its key West End outlet. Buchanan toyed with re-opening the Leicester Square Theatre as a variety hall but then leased it to GCF. With its excellent location and large capacity (1,760 seats), the Leicester Square Theatre only needed the right films to become highly profitable. GFD was able to provide a stream of important releases, including those early Deanna Durbin pictures from Universal. The London-region properties and the west of England and Welsh holdings in the GCF portfolio included a high proportion of large, modern cinemas in densely populated areas that gave J. Arthur Rank and his fellow directors an important stake in British film exhibition. The managing director of the two London circuits was S. F. Ditcham and the theatre controller was W. H. Attrill.

In April 1938, Rank became chairman of the GCF, at which time he owned around a quarter of the company.

Rank and Odeon

GCF made a substantial purchase of Odeon shares, resulting in Rank becoming a director in January 1939. Oscar Deutsch, the Odeon chief, remained firmly in charge and continued his discussions about taking over the rival Gaumont chain (these were suspended in November 1939 following the outbreak of war). He made his own private investments in British film production, as Odeon itself had promised shareholders that it would not risk the company's money in that field. As noted in the first volume of this Odeon history, Deutsch's last major production venture was to form British Film Makers in 1941 with C. M. Woolf and J. Arthur Rank.

Deutsch had long battled with cancer and by 1939 knew that his days were numbered. To safeguard the future of Odeon and keep it in British hands, Deutsch formed a new company with

Rank in 1940 called Foy Investments which took control of Odeon Cinema Holdings, the company jointly owned by United Artists that in turn controlled Odeon Theatres. Very clearly, Oscar was nominating J. Arthur as his successor.

On 23 October 1941, on behalf of GCF, C. M. Woolf purchased control of the Gaumont-British Picture Corporation from the Ostrer family. Woolf must have received great satisfaction in gaining control of the company from which he had been ousted in the middle of 1935. He resumed his old role of joint managing director with Mark Ostrer while J. Arthur Rank became chairman of the company and of its key subsidiaries, Provincial Cinematograph Theatres and General Theatres Corporation.

On 2 December 1941, just three days before Oscar Deutsch's death, Rank took the Odeon chief's place to chair the fourth AGM of Odeon Theatres. Deutsch's associate, John Davis, recalled in 1990:

> Arthur Rank became associated with Oscar Deutsch only twelve or eighteen months before Deutsch's death and it was agreed in principle that when Oscar died his estate would sell his interest to Arthur Rank. When Arthur realised how important film was in the life of a nation, and that the American film industry had a stranglehold throughout the world, he decided to take them on to show the British way of life as compared with the American.

John Davis and F. Stanley Bates became joint managing directors of Odeon on 19 December 1941 with J. Arthur Rank as acting chairman. Davis had been the financial director while Bates was one of Deutsch's closest business associates in the creation of the Odeon circuit.

During 1942, Rank used a company he owned, Manorfield Investments, to acquire all Deutsch's shares in Foy Investments and so gained control of Odeon Cinema Holdings and Odeon Theatres. Rank also began to enlarge his quarter share in GCF from April 1942 and gained a majority interest within a year.

There were some serious personality clashes within Odeon. W. G. Elcock, Deutsch's other main partner along with F. Stanley Bates, wanted to run Odeon. Rank wouldn't have it and bought out Elcock's interest in Odeon, leading to his resignation from the board in January 1942.*

---

* Elcock took with him Scophony, Deutsch's cinema television company, and started a new cinema circuit called Mayfair on 5 December 1942 to acquire a motley assortment of thirty-nine properties. Elcock's fellow director and booking manager was veteran exhibitor Arthur Cohen, who had been managing director of London and Southern Super Cinemas, now part of Odeon. Mayfair was soon acquired by British Luminous Industries, which made war munitions, with Elcock and Cohen joining the board. Mayfair expanded to fifty-five cinemas by mid-1943. The company then sold all but a dozen, including a batch of small town R e g a l s ,

Another of the old guard who didn't fit in was Wilfred Phillips. A cousin of Oscar Deutsch, he had been appointed chief film booker by the Odeon chief on a seven year contract from September 1939 at an annual salary of £2,080. After Deutsch's death, Phillips declared that John Davis, as the new joint managing director, wanted him out. The Odeon board issued instructions that he should report to them all his negotiations for first feature films before making a decision on whether or not to book them. He was also instructed to take with him Richard Hamer, the booker for the GCF circuits, when discussing the renting of films, as Hamer had been appointed to carry out Phillips' duties when he was called up for Army service. On Tuesday 12 May 1942, J. Arthur Rank told Phillips that he had disobeyed the board's instructions and he was invited to resign. Phillips asked for £10,000 in compensation and refused to resign after he was offered only £7,000, resulting in his dismissal. Hamer took over as Odeon's booking controller on Friday 15 May 1942.

Phillips' suit alleging wrongful dismissal came to court in September 1944. He pointed out that his instructions to report booking negotiations to the board were impracticable but he had to admit that he had only once taken Mr. Hamer along when visiting distributors. The case was dropped when Phillips accepted a renewed offer of £7,000 plus his costs. Richard Hamer was now the permanent booking manager.

Rank had a major setback when his most trusted associate, C. M. Woolf, died at the age of 63 on 31 December 1942 after a brief illness. "A heart ailment is blamed for his sudden death, which shocked film industry circles because he appeared in good health only last summer," reported *Variety*'s London correspondent. Rank's inner circle of advisors now consisted of Leslie Farrow, his lawyer G. L. Woodham-Smith – and John Davis.

The war years turned into a boom period for the Odeon circuit. The 53-week year ending 27 June 1942 produced a record profit of £1,530,539, massively up on the previous year's £643,287, and enabled the resumption of a dividend (10 per cent) on the ordinary stock.

The small Town Theatres circuit was taken over early in 1942 and negotiations may well have commenced during Oscar Deutsch's lifetime. This added the following rather nondescript batch of properties:

Camden Town Plaza
East Molesey Court
Hayes (Kent) Rex

to ABC as early as August 1943 (see *ABC The First Name In Entertainment*, page 66). The company ceased operating during 1950 and a winding up order was made on 17 December 1952. Elcock was later involved in an unsuccessful theatre group that leased the Regent King's Cross.

Kentish Town Gaisford
Putney Bridge Kinema

The Putney Bridge Kinema was closed at the time of take-over and the license had been allowed to lapse. As Odeon already had the larger and better located Hippodrome on the other side of the bridge, it was never re-opened. Only the Hayes cinema would be renamed Odeon and this became a loss maker and early closure. The Camden Town Plaza had the greatest potential of the group as it could play the Odeon circuit release first-run in this populous inner London area but it had only 731 seats (dwarfed by the 2,742 seats at the close-by Gaumont).

Back in November 1939, Oscar Deutsch had signed the agreement to lease the Paramounts at Leeds, Manchester and Newcastle-on-Tyne, plus the four London suburban Astorias at Brixton, Finsbury Park, Old Kent Road and Streatham. Paramount had disposed of the three provincial cinemas because Oscar Deutsch was well advanced in plans to build large new Odeons in direct competition with them but the American company had held onto the other four – at Birmingham, Glasgow, Liverpool and London's Tottenham Court Road – until now, no doubt haggling for an increased offer (although it had generously agreed that the annual payments for the earlier group could be suspended until after the war). In August 1942, the leases of these remaining four Paramount cinemas were acquired by Odeon. The American company retained only its two West End outlets, the Plaza Lower Regent Streeet and the Carlton Haymarket, for launching its releases. The deal consolidated t h e arrangement by which Paramount pictures played the Odeon circuit.

The Paramount takeover, on top of Rank's control of both the Odeon and Gaumont chains, alarmed the war-time coalition government. Dr. Hugh Dalton, President of the Board of Trade (BoT), sent for Rank and threatened that legislation might be introduced to stop further expansion unless he gave an assurance that he would buy no further cinemas in Britain without BoT approval. Dalton then allowed the Paramount deal to go ahead. Learning that the other national circuit, ABC, would be asked for a similar undertaking, Rank settled on a maximum of 607 cinemas (the same number was accepted by ABC in February 1944). The agreement was made public in July 1943 but Rank (according to his biographer, Alan Wood) had told Dalton, "I'd have liked to have had a few more" (although he never reached the permitted total).

With the latest Paramounts, Odeon obtained first-class city centre representation in the six key British cities outside London. The cinemas were quickly renamed Odeon and became the most important ones on the circuit because of their size, location and huge grosses (helped by higher ticket prices). They played the weekly circuit release on exclusive first run in their areas with occasional holdovers for the biggest draws. As part of the deal, they continued showing British Paramount News. (The flagship Odeon Leicester Square charged even higher prices but, because of West End competition, played fewer films for longer runs, usually three weeks or more, and its grosses were lowered by the much reduced takings later on.)

Another addition to the circuit in 1942 was the Marlborough Holloway. Dropped as redundant by Gaumont in 1940, it re-opened to give Odeon a valuable outlet in this inner north London area. In Croydon, the lease of the Hippodrome, which had been the town's second ABC hall, was taken over by Odeon. With a capacity similar to the 1,280 seats of the town's existing Odeon, it strengthened the circuit's position considerably, enabling the two cinemas to play the weekly Odeon release simultaneously for many years, although the huge Davis Theatre took some of the bigger films concurrently with the Odeon until the early 1950s.

At the end of 1942, two attractive cinemas opened by John Buckley and run by Anglo-Scottish Theatres were acquired to strengthen Odeon's weak representation in the Manchester area: the Lido Burnage and the Pyramid Sale. These were soon re-branded as Odeons.

As previously mentioned, the Eastern Counties (GCF) and Kessex circuits, associated with J. Arthur Rank since 1937, were brought into Odeon at the end of February 1943. These had not grown over the past six years but their generally well-positioned cinemas considerably strengthened the circuit.

At this time, many picture houses were available for purchase, especially in inner London where proprietors had seen attendances plummet because of the Blitz, the call up and widespread evacuation. They were losing money or uncertain of the future but Rank did not hesitate to expand the Odeon circuit. Certainly Odeon was in the driving seat when (after receiving BoT approval) it acquired the Metropole Victoria in the autumn of 1943 from the Hyams brothers who had already sold their other large inner London properties, fearing their vulnerability in bombing raids. The Hyams wanted to dispose of the small Biograph at Victoria along with the Metropole but backed down when Odeon refused to take that as well. Rank soon linked the Metropole with the Paramount Tottenham Court Road to show the Odeon release for a week just before it went into the suburbs.

Some further valuable additions were made in 1943. There were the Majestics at Darlington and West Hartlepool (to be followed by the Majestic Bishop Auckland, from the same group, late in 1944). Also circa 1943 Odeon took over three of Max Corne's four cinemas in Wales: the Majestic Port Talbot (which

In 1943, the Palladium Paignton has the words "This is an Odeon Theatre" mounted on the trademark-style "O" between the centre columns. (CTA Archive.)

The auditorium of the Majestic Bishop Auckland, taken over by Odeon in 1944 and renamed the following year.

had been, in its planning stages, an Odeon scheme until Odeon exchanged it for Corne's cinema in Cardiff town centre), the small Regent Taibach in the same area, and the Maxime Sketty, a large, modern cinema in the Swansea suburbs (the one that Corne retained was the Maxime Blackwood). Other apparently isolated additions in 1943 were the Roxy Barrow-in-Furness (a single hall from James Brennan's circuit with a faience-tiled exterior in 1930s Odeon style); the Plaza Blackfen, near Bexley-heath, Kent (of dubious value, as Odeon were well represented in the area); the Plaza Crosby, near Liverpool (only opened the day before war broke out in September 1939); the Cavendish at Normanton, Derby; Black's Regals at Gateshead and South Shields (but not, at this time, any of Alfred Black's other four halls in the region); the Palladium Paignton, peculiarly sited halfway to Torquay; and the Majestic Sevenoaks (from Cohen and Rafer, leaving the partnership with the Plaza Sevenoaks and Regal Kettering, sold to Granada in 1947).

There was some competition for the small but valuable Joseph Mears circuit, comprising The Kensington, The Rich-mond, The Sheen and The Twickenham Cinemas (called after the affluent west London areas in which they were located but temporarily re-named during the war to avoid helping any German parachutists identify their whereabouts), plus additional cinemas at Richmond (the Royalty) and Twickenham (the Luxor). Mears had found the going difficult because The Kensington and The Twickenham had been requisitioned by the government for other uses but Rank, with his deep pockets, could take a long-term view. The Mayfair circuit, with which Oscar Deutsch's close associate George Elcock was associated, competed for the group but a Rank bid of circa £700,000 was accepted in early October 1943, although the handover did not take place until 3 January 1944. Rank was able to re-open The Kensington as an Odeon later in 1944 with its Christie organ playing (Cyril Martin was soon appointed resident organist). The Twickenham followed at the end of 1945 (this kept its war-time name of the Queen's as the Odeon name was bestowed on the larger Luxor). The Richmond and The Sheen also took the Odeon name. It is indicative of their high value that the Odeon Kensington and Odeon Richmond remain open as profitable Odeon cinemas to this day.

Also in 1944, Odeon took over the Regal Stockton-on-Tees and the large and modern Ritz cinemas at Park Royal, north London, and Whitton, west London. The two Ritzes were very similar properties (same architect: Major W. J. King) that had been leased to the small London and District circuit from opening but were withdrawn after a receiver was appointed to that company in July 1939. (Odeon seem to have had a deal at one time to run Park Royal before it opened, to judge by the listing of a site there in the October 1937 memorandum reproduced in *Odeon Cinemas 1*, page 157.) They proved to be lacklustre additions to the Odeon circuit. A more worthwhile acquisition in this same year was the Regal Accrington, the town's only large, modern cinema.

Rather surprisingly, Odeon took on the huge Regal Marble Arch, on the edge of London's West End, which the ABC circuit had dropped in January 1945, defeated in its efforts to run the place successfully on lease from its owner, A. E. Abrahams.

In addition, the circuit name was bolstered by the renaming of many takeovers as Odeons, with the others proclaiming an association with Odeon on their frontage and in press advertising where they used the trademark style of lettering for their names.

Bomb damage

J. Arthur Rank's pre-Odeon cinema interests experienced the winds of war when the Leicester Square Theatre suffered severe damage to its frontage during a raid on 17 October 1940. "Partition walls, box offices, furniture and decorations were destroyed but fortunately the auditorium and stage were not damaged," recalled manager E. S. Luke in September 1941. "The theatre was within six days of re-opening when, on 16 April 1941, the upper circle café was hit during a very heavy raid that night. Reinstatement was begun at once and the theatre re-opened on 11 July 1941 with Marlene Dietrich in *The Flame Of New Orleans*. The result is a great testimony to the resisting powers of steel and concrete."

Serious bomb damage to several Odeon properties during Oscar Deutsch's lifetime has been detailed in the first volume of this Odeon history. To these should be added the South Hackney Picture House, closed by enemy action on 17 April 1941, and the Odeon Haverstock Hill, closed in October 1941. Bob Narduzzo has written to me:

I was a junior projectionist at the Odeon Colindale in 1941 and during that time the Odeon Haverstock Hill was bombed. The manager at Colindale was a very go-ahead chap and we, at the time, staged cine-variety shows. He obtained permission from head office to transfer any stage drapes and so one Sunday morning a few of us went to Haverstock Hill and I will always remember the devastation there. The bomb fell near the right hand side of the front stalls making a huge dent in the massive safety curtain but all the stage drapes survived. The festoon tabs that we took back and installed at Colindale are clearly shown in the picture of Haverstock Hill on page 45 of *Odeon Cinemas 1*.

The onslaught continued. In his book *The Picture House In East Anglia*, Stephen Peart noted:

Wartime devastation affects the Odeon at Lowestoft in January 1942. (Photograph by Ford Jenkins.)

Below, the Odeon displays news of victory in October 1944.

A terrible tragedy involving Lowestoft's Odeon occurred in 1942. On the 13th January a Dornier aircraft dived into the town and dropped four bombs on several premises in London Road opposite the cinema. It was tea-time and Wallers restaurant was packed. Altogether seventy-four people lost their lives and 124 were injured. The Odeon's facade was badly damaged but its large main foyer served as a casualty centre. Somehow the film being screened at the time held a poignant meaning for the tragic occasion: *Hold Back The Dawn*.

Peart notes that, during the peak of the Blitz in 1942, another bomb penetrated the Odeon Norwich as far as the manager's office but failed to explode. The cinema had to be closed for urgent repairs but the Odeon release played concurrently at the much more central Carlton (a former County house) and so remained available to local cinemagoers.

The Odeon Exeter was damaged during a devastating seventy minutes of dive bombing by the Germans in a so-called "reprisal raid" with high explosive and incendiary bombs that rained down on the town early on Monday 4 May 1942. The Odeon was able to re-open four weeks later but its frontage was never fully restored.

Stephen Peart recorded the recollections of an attendant at the Odeon Clacton when incendiary bombs fell on the town on 13 February 1944:

I heard the crack and someone said there were bombs in the cinema. Two fell in the circle, one in the stalls and two in the projection room. One fell between a soldier and his companion, and he just got up, fetched some sand which we had handy all over the cinema, and that was that! When I ran for buckets of sand, a soldier said, "All right, Dad, we'll do that" – and they did. Afterwards the audience asked for the performance to go on and it did. A number of people filed out in an orderly fashion when the bombs fell, but there was no panic.

The menace of the V1 flying bombs or "doodlebugs" was first felt during eighty days of intensive raids on southern England that began in June 1944. On the morning of 16 June, the Odeon Deptford, south east London, commenced more than six years of closure after a bomb caused severe structural damage, particularly to the roof and the stage area including the rear wall. The front was scarcely affected. In nearby Sidcup, Kent, one of the flying bombs hit an elm tree and exploded in the air during the early hours of Monday 16 October, causing severe damage to a parish church opposite the Odeon. The cinema frontage, along with the flanking shops and flats, was struck by the blast and a firewatcher in the cinema received cuts. The extent of interior damage was unspecified but the Odeon remained closed for almost ten years.

Less serious damage happened at many Odeons. As CTA member Spencer Hobbs notes, from researching Southwark cinemas:

Quite a few Odeons seem to have suffered slight or minor blast damage that would be quickly patched up, so that it would not be indicated by a break in weekly film advertising. The Camberwell Odeon suffered what was classed as damage of a "rather serious nature" when, on 23 June 1944, about half its roofing sheets were blown off in a blast. In addition, minor damage was caused to doors, windows, plasterwork etc. though the roofing frame itself was said to "practically undamaged". The cinema sustained further slight damage on 2 and 3 July 1944, and again on 28 October, being quickly patched up each time.

At Stockton, barely had the Regal been renamed Odeon than it became "temporarily closed" in late March 1945 with patrons being advised to look out for a re-opening date that finally arrived sixteen months later. "No news item explains this closure which, coming midweek and less than two weeks after a name change, must surely have been unplanned," comments CTA member Richard Lacey. "There is no record of any enemy action on Stockton this late, so I assume it must have been an earlier problem which had become more serious." Indeed, two months later, plans were passed for the reconstruction of the roof truss.

One of the last V bombs of the war struck the Regal Marble Arch while Odeon was in the process of refurbishing it, delaying the re-opening until peacetime.

Some Odeons were directly involved in the fight against Hitler. General Montgomery used those at Folkestone and Plymouth to address troops preparing for the invasion of France in 1944. Many others hosted special shows for troops in their area: the Odeon Kingstanding often functioned as a garrison cinema for American troops early in the morning. The most illustrious of all the troop shows took place on the Sunday afternoon of 1 August 1943 when Bob Hope, Adolphe Menjou and the Glenn Miller Orchestra performed on the stage of the Odeon Leicester Square before an audience that included Winston Churchill, General Eisenhower and American servicemen.

The merger

Now that he controlled both Odeon and Gaumont, J. Arthur Rank was keen to merge the two companies administratively, but there were obstacles. In the case of Gaumont, 20th Century-Fox had the right of veto through its holding in the controlling Metropolis and Bradford Trust. By May 1944 Rank managed to obtain the agreement of Fox head Spyros Skouras and the consent of the Treasury. Next he had to win over the Board of Trade...

Just as Rank had been offended by the failure of Gaumont to

obtain a proper release for *Turn Of The Tide*, so Michael Balcon, the head of Ealing Films, had been disturbed by the refusal of the major circuits to take some of his war-time productions, such as *They Came To A City* (a stolid version of J. B. Priestley's socialist vision of Utopia, featuring the cast of the West End play). Balcon was largely responsible for Hugh Dalton, President of the BoT, commissioning a report, *Tendencies To Monopoly In The Cinematograph Films Industry*, from a committee headed by Dr. Albert Palache. This was published in July 1944 and one of the points it made was that no British production could recover its costs without a release on one of the three major circuits.

The vision

Long before the war ended, J. Arthur Rank had a vision that the film markets of liberated European countries, including Germany itself, could be conquered by British rather than American films, and that even North America could be persuaded to accept them.

He dispatched John Davis to finalise a deal to buy into the Canadian Odeon circuit in 1944 and to make arrangements to build a cinema in New York. Davis was also sent to Cairo where he acquired a site for a new 2,200-seat cinema to act as a shop window for Rank films in the Middle East (he also envisaged opening cinemas in Tel-Aviv, Haifa and Jerusalem).

In November 1944, Rank bought a half interest in the Odeon circuit of Canada with 102 cinemas. Formed in 1941, this had no prior connection with Oscar Deutsch and Britain. Consisting of several independent regional chains of modern movie theatres and some purpose-built additions, it was headed by industry veteran Nathan L. Nathanson, who had been president of Famous Players, the principal Canadian circuit controlled by the major American company, Paramount. He died in 1943 and was succeeded by his son, Paul.

The announcement in the same month that Rank had secured a site for a 2,000-seat cinema in the heart of New York City's entertainment district caused a shock wave to go through the American film industry. The site seems not to have been revealed, although the *Daily Film Renter* (13 November 1944) reported that it might be adjacent to Radio City at 52nd Street and Sixth Avenue. It was stated that the cinema would not be exclusively devoted to British films but would also play some American product.

Closer to home, the *Kine Weekly* (7 December 1944) reported that Rank was after a circuit of key cinemas in France (Gaumont perhaps?), although nothing came of it.

In January 1945, the *Kine Weekly* published J. Arthur Rank's vision of the future. "Our slogan is that we are establishing British pictures on the screens of the world", he declared. "At the same time I realise that our films must be tailored for overseas sale. We have to present our wares in such a way that the patrons are interested in them first, and they will find they understand Great Britain all the better. The big films of universal appeal cannot be denied exhibition throughout the world."

Booking

While the Odeon circuit was being built up, several major films were jointly booked to both Odeon and Gaumont circuits (see *Odeon Cinemas 1*, page 214). There were two more examples of this in 1942 *(Suspicion* and *Coastal Command)*, one partial instance in 1944 *(The Song Of Bernadette)*, then only the special cases of *Caesar And Cleopatra* in 1946 and *A Queen Is Crowned* in 1953.

By 1942 Odeon had established itself as the equal of the other two national circuits with its own weekly release outside London's West End. A photocopy of a single page from a file of "Circuit Grosses", unearthed by former Rank film booker Michael Fisher, covers the period from June 1941 to the beginning of April 1942 and reveals that Odeon paid to the distributor a percentage of the total gross achieved by the main feature outside London's West End (in 1942 the number of Odeon cinemas each release played ranged between 226 and 247). The percentage of the gross that was paid varied – from 25 per cent for totals of under £122,500 to 50 per cent when films took over £185,000. This method of arriving at a payment was unusual – cinemas normally had individual contracts – and may have been a simplified procedure occasioned by the War. Paramount films shown in 1942 – *Birth Of The Blues*, *Sullivan's Travels*, *Hatter's Castle* and *Louisiana Purchase* – are noted as receiving better terms, perhaps as part of the cinema takeover deal.

Grosses ranged from a low of £74,167 for *Cheers For Miss Bishop* to a high of £190,667 for *49th Parallel*, a confirmation of the enormous popularity of the latter production and a reminder of the considerable variations in appeal of different films even in the boom years of cinemagoing. Other major successes were *Nice Girl*, *Pimpernel Smith*, *Major Barbara*, *That Night In Rio*, *Lady Hamilton*, *Hold Back The Dawn*, *Aloma Of The South Seas*, *Moon Over Miami* and *Blood And Sand*. The escapist appeal of musicals and Technicolor is evident in many of these titles.

A single carbon copy of a page of London grosses has also survived, covering the last week of December 1941 to the end of May 1942. This shows that north London normally outgrossed south London (if only because it had more theatres) and that the number of Odeons showing the release ranged between 62 and 68. The outstanding performers were *Babes On Broadway*, grossing £41,961, and *Blood And Sand*, grossing £41,605, followed by *Song Of The Thin Man*, *Louisiana Purchase* and *Keep 'Em Flying*. The lowest total came from *Unfinished Business*: £25,199.

ODEON
telephone 547 WEYMOUTH

Doors Open 1.30
Start - - 2.0

MONDAY, June 12th and ALL THE WEEK
IN GLORIOUS TECHNICOLOR

THE PHANTOM OF THE OPERA

(A) STARRING—
CLAUD RAINS , NELSON EDDIE . SUSANNA FOSTER

Showing Daily at 1.45• — 4.5 — 6.20 — 8.30

Also March of Time, No. 8 and Disney Cartoon

News—Special FIRST PICTURES OF INVASION

Showing at 3.40, 6.0, 8.15

| Sunday, June 18
Doors Open 1.30
Start at 2.0 | MARLENE DIETRICH in **PITTSBURGH** (A)
ROBERT PAGE in **HI, BUDDY** (U) |

This 1944 advertisement shows the importance of the newsreel in showing war news. There is no B feature to allow the strong main film to play four times daily, only a cartoon and a documentary from the American March Of Time *series. A pity that two of the three stars have their names misspelled. (Courtesy of John Yallop.)*

The manager encourages the children to wave their arms to promote the launch of the Odeon National Club at the Grand Palace St. Albans in 1943. (St. Albans Museums. Copyright reserved.)

The key Odeons in the larger towns would retain a hit film like Paramount's *For Whom The Bell Tolls* for a second week. In September 1944, this Spanish Civil War drama-cum-romance clocked up an unprecedented total of over 50,000 admissions in its first week at the Odeon Plymouth (the 50,000th patron, able seaman H. Jenkins, was presented with a free ticket by the manager). A huge capacity of 3,245 seats helped this Odeon achieve such a high total.

To save celluloid by reducing the number of general release prints required on all three of the major circuits, north London was divided up into two areas instead of one from 10 May 1943 – northwest and northeast – and films took longer to complete their run. "Northeast" didn't immediately provide enough outlets, so Odeon cinemas in south and west London – at East S h e e n, Hounslow, Kingston, Richmond, Shannon Corner, Southall, Surbiton, Twickenham, Walton-on-Thames and Whitton – were put into the second week area and in group advertising became part of northeast London. Gaumont and ABC cinemas in the same areas were similarly misplaced. They did have the advantage of playing programmes a week before cinemas in adjacent parts of south London.

At the end of 1944, Odeon had 318 cinemas which recorded 180 million admissions annually, and there were eighty-five restaurants in operation.

Of children and religion

Saturday morning shows for children at Odeons, which were suspended at the outbreak of war, resumed after the decline in daytime bombing raids made cinemas reasonably safe. According to Terry Staples, in his history of children's shows *All Pals Together*, J. Arthur Rank was disturbed by the rise of anti-social behaviour among youngsters due to lack of parental supervision and decided to re-organise the clubs at his Odeons and Gaumonts in an attempt to improve standards of conduct. On 17 April 1943, the Odeon National Cinema Club was launched at 150 cinemas. J. Arthur Rank attended the opening at the Odeon Morden. Short rhymes about the virtues of regularly cleaning teeth, washing hands or going to Sunday school were now presented by slides on the screen. The cinema manager (the "club chief") read out pledges of good behaviour like "I promise to tell the truth, to help others and obey my parents" to which the children were expected to reply "I promise". It seems that the song (starting "Is everybody happy? Yes!") quoted in *Odeon Cinemas 1* on page 218 was, in fact, introduced at this time. Some children had fun responding "No!" to the song's questions.

Activities by the clubs ranged ranged from local campaigns to circuit-wide initiatives like "Odeon Safety Forces" – where red, amber and then green badges were awarded as members passed increasingly difficult tests of road safety knowledge. Local initiatives included members at Middlesbrough collecting books to send to the troops (seventy-five boys and girls received field marshal badges for contributing 250 volumes) and those at Sutton Coldfield gathering fruit, flowers and groceries for local hospitals.

By the start of 1945, there were 225 clubs (out of the 318 cinemas in all) with an average of one thousand children attending each week.

One result of J. Arthur Rank's control of Odeon was the introduction of five-minute films entitled *Sunday Thought For The Week*. These were made by Rank's religious film unit, GHW, formed in 1940 and named after three of its directors (Dr. B. Gregory, R. J. V. Hake, and film director Norman Walker). They were screened twice on Sundays at Odeon cinemas from the autumn of 1942 with the dual purpose of promoting Christ and helping to justify the showing of films on the Sabbath. Rank brought former British film star Stewart Rome out of retirement to portray a character called Doctor Goodfellow who leaned over a farm gate and told the audience what to think about and what to do during the following week.

Brian Gauntlett remembers his Sunday visits to the Odeon Portsmouth:

> The screening of the *Sunday Thought* seemed to act as some sort of signal for the fatherless youth of the day (their Dads away fighting the war) to call out across the auditorium to their pals and chat up the girls in very, very loud voices. The series was definitely not popular. The *Thoughts* went on for quite a few years but after a Sunday night at the Odeon Edgware Road when the youthful audience went berserk and started to throw things at the screen, they ended.

GHW also made the worthy feature-length biopic *The Great Mr. Handel*, without star names but featuring Handel's "Messiah" and Technicolor. Unlike *The Turn Of The Tide*, this encountered no release problems: distributed by Rank's own GFD, it went into GFD's own West End outlet, the Leicester Square Theatre (not yet part of Odeon) in the autumn of 1942, and had no difficulty in obtaining a full Odeon circuit release.

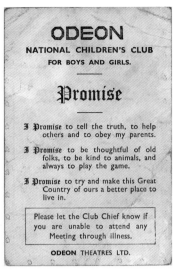

Membership card showing J. Arthur Rank as president of the Odeon National Cinema Club. (CTA Archive.)

J. Arthur Rank with staff and youngsters poses on the stairs to the balcony of the Odeon Leicester Square on an unidentified occasion. (CTA Archive.)

AFTER THE WAR (1945-1953)

Helped by postwar euphoria and the lack of many alternative leisure pursuits, 1946 was the best year ever for British cinemas with attendances of 1,635 million. Odeon's share of those admissions was around 12 per cent.

Odeon seems to have had 308 operating cinemas at the end of the war. The following were closed, having been totally destroyed or seriously damaged by enemy action (except where otherwise noted):

Bloomsbury (London) Super
Broadstairs Royalty (while on lease to an independent)
Canning Town Odeon
Coventry Rialto
Deptford Odeon
Devonport Hippodrome
Dover King's Hall (pre-war fire)
Haverstock Hill Odeon
Margate Regal
Putney Bridge Kinema (closed when acquired)
Sidcup Odeon
South Hackney Picture House

No attempt seems to have been made to revive cinema use at Bloomsbury, Coventry Rialto, Devonport, Putney Bridge or South Hackney.

For some time, Odeon continued to harbour hopes of re-opening at Canning Town in east London. A note dated 17 February 1948 regarding the bombed cinema, attached to the company's licensing files, reads: "No obvious damage but building cracked and Authority will not grant licence." Permission to reinstate the Odeon Sidcup was refused on at least two occasions, in 1946 and 1950, and the company was only able to proceed here and elsewhere when restrictions on expenditure were sufficiently relaxed in 1954.

In addition, the company classified the following Odeons as still being "under construction":

Doncaster
Gloucester
Highgate (north London)
Morley
Sheffield
Westbourne Grove (west London)
Worcester

All of these schemes, except Morley, were revived with the easing of restrictions in 1954.

Odeon was cash rich as a result of the huge surge in attendances (allowing it to pay big dividends to shareholders who had seen the price of shares rise by 1,000 per cent on 1940); and it gained further income from disposing of unwanted sites (the one for a Leeds Odeon went for use as a bus station in September 1945; that for the Odeon at Morley was sold off in April 1950).

Sites
Internal property lists dated 23 November 1950 and 22 January 1951 record many sites on which no work had ever started. In the Odeon Theatres Group in London and the South, these were listed as follows (without any further details): Grange St. Albans; Barking; Barnet (Hatfield); Becontree Heath; Elm Park (Hornchurch); Gallows Cr [Corner] Romford; Leytonstone; Newbury Park [Place?] Ilford; Potters Bar; West Ham; Banstead; Kennington; a "property" in Clapton [identifed as an Odeon site on an earlier 27 June 1949 list]. In the Northeast: Wakefield. In the Western area: Swansea and Plymouth. In Scotland: Bridgeton, Partick, Townhead, Edinburgh, Falkirk. The list also includes the Worthing Plaza ("let") and the Bromley New Theatre.

A list of the Odeon Associated Theatres Group includes the Ilford Hippodrome (a Frank Matcham theatre bombed in 1941) as a "site" and notes the Kingsland Empire, Stoke Newington Ambassador and Forest Hill Capitol as being "let". The Empire had closed in 1937 to be reconstructed as the Classic Dalston (the Rio in 2005), so its appearance under the old name is somewhat odd. The Ambassador showed the Odeon release while the Capitol was operated by ABC and played its weekly programme.

Most, if not all, of the sites cropped up before the War (see pages 201-204 in *Odeon Cinemas 1*). No cinemas were built on any of them, although Odeon did attempt to proceed with some, especially in Scotland. The scheme in Edinburgh was for a 3,500-seater at the corner of Leith Street and Greenhill, near the independent Playhouse. This was active in mid-1953 when revised plans (reducing the number of seats to 1,500) were approved, although a building permit was still unavailable at that time. And, in 1949, the company pushed hard to advance its pre-war Scottish schemes, receiving the planning go-ahead at Townhead and Falkirk, a deferment at Bridgeton, and a thumbs down at Partick. By the time construction was possible, Odeon had lost interest in all these schemes.

In south London, the Kennington Theatre had been purchased pre-war for replacement by an Odeon designed by George Coles. Derelict at the outbreak of war, the old theatre was so badly shaken by bombs that work on demolition commenced in April 1943. In March 1949 Coles applied unsuccessfully for a building licence and in May 1950 Odeon itself sought permission to build on the cleared site. But over 3,000 people were on Southwark Council's waiting list for homes and it obtained a compulsory purchase order and built a block of thirty-two flats called Kennington Park House. In January 1951 Odeon sought £2,500 compensation from the Council for the cost of surveys and preparations to build its cinema there. Whether the money was handed over is unclear.

Some schemes definitely originated postwar. Rank made arrangements to take over, from 1 November 1946, the Picture House in Royal Avenue, Belfast, an 850-seat first-run hall, along with adjacent property on which it was proposed to build a 3,000-seat Odeon. (Another report at this time referred to a new £600,000 Rank cinema in Royal Avenue and Garfield Street in central Belfast, which would seat 5,000 and be the largest in the UK, including a ballroom and café: perhaps this involved demolishing the Picture House to enlarge the site?). The only existing large cinemas in Belfast were Gaumont's Classic (1,800 seats) and ABC's Ritz (2,200 seats). The deal for the Picture House fell through and the Royal Avenue schemes were superseded by early 1948 plans for a 3,000-seat Odeon at the corner of Castle Street and Fountain Street, designed by Harry Weedon and Partners, the practice that had handled so many pre-war Odeons. But, in the end, Rank found it easier to take over existing cinemas in order to expand in Northern Ireland.

In 1948, Odeon put forward a plan to replace the disreputable Gaisford Kentish Town, north London, a late-run hall located up a side street, with a larger cinema that took in adjacent property to gain a frontage on the main road. Here again, by the time progress was possible, Odeon lost interest or patience.

Two north London exteriors from a circuit survey in November 1949. Above, the Foresters at Bethnal Green, smartened up after repairs to wartime damage, plays Gaumont releases and advertises as "A Gaumont Theatre" while, below, the battered Gaisford Kentish Town was a candidate for total replacement. (Both courtesy of Derek Knights.)

Odeon Broadstairs, undated exterior and auditorium in 1950 (latter courtesy of Linton Culver).

Re-openings

One cinema that made an early postwar return was the Odeon (ex-Regal) Stockton. The plans for "reconstruction of roof truss" had been passed by the Plans and Town Planning Committee on 28 May 1945 but it was not until 2 July 1946 that they were advised by the borough engineer that he had certified the completed work as safe. Re-opening followed on 22 July 1946 with Florence de Jong at the organ. However, the recurrence of structural defects eventually brought about the complete reconstruction of the cinema.

Then the King's Hall at Dover resumed life in July 1947. Gutted by fire ten years previously, it had been about to re-open in 1940 when it was requisitioned by the Navy for training purposes. Acquired by Odeon in 1943, it was re-launched with the Rank production *Frieda* and a personal appearance by the film's co-star, David Farrar.

Fire severely damaged one of the smallest cinemas on the circuit, the Victoria at Dursley, in the early hours of 25 January 1947. A little surprisingly, the 300-plus seater was done up and re-opened eighteen months later as an Odeon. However, it only survived another six years before closure on economic grounds.

On Monday 10 October 1949 came the re-opening of the Bethnal Green Foresters in east London. This had closed two-and-a-half years earlier to deal with damage sustained during the very heavy wartime bombing of the immediate area. Work included a new side wall and a completely new roof, plus a bland new facade. The Foresters re-opened with a special evening stage show to reflect the building's early history as a music hall, with Vic Hammett performing on an electric organ, a personal appearance by rising Rank star Dirk Bogarde, and the week's Gaumont release main feature, *Chicago Deadline*.

The Royalty Broadstairs was on lease to an independent when closed by bomb damage in November 1940. It was re-opened by Odeon with (for the first time) the Odeon name on 3 August 1950, playing films well after Margate and Ramsgate. At this time, the circuit seemed intent on running the maximum number of cinemas possible. Like the Odeon Dursley, this small cinema (794 seats) only lasted a few more years.

Work started on repairing the Odeon Deptford in April 1951 under the supervision of its original architect, George Coles. Because of severe restrictions on how much could be spent, Coles was confined to reinstating his 1938 scheme although, in redecoration of the auditorium, sea green gave way to peach and beige colours with red and gold highlights. The wide entrance foyer received a new sales kiosk and paybox with new flooring while the faience-clad front elevation was cleaned. Petula Clark made a personal appearance and performed some popular songs on the invitation-only re-opening night of 17 December. The week's south London Odeon release programme, *Too Young To Kiss* plus *The Man With The Cloak*, was also shown and this continued for the rest of the week.

Some other small scale work was done elsewhere, as at Wembley where the rather superficial "atmospheric" interior of the Majestic received attention. Ian G. Dalgliesh recalled in *Picture House* no. 4, page 8 (Winter 1983):

> During the run of *Scott Of The Antarctic* in the spring of 1949 I found the walls covered in scaffolding and huge dust sheets, so I couldn't wait for the next week to see what had happened. To my sorrow they had removed the atmospheric decor completely. All that was left of the original decor was the splendid proscenium arch and three sets of classical columns on each of the side walls. The organ grilles were new, the right side actually fronting the chambers of the 2/6 Compton Kinestra. Naturally there was a dummy grille made to match on the other side.

Two openings

One of the cinemas being built before the War managed to open in 1950 because it had been so nearly completed. Requisitioned at the outbreak of hostilities by the authorities, the Odeon Worcester was returned to Rank in June 1948 after having been used first by the Ministry of Aircraft Production to store special alloys in transit between Birmingham and Bristol and then from 1945 to 1947 to hold surplus government goods. A side wall had been broken through to provide access to the adjacent railway station. Some work commenced in February 1949 to repair the damage. Modifications to the original Harry Weedon scheme were made by Robert Bullivant, a partner in the practice. After a licence was finally granted to proceed, the building opened on 2 January 1950 with 1,674 seats – only fourteen less than had been planned pre-war. This had an exterior in brick with two large wings relieved only by a small window and diapering. The standard Odeon sign was perched on a pediment with tall windows behind. The unusual round-fronted canopy seems to have been designed to be crossed by neon bands at intervals. Programme information was displayed in frames mounted on the canopy.

The dreariness of the Odeon Worcester's auditorium seemed to reflect postwar austerity with an absence of decorative grille-work and only the two suspended light fittings giving a hint of luxury.

No Ministry of Works licence was required on the Channel Islands and this enabled the Odeon at St. Helier, Jersey, to become the first newly designed cinema opened in Britain after World War Two. It made its bow on Whit Monday 2 June 1952 with the world premiere of Rank's new production of *The*

Repairs to the dome at the Astoria Brixton, now calling itself the Odeon Astoria, in November 1949. The café restaurant is prominently advertised while the title of the current attraction is mounted on the scaffolding. (Courtesy of Derek Knights.)

Odeon Worcester. Exterior in 1950 (CTA Archive). Patrons arriving by car could use the car park behind the Gaumont opposite. Wide posters mounted on the canopy, angled in each direction along the street, replace the use of lettering slotted into the front edge of the canopy. For the auditorium, see colour section.

Odeon Jersey, 1953. The planners stipulated the entrance had to be in a specially created side road but the Odeon sign was placed on the main road.

Importance Of Being Earnest and personal appearances by Joan Greenwood, Margaret Rutherford, Kay Kendall and Anthony Steel.

Designed by T. P. Bennett and Son (which had handled a few pre-war Odeons), the cinema was located some distance from the town centre with its entrance down a side road rather than on the corner with the main road. The side of the auditorium along the main road carried the only prominent name sign, a vertical Odeon sign, attached to a projecting flat hood and tower feature that paid homage to the 1930s circuit style. Also reminiscent of 1930s Odeons, just below roof level, was the rounded corner with a corridor enclosed by glazing at the corner (cf. Shannon Corner, Morecambe) which continued along the front elevation (cf. Redhill). The chequered pattern of the main facade recalls the faience squares of previous Odeons and the basketweave alternations of tiles. The line of tall recessed windows above the entrance and the horizontal banding at ground level were also familiar from pre-war Odeons but the decorative motif (like racked billiard balls) above the windows was a new touch, along with the use of strip neon along the edge of the canopy instead of slotting in film titles.

Some interior details of the foyers and staircases were in the spirit of the Festival of Britain, particularly the wood handrails. Designed with large-screen television in mind, the auditorium was slightly smaller than most pre-war Odeons, seating 1,359 in total with almost the same number in the stalls as in the balcony. It presented a pleasing composition of gentle curves with a stage extending forward in place of an orchestra pit and two bands of concealed lighting in the ceiling echoing the curve in the proscenium arch. The walls and ceiling were plain, relieved only by raised acoustic tiles on the side walls and ceiling, arranged for decorative effect in matching patches (rather like bits of a jigsaw puzzle), and by the pronounced patterns of openings for ventilation and the public address system. Grey (rather than black) screen masking was used and apparently caused quite a stir in industry circles.

Elsewhere in the Channel Islands, Odeon had acquired representation on Guernsey by taking over the Regal at St. Peter Port and renaming that in 1950.

Acquisitions and disposals

The Regal Marble Arch finally re-opened on 9 September 1945, still with 2,400 seats, renamed the Odeon. The main film was *A Bell For Adano*, which had premiered at the Leicester Square Theatre. The Odeon made weekly changes of films already shown in the West End until it was turned into a first-run house for the world premiere presentation of Rank's epic *Caesar And Cleopatra* from 13 December 1945, with reserved seats and

 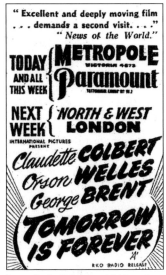

Rank's epic seems to be showing continuously in February 1946 on its West End premiere run. The Metropole Victoria and Paramount Tottenham Court Road are showing the Odeon circuit release a week ahead of the London suburbs.

Odeon Guernsey in 1950. (Courtesy of Bruce Peter.)

higher prices. The cinema, which already had a Roman motif in its interior decorations, received additional touches to dress it up for this vitally important presentation. (It was heavily fined for unauthorised external alterations.) J. Arthur Rank had been unable to curb the profligacy of producer Gabriel Pascal and the film had gone vastly overbudget to cost £1.25 million in all, a mistake that Rank's critics never forgot. He was left hoping for a *Gone With The Wind*-style hit – it did have the same female lead, Vivien Leigh.

The Observer's critic, C. A. Lejeune, seemed to praise the cinema more than the film as she referred to the interior as "newly conditioned as an Egyptian temple, with figures of gods in niches, and drop-curtain enscrolled with a map of Alexandra" (see *Picture House*, no. 9, Winter 1986, page 29, for a black-and-white photograph of this new curtain). John Fernee recalls a three-dimensional stage set, featuring the Sphinx and backed by gauze, which was flown before the film started.

As it stayed at Marble Arch until 27 July 1946, *Caesar And Cleopatra* seems to have been a reasonable success. Thereafter, the Odeon reverted to weekly changes for a short while before becoming a permanent first-run house, premiering some notable films including *Oliver Twist* in 1948 and *The Lavender Hill Mob* in 1951. In 1949, on the evening of 17 November, it was chosen to host the Royal Film Performance instead of the Odeon or Empire Leicester Square, but only because of its lift: King George VI was in bad health and used it to reach the circle lounge where the star guests were lined up to meet him. Some improvements had been carried out at this time to tidy up remaining war damage. The Royal party was treated to a live stage show, *Cinderella Meets The Stars*, which featured such names as Margaret Lockwood, Gregory Peck, Anna Neagle, Rosalind Russell, Walter Pidgeon and Michael Wilding, before viewing the feature, MGM's *The Forsyte Saga* (which had its public run some weeks later at the Empire).

There was one curious takeover in the immediate postwar period. By October 1945, Odeon Theatres had bought control of the Winter Garden Theatre in London and made an offer for the outstanding shares. Quite what Odeon had in mind is unclear but this live theatre was never used as a cinema and sold off in 1959. Possibly Rank wanted it to give stage experience to the contract artists in its "charm school" instead of the Connaught Worthing which was used for that purpose?

In December 1945, the Odeon war-time offices at Cookham and Marlow were closed and staff moved into new headquarters in Albion House in the centre of London at 59 New Oxford Street. The offices established by Oscar Deutsch at 44 Park Lane were vacated.

The Leicester Square Theatre was transferred into the Odeon group in July 1946. Large and centrally located, this became the second most desirable place to open a film among Rank's West End group, after the Odeon Leicester Square.

The number of Odeon disposals was negligible during this period. Rank had both an Odeon and Gaumont in Derby and the large Hippodrome (part of the former County chain) was relinquished in late 1950 and returned to live show use. The very small Court at East Molesey (472 seats) was sold to an independent at the end of 1951 and survived another seven years. The lease of the even smaller Headgate at Colchester (320 seats), a former County property, was not renewed but it continued in other hands for many years: Odeon retained the large Regal (also ex-County) in the town while Rank had the Hippodrome to play the Gaumont release. The St. Johns at Worcester was no longer required after the Odeon opened in 1950 and this went to a small operator.

More notable was the first sale of an original Odeon, although it had long been a problem theatre. The Odeon at Lancing, West Sussex, had seemed an odd venture when it opened in 1933. Renamed the Regal, it had been leased to two independents who couldn't make it pay, then taken back during the war. It was renamed Odeon in March 1945 but could not compete with the better located, more modern Luxor, opened in 1940. A small but significant regional circuit, Shipman and King, arranged to take over both cinemas on 21 January 1952, closing the Odeon without ever operating it to concentrate on the Luxor. S&K put the building up for sale with a restrictive covenant preventing further entertainment use, and it became industrial premises. First run in the area was at Worthing where Rank retained a large Odeon.

Overseas expansion

If J. Arthur Rank was thwarted in his attempts to build new Odeons at home, there were few restrictions overseas. He expanded his interest in Canadian Odeon to a major stake by the end of February 1946. The movie palaces of the main Canadian circuit, Famous Players, were mostly built in the 1920s and Canadian Odeon daringly set about building modern cinemas in direct competition after wartime restrictions were lifted. Rank invested over half a million pounds in the financial year 1948/49 and at least twenty Odeons were opened between April 1948 and May 1949, including city centre theatres in Victoria, Toronto and Ottawa. All carried the Odeon name in the British style of lettering and gave priority to booking J. Arthur Rank's British productions.

The largest and most spectacular of the new Odeons was the one in Toronto which styled itself "The Showplace of the Dominion" and seated 2,318 (or 2,221 – sources vary). It opened

Odeon Toronto, Canada, in 1948. "The Showplace Of The Dominion" was later known as the Carlton. The organ console was subsequently moved to a lift in the centre of the pit and was played regularly on Friday and Saturday nights until the cinema closed down *in 1984.*

on 9 September 1948 with the North American premiere of Rank's *Oliver Twist* and personal appearances by Trevor Howard and Patricia Roc.

With its rounded corner and a towering vertical name sign, its sleek foyers and the cove-lit stepped-down ceiling of the auditorium, it had clear links with the British Odeon style of the 1930s, although the vast contoured main curtain was a North American touch. This was the last cinema auditorium of its size to be built in North America and the last to have an organ specially made for it (a 3/19 Hillgreen Lane).

The architect had the somewhat appropriate surname of English. Having previously designed cinemas for Famous Players, Jay I. English visited Britain in 1945 to look at Odeons and then designed nineteen cinemas for the Canadian circuit. Only one had opened by the time of his death, from a heart attack, at age 45. He designed several lively Odeons for the Toronto suburbs but these bore little resemblance to British equivalents. The only known British involvement in Odeon Canada design came about when Leslie H. Kemp was engaged to oversee the completion of English's work. (The architect of many pre-war cinemas, Kemp had never designed a purpose-built Odeon but some of the cinemas from his practice were now part of the circuit, including the former Havana Romford.)

The 1,539-seat Odeon Ottawa completed the expansion programme and opened with *The Red Shoes*. The cinemas proved that British films could draw large audiences in North America. As there was no substantial difference in the tastes of Canadian moviegoers and those in the United States, this encouraged Rank to seek playing time on the major US circuits on purely commercial grounds. He hoped to block book British films along with American ones but the US government stepped in to outlaw the selling of films in groups rather than individually. Nevertheless, Rank was able to set up an almost complete network for the distribution of British films in the free world outside North America by 1948.

In November 1945, for example, Rank took a half interest in Greater Union, a major Australian circuit with seventy-two cinemas. Under Rank's impetus, Greater Union embarked on expansion and modernisation. At least one new cinema at Port Kembla was called Odeon and some older ones were re-named.

In January 1946, Rank acquired an interest in Irish Cinemas, run by the Elliman family, the only substantial chain in the Republic of Ireland with halls that included the huge Savoys in Dublin and Cork and the Theatre Royal in Dublin.*

* Rank soon took over full control and renamed the company Odeon (Ireland) Ltd. Louis Elliman remained as managing director with J. Arthur Rank as chairman. The sixteen properties it operated were in Dublin (Metropole, Corinthian, Phipsboro Picture House, Theatre

In March 1947, Rank acquired a non-controlling interest in the Schlesinger group in South Africa through a reciprocal arrangement which allowed the foreign outfit to acquire a holding in Rank's British enterprises. The Schlesinger chain, African Consolidated Theatres, operated or managed over four hundred cinemas and it was planned to build new ones in due course. Rank linked up with Universal to supply the chain (and other South African cinemas) with its British productions.

Rank also gained control of cinemas in Jamaica, Ceylon (now Sri Lanka) and Malaya. He opened an Odeon in Singapore in conjunction with the Cathay organisation in 1953. It was influenced by the 1930s Odeon style, featuring a tall slab tower on which the name appeared in italic across the top and upright in trademark style on a vertical sign underneath. Another cinema was built at Kota Bharu. Also in July 1947, Rank acquired a one-third holding in the recently merged Tuschinki and Royal circuits that ran seventeen cinemas in the Netherlands.

In New Zealand, Rank bought into the Kerridge circuit and soon became the principal partner in a circuit of 143 cinemas.

In other countries, Rank did not purchase circuits but set about establishing flagship cinemas to launch British films. The Tivoli Cairo was designed by British architect Leonard Allen to harmonise with adjacent buildings and built at a cost of £250,000 in association with a local company. It opened in February 1948 with a British manager and a Compton cinema organ, inaugurated by Gerald Shaw. (In January 1952 it was seriously damaged in anti-British riots and sold by Rank at a loss of £120,000.)

In Portugal, Rank went into a local partnership to erect the lavish Sao Jorge in the centre of Lisbon (use of the Odeon name was ruled out as it had been taken by a theatre). Seating 1,827 and fitted with a Compton organ, the Sao Jorge was the largest cinema on the Iberian peninsula when it opened on 24 February 1950 with Rank's *The Red Shoes*.

Rank was not able to buy cinemas in North America. "I want theatres in America," he said in 1948 (*Kine Weekly*, 17 June), "and it is the British Treasury which refused to let me spend dollars on buying these theatres." The idea of building a new single shopwindow cinema in the heart of New York was dropped in October 1945 in favour of an arrangement with United Artists by which the American company (which, of course, had a substantial interest in British Odeon) leased the Winter

Royal, Regal Rooms, Queens, De Luxe, Savoy, Broadway and Camden Picture House); Cork (Savoy); Limerick (Savoy); Dun Laoghaire (Pavilion, Picture House); Bray (Royal); and Blackrock (Regent). To these was added in April 1949, the 1,500-seat Grand at Cabra, Dublin, which was taken over while under construction.

Garden, a live theatre in New York, to showcase Rank's British films including *The Life And Death Of Colonel Blimp*, *Henry V* and *Caesar And Cleopatra*. The Winter Garden became a movie house before the end of 1945 but reverted to live shows in 1948.

The product crisis

In early 1947, Britain endured the Big Freeze, the worst weather for decades with blizzards creating a fuel crisis and snowfalls paralysing the country. There were many power cuts and cinemas were not allowed to open until 4pm in some areas. The Odeon Leicester Square was forced to drop two of the five daily screenings of its current hit, *Odd Man Out*, which was playing to capacity.

But this was just a mild prelude to the financial storm which started on 6 August 1947. J. Arthur Rank provided Odeon shareholders with a very fair and candid account of the events that brought the company to a state of crisis, its very survival at stake:

At the beginning of [August 1947] a Statutory Order was made, S.R. & O. No. 1690 of 1947, which imposed a heavy import duty on all foreign films entering this country. Although this duty remained in force for nine months, no revenue was collected under it, because producers of American and other foreign films regarded it as a confiscatory measure and withheld their films.

Not a single first feature film entered the country from the 6th August, 1947 to the 14th June, 1948, and it was between these dates that the decision was made to step up British production in our studios in order to fill the gap so unexpectedly created.

You may remember that at that time the Government was insistent that the national economy was such that only a small proportion of the dollars which had been spent in the past on films could be made available in the future.

The British Industry was thus called upon to produce films so that dollars could be saved, and entertainment could nevertheless be provided for the millions of people who go to cinematograph theatres every week. It was a duty and an opportunity; and in the circumstances in which decisions then had to be made there seemed to me only one answer.

Events may well have proved that the decision was wrong; it may be that we should have foreseen that the Government would repeal the import duty; but the decision was made and I accept full responsibility for it.

It will be appreciated that we had 559 theatres in this country for which no new product was coming forward, and had no idea how long this situation would continue. Indeed it was not until the spring of 1948 that the American Industry sent its representatives to London to hold discussions with the Government and negotiated a settlement.

Thus for eight months while no new American features entered this country, there was no sign that a solution to the international impasse could be found. This meant that if the level of British production remained the same as before this crisis our theatres would have to rely perhaps indefinitely on re-issues of old films and some of the theatres would have to close.

We therefore made plans to increase the number of films we would have in production. The effect of such plans in the production field are necessarily long-term and the consequences, whether successful or unsuccessful, cannot be fully assessed for eighteen months or two years after the decisions are made.

As you know, the settlement reached in March, 1948 between the American industry, assisted by the diplomatic resources of the United States on the one hand, and the British Government on the other, concerning which the British Film Industry was not consulted, resulted in the repeal of the import duty and the re-entry of American films into this country in June, 1948.

The terms of the settlement which placed controls on the amount of sterling which the American companies can convert into dollars imposed no restrictions on the number of American films to be imported.

As a result a large part of the increased number of British films had to be released in competition with almost two years' output of the American studios, for the best of the American films which had been withheld and [the] best of the new product came forward together. Even if all our films had been of the quality that we had hoped, this unusually strong competition would have made it difficult to achieve satisfactory results.

Unfortunately many of the films we produced were not of a quality to ensure even reasonable returns. It can now be seen that our plans to meet an unexpected and critical situation were too ambitious, that we made demands on the creative talent in the industry that were beyond its resources, and that as a result we spread our production capacity, in which I still have unshaken faith, too thinly over the films we made.

[...] Before, however, I leave this sorry account of the past there is one other factor which has made an important contribution to the losses which are reflected in the accounts.

By August 1947 we had made substantial progress in securing profitable distribution for our films in the United States, and when I returned from New York in July of that year I brought with me promises of support from our friends there that made the future look very bright. Unfortunately my hopes were short-lived. The imposition of the import duty in August changed the attitude of the American Industry overnight. Great resentment was expressed not only by the American production companies who were immediately affected, but also by exhibitors from coast to coast. This had an immediate effect on our business and instead of increasing our ability to earn dollars with our films we were unable to maintain the level of the past. It has been only during the last twelve months that we have started to make progress again. This has been real progress, and has been best evidenced by the overwhelming success of films like *Hamlet* and *The Red Shoes*.

The postwar Labour government needed to cut imports to reduce a huge balance of payments deficit – but it never intended to cut off the supply of Hollywood movies completely. Even allowing for the benefit of hindsight, there can be no doubt that the government's handling of the whole affair was utterly inept. According to Rank's biographer, Alan Wood, the blame for this should be attached to Dr. Hugh Dalton as Chancellor of the Exchequer and Sir Stafford Cripps at the Board of Trade.

In the first place, the government demanded that distributors of American films pre-pay no less than a 75 per cent duty on each film they brought into Britain, based on estimated box-office income. The American companies were prepared to freeze part of their earnings in Britain but the amount demanded was so outrageous that no negotiation was possible. Had the government asked for 25 per cent, as it had originally planned, the scheme might well have been accepted. The Americans had a stockpile of 125 unreleased films (sixty of them main features) to tide them over for a while and Labour's calculations that Hollywood would cave in to keep its most important foreign outlet proved quite mistaken, although the loss of the British market (which represented 50 per cent of foreign income) had an impact in that some expensive films were postponed and some budgets cut back.

In the second place, Rank was, as he stated, making real progress in obtaining bookings for his British pictures in major cinemas. *Great Expectations* did five weeks of excellent business in the summer of 1947 at Radio City Music Hall in New York and was the biggest draw of the week at Loew's State, Louisville, Kentucky. The Loew's chain as a whole booked *A Matter Of Life And Death* (released by Universal as *Stairway To Heaven*) and it didn't even have the incentive of the Fox, Paramount and RKO circuits to please Rank because his circuits showed their films in Britain (Loew's production company, Metro-Goldwyn-Mayer, was linked to the rival ABC circuit.)

The British government urged Rank and other producers to fill the gap in film supply. In November 1947 Rank obliged by announcing plans to make forty-seven films at a cost of £9,250,000. To finance these films, Rank proposed that Odeon Theatres should buy General Cinema Finance Corporation and bring all Rank's film interests under one roof. Odeon could guarantee the production loans from its assets. But in 1937 Oscar Deutsch had encouraged the public to invest in Odeon with the promise, expressed in capital letters in the prospectus, that THE COMPANY WILL NOT ENGAGE IN FILM PRODUCTION, EITHER BY ITSELF OR ANY SUSIDIARY COMPANY. Odeon had remained hugely profitable but the GCF deal would bring Gaumont-British under its control – the cinema circuit was worthwhile but Gaumont's record in film-making was not

encouraging: there had been a loss of £1,667,070 on film production in the year to 28 September 1946, with losses of £179,412 and £378,293 in the preceding two years.

Rank was heavily criticised in *The Financial Times* – and, it would seem, by the financial press as a whole – for endangering the income of Odeon shareholders and breaching Oscar Deutsch's promise. Alan Wood points out in his biography of J. Arthur Rank that these shareholders had been amply rewarded over the years and could have sold their shares at a considerable profit if they did not like the direction the company was taking. As shareholders in Odeon, the American distributor United Artists was among those displeased. The company's Edward C. Raftery summarised the position in a memorandum to American headquarters: "Odeon shareholders, then reaping rich dividends from exhibition, were to have their money invested in the much more risky business of production. Again, Odeon Theatres was a public company, with a great deal of public money invested in it; GCF was a private company, under no obligation to publish accounts. So Odeon shareholders would be paying Rank for the shares… in a concern of unknown financial prospects." UA further opposed the Odeon-GCF merger because it would bring the Odeon and Gaumont chains together, reducing competition and the number of opportunities for UA to gain a circuit release for its films.* It took Rank's casting vote to gain a majority vote of Odeon's directors and Odeon bought GCF at the end of December 1947.

Of course, as a cinema owner, Rank had a particular incentive to increase production – to fill the gap left in the weekly schedules by the loss of Hollywood's output. The extensive number of re-issues that Rank and ABC had been forced to book were not drawing audiences in the same numbers as new films and threatened to wreck the frequency and perhaps the very habit of cinemagoing. The shortage of Hollywood films contributed to a

* Despite its 50 per cent non-voting stake in Odeon Cinema Holdings, which controlled Odeon Theatres, United Artists had found it increasingly difficult to obtain a circuit release for its weak array of product. Odeon rightly argued it had very few pictures worth showing. In September 1947, UA talked about creating a separate circuit to show its films, spearheaded by Southan Morris's SM Super cinemas, but this was dropped when it obtained a series of dates from the Gaumont chain during the product crisis. In December 1947, the British UA company had to sell 82,000 Odeon Theatres shares to make ends meet. In May 1949 it tried to sell its half share in Odeon Cinema Holdings. Rank offered £800,000 plus more playing time for UA's releases on the Odeon and Gaumont circuits. In July 1953 United Artists finally sold its entire shareholding to the Schlesinger Organisation of South Africa, a Rank ally which then sold all the shares to the Rank Charity Trust in December 1958, leaving control of Odeon in the hands of the Trust.

dramatic drop in UK 1947 attendances of 173 million admissions – nearly ten per cent down on 1946 and the lowest total in six years.

Had it been realistic to expect that the Hollywood boycott would last long enough for Rank's rushed programme of British films to have a clear run? Hollywood became increasingly desperate to get back into British cinemas as time went by. And was it realistic to expect that such a huge increase in British film production would result in films of more acceptable quality than the reissues which had plugged the gaps? It seems that J. Arthur Rank could not resist an opportunity to have British films dominate the screens of British cinemas.

Of course, Rank could ensure that his admittedly substandard productions were booked into Odeons and Gaumonts in preference to the more appealing Hollywood films and he was helped when the Government, represented by Harold Wilson as the new President of the Board of Trade, on dropping the ad valorem tax increased the exhibitors' quota of British main features from 20 per cent to 45 per cent. This helped to ensure that the flood of British main features were shown but it did nothing to protect these offerings from the best of the unleashed Hollywood backlog.

1948 showed a partial recovery of 52 million more admissions over the preceding year, held back by the exceptionally mild spring and poor selection of films but reflecting the top American pictures shown in the last half of the year. (Thereafter, a decline set in with admissions nationally dropping by 84 million in 1949, 34 million in 1950, 30 million in 1951, 53 million in 1952 and 28 million in 1953. Perhaps the dispute did have a lasting effect.)

In mid-1948, J. Arthur Rank told the trade press (*Kine Weekly*, 17 June) that the Odeon and Gaumont circuits would be playing between 60 and 65 per cent British pictures that year. Rank also vented his anger at the increasing number of exhibitors who were not showing the full quota: "The *Kine* put out that in spite of there being more British films, 356 more theatres defaulted. That statement completely turned me round. When I find that these people deliberately reject entertainment and have a vendetta against British films, then I must take action and get the highest possible quota imposed. [...] It is no good people refusing to play 45 per cent British pictures and saying 'We can't get pictures', because I am going to see that everyone plays 45 per cent with no excuses." Rank had no time for the excuse made by many defaulters that their audiences didn't like British pictures and wouldn't pay to see them! In addition, there was widespread dissatisfaction with the terms demanded by Rank's GFD. Representing film producers, Mr. Rank promptly became one of the ten members of the Quota Relief Committee set up to deal with 2,600 applications for reduction or exemption that had been filed by independent exhibitors.[*]

The high quota also infuriated the American distributors who, in October 1948, banded together and refused to allow Rank and ABC to book attractive Hollywood films in support of poor quality British features. The preferential treatment given by the Odeon and Gaumont circuits to Universal's output (distributed by Rank) and that of 20th Century-Fox (because of its holding in Gaumont) further squeezed the playing time available for companies like RKO, Paramount, Columbia and United Artists, and so they released many important pictures to the independents, providing a temporary bonanza which must have reduced attendances at major circuit halls. According to Connery Chappell (*Kine Weekly*, 3 June 1948), "It is known that two companies which have previously used the Rank group as their main outlet have lately attempted to switch to the ABC circuit. Another company is reported to have revived its interest in that old idea about a fourth circuit."

The poor box office figures achieved by Rank's rushed slate of new films resulted in the Odeon group owing £15,589,858 by October 1948 in bank loans and overdrafts. This rose to £16,286,581 a year later.[**] The amount had to be reduced and John Davis reached the height of his powers as J. Arthur Rank stepped back to let him wield the axe. Not only managing director of Odeon but a director of numerous other Rank companies, John Davis had been described as "Rank's Number 1" in a *Daily Express* profile (12 December 1947) that noted he was now replacing Rank on the sound stages, keeping a close eye on films in production.[**]

This marked the end of Rank's close involvement with the great talents of the British film industry like David Lean and Michael Powell & Emeric Pressburger and a move towards routine commercial fare more to John Davis's liking. J. Arthur Rank told the *Kine Weekly* (17 June 1948): "We are getting production costs down. You will notice that certain producers and directors

---

[*] The Rank circuits were not above seeking relief. Booking controller Robert Hamer applied for a "certificate of exemption" on behalf of the three Odeons at Bloxwich, Dunstall and Spalding that had failed – narrowly – to meet the 25 per cent quota for British second features in the year to 30 September 1952. All three were late run halls changing programmes midweek.

[**] Because of their political differences, Rank being a capitalist and Conservative Party supporter, there was little or no sympathy in the Labour government camp for his difficulties. The problem was compounded by the fact that Entertainments Tax (originally introduced as a short-term measure in World War One), took 38 per cent of box-office receipts, a bigger share than exhibitors retained after handing distributors their percentage.

are no longer with us. I have told our creative artists that they must realise that their creative freedom must be related to the economic side. The two must be blended."

Rank still provided finance for the Ealing Studios output in exchange for distribution rights: this tie had provided such hits as *Frieda* and *The Blue Lamp* for distribution through GFD. Ealing head Michael Balcon became a director of Odeon in June 1950.

Odeon issued no dividend in 1950. Fortunately, a reduction in the main feature quota to 30 per cent in 1950 (following a small reduction to 40 per cent in 1949) relieved the need for Rank to make so many films. Davis sought to restrict budgets to £150,000 – less than half the cost of earlier big productions. Of course, the runaway cost of productions like *Caesar And Cleopatra* and the £1 million musical *London Town* remained a major embarrassment (although *C&C* had been a big success in North America). This also meant an end to the kind of expensive films like *Hamlet* and *The Red Shoes* that J. Arthur Rank had described as achieving "overwhelming success". *The Red Shoes* had ended up costing £700,000 and its director, Michael Powell, claimed in 1987: "When J. Arthur Rank and John Davis saw the film for the first time, they thought they had lost their shirts, collective and individual." Powell left Rank to work for Alexander Korda.

After Rank gave Davis full powers to apply drastic cutbacks and reduce the huge overdraft of mid-1949, it was nearly halved – to £9.5 million – in three years. This was regarded in financial circles as a great achievement. Then Rank's older brother, J. V. Rank, died in 1952 and J. Arthur became responsible for the family flour-milling interests, considerably reducing the amount of time he spent on his film empire.*

In June 1952, to further reduce debt, the Rank company sold all its 134,000 shares in Universal, representing a 12 per cent stake, for over half a million pounds. J. Arthur Rank, John Davis and Woodham Smith resigned their seats on the board. Rank's lucrative contract to distribute Universal's output through GFD was not immediately threatened – it had four-and-a-half years to run – but it meant that subsequent renewals could not be taken

* An early example of Davis's interference is described in the book *J. Arthur Rank And The British Film Industry* (pages 158-160), concerning Davis's attempts to halt production of Jill Craigie's low-budget documentary-style drama *The Way We Live*, about a Plymouth family's recovery from the war, on the grounds that it was uncommercial. Craigie had persuaded J. Arthur Rank to back the film and she successfully appealed to Rank who overruled Davis. It is alleged that Davis then arranged test bookings at the wrong time and in the wrong places so that he would have an excuse to shelve it. However, it was rescued by the critics and won a full Odeon release as second feature to the Hollywood weepie *To Each His Own* in September 1946.

for granted. And it meant that the British film industry's only major stake in Hollywood had ended. Although Universal had been making losses, the sale may have been a mistake as the studio became immensely profitable during the later 1950s and 1960s.

Booking

The Odeon circuit scored a particular triumph in the first months of peace with its booking of *The Seventh Veil*, the psychological drama starring Ann Todd and James Mason. In the *Motion Picture Herald* (12 January 1946), London correspondent Peter Burnup noted: "*Seventh Veil* was in a class by itself. Heralded by no special ballyhoo and not particularly highly regarded by its distributors [Rank's GFD] prior to the unveiling, the picture hit the public heart-strings from the outset. By long chalks, it will be the biggest grosser not only for 1945 but for many years past."

It remains questionable whether the circuit fared well when Laurence Olivier's *Henry V* went out nine months after its London West End opening. Film-maker Jill Craigie recalled (in *J. Arthur Rank And The British Film Industry*) an East End manager telling her that audiences had thrown tomatoes at the screen.

Laurence Olivier's production of *Hamlet* stayed more than five months at the Odeon Leicester Square in 1948 – the longest run ever at this cinema. By the time it went out on full Odeon circuit release, it could advertise "5 American Academy Awards including Best Picture of the Year". It played, as usual, with continuous performances but, of course, was ill-suited to be watched from the middle and advertisements gently added: "It will be appreciated if patrons take their seats prior to the commencement of each performance". Like *Henry V*, this may have had problems on its release as Brian Gauntlett recalls a scheduled second week at the Odeon Portsmouth being cancelled and a previously seen Richard Widmark film substituted at short notice. However, at the Odeon Dalston two extra separate performances at 9.45am were advertised for the Tuesday and Thursday of the week's run – perhaps the cinema had spare seats to fill from school bookings. The film was certainly pushed for maximum income, playing at Rank's surplus Guildford hall, the Plaza, for a full six days a fortnight after finishing a week at the town's Odeon.

Rank also maximised the return from its own biggest pictures by playing them on one circuit and concurrently at as many non-competing cinemas of the other circuit as possible. *Great Expectations* was primarily released on the Gaumont circuit but it also played at as many Odeons as possible. Rank's hugely expensive *London Town* did not warrant such wide exposure and was confined to the Odeon circuit but another technique, frequently applied to boost takings of major attractions, was brought into action: the second feature was eliminated so that it could be screened four times a day instead of the usual three showings.

Quite apart from *The Seventh Veil*, the success of British films in the mid- to late 1940s is astonishing. Rank's GFD releases of *Odd Man Out*, *Frieda* and *Jassy* (the last in Technicolor) were the three top draws to go out onto the Odeon circuit in 1947 after the Hollywood Technicolor musical *Blue Skies*, which started playing in late 1946. In 1948, Odeons played no less than six of the year's ten biggest attractions: among the six, Hollywood again led with *The Best Years Of Our Lives* but the GFD releases *Oliver Twist* and *It Always Rains On Sunday* (which was re-run at Gaumonts three weeks later during the product crisis) were among the other five. In 1949, Odeon had four of the top ten, led by GFD's *Scott Of The Antarctic* but closely followed by Hollywood's *The Paleface* and others. In 1950, Odeon played three of the big draws, including GFD's *The Blue Lamp* – the biggest, or second biggest, hit of the year (sources vary). But, in 1951, GFD's *White Corridors* was the only British film among Odeon's four in the top ten. In 1952, Odeon had three, including the top draw, *The Greatest Show On Earth* – but none of them British. In 1953, Odeons and Gaumonts combined to show Rank's Royal Coronation documentary, *A Queen Is Crowned*, which was the year's box-office champion by far, while Odeon also had GFD's *Malta Story* and the British-made *The Red Beret* in the top ten.

"One large family": CMA

The need to cut Odeon's overdraft enabled Rank to merge the Odeon and Gaumont circuits administratively now that Gaumont was under Odeon control. A letter dated 24 June 1948 and addressed to employees read: "A new company known as Circuits Management Association Limited (CMA) has been formed for the purpose of operating all theatres at present forming part of the Odeon and Gaumont circuits. The scheme will come into operation on Sunday, 27th June, 1948... The new arrangement permits complete co-operation between all theatres now operated by Odeon and Gaumont and will enable the house staffs to feel they are now – as never before – part of one large family." This feeling was not going to be shared by those four hundred whose jobs were eliminated.

J. Arthur Rank was chairman of CMA and John Davis managing director with the other directors being J. A. Callum (an Odeon director), L. W. Farrow (a director of Odeon and joint managing director [finance] of Gaumont-British), L. Kent (an American director of Gaumont, representing 20th Century-Fox's stake) and Mark Ostrer (the other joint m.d. of Gaumont). The formation of CMA eliminated the position held by F. Stanley Bates of co-managing director of Odeon Theatres (with

This April 1950 advertisement shows the cinemas taking an average Odeon release in the three London areas. Odeon cinemas (not all named Odeon) and surplus Gaumonts are so plentiful there is limited scope for non-Rank halls to join in. In the first week, the ABC circuit features at Hammersmith, North Kensington and Walham Green while Essoldo comes in at Chelsea and Queensbury. In the second week, Granada pops up at Leyton, Loughton and West Ham while cinemas at Grays, Stoke Newington, Stamford Hill, Tottenham and Walthamstow get a look in. (The Odeon Ilford is mistakenly listed under its old name of Savoy.) In the third week (south London), independents feature at Bexleyheath, Crofton Park, Lee Green, Orpington and Sutton while Granada appears at Dartford, Leytonstone (a week late) and Sydenham.

Below, the Capitol Cardiff, a key theatre seen in 1952.

John Davis), although he continued as a director of Odeon companies until mid-1950.

Encompassing 564 operating cinemas, plus various sites, closed cinemas and other property interests, CMA immediately established Odeon as the superior circuit: it had a 58.5 per cent interest in the new company compared to 41.5 per cent for Gaumont. No doubt this accurately reflected the value and earnings potential of the two circuits (Gaumont had approximately 250 cinemas to Odeon's 310).

The first decision made by CMA was to abolish almost all live shows.* Cine-variety had still been featured at some of Gaumont's larger halls but it was now deemed uneconomic. This decision may have contributed to the rapid departure of Gaumont booking chief Arthur Brown. The BoT had initially insisted that the two circuits had to be booked separately but it allowed their booking departments to be merged into one in October under Odeon's chief booker, Richard Hamer, instead of competing with each other. The Odeon and Gaumont circuits became indistinguishable as far as film booking arrangements were concerned. The Labour government therefore allowed Hamer to become the final arbiter (always excepting any edict from John Davis) on what would be shown on both circuits, leaving the producer and distributor of a British film with only one other port of call, ABC, to secure a national release.

A more daring left-wing government would have nationalised one of the circuits, as was often suggested, but of course it was strapped for cash to pay compensation. It did not even implement the recommendation of the Plant Report, the latest investigation it had commissioned of the film industry, that there should be competitive bidding for each new picture ("The introduction of more active competitive trading at each stage in the process of film distribution and exhibition is an essential condition for any real revival of prosperity in the industry").

In theory, the whims and tastes of Hamer and his counterpart at ABC did not constitute the final word. Under the 1948 Cinematograph Films Act, the Board of Trade could compel the three major circuits to show British productions deemed by a selection committee as having sufficient entertainment value to deserve a circuit release. The aim was to overcome discrimination by Rank or ABC against an independent producer.

Several films were submitted to this committee but in only one case did the BoT use its powers to force a circuit release.

* The use of organs had been severely reduced the previous year. In November 1946, Odeon had thirty-four organists but a year later the number had been cut down to ten. Gaumont, which had many more organs, still retained thirty-eight organists in November 1947, down from fifty-five. CMA cut back much further: only five organists were still employed by 1951 to cover the two circuits.

The film was *Chance Of A Lifetime* (1950), co-directed and co-written by Bernard Miles who also starred with Basil Radford, and released by British Lion. It is a mild comedy about a boss giving his workers the chance to run a factory their way which ended up suggesting that co-operation between both sides was the best route forward. It is certainly well made, reasonably entertaining, and now seems not at all radical or provocative – just sensible. The circuits claimed to have rejected the film for its lack of entertainment values rather than its politics. Because the film had no chance of getting its money back without a circuit release, Bernard Miles wrote to the BoT declaring that the production company faced bankruptcy if it wasn't shown. The three circuits were invited to sort out between themselves which one of them would take the film: a draw was held and Odeon had the short straw.

Chance Of A Lifetime was doomed because of the widespread publicity about its compulsory release. The London critics praised it and castigated the circuits for their poor judgement in turning it down. This did not help: probably it hindered. The public stayed away in droves, clearly determined that the government wouldn't tell them what to see and obviously suspecting the film contained heavy-handed political propaganda. Its Odeon release started with a West End opening at the Leicester Square Theatre where it took only a fifth of the amount earned by the same distributor's British thriller *State Secret*, which made its bow at a cinema of similar size, the Plaza. It stayed a second week at the BoT's insistence and then went out on general release where Rank claimed to have incurred a "substantial operating loss" after it was fully shown, down to the late run three-days halls and including fifty-eight Gaumont situations that normally tapped into the Odeon release (such as the Gaumont Leeds and Scala Ilfracombe). The outcome offered no encouragement to other aggrieved producers to follow Bernard Miles' example.

Although large numbers of cinemas not owned by Odeon regularly played the Odeon release in the absence of an Odeon theatre in their locality, several others in less clear-cut circumstances sought to join their number by applying to the Cinematograph Exhibitors' Association which ruled on bars and concurrencies. Few applications became public but one was mentioned in the trade press: in late 1952, the Danilo Stoke-on-Trent (part of the substantial SM Super circuit) was refused a concurrency with the Odeon Hanley. The Danilo was a first-rate cinema, the best in Stoke – slightly larger than the Odeon, nearly three years younger, and some distance away (many Odeons that were closer together played the Odeon release). The Danilo couldn't play the Gaumont or ABC release because these circuits had inferior halls in the town. It deserved access to a major circuit release but survived nonetheless, partly through latching onto the Fox CinemaScope bonanza described in the next chapter.

In striking contrast to the petty restrictions that were imposed on Rank is the far tougher anti-monopoly stand taken by the American government through the Paramount consent decree of 1948 which forced the five major film producer-distributors that were also major exhibitors (Paramount, 20th Century-Fox, Warner Bros., Loew's [MGM] and RKO Radio) to sell off their circuits (this was called divorcement) because these gave an unfair competitive advantage. In Britain, Rank and ABC similarly gave booking priority to their own films to gain the maximum return but, without this guarantee of playing time and the necessity as exhibitors to meet British quota obligations, they would have been less active in film production or have withdrawn from it completely. None of the American combines had had anything like the national spread and market share of Rank in Britain, although they were dominant in particular areas.*

After CMA was established, a handful of Odeon cinemas were renamed Gaumont in situations where the Odeon circuit had two cinemas in close proximity and one of them customarily played the Gaumont circuit release. The change, of course, made it much easier for picturegoers to know what they would be showing. Thus the Odeons at Eltham Hill and Kingsbury, the Heathway Dagenham, Plaza Romford, Regal Wimbledon and King's Hall Dover were among those renamed and then listed as part of the Gaumont circuit, although they were never owned by Gaumont. Similarly, when the Bethnal Green Foresters re-opened in 1949, its facade proclaimed that it had become "A Gaumont Theatre" for the same reason (there may have been a restriction on any name change). However, in the London area alone, Odeon cinemas at Sudbury, Temple Fortune and Weybridge, as well as the Playhouse Guildford, Dominion Hounslow and others, regularly played the Gaumont release without under-

* In fact, once relieved of the pressure to feed their own circuits, the five American studios produced fewer films. The smaller non-theatre owning companies – Universal-International (as Universal had become), Columbia and United Artists – expanded production to take advantage of the far better opportunities to place their product in the leading theatres and became full-fledged rivals to the old five. Individual theatres, particularly in city centres, suffered from the loss of old ties: the closures of the Roxy and Paramount in New York City were hastened when they had to compete for product instead of having automatic access to the best pictures from 20th Century-Fox and Paramount respectively. By the late 1950s, there was a general shortage of new Hollywood films that seriously affected British cinemas. (From 1986, Hollywood companies were again allowed to buy cinema chains.)

A small queue at the Odeon West Wickham in November 1948. The cinema was renamed Gaumont in 1951 to reflect the fact that it played the weekly Gaumont release. The Odeon sign covers up the original Plaza name, which was exposed after the cinema's closure in 1957 (see Gaumont British Cinemas, *page 144.) (Courtesy of Spencer Hobbs.)*

Odeon York, spring 1951. This splendid shot shows Robert Bullivant's fully realised scheme with its integral extension of shops and flats. (Compare with uncompleted view in Odeon Cinemas 1, *page 115.) (Courtesy of Carl Chesworth.)*

going a change of name. Indeed, the Playhouse continued advertising in the press as "An Odeon Theatre".

There seem to have been just two examples of Gaumonts being attached to the Odeon circuit. In Salisbury, Gaumont had two cinemas and the lesser of the two, the Picture House, was renamed Odeon as it took the Odeon release. And in Islington, north London, where the Angel and the Blue Hall/Gaumont were in close proximity, the former took the Odeon release concurrently with the local Odeon which was far enough away in Upper Street to make this practicable, although they retained their different names to avoid confusion.

As far as film bookings were concerned, a joint booking department negotiated circuit releases with the same distributors for both circuits. Whereas Paramount pictures had played almost exclusively on the Odeon circuit since August 1941 (with two insignificant exceptions), they now played either of the Rank circuits with *A Foreign Affair* in November 1948 becoming the first new main feature from the studio to have a Gaumont release in seven years.

Rather surprisingly, some MGM and Warner Bros. product filled Odeon and Gaumont screens under CMA – either there was no space at their normal home on the ABC circuit or there was genuine competition to book them. None of the films was a spectacular box-office draw but their appeal was not negligible. In 1950, the Odeon circuit played MGM's *The Duchess Of Idaho*, then in 1951 the same studio's *Crisis, Kim, Soldiers Three, You Belong To My Heart, The Law And The Lady* (with MGM B feature, *The Tall Target*), and *Too Young To Kiss* plus *The Man With The Cloak*. The MGM output then reverted solidly to the ABC circuit for several years. However, some Warner Bros. films continued to appear at Odeons after 1952 (*Come Fill The Cup, The Big Trees* plus *Inside The Walls Of Folsom Prison,* and *Room For One More*) and 1953 (*Trouble Along The Way,* and *South Sea Woman* plus *The City Is Dark*).

The BoT outlawed "cross booking", which I take to mean swopping programmes between Odeons and Gaumonts where they were in direct competition. This resulted in many a top box-office attraction playing at a smaller, inferior hall rather than the bigger and more attractive one of the other Rank circuit. Inevitably, this dented the box-office take of major attractions (although, arguably, it increased the potential take at second-run halls where these existed). Queues quickly formed outside a small cinema like the Gaumont at Balham, south London, especially for the cheaper seats, when a popular film like *Where No Vultures Fly* played, while there were often seats to spare up the hill at the larger Odeon. There was no question then of any film being held over for an extra week at a London suburban hall in response to full houses (the print was committed elsewhere and subsequent

run cinemas would have objected). Of course, if Rank's lesser halls had been deprived of their circuit's top draws, they might well have closed earlier than they did.

However, there were many instances under CMA of continuing the practice by which some major films on one circuit (usually, but not always, Rank GFD releases) would also play at as many non-competing cinemas on the other circuit as possible. Among Odeon releases, *Oliver Twist* was an early example while *XIVth Olympiad* was a Gaumont circuit release that many Odeons took. In 1953, the London-area Odeons at East Sheen, East Dulwich and Elmers End were among those that dropped a weak Odeon release in favour of the Gaumont release of Rank's hit war drama *The Cruel Sea*. And in Streatham, where the Gaumont was closed by war damage until 1955, Odeon's Astoria plucked many of the Gaumont plums.

Some Odeons and Gaumonts played new films late in their first release, mostly for three days (a strong attraction would command a full six days). Many of these cinemas were in small towns. In Trowbridge, Wiltshire, with a Gaumont and ABC's Regal as the two first-run halls, there was competition between them for top Odeon titles: the Regal rather than the Gaumont gained surefire winner *The Greatest Show On Earth* for a week's run in 1952.

In places where Odeons were thick on the ground, the inferior or less well located halls obtained the Odeon release three or more weeks later. These included the Odeons Kemp Town and Hove (both very secondary to the Odeon Brighton) and the Odeons Worcester Park and Blackfen in the London suburbs. In Birmingham, a three-tier pre-war pattern still operated: city centre played first; the Odeons at Perry Barr, Sutton Coldfield and Warley came next with concurrent full week runs; then, after a further interval, the Odeons at Blackheath and Kingstanding followed, usually with three-day runs (filling out the week with a Gaumont or other programme).

Many independent cinemas found that foreign films could draw good audiences, both subtitled and dubbed, especially if they had sensational elements. No such releases were given an Odeon circuit booking at this time but some replaced B features in more sophisticated areas, as had happened before the War. The acclaimed Italian film *Miracle In Milan* was spot booked into the Odeons Kensington, Swiss Cottage, Haverstock Hill, Putney, Richmond and Streatham in 1950. When Rank's GFD released a well-received French comedy *Plus de vacances pour le Bon Dieu* in 1951, this replaced the routine Hollywood support for GFD's British hospital drama *White Corridors* at many of the same theatres as well as Southgate.

One area where the CMA amalgamation worked adversely for Gaumont was London's West End. The two circuits' cinemas were pooled for premiere runs and there was no requirement that a Gaumont circuit release had to have its premiere run in a hall belonging to that circuit. The large Odeons at Leicester Square and Marble Arch and the Leicester Square Theatre took most of the top new releases at the expense of the three smaller first-run Gaumont halls – the Gaumont Haymarket, Marble Arch Pavilion and New Gallery (although the first two were later combined to improve their appeal). There was an excess of seats in the West End generally and in 1952 these six Rank properties lost £120,000 as a group with the Gaumont Haymarket and the New Gallery identified as the worst performers.

Six other West End CMA cinemas pre-released the three major circuits' general release programmes (including the supporting feature usually omitted from the premiere run). These programmes played for a week immediately prior to the start of their run through the London suburbs in the northwest area. The two Odeon properties – the Odeon Tottenham Court Road and Metropole Victoria – continued their practice of showcasing the Odeon release. The Dominion and New Victoria presented the Gaumont choice, and the Astoria and Tivoli took the ABC programme (ABC had no West End cinemas). Some main features denied a proper West End run (because they were too unsophisticated to appeal or were rushed into release to fill a gap) had their first showing via the pre-release week at these theatres. (The Odeon Kensington at this time was grouped with the northwest London theatres.)

The British Board of Film Censors introduced the X certificate in January 1951 to exclude under-sixteens from pictures of an adult nature. This replaced the H certificate which had only applied to horror films. Earlier, in 1949, faced with Fox's *The Snake Pit*, a serious film about mental illness, the BBFC had applied an A certificate with a special condition that under-sixteens should not be admitted (an A certificate normally allowed children to attend in the company of a parent or adult guardian).

Thanks to its controversial subject matter, *The Snake Pit* played to six weeks of huge business at the Odeon Marble Arch and then transferred to the Marble Arch Pavilion for thirteen weeks. It went out on Odeon release with many places like Southampton keeping it for a second week. It was by far the biggest attraction of 1949 at the Gaumont Sheffield, which nabbed the film in the absence of an Odeon. However, it was banned in such towns as Bath and Taunton and required "modifications" to play in Chester.

Paramount's *Detective Story*, a drama with a subplot concerning abortion, was given the X certificate in 1951. This also was circuit-released through Odeon and seems to have caused little fuss. But, clearly meaning this and *The Snake Pit* when he referred to pictures restricted to adults, J. Arthur Rank subsequently declared: "We have tried out two of these films and have found the policy seriously hurt family business." John Davis ruled in September 1952 that no more X films would be booked.[*]

The rival ABC circuit displayed no such qualms and had taken six X certificate main features from its normal suppliers by the end of 1953. As a result of Davis's edict, two important releases from Rank's regular sources, RKO Radio's *The Thing From Another World* (1952) and Paramount's *War Of The Worlds* (1953), were eagerly snapped up by the independents and proved to be the biggest off-circuit draws of their respective years. Rank and Davis may well have been correct over the longer-term consequences of excluding a family audience but they gave away two well-made films that were certain winners – still, Rank's loss was the independents' gain and they needed such lucky breaks to stay in business.

What also affected attendances was the occasional pairing of an A certificate supporting feature with a U certificate main feature which prevented children from attending by themselves. As a kid, I was infuriated that a western I really wanted to see – *High Noon* (U) – was supported by *Edward, My Son* (A), a revival of an MGM British main feature for quota purposes. Fortunately, I was able to persuade my father to take me so it could be said that an extra admission resulted (later on, I would ask some stranger to take me in – this almost always worked and I never came to any harm). I found *Edward, My Son* a stodgy bore (especially as Edward was never seen!) and it may have been that the whole programme was geared to adult audiences. (Stan Fishman, working for Rank at the time, informs me that *High Noon* was not doing particularly well until the title song became a hit record.) It was noticeable that independent cinemas with access to a circuit release frequently provided an all-U programme by changing the support.

Subsidiary income

With patronage on the decline, there was an increased emphasis on selling items like sweets and ice creams as supplies became more readily available: in the summer of 1949, the decorative fountain in the inner foyer at the Astoria Brixton was removed to make way for a new sales kiosk. A small insight into this subsidiary income is provided by a handwritten note by CMA executive Dickie Dewes that Odeon and Gaumont patrons were spending on average 3.86 pence in the four weeks to 20 May 1950 (he notes that February to May were regarded as "fair" months, with June to September as "good" months and October to January as "bad" months). Ices accounted for 2.08 pence,

[*] This also avoided the minor problem of obtaining licensing permission for under-sixteens to work in the projection room or auditorium while X films were playing. This was usually allowed provided parents gave written permission.

Odeon Leeds, early 1949. Opened in 1932 as the Paramount, the cinema had a dignified frontage to suit its sensitive location in the Headrow. The canopy is the original Paramount one modified to take the Odeon name. Note also the tightly spaced Odeon sign at roof level and the publicising of organist Con Docherty on the canopy. In later years, a tall readograph covered the corner section with the main name sign mounted just above it, below the parapet. (Courtesy of Carl Chesworth.)

The Odeon Newcastle has the adapted vertical and canopy from its Paramount days in summer 1951. Note the restaurant entrance at right. Whatever was on the left has been airbrushed out. (CTA Archive.)

followed by cigarettes (0.76 pence), confectionery (0.54 pence), nuts (0.28 pence) and drinks (0.17 pence). A letter to all managers dated 17 December 1953 referred to a general decrease in ice cream sales and a more than corresponding increase in confectionery and cigarette sales but pointed out that the overall rise in sales volume was not satisfactory because ice creams were a high profit line and cigarettes were the lowest. Nuts were the second highest profit earner, followed by drinks and confectionery.

In view of the increasing significance of such sales, which were later said to provide all the profits at many cinemas, it would be nice to follow this area of activity through but an absence of data makes it impossible.

Lifting the gloom

To save power, even the use of electricity to illuminate name signs and light up exteriors was forbidden until one glorious Saturday evening – 2 April 1949. People turned out in their thousands at dusk to watch the lights come on as many cinemas made a big event out of it. (There were still weekday restrictions until 2 October 1949.)

The rival ABC circuit scored best with many of its new three-colour triangular signs installed and ready for the occasion. A new display for the Odeon Leicester Square was conspicuous among the world-renowned wall of advertising at Piccadilly Circus which drew the biggest crowds of all on that Saturday evening. The Odeon name appeared in 6ft.-high letters picked out by two rows of lamps on a dimmer to vary the intensity of the light (neon outline was to be added later) while, below, a poster for the current attraction was floodlit by fluorescent tubes and a giant animated arrow pointed in the direction of the cinema itself. Its frontage was ablaze with light but it was not yet able to illuminate the name of the current feature as the nearby Warner did. The Leicester Square Theatre featured an animated neon sign of the GFD symbol which outlined the man and created an impression of the gong-stick being raised and then the gong being struck (the sound conveyed by enlarging rings of neon).

The Odeon Brighton then (or soon after) featured one of the first "lightbox" canopies with lettering mounted on the front and ends to be silhouetted at night from the internal illumination. But there was no return to the pre-war neon outlining of Odeon frontages.

More excitement came the following year when Rank kept Odeons and Gaumonts open as late as 2am for news of the General Election results after polling had finished on 23 February 1950. In some places, applications for a special license were refused but elsewhere cinemas extended the film programme to end at midnight, and then offered tea and coffee along with

Above: J. Arthur Rank with Charles Chaplin, Mrs. Rank and Oona Chaplin at the world premiere of Limelight *in October 1952 at the Odeon Leicester Square. (CTA Archive.)*

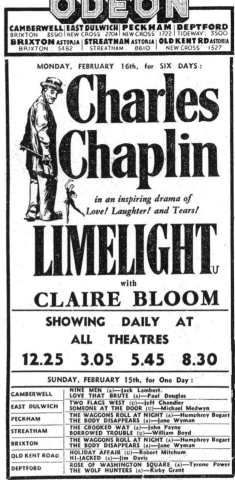

Limelight on general release in northwest London in February 1953 and south London group advertising.

such diversions as community singing, local talent shows and organ interludes until the results were announced. The victorious candidates sometimes came by to make personal appearances (the Labour government just scraped home to victory). The idea of making an event out of the General Election did not interest the ABC chain.

Television in cinemas

Television in cinemas had been tried out just before World War Two at the Odeon Leicester Square and elsewhere (see *Odeon Cinemas 1*, pages 218-9). Development continued in the late 1940s, with the Odeon Penge being used for tests. When between five and six million people sat down and watched the Cup Final at home on television in April 1950, attendances were seriously reduced at cinemas in the London and the Midlands area serviced by the BBC. Rank's subsidiary company, Cinema Television, thought it had the answer: show major sporting events live in cinemas to save people buying television sets and give them a community experience akin to being in the crowd at the match itself. As a demonstration, this very same football match was shown live at the Odeon Penge to Members of Parlament, the press, delegates to an international radio conference and film executives. The American trade paper *Variety* commented (10 May 1950):

> The Wembley Stadium, where the Cup Final was played, was enveloped in mist throughout the game. There had been heavy rainfall and condi-tions were anything but favourable for achieving first-class reproduction. The TV picture filled a screen 20 by 15 feet, with an amazing degree of light. Although using the BBC 405 line system, there was no evidence of a coarse grain and definition compared not unfavourably with rush newsreel jobs. The most interesting factor... was that, after the first two or three minutes, the invited audience completely forgot they were witnessing a new technical advance, but became thoroughly immersed in the game.

The men at the top

John Davis had his admirers. In 1971, retired executive R. H. "Dickie" Dewes offered these recollections of his former boss:

> One of the most noticeable characteristics of John Davis was his power of concentration. Successful men normally have this trait, but he possessed it to a quite abnormal degree. If he was leaving for a business tour covering almost the entire world he would work normally, and with his usual close attention to detail, until the exact moment when his car was timed to leave for the airport.

And, referring to the time in 1949 when the Rank empire was in greatest danger of collapse, Dewes recalled:

Critics were saying that the Rank Organisation could never carry on, and the 'knockers' of this world gathered together like vultures from afar. People on the inside knew how grim the situation actually was.

A few months before, CMA had been formed and the work of organising certain aspects of that amalgamation of exhibiting interests was still taking place. There came a morning when all the papers seemed to have us in their headlines prophesying doom. Outside, all the wolves appeared to be giving tongue together.

I attended two meetings at South Street that day. One was in connection with the group medical service arrangements and the other was concerned with the welfare scheme. John Davis presided at both. He handled the two detailed questions with thoroughness and complete sympathy. He never indicated by as much as the movement of an eyelid...that the future of us all was, as everyone knew only too well, in the balance. There was something bizarre – as there was something very grand – about that utter concentration, that complete detachment. It was like a man grilling a steak while riding in a runaway toboggan. The admiration which I felt for John Davis that morning will remain with me always.

And Mrs. Rowan, of Keyworth, Nottinghamshire, won a £5 note for this "Prize Letter" in her local paper dated 10 July 1983:

> In 1946 I got a job as a cinema usherette at our local Odeon in Stourbridge. There were eleven more ushers, all of whom had worked there for some years. I had worked there a fortnight when a patron came to the circle without an entry ticket, saying he was a friend of the manager. I politely told him I could not admit him without a ticket and advised him to get a complimentary ticket from the pay box. We argued and argued, with him saying he was a friend of the manager, and me standing my ground refusing him entrance without a ticket.
>
> The queue of patrons got bigger and bigger as this fellow and I became angrier and angrier. Then I really lost my temper, saying to him: "I don't care if you're the King, you're not coming in without a ticket." He asked me why. I told him: "If the Customs and Excise people caught any patron being admitted without a ticket (it was an offence in those days), you would, along with the manager and myself, be prosecuted. Eventually he went off, apparently in a huff, and a few minutes later I was called to the manager's office. "Oh, crumbs," I thought, "I've only been here a couple of weeks and I've got the sack." When I arrived at the office this fellow was also there. The manager asked me if I knew who he was. Imagine my surprise when the manager smiled and said, "Miss Hill, let me introduce you to your employer and mine, Mr. J. Arthur Rank."
>
> Instead of being sacked I was promoted to cashier by J. Arthur Rank. A few months later I was promoted again to secretary. I met him twice more afterwards and his greeting to me was: "No, I'm not the King yet."

THE WIDE SCREEN ERA (1953-1959)

John Davis continued to put Odeon back onto an even keel, reducing the overdraft to £4 million by 1954. Film production carried on with Davis personally approving each project and taking a close interest in scripting, casting, editing, publicity and release. The increase in earnings through Rank's exhibition and distribution interests abroad resulted in the company's pictures earning more than half their income outside the UK. However, Davis set about diversifying into other areas to relieve the dependence on film production, distribution and exhibition.

At the annual general meeting on 7 October 1955, a resolution was passed by which Odeon Theatres Ltd. was renamed The Rank Organisation Ltd. to reflect the fact that its interests by then extended far beyond running the cinema chain. The new company adopted as its logo "the man with the gong". This had been the trademark of General Film Distributors since it was formed in 1935. (GFD itself had recently undergone a change of name to J. Arthur Rank Film Distributors.)

More television in cinemas

In June 1952, Cinema Television's Cintel equipment was installed at the Odeon Leicester Square for a week to relay to audiences by closed circuit a fashion parade taking place in the circle lounge.

The first major public test came on 2 June 1953 when BBC Television's all day black-and-white coverage of the Coronation was shown live in several Rank cinemas including the Odeons Leicester Square and Leeds, the Marble Arch Pavilion, and the Gaumonts at Doncaster and Manchester. Tickets for the show at the Pavilion (with the chance to watch from the roof the actual Coronation procession pass by) were offered in a competition at Odeons and Gaumonts which started two months before, during the mid-programme sales interval, when audiences had to identify the stars who were heard talking about films to be shown later in the year.

Although the Coronation telecast caused a surge in the purchase of home television sets, J. Arthur Rank informed shareholders in 1954: "A most encouraging factor has been the continued rebound in our theatre business in certain of the larger television-saturated areas, where the novelty of television has fallen off and the period of instalment payments for the television sets has been completed." (Note the implication that it was the cost of paying for a television set that prevented people buying cinema tickets, not that they might prefer to watch television instead.)

On the afternoon of Wednesday 1 December 1954, large screen television was used experimentally to relay an England-versus-Germany match from Wembley to eight cinemas at the same time as it was watched by home viewers. With the exception of the Marble Arch Pavilion, the same Rank theatres that had shown the Coronation took part. The Odeon Leicester Square was sold out and, for the first time, ticket touts were observed outside the cinema. Some 13,000 people in all paid to see the match at the various cinemas with the provincial bookings estimated about 75 per cent full, way above normal matinee levels.

This seems to have been the last large screen televising of BBC programmes in cinemas. It appears that terms could not be agreed with the BBC. Future presentations would be exclusive events by closed circuit.

3-D

In 1953, the Odeon Marble Arch hosted the highly successful premiere run of the African adventure film *Bwana Devil* which launched a relatively brief vogue for three-dimensional films. Showing them was an expensive undertaking requiring the use of two projectors simultaneously (showing 5,000ft. reels), special silver-surfaced screens, and the sale or loan of viewing glasses. As a result, early 3-D films – including the most successful release of the entire cycle, Warner Bros.' *House Of Wax* – had a restricted release at the limited number of cinemas fitted out to show them. Various, mainly off-circuit Odeon and Gaumont cinemas showed 3-D films and one of those to benefit from *House Of Wax* was the Ritz Southend, the large and hard-to-fill surplus Odeon hall in the town. The ABC circuit later gave a full circuit release to several 3-D productions (showing them "flat" at some halls unsuitable for the process) but neither

Inferno *played only at the Odeon Marble Arch in 3-D.*

of the Rank circuits was equipped for the process. 20th Century-Fox used the 3-D installation at the Odeon Marble Arch to open its accomplished desert thriller *Inferno* but then decided to release it "flat" on the Odeon circuit rather than be limited to the 120 cinemas able to show it in depth. When Paramount gained an Odeon circuit showing for its adventure drama *Sangaree* in the flat version, the picture had already played in 3-D at the independent Eros Croydon and the local Odeon substituted an old Danny Kaye film.

Later important 3-D films given circuit releases, like RKO's thriller *Second Chance*, were seen only in the flat version, although tell-tale indications remained through sequences that were designed to exploit the illusion of depth, mainly by chucking objects towards the audience. Universal provided Rank's GFD with some 3-D films, including the popular A-certificate *It Came From Outer Space*, but this too had a restricted release.

Wide screen

The first announcement of a wide screen installation was made by the Empire Leicester Square, MGM's West End flagship. However, Rank quickly and surreptitiously got cracking with the result that the first wide screen to be seen by the British public was at the Odeon Leicester Square, where it was unveiled without prior announcement for the premiere on 14 May 1953 and subsequent run of the feature film *Tonight We Sing*. The newsreel and supporting programme were shown on the regular 1.33:1 screen which was then flown to dramatically reveal a new wide screen of 1.66:1 aspect ratio with its own frame in place of masking, bathed in pale blue light. The Odeon had closed for the whole day before the premiere to install the new screen. Whereas the newsreel image had occupied 390 sq.ft., the feature took up 1,200 sq. ft. The only patrons not to be impressed were those in the rear stalls where the front of the balcony cut off the top of the image. The Empire inaugurated its own wide screen nine days later and others soon followed. Many of the films that were proudly shown in "panoramic wide screen" had never been photographed with that in mind and therefore suffered badly from being cut off at top and bottom.

Rank fitted wide screens to the Odeon Marble Arch and the Leicester Square Theatre and elsewhere: the Odeon Burnley gained a new concave screen 34ft. wide by 21ft. 6ins. high in August 1954 (compared to an old screen size of 22ft. by 17ft.). But CinemaScope had taken such a hold in the United States that even wider screens now loomed as the way forward.

CinemaScope

20th Century-Fox launched CinemaScope and full stereophonic

sound both as a more practical and affordable alternative to Cinerama, which had been successful launched in New York in 30 September 1952 (but had not yet reached London), and as a means of distancing cinema from television which aped the established screen ratio. (In North America, movie theatre attendances had already been savaged by television.) The record-breaking box-office figures when the first CinemaScope release, the biblical epic *The Robe*, opened at the vast Roxy in New York City dispelled any doubts over its appeal and its potential value to the film industry.

The Fox company owned no cinemas in Britain and went to Rank, as its long-established outlet, for a large, centrally placed London auditorium in which to demonstrate CinemaScope to exhibitors. The Odeon Tottenham Court Road was chosen, with a trade audience being wildly impressed by a private pre-view of the process on 30 June 1953 on a 53ft. by 21ft. screen with a 3ft.-deep curve in the centre. In July, Fox put Cinema-Scope into the private Century Theatre at its Soho Square head-quarters.

At first, it seemed like business as usual as far as the release of CinemaScope films was concerned. *The Robe* was lined up for a full Odeon circuit release and the second CinemaScope feature, *How To Marry A Millionaire* (actually filmed before *The Robe*), was assigned to Gaumonts.

The Odeon Leicester Square was the obvious location for the European premiere presentation of *The Robe* and CinemaScope with full stereophonic sound. Fox wanted an October 1953 opening but was forced to wait out the run of Walt Disney's *Rob Roy The Highland Rogue* following its premiere as that year's Royal Film Performance. *The Robe* finally opened on Thursday 19 November and stayed for three months with five shows daily (except Sundays). The imported "Miracle Mirror" screen measured 52ft. by 27ft. and masked down to 50ft. by 20ft. for the 'scope ratio of 2.55:1. The B-TH Supa projectors were fitted with 'scope lenses and B-TH 4-track magnetic sound reproducing heads.

Even before *The Robe*'s opening, Rank had decided to install CinemaScope and stereophonic sound for the religious drama to be shown on extended runs, commencing 11 January 1954, at the key provincial Odeons at Birmingham, Glasgow, Leeds, Liverpool, Manchester and Newcastle (all former Paramount theatres, demonstrating the importance of that particular group) plus the Capitol Cardiff (larger than the town's Odeon) and the Odeon Brighton. At this time, all the screens had to be flown in from America and typical sizes were 51ft.9ins. by 21ft. at Liverpool and 52ft. by 20ft.6ins. at Newcastle. Rank insisted on showing the film at normal prices (whereas higher prices had been charged in America). *The Robe* drew 50,000 people in its

The first CinemaScope release, The Robe, *widens its run at the Odeon Leicester Square to play the key Odeon theatres including the Capitol Cardiff plus four independents where there are no Odeons.*

first week at the Odeon Glasgow while admissions totalled 190,615 over five weeks at the Odeon Newcastle.*

How To Marry A Millionaire opened in the West End at the Odeon Marble Arch, followed by twelve key Gaumont cinemas plus the Odeon Cardiff (which was more suitable for 'Scope than Gaumont's Empire, a former live theatre).

Once CinemaScope and stereophonic sound had confirmed their appeal to British picturegoers at the Odeon Leicester Square, Rank extended its commitment to installations at sixty Odeons and Gaumonts. Smaller exhibitors seized the opportunity to climb on board the bandwagon – especially in towns like Edinburgh, Hull, Sheffield and Swansea where they had major city centre halls that could play the Odeon release in the absence of an Odeon theatre.

However, in early February 1954, Rank announced that there would be no further installations of stereophonic sound. This cost even more than CinemaScope itself – £2,500 to £3,000 per cinema, largely because of the dozen or more speakers spread around the auditorium walls – but J. Arthur Rank (in a report to shareholders) gave a different explanation: "...from our experience the public do not take kindly to stereophonic sound in its present form". (Was this an echo of the early resistance by some patrons to the intrusive nature of talkies? I was only a kid but I thought stereophonic sound was exhilarating!) 20th Century-Fox retorted that no other country had quibbled about installing stereophonic sound and Rank did not remove the stereophonic sound systems that were already in place.

The Robe opened in further Odeons with full 'Scope and stereo on 4 March at Blackpool and Bournemouth, on 7 March at Southampton and Southend, and on 8 March at Aberdeen, Bolton, Bradford, Bristol, Hanley, Leicester, Nottingham, Plymouth, Rotherham and Wolverhampton.

Even before Rank had called a halt on stereo, there was one upset to the normal circuit release pattern when Essoldo installed CinemaScope and stereophonic sound at its 1,926-seat Troxy Portsmouth and showed both *The Robe* and *How To Marry A Millionaire* despite the presence of large Odeon and Gaumont halls in the town. Essoldo's other initial commitment, to show both films at the Essoldo Stockport, was uncontentious as Rank had no cinemas there.

It wasn't just the stereophonic sound issue that upset Fox. Because of the significant shareholding the company held in Gaumont, it continued to press for full installations throughout

---

* There was some trade criticism that long runs of *The Robe* would destroy business for subsequent-run houses and Fox publicised the fact that, in Newcastle, when the picture moved into the independently-owned, 800-seat Brighton cinema, normally a three-day house, its two-week run had to be extended to three.

that circuit but was not so insistent over Odeon. The real stumbling block – the only one, according to Fox chief Murray Silverstone in October 1954 – was Rank's refusal to agree to extended runs throughout its two circuits. A six- or seven-day run was the maximum in suburban and smaller town Odeons and Gaumonts although a second and even a third week was arranged in major city centres and seaside locations when business warranted. Fox maintained that everywhere else in the world was flexible but Rank believed that to hold on to the regular patronage at local cinemas, it was essential to change programmes every week.

Rank must have calculated that Fox would cave in, but it misjudged the company's head, the Greek-born Spyros Skouras (who pronounced his company's pride and joy as "Cinemascop", overlooking the final 'e'). Skouras approached ABC, which also refused Fox's terms, and then set up an entirely new release pattern for the company's output. Fox leased the Carlton Haymarket from Paramount and also (for a year) the Odeon Marble Arch to open its films in London's West End, and linked up with smaller circuits and independents – particularly the Granada and Essoldo circuits – that were amenable to showing its 'Scope films in full stereo with extended runs where justified. This move resulted in neither *The Robe* nor *How To Marry A Millionaire* being shown in any further Rank cinemas in Britain at this time and Rank capping its stereo installations at seventy sites out of 550.

Ironically, Rank's stand against stereophonic sound proved effective when the other Hollywood studios failed to insist upon it for their productions in CinemaScope. Even Fox made its releases available in mono sound as well as stereo but it now had committed itself to its grouping of independent cinemas and ruled out any reconciliation with Rank.*

While the new Fox or fourth circuit outlets enjoyed the bonanza of quality first-run Fox films, the financial implications for both Fox and Rank were severe. Fox's twenty-eight releases in 1954 (after *How To Marry A Millionaire*) included fourteen

---

* There is no doubt that the introduction of CinemaScope was greatly beneficial while its novelty appeal lasted. Although UK cinema admissions still declined, if only very slightly in 1954 (8.7 million down), the Granada circuit increased its admissions dramatically that year and in the following year still stayed comfortably ahead of 1953 (see figures in *The Granada Theatres*, page 159). Audiences were clearly flocking to the halls showing Fox's CinemaScope pictures at the expense of competing Rank cinemas. A further factor in the appeal of CinemaScope was that all its productions were in colour until 1957. However, there was considerable relief among exhibitors during 1954 when films like *From Here To Eternity* and *On The Waterfront*, as well as the British productions *The Belles Of St. Trinian's* and *The Kidnappers*, drew huge audiences even though they lacked both colour and CinemaScope.

CinemaScope attractions that could not achieve anywhere near their full box-office potential because of the patchy spread and lower capacity of its new circuit compared to Odeon and Gaumont, although extended runs made up some of the difference. Fox's Movietone newsreel organisation produced a full-length CinemaScope documentary of the Queen's post-Coronation tour of the Commonwealth, *Flight Of The White Heron*, which proved to be a huge box-office draw in June 1954. Fox opened it in the West End of London at the Carlton and the leased Odeon Marble Arch and at thirty-nine cinemas elsewhere but its total release was limited to about seventy-five independent cinemas whereas a full Odeon or Gaumont circuit release would have trebled this number in Rank bookings alone. Rank high-handedly refused to book the film at any of its seventy halls with 'Scope and stereo because it had been given to the opposition in many places and because bookings would have interrupted regular circuit programmes.

Although it was estimated that 500 cinemas would be equipped with 'Scope and stereo by the end of 1954 and therefore eligible to show Fox's films, a major draw would normally gain at least 2,000 bookings.

Rank's seventy installations of CinemaScope and stereophonic sound sat idle for around a year. Then, in late 1954, the Odeon Leicester Square played two historical adventures, *The Black Shield Of Falworth* and *Sign Of The Pagan*, in 'Scope and stereo, both made by Universal and automatically distributed by Rank through General Film Distributors. (Despite J. Arthur Rank's earlier declaration that people didn't like it, "full stereophonic sound" was prominently advertised at the Odeon Leicester Square.) The first of these pictures was generally released through Gaumonts and it wasn't until the second went out to Odeons that the circuit's other fully equipped theatres boomed again with stereo sound and motored their dusty masking out to 'Scope proportions.

Rank needed to install CinemaScope in all its halls to show the stream of films in the process that were coming from major suppliers like Columbia and United Artists as well as from Universal. (CinemaScope with optical, non-stereo sound had a 2.35:1 ratio. In the short term, some non-'Scope versions were available but obviously cinemagoers regarded them as inferior.) Some Hollywood studios preferred other systems that were compatible with a CinemaScope-to-wide-screen installation: RKO offered SuperScope (later called RKOScope), first demonstrated at the Odeon Tottenham Court Road at a 1.5:1 aspect ratio but later presented at 2:1. Paramount came up with Vista-Vision, which allowed the exhibitor to choose any ratio up to 2:1 and did not require the anamorphic lenses of CinemaScope which converted squeezed images on the film into a wide picture.

VistaVision films were photographed in horizontal double-frame and reduced to standard vertical 35mm, producing a much sharper image. However, the Odeon Leicester Square (along with Paramount's West End showcase, the Plaza) was specially equipped to show VistaVision prints in double frame at a speed of 180ft. per minute (requiring larger spools). In an obviously calculated snub to Fox, VistaVision was the wide screen system that Rank adopted for its own productions.★

When Universal's historical epic *Sign Of The Pagan* started its London area general release in January 1955, it became the first CinemaScope presentation at most local Odeons. A few resorted to the standard wide screen version. In the London area these were the Camden Town Plaza, Clapton Kenning Hall, Ealing Walpole and Islington Angel – probably because these older and mostly smaller cinemas created installation problems and had less priority. Many of the same cinemas could not play *Underwater!* in the SuperScope version but, by the time the next CinemaScope film, Columbia's *The Long Gray Line*, came along in April 1955, every London Odeon seems to have been fitted out.★★

Installation difficulties were caused by narrow proscenium openings (particularly found in pre-World War One halls) and the only way to fit CinemaScope within them was to reduce the horizontal masking so that films in the process had a much smaller picture area than those in standard wide screen, reversing the more spectacular impression they were supposed to make. This gave rise to the "letterbox" notion of CinemaScope and affected such a key site as the Odeon Birmingham, where the picture was masked down so far that, in the words of ex-projectionist J. A. Newey, "it spoilt the illusion". The Odeon Torquay was another, so pinched for width that the 'scope picture masked down top and bottom.

Rank more often got around the problem by the more expensive solution of placing a CinemaScope screen on a frame in front of the proscenium arch where the auditorium was wider. Curtains were then added, often completely or almost completely covering the end wall and creating a very plain effect. This happened at the Odeon Kensington (either in 1954 or in the 1960 refurbishment.)

★ Rank's initial production in VistaVision, the Diana Dors comedy *Value For Money* (with mono sound), began shooting in December and Rank went on to use the process extensively until switching to CinemaScope, initially for two spectacular 1959 releases aimed at the international market, *Ferry To Hong Kong* and *North West Frontier*.

★★ According to the *Kine Weekly*, 10 February 1955, Rank had by then equipped 450 halls with 'Scope, leaving another 92 to follow. Rank even installed CinemaScope at four places which used rear projection, despite the short throw. These included the Alhambra Barnsley, a former live theatre with a deep stage.

The Odeon Southampton. Exterior in 1949 with doctored background and foreground. The café is behind the tall windows. It had too narrow a pros arch to accommodate a larger CinemaScope image and eventually a new screen was placed further forward. (Exterior courtesy of Bruce Peter.)

From my own experience, CinemaScope was a major disappointment at Odeon's Astoria Streatham. This huge and important south London hall had virtually a square proscenium opening and a vast screen that filled the space. The CinemaScope picture seemed about half the size and really did give a letterbox impression. At a full house for the smash hit *Bridge On The River Kwai*, it was a particular anti-climax when the supporting programme, including the newsreel and trailers, had been shown on the regular screen and then the curtains parted to start the main feature on that much reduced area – but, of course, the audience quickly became absorbed by the film and forgot about it. The difference in screen size became even more evident when CinemaScope trailers were shown. They were only available in that format and the masking would be adjusted in full view for the short time it took to show one of these. The other Streatham cinemas – the Gaumont and ABC's Regal – had large Cinema-Scope screens with side-expanding masking which only served to emphasise the Astoria's shortcomings.

One inherent problem with CinemaScope which was never mentioned was the effect on sightlines from the stalls. Even though the stalls would have a sloping floor, it often became impossible to see the full width of the screen past the heads of people in front (whereas the old 1.33:1 image – which has become known as the "Academy ratio" – could usually be seen in full, even if it sometimes required leaning to one side). Of course, there was no problem from balcony seats as these had stepped seating.

The front rows of seats were also uncomfortably close to the CinemaScope screen (a cartoon in the fan magazine *Picturegoer* showed a couple busily reporting to each other what was happening at their end of the screen). Many rows were removed at this time, although this also happened in later years when declining attendances meant that there was little likelihood of these seats being needed.

A great advantage of the Odeon circuit was that most of its 1930s purpose-built properties had wide proscenium openings into which CinemaScope fitted quite comfortably. Why was this? It is unlikely that Hollywood's brief flirtation with wide screen in 1929-1930 had left cinemas contemplating the possibility of its return (although the Fox Grandeur process of that time formed the basis of CinemaScope). Odeons (and other 1930s cinemas) tended to be built on cheaper land at the edge of city centres on spacious sites. They could be built to ideal proportions (wide rather than long and narrow) with excess space used for parking. They would stay wide at the screen end to increase the seating capacity, although with some reduction via the splay walls.

Some 1930s cinemas did, as a matter of neat design, bring in the splay walls to provide a narrow proscenium arch that neatly enclosed the screen shape of the time, but at the Odeon Stafford it was the only way to fit the auditorium onto a particularly difficult site. Ray Faulkner, the chief operator from 1949, recalls "coffin-shaped" CinemaScope with drop masking being installed to show *Sign Of The Pagan* from 13 January 1955. This resulted in the loss of 170 seats that were too close to the screen as well as the removal of small light fittings on the side wall that were a distraction, being too close to the new screen. Another purpose-built Odeon at Worcester Park had (in the memory of a local patron) an "appalling" CinemaScope screen, while the Odeon Harlesden is also recalled as having reduced screen size.

By 1956, CinemaScope had lost its novelty impact and received a much reduced mention in advertising. Although it was taken for granted, the dispute between Fox and Rank remained.

New and re-opened Odeons

Until 1954, cinemas were restricted by the Ministry of Works to £1,000 of building works within a year at a time when factories and workshops were allowed to spend up to £25,000.

Rank made renewed appeals to be allowed to rebuild the bomb-damaged Odeon Canning Town, to have the unfinished Odeon Westbourne Grove derequisitioned and the similarly incomplete Odeon Highgate released from storage use by the Ministry of Works.

At Canning Town, West Ham's town planning committee passed revised plans for the "reinstatement" of the Odeon in March 1955 but the licence, which had been continually re-newed at the annual cost of £1, was allowed to lapse after expiring on 26 September 1956, showing that Rank had by then changed its mind or given up. In December 1954, Rank still spoke of rebuilding the Regal Margate, but this idea was also dropped and the site sold.

War-time damage caught up with the Odeon Exeter when it was suddenly forced to close in March 1954 (although the restaurant remained open, at least temporarily). The Gaumont went over to many split weeks to play the Odeon releases as well, including the programme that was interrupted by the Odeon's emergency closure. Most work needed to be done on the roof and much of the auditorium ceiling was replaced. However, the quaint lines of medieval figures (which seem to have been removed as a war-time precaution) climbing each of the side walls were reinstated and the cinema re-opened with a new wide screen. Externally, a new canopy replaced the intricate original and the four vertical bands of faience were capped and no longer curved back at the top.

Later in the year, Rank re-opened two Odeons that had been closed since the war: Sidcup on Monday 2 August and Haver-stock Hill on Monday 13 December.

Sign Of The Pagan at the Odeon Leicester Square before its general circuit release.

The Odeon Kensington with new curtains and pelmet in front of the CinemaScope screen. (CTA Archive.)

The Odeon Exeter, following repairs in 1954. Compared with the illustration on page 126 of Odeon Cinemas 1, *the ceiling is much plainer, the proscenium arch has been rebuilt and the bands on the front side walls no longer wrap around the sides of the opening. The front row of stalls seats has been removed at each side. The medieval figures have been picked out in several colours whereas before they were all one shade.*

The Odeon Sidcup returned on the Bank Holiday afternoon with a packed house for *Father Brown*, the week's circuit release in south London. The exterior at Sidcup appeared almost the same as before but the walls and ceiling of the auditorium were completely rebuilt in a very bland fashion, allowing a lively pattern on the tabs to take most of the attention. Modern chandeliers were suspended from a large ceiling recess and the splay walls became completely plain. A new wide screen was installed.

The Odeon Haverstock Hill returned with more pomp and ceremony, a special screening of the new Rank comedy *Mad About Men* being accompanied by personal appearances from Rank stars Donald Sinden, Diana Dors and Jack Warner with Rank supremo John Davis in attendance. The wide auditorium had been modified but the bands of sequenced cove lighting that so dramatically enclosed the screen had been largely reinstated.

In 1955, two pre-war schemes were finally realised. Planned in 1937 by the Andrew Mather practice, the Odeon Westbourne Grove, west London, opened on 29 August 1955, completed to a revised scheme by Mather's successor, Leonard Allen. The basic structure was complete and so retained the tower and the rounded corner to the shops extension but Allen eliminated all the faience cladding and the six fins that would have accompanied the five tall windows. The result was tepid. The interior was lavishly outfitted: the foyer had an island paybox and mosaic floor while the auditorium had a proscenium arch designed for Cinema-Scope with a wooden orchestra barrier and dado, and simple splay wall decoration. Capacity was reduced from the pre-war scheme but remained substantial with 1,726 seats.

At Highgate, in north London, the original architects, T. P. Bennett & Son, revised their scheme with seating reduced by 240 and the stage end redesigned to take a 44ft.-wide screen. Work started in March 1955 and the Odeon opened on 19 December. Externally, this had clear echoes of pre-war Odeons with its rounded corner and central tiled area but the tower feature was half-hearted, more of a stub than a statement. The narrow, canopied open-air walkway at the top of the facade extends almost all the way along the side of the building and recalls that of the Odeon Jersey by the same architects.

The auditorium aimed at complete blandness with no splay wall decoration at all. The ceiling descended towards the screen in gentle steps but there was no use of concealed lighting – illumination was direct but flush with the ceiling. A small stage replaced the orchestra pit with a raised front edge to conceal footlights.

Work resumed in April 1955 on the Odeon Sheffield that was only just begun when war broke out. It was still in the hands of the Harry Weedon practice where Robert Bullivant completely altered the pre-war design by W. Calder Robson. Most of the old steelwork was removed and the exterior became chunkier

This was one of the great places to view a film with superb sightlines in a fan-shaped, stadium-style auditorium with the four bands of concealed lighting designed to go off in sequence towards the screen before the film started. In the restoration, the fifth, innermost band of concealed lighting had been eliminated (even though the opening was not enlarged), while the ceiling was plainer with inappropriate new light fittings. And no Compton organ reappeared. (See Odeon Cinemas 1, *pages 44 and 45, for original photographs.)*

Odeon Haverstock Hill, as restored in 1954 after wartime bomb damage. Name signs were now mounted vertically to each side of a tall false window which replaced the original programme display while the space above occupied by the original, condensed Odeon sign was left blank. The edge of the canopy no longer carries slotted lettering. Tall frames of scene stills have given way to framed posters but the outside paybox remained. The V-shaped pair of wide, narrow posters mounted above the canopy were widespread across the circuit.

The new Odeon Westbourne Grove in 1955. Note the man with the gong displayed above the stairs to the balcony. The original exterior design is reproduced on page 158 of Odeon Cinemas 1.

Odeon Highgate, with Christmas tree on the canopy in 1955 and a Rank production advertised by two illuminated banners rather than by lettering on the edge of the canopy. The outer foyer photograph shows that there were three prices for stalls seats but only one for the circle, at a little under twice the price of the cheapest front stalls seats. The spray light fitting resembles those widely introduced to ABC cinemas. In the auditorium, there is an exit at the front of the balcony only on the righthand side and the matching extension on the left is for appearance's sake only.

The new Odeon Sheffield in 1956 and an artist's impression of the original 1938 design for the exterior. The auditorium is reproduced in the colour section.

The Odeon Doncaster in summer 1955 – the renamed Ritz. (Courtesy of Bruce Peter.) The auditorium appears in the colour section.

with rounded corners and brickwork replacing faience. The Odeon's frontage boasted a huge readograph for programme announcements above the entrance and glass side walls to the foyer block. It opened on 16 July 1956 with its original seating plan reconfigured to add three more seats to the stalls and remove ten from the balcony, giving a postwar record total of 2,319 seats in a new single cinema auditorium. In contrast to the plain splay walls at Sidcup and Highgate, there was some suggestion of pre-war Odeon design in the concealed lighting and decorative panels leading toward the proscenium arch. Much of the foyer and auditorium decoration displayed the influence of the 1952 Royal Festival Hall but the ceiling treatment was weak. The Odeon's opening was a blow to the independent Hippo-drome and Cinema House which had previously taken the circuit's releases (and to the Gaumont which had collared some of the plums as well).

In May 1956, the Falkirk Cinema was the victim of one of the fires to which Scottish cinemas were so prone (the town's Gaumont was closed for a month the following year by another blaze). Rank planned to build a new Odeon here (possibly on one of its pre-war sites rather than where the Cinema stood): this was still the intention in July 1958 but the scheme was dropped when Rank decided it only needed one hall and this would be the existing Gaumont.

A new area of housing development reportedly targeted by Rank from mid-1957 was the Roseberry Estate at Billingham-on-Tees where a 1,100-seat auditorium was promised to the plans of Lennox D. Paterson, a cinema specialist who normally practised in Scotland. What second thoughts occurred here is not known.

Rank was reported to have auctioned off a site at St. Helens at this time. Could this have been the one in Tontine Street for which Harry Weedon had prepared plans in 1937?

Acquisitions

In two instances, Rank abandoned plans to complete a pre-war Odeon scheme by taking over an existing cinema instead.

Work on the Odeon Doncaster was about to resume in 1954 on a site directly opposite the Ritz cinema in Hallgate. The Ritz was a 2,459-seat independent cinema, opened in 1934, which played Odeon releases and now faced the threat of a product shortage and a much more modern rival across the road. Under the circumstances, the owners were prepared to sell the Ritz for a price that made it worthwhile for Rank to drop its scheme. The Ritz was taken over in April 1955 and closed for improvements, re-opening the following month as the town's Odeon.

Similarly, in Gloucester, Rank announced the resumption of work on its Odeon scheme but instead, in January 1956, acquired the large but rudimentary Plaza in Barton Street, a development facilitated by Rank's minority interest in the cinema (dating from the 1930s and GCF). This too was modernised before taking the Odeon name a year later but still had such drawbacks as side exits that opened directly onto the outside, letting daylight flood in.

Rank, through CMA, also embarked on a buying spree of other existing cinemas on a scale not seen since the war years.

The makeshift post-war Regal Harlow was acquired solely to inherit the owner's option on the site reserved for a proper new cinema in the town. Then there was the takeover of the Wembley Hall Cinema, renamed Gaumont, to bolster that circuit.

Back in 1944, Odeon had taken over two of Alfred Black's four huge Regals in the north east of England, at Gateshead and South Shields. Now Rank greatly strengthened its position in the area by acquiring Black's other two Regals in July 1955: the biggest cinema in Sunderland, Black's Regal Theatre with 2,522 seats and attached café and ballroom; and Black's Regal Byker with 1,838 seats. In Sunderland, Black's smaller Theatre Royal followed in 1959.

In September 1955 Rank bought up the two cinemas operated by Burton-on-Trent Picturedromes, the New Picturedrome and Ritz. The slightly larger but unprepossessing Picturedrome became the town's Odeon while the more centrally located and prominent Ritz became the Gaumont shortly after the disposal of the existing Gaumont, a small and old-fashioned hall.

An odd takeover that same September brought the large and comparatively modern Plaza Dudley into the Rank net from independent operator Miles Jervis. As Rank already had an Odeon opposite on Castle Hill and two other cinemas elsewhere in the town – the Gaumont and Criterion – its interest in the Plaza is hard to fathom. Although it now had a monopoly in the town centre, Rank did not normally seek to blanket a town. Also, the Plaza had been part of the circuit showing Fox CinemaScope pictures, so its programming should have become more restricted.

Even more puzzling is the purchase in April 1955 of seven cinemas in the Glasgow suburbs from Glasgow and West of Scotland Cinemas and related companies, all of them previously booked by and associated with Sir Alex B. King's Scottish circuit since April 1945: the Astor Springburn, Astoria Possil, Avon Possilpark, Carlton Townhead, Roxy and Seamore at Maryhill, and Standard Partick. Apart from the huge Astoria, the second largest cinema in Glasgow, they were a poor bunch. None was ever dignified by being renamed Odeon or Gaumont. The Standard Partick shut down within a year. The others all closed as cinemas in the 1960s.

Rank showed far more enthusiasm for an isolated Scottish acquisition that same year at Greenock. The King's Theatre was

Odeon Byker – the former Black's Regal on 21 January 1957 (courtesy of Bruce Peter). Interior showing organ console taken on 12 June 1968. (CTA Archive/photograph by John D. Sharp).

closed for modernisation before re-opening as an Odeon early in 1956. The old Hippodrome in Leigh, near Manchester, was also acquired, improved and re-opened as an Odeon, although it still retained its rear projection system.

At the start of 1956, Rank scooped up the attractive Ritz Lincoln and gave that the Odeon name a few months later. With it came the smaller Astoria which closed within six months.

Two significant north of England acquisitions from related companies in Rochdale brought that town's Rialto Super Cinema and the important Rialto Blackburn into the Rank orbit. Technically, these were Gaumont properties but when their names were changed in 1959 they became Odeons.

In mid-1956 Rank also consolidated its hold on seven cinemas it rented from Paramount by agreeing to pay the American company £1,850,000 over twenty years to take over the three freeholds and four leaseholds involved.

The impact of television

The arrival of Independent Television hurt cinema attendances far more than the BBC had ever done because ITV offered more popular programming than the BBC had done while the latter dropped its elitist "policy of excellence" and chased viewing figures with less demanding programmes.

ITV took several years to spread all over Britain after its London-area opening in September 1955. When the Independent Television Authority (ITA) began granting regional licences to establish commercial channels in opposition to the BBC, the major cinema chains were at the front of the queue. The Rank Organisation teamed up with Associated Newspapers and The Amalgamated Press to form Southern Television and bid successfully for the franchise to transmit to an area stretching along the south coast from Weymouth to Brighton and inland as far as Newbury. On 30 August 1958, it began putting out ITV programmes from the Southern Television Centre created out of a former Odeon cinema, the Plaza at Northam (a particularly large second-run cinema in the suburbs of Southampton).

Although it was a promising business opportunity and, if Rank hadn't participated, some other company would have taken its place, the move into television nevertheless diluted Rank's commitment to cinema. Of course, other cinema groups, including ABC and Granada, also sought and gained a slice of the ITV pie and obviously Rank's experience in entertainment was a valuable qualification for running an ITV region. Nevertheless, Rank and partners eventually disappointed the ITA and lost the franchise at renewal time.

"It was possible to measure over the first six or seven months [of its arrival] a 10 per cent fall in attendances in the area covered [by ITV] compared with the rest of the country", said J. Arthur

Rank. Another report indicates that attendances at British cinemas dropped 20 per cent between March and the end of September 1956 compared to the preceding year, partly as a result of the spread of ITV outside London to the Midlands. The startling plunge in cinema admissions between 1955 and 1959 does tie in nicely with the spread and initial impact of ITV. (It should also be related to the end of the benefit from CinemaScope.)

Shedding lossmakers

As attendances declined, the previously reliable exhibition side of the Rank empire developed serious financial problems and attention turned to persuading the government to reduce the burden of Entertainments Tax, which had been introduced as a temporary measure during World War One and remained in force at different levels ever since.

As early as June 1953, in his report to shareholders, J. Arthur Rank pointed out: "We operate 550 theatres in this country and of these during the year under review 236 operated at a loss of approximately £725,000 before providing for interest on capital employed and excluding profits on the sales made in the theatres. Even allowing for profits on theatre sales an overall net loss was incurred in these theatres before charging interest on capital. This in spite of the fact that these same theatres paid £3,449,000 in Entertainments Tax. [....] Obviously if the present situation continues we must in the interests of the shareholders close many of these theatres in order to protect the activities of our business as a whole. If we do, the effect will be far-reaching. The Chancellor of the Exchequer will lose Entertainments Tax, British production would lose on these theatres alone film hire of approximately £500,000 per annum and we should have to dispense with the services of a large number of employees..."

Even though, according to Rank, nearly half of his cinemas were in trouble, there were only a few reductions of the number of Odeons before 1956. As mentioned earlier, the tiny Odeon Dursley shut just over five years after its reconstruction following a fire. The Astoria at Earlsdon, a district of Coventry, and the small Royal at Winchester were both taken over by independents (the latter was originally to be sold in 1949). Then, early in 1956, the Odeon Farncombe, Surrey, suffered the ignominious fate of being turned into a sausage factory (but locals had the superior Odeon at Godalming close to hand).

In September 1956, Rank had six fewer loss-making cinemas than in 1953. A total of 230 cinemas were in the red after paying £455,453 in Entertainments Tax (compared to only £316,870 for film hire). Of these, 184 were losing a total of £440,000 per annum. These included twenty-nine of the largest cinemas (seating over 2,000) which had lost £100,180 (Rank had nearly one hundred cinemas of this size).

At the end of August 1956, the Rank Organisation announced that forty cinemas were to be closed, twenty-six of them by the end of September. The statement said: "The forthcoming closures are a logical consequence of the Chancellor's refusal to reduce the tax."

The ridiculous aspect of the tax (which had been reduced but still took 28.8 per cent of gross box office receipts) was the absence of relief for the cinemas which it was making unprofitable, forcing them to close and depriving the government of further tax income. They might have paid a reduced tax but no sliding scale was ever introduced. Prices could not be increased for competitive reasons and in any case would have made some regular patrons give up or go less often.

J. Arthur Rank then called a press conference on 12 September 1956 to inform reporters that a further thirty-nine cinemas would be shut after Christmas. A total of 1,830 people would be thrown out of work. The news of the closures made national headlines. ABC added to the gloom with its announcement of shedding up to thirty cinemas.

Rank's motive in so heavily publicising its closures was clearly to put pressure on the Chancellor of the Exchequer to reduce the tax and perhaps to make a good impression of house cleaning on its shareholders. But it suggested to the public that cinemas generally were in serious trouble and that cinemagoing was going out of fashion. Nobody likes to be associated with something that is unfashionable and such publicity can have only accelerated the decline in attendances. It also exaggerated the situation as only fifty-nine Rank cinemas were closed over the next few months.* Nevertheless, Rank continued to make a habit of getting rid of cinemas in batches and making sure that the national press knew all about it... The positive news that it had also acquired fourteen cinemas and built or reconstructed seven others received little attention.

In fact, the fifty-nine closed cinemas were fairly insignificant – most of them elderly, rundown, off-circuit or secondary Gaumont properties. However, all had been fitted out with CinemaScope and some had been recently modernised (it became a joke among managers that if your cinema had just had a new boiler fitted and the auditorium redecorated it was almost certainly in line for the chop). These cinemas had their own appreciative (if small) audiences and their closure contributed to the overall decline in attendances as not all their patrons would go elsewhere, especially where it meant travelling some distance. It was

* Two unidentified halls were spared when the landlords refused to terminate the leases until alternative uses for the sites could be found. One seems to have been the Odeon Whitton.

The Royal Theatre Winchester, seen here in November 1949, went to an independent in 1954. (Courtesy of Derek Knights.)

The Globe Coventry, one of Oscar Deutsch's first cinema acquisitions, closed in 1956. It is seen here in November 1949. (Courtesy of Derek Knights.)

generally believed that a majority of visits were lost for good when a cinema shut down.

The first of the purpose-built Odeons to go at this time was at Worcester Park, Surrey. A local deputation of protest was informed at Rank's head office that the cinema had been running at a considerable loss, apparently since the War, and would still lose money if it paid no Entertainments Tax at all. This was one of those halls that played films three weeks later than the main Rank cinemas in the area but it had the satisfaction of drawing a full house for its last performance ever, the end of a seven-day run of Rank's smash hit World War Two drama, *Reach For The Sky*. Worcester Park's demise was closely followed by that of the Odeon Sudbury, an attractive hall which customarily showed the Gaumont release and suffered from a poor location. Among the other casualties, the huge Regal Golders Green, the Croydon Hippodrome and the Odeons at Blackfen and Hayes (Kent) were all cinemas like Worcester Park that had been denied the Odeon release on first run because of competing Odeons in their areas: they had either played off-circuit releases or circuit programmes some three weeks later, neither conducive to good attendances. Blackfen was a good example of premature building: anticipated new housing never came and the cinema still had undeveloped heathland on two sides when it closed. There were particularly heavy protests over the Hayes closure, as it made a huge dent in the town's amenities.

Elsewhere, the Odeon Bethnal Green, north London, was perhaps a surprising closure as it played the Odeon release on first suburban run. The demise of the Aldershot Pavilion, Camberley Arcade, Farnham County, Guildford Plaza and Weybridge County all left a second, better Odeon cinema in the same town. Similarly, the Taibach Regent left the Port Talbot Odeon nearby. At Broadstairs, the Odeon had already been leased out once and Rank's second attempt to operate it was now officially declared a failure. The cinema had suffered from playing films weeks after the Odeon Ramsgate. The Paragon Gorbals had been the runt of the Glasgow litter since it was taken over in the 1930s, so its departure was no surprise.

One of Oscar Deutsch's first picture houses, the Globe Coventry, also went. Four purpose-built Odeons were among the last nine to go, on 5 January 1957 – almost as though there was a sentimental move to keep them open for as long as possible and until after the Christmas holidays. These were the Odeons at Isleworth (near Hounslow) and Rickmansworth (near Watford) and two that were architecturally outstanding but seem to have been long-term white elephants – the Odeon Colwyn Bay (leaving two other more centrally placed cinemas seating 1,800 between them, so that film provision was well maintained) and one of the very last Odeons to open, the

Odeon Elmers End, which had the shortest operating life of any of Oscar Deutsch's building ventures other than the war-damaged Odeon Canning Town. Normally a south London release theatre, for a period in the early 1950s it had been relegated to second run status, playing circuit programmes three weeks later. It had been reinstated, then in its final months had usually exchanged programmes midweek with the West Wickham Gaumont (an Odeon property), thereby playing both the Rank circuits' releases in an attempt to improve business.

Rank's purge did seem excessive when both the Elmers End and West Wickham sites closed on the same day as they were only two miles apart and the closure of one ought to have benefited the other. But, in this area, the well positioned ABC Regal Beckenham was preferred by audiences (it has survived to this day – to become an Odeon).

In Twickenham, the closure of the Gaumont (an Odeon property which had recently had a new boiler installed) left the town's Odeon able to pick up any outstanding Gaumont programme. (There was something odd about Twickenham as ABC's modern Regal closed very early, in 1960, leaving the Odeon able to pick up an exceptional ABC release as well.)

Most of the fifty-nine cinemas were put up for sale, although Rank planned to convert a few to dance halls. Along with many other failed picture houses, they were boarded up, awaiting a buyer and creating a dismal impression on numerous High Streets. Although most of the buildings were stripped of their name signs (but usually left a telltale outline behind), the Odeon Isleworth still displayed all its signage three years later. (It was put to temporary use storing the discs of Top Rank Records, launched in January 1959 as a short-lived Rank diversification venture.)

When closed properties were sold, it was usually with a covenant that they could not be re-opened as cinemas. This made sense in that Rank believed in reducing the number of cinemas to help those that survived – but it also implied a belief that if Rank could not operate a cinema successfully then nobody else could, or should be allowed to try. (ABC took a different view and allowed independents to take over some of its unwanted cinemas, although none survived for long.)

The Odeon Colwyn Bay was the only one of Rank's 1956/7 closures to make an eventual comeback. After it had remained unsold for nine years, Rank were receptive to an offer from the Hutchinson group to buy it for ground floor bingo and an Astra cinema in the former balcony. The cinema ran for twenty years, outlasting the bingo.

Following this massive clear-out, a total of sixteen more Rank cinemas were shut without major fanfare by the end of 1957. These included the purpose-built Odeons at Radcliffe and Wallington, the County Bletchley, Odeon Fleet and Plaza

Odeon Elmers End in April 1956 (photograph courtesy of Derek Knights) and closure announcement. The Gaumont Penge would close less than two years later.

The Odeon Isleworth retains its vertical name sign on the corner and spaced out horizontally on the side of the auditorium in these April 1960 photographs taken after closure (by Allen Eyles).

The Odeon Fleet, seen here in November 1949, was an early closure. Note the Odeon shop next door. (Courtesy of Derek Knights.)

Northam (the last perhaps sacrificed for its new role as the Southern Television Centre) – all late-run halls. Then there was the Marlborough Holloway, a former theatre by Frank Matcham, which played the northwest London Odeon release (and featured shortly after closing in the British crime picture, *Gideon's Day*). In this case, Rank may have wanted to reduce competition now that the Odeon Highgate was operating and a decision had been taken to re-open the almost adjacent war-damaged Gaumont, although this would, in fact, play its own release rather than the Odeon one.

In 1958, the further casualties were yet again largely Gaumont halls but from the Odeon side came the off-circuit Tredegar Hall in Newport and the St. Helier Opera House on Jersey (leaving the Odeon). Rank did sell as a going concern the Clapton Kenninghall, a seedy Odeon property in northeast London with an often tenuous link to the circuit in press advertising.

Programming

Although, in general, Rank's film productions of the 1950s are not highly regarded today, many of them were hugely popular. J. Arthur Rank informed shareholders in 1955: "I am pleased to tell you that of the twenty-four best box-office attractions played on our two circuits during the year twelve were British and twelve were American, and the receipts from these two groups were almost exactly equal. This result was achieved in spite of the high box-office value of certain of the American pictures." A similar proportion applied to the previous year and the two following years.

Rank's films were made on tight budgets to equally tight schedules in an assembly line approach, using contract talent wherever possible. Some more ambitious projects like *Lawrence Of Arabia* and *The Mayor Of Casterbridge*, both with Dirk Bogarde, and a Laurence Olivier version of Shakespeare's *Macbeth*, were developed then cancelled. Michael Powell and Emeric Pressburger returned to the fold but their Rank films, including *The Battle Of The River Plate*, were uninspired.

However, Rank's many box-office successes were a considerable financial achievement and a credit to John Davis's stewardship. It was British comedies and war dramas that had the most appeal – with Rank's Norman Wisdom vehicles and *Doctor* series heading its comedy hits and *Reach For The Sky* topping the war pictures. *Doctor In The House* was said to have drawn over sixteen million admissions by the end of 1954.*

* Rank didn't always know when it had a potential hit. The vintage car comedy *Genevieve* was viewed by J. Arthur Rank and John Davis in the presence of the CMA booking controller, Richard Hamer, and considered a certain loser (its cast had no drawing power at that time). It was shelved and only given a West End run to fill a gap in May 1953

Rank also benefited from its continued investment in the Ealing Studios output for distribution rights, leading to hits like *The Ladykillers* and a stream of strong British quota titles. It was a loss when Ealing fell out with Rank and linked up with Metro-Goldwyn-Mayer which released its small output from 1957 to the ABC circuit – most of the pictures were mediocre but they included one enormous hit, *Dunkirk*.

And then, of course, there was the exceptional appeal of Rank's Coronation film in Technicolor, *A Queen Is Crowned*, which was played at almost all first-run Odeon and Gaumont cinemas simultaneously. The Coronation took place on Tuesday 2 June 1953 and the feature-length documentary had its world premiere before an invited audience on the following Friday evening at the Odeon Leicester Square. The film opened to the public on the following day there and concurrently (for an eight-day run) at the New Victoria and Odeon Tottenham Court Road, then started almost everywhere else on Monday 8 June for a six-day run, with a total of 308 copies being made (compared to forty for a normal release).

Major hold-outs were the Dominion and Metropole in central London which played an off-circuit Columbia double bill combining a western, *Hangman's Knot*, and a war film, *Eight Iron Men*. A few Gaumonts in close proximity to larger Odeons played similar Columbia fare, while at least one Odeon hall, the Plaza Camden Town, followed suit. Second-run Rank halls like the Odeon Kemp Town (a district of Brighton) still waited the customary three weeks before receiving the Coronation film. Curiously, Rank booked the same B feature support, *No Escape* (a United Artists release), to both its circuits instead of introducing an element of choice, thereby making this unremarkable Hollywood thriller the most seen B feature in British cinema history.

A Queen Is Crowned was a particular triumph for Rank as the rival ABC circuit fared disastrously with its *Elizabeth Is Queen* (in Warnercolor) which was double-billed with a Welsh comedy, *Valley Of Song*. Audiences clearly picked *A Queen Is Crowned* as the better record of the Coronation and the use of Technicolor seems to have registered in its favour.

Takings were boosted by special morning performances for organised school parties. Brian Gauntlett remembers arriving for duty as third projectionist at the Odeon Southsea past the large queues of children waiting for the 9am showing. And

A. I. Todd, the chief operator at the Odeon Erith, wrote into the CMA magazine, *The Circle*:

> I have just finished running a morning matinee of the film *A Queen Is Crowned*. During the procession scenes I stood at the back of the circle and experienced a feeling that I have never felt before in twenty-two years of showing films. The children were magnificent: the spontaneous cheers for the parades of armed forces were terrific. When 'The Mounties' came by I swear I saw the roof lift a couple of inches! And when the Queen came into the picture, I found myself nearly joining in as well. We have another three matinees to run and I am looking forward to them as much as the children. It was a very moving experience and one that I am glad I did not miss. What a wonderful way to start a day's work!

Some cinemas were showing *A Queen Is Crowned* when Her Majesty made tours of the London suburbs. Among those she passed, decked out in celebration, were the Odeon Camberwell and the Astoria Old Kent Road.

From early 1954, Rank had the previously discussed problem of replacing 20th Century-Fox's output. The last Fox non-CinemaScope main feature to have an Odeon release was the Marilyn Monroe-Jane Russell musical comedy *Gentlemen Prefer Blondes*. The rift with Rank was only relaxed when one of Fox's few non-'Scope-and-stereo films, a thriller called *A Life In The Balance*, did support duty to GFD's *Foxfire* in 1955 (others in this series of Leonard Goldstein's Panoramic Productions released by Fox, like *Three Young Texans* and *The Raid*, gained an ABC release).⋆

Although, even in the autumn of 1954, John Davis was asserting "Fox are the losers, not us" (*Kine Weekly*, 23 September), the dispute meant not only Rank losing business to many, often inferior opposition halls that had gained a new lease of life with Fox's CinemaScope output but also having to replace Fox's substantial contribution to the Odeon and Gaumont weekly release schedules at a time when Hollywood in general was reducing output. In 1953, Fox had supplied no less than twelve weeks of programming to Odeon and the same number to Gaumont. Many inferior films that Odeon and, more particularly, Gaumont (as the weaker of the two circuits) were forced to play from 1954 onwards are indicative of the damage that the dispute caused. (After the lesson of 1948, Rank did not increase the number of its own productions to fill the gap.) The Gau-

---

but then did well on Gaumont release, doing even better later on a perennially available double bill with *Doctor In The House*, the pair being promoted as "The Doc and the Crock". (The Odeon Kensington, however, revived *Genevieve* and *La Ronde* as a way of avoiding the week's new release, a plebeian Martin and Lewis comedy.)

⋆ There seem to have been some individual bookings of Fox Cinema-Scope films. In 1956 the Odeon Guildford played Fox's *Carousel* for a week, perhaps on the technicality that it was shot in CinemaScope 55, and Rank's second run hall in the town, the Plaza, showed several Fox CinemaScope films for three days without mention of CinemaScope in press advertising.

mont release suffered further because many non-Rank cinemas (particularly Granadas) which normally played it defected to the Fox output in the weeks when that was available. As it happened, the Odeon release was not so widely affected – although, at Clapham Junction, south London, where it most often went into the huge Granada, it was frequently shunted into one of the lesser halls by a Fox booking and occasionally not shown at all.

The pressure also showed in the number of revivals. Odeon re-ran *White Christmas* three years after its initial release and re-released two Gaumont circuit main features: *Doctor In The House* only eleven weeks after its first run and *The Lady And The Tramp* eighteen months later. *Doctor In The House* was clearly not regarded as a strong attraction the second time around because Odeons that could take the week's mediocre Gaumont offering did so (it was a double bill of *The Long Wait* and *Camels West*). Despite the product shortage, Rank's comedy *The Big Money*, starring Ian Carmichael, was shelved in July 1956, reputedly on John Davis's instructions after seeing a rough cut, writing off a £100,000 investment. A subsequent test screening at the Kilburn State produced a highly favourable response and it was given an Odeon release in summer 1958 to lacklustre results. Almost all the critics unhelpfully reminded readers that it had been shelved and damned it with faint praise. As in the case of *Chance Of A Lifetime*, the critics made people suspicious of seeing it.

Although Columbia, a reinvigorated United Artists and (briefly) Republic had product of adequate or better quality to help fill the gap left by Fox, the problem was soon exacerbated by the rapid decline of RKO Radio as a principal supplier. Most of its output became mediocre after Walt Disney terminated a releasing arrangement in 1955, forming its own British distribution company which supplied some of its best titles to the ABC circuit although eventually allying itself firmly with Rank.*

Rank inflicted further difficulties on itself by adhering to its ban on X certificate films. A few Odeons showed Otto Preminger's adult comedy *The Moon Is Blue* in 1954 in an odd week when others played revivals or took the Gaumont release, *Miss Sadie Thompson*. The ban was not fully lifted until 1956 when another Otto Preminger picture, *The Man With The Golden Arm*, starring Frank Sinatra as a drug addict, opened at the Odeon Leicester

* The ABC circuit seems to have enjoyed slightly too much Hollywood product at times as its distribution partner, Associated British-Pathe, supplied a few films to the Rank circuits including Billy Wilder's *Love In The Afternoon* to Odeon, while some MGM films, normally played by ABC, went to Rank as well. In particular, the latest reissue of *Gone With The Wind* (in Metroscope) went through Odeons in 1957, although a change of circuits might have been deemed a good idea as its previous four general releases had been through ABC.

Square on 12 January followed by a full Odeon circuit release. John Davis issued a statement that the film's subject was one which the public had every right to see and that Rank's ban applied to the horror and sex pictures commonly associated with the X certificate. Undoubtedly, there was considerable pressure on Rank to show this particular film, because it was a big attraction with a major star. Back in 1954, Columbia's undeniably excellent crime drama, *The Big Heat*, starring Glenn Ford and Gloria Grahame, was X-certificated for its violence and became another victim of Rank's policy but this was snatched up by the ABC circuit (which also played *The Moon Is Blue* quite widely). (Another Columbia X film also starring Ford and Grahame, *Human Desire*, had only a "floating" release from March 1955.)

Several Rank-distributed Hammer horror films were handed over to a very receptive ABC circuit, which also inherited some further American X films that the Rank circuits could have played, like Columbia's box-office draw *The Camp On Blood Island* (made by Hammer), *Cell 2455, Death Row*, and another British production, *Night Of The Demon*. Rank also distributed some X certificate titles from Universal, like *Abbott and Costello Meet Dr. Jekyll and Mr. Hyde* and *Creature From The Black Lagoon* (the latter shot in 3-D but shown flat), and these were barred from Odeon and Gaumont main circuit houses, leaving the accomplished *Creature* to become a winner for less sensitive halls.

It was more than two years after *Man With The Golden Arm* that another X film, Paramount's *Desire Under The Elms* (based on a respectable stage play) went out through the Odeon circuit, causing a problem in the south London area when its appearance had to be delayed by a week to avoid giving offence on Whit Sunday and Whit Monday in 1958. Partly as a reflection of its increasing difficulty in obtaining films, the Gaumont circuit resorted to slightly more X films in the 1950s.

Major foreign films continued to intermittently replace supporting features at such Odeons as Kensington, Swiss Cottage, Haverstock Hill, Putney, Richmond and Streatham. One remarkable example of this occurred in February 1955 at Odeon's Astoria Streatham when a gritty Technicolor war drama, *The Bridges At Toko-Ri*, an important Paramount release, was supported by a revival of the U-certificate subtitled Italian neo-realist masterpiece, *Bicycle Thieves*. In November of that year, the Astoria revived the delectable French period comedy *Les Belles de Nuit* in support of the British gangster film *Joe Macbeth*. Had audiences rebelled at these subtitled offerings, the practice would have stopped long before. It must have been felt that such a strong support would increase audiences in relatively up-market areas or at least avoid the negative reaction that the poor supporting feature shown elsewhere would have provoked.

But undemanding French films with English subtitles could

also play the entire Odeon circuit. *French Can-Can* and *Folies Bergere*, two saucy Continental offerings, were double-billed with weak Hollywood fare. Fernandel comedies such as *Fernandel the Dressmaker* and *Casimir* were shown as support, as was a Rank-distributed Jean Gabin drama, *Gas-Oil*. The acclaimed French short *The Red Balloon* accompanied the major Rank film *The Battle Of The River Plate*. A Spanish film, *Pepote*, supported *Gunfight At The O.K. Corral*. The foreign film given the most exposure by Odeon was the thriller *The Wages Of Fear* (*Le Salaire de la peur*) in 1954, following an immensely successful run at the Academy art house in Oxford Street. It played solo, supported by shorts, had comparatively few subtitles and some of the dialogue was in English. Even so, it was shown in advance to Odeon managers who were invited to request an alternative programme if they wanted. A check on London-area showings shows no sign of any Odeons opting out.

The film proved to be a huge success. Josh Billings, the *Kine Weekly*'s down-to-earth box-office commentator, reported (17 June): "*The Wages Of Fear* has exploded the stupid belief that average audiences are not interested in foreign fare. It's cashing in everywhere". And Gordon Sweeney, manager of the Odeon Deptford, a tough working-class area, still remembers his surprise at how well it did there.

One X film that infiltrated Odeon cinemas was *The Light Across The Street*, a subtitled drama with a briefly topless Brigitte Bardot that had enjoyed a long art house run in London's West End. Its first Odeon appearance was at the off-circuit Hippo-drome Croydon but it then played the key London Odeons at Kensington and Swiss Cottage as the main feature on its art house credentials, thereby enabling them to duck out of the weak regular circuit release, *Slightly Scarlet* and *Mohawk*. Then, rather surprisingly, it was brought in to drum up some business for certain Odeons afflicted with RKO Radio's U-certificated Ginger Rogers comedy *The First Traveling Saleslady* in the summer of 1956. Kensington and Swiss Cottage again went their own way with a revival of Garbo's *Camille* and the musical *Lili*, while elsewhere *Saleslady* started out with a B feature *Breakaway*, starring Tom Conway, which was dropped by the third week of London release in order to strengthen the pro-gramme. Several Odeons substituted an old RKO main feature, *Appointment In Honduras*, which had not received a circuit release, but the large Astorias at Brixton and Streatham paired Ginger Rogers with *The Light Across The Street*, clearly going after the adult audience which would be drawn to the latter to the exclusion of Rank's beloved family audience to which the comedy might have appealed (could anyone have enjoyed both pictures?). In one way or another, the Bardot film was spot booked into sixty Rank halls including the Odeons Bognor Regis,

Odeon's "opening book" trailer day-set titles were introduced in 1953 and replaced by a new design in February 1959 for use by both Odeons and Gaumonts. (Courtesy of Carl Chesworth.)

Boston, Erith, Exeter, Fleet, Henley, Lewes, Newport (Isle of Wight), Marlow, Ramsgate, Rickmansworth, Sevenoaks, Spalding and Stourbridge.

These foreign films were undoubtedly favoured because of the product shortage (and, perhaps, to see if a wider range of offerings could arrest the decline in attendances) but they nevertheless demonstrate that Rank, like the rival ABC circuit (but unlike the multiplex circuits of today), saw no insurmountable audience resistance to foreign and subtitled pictures.

When *The Bridge On The River Kwai*, clearly the top attraction of its year, was released to Odeon, Rank did experiment with two-week runs at some key suburban cinemas where one week was the firm rule. This involved the film starting a week ahead of other cinemas rather than opening simultaneously and staying on an extra week. The arrangement was facilitated by the same distributor's willingness to give up bookings of the preceding week's release, the low appeal *Bitter Victory*, to allow these cinemas to start *Kwai* early.

In addition, various Gaumonts not directly competing with an Odeon defected from their own release to show it. These included the London-area Gaumonts at Clapham, Cricklewood, Hackney (Pavilion), Kings Cross, Lewisham, Rushey Green, Stepney (Troxy), Stratford, West Norwood (Regal) and Wood Green. Such bookings were sometimes at the expense of the opposition halls on smaller circuits which normally played the Odeon release but they may have baulked at the stiff terms the distributor demanded. Also, in this instance, an Odeon hall, the Plaza Camden Town, stepped aside for the much larger Gaumont to play *Kwai*. Much the same group took up *Oklahoma!*, but this time including the Gaumonts at Edmonton (Regal), Leyton, Palmers Green, Shepherd's Bush, Sutton and Wandsworth. Similarly, many Odeons were in a position to access a particularly strong Gaumont release – including, in the London area, East Dulwich, Erith, Haverstock Hill, Highgate (until the re-opening of the Gaumont Holloway) and Twickenham.

Although Odeons and Gaumonts in direct competition were supposed to adhere to their respective circuit releases, there were some instances of programmes being exchanged. In the mid-1950s, the Odeon and Gaumont Edgware Road often swopped over, seemingly so that the much larger Odeon gained the top Gaumont releases. This didn't make life easy for the manager of the Gaumont, who still had nearly 2,000 seats to fill. Rank's major production *A Night To Remember* switched from the Odeons at Finchley and Bromley to larger Gaumonts as well as playing at the Gaumonts that had joined the *Kwai* line-up.

Sunday revival bookings began to be dropped in favour of seven-day runs from April 1955, beginning with the larger key cinemas and spreading more and more. Flat-rate Sunday pro-grammes had started as a protest over the compulsory charity levy and limited opening hours. They were very profitable for cinemas but distributors wanted to make money from new films on one of the busiest days of the week and there was a demand by cinemagoers for a change. However, revivals returned when Disney and other family-orientated programmes came along.

The rigid circuit release system may seem absurd today but it was taken for granted at the time. However, there was one occasion in 1956 when Rank foresaw that a major release was not suited to all locations. This was Laurence Olivier's version of *Richard III*. Unlike Olivier's previous Shakespearian films, it was not a Rank production, otherwise it might have played the full circuit regardless, to maximise takings. Instead, alternative lowbrow programming – mainly GFD's X-certificate *Revenge Of The Creature* – was introduced at such cinemas as the Odeons Deptford, Edgware Road, Harlesden, Islington, Kensal Rise, and at the Astoria Old Kent Road (where *Richard III* then became available to the independent Globe cinema which resourcefully promoted it as a horror film). Olivier's production did well enough to produce some queues outside my local cinema, the Astoria Streatham. Later on, following appalling reviews, Otto Preminger's *Saint Joan* was restricted to the posher Odeons while the others took the rare opportunity to play new X-certificate horror films from the same distributor, United Artists.

Greater London was so well supplied with large cinemas that there were outlets for all the major releases almost everywhere, resulting in six or seven day runs rather than an opportunity to split the week and show two of the programmes. Rank attempted to improve the box office at a few problem sites by pairing them to show the Odeon and Gaumont release for half the week and exchange prints. The Odeon Elmers End and Gaumont West Wickham soon closed despite following this practice, but the Odeons at East Sheen and Whitton lasted rather longer showing the Gaumont release for half of most weeks (a top Odeon attraction would still command a full week at both theatres). Following the demise of the Bethnal Green Odeon, the Foresters also went over to split weeks, often exchanging prints with the Odeon Stepney. It is doubtful whether any two independent cinemas would have been allowed to carry out this practice, but Rank could argue it didn't require extra prints and should increase the return for distributors.

The three-leg London release presented a problem at Christmas, especially in the final week in south London. The weeks beforehand were notoriously dire as people reserved their money for presents and were preoccupied by holiday preparations, so they became a dumping ground for poor films (thereby making people even less inclined to go out). I remember the Astoria Streatham playing a truly dismal double bill at Christmas 1955,

Flame Of The Islands and *A Yank In Ermine*, and thinking this was a waste of an opportunity to provide cinemagoers with a film they'd want to see when they were in festive mood – whereas northwest London Odeons had the perfect holiday attraction, Alfred Hitchcock's *To Catch A Thief*. But the problem under the rigid progress of each programme through the London suburbs was that for a top attraction to play south London at Christmas time, it would not have fulfilled its potential in the preceding two weeks.

In 1956, Rank got around the problem by initiating strong new releases simultaneously in all three areas: northwest London played the Martin and Lewis comedy *Hollywood Or Bust*, northeast took the Rank thriller *Tiger In The Smoke*, while south had the big Rank production *The Battle Of The River Plate*. The three were then swopped around until they had played the whole of London and no further new release was needed until mid-January.

Rank and Fox finally effected a reconciliation. It seems that the impending release of the smash hit *Peyton Place* focussed minds at the two companies: Fox wanted to realise the film's full box-office potential and Rank was keen to play it. However, this did not mean the end of the Fox release just yet. In January 1958, Fox agreed to allocate half its output to the Gaumont and Odeon circuits while promising its regular outlets the other half which would be qualitatively equal and include all Fox's British productions to help those cinemas meet their quota obligations.

In April 1958, *Peyton Place* became the first Fox main feature in over four years to play the Odeon circuit, while another big attraction, *The Young Lions*, went to the fourth circuit. In June, *The Long Hot Summer* was shared by the two circuits with some left-out Rank cinemas taking *The Young Lions* or Fox revival double bills including *3 Coins In The Fountain*. In December, the very first CinemaScope release, *The Robe*, belatedly obtained a full Odeon showing but Rank was denied Fox's attractive Christmas offering, the Kenneth More comedy *The Sheriff Of Fractured Jaw*, which counted for British quota as the final release of the fourth circuit (where it broke convention by opening on Boxing Day Friday for a nine-day run).

Fox's biggest attraction of the period, *The Inn Of The Sixth Happiness* (also British for quota purposes), had returned Fox films to the Odeon Leicester Square in November 1958 and it went on to a full Odeon general release in January 1959, playing for two weeks at many halls in the London area – Croydon, East Ham, Finsbury Park (Astoria), Ilford, Kingston, Peckham, Romford and Streatham – giving the kind of extended suburban run that Fox had always wanted from Rank, except that it was still pre-determined and not open ended, and the first week came

ahead of general release, as had happened with *Bridge On The River Kwai*.⋆

In one of the first instances of increasing flexibility generally, a children's film, *Noddy In Toyland*, was given special daily matinees at Christmas 1958 at the Odeons Ealing, Watford and Wealdstone and Astoria Finsbury Park and elsewhere.

Overseas

In June 1953, Rank had an interest in a grand total of 642 cinemas overseas compared to 550 fully owned in Britain. There were 136 in South Africa; 133 in Australia; 120 in New Zealand; 103 in Canada; 66 in Ceylon [now Sri Lanka]; 31 in the West Indies; 18 in Eire; 17 in Holland; 17 in Malaya and Singapore; and one in Portugal.

As previously indicated, in many countries the Odeon name and trademark lettering was used. From Rank's Australian partnership with Greater Union, an Odeon Melbourne appeared and, among numerous Odeons associated with the Greater Union subsidiary, Acme Theatres, could be found a 1,111-seat Odeon Ramsgate (did it exchange greetings with its Kent namesake?)

Rank had only one large Gaumont in central Belfast when in February 1955 it formed Odeon (Northern Ireland) Ltd. to buy twelve halls from George Lodge who remained in charge for a while as managing director. These cinemas were located in Belfast (Alhambra, Coliseum, Forum, New Princess, Mount Pottinger Picturedrome, Stadium, and a new cinema under construction at Finaghy which opened as the Tivoli on 17 June 1955), Coleraine (Palladium), Enniskillen (Regal), Larne (Regal), Lisburn (Picture House and a site for a new cinema) and Port Stewart (Palladium). At this time, Rank still planned to built an Odeon in Belfast at the corner of Castle Street and Fountain Street which had been scaled down from 3,000 seats to 1,750. Now the scheme quietly died.

Then, in December 1956, Rank took a majority interest in the more significant Curran Theatres circuit which brought in seven more Belfast cinemas (Apollo, Astoria, Broadway, Capitol, Lyceum, Regal and Regent) plus the huge Tonic Bangor, the Frontier at Newry, Majestic Portrush and two cinemas in Londonderry (the Strand and Midland). This group was apportioned 60 per cent to Odeon and 40 per cent to Gaumont.

Although, with twenty-four theatres, Rank suddenly became

⋆ Longer runs were proving the salvation of film exhibition in America, leading to the roadshow era. In the summer of 1958, film business in the United States was showing an improvement of between 4 per cent and 11 per cent nationwide, according to *Variety*, representing not so much an increase in business of the average film but long runs of a few box-office hits like *Rio Bravo*, *Some Like It Hot* and *Imitation Of Life*.

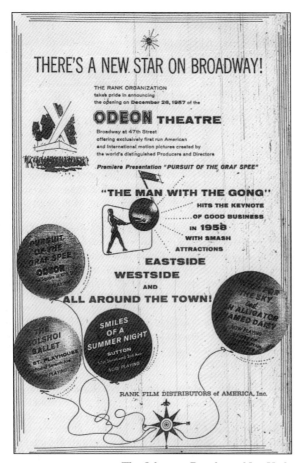

The Odeon on Broadway, New York.
Better quality illustrations were not available.

the dominant operator in Northern Ireland, there was very limited re-naming of these properties: the Strand Londonderry took the Odeon name around 1958 and the Tivoli Finaghy became the Gaumont in 1961.

Rank was still building isolated cinemas in Europe to help launch its films. In 1956 (or early 1957) it completed a new cinema in Hamburg and had a further cinema in Brussels expected to open in the late autumn of 1957. Rank had told shareholders in 1956, "in both cities we have encountered... grave difficulties in securing a regular outlet for our product, and in order to meet this situation we decided to build. It is not our intention to build extensively in either Germany or Belgium."

The Great American Adventure

Rank's pictures were performing well on the world market but John Davis was disappointed at the limited returns from the United States where they were released by Universal, Republic and other companies. And J. Arthur Rank was personally incensed at the reception given *A Queen Is Crowned* (distributed by Universal). He told shareholders: "We have, as you know, no theatre interests in that country. I believe that if we had and had been able to open this film in about fifty situations on reasonable terms it would have been as great a success there as elsewhere, since the American public who have seen the film are enthusiastic about it. Unfortunately until the film was seen by the public there was no confidence in its potential market value with the result that there was grave difficulty in booking the film in the United States of America both as to terms and the type of theatre in which it was to play. This position...would not have happened if we had been operating our own theatres. This has been an outstanding example of our problem in this market but there have been other cases during the year."

Eventually, John Davis decided to set up Rank Film Distributors of America to tackle the market head on and to lease outlets in the centre of New York to control the launch of its product. In contrast to the 1945 plans for a new 2,500-seat Odeon, Davis rented two existing theatres of modest size. First came the 561-seat Sutton, where in the summer of 1957 Rank had a disappointing run of just under five weeks with *Reach For The Sky*.

Then Rank sent up tent with an Odeon in the heart of New York, on Broadway at 47th Street. Formerly the closed Central, the 854-seat theatre re-opened on Thursday 26 December 1957 with Rank's *Pursuit Of The Graf Spee*, which had scored considerable box-office success in Britain under the more sober title of *The Battle Of The River Plate*. The Odeon was managed under contract by Charles Moss and the team that ran the Criterion nearby. *Graf Spee* ran at the Odeon for five weeks. It was followed by a five-week revival run of Olivier's *Henry V*, launched before an invited audience and presented for the first time in SuperScope (a version never shown in Britain). The two theatres booked some American films, teaming for the New York premiere run of Paramount's *Desire Under The Elms* in March 1958. Unfortunately, most of Rank's thirty-two US releases did very poorly everywhere and the two New York halls recorded heavy losses. After Rank's version of the Titanic disaster, *A Night To Remember*, failed to remedy the situation, the cinemas were dropped by the start of 1959, followed by the closure of the distribution organisation on 28 March. The Odeon then came directly under Moss management but the name continued to light up on Broadway until Monday 15 June 1959 when it became the Forum in time for a premiere two days later.

Rank also set about obtaining a beachhead in Mexico City and acquired a first-run hall, the Cine Metropolitan, in December 1957. How long Rank operated this property is not known but its distribution set-up all over Latin America was a huge success, largely because it handled the Walt Disney releases.

Roadshows

Extended runs ("roadshows" or "hardticket" engagements) with increased prices and (usually) separate performances had long been established as a way of maximising income from occasional outstanding attractions in city centres. To this had been added the idea of massive screens, initiated in America with Cinerama in 1952 (London did not see it until 1954) and followed up by Todd-AO (the partnership of entrepreneur Michael Todd and scientific manufacturers American Optical). When *Oklahoma!*, the first film to be shot in Todd-AO, became available in 1956, the alternative CinemaScope version was chosen for release in this country, opening on 6 September 1956 for a run of nearly eight weeks at the Odeon Leicester Square followed by three months at the Odeon Marble Arch and a general circuit release starting 11 March 1957.

The first Rank cinema to be converted to roadshow use was a central London Gaumont house, the Astoria Charing Cross Road, which opened another Todd-AO production, *Around The World In 80 Days*, on 2 July 1957 – not in Todd AO, not even in 35mm – but in 34mm. Shaving 1mm off the print was a successful ruse to ensure an unbroken run, relieving the Astoria of its British quota requirements which only applied to 35mm. (Non-35mm presentations were "quota neutral", i.e. did not count one way or the other in quota calculations.)

Rank overcame its differences with 20th Century-Fox to install 70mm projectors and giant screens in 1958 at two Gaumont theatres – the Dominion Tottenham Court Road, London, and the Gaumont Manchester – for record-breaking runs of *South Pacific*. And the Odeon Tottenham Court Road,

on the northern extremity of the West End, was fitted out for Cinemiracle, a three-strip rival to Cinerama developed by the American chain, National Theatres, and installed in its New York Roxy in April 1958 to show the first and only feature in the process, *Windjammer*. At the Odeon, a huge 71ft. by 28½ft. screen, claimed to be the largest in the country, extended beyond the proscenium arch into the auditorium. Three projectors were installed at the back of the stalls for a nearly level throw and seating capacity was reduced by over 700 to 1,700. *Windjammer* opened in May 1958 but only lasted until the end of October, after which the Odeon reverted to weekly changes of circuit releases just before they appeared in northwest London, along with live shows that including a two-week variety presentation at the end of 1958. It seems never to have recovered its old audience and closed in March 1960 to be promptly demolished.

Roadshows at this time also took advantage of a concession in the 1950 Budget reducing Entertainments Tax for cinemas which featured a live element as well as films. Performances were therefore prefaced by a live organ or small orchestra show. (In 1958, the Chancellor halved the rate of the tax to approximately 15 per cent of receipts. All other forms of entertainment were completely untaxed. Once the tax was abolished in 1960, the live musical prologues were discontinued.) Until 1963, roadshows did not contribute to the Eady levy to aid British production.

Roadshows were at first confined to larger cities. *Around The World In 80 Days* spread from London to six "specially equipped" cinemas for an indefinite (minimum of four weeks) run commencing 23 December 1957: the Odeon Cardiff, four Gaumonts (Glasgow, Leeds, West End Birmingham and Queens Newcastle) plus an independent (the Oxford Manchester, which would soon be taken over by Rank). In the spring of 1958, the same film opened at the Odeons Aberdeen, Middlesbrough, Sunderland, Leicester, Nottingham, Hanley, Plymouth and Bristol. Then it played at various coastal Odeons during the summer holiday period: for four weeks (at normal prices) at Brighton and Folkestone, three weeks at Ramsgate, two weeks at Worthing, Torquay and Weston-super-Mare, plus an indefinite run at Ayr. Gaumonts at Bournemouth and Weymouth were also included.

The next roadshow attraction was Cecil B. DeMille's epic in VistaVision, *The Ten Commandments*, released by Paramount and premiered in London at its West End showcase, the Plaza. The Odeon Cardiff and four provincial Gaumont halls commenced engagements in the summer of 1958. The preponderance of Gaumonts reflected the fact that this company had excess centrally-located cinemas in the big cities while Odeon ran just one outlet (except for Cardiff where it had both the Capitol and the Odeon).

ODEON
Leicester Square
PHONE: WHI. 6111

TONY CURTIS · SIDNEY POITIER
THE DEFIANT ONES 'A'
Weekdays showing at: 1.35, 4.05, 6.35, 9.10.   Sunday at 5.25, 8.20.
Weekday programmes at 1.15, 3.15, 5.45, 8.20.   Sunday progs: 4.30, 7.20.

ODEON
Marble Arch
RESTAURANT PAD. 8013
THEATRE PAD. 8011

KIRK · **TONY** · **ERNEST** · **JANET**
DOUGLAS · CURTIS · BORGNINE · LEIGH
THE VIKINGS 'A'
TECHNIRAMA® and TECHNICOLOR®
Weekday showing at: 1.10, 3.40, 6.10, 8.45.   Sunday showing at: 5.15, 8.5.
Weekday progs. at: 12.55, 3.5, 5.35, 8.5.   Sunday progs: 4.40, 7.30.

Leicester Square
THEATRE
AN ODEON THEATRE
PHONE WHI. 5252

VIRGINIA · **BILL** · **YVONNE**
McKENNA · TRAVERS · MITCHELL
PASSIONATE SUMMER
ALSO STARRING **ALEXANDER KNOX · CARL MOHNER** EASTMAN COLOUR 'A'
Weekdays showing at: 1.15, 3.50, 6.25, 9.5.   Sunday at 5.35, 8.35.
Weekday programmes at: 1.0, 3.0, 5.35, 8.15.   Sunday progs: 4.30, 7.25.

GAUMONT
HAYMARKET
PHONE WHI. 6655

THE NAKED AND THE DEAD
TECHNICOLOR® RKO-SCOPE 'A'
ALDO · **CLIFF** · **RAYMOND**
RAY · ROBERTSON · MASSEY
Weekdays showing at 12.55, 3.30, 6.5, 8.35.   Sunday at 5.10, 8.5.
Weekday programmes at: 12.35, 3.5, 5.40, 8.15.   Sunday progs.: 4.30, 7.25

ASTORIA
CHARING CROSS Rd.
PHONE GER 5385

2nd. YEAR MICHAEL TODD'S
AROUND THE WORLD IN 80 DAYS 'U'
STARRING **DAVID NIVEN · CANTINFLAS · ROBERT NEWTON**
SHIRLEY MacLAINE   FEATURING 44 "CAMEO" STARS
TECHNICOLOR® ALL SEATS BOOKABLE
Screenplay by JAMES POE, JOHN FARROW and S. J. PERELMAN
from the Classic by JULES VERNE Directed by MICHAEL ANDERSON
Daily at 2.30 and 8.0 p.m.   Sunday at 4.30, 7.40.
Orchestra 1.30, 7.0.

Dominion
TOTTENHAM COURT ROAD
PHONE MUS 2176

BOOK NOW! NOW-FOR THE FIRST TIME IN BRITAIN-BREATHTAKING **TODD-AO!**
RODGERS and HAMMERSTEIN'S
NOW SHOWING EVERY SEAT BOOKABLE Prices 15/6 to 7/6
Colour by Technicolor
SOUTH PACIFIC 'U'
HERMANOS DENIZ CUBAN BAND Playing Evgs. 6.45, Sun. 8.0, Mats. 1.30.
SOUTH PACIFIC: Evgs. 7.45. Sun. 6.0. Mats., Tues., Wed., Thurs., Sat., 2.30.

ODEON
Tottenham Court Rd.
PHONE EUSton 8451

THE FIRST CINEMIRACLE PRODUCTION
EXCLUSIVE ALL SEATS BOOKABLE 15/- to 5/-
7-Track Hi-Fi Sound!
WINDJAMMER 'U'
TWICE DAILY 2.30 and 7.45. **SUNDAYS** 6.45.
in EASTMAN COLOUR
ORCHESTRA WEEKDAYS 1.45, 7.0. Sunday doors open 6.0. CHILDREN SPECIAL RATES.

Left, the London West End line-up of Rank cinemas in early October 1958 with the top four cinemas on regular runs with continuous performances and the last three on roadshows with bookable seats and separate performances.

In 1958 The Ten Commandments initiated a new form of release whereby the Cecil B. DeMille spectacular played small batches of London suburban cinemas for extended runs at advanced prices two months after its West End premiere run at the Plaza had finished. This was the first London group.

STARTS OCTOBER 12th
EXCLUSIVE
4 WEEK SEASON

PARAMOUNT PRESENTS
Cecil B. DeMille's
PRODUCTION OF
The Ten Commandments
TECHNICOLOR (R) & VISTAVISION (R)

CHARLTON HESTON as PRINCE MOSES

YUL BRYNNER as RAMESES II

MAGNIFICENT UNPRECEDENTED SPECTACLE ...

SEE IT AT
GAUMONT, Hammersmith
RIV 4081
Twice Dly. 2.05 & 7.10 p.m. Suns. 6.35 p.m.
ODEON, Croydon
CROYDON 4086
Twice Dly. 2.05 & 7.10 p.m. Suns. 6.35 p.m.
ODEON, Swiss Cottage
PRIMROSE 3424
Twice Dly. 2.05 & 7.10 p.m. Suns. 6.20 p.m.
ODEON, Mile End Road
ADVANCE 2034
Twice Dly. 2.05 & 7.10 p.m. Suns. 6.20 p.m.
SEATS MAY BE BOOKED IN ADVANCE at the Theatre Box Offices.
(Postal Bookings Accepted)
PRICES: 3/6, 5/6 and 7/6.

In the London suburbs, Fox had really shaken up the traditional release pattern by opening its major musical *The King And I* in October 1956, while still playing in the West End, for simultaneous two-week runs at increased prices at twenty-five halls on its fourth circuit all over the capital, ignoring the standard progression by area (see *The Granada Theatres*, page 162). It was not until two years later that some Rank cinemas breached the established pattern for a roadshow engagement. *The Ten Commandments* opened at the Odeons Croydon, Mile End and Swiss Cottage, along with the Gaumont Hammersmith, on 12 October 1958 for four weeks at advanced prices with two separate performances daily (one on Sunday). This meant that the regular circuit releases during those weeks were displaced to lesser cinemas or not shown at all, which cannot have pleased the distributors concerned.

But these bookings of *The Ten Commandments* seem to mark a recognition by Rank of changing conditions. No lasting damage was likely to be done to future attendances by a four-week run as habitual weekly visits to a particular cinema were pretty much a thing of the past: audiences had become more selective, partly because of changing lifestyles and television as a ready source of routine entertainment, and partly because the range of subject matter in films had widened so considerably that no-one could possibly want to see everything a local cinema presented.

In another breakthrough, Rank spot booked its own specialised release, *The Bolshoi Ballet*, for six-day runs in the spring of 1958, pre-empting a regular circuit programme at suitably upmarket locations that included the Odeons Barnet, Bournemouth, Epsom, Sidcup and Temple Fortune.

Film booking was at last becoming more flexible. But the end of the weekly circuit release was still a long way off.

Live shows

Pop concerts became a significant activity at suitable Odeons. The Odeon Plymouth featured Guy Mitchell in two shows on Sunday 20 June 1954. In 1956, an impresario called Ed. W. Jones hired the Odeon Barking on Sundays about once a month for variety shows even though the Granada East Ham was more geared to live show use in the area – these included a Joe Loss Band Show with Benny Hill and such artists as Max Wall, Frankie Vaughan and Dickie Valentine.

It was a simple matter to replace films on Sundays as this day was usually reserved for revivals and there would be no interruption to the run of a new film. When concerts took over on other days, it was a sign of how weak the film side was becoming.

In response to the huge appeal of *Rock Around The Clock*, Bill Haley and the Comets came over to perform live in this country. They did four days in early February at the Dominion

Tottenham Court Road and are said to have been the first pop group to perform at the Odeon Birmingham (on Tuesday 12 February 1957 for two shows at 6.15pm and 8.30pm).* Among the performers who followed them onto the Birmingham stage were the Rolling Stones, Genesis, ELO, The Beatles, Diana Ross, Queen, David Essex, David Bowie...

Elsewhere in London, in 1957 the Astoria Brixton dropped films for a week-long stage show. The Gaumont Wimbledon (an Odeon property) was a favourite with local amateur groups for week-long runs.

The Odeon Leicester Square was taken over on Saturday 12 April 1958 for two concerts starring Sara Vaughn but live shows of this sort were a very rare occurrence here.

In another form of live use, certain north London cinemas were regularly hired as synagogues for the Jewish New Year and the Day of Atonement in September/October. The particular halls varied slightly from year to year but included the Odeons at Haverstock Hill, Hendon, Southgate, Swiss Cottage and Temple Fortune.

Dance halls

Rank had stated that some of the cinemas closed in the 1956/7 purge would be turned into dance halls. The Globe Coventry became a Majestic Ballroom ten months later. The Tredegar Hall at Newport, Gwent, and the Palace Aberdeen seem to have been closed at later dates with this use in mind. In Aberdeen, the stalls floor was levelled and a false ceiling extended from the balcony front to the stage end of the building. Here the name used was New Palace Ballroom. Most of the subsequent conversions affected small, old Gaumont properties.

Victor Silvester Dance Studios took over the restaurant areas of many Rank cinemas through a joint venture with the veteran band leader. It was mostly Gaumonts that had the space because Oscar Deutsch never favoured restaurants in his purpose-built Odeons. But the taken over Odeons at Rochdale and Wembley featured on the Silvester circuit.

And photocopying

Since there was no way of guaranteeing substantial profits from film production and exhibition was now faltering, Rank had every incentive to diversify. By 1956, 30 per cent of profits came from

---

* This tour coincided with the showing in London's West End and at the Gaumont Birmingham of the Bill Haley film *Don't Knock The Rock*, the follow-up to *Rock Around The Clock*. That week, the Odeon Birmingham was showing the Rank production *Tiger In The Smoke* which was still screened twice on the day of the concert, at 10.30am (the Odeon's normal starting time) and 2pm, with one screening in between of the supporting film.

manufacturing, which including making radios and televisions as well as optical instruments. Rank's involvement in Southern Television, a local ITV company, has already been mentioned. Then came an investment which was to pay dividends out of all proportion to the results achieved by Rank's other endeavours. This was the partnership the Rank Organisation formed with the Haloid Company of America on 19 December 1956 to exploit the potential outside of North America of the new process of xerography or photocopying (before which offices had relied on carbon paper).

"The deal was brought to Davis by Rank Precision Industries, the scientific instruments arm of the group," recalled John Bell in *The Sunday Times*, 21 September 1975:

It was a straight venture capital operation. And to Sir John's eternal credit, he decided to stump up some cash, even though giants like IBM and RCA had long since looked, assessed and firmly declined.

It appeared a high risk investment, for the Xerox process was then not even at the commercial stage. Yet Davis, seeking to divert cash away from an ailing cinema industry, took a bold decision that paid off brilliantly. He agreed to put roughly £1m, a lot of cash in those days, in the Haloid Company, which became the Xerox Corporation, undoubtedly one of the major post war business successes. The fruit of the liaison was Rank Xerox, which grew furiously under Davis's stewardship.

Rank set up a new factory at Elstree which commenced manufacturing the copiers and related supplies in August 1957. The company made distribution arrangements for Xerox equipment throughout the world. For many years, "make a xerox" was synonymous with making a photocopy just as hoovering meant vacuum cleaning. "It will not be too long before profits from non-cinema interests exceed those from cinema activities," prophesised Lord Rank in September 1959.

A Sunday live show at the Odeon Barking in 1959.

The Odeon Tottenham Court Road has been sold in April 1960, a month after closing. (Photograph by Allen Eyles.)

ONE MAIN CIRCUIT (1959-1964)

By the start of 1961, Rank had agreed to pay £4 million, spread over eleven years, to Fox for its interest, dating from July 1929, in the Metropolis and Bradford Trust which controlled Gaumont. This acquisition made it possible to absorb Gaumont into the Rank Organisation rather than maintaining it as a separate subsidiary company. By January 1962, all activities (including non-cinema interests) were under the Rank Organisation name.

The Rank Organisation held a 56½ per cent interest and the Gaumont companies 43½ per cent in the combined group. Circuits Management Association became the Rank Theatre Division from November 1963 (then simply Rank Theatres from 1966).

In October 1962, J. Arthur Rank retired as chairman of the Rank Organisation and turned over to John Davis the first floor office which he had used every weekday at the South Street, Mayfair, headquarters. Aged 73, Rank still remained chairman of the family flour concern (he had succeeded his brother in October 1952) and he accepted the newly created position of president of the Rank Organisation. John Davis, who had been both deputy chairman and managing director, took the positions of chairman and chief executive and replaced J. Arthur Rank for the first time in the address to shareholders at the 1963 Annual General Meeting.

Rationalisation

After shutting down almost sixty cinemas in late 1956/early 1957, John Davis addressed the annual conference of the Cinematograph Exhibitors' Association (CEA) at Gleneagles in May 1957 with a proposal for further cuts by the industry as a whole. Rank executive R. H. ("Dickie") Dewes later recalled Davis's speech and its impact.

> This forecast that in the next few years a very large number of cinemas would be forced to close, and did this in considerable detail. The prophecy came as a great shock to his hearers, but proved in course of time quite uncanny in its accuracy.
> The scheme suggested to the CEA was that the Industry should rationalise by a comprehensive and carefully compiled

plan, operated by agreement within the Trade itself, and not by chance, and [not by] the rough and ready application of jungle law. Very broadly it proposed that the cinemas of each district should be scientifically assessed by a Committee, and classified as viable or redundant. The latter would then be closed subject to compensation paid by the former.

> The response was not enthusiastic. Many proprietors appeared to think it was an effort to push them out of the Industry with compensation which they imagine[d] would be inadequate. Eventually, in the absence of any concrete development, the Rank Organisation went ahead with a rationalisation scheme of its own. Later the CEA set up a special committee to consider the original proposal, but it was too late.

> The scheme was a bold and realistic approach to a grave and urgent problem, and the fact that it was not operated undoubtedly caused hardship in numerous spheres of exhibition. In the event many owners of closed cinemas were fortunate as the unanticipated and rocket-like rise of property values in the High Street cushioned the blow.

That the proposal had no effect is not surprising. There was too much suspicion that Rank would gain the most and lose the least from any such arrangements.

Following an unprecedented fall in cinema attendances in the second half of 1957 that continued into 1958 (during 1957, the number of television viewers able to receive both ITV and BBC channels almost doubled to nearly five million), J. Arthur Rank took up the "orderly closure" theme in his annual report to shareholders:

> It is our belief that the Industry is faced with a material change in working conditions in that the loss of attendances has been caused not only by television but by many other factors, such as the demand for semi-luxury goods – washing machines, refrigerators, motor-cars and so on, all of which affects the spending power of the public.

Rank went on to note the disturbing decline in the number of Hollywood films being made and the lack of sufficient main features to support four national weekly releases (although the Fox one had always been intermittent).

The inevitable result is that there will have to be a material change in the pattern of exhibition and distribution involving the further closing of a considerable number of theatres. These factors clearly establish the necessity for rationalisation of the present exhibition and distribution patterns. This rationalisation can develop one of two ways, either by a soundly based scheme operated by the Industry, or by the application of the natural economic laws forcing the weaker theatres to close first, with the result that the new pattern may not give the best service to the public. This in turn would not be in the best interests of the Industry. In as far as this Organisation is concerned, we would like to participate in a national rationalisation scheme. At the moment it does not appear that the Industry will approach the problem on this basis, consequently we are pursuing the rationalisation of our circuits by closing uneconomic theatres.

At the time, Rank operated 516 cinemas in Britain, down thirteen on the previous year and fifty-nine on the year before that.

In October 1958, John Davis described the go-it-alone rationalisation policy that had been decided:

...we are creating a Rank releasing circuit of approximately 300 theatres which will have a booking strength of approximately that of the Odeon release at its peak... In addition we shall have approximately eighty theatres available for the handling of films on a specialised basis such as the Todd-AO films, for extended runs and move-overs for films that need them, and...to materially strengthen the Fox booking release.

There were an additional eighty Rank theatres which would either be converted to other uses or sold to developers but which would be available in the short term for use in the same varied ways as the eighty that Rank intended to keep. Rank was already booking films for its new circuit and expected Fox to set the pattern for the Fox release, revised to include other companies' films.

Davis even forecast that the new third circuit would have 306 outlets compared to 300 for the "Rank Release" and 272 for the ABC release. However, its effectiveness was undermined from the start by the plan to use outlets for roadshows during which time they would not be available to take the third release and by Davis's revelation of the eighty halls, unidentified to avoid reducing their value but presumably for the most part attached to the third release, that would close within the next three years, as soon as they could be "sold successfully". One can compliment the Rank Organisation on its candour but it wasn't helpful in launching the third release. Furthermore, Fox did not organise the programming or even commit all its films. The company preferred to sell its best product to the Rank Release.

Davis's scheme came into effect without any apparent opposition from the government or the CEA. It broke down the barrier between Odeons and Gaumonts that Rank had previously been obliged to maintain. It can't be said that the new Rank Release was the Odeon release under a new name because the single most important aspect of it from the Rank point of view was the rescue of important Gaumont cinemas at such places as Hammersmith, Lewisham and Wood Green in London, along with others elsewhere, which had suffered from the increasingly weak Gaumont release (John Davis estimated that only six of the Gaumont releases in the past year would have been good enough for the new circuit). Conversely, the new arrangement resulted in many Odeon cinemas which had enjoyed a strong weekly release becoming attached to the third circuit and what was called the "National Release". Davis was accurate when he stated that combining the best of the Odeons and Gaumonts to show the new Rank Release would result in the equivalent of the old Odeon release at its peak. As Odeon cinemas were now spread between the two releases, they will both be considered.

The new releases

In the initial list of 298 cinemas making up the new Rank circuit (reproduced in *Gaumont British Cinemas*, page 151), there were more than twice as many Odeons as there were Gaumonts. (The Monopolies Commission's 1966 *Report on the Supply of Films* states that the Rank Release started out with 286 Rank cinemas.) Cinemas that were not selected for the Rank Release were generally assigned to the third or National Release.

When choosing between Odeons and Gaumonts in direct competition, it was usually quite evident which was the better cinema (i.e. more modern and larger) and this was allocated the Rank Release. In some large towns, though, like Bristol and Portsmouth, the more modern Odeon was refitted for primarily roadshow use and the older Gaumont took the Rank Release.

Sometimes the better Rank site was hard to call, as in Wolverhampton where the Gaumont lost out to the Odeon which was slightly better located, or Worcester where the postwar Odeon lost out to the slightly larger Gaumont opposite, or in the London suburbs where perhaps a bias towards Odeon tipped the balance in favour of the Odeon Well Hall over the Gaumont Eltham Hill and in favour of the Odeon South Harrow over the Gaumont Rayners Lane (although all four were originally Odeon properties). The Gaumont Bromley won out over the Odeon, presumably because of its larger size and better location. The choice of the Gaumont Peckham over the Odeon is harder to explain.

In general, Rank seems to have imposed its new Rank Release line-up with little consideration for rival independent cinemas. Of course, Odeon release outlets like the Rex Lewisham and the Rex Wood Green in the London area could hardly argue that they were in the same league as the Gaumonts which took the new Rank Release. But Rank exercised its muscle in Bath and Croydon in favour of inferior Odeons at the expense of the much larger and better appointed Forum and Davis respectively. Whereas the Forum at Bath held 2,000, the Odeon there seated only 789 and was so old fashioned it had a pull-down shutter instead of front doors (as well as being prone to flooding). The Odeon in Croydon was larger but little better. Here the Davis Theatre was a huge super cinema with 3,678 seats which had been choosing between Gaumont, Fox and off-circuit programmes. As managing director Alfred Davis wrote in his unpublished autobiography: "The large Davis Theatre was no longer viable. The Rank Organisation... had received permission from the Board of Trade that they could merge into one big circuit, which to all intents and purposes meant the death of the Davis Theatre. Reluctantly, I came to the conclusion that we had to get out when the opportunity arose."* Closure of the Davis was announced in mid-December 1958, two months after Rank had publicly listed the Croydon Odeon as part of its new main circuit. The Davis shut down in May 1959 after four months of combining the National Release with second runs and live shows, to be demolished for an office block. It seems reasonable to conclude that the Rank Organisation forced the closure of this outstanding building which might otherwise have survived (like its near-sister theatre at Hammersmith, the former Gaumont, now the Apollo). In Bath, the Forum clung on until 1968 when bingo gave it a further lease of life, since extended by listing and sympathetic church use (Rank may still have held its interest in the property dating from the 1930s, complicating the situation).

In Edinburgh, the 3,048-seat independent Playhouse – a well run, centrally located cinema – had been accustomed to playing the Odeon release while the widely separated 1,857-seat New Victoria and 2,000-seat Gaumont had both screened the Gaumont release. When the new release pattern was introduced, the New Victoria was on an extended run of *South Pacific* and the Gaumont and Playhouse split the Rank and National programmes. Two years later, the same split applied except that the New Victoria was also taking some of the Rank Releases (including *Tunes Of Glory* which ran four weeks because of its Scottish setting and characters) until it embarked on a roadshow booking of *Spartacus*. The Gaumont was permanently closed by fire in 1962 but the New Victoria (renamed Odeon in 1964) took an increasing share of the best films and the Playhouse was forced to close as a cinema in 1973.

* Alfred Davis's description of his career in film exhibition is published in the summer 2005 edition of the Cinema Theatre Association's magazine, *Picture House*.

Rank was less able to ride roughshod over ABC, as former ABC manager Ray Dolling recalls with regard to the circuit's Ritz Chatham in the Rochester-Chatham area:

The Ritz had always played the Odeon release while the Gaumont release played concurrent at the Gaumonts Rochester and Chatham. When the Rank Release and National Release came into being, a split was devised whereby 50 per cent of the Rank Release and 50 per cent of the National Release went to the Ritz and the remainder to the two Gaumonts (although the Gaumont Chatham – which to all intents and purposes was in Gillingham – closed about this time). When the National Release faded out, off-circuit product had to be found for the spare weeks which meant that both the Ritz Chatham and Gaumont Rochester (re-named Odeon) would one week be playing a strong feature from United Artists or Rank Film Distributors and the next cheap product from Compton-Cameo or New Realm – a quite incongruous situation which is why these two large, well-appointed cinemas were both used for live shows and, in time, 70mm roadshows.

At Fulham, west London, ABC's large Regal Walham Green, which had played the Odeon release, inherited the Rank Release while Rank's older and smaller Gaumont took the National Release. However, in nearby Hammersmith, ABC's large Regal had to settle for the National Release as the Rank Release naturally went into the enormous Gaumont.

Sidney Bernstein, head of the small but powerful Granada circuit, seemed to accept the new release set-up while ruefully noting that his chain would be badly hurt. Here Rank made some concessions: in Greenwich and Kingston, the larger Granada took the Rank Release and the Odeon was consigned the National Release (the same applied to Sutton, where the Rank cinema was a Gaumont). In Harrow the centrally placed Granada took over the Rank Release along with the outlying Odeon South Harrow and Gaumont Kingsbury. But in Woolwich – and, to a lesser extent, Welling – Granada was hard done by when the Rank Release went to the competing Odeon. Had any court of redress existed, these would have been good cases to bring before it – not that the Odeon Woolwich wasn't a large and attractive cinema but the Granada had many more seats to fill and was on a grander scale. At Epsom, however, the Odeon obtained the Rank Release and deserved it more than the Granada. At East Ham, where the huge Granada had enjoyed the Fox output, the Rank Release went to the Odeon and the National Release to the Gaumont, but the Granada eventually obtained a small proportion of Rank Releases.

It was, of course, bad news for the Odeons that were assigned the National line-up. Although initially announced for the Rank Release, the Astoria Finsbury Park was used to bolster the

National one, being midway between the Holloway and Wood Green Gaumonts which were deemed to give the Rank Release sufficient coverage. The Astoria was one of those cinemas which did gain roadshows and pre-releases, while its sister Astoria at Old Kent Road, though similarly afflicted, gained a lengthy respite on the Rank Release while the replacement cinema for the Elephant and Castle Trocadero was being built. Other London area Odeons on the National Release included those at Colindale, Finchley, Kenton, Wealdstone, Whalebone Lane and Wimbledon.

Booking

The last Odeon release was Rank's romantic comedy *Bachelor Of Hearts* while *The 7th Voyage Of Sinbad* ended the Gaumont one. The new Rank Release and National Release were introduced in the northwest London area on 25 or 26 January 1959 according to whether cinemas started their runs on Sunday or Monday. The Cary Grant-Sophia Loren comedy *Houseboat* played at all but six Odeons and at thirteen Gaumonts as the first Rank Release. The Fox musical *Mardi Gras* was the first National Release, playing at the six Odeons and all the other Gaumonts. The next Rank Release was *The Captain's Table* with *Stranger In My Arms* as the competing National Release.

The Rank Release took all the really major films made by Rank (like its big-budget *Ferry To Hong Kong* and *North West Frontier* and latest Norman Wisdom, *Follow A Star*). It also played the biggest and most important films from its regular suppliers. Solid draws would occasionally be directed towards the National Release, but it principally received the dregs.

The ban on X certificates was considerably relaxed. Whereas, between 1951 (when the X was introduced) and 1958, Odeons as a whole showed only three programmes with an X film (with a partial release of *The Moon Is Blue*) and Gaumonts took six (two of them double bills), the rival ABC circuit had accepted thirty-eight programmes with one or two X films without seeming to suffer commercially as a result.

The new Rank Release played two X films in 1959, four in 1960, seven in 1961 and eight in 1962. The National Release took a similar number. In 1961, Rank even financed and distributed two X-certificate dramas, *No Love For Johnnie* (about an unsavoury Labour, not Tory, politician) and *Victim* (which examined the blackmailing of homosexuals), followed by a university drama, *The Wild And The Willing*, in 1962 – all of which had a full Rank Release. The producer of *Victim* declared in *Films and Filming* that John Davis had enthusiastically helped with the financing of the film, but there remained limits to what Rank cinemas could show. Early in 1961, 20th Century-Fox issued its X-certificate drama, *The Mark*, which was selected by a committee of British film producers to be the official British

entry at the Cannes Film Festival and which earned leading player Stuart Whitman an Oscar nomination as best actor for his portrayal of a convicted paedophile. Although it was widely praised by the British critics, John Davis told *The Daily Herald*, "I have seen it and I disliked it intensely" – which was fair enough, but he then added: "It will not be shown in our cinemas." No other circuit had any problem with showing the film and this writer saw it at the Granada Brixton.★

One daring, popular and critically applauded X certificate film, *Anatomy Of A Murder*, starring James Stewart, brought the Rank Organisation into dispute with its redoubtable producer-director, Otto Preminger, for reasons unrelated to its subject matter and language. *Films and Filming* (*F&F*) reader Stanley G. Stewart complained in the letters column of the March 1960 issue that, having viewed the 160-minute film during its West End premiere run, he had then seen it again at the New Victoria (just prior to its general Rank Release) where 20-25 minutes of running time had been removed, introducing many plot inconsistencies (which he carefully itemised), while a ten-minute interval had been introduced, adding "insult to injury". He c o n - cluded: "As long as such acts of vandalism remain unchecked, how dare film companies talk of the decline in cinema attendances."

The following issue of *F&F* produced a much longer letter from Alan Tucker of Columbia Pictures, the distributor, within which he declared:

> The re-editing of *Anatomy Of A Murder* since its original presentation at the Columbia Theatre [operated by the distributor] was undertaken as a result of numerous comments received from members of the public about what they considered its excessive length. The cuts were personally selected and made by Mr. Preminger, who would be the last person to prune his own work of art in a ham-fisted manner. The picture has been shortened by 19 minutes 47 seconds to be exact, but I should like to make it clear that this was a decision made by Mr. Preminger and Columbia, and had nothing to do with the Rank Organisation.

★ It is not as though John Davis was a man above moral reproach. When his fifth wife, the actress Dinah Sheridan, gained a divorce on the ground of cruelty in 1965, Davis did not defend the petition and Lord Justice Willmer commented that if her allegations were only approximately true, her husband was shown up in "a very bad light" (*London Evening Standard*, 24 October 1966). After I wrote a short editorial for a university film magazine criticising Davis's decision to ban *The Mark*, the printers set it in type and proofed it, then apologetically declared that they could not run the page. Having printed Derek Hill's provocative summary of J. Arthur Rank's career in the film industry, "Where the Holy Spirit Leads", for another magazine called *Definition*, this small company remembered that it had been threatened with serious legal action if it ever printed anything critical of Rank again.

RANK
RELEASE ☐ THEATRES
NEXT WEEK
SOME THEATRES NOW COMMENCE THEIR
PROGRAMMES ON SUNDAY — SEE LOCAL PRESS

NORTH & WEST

THE BUCCANEER 'U'
TECHNICOLOR® VISTAVISION

RIVERS OF TIME 'U'
EASTMAN·COLOUR

ACTON Odeon	KENSAL RISE Odeon
BARNET Odeon	*KENSINGTON Odeon
*BURNT OAK Odeon	KILBURN State
CAMDEN TOWN Gaumont	*KINGSBURY Gaumont
CHELSEA Gaumont	KINGS CROSS Gaumont
*CRICKLEWOOD Gaumont	MUSWELL HILL Odeon
EALING Odeon	PALMERS GREEN Gaumont
EDGWARE ROAD Odeon	PARK ROYAL Odeon
EDMONTON Regal	SHEPHERDS BUSH Gaumont
*FINCHLEY Gaumont	SOUTHGATE Odeon
HAMMERSMITH Gaumont	SOUTH HARROW Odeon
*HAVERSTOCK HILL	ST. ALBANS Odeon
Odeon	STAMFORD HILL Regent
HARLESDEN Odeon	*SWISS COTTAGE Odeon
HENDON Odeon	*TEMPLE FORTUNE Odeon
HIGHGATE Odeon	WATFORD Odeon
HOLLOWAY Odeon	*WESTBOURNE GROVE Odeon
ISLINGTON Angel	WOOD GREEN Odeon
ISLINGTON Odeon	

NORTH & EAST

SAPPHIRE 'A'
EASTMAN COLOUR

JACQUELINE 'U'
(ABRIDGED VERSION)

BARKING Odeon	ILFORD Odeon
BRENTWOOD Odeon	LEYTON Gaumont
CHADWELL HEATH Gaumont	MILE END RD. Odeon
CHINGFORD Odeon	RICHMOND Odeon
COMMERCIAL RD. Troxy	ROMFORD Odeon
DAGENHAM Gaumont	SHANNON CORNER
DALSTON Odeon	Odeon
EAST HAM Odeon	SOUTHALL Odeon
EAST SHEEN Odeon	STRATFORD Gaumont
FOREST GATE Odeon	SURBITON Odeon
HACKNEY RD. Odeon	TWICKENHAM Odeon
HACKNEY Pavilion	UXBRIDGE Odeon
HAYES Ambassador	WALTON Odeon
HORNCHURCH Odeon	WHITTON Odeon
HOUNSLOW Odeon	

JUNE 7 for 4 days — BETHNAL GREEN Foresters

JUNE 11 for 3 days — STEPNEY Odeon

SOUTH

IT HAPPENED TO JANE 'U'
IN EASTMAN COLOUR

GUNMEN FROM LAREDO 'U'
IN COLOUR

BALHAM Odeon	PENGE Odeon
BRIXTON Astoria	PUTNEY Gaumont
BROMLEY Odeon	REDHILL Odeon
CAMBERWELL Odeon	RUSHEY GREEN Gaumont
CROYDON Odeon	SIDCUP Odeon
DEPTFORD Odeon	SOUTH NORWOOD Odeon
EAST DULWICH Odeon	STAINES Majestic
ELEPHANT & CASTLE	STREATHAM Astoria
Trocadero	WANDSWORTH Odeon
EPSOM Odeon	WELL HALL Odeon
GUILDFORD Odeon	WELLING Odeon
*LEWISHAM Gaumont	WIMBLEDON Gaumont
MORDEN Odeon	WOKING Odeon
PECKHAM Gaumont	WOOLWICH Odeon

*Supporting feature varies. See Local Press.

---

national
RELEASE ☐ THEATRES
NEXT WEEK
SELECTED THEATRES NOW COMMENCE THEIR
PROGRAMMES ON SUNDAY — SEE LOCAL PRESS

NORTH-WEST

BEYOND THIS PLACE 'A'

CARRY ON ADMIRAL 'U'
SPECTASCOPE

BARNET Gaumont	KENTON Odeon
CAMDEN TOWN	KILBURN Grange
Plaza	NOTTING HILL
*COLINDALE Odeon	Gaumont
EALING Walpole	RAYNERS LANE
EDGWARE RD.	Gaumont
FINCHLEY Odeon	ST. ALBANS Gaumont
FINSBURY PARK	TOTTENHAM Palace
Astoria	WALHAM GREEN
HENDON Gaumont	Gaumont
ISLINGTON Gaumont	WATFORD Gaumont
	WEALDSTONE Odeon
	WEMBLEY Gaumont

NORTH-EAST

ALIAS JESSE JAMES 'U'
EASTMAN COLOUR

TEN DAYS TO TULARA 'A'

DAGENHAM Grange	ROMFORD Gaumont
DALSTON Gaumont	SOUTHALL Gaumont
EAST HAM Gaumont	UPMINSTER Gaumont
HOUNSLOW Dominion	WHALEBONE LANE
KINGSTON Gaumont	Odeon
RICHMOND Gaumont	WEYBRIDGE Odeon

JUNE 7 for 4 days — STEPNEY Odeon

JUNE 11 for 3 days BETHNAL GREEN Foresters

SOUTH

AL CAPONE 'A'

WOLF LARSEN 'A'

BALHAM Gaumont	OLD KENT RD. Astoria
BROMLEY Gaumont	PECKHAM Odeon
CLAPHAM Gaumont	PUTNEY Hippodrome
ELTHAM HILL	ROSE HILL Gaumont
Gaumont	(Carshalton)
ERITH Odeon	STREATHAM Gaumont
GREENWICH Odeon	WEST NORWOOD
GUILDFORD	Regal
Playhouse	WIMBLEDON Odeon
NEW CROSS Gaumont	WOKING Gaumont

*Supporting feature varies— See Local Press.

Left, the division of London-area Odeons and Gaumonts into Rank and National Release theatres is shown for the week commencing Sunday 7 June 1959. There is only one black-and-white film (a reissue) on the Rank Release and only one colour film on the National Release. The Odeon Stepney and Bethnal Green Foresters are showing both programmes for half a week, swopping prints.

ODEON
LLANELLY PHONE 4057
Monday, Jan. 18. For 6 Days.
From 2.15 p.m.
David NIVEN, Shirley MacLAINE
Gig YOUNG
ASK ANY GIRL
2.35 5.35 8.35 (U)
Colour and CinemaScope
Leslie Phillips, Susan Beaumont
THE MAN WHO LIKED FUNERALS
4.10 7.10 (U)
Patrons may book in advance for
8/9 seats, from Mon. to Friday
(incl.). Call or Phone 4057

ODEON
SKETTY
THE SWANSEA
23955
Free Car Park. Today: Brian Rix.
Cecil Parker. **The Night We
Dropped A Clanger.** 2.5 5.20 8.40
(U). John Saxon. **Cry Tough** 3.30
6.50 (A). Tomorrow, Sun. Open
5.20: Jeff Chandler, Joanne Dru.
Drango. 5.35 8.25 (U). **Harbour of
Missing Men.** 7.10 only.
Monday, Jan. 18. For 3 Days
Sal Mineo, Gary Crosby. Terry
Moore
A PRIVATE'S AFFAIR
5.10 8.35 (U). Eastman Colour.
CinemaScope. The Award winning
Swedish drama: **Wild Straw-
berries.** 6.45 (A). Patrons may
book in advance 3/9 seats Mon.-
Fri. (incl). Call or Phone 23955

Above, in early 1960, the Odeon Llanelly is showing a Rank Release programme while the Odeon Sketty, the only Rank cinema in the Swansea area, plays three day runs of films weeks after their screening in the town centre. In an eye-popping move, this large suburban hall is propping up a weak Hollywood service comedy on National Release, A Private's Affair, with Ingmar Bergman's subtitled art house masterpiece Wild Strawberries in place of the regular B feature.

Anatomy Of A Murder is released with no mention of cuts while Saul Bass's celebrated title design of a dismembered body gives way to a conventional image of star James Stewart.

"A BRILLIANT FILM...DIALOGUE THAT WILL ASTONISH YOU, ACTING
THAT WILL THRILL YOU, AND A COURTROOM TENSION THAT WILL
DEVASTATE YOU" DONALD ZEC DAILY MIRROR

JAMES STEWART
LEE REMICK
BEN GAZZARA
ARTHUR O'CONNELL
EVE ARDEN
KATHRYN GRANT

IN OTTO PREMINGER'S
ANATOMY OF A MURDER
'X' CERTIFICATE ADULTS ONLY
and JOSEPH N. WELCH as Judge Weaver
GEORGE C. SCOTT/ORSON BEAN/RUSS BROWN/MURRAY HAMILTON/BROOKS WEST
screenplay by WENDELL MAYES from the best-seller by ROBERT TRAVER photography by
SAM LEAVITT/production designed by BORIS LEVEN/produced and directed by OTTO
PREMINGER/a Columbia release ▪ music by Duke Ellington ◄

NOW SHOWING AT POPULAR PRICES
AFTER 4 MONTHS WEST-END RUN
RANK
RELEASE ☐ THEATRES
AND OTHER SELECTED CINEMAS

NORTH & EAST LONDON

BARKING	—Odeon
BRENTWOOD	—Odeon
CHADWELL HEATH	—Gaumont
CHINGFORD	—Odeon
CLAPTON	—Kenning Hall
COMMERCIAL ROAD	—Troxy
DAGENHAM	—Gaumont
DALSTON	—Odeon
EAST HAM	—Odeon
EAST SHEEN	—Odeon
ESHER	—Embassy
FOREST GATE	—Odeon
GERRARDS CROSS	—Playhouse
GREENFORD	—Granada
HACKNEY	—Pavilion
HACKNEY ROAD	—Odeon
HAYES	—Ambassador
HIGH WYCOMBE	—Odeon
HORNCHURCH	—Odeon
HOUNSLOW	—Odeon
ILFORD	—Odeon
KINGSTON	—Granada
LEYTON	—Gaumont
LEYTONSTONE	—Rialto
MILE END	—Odeon
RICHMOND	—Odeon
ROMFORD	—Odeon
RUISLIP	—Astoria
SOUTHALL	—Odeon
SOUTH WOODFORD	—Plaza
STOKE NEWINGTON	—Ambassadors
SURBITON	—Odeon
TWICKENHAM	—Odeon
UXBRIDGE	—Odeon
WALTHAMSTOW	—Granada
WALTON-ON-THAMES	—Odeon
WHITTON	—Odeon

In the next month's *F&F*, the dispute moved to the editorial pages as the magazine reported that Otto Preminger "is furious that *Anatomy Of A Murder* was cut for general distribution in Britain. And he blames the Rank Organisation for it." Preminger is quoted as saying:

...I made several cuts in the picture at the urgent request of Columbia Pictures on the condition that this cut version would only be shown in very small provincial theatres but nowhere in a large town, much less in London... I have been in touch with Abe Schneider, President of Columbia in New York. I have a letter in which Mr. Schneider asks Kenneth Winkles [Winckles] of the Rank Organisation to re-instate the uncut version of the picture at my request. Mr. Winkles refused to do so, so if Mr. Tucker in a statement says that the Rank Organisation has nothing to do with this, it is a lame attempt to whitewash the Rank Organisation which has deliberately shown the picture in the worst possible way.

I feel just like Mr. Stanley G. Stewart, who wrote to you, that to show a picture in one theatre, to have this picture reviewed – and this particular picture got very good reviews in London – and then to show it at other theatres in London in a distorted version, comes very close to cheating the public and certainly [is] very unethical...

This picture... has been shown all over the world in the original version without any complaints from critics or public. Incidentally, I never authorised an intermission and it has never played with an intermission anywhere in the world except here in England.

As in the cases of John Davis's earlier stand against X films and Fox's 1954 declaration that Rank was the only circuit anywhere in the world that refused to allow extended runs, this story raises an image of Rank as a company stubbornly and even arrogantly out of step with the changing times.*

At the CEA Conference in June 1960, John Davis continued his criticism of X certificate films, railing against their number (to which his own company had contributed a violent thriller, *Never Let Go*, the premiere of which Davis had just attended at the Odeon Leicester Square). "There are far too many X certificate films of the wrong type today," he told delegates. "Some of you have made money out of them. But will you go on making money? There is doubt on that issue... how many people are stopping away from the cinema because they don't like seeing too much of a certain type of product. We have evidence to support this view... In the mass entertainment areas are we right in playing so many X films?" He claimed that family audiences were still attending cinemas in suburban and industrial areas

* Rank had been scrupulous in advertising "Abridged version" when some of its own productions were re-released as second features with cuts to reduce the overall programme to a standard length.

and referred to clear indications of "a silent revolt", stating that Rank had played more mass audience films than most and seen an improvement in trade above the national average. He admitted that he had gone reluctantly to see the hit drama *Suddenly Last Summer* (based on the Tennessee Williams play, featuring homosexuality and cannibalism), would not like Rank to make such a film, but felt it had been well handled and justified the X certificate. (It received a full Rank Release.) Veteran exhibitor Jim Poole commented that a major reason for X films being shown so extensively was that they bridged the product shortage.

In October 1959, during its first year, a Rank Release was daringly granted to the Jacques Tati comedy *My Uncle (Mon Oncle)*, which played with subtitles (although they were few in number and the film's humour was essentially visual). The film came from a minor distributor, was not double-billed but stood on its own feet, supported by a B feature western. It had been a huge success in West End art houses but played "with disastrous results to ourselves" according to Rank's Kenneth Winckles (letter to the author), although it drew a good audience to the Streatham Astoria and the *Kine Weekly's* box-office observer Josh Billings described it as "a hit in good and high class halls, flagging badly in industrial areas".

The practice continued at some cinemas of boosting the main feature with a top subtitled foreign film in place of a B feature. They became a very frequent part of programming at the Odeon Kensington resulting in such improved value double bills as *The Greengage Summer* plus Fellini's *Lights Of Variety* and Rank's *Flame In The Streets* plus Bondarchuk's *Destiny Of A Man* (distributed by Rank).

The National Release

The Monopolies Commission's 1966 *Report on the Supply of Films* indicates that, at the outset of the National Release, Rank felt that it would only have enough films for half the year at most, and that the other half would have to be used for extended runs of special attractions. In fact, the National Release found new films weekly for nearly three years (with the exception of two weeks of reissues and some other revivals as supporting features).

Although the National Release involved several circuits, it was in practice left to Rank to choose the films. While no production with smash hit potential was going to receive a National Release, Rank did locate some worthwhile titles. The Kirk Douglas western *Last Train To Gun Hill* was a strong alternative to the Rank Release of *I Want To Live!* The Doris Day comedy *Pillow Talk* provided a fluffy counter-attraction to *Anatomy Of A Murder*. *Journey To The Center Of The Earth* was more mass-market than *On The Beach*.

The Astoria Old Kent Road was a National Release cinema as advertised on the canopy in the photograph above where manager Maurice Cheepen promotes Journey To The Centre Of The Earth *in 1960. Top right, taking advantage of roadworks to promote* Whirlpool. *Note advertisement in lower picture for the children's Saturday club. (CTA Archive.)*

BALHAM ODEON	MORDEN ODEON
BATTERSEA 7931	MITCHAM 2900

BALHAM ODEON — BATTERSEA 7931

MONDAY, MARCH 16th   FOR 6 DAYS
Doors open 1.25
GREGORY PECK   JEAN SIMMONS
CARROLL BAKER CHARLTON HESTON
BURL IVES
THE BIG COUNTRY (A)
Technicolor — Technirama
1.40 4.45 7.50

SUNDAY, MARCH 1?...   DAY
lbert
sing

MORDEN ODEON — MITCHAM 2900

MONDAY, MARCH 16th   FOR 6 DAYS
Doors open 1.20
GREGORY PECK   JEAN SIMMONS
CARROLL BAKER CHARLTON HESTON
BURL IVES
THE BIG COUNTRY (A)
Technicolor — Technirama
1.40 4.45 7.50
SUNDAY, MARCH 15th   1 DAY ONLY
Doors open 4.15
Rock Hudson   Arlene Dahl
Ursula Thiess
BENGAL RIFLES (U)
Colour by Technicolor
Edward G. Robinson   George Raft
Audrey Totter
A BULLET FOR JOEY (A)

SOUTH NORWOOD ODEON — LIVINGSTONE 1440

MONDAY, MARCH 16th   FOR 6 DAYS
Doors open 1.00   Last Prog. 7.35
GREGORY PECK   JEAN SIMMONS
CARROLL BAKER CHARLTON HESTON
BURL IVES
in
THE BIG COUNTRY (A)
Technicolor and Technirama
1.30 4.40 7.50

SUNDAY, MARCH 15th   FOR 1 DAY
Doors open 4.15 Last Perf. 7.20
Maureen O'Hara and Anthony Quinn in
THE BRAVE AND THE BEAUTIFUL (A)
CinemaScope
Arthur Lucan and Bela Lugosi in
OLD MOTHER RILEY MEETS THE VAMPIRE (A)

From October 1956, much Odeon local press advertising went to dreary directory-style listings combining Odeons and Gaumonts that relied on extensive typesetting rather than eye-catching artwork. When a small number of cinemas was involved, the ad went from double column to single column and often lost a prominent position on the page. Large numbers of cinemas used far more space than before, repeating the same information with only a slight variation in showing times. How many admissions were lost as a result of this dreary approach?

The most successful film to play the third release was the Steve Reeves epic *The Last Days Of Pompeii* (summer 1960), closely followed by the racy Greek comedy *Never On Sunday* (early 1961), both provided by United Artists.

Rank also contributed several of its British pictures to the National Release – *Too Many Crooks, Whirlpool, Blind Date, The Night We Dropped A Clanger, Desert Mice, The Shakedown, Very Important Person.*

Unfortunately, outlets also had to contend with too many films, British and American, that had negligible appeal – films such as *The Blue Angel, The Last Angry Man, The Gallant Hours* and *Five Golden Hours.*

Roadshow bookings only provided significant relief in the big cities. In Bristol and Sheffield, the Gaumonts took the Rank Release but the Odeons only bothered with the National Release in occasional spare weeks between extended runs. In Cardiff, though, the Odeon was dependent on the National Release and even this had priority at the Gaumont (Rank's Capitol took the Rank Release or played 70mm roadshows with the Gaumont acquiring the Rank Release, displacing the week's National programme to the Odeon).

In the London suburbs, the shorter roadshow engagements often played Rank Release cinemas rather than National ones, but this had the advantage that the latter then took over the Rank Release temporarily (while further weakening the National line-up). Similarly, when the Rank Release cinema in Wimbledon, the Gaumont, was hired out for a week of live use, its programme transferred to the Odeon (which thereby gained a major hit, *The Big Country*).

When Rank began closing more cinemas, presumably among the eighty it had announced for gradual disposal, they included some taking the Rank Release – such as the Gaumonts Bromley and Peckham, the Odeon Southall – but this improved the lot of the Odeons at Bromley and Peckham as well as the Gaumont Southall when these dropped the National Release for the Rank Release.

Besides these defections, it was the National Release outlets which Rank closed in 1960 and 1961 that fatally reduced its strength. The biggest hole was in the London area where the National Release had half the value of an ABC or Rank Release. The Odeons at Colindale, Kenton and Wealdstone closed in north London but the situation became farcical in south London. Rank started out with about fifteen cinemas firmly committed to the National Release (as compared to twenty-seven for the Rank Release). On top of transferring the Odeons at Bromley and Peckham, Rank closed the Odeons at Greenwich, Putney (Hippodrome), Weybridge and Wimbledon along with Gaumont outlets at Balham, Clapham, New Cross, Rose Hill, Streatham, West

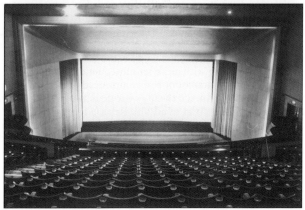

The Odeon Bristol in 1959. In Bristol, the Odeon became the roadshow and National Release outlet while the Gaumont played the regular Rank Release. The advertising space on the side wall promotes a local hotel. Inside, the proscenium surround has been completely modernised and these interior photographs show the size of picture for standard wide screen, 'scope and, largest of all, 70mm. Compare with earlier images on page 188 of Odeon Cinemas 1. (Photographs by Andrew Linham via Giles Woodforde.)

Norwood (Regal) and Woking.* In addition, the Playhouse Guildford often defected to the ABC programme. Eventually, only two Rank cinemas in south London played the National Release through thick and thin – the Astoria Old Kent Road and the Gaumont Eltham Hill (although the Odeon Whalebone Lane generally joined them a week late from northeast London). If Rank had been serious about maintaining the National Release, it would have bolstered it with some of the Rank Release outlets.

Rank faced the problem that the same distributors supplied both the Rank and National circuits and all of them clamoured for a Rank Release. In June 1961, John Davis referred to "certain distributors and producers refusing, point-blank, regardless of the circumstances, to play their product on the National Release. They did this long before as many theatres were closed as today. In fact, their actions have hastened the closure of further theatres."

The refusal of a Rank Release to MGM's *Cimarron* and Paramount's *All In A Night's Work* proved costly to Rank. In 1958, the company had made a deal with MGM by which the distributor split its new releases equally between the Rank/National circuits and its customary outlet, ABC. This brought one particular plum, Alfred Hitchcock's *North By Northwest*, which was experimentally given a Rank Release that started in the London suburbs at the end of November 1959 to test whether a strong film could draw cinemagoers in the run up to Christmas. Apparently, the results were more than satisfactory, suggesting that it was poor films that created the poor business at this time of year. Even more experimentally, *North By Northwest* was shown at both the Odeon and Gaumont Wimbledon to see which hall cinemagoers preferred (and, by inference, which should survive). The results were deemed inconclusive but the Odeon (which normally took the National Release) closed a year later.

The MGM deal also resulted in a Rank Release for such films as *Ask Any Girl*, *Libel*, *Never So Few* and *The Four Horsemen Of The Apocalypse*. MGM settled for a National Release for its Doris Day comedy *Please Don't Eat The Daisies* and the unpromising *All The Fine Young Cannibals* but objected to its big-budget landrush western *Cimarron* going the same route and gave it to ABC in March 1961, along with all of its subsequent releases.

In June 1961, Paramount also commenced giving all its films to the ABC circuit, ended a twenty-year tie between the distributor and Odeon. The refusal of a Rank Release for the Dean Martin/Shirley MacLaine comedy *All In A Night's Work* had been the final straw. The loss of MGM and Paramount pictures torpedoed the National Release.

* The Hippodrome Putney remained standing for several years, during which time it featured extensively as a setting in the black comedy *Theatre Of Blood*. The Odeon Weybridge had swopped some programmes midweek with the Odeon Walton (on the Rank Release).

Once distributors had decided there were only two main circuit releases worth supplying, some readjustment of ties in ABC's favour was needed to create a better balance in supply. Rank now generally provided a release for the output of Columbia, United Artists, 20th Century-Fox, Buena Vista (Disney) and its own Rank-Universal product. ABC now served as the conduit for the films of Paramount, MGM, Warner Bros. and its own distribution set-up.

Even with this readjustment, by early October 1961 there were so few new films available that both ABC and Rank were struggling to fill all their November and December dates, and the National Release effectively ended when it was forced to show three consecutive weeks of reissues.

A third circuit release persisted with a combination of new films and revivals for another year, then functioned intermittently with pictures usually of dubious appeal. An offering like Fox's *The Condemned Of Altona* – of art house appeal but hopeless for large cinemas – went out in November 1963 for a token appearance at an absolute minimum of Rank outlets: the Walpole Ealing, Gaumont Hendon and Odeon Haverstock Hill in north London, and just the Gaumont Eltham Hill and the Odeon Whalebone Lane the following week (the Old Kent Road Astoria was temporarily on the Rank Release).

Changing release patterns

Rank displayed a new flexibility by an increasing willingness to drastically reduce the number of its cinemas playing the Rank Release in favour of a more promising third release. In this way, the acclaimed French thriller *Purple Noon (Plein Soleil)* played at fourteen halls in northwest London alone, including the Odeon Kensington, in January 1962.

In June 1962, *Two And Two Make Six*, a British romantic drama released by British Lion, did so poorly that it had to be withdrawn after the first two weeks. Although a revival of the same distributor's *A Taste Of Honey* was drummed up for south London, a majority of Rank cinemas switched to a current third release, the routine western *Geronimo*.

A month later, the third circuit took the saucy, X-rated *Jessica* at the same time as the "important" production of *Judgment At Nuremberg* was on Rank Release. *Jessica* actually played at slightly more London Rank cinemas than the war crimes drama, an arrangement facilitated by both films having the same distributor, United Artists. Similarly, American political dramas were a difficult sell and there were many defections to the third circuit's release of a British drama, *The Boys*, when Columbia's Otto Preminger production *Advise And Consent* was given a Rank Release.

In December 1963, the third circuit's weak but up-market

Odeon Wrexham, early 1964. The name sign atop the fin has been removed, leaving crudely visible marks, while the main name sign has been mounted on the top edge of the frontage to make way for a programme display. Compare with picture on page 117 of Odeon Cinemas 1.

Odeon Llandudno, circa 1964. This overpowering and rather ugly Odeon reveals its former name on the upper side wall. The cinema entrance has been modernised but the matching area at the far end has its original canopy and serves as offices for Cream's Coach Tours. It still included a large ballroom reached through the furthest right of the three doorways on the cinema side.

Odeon Rochdale, summer 1964. The new canopy fits awkwardly on the 1928 exterior of the former Rialto. The two lower extensions carrying the cinema name had advertised the Top Rank Victor Silvester Dance Studios on the first floor until their recent closure.

Odeon Oldham, late 1964. This former variety theatre has a modernised entrance area and canopy but reveals its age everywhere else externally. The auditorium was entirely rebuilt when Odeon took over. See page 82 of Odeon Cinemas 1. *(All photographs courtesy of Carl Chesworth.)*

Toys In The Attic plus *War Hunt* was up against the Rank Release's down-market double bill of *Diary Of A Madman* plus *Sword Of The Conqueror*. All the films were distributed by United Artists which enabled an amicable adjustment by which the two programmes were divided almost equally between Rank cinemas in the London area (with a record number of twelve splitting the week to play both of them).

This was a foretaste of a later practice, after the third release completely petered out in April 1964, by which Rank cinemas would occasionally screen two poor programmes in the same week in the London area, split fairly evenly in number of bookings.

Many Odeon and Gaumont cinemas denied the Rank Release were helped by closures of ABC halls, enabling them to take that circuit's release. Those in the London area that came to rely heavily on the ABC programme included the Plaza Camden Town, Odeons Finchley, Peckham, Southall and Whalebone Lane and the Playhouse Guildford as well as the Gaumont St. Albans. Others that would clamber aboard a strong ABC release included the Odeons Barking, Chingford, Deptford, Haverstock Hill and Twickenham. The Odeon Becontree also tapped into the ABC release but subsequently specialised in horror films.

New names, new release patterns

For a while Rank experimented in promoting its chain as "Top Rank" cinemas rather than Odeons or Gaumonts to link up with its use of the Top Rank name in other leisure areas: bingo clubs, bowling alleys and on its shortlived record label. From late 1961 to 1963, group advertisements in the local press were headed "Your Guide to Top Rank Entertainment" while distributors promoted films as showing at "Top Rank Release Theatres and other important theatres" (the last four words in much smaller print). Rank dropped references to the National Release in advertising from October 1961, calling the group of halls "Selected Odeon and Gaumont Release Theatres".

A faster playoff of new films had been inhibited by the high cost of making prints – around £300 for a colour film. But the regional structure of the ITV network led to the idea of an area mass release backed by television advertising (which would only be cost effective if the film was showing simultaneously all over the area, doing away with barring delays). And in London, experiments were made to end the three-leg release, introduced in wartime to reduce the number of prints needed, by reverting to the pre-war arrangement of north London playing first, followed a week later by south London. The two north London areas were merged experimentally for the Walt Disney attraction *Bon Voyage!* and the Rank production *Tiara Tahiti* in the summer of 1962, and then permanently from the booking of Rank's Norman Wisdom comedy *On The Beat* at the end of the year. As many as

fifty-six prints were now required for a top attraction in north London (compared to around thirty-two for a northwest London Odeon release in the mid-1950s).

In fact, one hundred prints of *Tiara Tahiti* were put into circulation. Backed up by a major publicity push on posters, three different records of the title song, Miss Tiara Tahiti contests on the stages of cinemas, and television appearances and personal appearances across Britain by female lead Rosenda Monteros, Rank Film Distributors opened the film in the various ITV regions in turn with television commercials, mostly at peak time. Rank halved the number of prints required for support by dividing two new B features between the sites, the prints being swopped over to play with another main picture at a later date (a device that was occasionally repeated in later years).

An interesting situation arose in July 1964 when Columbia's Winston Churchill documentary *The Finest Hours* was released as a main feature but withheld from the London-area Odeons at Balham, Barking, Camberwell, Dalston, Harlesden, Islington and (Astoria) Old Kent Road – all working class areas clearly deemed unlikely to support this eulogy of a Tory politician. (It was, in any case, very rare for a straight documentary to play as a main feature.)

Rank's British picture *Seance On A Wet Afternoon* had a similarly half-hearted Rank Release the following week. This critically praised but "arty" drama bypassed the London Rank outlets in less sophisticated Brixton, Dagenham, Deptford, East Ham, Edgware Road, Harlesden, Mile End Road, Old Kent Road, Shepherd's Bush, Southall, Tottenham and Woolwich, all of which substituted revival double bills – either the first Bond film, *Dr. No*, with various features or Paramount's *Gunfight At The O.K. Corral* plus *Hell Is For Heroes*. This was a precursor of the time when better business could often be achieved by bringing back old hits rather than playing new films.

Although, by 1962, London Rank cinemas had almost always moved to Sunday starts and seven day runs (except for children's attractions like Disney's *The Three Lives Of Thomasina)*, the Odeons at Deptford, Kensal Rise and the Gaumont/Odeon King's Cross retained separate Sunday bookings almost every week, obviously beneficial in their downmarket locations.

Roadshows and London waves

The Metropole Victoria, London, installed Todd-AO at the end of 1959 and played the big screen version of *Oklahoma!* followed by the premiere of the Fox musical *Can-Can*. The Odeon Tottenham Court Road might have been as suitable a venue but, of course, Rank had two theatres to programme at Victoria. These had previewed the Odeon and Gaumont release the week before the suburbs. Making the Metropole a roadshow house left the New Victoria to take the Rank Release (or a superior National Release) prior to the suburbs. At the Metropole, a much larger screen was installed in front of the old proscenium with a plain surround that covered the old organ grilles and seating was reduced by over 500 to 1,394. The roadshow policy of extended engagements with separate performances continued with productions like *El Cid* and *Lord Jim* while some like *Lawrence Of Arabia* were broken in at the Odeon Leicester Square and then transferred to the Metropole (Lean's epic stayed for ninety-eight weeks from February 1963).

Todd-AO was installed in twenty cinemas in all. The Odeon Portsmouth received a huge Todd-AO screen within a new proscenium arch during a two-week period of closure in September 1960, re-opening with *South Pacific*. There were 200 fewer seats. Other Todd-AO installations were at the Odeons Bristol, Glasgow, Sheffield, and the Capitol Cardiff as well as many Gaumont halls like the New Victoria Edinburgh. The Odeon Southampton closed for three months so that its narrow pros arch could be enlarged and a much bigger screen fitted for 70mm use, although it re-opened with regular Rank Releases, beginning with *HMS Defiant* in May 1962.*

When roadshow films were released in Todd-AO/70mm there were only a limited number of cinemas equipped to show them and they could obtain bookings that crossed traditional boundaries. This gave some independents a chance to put on roadshows. When the huge London hit *South Pacific* gained a wave of indefinite runs by mid-1959, most of the bookings were at Rank cinemas (Odeons Bournemouth, Bristol, Nottingham, Sheffield) but some were at ABCs (Leicester, Southampton, Astoria Brighton) where Rank either had no 70mm halls or they were busy with another film, and others were at independents like the Palladium Blackpool. In Brighton, the Astoria had a monopoly on 70mm films until Rank carried out structural alterations in 1962 to enable the Regent (a Gaumont house) to play them.

The extended runs in big cities were followed by shorter runs in suburban and small town situations. These were usually from two weeks to four weeks and cut across the regular circuit release. Thus the Odeon Chichester (a National Release theatre) played *Around The World In 80 Days* for two weeks.

The first batch of London suburban engagements of *The Ten Commandments* in 1958, mentioned in the preceding chapter, did well enough for another four cinemas to play the religious

epic for four weeks from mid-February 1959.* Three of the halls were otherwise attached to the new National Release: the Odeon Kingston and the Gaumonts at East Ham and Wembley while the selection of the Gaumont Peckham resulted in the nearby Odeon temporarily defecting from the National release to pick up the Gaumont's Rank Release programmes. Four more cinemas dropped out of the National Release for a month with the same film in late June: the Odeon Bromley, Dominion Hounslow, Gaumont Streatham and the Astoria Finsbury Park. The next quartet two months later, comprised the Odeons at Hendon, Whalebone Lane and Woolwich plus the Essoldo Clapham Junction from a rival circuit. The Odeons at Hendon and Woolwich were Rank Release outlets but gave the Gaumont Hendon and Granada Woolwich the opportunity to take over the Rank Release programmes for a period. By September 1960, *The Ten Commandments* was playing mere two week runs at the Odeons Edgware Road, Forest Gate, Twickenham and South Norwood, all Rank Release outlets. (South Norwood audiences thereby missed *Doctor In Love* and *Psycho*. Such was the rigidity of the release system that the Odeon returned to the Rank Release to play the unpopular *Inherit The Wind* rather than backtrack to catch either of those very successful films.)

Around The World In 80 Days played in similar three-week waves through the London suburbs in 1960 after its West End run had finished at the Astoria.

However, *The Guns Of Navarone* initiated a slightly different approach – opening in the suburbs while it was still playing in the West End. This smash hit started with a two-month run at the Odeon Leicester Square from the end of April 1961, then transferred to the Columbia. It was first seen in the London suburbs at seven cinemas in October 1961, then played at further groups of predominantly Rank cinemas for four week runs.

After the Dominion Tottenham Court Road's amazing four-and-a-half year run of *South Pacific* ended on Sunday 30 September 1962, the musical at long last became available to other London-area cinemas: it opened the very next day for four week runs at the Odeons Haverstock Hill, Kingston, Mile End Road and Streatham, plus the Finsbury Park Astoria, Gaumont Hammersmith and Granada Harrow.

In October 1963, the Leicester Square Theatre was just ending an eleven-month run of *The Longest Day* when it opened for three week runs at twelve Rank halls: the Odeons at Bromley, Finsbury Park (Astoria), Hammersmith, Ilford, Kingston, Lewisham, Mile End Road and Streatham, plus the Gaumonts Finchley, Rayners Lane and Watford and the State Kilburn.

* I am indebted to James E. Tilmouth for this information: "Before the start of the programme on the re-opening day, a recorded message of good wishes for the relaunch was played to the audience. This was from Captain Warwick aboard the Queen Mary in mid-Atlantic. Passengers from both the Queen Mary and Queen Elizabeth were frequent Odeon film fans, and for that reason we accepted American dollars."

* The ABC circuit followed Rank's example with four-week runs at four London cinemas of Warner Bros.' *The Nun's Story*. It matched Rank's involvement in roadshows throughout the era they were shown.

The Guns Of Navarone. *Three London waves. Top: October 1961. Above: December 1961. Right: February 1962.*

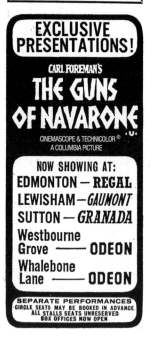

The following month, *West Side Story* appeared at virtually the same dozen London suburban halls while continuing its premiere run at the Astoria Charing Cross Road. These presentations lasted two weeks (three at the Carlton Watford), included the Granada Harrow (instead of the Gaumont Rayners Lane), and allowed the Gaumont Hammersmith a Saturday off for a live show.

Rank had an important stake in the roadshow market as a distributor through a deal with Spain-based producer Samuel Bronston by which it invested in and received widespread distribution rights for a series of epics: *El Cid* (1961), *55 Days At Peking* (1963), *The Fall Of The Roman Empire* (1964) and *The Magnificent Showman* (1964). These were supplemented by the purchase of films like *Sodom And Gomorrah* in 1961 for distribution in the UK and many overseas territories and by Rank's role as distributor for Universal of *Spartacus* (1960).

Some hit films were deemed more suited to a quicker playoff and a new technique was devised to reap more financial benefit from the James Bond productions released by United Artists. Both the distributor and Rank had been caught off guard by the first 007 adventure, *Dr. No*. This opened at the London Pavilion, a home of lesser product, on Friday 5 October 1962 and then went for rapid playoff into London general release from the following Sunday (when eight of the best cinemas were tied up with the first suburban runs of *South Pacific*). However, outside London there was more flexibility and cinemas like the Odeon Southend, where *Dr. No* opened on 7 October, were able to respond to demand by holding the picture for a second week.

No mistakes were made with the second Bond film, *From Russia With Love*, which opened a year later on 10 October 1963 at the Odeon Leicester Square. It was rushed into wider London release from 27 October even though it was still playing at the flagship (and, by now, at the Odeon Marble Arch as well) to capitalise on the huge public interest. A late decision was made to drop a second feature, *Stowaway In The Sky*, and substitute the short *This Is Jordan* to enable more showings daily and it played two weeks at many of the top London suburban cinemas (four weeks at the Odeon Watford).

A year later, with the third Bond film, *Goldfinger*, an even faster London release pattern was tried out. A group of large suburban cinemas (modelled on the "Red Carpet Theatres" in New York City) played the film at "popular" (i.e. slightly increased) prices almost concurrent with the West End premiere. These were labelled "Premiere Showcase Theatres" and they opened the new Bond film just three days after its world premiere on Thursday 17 September 1964 at the Odeon Leicester Square. Rank cinemas predominated and the choice provided a good geographical spread of large, high grossing cinemas – the New

Victoria, the Odeons at Bromley, Hammersmith, Ilford, Streatham and Watford, and the Astoria Finsbury Park (relieving it of its normally inferior programming). The two leading independent chains also participated, Granada at Kingston and Shipman & King at the Astoria Purley – because they might otherwise have opposed this radical break with tradition which elevated some cinemas above the rest. Runs generally extended to three weeks. Co-star Honor Blackman made personal appearances at many of the cinemas. A week after the runs finished, the film started playing the other Rank Release outlets for seven days at normal prices.

More closures*

Helping to undermine both the newly launched National Release and staff morale, Rank collared more newspaper headlines in March 1959 when it announced that it was putting fourteen cinemas up for auction on 22 April while they were still open and converting at least two others into bowling alleys (see later). These were the first disposals in two years. Once again, it was older properties of the Gaumont side that were principally involved. Four of the fourteen cinemas (all Gaumonts) were closed before the auction when a property company took them for replacement by shops and supermarkets. Among the other ten were three Odeon properties: the Gaumont Barnet, Odeon Bloxwich and Odeon North Watford. The Odeon North Watford was the only 1930s building in the batch, but it was very subsidiary to the Odeon and Gaumont in the centre of Watford and played their films several weeks later. A fine building architecturally, it closed in May 1959 to be converted into a supermarket.

Rank also dropped the Odeons at Henley and Marlow on the same day in March 1959, although both continued in independent hands, Marlow immediately and Henley when it re-opened in 1960. The Odeon Newport (Isle of Wight) was also taken over as a going concern in 1961, by a local circuit.

The shedding of the Odeons at Brierley Hill and Tolworth caused little commotion as these were late-run, secondary cinemas. Similarly, the subsequent departure of the Odeons Blackheath, Cleveleys and Dunstall, the Gaisford Kentish Town and Bethnal Green Foresters in London, and the Regal Coventry, Cavendish Derby and Rialto Southampton seems to have caused no great stir. In Islington, having two outlets in one London suburb was no longer practicable and the Odeon Islington went, leaving the

* The Monopolies Commission's 1966 *Report on the Supply of Films* differentiates between Rank cinemas that were shut because they were losing money (189 between 1954 and 1963) and others closed by "programme difficulties" (25 between 1956 and 1963, peaking at seven in 1961). Unfortunately, the locations are not identified.

This innovatory release of Goldfinger *placed nine suburban cinemas on a temporary par with the Odeon Leicester Square. It meant that these halls missed the normal circuit release for three weeks, although one might have been played later during the week when the Bond film had its normal run.*

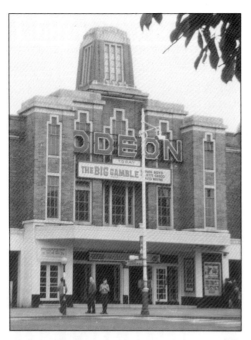

*Two lesser Odeons. Top: Odeon Whitton in May 1961.
(CTA Archive/photograph by Kevin S. Wheelan.)
Above: Odeon East Sheen in April 1960. (Photograph by
Allen Eyles.) For many years, these two cinemas exchanged
weaker Odeon and Gaumont programmes midweek.*

better placed Angel to continue playing the Rank Release (and inherit the Odeon name in due course).

However, the loss of the Odeon Shannon Corner, New Malden, at the beginning of 1960, came as a surprise because this was a well-placed cinema (at least in terms of road access) that reputedly did good business, having the advantage of playing the Rank Release a week before many of its nearby rivals (being part of north east London for release purposes). It seems that its neighbour, Decca Navigation, wanted the building for storage and put in an offer that Rank couldn't resist. George Coles' splendid building remained standing, to have holes punched in its walls for windows and other ignominious changes.

Similarly unexpected was the closure of the Odeon Sidcup less than seven years after its postwar re-opening. This played the main Rank Release but had obviously not caught on. It was outlived by ABC's Regal, which was an older property but better sited. The proximity of other Rank Release cinemas like the Odeon Well Hall had not helped.

The Odeon East Sheen was an important cinema architecturally (designed by Leathart and Granger) but too close to the Odeon Richmond (by the same architects, and even more distinguished). It had fluctuated between Rank and National R e l e a s e s until closed in June 1961 to be replaced by a supermarket.

A few months later, Rank was relieved to dispose of the Odeon Whitton in the same area. This over-sized property lay between Twickenham and Hounslow. It had been leased with two others (one being at Park Royal) and the owners for a long while refused to allow its closure. It was on restricted opening in 1956, by which time it most frequently swopped prints of the current Odeon and Gaumont releases midweek with the East Sheen Odeon. It eventually adopted a policy of reduced evening prices for latecomers who only wanted to see the main feature – a "bargain" approach that went against the up-market image of Odeon and smacked of desperation. It remained a problem building for new owners, Tesco: their lawyers failed to take seriously a restrictive clause that prevented its conversion to a supermarket. It was not demolished until 1972 – for flats.

For other Odeons, the switch from their own circuit release to the National one seems to have been quickly fatal. The casualties in south London have already been mentioned. Others in the London area included the Odeons at Colindale and Kenton, and the Grange Dagenham. Outside London, the Alhambra Barnsley and the Odeons at Chichester and Salisbury had similarly hastened ends. With three circuit cinemas, Chichester was heavily over-seated and the Odeon was the first to go, although soon followed by the Gaumont.

John Davis's call for a co-operative approach to reducing the number of cinemas in competition struck a responsive chord with Granada and a deal was reached by which the circuits each dropped cinemas to benefit the other. In October 1960, Rank closed the Gaumont Chichester and Odeon Welling in favour of Granada while Granada withdrew from Epsom and Sevenoaks, leaving Odeon with a clear field. The closure later that month of the Odeon Kettering and Granada Hounslow may have been a coincidence or a third example of this arrangement at work. Rank went from having had two cinemas in both Chichester and Kettering to none. Kettering had become notorious in the film trade for its apathy toward cinemagoing.

In Watford, Rank had, a little surprisingly, allocated the Rank Release to the Odeon rather than the equally large and more modern Gaumont. However, the Odeon was sold for redevelopment and the Gaumont inherited the Rank Release and the Odeon name.

Some Odeon closures seem to have been involuntary. The Majestics at Wembley, Staines and High Wycombe were large and well placed ex-County halls held on leases (only Staines had not been renamed Odeon). Either the owners were not interested in renewing the leases or the terms were too exorbitant for Rank to accept. Wembley and Staines closed on the same day in May 1961. The High Wycombe cinema continued until early 1969. Only at Wembley did Rank have a second hall, acquired in 1955 and eventually taking the Odeon name.

Regrettably, I can offer no comment on the closures of the Odeons at Alfreton, Guide Bridge, Hinckley and Prestwich. The Odeon Finchley shut in 1964, access to the ABC release having evidently proved of insufficient benefit. However, the Gaumont Finchley was able to tap into this alternative source of programmes alongside playing the Rank Release.

On top of all these closures come the many cinemas turned over to potentially more profitable uses by other divisions of Rank.

Closed for other uses: Bowling

Observing the success of ten-pin bowling alleys in North America and other plans to build them here, Rank announced in March 1959 a pilot venture adapting two cinemas. One was the former Regal Golders Green, which was ideal for the purpose as it had not been sold since closing in December 1956 and, having been built as a skating rink, offered a huge single-level floor for bowling lanes. The other was the Ambassador Hayes (Middlesex), with a useful stadium-style auditorium. Rank's partners were to be two New York businessmen, the brothers Stuart and Herbert Scheftel, and equipment would be supplied by the Brunswick company of Chicago from a new factory in Dublin.

The rival ABC circuit started the ball rolling in January 1960 with a bowl in a former cinema at Stamford Hill, north London. Even before opening one itself, Rank was so confident of the fortune it was going to make that it spoke of converting sixty cinemas.

The first Top Rank Bowl started up in March 1960 at Golders Green and was a great success initially. Anxious to lock in areas before its ABC rival, Rank announced seven more bowling alleys at the end of 1960. An obvious choice for adaptation was the Odeon Hove, the twin of the Regal Golders Green. Though the cinema was reputedly still profitable, it was not brilliantly positioned to serve the Brighton area for bowling. To cover west London, the Odeon Southall replaced the earlier choice of the Ambassador Hayes and was gutted for bowling on two floors. Its closure had the knock-on effect of saving the Gaumont Southall from imminent conversion to a warehouse. (The Ambassador Hayes closed anyway in June 1961; the Gaumont Southall inherited the Rank Release, later the Odeon name.)

In the West Country, the Odeon at Kingswood, Bristol, succumbed to bowling even though it had been very extensively modernised in recent times and was in tip-top condition.

In the Midlands, the late Oscar Deutsch's local, the Odeon Warley, fell victim to the craze. The imposing frontage survived but the auditorium was demolished and rebuilt.

In Manchester, the once "atmospheric" Odeon Cheetham Hill, with a convenient and vast single floor, was sacrificed to bring bowling to Manchester.

Gaumonts at Chatham, Chester, Oldham and Streatham (south London) were also turned into Top Rank Bowls. Plans to convert the Gaumont Leeds were shelved when it was learned the building might be threatened by a road widening scheme.

The success of bowling alleys was short-lived. By 1962, Rank had begun to realise its mistake and plans for further bowls were dropped.

Closed for other uses: Bingo

If bowling was a costly mistake, bingo was both a less expensive option and one that caught on almost everywhere, in all but the most affluent areas.

Rank made its first substantial step into bingo by launching Top Rank Clubs in May 1961. Two London cinemas were chosen: the Gaumont at Peckham came first, followed four days later by the large Odeon Hackney Road which changed use overnight. Initially, these two buildings opened for bingo on four nights a week but this gradually extended to every day. The Hackney Road building remains on bingo in 2005 but has been so substantially altered internally that only traces remain of its appearance as a cinema.

At the same time, eighteen cinema ballrooms introduced bingo on certain evenings and afternoons. In addition, bingo was set up on Saturday mornings at the Odeons Doncaster and

Oldham and on Sunday afternoons at certain other cinemas, including several in the London area and the Odeon Burnley in Lancashire. A certain percentage of the takings had to be returned as prizes. James Bettley recalls:

A Top Rank bingo session was held at Romford every Sunday afternoon with all available personnel, including myself, selling the various cards from tables in front of the orchestra pit rail with the caller, Danny King, and his equipment being on stage. The takings had to be rapidly computed in order that prizes could be calculated, announced and paid out from half-time onwards.

Bingo was tried out every weekday morning from July at many Odeons, mostly at the seaside – Ayr, Blackpool, Bognor, Clacton, Falmouth, Herne Bay, Llandudno, Morecambe, Paignton, Ramsgate, Rhyl, Southend (Ritz) and Worthing. The Kinematograph Renters' Society made it clear that if any film performances were replaced by bingo, the distributors would demand financial compensation for lost takings. Of course, these sessions could not compete with local clubs offering afternoon and evening bingo and usually had to be dropped. However, at Paignton (which had only been viable as a cinema in the holiday season), bingo took over full-time in January 1962. For the launch there, cinema staff were called in from as far away as Chichester, Bournemouth and Weymouth to help leaflet the area, while coach trips for players from Exeter and Plymouth were later organised until these towns gained their own bingo clubs.

Bingo also provided a lasting new use for the closed Odeon at Welling, Kent, as well as the disused Odeon Kemp Town, Brighton. Rank did well out of agreeing to close Welling to help Granada, as its bingo club went on to outlast Granada's cinema and preclude it from going over to bingo.

As bingo showed it was more than a passing craze, further cinemas were specifically closed to be turned over to the eyes down brigade over the next twenty years.

The Gaumont Upminster, a former Odeon property, was the third Rank cinema to be closed for bingo, two months after Hackney Road, and the first of a group of seven that included the Odeon Bedminster in the suburbs of Bristol. Besides the Odeon Paignton, mentioned above, the Odeon Whalley Range (suburban Manchester) and the Dominion Hounslow (ex-Odeon, former National Release outlet) were among a further seven that crossed over to bingo during 1961.

In 1962, the huge Odeon Sketty, which showed films weeks after the cinemas in Swansea, made the switch along with the Odeon South Shields, the vast Astoria at Possil, Glasgow, and the Odeon Kingstanding, a key cinema in the evolution of the Odeon style.

Rank even ran a "bingo ship" to Calais in June 1962. At the same month's Methodist Conference, the company's chairman was criticised in a report on gambling and leisure made by the Christian Citizen Department: "The Department is fully convinced of Lord Rank's integrity, and that his opinion that bingo is a harmless amusement is a sincere conviction... At the same time, we claim the right to express our own conscientious conviction that Lord Rank is mistaken in his judgment." A company spokesman responded that Lord Rank did not want to elaborate on his views.

The conversions continued. The Odeon Coventry became a Top Rank Club in 1963, followed by the Odeon Bilston and Theatre Royal Sunderland in 1964.

Marketing manoeuvres

In 1960, Rank made its first tie-in promotion, called "Swop Tops", with Canada Dry under which free seats to Odeons and Gaumonts were offered in exchange for twenty-four bottle tops. The soft drinks manufacturer fully reimbursed Rank for the price of the tickets and promoted the offer with press, TV and cinema advertising. The scheme was reintroduced for a further two months, halving the number of tops required.

Minor experiments of this period included starting films a day later, to run from Monday to Sunday from July 1960 at nine London suburban cinemas, including the Odeons at Southgate, Hornchurch, Chingford, Weybridge, East Dulwich and Peckham. This was a shortlived attempt to capitalise on favourable word-of-mouth so that cinemas would improve their weekend business. And at the Odeon Stockton, separate weekday afternoon shows heavily publicised as "Housewives Matinees" were introduced in February 1960 with the main feature and a special supporting show, finishing early enough for ladies to "Be home in time for Tea".

Gaumonts into Odeons

With the end of the Gaumont circuit release, there was no longer a powerful reason to keep the Gaumont name. In addition, Gaumont British had just been integrated into the Rank Organisation and was powerless to object to a wider use of the Odeon name at the expense of its own.

The last cinema to be branded Gaumont was the Broadway in Peterborough in November 1961. A little over a month later, Gaumonts started being renamed Odeons at Southall and Wembley. In both places, sufficient time had elapsed since the loss of earlier Odeons to avoid giving rise to confusion.

These were suburban halls but the change was really rubbed in when, in 1962, the new basement cinema in the West End of London replacing the former Gaumont Haymarket in a complete remodelling of the existing building was named Odeon and when the fire-damaged Gaumont Lewisham re-opened as an Odeon after extensive modernisation (among other changes, false walls reduced the size of the huge old foyer).

Similarly, after a considerable sum was spent subdividing the Gaumonts at Plymouth and Preston in 1962, the new cinemas in the extended circles took the Odeon name (the former stalls areas became dance halls). At Plymouth, the existing Odeon closed just two days before the new one opened.

The more routine change of name from Gaumont to Odeon at twenty-four other sites between September 1962 and January 1963 reaffirmed beyond doubt that Odeon was the preferred name and "Gaumont" was being phased out. The war-damaged cinemas that had been rebuilt or replaced at Barnsley, Holloway and Shepherds Bush were re-branded after only a few years as Gaumonts. The key London Gaumonts at Chelsea, Hammersmith and Wood Green followed, along with other longstanding purpose-built Gaumonts at Barnstaple, Chippenham, Cheltenham, Stroud and Trowbridge. At Burnt Oak, the Gaumont reverted to the Odeon name under which it had traded between 1937 and 1949. At Stamford Hill, the Gaumont signs had been up for less than three years at the former Regent before being replaced. At Wimbledon, the Gaumont was an Odeon property that assumed the name two years after the original Odeon had closed. Other affected halls were at Allerton, Ashton-under-Lyne, Falkirk, Grimsby, King's Cross, Kirkcaldy, Perth, Putney, Rochester and Southport – all introducing the Odeon name to places where it had not been seen before. Much as these changes were resented by some Gaumont veterans, they represented a gesture of confidence in the future of these buildings.

Later in 1963, the Gaumont Swindon and Angel Islington adopted the Odeon name. Then, during the first five months of 1964, another thirteen Gaumonts were rebranded: Anniesland, Bootle, Camden Town, Carlisle, Chadwell Heath, Dagenham, Edinburgh (New Victoria), Eglinton Toll (New Cinerama), Kingsbury, Leyton, Northampton, Rayners Lane and Wednesbury. (Eglinton Toll had to be renamed to avoid confusion with the Cinerama process installed at ABC's Coliseum in Glasgow.) Later in 1964 the Gaumonts at Alloa, Salisbury and Watford followed. The Dagenham, Kingsbury and Rayners Lane cinemas were actually Odeon properties (and the latter two had been Odeons until 1950). At Salisbury, as at Watford, the closure of the existing Odeon enabled the change to take place.

Over the next couple of years, the Gaumonts at Derby, Walsall and Burton-on-Trent followed suit, but no changes of name occurred in 1967 and 1968. There were still many towns where Rank operated both an Odeon and Gaumont, keeping both names alive.

Odeon Preston, early 1964. The former New Victoria/Gaumont is a Top Rank Entertainment Centre with Dancing on the ground floor and an Odeon upstairs, plus a first floor Restaurant. The entrance at ground level has been throughly modernised and the central window lost above, while the tilework is pockmarked from the removal of the original name sign above the parapet. (Courtesy of Carl Chesworth.)

The Gaumont Bootle has recently been renamed Odeon in this summer 1964 photograph. This cinema was an experiment in economical cinema construction – and looks it. The shadow of the old name sign remains on the left. Compare with photograph on page 138 of Gaumont British Cinemas. *(Courtesy of Carl Chesworth.)*

Through the wholesale expansion of the Odeon name, a much enlarged Odeon circuit had been created and films which had been advertised as playing "At Principal Odeon and Gaumont Theatres" were from June 1964 to be found "At Odeon and Other Important Theatres" or "At Principal Odeon Theatres". The Gaumont name held on at a few sites and it was not until 1987 that the very last Gaumont at Doncaster became an Odeon.

Live shows

One result of the fall in attendances was that Rank's large cinemas with stage facilities became increasingly available for hire for one night two-performance stands by touring pop groups, even at weekends. Distributors did not like their films sitting idle for a day, perhaps the best day of the week, but were given little choice. The tours typically mixed Rank theatres with Granadas, ABCs, independents, live theatres and municipal halls and so are not specifically relevant to the history of Odeon. However, these shows sometimes provide the most vivid memories of visiting particular cinemas, and were among the few occasions when their huge seating capacities were really required and when they sprung to life as they had in the boom years of cinemagoing. In some towns, like Romford, a rival ABC and Odeon were both available for live shows. In other towns, such as Liverpool and Newcastle, a non-cinema venue seems to have been preferred to the Odeons.

Here are some instances of Odeons on live shows. Roy Orbison and Freddie and the Dreamers headlined a three-week tour in September-October 1963: their twenty-two engagements included the Odeons at Nottingham, Glasgow, Manchester, Birmingham and Leeds as well as the Gaumonts Hanley, Southampton and Rochester. In April-May the following year, the same top acts, with different support, did another tour and the twenty-seven venues included the Odeons at Southend, Birmingham, Bolton, Manchester, Leeds, Glasgow and Stockton as well as the Gaumonts at Southampton, Hanley, Ispwich, Nottingham, Worcester and Doncaster (at Southend and Worcester, Freddie and the Dreamers were replaced by Brian Poole and the Tremeloes).

A live appearance by the Beatles is a noteworthy event in the history of any building and Mark Lewisohn's *The Complete Beatles Chronicle* (1992) provides a useful record of the pop group's involvement with Rank properties. The first such booking was at the Majestic Ballroom, Birkenhead (a former Gaumont cinema), on Thursday 28 June 1962, and over the next year they played twelve more Rank ballrooms (mostly other ex-Gaumont halls), concluding at the Majestic Newcastle in June 1963.

The Beatles went on tour supporting Helen Shapiro and others in early 1963 and the one-day bookings took them to the Gaumonts at Bradford, Doncaster, Taunton and Hanley and the Odeon (former Gaumont) Southport. The quartet then went out on a second package tour which they dominated, despite top billing being given to two American artists, Tommy Roe and Chris Montez. This tour called at the Odeon (former Gaumont) Lewisham, south London, on Friday 29 March 1963. For a third tour in May-June, they took top billing ahead of Roy Orbison, the mix of cinemas including the Gaumonts Hanley, Southampton, Ipswich and Worcester; the Odeons Nottingham, Manchester, Southend, Leeds and Glasgow; and Odeon's Capitol Cardiff.

The Odeon Romford featured the Beatles on Sunday 16 June 1963 as part of another, truncated tour. "This was a truly remarkable booking for, in what may be the only time in popular music history, the show's three main acts – the Beatles, Billy J. Kramer with the Dakotas, and Gerry and the Pacemakers – occupied numbers one, two and three in that week's British singles charts", observes Mark Lewisohn. The Odeon Guildford had the Beatles on Friday 21 June.

The Beatles' tour of seaside resorts in the summer of 1963 brought them for six day runs to the Odeon Weston-super-Mare (22-27 July), Odeon Llandudno (12-17 August), Gaumont Bournemouth (19-24 August) and Odeon Southport (26-31 August).

A mini-tour in early September included single nights at the Gaumonts Taunton and Worcester and at the Odeon Luton. *The Beatles' Autumn Tour* started at the Odeon Cheltenham on 1 November and visited the Odeons at Leeds, Liverpool, Lewisham and Nottingham, plus the Gaumonts Wolverhampton, Doncaster and (for the last night, Friday 13 December) Southampton. *The Beatles' Christmas Show* had a pared-down preview at the Gaumont Bradford on Saturday 21 December and opened on Tuesday 24 December at the Astoria Finsbury Park for the team's longest run at any cinema: sixteen nights ending on Saturday 11 January 1964 (three nights were excluded). Lewisohn notes: "One hundred thousand tickets for the 30 shows went on sale on 21 October. By 16 November they were all sold."

1964 was the year the Beatles conquered America in two tours and Australasia in one. In the UK, they filmed *A Hard Day's Night*, locations including the iron staircase at the back of the Odeon Hammersmith. This cinema provided the venue for *Another Beatles' Christmas Show*, from 22 December to 16 January 1965. Before that, the Odeon Glasgow hosted the quartet on Thursday 30 April; they attended the northern premiere of *A Hard Day's Night* at the Odeon Liverpool on Friday 10 July; they appeared at the Gaumont Bournemouth on Sunday 2 August; and their one British tour of the year in October-November included the Gaumont Bradford, Odeons Birmingham, Glasgow, Leeds and Nottingham, Capitol Cardiff,

Gaumont State Kilburn and Gaumonts Bournemouth, Ipswich and Southampton.

The Beatles' last, brief British tour opened at the Odeon Glasgow for the one night of Friday 3 December and concluded at the Capitol Cardiff on Sunday 12 December, intervening venues including the Gaumont Sheffield, Odeons Birmingham and Hammersmith and the Astoria Finsbury Park.

But it wasn't all pop music: after the Beatles played their week at Llandudno, the Odeon presented a week of the Welsh National Opera Company.

The Gaumont Hammersmith, the New Victoria, the Regal Edmonton and the Astoria Finsbury Park seem to have been the Rank theatres most used for live shows in London. The Astoria Brixton, Odeon Streatham and Gaumont Watford were other occasional venues by 1963/4.

One remarkable development occurred when the Royal Philharmonic Orchestra needed a new home after the Royal Festival Hall on London's South Bank closed at the end of May 1964 for seven months of renovation. The Odeon Swiss Cottage was chosen for a series of nine Sunday night concerts, which began on 24 May 1964 with Sir Malcolm Sargent conducting a programme of works by Rossini, Mozart, Britten and Sibelius. Rank went to the trouble of erecting a new acoustic "shell" on the stage to project the sound into the auditorium. The cinema followed up the first series of concerts with a Sunday booking of the film *Der Rosenkavalier*. The concerts were so popular that the Royal Philharmonic returned for many more series, switching to Tuesdays and then back to Sundays, with Rank continuing to add numerous one-day specials of ballet and opera films on the same days between the seasons of live shows. The concerts continued at least until the end of 1969. Audiences only faded when the orchestra performed too many pieces by less popular composers under pressure from its sources of funding.

New cinemas

Against the stream of closures came a trickle of openings. The New Towns with their rapidly expanding, generally affluent populations were prime targets for new cinemas. Even though Crawley and Hemel Hempstead had pre-war halls serving the old towns, Rank decided to build Odeons. At Harlow, the independently-run Regal had opened in 1952 as the first completely new postwar cinema designed and built in England. Belying its name, the 650-seater was a utilitarian adaptation of a standard factory unit at an out-of-the-way location, arranged as a temporary measure by the Harlow Development Corporation after it was unable to obtain a building licence for a proper cinema in the town centre. Otherwise, there would have been no cinema within seven miles and the population of Harlow, between 7,000 and

Live shows. The Beatles at Finsbury Park (Courtesy of Stan Fishman.)

This 1964 advertisement shows the Odeon Swiss Cottage embarking on its long series of one-day classical concerts.

ODEON THEATRE, Swiss Cottage, N.W.3
Sunday, May 24th at 7.30 p.m.
ROYAL PHILHARMONIC ORCHESTRA
Overture, A Journey to Rheims ...... Rossini | Young Person's Guide to the Orch. ... Britten
Piano Concerto in E flat, K.482 ...... Mozart | Symphony No. 2 in D .... Sibelius
Conductor: | Soloist:
SIR MALCOLM SARGENT | **IDIL BIRET**
21/-, 17/6, 15/-, 12/6, 10/-, 7/6 from Theatre Box Office (PRI 3424) and local Agents

Odeon Harlow, 1960. Although freestanding here, this became part of a parade of buildings as always intended. The illuminated star above the roof was not a fixed feature but one of many placed around the town to promote the opening film, Follow A Star. *The style of name sign with the letters backlit in individual boxes had been tried out at the new Gaumont Barnsley in 1955 but was introduced at many Odeons from 1960. They had none of the impact of neon at night. The wide proscenium opening with its colourful tabs and giant wide screen ensured a maximum impact on cinemagoers. The side walls join the tabs in a smooth curve without the distinctive break found in earlier Odeons. (Exterior from CTA Archive.)*

8,000 in 1952, was growing by 2,000 annually. The lessee of the factory building had to outfit it as a cinema but gained an option on one of two sites that the Corporation had designated for new cinemas – on which, it was hoped, work could be started in 1959. In 1955, Rank took over the seven-year lease of the Regal solely to inherit the option on the central site.

Construction did indeed start in 1959 and the Odeon Harlow opened in February 1960. No rival cinema appeared on the other site. Designed by T. P. Bennett & Son, this was the first completely new Odeon to open on the British mainland since 1939. The high show frontage featured a brown brick panel recessed within a stone frame, lit up at night by sodium floods concealed behind the Readograph sign on the canopy. The name sign appeared high up, in the trademark letters, each in red on its own backlit box. (Replacing neon, this style had been introduced by Rank at the new Gaumont Barnsley in 1955 and was used for new name signs until the 1980s.)

The Odeon accommodated 1,244 on a single floor with wider-than-customary seats upholstered in almond green and a minimum of 3ft. 3ins. between rows. There was a low barrier between the stepped rear section and the front rows on a slope towards the screen. The cinema was fitted out with six-track magnetic stereo and mono sound, a huge screen (59ft. by 27ft. 6ins) with variable masking for Todd-AO/70mm presentations and almost level projection from a box suspended from the main ceiling over the rear seats. Six spray-type suspended light fittings hung from the auditorium ceiling with the curtains floodlit from a break in the ceiling line. The curtains, which extended the entire width of the stage end and over the side exits, had the only striking decorative feature: small, repeated appliquéd depictions of heraldic dragons brandishing scimitars.

The opening presentation was Rank's latest Norman Wisdom comedy, *Follow A Star*, with a personal appearance by one of the other leads, Michael Craig, preceded by Gerald Shaw at an organ brought in for the occasion.

During 1955, the same year it secured the Regal Harlow, Rank reached an agreement with Hemel Hempstead Development Corporation to build an Odeon there. It was designed by Robert Bullivant of the Harry Weedon partnership whose work included pre-war Odeons at Chester, Leicester, Rhyl and York as well as the postwar Odeons at Worcester and Sheffield. Subsoil problems temporarily halted work in spring 1959 but the foundation stone was laid later that year by actress Lauren Bacall (then starring in Rank's adventure film, *North West Frontier*, opposite Kenneth More).

The Odeon opened in August 1960 with a screening of the Rank comedy *Doctor In Love* attended by two of the stars, Leslie Phillips and Virginia Maskell. A low entrance led to a compact

Odeon Hemel Hempstead, 1960. The vertical name sign looks rather awkwardly hoisted. The Presto fast food restaurant/coffee bar fills in the corner of the site in right background and was the first Rank venture of its type, operating independently of the cinema from 10am to 10pm Monday to Saturday with capacity for seventy customers.

The tall, spacious auditorium with its huge screen had an elegance that eludes the modern multiplex. The front and back seating areas were separated by a low barrier. The tabs did not open completely for standard wide screen, reducing the area of masking on view.

Odeon Merrion Centre, Leeds, 1964. When really big name signs were needed, the Odeon name was put up in red individual shaped letters that were lit from within, requiring less maintenance and making less impact than external neon. (CTA Archive.)

foyer (managers regarded their office on one side as overly accessible). A Rank-operated Presto coffee bar stretched alongside, to the corner of the site, masking the width of the single-floor auditorium (visible down the side street). 1,148 seats were provided with generous spacing between rows – half on a raked floor and half on 5ft. steppings at the back. There was an almost horizontal throw to the huge screen in the 63ft.-wide proscenium opening, and ten effects speakers were placed on the side and rear walls of the auditorium. The result was an elegant and pleasing viewing environment. Eighteen months on, the Odeon became the town's only cinema after Essoldo's ancient Princess in the same street was closed by a Compulsory Purchase Order for further development of the new town.

The Crawley Odeon was announced in March 1955. Rank rejected the site initally offered because it was at the other end of town from the existing Embassy (part of the Shipman & King circuit). A site adjacent to the Embassy was much more acceptable and, in November 1957, Rank announced that construction would start in early 1958. The Odeon would seat 850 and cost £150,000. But the scheme was abandoned in 1959 and another company put a bowling alley on the site.

The new Odeon Haymarket in the West End of London was the long gestating replacement for the Gaumont, probably included to obtain planning consent. However, when it arrived in 1962 it fitted in well with the need for roadshow houses and began with an exclusive run of *Barabbas*.

The building, which had always had offices in the upper portion, was gutted internally and its exterior drastically simplified. Opened in 1962, the cinema had a minimal entrance with a bank taking most of the frontage along with the better corner facing up towards bustling Coventry Street. The cinema may not have been necessarily intended for Rank as the architect was Leslie C. Norton who had no track record with the company (he designed such pre-war cinemas as the Ritz Lincoln, an Odeon takeover, and later handled the ABC 2 in Sauchiehall Street, Glasgow).

Once past the Odeon's cramped entrance hall and narrow winding staircase (with the alternative of a lift), patrons reached a slightly more generous foyer before descending further to the unexpectedly spacious auditorium that occupied the basement of the entire island site. Its twin set of festoon curtains (top and bottom lit), its huge screen, its flat but lofty ceiling pierced by large circular openings, its side walls covered by damask silk and sloping in towards the ceiling, all helped to make it a most attractive place to view a film.

On the fringe of the West End, the Odeon Marble Arch had become very run down and in need of restoration by the early 1960s. It was also out on a limb as far as the West End was concerned. It did its best business with lowbrow product that attracted audiences off the Edgware Road. In 1959, it showed Rank's major production *North West Frontier* concurrently with the Odeon Leicester Square but rarely obtained big attractions on its own. It often played second run after films had premiered at more central Rank sites. T. P. Bennett & Son drew up plans to replace it with a new cinema attached to shops and an office tower on an expanded site. It closed in 1964 and its successor, opened almost three years later, is discussed in the next chapter.

In August 1964, Rank pioneered the concept of the cinema in a shopping centre: the Odeon Merrion Centre, Leeds. Designed for extended runs, this new first-floor cinema (over a supermarket) had a somewhat oppressive ceiling and plain, curtained side walls, with concealed lighting that changed colour. There were 900 seats on one floor. It opened as a roadshow house with Rank's *The Fall Of The Roman Empire*.

In the same year, the large Gaumont Leicester was demolished behind its facade and a new, exceedingly dull Odeon seating 822 on one floor appeared above a shopping arcade. This, too, was designed for extended runs although it opened with the mass release hit of the moment, *Goldfinger*.

The "zing" treatment and other makeovers

From mid-1959 to mid-1965 Rank modernised many of its more profitable cinemas. Some, like Bristol, were upgraded for roadshow use, with the proscenium area being remodelled to take a much larger screen. There was a widespread move to cut out concealed or cove lighting which was expensive and difficult to maintain, along with battens and footlights. Instead, banks of lights were mounted on the balcony front to flood curtains which were often new with reflective decoration.

At original Odeons such as Aylesbury, Brighton and Peterborough, the distinctive buff/cream exterior tiles and panels were removed around this time rather than repaired or replaced. At Peterborough, the balcony lounge was reduced in size for offices and further toilets. Pendant light fittings over the circle were replaced by much shorter, plainer ones.

The bigger makeovers received what was known as "the zing treatment". The Odeon Bradford closed in 1961 for one month during which £20,000 worth of alterations were carried out, extending from armour plate glass doors to an enlarged screen. But perhaps the major change was to the inner foyer where half the circle lounge went to open up more space on the ground floor with twin staircases up to the circle replacing the old side stairs. Re-spacing of the stalls removed 266 seats.

When the art teacher at my grammar school at Streatham, south London, asked me what I thought of the Egyptian murals at the Astoria, I had to confess I had never noticed them. The next time I visited the Astoria, I realised why. To save money, I never sat upstairs but, by walking forwards to the front of the stalls, I found I could look up and see the huge and splendid friezes, different on each side wall of the balcony. On a visit soon after, in 1961, scaffolding had been erected at the sides of the auditorium and vandalism soon prevailed: the cinema became a "Top Rank Luxury Theatre", now called Odeon, covering up or obliterating as much of the original Egyptian decoration as was in easy reach, such as those murals, leaving the pergola ceiling intact but unlit. A unique decorative scheme had been ruined.

The Odeon Woking also became a Top Rank Luxury Theatre a month or so after Streatham, but there was little to be lost there in terms of original decoration. However, the same cannot be said of the Odeon Swiss Cottage which, around this time, lost one of the most elegant and elaborate of the circuit's 1930s interiors. Further desecration removed the striking bas-reliefs on the splay walls at Halifax and the distinctive light fittings at Ipswich as well as the twee figures perched high on the side walls at Exeter.

In spring 1964 the Odeon Colchester had "unnecessary ornament" removed – a ridiculous half-measure that left odd pieces of Spanish-style decoration in the midst of new areas of blandness. The Odeon Woolwich was deprived of its striking side wall decoration. Yet sometimes the wave of modernisation was less thorough – at the Odeon Blackpool, the proscenium arch was widened but the side wall decoration and light fittings remained.

Takeovers

A rather surprising takeover at the expense of the independent sector concerned the Oxford in central Manchester, on the same street as the Odeon and Gaumont. This had long been part of the Harry Buxton circuit but Rank moved in on 12 June 1960 and the following year offered the first roadshow run in the area of *Ben-Hur*, an MGM film not normally found on Rank screens. It continued as a roadshow house along with the Gaumont while the Odeon took regular releases.

And, demonstrating how old wounds between Fox and Rank had healed, Rank took over the distributor's Drake Plymouth in 1961, less than three years after it had been opened as a defiant gesture in support of Fox's fourth circuit. This gave Rank a surplus of large cinemas in the town. It soon closed the huge Odeon, transferring the name to the new cinema within the former Gaumont and eventually turning the Drake into its main outlet in the town, calling that the Odeon Drake.

In Watford, Rank began actively running the Carlton from April 1962, having taken a lease on the hall, an awkwardly-shaped former roller skating rink, in 1950. It seems that when the company was unable to overcome existing bars on film booking, the cinema had been sub-leased to an independent. Once Rank had sold the town's Odeon for redevelopment, the Carlton was taken back to be upgraded for roadshow use. It closed for two months in 1963 for an elaborate makeover. The Odeon name passed to the Gaumont in 1964 while the Carlton's went unchanged.

Overseas, too, there was some expansion. On 28 November 1960, Rank took over the Hippodrome and Grand Opera House on Great Victoria Street in Belfast to add to the numerous other cinemas it operated in the city. In March 1961, Rank bought land around one of these, the Regent (ex-Picture House) in Royal Avenue, leading to a surmise that it was once again planning to build a new cinema there. (This had been one of two post-war announcements of new Odeons in the centre of Belfast.) But Rank simply modernised its two acquisitions. The Hippodrome was closed for three months of alterations before re-opening in October 1961 as the Odeon Belfast with a new box-like exterior and vertical name sign and 1,150 seats inside. The immediately adjacent Grand Opera House closed at the same time for three weeks of severe alterations to the foyer by local architect J. McBride Neill, re-seating of the auditorium, and a new projection box at the back of the gallery. With ABC's huge Ritz on the other side of the Odeon, these formed the main concentration of Belfast cinemas.

Odeon Colchester (March 1981 photographs by Allen Eyles). Interior shows the rich ceiling and bland walls and pros arch after modernisation.

Diversification

At a time when cinemagoing was in such sharp decline, it is only natural that Rank should have thought of turning to other areas. But was the company right in assuming that its experience in cinema automatically suited it to other fields of entertainment and leisure? Most of Rank's diversifications were failures. Rank Records was launched in early 1959 but its Top Rank label struggled to gain effective distribution (discs were played at Odeons and Gaumonts and offered at half price). After eighteen months the business was handed over, free of charge, to EMI. Rank went into health clubs in 1960, promised rapid expansion in 1961, then gave up on them in 1962. It also took a half interest in Choiceview, a pay-TV company, for which it was heavily criticised by elements in the CEA. However, while Rank was often attacked for not trying harder on the film side and, with more effort, might have delayed the decline, it could hardly have halted or turned round a trend that affected so many countries.

In the year 1959/60 Rank Xerox made a small profit for the first time from making and selling photocopiers. Whereas in 1958/9 Rank's UK cinemas contributed 40 per cent of sales and almost 60 per cent of profits, in 1964/5 this had shrunk to 22 per cent of both sales and profits, the latter only slightly ahead of Rank Xerox and other manufacturing interests.

Odeon Woking. (CTA Archive.)

TWINS AND TRIPLES (1965-1975)

The Rank Organisation became badly distended by the huge return from the Rank Xerox photocopying side which provided nearly 90 per cent of profits pre-tax by 1967. Rank's policy of diversification had run into further snags. Its twenty-four bowling alleys (which had claimed so many cinemas) were doing badly by 1965 and nearly half had been shut down or sold by the end of 1967. Rank was out of bowling entirely by 1970, only ten years after entering the field (it was reintroduced at holiday camps and at some leisure parks in the 1990s). Rank's hotel division was also making heavy losses by 1966.

On the film side, Rank gave up production in the late 1960s and turned Pinewood Studios into a rental facility while continuing in distribution.

Rank Theatres became a division of Rank Leisure Services from 1 January 1969, lumped together with Dancing, Catering, Top Rank Clubs (bingo) and what was left of Bowling. (Motor service areas were added by 1974.)

Rank cinema attendances got off to a bad start in the 1970s when the combination of a flu epidemic, fine summer and the World Cup series, together with the increasing spread of colour television sets, brought about a 10.6 per cent decline in 1970. Almost every year showed a further drop and by 1972 the cinemas fell well behind Rank's radio and television interests in profits before taxation. Although twinning and tripling cinemas helped figures in 1974 (despite the three-day week and the energy crisis), the following year John Davis declared that, apart from the London West End sites, Rank's cinemas were making almost no profit at all.

A new broom

In 1967, Bryan Quilter succeeded Kenneth Winckles as managing director of the Rank Theatre Division. Then aged 39, Quilter had joined the Theatre Division as assistant managing director in 1964 – a rare appointment from outside the film industry, as he had been a market controller at Beecham's specialising in toothpaste. He introduced the concept of market research into cinemagoing.

Quilter was given £2 million by the main board to spend in a year on fourteen cinemas – mostly on subdividing big city sites into two, one screen being for roadshows, the other for general releases. A similar amount was allocated for the following year.

"Two-thirds of today's cinemagoers are under thirty-five. They are young – we must be youthful, too," Quilter declared in May 1967. "They don't want in their cinemas domes and organs and mock decorations. They want compact theatres with comfortable seats, plenty of leg room, pleasant decor, and car parks."

"Suburban cinemas are not so important any more," he told *The Sunday Times* (8 October 1967), singling out South London as "a terrible problem" and wishing he could have £70 million to knock old cinemas down and start again. He continued:

> The trouble with the industry is that it regards itself as a kind of custodian of the Thirties. Whether you measure it by our share of the leisure £ or by the cinema itself we just haven't been competitive. We have an ageing management force and a dire shortage of top and middle managers. The reason why we can't attract graduates is that most cinema managers are not busy enough. What sort of people are going to spend two-thirds of their working lives waiting for the show to finish?

Quilter had already announced his solution to the apparent idleness of managers in August 1967. Gerry Crane, manager of the Odeon Norwich, recalled (in *The Mercia Bioscope*, May 2004):

> When Bryan Quilter...was made assistant managing director of Odeon Cinemas he spent some time as my assistant manager getting to know how everything was done – except, that is, getting a queue in, as it was during a scorching hot summer! It was during this period that 'BQ' whilst standing at the front of house suggested, "I think you chaps could manage two theatres in towns where they are reasonably closely situated."

Quilter instituted the Town Management scheme, later called Multiple Unit Management (MUM for short), making one manager responsible for two or more cinemas. Some managers enjoyed it – in Southampton, the Gaumont's many live shows offered an exciting challenge on top of running the Odeon. And it enabled concessions stock to be pooled and easily transferred, along with moving staff in busy periods. It even applied to

Odeons as Classics:
Herne Bay (above),
Ramsgate, split with
Mecca bingo (right) and
Chingford (below).
(Photographs by
Allen Eyles.)

London's West End where the Odeon Leicester Square and the Leicester Square Theatre came under one manager, as did the Dominion and Astoria, and the Metropole and New Victoria.

Quilter demanded that managers spend less time in front of house and more on filling in paperwork. But he did involve managers in "profit planning", giving them information about their theatres' profits and involving them in seminars and group debates on cutting costs.

Sold as going concerns

Of all Quilter's moves, the most startling was in July 1967, putting up for sale forty-seven Odeon and Gaumont cinemas as going concerns at an asking price of £1.75 million. Among the companies that expressed an interest was Granada, which received a record of the cinemas' box-office takings for the past two years in order to better assess their potential.

Listed by their takings in 1966, the cinemas were the Odeons Ramsgate (top at £43,999), Llanelly, Allerton, Morecambe, Horsham, Crosby, Chingford, Loughborough, Accrington, Barrow-in-Furness, Weymouth, Boston, Gillingham, Falmouth, St. Austell, Barnstaple, Stroud, Bridgwater, Chippenham, Camberley, Leigh, Erith, Littlehampton, Andover, Park Royal, Spalding, Farnborough (Rex), Alloa, Hawick, Sittingbourne, Herne Bay, Deal, Hatfield, Godalming, Burnage, Taunton, Faversham, Wishaw and Skipton (£12,877). The Gaumont halls were at Partick (Tivoli), Wallasey, Yeovil, Tottenham (Palace), Hinckley, Airdrie (Pavilion), Frome and Redditch.

What the properties seemed to have in common was that they were run down and needed investment to carry on. Clearly, none had sufficient potential to interest Rank any longer but there was a surprising range in their takings which suggests that not all of them were chronic loss-makers. Perhaps one or two plums were included to encourage buyers? Granada did express an interest in thirty-eight of them, but by that time (October 1967) Classic had made a successful bid of £1.6 million for the lot (except the Tottenham Palace, which seems to have been withdrawn). Managing director Eric Rhodes told me in 1988:

> By and large, that was a very good deal. I never saw Rank's figures, I didn't ask for their figures. I put my own valuation on all of those properties and it was considerably above what we paid. When I told Max Joseph [chairman of Classic] what they were asking, he said, "Marvellous." That was all he said – "Marvellous." Mostly they were in bad condition. We had to spend money on most of them. They used to have black or dark brown walls!

We took on all the staff, including all the managers and manageresses. There were forty-nine managers and in less than forty-nine days we only had about nine left. I have always said that I do not particularly like circuit managers. I am sorry if I'm treading on anybody's toes but I have always found that circuit managers are not generally good to have. They don't like working, they neglect the theatres.

When I took over, Bryan Quilter called a meeting with the managers at the Royal Garden Hotel. He apologised to them for selling, etc. etc., and he hoped they'd be happy, blah, blah, blah. I told the managers they had nothing to be worried about, their jobs are there, all we want is a good day's work for a good day's pay. They should be very pleased to be going into a company that is doing the buying and not the company that is selling. Then they came in and with the few odd exceptions they were all out. The few good ones remained...*

The Classic company was associated with repertory and cartoon (ex-newsreel) theatres paying low film rentals but the takeover of the Rank cinemas in December 1967 made it predominantly a first-run chain paying percentages. Eric Rhodes later regretted that the cinemas were all renamed Classic rather than given the circuit's reserve name of Curzon. He declared that all of them would continue, with a more flexible booking policy, and that £500,000 had been earmarked for improving them over the following two years. Few, however, survived for any length of time as Classic cinemas, being switched to bingo or sold off for redevelopment.

Classic's takeover of the Odeons at Taunton and Weymouth paved the way for those towns' Gaumonts (retained by Rank as the better cinemas) to inherit the Odeon name after a decent interval. In Yeovil, Rank followed its sale of the Gaumont by letting Classic take over the Odeon as well in 1972. The company promptly tripled it, turning the former Gaumont over to bingo. The ex-Odeon continued until 2002.

Rank also sold some Odeons in north Wales to the Hutchinson Leisure Group. Colwyn Bay came back from the dead after ten years of total disuse when Hutchinson's re-opened it as the Astra Entertainment Centre, split for bingo in the stalls area and cinema in the circle with a new screen. "Renovation involved removing a tree which was growing in the stalls [but] the boiler, which had been flooded, needed only a new burner before being ready for instant service," recalls Charles Morris, now an independent cinema owner. Rank had prohibited further cinema use of the properties it closed in 1956/7 but no doubt removed the covenant in this case to get rid of the property, even though its Odeon at Llandudno might be adversely affected. In fact, this soon became Hutchinson's problem as it acquired that Odeon, too, for £84,000 in September 1969, along with the Odeon

* Quoted from "Eric Rhodes: Mr. Classic", *Picture House* no. 12, Autumn 1988, pages 3-6.

Rhyl, removing Rank from north Wales altogether. (Hutchinson's also bought former Odeons operating as Top Rank Clubs at Bilston and Dunstall in the West Midlands on 2 September 1971 and continued bingo under its Surewin name.)

In 1971, the Star circuit took over the Odeons at Lancaster and Winchester and subdivided them, using the stalls floor for bingo and putting twin cinemas in the balcony (plus a third at Winchester in disused space elsewhere).

There were further instances of Rank cinemas continuing in other hands. Closed in 1970, the Odeon (ex-Gaumont) King's Cross re-opened as an independent, initially as a club for sex films during the day with evening performances of specialised films by The Other Cinema. The stalls eventually went over to snooker with the steep balcony serving as the second home of the well-known Scala Cinema Club for twelve years. In North Shields, the former Gaumont had been renamed Odeon for less than two years when it was handed over to another operator.

Then there were cinemas in areas suitable for showing Bollywood. Several were leased to the Liberty chain for that purpose: the Odeons Balham, Edgware Road, Harlesden, Leicester (Market Place), Mile End and Wembley (ex-Gaumont). Balham even showed some mainstream films while under the Liberty banner. The former Odeon (ex-Gaumont) Southall later became part of the Liberty chain, after being renamed Godeon by another independent operator. However, the new leases of life were only temporary as most Liberty sites closed in May 1977. The large Odeon Stepney also went to Indian films for a few years, but under the name of Naz.

The Odeon (ex-Gaumont) Wednesbury was taken over by a local chain and operated as the Silver cinema for another two years before bingo reigned.

The year ending 31 October 1975 was grim, according to John Davis who told shareholders at the AGM: "Overall, the profit from United Kingdom film exhibition, outside of the West End of London, was virtually nil." His response to this, he announced, was to shed twenty-five cinemas, letting out nine of them at profitable rentals. Like the batch sold to Classic eight years earlier, these were rundown properties that needed some attention and were the wrong shape to be economically tripled, except for the Odeon Sevenoaks which had already been subdivided with disappointing results.

Brent Walker took over the Odeons at Bury St. Edmunds, Crewe and Hereford. Built in the 1930s for Oscar Deutsch, all three were on the smaller side. Crewe, with its stadium layout, had a magnificent design inside and out from the Harry Weedon office that had been little altered. The new owners kept it going for another seven years. They passed the Hereford cinema to Classic in 1983 and it closed within nine months. A last minute

Leicester Square Theatre. Organ concert before complete modernisation. (Photograph by John D. Sharp, taken 28 January 1968. CTA Archive.)

visit revealed a thrilling auditorium with all the concealed lighting in the bands across the ceiling still working at full strength. As well as Sevenoaks, the Brent Walker batch further included the Odeon Grimsby (the recently renamed Gaumont) and the Gaumont South Shields. All were renamed Focus while operated by Brent Walker. In 2005, Sevenoaks is the only one still showing films – in the two small auditoria downstairs, the extended balcony having become a live theatre.

Rank also let go at this time the Odeon Rotherham, renamed the Scala by the independent who ran it for a further nine years.

Smashing time

In 1967 one of the most shameful episodes in Rank's history took place – as the culmination of the "zing" treatment, the style of sweeping modernisation introduced in the Kenneth Winckles era. Now it was the turn of the Odeon Leicester Square.

The main frontage underwent drastic simplification. The remarkable etched glass doors were slung on a skip. The elegant high canopy was replaced by a much wider low-level canopy with the Odeon name in the centre on the front edge. A huge lightbox was placed just above the new canopy, the lower part covering up the balcony lounge windows (which had been blocked in by advertising displays for many years). The lightbox left an empty recess of similar dimensions higher up where the current programme had been previously advertised in changeable lettering. It looked as though this new readograph had slipped out of its proper position. The tower was left alone except that one of the two lines of red neon in the name sign was replaced by blue, giving an overall mauve effect.

The auditorium suffered much worse treatment. It was gutted and the flying ladies of the auditorium splay walls and the leopard skin seat covers were tossed out to be replaced by an almost completely new decor of stupefying blandness. The title of the re-opening attraction said it all: *Smashing Time*. The changes were a matter of regret to every Rank executive and manager who has mentioned it to me since, and several delighted in relaying the devastating comment of the Queen on her first visit to a premiere afterwards: "It is not an improvement."

Over the succeeding years, various attempts were made to introduce a decorative device that could be spotlit at intervals to fill the blank space left by the flying ladies: the first of these was an absurd fountain-like (or cactii-like) feature in low relief which had appeared on each side wall by the early 1970s. Then on 19 November 1975 the Odeon closed for £60,000 worth of alterations, re-opening after a month with a simple rolling form on the side walls that recalled the waves once ridden by the dancing ladies and that were nicknamed "the snails".

In 1968 the Leicester Square Theatre, which still had two

balconies, side boxes and a generally theatrical atmosphere in its auditorium, closed for eight months to be gutted and the upper circle sealed off (with its own side entrance blocked in). The new auditorium seated 1,402 and, although on the plain side, had concealed lighting around the side walls of the balcony that extended to the rear stalls area underneath and made it seem to float. The scheme was enlivened by seats in five colours – mauve, blue, green, orange and shocking pink. The stage end was rebuilt so that the screen could be set 50ft. further back but this area was never finished off externally and has looked an eyesore ever since. A week after the re-opening, another West End hall, the Astoria Charing Cross Road, also returned to reveal its completely new, reduced size interior.

New builds

Opened in 1930 with nearly 3,500 seats, the Elephant and Castle Trocadero possessed one of the finest American-style classical picture palace auditoria in the country (the later Gaumont State Kilburn by the same architect, George Coles, was a simplified imitation). The "Troc" was forced to close in 1963 for road widening and the hideous, pedestrian-unfriendly roundabout we see today. As usual, the planners had insisted on a replacement cinema. And, thanks to the engagement of a major architect, Ernö Goldfinger, the resulting Odeon Elephant and Castle was the most accomplished and innovative postwar cinema development in this country. Goldfinger also designed the adjacent office block, the less interesting Alexander Fleming House, which was quite distinct from the cinema (but his competition entry for the shopping centre was unsuccessful). The cinema was built on the end of the Troc's site, giving the most prominent position to the offices. It opened at Christmas 1966, opposite the ABC cinema.

Goldfinger's brutalist approach did not appeal to everyone but, along with the spartan character of the auditorium, it seemed an appropriate response to the rough character of the area. Inside and out, this was a building that eliminated all frills; it was design stripped back to the essence. Externally, the back wall of the stadium auditorium, the projection box and the tower (for the air-conditioning) were clearly expressed above a glassed-in foyer and two exit staircases. The unusual Odeon signage with the individual letters projecting outwards was part of Goldfinger's concept but Rank added the unnecessary red name signs nearby on the side walls.

The stadium-style auditorium was entered in the centre, at the cross aisle, and seated 1,040. The ceiling was dark and featureless. The side walls displayed illuminated vertical ribs above dado level that extended behind the exposed 'scope screen which was 50ft. wide by 23ft. tall. There were no screen

tabs: a changing, shell-like pattern was projected onto the screen during intervals. The screen stood out against the lighting of the wall behind, seeming to float in the absence of visible support.* There was no side masking but, following complaints, a specially designed contraption (rather prone to breakdowns) was later fitted at each end to swing round and mask the edges of the screen for the standard wide ratio. The rows were well spaced and the seats particularly robust to withstand the pressure of feet on their backs. The floor covering was more vinyl than carpet, adding to the impression of a somewhat chilly, utilitarian environment, although sightlines were excellent.

Two months after Elephant and Castle, another high quality replacement cinema appeared in London: the new Odeon Marble Arch, at the corner of Oxford Street and Edgware Road. The £2 million scheme designed by T. P. Bennett and Son provided shops at street level with the cinema above and an office tower at the back. The auditorium dominated the corner of the site as a large raised box with green sides that glowed in the dark and red Odeon name signs set into the top edge of each face.

The entrance was down the Edgware Road side rather than on the more valuable Oxford Street frontage, with the auditorium arranged so that the screen end was above Oxford Street. Still taking as little ground floor space as possible, the entrance had only the box office plus an escalator and fixed stairs leading up to the foyers. This was the first use of an escalator in a British cinema.

The main foyer was lofty and impressive, with doors to the back of the stalls on the right, a spiral staircase to a balcony landing at back left, and a fish pond alongside the bar in the far corner.

Designed for roadshow presentations, the Odeon seated 1,360 with the projection box at the rear of the stalls to provide an almost level throw onto what was, for 70mm presentations, one of the largest screens in the country: 75ft. by 30ft. at maximum, with a depth of curvature of 17ft. (Behind the masking, the screen was actually 76ft. x 32ft. The Gaumont Birmingham, fitted out for Cinerama, claimed Europe's largest screen: 84ft. by 33ft.)

Unlike the Elephant and Castle, the screen at Marble Arch was covered by side-opening curtains. The tall auditorium had some of the cool, cave-like atmosphere of the Curzon Mayfair opened ten months earlier. The cliff-like side walls were decorated with rough-surfaced panels leaving irregularly spaced horizontal openings backed by drapes (ventilation grilles were inconspicuously built into the design). The lighting at the rim of the flat ceiling

---

* There had been attempts to introduce a floating screen in the early 1950s, as at the Essoldo Penge, but these had been dropped with the arrival of wide screens and CinemaScope.

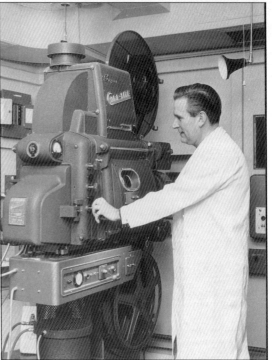

The new Odeon Marble Arch in 1967. The outside box glowed green at night. Note (top right) the fixed stairs through the door marked "Exit" to the right of the top of the escalator. House engineer Jack Isaac is seen with one of the giant Cinemeccanica projectors. (CTA Archive.)

Odeon Marble Arch, continued. This is the later D-150 screen which was installed on a 120 degree radius with programmed motorised masking to change aspect ratio rapidly. It was supplied by Andrew Smith Harkness, the marketing arm of Rank Audio Visual. (CTA Archive.)

changed colour and made the ceiling seem to float (an idea pioneered by the same architects at the Gaumont Streatham in 1955).

In practice, the best seats (but not the most expensive) were about ten rows back in the stalls, from where the screen engulfed the field of vision, as in Cinerama but without the distracting joins. When the full curved screen was in use for 70mm presentations, this was the most spectacular place to see a film in London. The sharpness of definition all over the screen from 70mm prints made epic films a joy to behold. Unfortunately, the cinema's isolated, fringe of West End location and some inappropriate choices of up-market exclusive runs counted against it, and it largely declined into extending runs of films launched in Leicester Square. (The late photographer Graham Nowell once told me of rushing down there to photograph a full house for Rank because it was such a rare event.)

Four months after Marble Arch came the Odeon Swansea, designed by Cassidy, Farrington and Dennys, and built at a cost of £300,000 on the site of the 3,000-seat independent Plaza, bringing an Odeon to the town thirty years after Oscar Deutsch had first planned one. Externally, the auditorium was an angled concrete box with a glazed and brick upper foyer set in the wedge above the flat base. It was an interesting conception but lacked the compact authority that Ernö Goldfinger had brought to the Elephant and Castle. Inside, a mirrored staircase led to a stadium style of auditorium seating 1,378, with a bare suspended screen like that at the Elephant.

The Odeon Swansea opened with *The Sound Of Music* on an extended run of twenty weeks. It was here than Rank first renamed usherettes "receptionists" and introduced a new uniform, replacing a military-style outfit with a lightweight grey jacket and dress with green trimmings for women and a dinner jacket-style suit with bow tie for men. Staff were given free hair-dos and manicures and taught how to answer the telephone.

Opened in October 1967, the Odeon St. Martin's Lane was a 737-seat underground cinema in a new office block, unusual in being built where there had been no cinema before and deep in London's theatreland (although the nearby Coliseum was on films at that time). Designed by Casson, Condor and Partners, this Odeon attempted to overcome a narrow, inconspicuous entrance with a huge canopy jutting out over the pavement. A small foyer contained a cash desk in a side wall while an advance booking office was sited at the back, behind a wide staircase leading down to the auditorium in the basement – which was attractive and spacious but bland compared to that of the Odeon Haymarket. Rank fitted another exposed floating 'scope screen, adding from the start wrap-around masking that gave a hard edge to standard wide screen images. This became

Top: Odeon Swansea. Even though the cinema has been open for several months, the shop units have not been let. (CTA Archive.)

Below: Odeon St. Martin's Lane, October 1967. Note the unusual way the illuminated Odeon sign, not in the standard style, is set into the canopy to light up at night. (CTA Archive.)

Odeon St. Martin's Lane. Top, the attractively illuminated staircase continues down to the auditorium past a pattern projected on the wall. (CTA Archive.) Below, the auditorium is well stepped and the floating screen has side masking.

another of Rank's West End roadshow outlets, making a successful start with an exclusive ten-month run of *Thoroughly Modern Millie,* but the cinema later housed short runs of unpromising new films and continuations of successful runs started elsewhere. At some point conventional curtains were fitted in front of the screen – perhaps in July 1975 when the cinema was leased to Walt Disney to became a showcase for its old and new films with doormen dressed up as cartoon figures and the interior decorated with Disney motifs. It was known as the Odeon Disney and the policy worked a treat for a few years.

In April 1968, an Odeon opened at Stockton-on-Tees, built at a cost of £150,000 to replace the old one which had closed in 1966, seemingly because of structural problems dating back to World War Two damage. The new building was described by Bill Altria, technical editor of the *Kine Weekly,* as "a breakthrough in the present-day economics of cinema construction." It was far superior to the Gaumont Bootle, the last experiment in low-cost construction. Like the Odeon St. Martin's Lane, it opened with *Thoroughly Modern Millie.* James Bettley, who later managed the cinema, recalls:

> Constructed for what was something of a record in terms of low construction costs for a cinema, the Odeon Stockton was designed as an average capacity provincial single-screen Odeon but with 70mm capability and facilities including licensed bar and advance booking office. The cinema was in its basic design really a larger version of the Leeds Merrion Centre Odeon of a few years earlier.

Rank had decided to build an Odeon in the new town of Stevenage, Hertfordshire, to follow those at Harlow and Hemel Hempstead, and obtained a site originally designated for a hotel. The Astonia cinema in the Old Town fearfully moved over to bingo in March 1969, just before preliminary work began on Rank's 850-seater, due to open in December at a cost of £150,000. Then Rank considered putting in two auditoria rather than one and otherwise re-examined the project before abandoning it in April 1970, concluding that rising costs and declining attendances made it no longer viable. The ABC circuit opened two new cinemas above a supermarket in 1973.

When a new Odeon opened in Norwich during the summer of 1971, it was part of a deal by which Rank had given up its existing 1938 Odeon in exchange for a cash payment and the shell of the replacement cinema on an adjacent site, leased at low cost. The Odeon was built for £300,000 on a concrete deck above a new shopping precinct with its own car park, the whole edge-of-town development being called Anglia Square. Alan Cooke's design was quite striking by 1970s standards if no match for the old building designed by Harry Weedon which

The new Odeon Stockton in April 1968. (CTA Archive.)

continued until two weeks before its successor opened and was then promptly demolished. The new cinema had a stepped auditorium seating 1,016 with a plain ceiling and beige curtains and wall drapes. The very large (48ft. by 20ft.) screen filled the end wall and had curtains in front. Outfitting the cinema was said to have cost Rank £146,000. At this time Rank also had the more central Gaumont and the new Odeon was envisaged principally for 70mm roadshow presentations, although it opened with a minor standard release, *Valdez Is Coming*. As so often happens, the old Odeon need not have been torn down as redevelopment stalled and the site remained vacant into the 1990s.

In 1973 a new Odeon opened on the South Coast in Brighton – but only because of the failure of Rank's bowling alley and ice rink/conference hall in its notoriously ugly seafront Top Rank Centre. The company spent over £1 million converting the vacant spaces into a three-screen Odeon which replaced the three Rank cinemas in Brighton: the Regent and the Academy, both Gaumont houses, and the Odeon, a few doors away on West Street.

The old Odeon had been mutilated over the years. Its exterior had been crudely modernised in the spring of 1969. The original tiles on the frontage were replaced with ground stone in different colours above new tiles at street level. A modern name sign appeared in five vertical boxes illuminated from within. The auditorium had also been altered: the splay walls had been made much simpler with plain ventilation grilles, the Odeon clocks had disappeared, a new rectangular proscenium opening had removed the curved top of the old one, and all the concealed lighting around the proscenium arch and across the ceiling was replaced, along with the stage footlights, by amber floodlighting of the tabs from the balcony front, for much simpler maintenance.

Restricted by the existing layout of the Top Rank Centre, the new Odeon had an inconspicuous first-floor entrance at the back, off West Street, reached by stairs or by an escalator (which, being outdoors, was prone to failure). The Odeon signs on the two street facades on West Street and Kings Road competed with those of the other attractions on the outside of what was renamed the Kingswest Centre and the Odeon was obliged to advertise in the press attached to the other attractions until the early 1990s. The three cinemas were large with total seating for 1,779, and characterless apart from colour coding. Odeon 3 (sea green, with 504 seats) had 70mm capability while Odeons 1 (blue, 390) and 2 (buff, 885) could be linked to show the same print.

The new Odeon opened a week before Bryan Quilter's departure from Rank Leisure Services. In its issue dated 23 February 1974, *CinemaTV Today* reported that Quilter had received a £44,000 golden handshake as compensation for loss of office, plus a Daimler. And, earlier (5 May 1973), the same trade paper quoted him as saying, "If I have to have a monument I think I would like it to be Kingswest. It is as good a centre as I think you can make at this moment." There's no accounting for taste.

Takeovers

There were a few acquisitions of existing cinemas. In 1970 Rank took over from the Compton group two recently opened 600-seat cinemas which a Rank subsidiary had equipped and outfitted (reputedly, cancellation of amounts outstanding was a large part of the deal). The Scala Superama in Birmingham had been the modest replacement for the old Scala within an office block known as Scala House. The Superama at Derby was attached to Rank's Pennine Hotel development. Both cinemas were put primarily to roadshow use: the one in Birmingham becoming the Odeon Ringway (adjusted to Odeon Queensway in 1972) and the one in Derby becoming the Odeon Pennine. These names distinguished them from the towns' existing Odeons.

A more surprising takeover was the 487-seat Classic on Shepherd's Bush Green, a cinema that had been completely modernised in 1968/9 and was almost adjacent to the Odeon. While Rank's desire for a second screen is understandable, the expanding Classic group was not in the habit of selling off cinemas as going concerns. Perhaps the cinema was doing badly or some trade-off was involved. Under Rank, it became Odeon 2.

However, Rank principally added screens by subdividing its existing sites.

Twins and triples

One of our own cinemas seating some 3,000 people no longer has a public to fill it in its particular district, but there is a public to fill a 1,500-seater. Our plans are far advanced; we are to put in a false floor and ceiling and convert the balcony into a modern up-to-date cinema. The ground floor is going to be converted into a big, self-service supermarket which we shall make available for renting, or even run it ourselves.

This was John Davis giving a solution to the problem of "mammoth" cinemas in his address to the Cinematograph Exhibitors' Conference back in May 1957. But nothing happened.

What cinema was he talking about? Possibly the Odeon Southend, where such a scheme was implemented in 1970. Plans for reducing the London New Victoria, were drawn up later in 1957, but these envisaged a ballroom below a smaller cinema. This scheme was also never carried out.

Rank did divide cinemas to incorporate its own dance halls: in the rear stalls area of the vast Gaumont State Kilburn in 1960; and on the stalls floor of the Gaumonts at Plymouth and Preston in 1962, opening the cinemas above as Odeons.

Rank's first twin, the Odeon Nottingham in July 1965.
Top, the canopy prominently features the man with the gong device.
An illuminated sign for the Carola Restaurant can just been seen
under the canopy. Below, the elegant divided staircase was inherited
from the original design. (CTA Archive.)

Odeon 1, the upstairs auditorium at the new Nottingham twins, and one of the automated projections rooms. (CTA Archive.)

Then, in 1964, Rank started an expensive and elaborate conversion of the Odeon Nottingham into two cinemas. Taking eight months, this attracted considerable worldwide attention when completed in July 1965 and seems to have been an innovation. The idea was that one screen would be equipped with 70mm for roadshows and the other would play regular circuit releases.

One cinema (seating 1,446) occupied the former stalls while the other (with 924 seats) was an extension of the old balcony. The total seating capacity of 2,370 was only fifty-six less than when the building had first opened in 1933 as the Ritz. There were two projection boxes, one above the other, with an automated system, Cinemation, developed by Rank, that operated the projectors, sound equipment, curtains, heating and ventilation, even the focussing of the image on the screen. A restaurant called the Carola, with 120 places, was tucked under the staircase to the upper Odeon while a basement space was turned into the Trent Room, with a stage and dance floor to accommodate up to 150 people for private functions. Whereas the original single auditorium had been tall and richly decorated, the new cinemas had low ceilings and minimal decor with much use of plain drapes on the side walls. The tall, narrow exterior of the cinema was also modernised in a stark fashion.

It was not until 1968 that more conversions in the Nottingham style were undertaken. Towards the end of this year, the key Odeons in Liverpool and Leeds closed, to re-open as twins in 1969. In both cases, charming but faded interiors of nearly forty years' standing were completely discarded.

At Liverpool, the £340,000 scheme took nine months. The corner facade was covered in galvanised steel in two vertically ribbed panels framed in white and separated at the corner by a vertical strip on which was mounted the Odeon name sign in red and the man-with-the-gong device below. Canopies with readographs projected from each elevation, with red lettering for Odeon 1 and blue for Odeon 2. Colour coding for the two auditoria continued on different sides of the island paybox, at the separate advance booking office, and in publicity frames and the signs in the foyer. The upstairs Odeon 1, designed for separate performances and extended runs, had a red carpeted foyer with a licensed bar in a former dance studio area. The 983-seat auditorium had a cave-like appearance with arches backed by white curtains like the screen tabs. Lighting on a cycle of reds and yellows added warmth. Sixty-six "Pullman" seats were included just behind the central crossover, in rows set 4ft. 3ins. apart giving generous legroom. The downstairs Odeon 2 had 1,405 seats upholstered in blue, with white curtains and white plaster on the upper side walls coloured amber by lighting, plus deep purple carpet on the lower side walls. This had a new

Odeon Liverpool.
Exterior in early 1964.
The two large advertising
panels on the side wall
have been effectively
abandoned with permanent
notices "Odeon Theatre
Fine Films In Luxurious
Surroundings" and (half
cut off) "Odeon Theatre
Always The Best I n
Entertainment". (Courtesy
of Carl Chesworth.)
Below, the uppper auditorium,
Odeon 1, after twinning
on 20 March 1969.
(CTA Archive.)

Odeon Liverpool. Two 1969 views of the new Odeon 2 on the old stalls floor with its low ceiling. (CTA Archive.)

projection box at the back and, like the upstairs auditorium, could project 35mm and 70mm prints. The biggest drawback to the scheme was the vast, oppressively flat ceiling of the lower auditorium – which was unavoidable. The new Odeon Liverpool was launched with the musicals *Oliver!* and *Chitty Chitty Bang Bang*.

The £320,000 conversion of the Odeon Leeds by a different team of architects and designers took eight months. Here the centre section of the corner entrance was covered by a new readograph surmounted by a horizontal Odeon sign while the stonework of the neo-Georgian facade to either side was cleaned. The curving staircase survived to lend a touch of elegance to the main foyer. The subdivision into two auditoria led to even duller results than at Liverpool ("uncluttered simplicity", according to the Rank press release). Odeon 1 upstairs had twenty-eight Pullman seats with the other 952 seats in turquoise blue, a blue-mottle carpet extending up the side walls to head height, blue-lit screen curtains, and red lighting of the plastered upper walls and ceiling. The larger Odeon 2 downstairs had rust-red curtains and gold-coloured seats with concealed lighting on the lower side walls to distract from the low ceiling. Again both cinemas could project both 35mm and 70mm. Odeon 1 opened with *Funny Girl* on 70mm while Odeon 2 offered *Mackenna's Gold* on 35mm. Of course, Rank also had its single-screen Odeon Merrion Centre for further roadshow use. This was fitted out for single-screen Cinerama in 1969 with a larger screen forward of the old one, but the only film shown in the process was *Ice Station Zebra* and this was a 70mm adaptation.

In Bradford, Bournemouth and Sheffield, it was the Gaumonts that were twinned in 1968/9. (Bradford, which also included bingo, re-opened as an Odeon since the previous Odeon had gone; the Bournemouth and Sheffield schemes led to the eventual closure of the towns' single screen Odeons.) As previously mentioned, in Southend, a somewhat smaller centre, the huge Odeon was subdivided in 1970 with a supermarket taking over the ground floor and entrance. The new cinema in the extended balcony held 1,235 people and could show 70mm prints while a second screen, seating 455, was created in the former café/dance studio area. A new entrance was created down a side street, Elmer Approach. (Rank's other Southend cinema, the Ritz, carried on for a further eighteen months.)

Southend was closely followed by the subdivision of the Odeon in the centre of Glasgow where the site, bounded on three sides by major streets, encouraged the conversion of the stage into a third cinema (with a balcony) as it could have its own separate entrance on West Regent Street. This actually increased the total seating to 2,939, with 1,138 in the 70mm auditorium, 1,243 in the one usually reserved for general releases,

Odeon Leeds. Exterior in March 1984. (Photograph by Allen Eyles.) Above, auditorium prior to 1968/9 twinning. (CTA Archive.) Right top, the new main foyer with advance booking office to the right and double staircase inherited from the original design. Right centre, Odeon 1 upstairs, with 980 seats and a higher ceiling. Right, Odeon 2 downstairs with 1290 seats.

Advertisement for the new Odeon Southend with sketch of displaced entrance and a widely used device of the man with the gong and the words "The Big Screen Scene". (Courtesy of Robin Dakin.)

and 558 on the stage. At the same time, the corner entrance with its elegant fins alternating with tall windows disappeared behind ugly grey corrugated sheet metal surrounding a readograph detailing the current attractions. This enabled Rank to close the Gaumont, its former home of roadshows, a little over a year later.

Three particularly large London suburban halls were split into two, with cinema use continuing in an extended balcony and the stalls floor given over to Top Rank Bingo. This entailed several months of closure, after which the Odeons at Camden Town and Edgware Road re-opened almost simultaneously in February 1968 with dreary auditoria seating well over 1,000 people. In both cases, the cinema retained the high street entrance while the bingo hall was entered via a side street. The Odeon Shepherd's Bush was the third of these conversions in 1970 – here cinema split the main entrance with bingo.

An experiment took place at Preston in 1970 when a second screen was opened in a former restaurant, seating only 105 and using 16mm prints. This initially showed reissues, titles being announced up to eight weeks ahead, but it soon went over to 35mm and new releases. Almost simultaneously, the Trent Room at the Odeon Nottingham was converted into a third cinema, with an initial emphasis on art house films. The new screens opened with names suggested by the public: Preston now boasted the Odeon 2 Cine Lounge while Nottingham offered the Odeon Mini Cine.

The elaborate conversion of major sites was too expensive for small town and suburban cinemas. But a more modest trial conversion of the Odeon at Sutton Coldfield in 1972 paved the way for reviving these halls. The rear stalls area was blocked off and then divided into two small 132-seat cinemas side by side with a new joint projection box at the back while the 594-seat balcony continued as the main cinema using the existing projection room and screen. Not only was this procedure comparatively inexpensive, it could be completed with the balcony remaining open for business on weekday evenings and full time at weekends. This intervention became known as "tripling" by "drop wall conversion" although sometimes the downstairs cinemas extended beyond the balcony front in an unsightly manner.

The resulting three-screen cinema was called a "film centre". Advances in automated projection helped make such schemes feasible as there was no need to increase technical staff. Entire shows could be run off a platter (or "cakestand") through a single projector without anyone in continuous attendance. (The more compact "turret" or "tower" system with huge reels was not favoured by Rank.) As in present day multiplexes, simple faults like loss of sharp focus or an out-of-rack image could take time to be noticed and rectified.

Odeon Renfield Street, Glasgow. Exterior, circa May 1960.
Top right, auditorium on 16 November 1962 and (above) before that date when there was concealed lighting in the ceiling, light fittings in front of the side grilles, and small grilles over the pros arch. The 1968/9 twinning covered the fins and windows over the corner entrance with a tall central readograph and plain cladding to each side.
The two-sided vertical sign seen at the very end of the building to the right survived until the 1990s when the original frontage was largely reinstated. Above, the modernised inner foyer in 1971.
(All courtesy of Bruce Peter.)

Odeon Renfield Street, Glasgow. Top left, the outer foyer after tripling in July 1971. Below left and above right, the large upstairs auditorium. Below right, the large downstairs auditorium. A third cinema occupied the old stage. (All courtesy of Bruce Peter.)

The tripling of the Odeon Sutton Coldfield proved such a success that Rank converted the Odeons at Exeter, Harrogate, Bolton and York to three-screen operation four months later. (Although Harrogate was identical to Sutton Coldfield, its minis seated only 108 each.) However, the Odeon Croydon was an old, narrow hall that had to be closed for three months to enable two cinemas of almost equal size to be created one above the other. At the end of 1972, the Odeons at Wimbledon, Salisbury, Dalston and Sevenoaks all became triples. Sevenoaks was the one inexplicable failure of Rank's entire tripling programme, leading to its early sale to Brent Walker. The inner-London Odeon Dalston was tripled to compensate for the recent closure of the nearby Odeons at Mile End and Stamford Hill.

In 1973, twelve Odeons became triples: Cheltenham, St. Albans, Swiss Cottage, Peterborough, Holloway, Guildford, Portsmouth, Aylesbury, Wolverhampton, Weston-Super-Mare, Wood Green and Richmond. At Holloway, the sheer size of the building enabled each of the minis to seat 216. In conversions at three narrower cinemas – Well Hall, Bishop Auckland and the Plaza Dudley – there was only room for a single screen in the rear stalls area.

In 1974, the tripling programme reached sixteen sites: Peckham, Leicester, Worcester, Barnet, Romford, Aberdeen, Burton-on-Trent, Colchester, Muswell Hill, Bristol, Watford, Worthing, Middlesbrough, Luton, Barking and Derby. The minis at the Odeon Barking were larger than most, each seating 190. The smallish Odeon Torquay became a twin over five winter months, out of the holiday season.

The Odeon Manchester was such an important theatre that it warranted a twinning on the lines of Leeds and Liverpool. This took six months and provided cinemas with 1,030 seats in the stalls and 629 seats in the balcony. Carl Chesworth was there:

The conversion to a twin theatre operation was marred by a change of managing director. He was aghast at the money his predecessors had been ploughing into similar schemes and persuaded the Rank board to convert Manchester as a cheap scheme.

The bulk of the capital expenditure went on the massive steel girders which supported the front circle extension, which in turn were anchored in tons of concrete in the sub-basement. Similar steel cross-girders were used at the rear of the new Odeon One screen, which then effectively became a huge roof void. Massive supporting ties were knocked through the original ceiling and held the new false ceiling above the former stalls area (Odeon Two). Many aspects of the beautiful original plasterwork which could have been incorporated in the auditorium in Odeon One were stripped out, and the finished result was bland in the extreme. No attempt was made to hide architectural features which couldn't be removed:

The 1972 tripling of the Odeon Harrogate. (Courtesy of James Bettley.)

The Odeon Manchester after twinning with a Saturday late night show advertised on the corner of the canopy. (Courtesy of Carl Chesworth.)

*Odeon Birmingham remains a single screen in autumn 1974.
(Photograph by Allen Eyles.)*

*The Odeon Newcastle after tripling in 1975. Elements of the lavish
original decoration remain. The minis downstairs protrude beyond the
balcony front. The stalls floor retains seats. (Courtesy of Bruce Peter.)*

basic plaster was just applied up the feature, which was left.
The original projection room was used and 70mm facilities
installed for a new larger screen. As the projectors now had
to be raked upwards (the new screen being just beyond the
old circle line), the 70mm picture caught an architectural
beam just beyond the projection ports. Consideration was
given to cutting a section of the projection room floor away
to lower the projectors a little but, after the projected size of
the picture was reduced to compensate for the girder problem,
the picture didn't look a great deal larger than CinemaScope,
so 70mm was abandoned.

The former mezzanine became home to a breezeblock projection room for Odeon Two in the former stalls. The original
screen and frame on the stage were used for this cinema. The
screen was still set at the rake for the original single screen
cinema. The focus was appalling and the wrong lenses were
used to fill this vast screen with much cropping of the projected picture. The projectionists enjoyed the brightest image,
the light being reflected straight back into the mezzanine
level. Because of budget problems, a decent lamphouse
couldn't be found to provide an acceptable light coverage, so
we had to make do with secondhand equipment from a closed
London mini-cinema. As the stage was 'open' (the screen
was suspended on the counterweight system), the auditorium
was always cold as heat would escape into the vast void
behind the screen up to the stage lantern high in the roof.

As a side issue, the new managing director had a passion for
the colour blue and instigated blue felt category boards instead
of the traditional black.

Over the years a little more money was found from various
budgets to instigate some improvements.

The brake on spending would explain why the pace slowed
down in 1975. Three-screen Odeons opened in March at Sunderland, Newcastle and Plymouth (Drake). Two more followed
towards the end of the year at Blackpool and Coventry with
large minis. The Gaumont State Kilburn added a second, 202-
seat cinema in former restaurant space.

Newcastle was one of the giant former Paramounts in a key
city. In the new mood of economy, it received a dropwall tripling rather than the thorough makeover of Leeds, Glasgow and
Manchester. At this time or perhaps earlier (in a zing treatment?), it underwent drastic alterations that took away much
but not all of its original decorative scheme. The proscenium
arch was simplified and the faded delicate detail in the panels on
the side walls of the auditorium was removed or hidden but the
fluted pilasters with their capitals were retained, along with their
art deco lampshades in the balcony. The ornate seat standards
still hinted at the original glory of the interior. Sitting in the
balcony, the result was an ugly compromise. This was one of the
places where the roof of the downstairs minis projected forward

several feet from the balcony front.* At least, at Sunderland, the attractive bas reliefs of gypsy dancers on the side walls of the auditorium were left intact.

At Plymouth, tripling took the unusual course of the balcony being divided down the middle to create two smaller cinemas while the stalls served as the largest auditorium.

At Blackpool, the two downstairs minis both seated 190 with an intervening passage that connected their new projection suite to one built in mid-stalls for the main screen. However, the throw was so short that it became difficult if not impossible to obtain a sharp image at the sides of the huge 'scope screen (as was demonstrated to me during a showing of *A Bridge Too Far*).

There were disadvantages to the drop wall conversions. The balcony seemed remote from the screen once the front stalls weren't in use and cinemagoers who wanted to sit nearer the screen no longer could (except at a few sites where the front stalls remained accessible and seats were retained). Usually, the stalls seats were removed and underfelt was often laid on the floor to absorb the echo; the area was kept as dark as possible, although clocks and side exit signs often remained illuminated to create an impression of use. Although audiences were sitting in the former "best seats in the house", this was no longer from choice. The downstairs cinemas were disconcertingly small, the sightlines were poor because of the slight rake, and the screens were restricted in size by the low ceilings and the need for the projection beam to clear the heads of patrons. At some sites (Aberdeen and Barnet among them), the projection was from behind, or alongside, the screen via mirrors in order to leave more space for seats. At times, the low capacities suited films of specialised appeal or films that had moved down to continue their runs, and it was possible to run a single print through both downstairs projectors to show the same film (at Blackpool, it could be shown on all three screens), but too often managers were faced with insufficient seats downstairs and too many empty ones upstairs. Soundproofing between auditoria was sometimes inadequate with seepage from one to another, especially when quiet scenes in one coincided with loud spots in another.

In contrast to Rank, the ABC circuit closed most of its cinemas for more extensive conversions, making its downstairs cinemas larger by extending them forward and putting up a new screen and splay walls close to the old balcony front for upstairs. This meant that ABC achieved a better balance of seating capacities and all the auditoria looked more modern. The original decor was largely removed or hidden from sight while Rank's drop

* For the Odeon as it looked on opening as the Paramount in 1931, see the rich array of illustrations in *Picture House*, no. 26, Summer 2001, pages 3-13 and back cover.

wall conversions preserved the existing decorative features and the view from the balcony was the same as before.

In many smaller places where Rank and ABC were in competition, one cinema was subdivided and the other closed, as to follow suit would have created a surplus of screens. In Muswell Hill, north London, ABC would have been first to triple but couldn't easily overcome problems associated with a steeply sloping site. Only by default did the Odeon become the survivor, eventually being tripled. However, in some larger towns, Odeon and ABC both operated three-screen cinemas: at Luton the Odeon was tripled three years after its rival while at Wolverhampton the Odeon came first and the ABC followed a few months later.

Whereas ABC would sometimes split a cinema into smaller auditoria plus bingo or a Painted Wagon bar, Rank's triple conversions were confined to film use. However, when Gloucester City Council refused a change of use to bingo at the Odeon because it objected to the loss of the cinema facility, Rank did propose in 1973 to convert the balcony into twin cinemas if the stalls could be used for bingo. ABC then tripled its hall in 1974 and Rank finally won approval for bingo on appeal, ending films in August 1975 as soon as it had a gaming licence.

The conversion of one Rank cinema often led to the closure of any second Rank hall in the same town. Inevitably, programming favoured the cinemas in which a substantial investment had been made while large single halls were not needed with the end of roadshows. The re-opening of the twinned Odeon Manchester cued the immediate closure of the much lamented single-screen Gaumont across the road although the Odeon Bournemouth went on for four and a half years after the more central Gaumont had been twinned. The Odeon in Market Place at Leicester was leased to an Asian operator a year or so after the main Odeon had been tripled. The Odeon Hanley went eighteen months after the Gaumont tripled. The Odeon Dudley lasted less than two years after the Plaza twinned. In Bradford, Rank knew from late 1968 that the Odeon would be compulsorily acquired by the Corporation for a redevelopment scheme and brought forward plans to twin the Gaumont and keep two screens in the town.

A few post-1975 Odeon triplings and twinnings are covered in the next chapter.

Booking: general releases

In 1966, the Monopolies Commission's *Report On The Supply Of Films*, after two years of deliberation, essentially found restrictive practices but offered no solution, fearing that any alternative might be worse: "To give the industry a new and competitive structure would mean breaking up the circuits, but that would be a drastic step, the results of which would be uncertain." It made several recommendations including one that Rank and ABC should be more flexible in booking, "giving trial runs to films whose appeal to the public is in doubt and giving limited or partial circuit bookings to films of limited appeal".

In fact, the rigidity of the circuit release had lessened but the main problem was that attendances were increasingly focused on a few must-see films with too many other releases having negligible appeal, shown to keep screens occupied (and prove to distributors that they were duds). Such flops as 20th Century-Fox's *Decline And Fall...Of A Birdwatcher* in 1968 and Rank's own *Some Girls Do* in 1969 were withdrawn or continued in release at a reduced number of sites. Two Fox disasters, *Che* and *Star!*, were split between certain Odeons in the London suburbs in 1969 while the better Odeons escaped altogether by launching into a roadshow. A new flexibility was evident, for example, when *The Pawnbroker*, with its appeal to a Jewish audience, played at the Odeons Swiss Cottage and Temple Fortune instead of the week's Disney picture *Follow Me, Boys!* in March 1967, even though this entailed depriving a major distributor of two important bookings in favour of the small distributor of the highly praised art house film. Two months later, Rank didn't fancy the chances of *A Funny Thing Happened On The Way To The Forum* at the Odeons Deptford and Erith on general release and put in revivals instead. And, in another form of flexibility, *Thunderbird 6* played at Odeons in the afternoon during school holidays in 1968 with a double-bill revival programme in the evenings.

As demonstrated by the attendances at the Odeons Gloucester and Southampton, it was a few staple types of film that drew in the crowds.

Rank enjoyed considerable success with its Norman Wisdom comedy *Press For Time* but this ended a fourteen-year association with the comedian in 1967. Fortunately, the company was able to tap into another well established comedy series as it took over the distribution of the *Carry Ons* in spring 1968 with *Carry On Doctor*. They had been released through the ABC circuit and it was a coup for them to play at Odeons. Their continuing popularity, especially *Carry On Up The Khyber*, kept them among the most popular attractions for several more years. Rank's distribution arm also obtained many of Hammer's horror output and, beginning with *Countess Dracula* (1971), these found a home in Odeons rather than at rival ABCs.

And the James Bond films remained immensely popular with *Thunderball* achieving the most admissions in the entire series and *You Only Live Twice* and *Live And Let Die* also featuring among the top one hundred best attended films in British cinemas according to the British Film Institute's 2004 compilation on the subject. The other Bond films of the 1965-75 period – *On Her Majesty's Secret Service*, *Diamonds Are Forever* and *Live And Let Die* were high in the Top Ten lists of their respective years. All the Bond films enjoyed repeat bookings, often paired.

Disney films – both new and reissues – remained surefire attractions. *The Aristocats* was easily the top attraction of 1971 at the Odeon Gloucester and, at the end of February 1971, it broke the (all-time?) admission record at the Odeon Stafford when 2,308 attended in one day (the previous record holder was *Chitty Chitty Bang Bang* with 1,938). Another notable achievement by *The Aristocats*, according to Rank's house magazine, was 3,575 admissions in one day at Dudley. Of course, Disney films could be revived for each new generation and *The Jungle Book*, first shown in 1967, warranted a further two-week run at local London Odeons at Christmas 1975. It is ranked seventh in the British Film Institute's 2004 list of the most attended films, beaten only among Disney films by *Snow White And The Seven Dwarfs*.

Reissues and a few sex films proved to be bigger draws than most routine new pictures, especially in the 1970s, with the Kung Fu or martial arts cycle revitalising the box office from 1973.

Reissue programmes usually combined two top attractions. Fox's inspired and unlikely coupling of *Butch* and *Brodie* – *Butch Cassidy And The Sundance Kid* together with *The Prime Of Miss Jean Brodie* – proved its worth at the Studio One in London and did huge business at many Odeons, including Newcastle where it doubled the average take in March 1971. At many sites the double bill held for a second week.

Another Fox double bill proved the potency of sex films – *Myra Breckinridge* and *Beyond The Valley Of The Dolls* was reported in the Rank house journal, *Gongbeats*, as doing tremendously well, with the Odeon Elephant and Castle recording the top business in the London area (this was a cinema where a special showing of *Der Rosenkavalier* the year after it opened had to be cancelled through lack of advance bookings).

Soft porn played a large part in the programming of cinemas in down-market areas and off-release halls, spot-booked rather than circuit released. This kind of film was the staple diet of smaller non-Rank halls in London's West End but it was rather sad to find them infiltrating all the major Rank screens outside the West End on occasion in the days before tripling became widespread (when such films principally found a home in the minis). The British examples, at least, had the benefit of helping meet the high quota obligations. Perhaps a cut above these, the smutty X-certificate series of *Confessions* sex comedies –*Confessions Of A Window Cleaner* (1974), *...Of A Pop Performer* (1975) and

ODEON GLOUCESTER: TEN MOST POPULAR FILMS

These numbers refer to admissions, not takings. The Odeon Gloucester screened the Rank releases while the competing ABC Gloucester played its circuit's programmes. Both were single screens during this period.

1967
The Sound Of Music
  (8 weeks 6 days*) 64,296
You Only Live Twice
  (2 weeks) 15,860
Press For Time
  (2 weeks) 15,543
Bambi 12,265
Casino Royale 8,568
Batman 8,459
Thunderbirds Are Go 8,363
** *Lady And The Tramp* 7,937
Follow That Camel 7,889
Tom Jones 7,042
  Total 156,222

* The highest admission figure was reached in the second week: 10,148.

** Played six days but total includes a Sunday booking of *Goliath And The Vampires* (separate figures not recorded). Even if *Goliath* did well, the eleventh most popular film, *The Return Of The Seven* with 6,828 admissions, is unlikely to have overtaken *Lady And The Tramp*

1968
Jungle Book (2 weeks) 25,579
Carry On Up The Khyber
  (10 days) 11,133
The Good, The Bad And The Ugly
  8,958
*Here We Go Round The Mulberry
  Bush* 8,067
Planet Of The Apes 8,036
Carry On Doctor 7,440
Prudence And The Pill 6,867
Bonnie And Clyde 6,652
The Charge Of The Light Brigade
  6,638
The Bible (6 days) 6,461
  Total 95,831

1969
Chitty Chitty Bang Bang 23,274
Carry On Camping 13,437
Doctor Dolittle 13,266
Carry On Up The Khyber 11,133
One Hundred And One Dalmatians
  10,871
The Love Bug 8,851
Cinderella 7,722
Thoroughly Modern Millie 7,451
Fanny Hill 7,028
The Magnificent Seven 7,003
  Total 109,576

1970
The Battle Of Britain 22,144
On Her Majesty's Secret Service
  16,909
*Butch Cassidy And The Sundance
  Kid* 12,651
The Virgin Soldiers 8,912
The Love Bug 7,783
Carry On Up The Jungle 7,000
Carry On Again Doctor 6,913
The Graduate 6,788
Alice In Wonderland 6,414
20,000 Leagues Under the Sea
  6,079
  Total 101,593

1971
The Aristocats 24,786
Anne Of The Thousand Days
  17,496
Soldier Blue 15,956
Cromwell 9,122
Doctor Zhivago 8,469
Oliver! 6,983
Butch Cassidy/Jean Brodie 6,606
Carry On Loving 6,192
When Eight Bells Toll 6,128
Pinocchio 5,721
  Total 107,459

1972
Diamonds Are Forever 25,229
Bedknobs And Broomsticks 13,322
Sleeping Beauty/Treasure Island
  6,503
The Love Bug/Robin Hood 6,459
Carry On At Your Convenience
  6,293
Living Free 6,013
Carry On Matron 5,485
Dumbo/Napoleon And Samantha
  5,414
The Song Of Norway 4,693
Straw Dogs 4,658
  Total 84,069

1973
Live And Let Die 29,001
Snow White And The Seven Dwarfs
  14,675
Mary Poppins 11,397
Sword In The Stone 6,091
Last Tango In Paris 5,155
*Butch Cassidy And The Sundance
  Kid* 4,306
Tales From The Crypt 3,886
Alice's Adventures In Wonderland
  3,731
The Naked Countess 3,459
The Aristocats 3,352
  Total 85,053

ODEON SOUTHAMPTON: TEN MOST POPULAR FILMS

These are financial years to the end of October. Total attendances of all films are given in square brackets at end. The number of weeks each film played is shown in round brackets after the title with number of weeks played by all the top ten films in round brackets before the total for each year. Many films played at the Gaumont Southampton instead of the Odeon. The ABC Southampton showed the ABC releases.

1972/3
Alice's Adventures In Wonderland (3)
  21,203
Mary Poppins (2) 12,810
Lost Horizon (3) 12,569
Sword In The Stone (2) 11,380
The Great Waltz (4) 11,356
Cabaret (2) 8,810
Soldier Blue/Carnal Knowledge (1)
  5,588
Butch Cassidy/M.A.S.H. (1) 5,104
Ooh, You Are Awful (1) 4,577
*When Eight Bells Toll/Puppet On A
  Chain* (1) 4,567
  **Total (20 weeks) 97,964
  [205,250]**

1973/4
Robin Hood (4) 51,651
Papillon (4) 23,395
Gold (3) 18,105
Zardoz (2) 9,690
Don't Look Now (2) 8,748
The Way We Were (2) 8,455
Snow White And The Seven Dwarfs
  (1) 7,576

*Diamonds Are Forever/From Russia
  With Love* (1) 7,086
Song Of The South (1) 6,469
Live And Let Die/O.H.M.S.S (1)
  6,127
  **Total (21 weeks) 147,302
  [274,935]**

1974/5
Island At The Top Of The World (4)
  34,148
Tommy (7) 30,480
Escape To Witch Mountain (3)
  18,753
The Odessa File (3) 12,680
Lady And The Tramp (2) 12,184
The Night Porter (3) 10,730
Funny Lady (3) 10,699
Planet Of The Apes (1) 9,502
Shampoo (2) 7,783
A Reason To Live (1) 5,321
  **Total (29 weeks) 152,280
  [246,910]**

Source: James E. Tilmouth, former manager.

This is Benjamin... He's a little worried about his future

JOSEPH E. LEVINE PRESENTS A
MIKE NICHOLS-LAWRENCE TURMAN PRODUCTION
THE GRADUATE

ACADEMY AWARD WINNER—BEST ACHIEVEMENT IN DIRECTION MIKE NICHOLS

STARRING
ANNE BANCROFT AND DUSTIN HOFFMAN · KATHARINE ROSS

SCREENPLAY BY
CALDER WILLINGHAM AND BUCK HENRY
SONGS BY PAUL SIMON
PERFORMED BY SIMON AND GARFUNKEL

PRODUCED BY LAWRENCE TURMAN
DIRECTED BY MIKE NICHOLS
TECHNICOLOR· PANAVISION· United Artists

SPECIAL PRESENTATION FROM **SEPT 15th** FOR TWO WEEKS

BROMLEY Odeon	GUILDFORD Odeon	PURLEY Astoria	STREATHAM Odeon
CAMDEN TOWN Odeon	HAMMERSMITH Odeon	RAYNERS LANE Odeon	SWISS COTTAGE Odeon
EPSOM Odeon	ILFORD Odeon	RICHMOND Odeon	WATFORD Odeon
GOLDERS GREEN Odeon	KINGSTON Granada	SLOUGH Granada	WALTHAM CROSS Embassy

STILL SHOWING LONDON PAVILION

Above, The Graduate *is given a two-week pre-release at London suburban cinemas, mostly Odeons, in September 1968.*

Far left, this 1966 advertisement shows the London-area Odeons that regularly took the main circuit release. Those with a round blob next to their names were on restricted opening, i.e. not open every weekday afternoon except in school holidays. Only the Odeon Deptford has a separate Sunday programme. Swiss Cottage had a concert on the Tuesday and three other cinemas had one-day specials.

Left, this advertisement covers off-circuit London-area Rank theatres in July 1966. Those playing Wonderful World of the Brothers Grimm *and* The Glass Bottom Boat *are tapping into the rival ABC release. Watford's two Rank halls typically played out of sync with London during this period. The Odeons at Erith and Hornchurch usually accessed the Rank release. Friday starts were a recent innovation at all cinemas.*

...Of A Driving Instructor (1976) – were popular draws on Odeon screens.

In Salisbury, the Watch Committee refused to allow the Odeon to advertise the title of *Do You Want To Remain A Virgin Forever?* in the press or outside the cinema. The cinema could only refer to "our unusual programme" and invite people to telephone for details – but publicity over the ban in *The People* and *News Of The World* resulted in extremely good business.

Bruce Lee was the big star of the shortlived Kung Fu cycle of films from Hong Kong. His *Fist Of Fury* achieved a half-release at Odeons in 1973. After the ABC circuit scooped box-office gold with *Enter The Dragon* early in 1974 Rank followed up with a full release of *The Way Of The Dragon* later in the year.

At Christmas 1973, the ABC circuit adjusted the time-honoured London suburban release pattern. It showed two major films, *Holiday On The Buses* and *Take Me High*, first in twenty-one sites across the whole of surburban London, then at the remainder. This had the effect of creating a first and second tier of cinemas, increasing business at some sites at the expense of others.

Rank continued with a north and south London split but within each area it often divided up two less promising programmes among its halls, particularly in a clear out during the pre-Christmas "graveyard slot", often placing a more sophisticated film in up market districts and a more down-to-earth attraction elsewhere. Usually, it was the downmarket title that did the better business. In 1971, for instance, *The House That Dripped Blood* managed average business while the romantic *Say Hello To Yesterday* was "disappointing". Many new releases proved disastrous and were dumped in favour of reissue double bills.

When tripling became widespread, it seems to have been general practice to maintain continuous performances in the upstairs screen and to have separate shows in one or both of the minis. The smaller screens seemed a suitable place to try out films of specialised appeal. A difficult but acclaimed subtitled film, the Russian *Solaris*, was booked into the Odeons at Guildford, Exeter, Brighton, Wimbledon, Gaumont Doncaster and the single screen at the Odeon Merrion Centre Leeds. But bookings of such films faded as the major distributors demanded the minis to extend the runs of films that had proven popular in the larger auditoria and this was a surer source of box-office income than an untried new film. Thus the run of popular titles like *A Touch Of Class* could be extended for ten weeks or more.

There were indications that Rank's bookers were losing touch with audience tastes. As a Columbia release, the biker movie *Easy Rider* should have found a West End berth with Odeon in 1969 but it went into the Classic Piccadilly Circus where it proved a phenomenal hit. (Of course, the Classic only seated 270 and its location was ideal for drawing in teenagers.) The Classic circuit also gained *Easy Rider* on first run in such places as Brighton, Glasgow, Leicester, Nottingham, Sheffield and Southampton, while Star and other independents took it elsewhere.

The ABC circuit was more receptive to offbeat fare. It played *Easy Rider* in the London suburbs in March 1970. And that same year it gave a circuit release to three United Artists pictures that had, as usual, been offered to Odeon. George Pinches, Rank's booking controller, was not enthusiastic about any of them and UA itself was uncertain of their potential – especially *Kes*, which Pinches felt needed subtitles to overcome its Yorkshire accents. It was amicably agreed that the films would be offered elsewhere. Ken Russell's *Women In Love* opened at the Prince Charles in November 1969 to rave reviews. It then went out for a two-week booking on ABCs and became one of the major box-office hits of the year. It was almost immediately followed on circuit by *Alice's Restaurant*, then by *Kes*, which had become a surprise West End hit at the Academy art house. However, Ken Russell's next extravaganza for United Artists, *The Music Lovers*, was given the roadshow treatment at Rank cinemas in 1971.[*]

A late attempt to compete with television on a topical subject occurred when Rank made a documentary, *A Prince For Wales*, about Charles's formative years and investiture, featuring an exclusive interview by David Frost: this replaced the second feature at most London Odeons for a week in July 1969.

Rank's long-standing relationship by which General (later Rank) Film Distributors had handled Universal's product in England since May 1936 came under strain when Odeon's film booking department declined to give substantial showings to some of the limited appeal British productions that Universal was churning out, such as *Work Is A 4-Letter Word* (1967), *The Bofors Gun* (1968), *Charlie Bubbles* (1968), *Secret Ceremony* (1969) and *Can Heironymus Merlin Ever Forget Mercy Humppe And Find True Happiness?* (1969, "See it – to hell with the title", said the ads in desperation). Indeed, Universal had to hire the Odeon St. Martin's Lane to give the films a West End premiere run.

Before this, Universal had bravely but (as it turned out) foolishly given Charles Chaplin the opportunity to make a lavish swansong, *A Countess From Hong Kong* (1967) with Marlon Brando and Sophia Loren. Although Chaplin used Rank's Pine-

---

[*] ABC had its blind spot. In 1973, the circuit was not allowed to show MGM's *Hitler: The Last Ten Days* on the instructions of Bernard Delfont. It played Odeons instead.

wood studios, he remembered that Rank had refused to play his last film, *A King In New York* (1957), and insisted that his new work should not premiere in a Rank cinema.[*] It went into the Carlton Haymarket before playing the Odeon circuit.

Early in 1972, Universal transferred its product to the ABC circuit even though it was still distributed by Rank, and Odeon lost such films as Clint Eastwood's *Play Misty For Me* and *Joe Kidd*. Rank's franchise was terminated on 3 December 1972 but films that had been delivered by that date continued to be handled by the company until 3 June 1973. To make up for the impending shortfall in releases, Rank's distribution arm merged with 20th Century-Fox to form Fox-Rank Distributors from 3 December 1972. This followed similar tie-ups between other big distributors in response to the shrinking UK market.

The loss of the Universal output may have been inevitable with the formation of Cinema International Corporation as an overseas distribution partnership with Paramount, but it had a serious effect on the Rank cinemas as the rival ABC circuit gained enormously from first call on such films as *The Sting* (1973) and *Jaws* (1975). Furthermore, both opened in London at the Plaza rather than benefiting one of the Rank West End outlets. Had Rank held onto its shares in Universal instead of selling them in 1952, it might have retained the Hollywood major's output.

However, the adjustment did divide the releases of the eight principal American studios evenly between the two major circuits: Rank's cinemas played the output of Disney, Columbia, United Artists and 20th Century-Fox (in addition, Rank normally had first choice of films from some of the newer and smaller distributors that sprung up, such as Avco-Embassy, Hemdale and Scotia-Barber). ABC took the films of Warner Bros., MGM, Paramount and Universal. With the large number of closed cinemas, many Odeons and ABCs were in solo situations able to pick from all the new releases, but they still gave preference to their main suppliers, sometimes to an absurd degree.

Roadshows

The roadshowing of films continued with *The Sound Of Music* (which premiered at the Dominion in London on 29 March 1965) and became the top-grossing picture of 1966, 1967 and

1968 even though it was restricted to special engagements. This was shown at the Dominion and elsewhere on what may have been the first instance of a 90-10 split above the house "nut" – by which the distributor took 90 per cent of the box-office receipts after the agreed cost of operating the cinema had been met (but did not share in the income from ice cream and other sales). Some of the runs were quite extraordinary: 82 weeks and 1,066 performances at the Odeon Bournemouth, for example. At Portsmouth, it lasted eleven months. It was not until 1969 that the Fox musical went on wider general release to mop up any remaining business.[*]

Major big-budget musicals such as *Oliver!* (1968), *Chitty Chitty Bang Bang* (1968), *Funny Girl* (1969), *Hello, Dolly!* (1970), *Fiddler On the Roof* (1971), *Bedknobs And Broomsticks* (1971) and *Lost Horizon* (1973) generally opened on extended runs with bookable seats at between eight to sixteen key city Rank halls a few days after starting their West End run. It wasn't entirely musicals that were roadshown. There were films like *Those Magnificent Men In Their Flying Machines* (1965), *Lord Jim* (1965) and *Young Winston* (1972), along with more specialised titles like Olivier's *Othello* and *Doctor Faustus*.

There was little room for independent cinemas. *Chitty* played exclusively at sixteen Rank cinemas outside London. *Bedknobs* played at eleven Rank cinemas outside London and only one independent, the Playhouse Edinburgh. Of course, in many towns Rank had invested heavily in twinning cinemas to create a house specifically for roadshow releases, besides which the number of independents had dwindled. But there were exceptions: by installing 70mm, the Scala Worcester played extended runs of *The Sound Of Music* and *Doctor Dolittle,* films that would otherwise have opened at the Odeon. And the Blackpool Palladium obtained *Lost Horizon* and others.

Rank and ABC's hold on the 70mm roadshow market was heavily criticised by Philip Refson, chairman of the important Essoldo chain. Asked in an interview with John Deighton (*Today's Cinema*, 1 December 1969), "Are you happy with the speed you get new films?", Refson replied:

Insofar as 35mm is concerned, the release pattern is reasonably satisfactory, except of course in those cases of exceptional attractions which are retained by the Duopoly for extended runs. On the other hand, the 70mm market – No! that is certainly the wrong word: How can there be a market when a buyer cannot buy no matter how much he is prepared to pay? At the time of the Monopolies Commission the

---

[*] In fact, *A King In New York* had premiered on 12 September 1957 at Rank's Leicester Square Theatre and at the art house Cameo-Poly Oxford Circus (a very unusual combination) for a good five-week run at the former and a sixth week at the latter. However, it did not then receive a general release on the Odeon or Gaumont circuit, instead going into some Essoldos, Granadas and others. There were later bookings of the film in some Rank halls in February/March 1958. It was released by a small distributor, Monarch, not one of Rank's major suppliers.

[*] "Four walling", by which distributors hired the cinema and received all the proceeds, was a rare occurrence but Stan Fishman, later Rank's booking controller, recalls that Paramount took over the Astoria Charing Cross Road to launch *Paint Your Wagon* on that basis in 1970.

barring period was agreed at 16 weeks and the industry accepted it on good faith. Some exhibitors, including ourselves, installed the necessary expensive equipment only to find after the 16-week period it was true we were not barred at all, but unfortunately there was no print available; and even when the run ended in that particular Duocentre, it immediately found its way into another one. So the merry game of 70mm checkers continues to this day with the Duopoly having every reason to be content but with other exhibitors finding the 16 week bar to be a nonsense. To aggravate the position still further we now have 35mm films (such as *Winning*) being converted to 70mm to the further benefit of the Duopoly and loss to other exhibitors when the films prove successful. Believe me, with 70mm it is not the speed of obtaining the new films – it is getting them at all that is the problem.

Winning was a car racing drama from Universal, released by Rank, and initially blown up to 70mm to fill the Cinerama screen at the independently-run London Casino. Refson was asked, "Do you think anything can be achieved by a rough grouping of independents – say Essoldo with Star and Granada?", and responded:

No. With the present-day arrangements no combination could ever hope to compete with the Duopoly now that it has been permitted to become so powerful and is so protected. At the time of the Monopolies Commission I advocated bidding because it appeared to be the only practicable way to introduce an element of competition into the business. Unfortunately, no one else agreed with this and our meetings with some of the pundits of the industry resulted only in pitying looks, and exclamations of horror that the renter [distributor] might also benefit [...] [I]f the introduction of competition meant that we paid more to the renter we would have been happy to do so provided our share was also improved. After all, it's what you are left with that matters. At the time bidding was stillborn; so died competition.

In fact, a third force would arrive. Classic, the former repertory chain which had moved into first-run exhibition with its acquisition of forty-six Rank cinemas in 1967, acquired Essoldo's cinemas in April 1972 and then other circuits. Although Classic premiered films in its West End halls, it did not have its own circuit release but played the Rank and/or ABC release as local circumstances permitted.

Programming at Rank's West End halls had changed by the late 1960s. The big roadshows occupied the Astoria, Dominion and Leicester Square Theatre. More specialised roadshows played the Odeon Haymarket while the Odeon St. Martin's Lane was sub-leased to Universal and Disney. The Odeon Marble Arch was largely into move-overs but still opened some roadshows

including *Hello, Dolly!* The Odeon Leicester Square continued to break in roadshows for early transfer elsewhere and played top attractions for general release. The Odeon Kensington moved into first runs while the New Victoria also opened many lesser films as did the Metropole when not in roadshow use.

In certain smaller seaside locations, Rank presented the same summer blockbuster on alternate weeks, e.g. *The Longest Day* at the Odeon Weymouth, with regular releases in between, providing a service to both visitors and local picturegoers. The print would have been shared with another cinema on the same policy.

Of course, not all roadshows were successful: the lethal reviews of the musical version of *Lost Horizon* scuppered its chances of doing much business. And, by the end of 1973, the roadshow was virtually dead. Hollywood was no longer regularly producing the big-budget big-subject spectacles which warranted higher prices. To some extent these had been replaced by smaller, more intimate historical pictures that had rave reviews and "quality" written all over them, like *A Man For All Seasons* (1966) and *The Lion In Winter* (1968).

One of the few new films on the right epic scale was *The Wind And The Lion*, which looked terrific on the huge 70mm screen at the Dominion Tottenham Court Road in 1975. It opened a few days later at the Odeons Brighton, Hanley, Leeds Merrion Centre, Liverpool, Manchester, Norwich, Plymouth and Southampton as well as the Capitol Cardiff and at some Gaumonts.

In contrast, *Tommy* was a film that seems to have propelled itself into the special attraction category. Released by a smaller distributor, Hemdale, Ken Russell's film version of The Who rock opera opened at the Leicester Square Theatre on 27 March 1975, seemingly on a test basis. It became the top West End draw for seven weeks, briefly gave way to *The Godfather II* and *The French Connection II*, then reclaimed the number one spot for several more weeks. No out-of-London engagements had been lined up and the first booking to be arranged was at the Odeon Blackpool. It was not generally released to the London suburbs until the end of October 1976.

London Waves

In 1964 United Artists had turned the Odeons at Bromley, Finsbury Park (Astoria), Hammersmith, Ilford, Streatham and Watford into Premiere Showcase Theatres to show *Goldfinger* concurrently with the West End at higher than usual prices. In 1965, exactly the same format was used for two Peter Sellers comedies released by UA: *A Shot In The Dark* at the end of January and *What's New Pussycat?* at the end of August. Rank used the Premiere Showcase set-up for a two-week run of its war picture, *The Heroes Of Telemark*. UA next revived it for the new James Bond picture *Thunderball*, which opened in the West

End at the end of the year (at the London Pavilion and Rialto, not the Odeon Leicester Square). *Thunderball* played a phenomenal four weeks at the nine Premiere Showcase cinemas, quickly followed by a one-week general release at the remaining Odeons.

However, during 1965, other films – *Mary Poppins*, *Cleopatra*, *Genghis Khan* – were pre-released at different and more numerous groups of suburban London cinemas, somewhat diluting the elite standing of the Premiere Showcase sites (some of which featured in these runs). In fact, the Odeon cinemas at Brixton (Astoria), Croydon, East Ham, Guildford (Playhouse), Haverstock Hill, Holloway, Kingston, Lewisham, Mile End Road, Rayners Lane, Romford and Southall were included in one or more of these waves which varied from two to four weeks and, of course, removed the sites from playing the regular release. *Mary Poppins* was still playing at the Odeon Haymarket (having opened in December 1964 at the Leicester Square Theatre) while these runs took place.

In an alternative approach, Columbia's Bond spoof *Casino Royale* claimed a fixed two weeks in 1967 on general release everywhere – but, after a bad first week, the second was cancelled at some cinemas. The year's genuine 007 outing, *You Only Live Twice*, opened at the Odeon Leicester Square in June and went out to the London suburbs in September for one week only.

UA used the Premiere Showcase cinemas but only referred to a "special presentation" of *The Graduate* in September 1968 when the line-up widened to bring in the Odeons at Camden Town, Epsom, Golders Green [Temple Fortune], Guildford, Rayners Lane, Richmond and Swiss Cottage along with two Granadas and two S&K halls. The Finsbury Park Astoria was no longer part of the grouping.

In January 1969, UA had detailed plans to showcase *The Thomas Crown Affair* but decided at the last minute to give it a standard release instead, perhaps fearing it was not special enough to make audiences pay higher prices. However, both *Chitty Chitty Bang Bang* and *Midnight Cowboy* had two-week waves similar to that of *The Graduate*.

But distributors could give special treatment to the wrong films. 20th Century-Fox attempted a two-week run of *Staircase*, its poorly reviewed comedy starring Richard Burton and Rex Harrison as gay hairdressers, at eleven London suburban Odeons (four of the usual pre-release halls – Ealing, Ilford, Bromley and Streatham – plus seven others in sophisticated areas) and the film had to be withdrawn after the first week.

The next 007 outing, *On Her Majesty's Secret Service*, was treated a little cautiously because it introduced a new lead, George Lazenby, in place of previous star Sean Connery. It premiered at the Odeon Leicester Square in December 1969

and played one week only runs in the London suburbs in March 1970.

The Columbia films *Cromwell* and *Waterloo* received special engagements in 1971. UA's next James Bond, *Diamonds Are Forever*, opened at the Odeon Leicester Square on 30 December 1971 and waited until 27 February 1972 before going into a three-week suburban wave. It received a two-week run at other London Odeons a fortnight later.

The next Bond, *Live And Let Die* opened at the Odeon flagship in July 1973 and had the regular delayed suburban release in September but played for two weeks everywhere, first north of the river, then south. *The Man With The Golden Gun* followed the same pattern, opening in December 1974 at the Odeon Leicester Square, followed by two weeks on local release in March 1975. All local cinemas were playing the films simultaneously within the two London areas.

Some West End runs could still bar all other cinemas for miles around, even when they lasted longer than anyone had expected. Astutely placed in the Odeon Haymarket at the end of 1968, *The Lion In Winter* ran for 79 weeks exclusively as probably the cinema's greatest hit. Londoners either had to fork out West End prices or wait, and wait, and wait...

Extra activities

One day bookings of opera, ballet and Shakespeare films had demonstrated their worth but from circa 1970 the arrival of pop concert films, beginning with *Johnny Cash! The Man, His World, His Music*, proved to have substantial appeal to the young, filling the gap caused by a decline in live tours by pop groups. *Monterey Pop* (featuring The Who, Otis Redding, Janis Joplin, Jimi Hendrix, etc.) coupled with *Cream Last Concert* did turnaway business at the Gaumont Aberdeen in November 1970 and a week later took more in one day at the Odeon Eglinton Toll that the programme showing the whole of the following week. It set one-day records at the Odeons Barnsley, Hartlepool and Northampton in March 1971 and seems to have played at most Rank halls over the next few months (including a late night show at the Kilburn State). The next one-day special was *Don't Look Back* (Bob Dylan, Joan Baez) which raised concerns that an anti-Vietnam slant might limit its appeal. These films were not exclusive to Rank's cinemas.

Odeons of this period put on numerous special film shows: the records for Gloucester in 1971-3 reveal that these accounted for around 10 per cent of admissions.

These "extra activities" at the Odeon Southampton seem to have been typical for Rank cinemas. During the financial year ending 31 October 1974 eleven one-day special presentations resulted in 8,517 admissions: *Fantasia* (2,617), *Macbeth* (1,046),

Elvis – That's The Way It Is (821), *Death In Venice* (571), *Wood-stock* (701), *Oh! What A Lovely War* (334); *Jimi Hendrix* (489); *Glastonbury Fayre* plus *When Comedy Was King* (452); *Little Women* (744); *Jane Eyre* plus *Lord Of The Flies* (744); and *Johnny Cash! The Man, His World, His Music* (339). Some of these were return engagements.

Three special Saturday matinees (during weeks when X-certificate films were playing) drew 897 admissions: *The Great St. Trinian's Train Robbery* plus *An Elephant Called Slowly* (275); *Pure Hell Of St. Trinian's* plus *Blue Murder At St. Trinian's* (138); and *Batman* (484).

Eleven "educational" performances produced 6,939 admissions: *It's A Mad Mad Mad Mad World* (425); *Kes* (1,824); *Lord Of The Flies* (149 + 695): *Animal Farm* (811); *Becket* (546); *West Side Story* (166); *Living Free* (306); *A Town Like Alice* (297); *Macbeth* [Polanski] (780); and *A High Wind In Jamaica* (940).

Sixteen midweek matinees aimed at children in holiday periods yielded 3,941 admissions: *The Incredible Mr. Limpet* (135); cartoon comedy programmes (632 + 195 + 269);*Attragon* (39); *Alakazam The Great* (101); *The First Spaceship On Venus* (200); *Bugs Bunny No. 6 Show* (267); *Master Of The World* (151); *Tickle Me* (332); *The Square Peg* (292); *Son Of Captain Blood* (338); *The Bulldog Breed* (241); *Spare A Copper* (193); *The Flight Of The Lost Balloon* (230); and *Men Of Sherwood Forest* (326).

Late night shows were featured at most Odeons. Major attractions like the James Bond films were widely given extra late night performances. An unusual development was the late-night screenings on Saturday 21 June 1969 of Columbia's western *Mackenna's Gold* at several Odeons (Mile End, Finsbury Park Astoria, Golders Green, Woolwich) before it opened for a two-week special run. In the London area, at the end of 1969, separate horror or gangster programmes played Fridays or Saturdays at the Odeons Acton, Edgware Road, Harlesden, Lewisham, Mile End, Southall, Stamford Hill as well as the Gaumont Finchley. In 1971, separate late night shows were to be found at the Odeons Lewisham, Muswell Hill, Peckham, Putney, Romford, Shepherd's Bush, Stamford Hill, Surbiton and Wood Green as well as the Regal Edmonton, Gaumont Notting Hill and Kilburn State. In 1972, the Odeon Shepherd's Bush was putting on shows every night at 11.15pm: these were distinct from the regular evening show and covered various categories, not just violence and sex.

Live shows

In the mid-1960s, Rank issued a brochure listing fifty-five cinemas with facilities for live shows together with details of seating, stage dimensions and dressing rooms. The New Victoria was the one in the West End (where other cinemas were "occasionally available"). In the London suburbs, Rank offered the Odeons at Barking, Brixton and Finsbury Park (Astorias), Hammersmith and Lewisham, Streatham and Wimbledon along with the Regal Edmonton and Gaumont State Kilburn. The Odeon Swiss Cottage was not listed, despite its continuing series of classical concerts.

Outside London, available Odeons were at Birmingham, Blackburn, Blackpool, Bolton, Canterbury, Cardiff (Capitol), Chelmsford, Cheltenham, Colchester, Derby, Exeter, Folkestone, Glasgow, Guildford, Halifax, Hanley, Ipswich, Leeds, Leicester, Liverpool, Llandudno, Luton, Manchester, Newcastle, Rochester, Romford, Salisbury, Southend, Southport, St. Albans, Sunderland, Swindon, Trowbridge, Watford and Weston-Super-Mare. (The Gaumonts were at Bournemouth, Bradford, Doncaster, Hanley, Ipswich, Norwich, Sheffield, Southampton, Taunton, Weymouth, Wolverhampton and Worcester.) Dressing rooms ranged from two at Halifax and Luton to fifteen at Southend and seating capacities varied from 1,124 at Canterbury to 3,483 at Hammersmith.

Cinemas were usually hired out. In some instances, the Rank Theatre Division took a presentation credit for live shows but this was normally in partnership with a promoter.

The unsubdivided Odeons at Birmingham and Glasgow were increasingly used for live shows. In his book *100 Years Of Glasgow's Amazing Cinemas*, Bruce Peter quoted former assistant projectionist Bill Beattie: "The most memorable concert was given by Duke Ellington and his Orchestra in the autumn of 1969. He complained about the cold all day, but gave a terrific show at night, as usual telling the audience that he 'loved them madly' and doing many encores. By then the concerts were making more money than films."

Beside pop concerts and other musical events, the 1970s was the peak period for live closed-circuit television presentations of championship boxing matches from North America, Africa and the Caribbean. The cinemas used did not need stage facilities: a large seating capacity and the right location were the key factors. And these sports relays were usually in the middle of the night, so there was no loss of normal film performances. As with pop concerts, Rank's sites participated along with those of other operators.

In March 1971, the Cassius Clay-Joe Frazier bout in New York was relayed live to twenty-nine Rank halls. These included the Dominion Tottenham Court Road and Odeon Kensington while in Glasgow, Cardiff, Manchester, Liverpool, Birmingham, Leeds and Nottingham, additional cinemas had to be added to meet the demand... The British heavyweight championship match of Henry Cooper versus Joe Bugner in the same month involved the Odeon Leicester Square, the New Victoria, Capitol Cardiff,

ODEON FILM CENTRES

CROYDON:681 2491
1. LIGHTNING SWORDS OF DEATH (X)/CRAZY JOE (X)
2. VAMPIRA (AA)/THE GRAVY TRAIN (X)

GUILDFORD:0483 4990
1. LIGHTNING SWORDS OF DEATH (X)/CRAZY JOE (X)
2. THE NINE LIVES OF FRITZ THE CAT (X) / WEEKEND WITH A
3. A TOUCH OF CLASS (AA)   BABY–SITTER (X)

HOUNSLOW:570 2096
1. LIGHTNING SWORDS OF DEATH (X)/CRAZY JOE (X)
2. THE THREE MUSKETEERS (U)
3. VAMPIRA (AA) / THE GRAVY TRAIN (X)

PECKHAM:639 1722
1. CHINATOWN (X)
2. THE NINE LIVES OF FRITZ THE CAT(X)/ WEEKEND WITH A
3. VAMPIRA (AA) / RED SUN (AA)   BABY–SITTER (X)

RICHMOND:940 5759
1. CHINATOWN (X)
2. THE GREAT GATSBY (A)
3. THE THREE MUSKETEERS (U)

WELL HALL:850 3351
1. CHINATOWN (X)
2. THE NINE LIVES OF FRITZ THE CAT (X)/WEEKEND WITH A
                                           BABY–SITTER (X)

WIMBLEDON:542 2277
1. LIGHTNING SWORDS OF DEATH (X)/CRAZY JOE (X)
2. VAMPIRA (AA)/ RED SUN (AA)
3. THE DAY OF THE JACKAL (A)

* Please note
Super Saturday Shows at these Theatres will now be on Saturday Afternoon

OTHER ODEONS

* BROMLEY (460 4425)
The Way We Were (A) / The Hireling (A)
CAMBERWELL (274 3590)
Lightning Swords of Death (X)/Crazy Joe (X)
ELEPHANT & CASTLE (407 1991)
Lightning Swords of Death (X)/Crazy Joe (X)
* LEWISHAM (852 1331)
Lightning Swords of Death (X)/Crazy Joe (X)
PENGE (778 5694)
Vampira (AA)/The Gravy Train (X)
* REDHILL (71 61563)
Lightning Swords of Death (X)/Crazy Joe (X)
* RICHMOND Gaumont (940 1760)
Magnum Force (X)/Dirty Harry (X)

STREATHAM (769 3346)
Lightning Swords of Death (X)/Crazy Joe (X)
* SURBITON (399 3884)
Vampira (AA)/The Gravy Train (X)
* TWICKENHAM (892 5005)
Lightning Swords of Death (X)/Crazy Joe (X)
* UXBRIDGE (89 34381)
Lightning Swords of Death (X)/Crazy Joe (X)
WALTON (98 20870)
Chinatown (X)
* WOKING (04862 61275)
Lightning Swords of Death (X)/Crazy Joe (X)
WOOLWICH (854 2255)
Lightning Swords of Death (X)/Crazy Joe (X)

ENQUIRIES? RING INDIVIDUAL ODEONS OR ODEON INFORMATION CENTRE 930 3774 9 a.m. to 8 p.m.

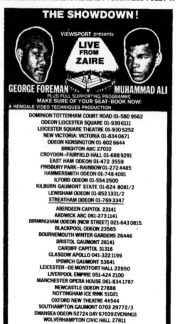

In this centre spread for the South London Odeon weekly programme in November 1974, the single screen cinemas are treated as also rans. The twinning and tripling programme will extend to Bromley, Streatham and Uxbridge but the others are doomed to closure sooner or later. A more sophisticated ABC circuit release, Chinatown, *is playing in several Odeons rather than the week's Rank releases,* Lighting Swords Of Death *and* Vampira.

The list of sites showing a major boxing match by closed circuit TV in October 1974 is dominated by Odeon and Gaumont cinemas.

and the Odeons Birmingham, Manchester, Leicester (Queen Street), Eglinton Toll (Glasgow) and Ilford.

At the end of October 1974, the George Foreman versus Muhammad Ali (formerly Cassius Clay) "showdown" in Zaire was seen in the early hours of the morning at all Rank's large West End venues – the Odeon Leicester Square, Dominion Tottenham Court Road, Leicester Square Theatre, New Victoria, Odeon Kensington – as well as at the Odeons East Ham, Hammersmith, Ilford, Lewisham and Streatham, plus the Gaumont State Kilburn (Rank had a near monopoly on the event in the London area as the only other venues were the Fairfield Hall Croydon and a former Odeon house, the Rainbow Finsbury Park). Outside London, the match played a wider range of outlets but Rank contributed the Odeons at Birmingham, Blackpool, Newcastle and Swansea, the Capitol Cardiff, plus the Gaumonts Bristol, Ipswich and Southampton. The ABC circuit participated only at Brighton and Manchester (Ardwick).

In February 1978, another Muhammad Ali fight – versus Leon Spinks – was relayed to the Odeon Leicester Square and other sites.

Live wrestling was more a speciality of Granada's stages but it was tried out at some Odeons, including Brighton, Romford, Temple Fortune and the Astoria Brixton. James Bettley recalls:

During 1970/71 I was acting manager of the Romford Odeon. On the fourth Saturday of the month, wrestling replaced the usual evening film performance with Dale Martin Promotions providing ring, wrestlers, referee, microphone and ring lights. The screen was always set well back on a deep stage and Rank provided black masking drapes which were hung in front of the screen tabs. The ring was erected at the front of the stage and the old (original?) house tabs were brought in a few yards on either side to provide changing space for the wrestlers. This was, by now, the only time these curtains were used and, though actually plain, they had acquired murky vertical, stripes through having hung gathered up at the side of the arch for so long amid nicotine and dust. Bottled beer was sold on wrestling nights from trestle tables in the circular balcony lounge. A separate late night presentation of an X certificate film took place every Saturday night and the wrestling equipment was often still being dismantled on stage as the first patrons took their seats.

Pantomime was staged at Christmas 1968 and 1969 at the Odeon Temple Fortune and, unusually, the Odeon Streatham. There may have been similar shows elsewhere.

Of course, twinning and tripling gradually removed most of the cinemas from the special events line-up.

The "enemy within"

In 1970, a new threat to the cinema estate emerged. Rank Property Developments was formed to handle all existing and planned redevelopment of properties owned by the Organisation – principally cinemas, of course – with a view to expansion of such activity. The ownership of many cinemas (such as the New Victoria) was transferred to the property company which then leased them back, resulting in an additional and much resented financial burden of paying rent.

One of the property company's major schemes was the replacement of the Gaumont and former Savoy cinemas in Glasgow. Together, they created an L-shaped site with frontages on two different streets for a new Savoy Centre, a nine-storey block containing a ground floor shopping precinct and a second floor Top Rank Suite with offices above (it took until 1981 before all the retail space was let). This followed the tripling of the city centre Odeon which made the Gaumont redundant.

Another major scheme – the destruction of the profitable Odeon Kensington – hit planning problems. Along with adjacent properties, it was to be superseded by a 1,000-room hotel and shops with a standard replacement gesture of two smaller Odeon cinemas. When permission was denied for a hotel of the size envisaged, Rank declared that was no longer a viable proposition and put forward a proposal for shops, offices and flats instead. (Rank did build and operate the 570-seat Gloucester Hotel in South Kensington.)

City Wall Properties was then acquired in 1971 to add more experienced management. This enabled many major developments to take place overseas. But City Wall could not bring off the Kensington scheme and Sir John Davis declared in the 1972 annual report to shareholders: "The development of the Odeon Kensington site has made no progress since my last report as the numerous schemes we have drawn up have all been rejected." Then he observed more generally: "There is one aspect which is disturbing – that we find that local authorities are inclined to ask for inclusion of a cinema in a redevelopment scheme which they contend meets a local demand, whereas our experience shows clearly that the cinema we are wishing to redevelop has been a 'loser' for some years through lack of public support." Once again, Sir John expressed the highly debatable view that if Rank could not run a cinema profitably, then no one else could and, therefore, film entertainment had no future in that particular area.

However, City Wall did redevelop the Odeon Burnt Oak and the Angel Islington, bringing about the closure of both in 1972. At the latter, it demolished a remarkably intact 1912 auditorium while leaving the landmark entrance tower which was found worthy of listing in 1991 (the staircase from the street up to the foyer has been removed). How much better if the entire building had been listed twenty years earlier!

Top, the tower of the Odeon Islington. (Photograph by Allen Eyles.)
Below, the auditorium being stripped after closure in 1972. The framework which carried the new curtains for the wider CinemaScope screen from the mid-1950s can be seen, along with the original tall narrow proscenium arch behind, including urns in niches on each side of where the old screen stood. The colonnades down each side of the stalls are also evident along with the lofty ceiling which was concealed from audience view by powerful suspended downlights at intervals. (Courtesy of former GLC Historic Buildings Division.)

In 1972, Rank Property Developments also pulled off a £450,000 destruction and reconstruction of the huge Odeon Chelsea. This reduced cinema to a single 739-seat screen in the old balcony, retaining some of the balcony foyer and a former exit staircase onto the main King's Road to provide the modest new entrance. The full original entrance was used by Habitat for a new store. The flytower was converted into flats. Rank estimated that the scheme would bring in five times as much annual revenue as the old cinema; but this did not take into account the fact that its new cinema would become a failure – at least as run by Rank.

The *Daily Telegraph* (1 April 1972) reported that Rank "reckons that at least one-third of its 235 cinema sites will be eliminated from the circuit and put to more profitable use as mixed commercial redevelopments over the next five to 10 years" and asserted that Rank was disappointed in the slow return on its twins and triple cinemas and by the further 10 per cent decline in attendances over the past three years.

Two last nights

I had little enthusiasm for attending the last night of any cinema but I did make the effort for a couple of original Odeons in September 1972.

By this time cinemas tended to die quietly amid the same public apathy that brought about their closure. But events at the Odeon Southgate recalled the 1950s when the loss of a cinema shocked the community. Here, with only a couple of weeks' notice, junior cinemagoers from the Odeon's highly successful Saturday club marched through the town waving banners of protest and the usual petition was organised. Nevertheless, on Thursday 7 September the Odeon gave its last film performance (being let for Jewish services on the Friday and Saturday).

The last programme consisted of *Junior Bonner* plus *The Moon And The Sledgehammer*. Manager John Hooper had hoped to obtain *The Last Grenade* as being more entertaining and having an appropriate word in its title. He arranged for an extra afternoon show at 3.45 on the last day, the only matinee of the week. In the evening, *The Moon And The Sledgehammer* concluded to a small round of applause. The curtains did not close but the screen, bathed in pink light, opened out to CinemaScope and music was played on the non-sync. Mr. Hooper came on stage to help a little girl present a bouquet of flowers to two elderly ladies who had attended the very first performance when the Odeon opened in 1935. The manager pointed out that the cinema was being closed for one reason only: lack of support. And, even on the final night, this was clear enough: a fairly sparse number of patrons had come (although the main feature, a story of rodeo life, was a dud in terms of audience appeal and barely shown in many parts of this country). Before leaving the stage, Mr. Hooper asked for and obtained a round of applause for the projectionist, who had been at the cinema for forty years. From one side, a coffin was carried to the centre of the stage and four cadets from the Air Training Corps marched on and played "The Last Post". Local press photographers were on hand to record the events. Then the censor's certificate for *Junior Bonner* came up on the screen and its conclusion 103 minutes later was followed by the National Anthem.

The cinema had been barely altered since its opening. It was a dull design by theatre architect Bertie Crewe, quite without the flair of the best Odeons and probably initiated by another promoter. The future of the building was uncertain. Apparently a new road scheme could claim much of the frontage and a multi-purpose redevelopment of the rest of the site, without a cinema, was likely. It was said that the rival ABC cinema at Bowes Road, New Southgate, which had been extensively modernised to dis-appointing results, had been under consideration for bingo but was now reprieved by the Odeon's demise, but this, too, closed fifteen months later. After more than three years of disuse, Rank was happy to let the Odeon to an independent on a five-year lease: it re-opened as the Capitol, using only the stalls, but did well enough for the front of the circle to be re-seated and brought in as well. However, during those five years Rank sold the building to a developer. When the five years were up, the developer would only renew the lease for very short periods at a time, making its continued operation as a cinema too dubious for the lessee. It was demolished and replaced by offices.

In complete contrast to Southgate's dignified finale as an Odeon, there was a packed house for the last night of the Odeon Haverstock Hill, the manager was invisible, and the presentation was shoddy.

This Odeon was a superb building that had long struggled in the shadow of the nearby Odeon Swiss Cottage: in recent years, it had played a mix of Odeon and ABC releases (seemingly, the Playhouse Hampstead had first call on the latter but often didn't take it); it had also shown many foreign films and reissues, including an exclusive two-week re-release of Al Jolson's *The Singing Fool*, the picture that launched talkies in this country, shown four times daily when only evening shows was normal practice.

Whether or not it was operating profitably, this Odeon's trading figures must have been adversely affected in its later years by a factor unique in my extensive experience of attending Rank cinemas: rotten projection. I remember seeing a revival of *The Big Country* where the change-overs were repeatedly bungled and watching the entire trailer for a film in standard wide screen stretched out through an anamorphic lens.

The last programme was the Michael Caine comedy-thriller *Pulp* with a minor supporting feature. As the main film appeared to have only moderate appeal, I was surprised to find the cinema so full on that last evening: was it the film, a desire for a last look at the building, or a bit of both? Or was this a regularly well-attended cinema being sold for its site value? Even at the last picture show, the projection crew couldn't get it right: the image on the supporting feature became fainter and fainter and disappeared completely at one point while the sound continued. Overhearing staff who were buzzing about the crowded foyer during the interval, it seemed they were more concerned with gathering enough food and drink for their party afterwards than in putting on a good final performance.

A Budgens supermarket replaced the Odeon but space was allocated for a token replacement cinema on one side of the redevelopment (a condition of planning consent?), reached through what had been one of the adjacent shops. It took five years to open, not operated by Rank but as the art house Screen on the Hill.

Over to bingo

Bingo still took its toll, usually by cinemas passing to the Top Rank Clubs division but sometimes being leased or sold to a local group.

The Odeon Burton-on-Trent went to the eyes-down brigade in 1965, enabling the Gaumont, the better property of the two, to inherit the Odeon name and remain the town's only cinema, with a single screen until being tripled in 1974.

Most of Rank's major Odeons in the Glasgow suburbs went over to bingo: Scotstoun in 1967, Shettleston in 1969, Rutherglen in 1974 and Anniesland (ex-Gaumont) in 1975. Closed on the same day as the Odeon at nearby Motherwell (also destined for bingo), Anniesland was eventually listed but the Scottish authorities showed characteristic feebleness in allowing all but the facade to be demolished for flats. Rank's only remaining suburban cinema was the Odeon Eglinton Toll, an old ex-Gaumont property which increasingly relied on live shows.

The huge and relatively new Odeon Sheffield, put into an inferior position by the twinning of the Gaumont, passed to Top Rank bingo in 1971. In 1972, Rank bingo took over the Odeons at Stamford Hill and Whalebone Lane in the London area. The latter's twin, the Odeon Hornchurch, went to Rank bingo the following year but the Odeon Romford remained open in the area, soon to be tripled.

Then, in 1974, Top Rank Clubs claimed two former Gaumont halls, the Odeons at Northampton and Swindon, leaving ABC to carry on with triple cinemas in both locations. The Odeon Halifax went in 1975. Its departure from the film scene encouraged ABC to triple its Halifax cinema the following year.

In 1975, the huge Odeon Gateshead, the former Black's Regal, closed – but it was three years before this was turned into a Top Rank Club. Rank's success in putting bingo into the Odeon Gloucester this same year has been mentioned earlier.

At a few places, bingo was introduced for part of the week. At Wrexham, the Odeon surrendered three nights to bingo in 1972 and Rank sought to drop films entirely by November 1974 when weekly attendances were stated to be averaging 1,000. In April 1975 Rank declared:

> The Odeon Wrexham has been losing money for some time, quite simply because not enough people visit the cinema. Rather than close the Odeon we chose to introduce bingo on three days a week, hoping that bingo and a four-day film operation would each become profitable. We immediately encountered problems in obtaining the right films for the theatre as many film distributors are not over interested in four-day bookings. As a result, we have not been able to show the best choice of films and audience levels have fallen from bad to almost non-existent. Bingo, on the other hand, has attracted steadily rising attendances and we have therefore taken the decision to apply for full-time bingo at the Odeon.

From its 1960 opening, the Odeon Hemel Hempstead had suffered in playing films later than the Odeons at Watford and St. Albans (which were considered part of the London release area). Rank sought permission in 1973 to switch over to bingo on Thursdays, Fridays and Saturdays while the Borough Council suggested Mondays, Tuesdays and Wednesdays! After much negotiation, consent was forthcoming for bingo from Wednesday to Friday, giving films a four-day run from Saturday.

Bingo also began taking evenings away from film at the Odeon Shirley during this period.

Other last picture shows

The Odeon South Harrow was set to become a Top Rank Club but its scheduled closure on 23 March 1968 was cancelled during the preceding month because the bingo division's budget wouldn't stretch to the adaptation needed and there were higher priorities. The Odeon lost its access to the main Rank release (to the benefit of the Odeon Rayners Lane) and lingered on for nearly four years with the often desperate and highly eclectic assortment of programmes available to an off-circuit house, varying from an Andy Warhol film to a revival of the John Wayne epic *The Alamo* which I attended on a busy Saturday evening to find that the cinema was remarkably unaltered inside and out and that all the auditorium's red cove lighting was still working forty years on. This was a really pleasant, welcoming place, of comfortable size. And, being the Odeon that so

dramatically launched the circuit style in 1933, it was a highly significant property. Had bingo gone ahead, it might have survived long enough to become a listed building. Instead, the auditorium was replaced with flats which filled in the deep recess over the entrance so that the new frontage was flush with the surviving corners of shops and flats clad in buff faience. The developer lacked the respect to match the 1933 tilework in the new frontage.

The Odeon Kirkcaldy was destroyed by an overnight fire, Scottish cinemas having always been particularly vulnerable to a good blaze. However, the same fate also brought about the end of the Odeon (ex-Gaumont) Walsall in the West Midlands.

Occasionally, successful cinemas were closed when the leases could not be renewed, at least on acceptable terms. Rank had lost two of the three former Majestics at Staines and Wembley in 1961 and the third at High Wycombe was sold in 1967 by its owner, along with the adjacent hotel, to become the site of a new Woolworth's. However, the cinema remained open for nearly two years until the scheme was ready to proceed.

In 1970 the London suburban Odeons at Deptford and Kensal Rise ended their days. In 1971, thinning out removed the Odeons at Dagenham, Dover, Epsom, Lewes, Port Talbot, South Norwood and Trowbridge. The Odeon Dagenham was the last cinema in this large industrial town, its closure attributed to a sharp reduction in the number of young people living in the area. Vacating well-heeled Epsom seems to have been a case of sacrificing a profitable cinema for a generous offer from a supermarket chain. Like South Harrow, South Norwood was a particularly fine example of the 1930s Odeon style, rundown but intact, and it made way for another supermarket.

In Putney, Rank agreed to sell its profitable Odeon to help the rival ABC circuit – for a price. ABC wanted to replace its almost adjacent cinema with a new three-screen one as part of a big redevelopment scheme that extended over the Odeon's site and included offices. Rank consented to pull out after ABC sweetened the deal by agreeing to close its cinemas at Richmond and Walton-on-Thames to give a clear field to both towns' Odeons. (How the new Putney ABC has become an Odeon is outside the scope of this book.)

The huge Astoria Old Kent Road lasted until mid-1968, having continued on alternative programming a further eighteen months after the new Odeon Elephant and Castle had taken away the main Rank release. It closed down as a faded, melancholy hall that had never once been redecorated... the landscapes painted on the splay walls could still be seen.

And 1971 saw Rank drop its more notable sister theatre on the other side of London, the Astoria Finsbury Park, less than year after going to the trouble of renaming it Odeon. This vast and wonderful "atmospheric" hall had done well to survive so long on last-ditch film programming insufficiently relieved by live shows and pre-release engagements of new pictures.★

Besides property development, there was another wheeze for making use of very large cinemas. In 1972, Rank Leisure Services invested almost £500,000 in converting three cinemas plus a former ballroom and the closed Old Trafford Bowl into pop concert halls. Two of the cinemas were in rough areas of London: the Astoria Brixton and Odeon Mile End Road. (As recently as 1968, the latter had closed for two months to undergo an £85,000 facelift. This included new aluminium-framed entrance doors, suspended ceiling bars across the main foyer and circle lounge, and new blue seating in the auditorium with red curtains. The investment clearly hadn't paid off.) The two were re-launched as Sundown Discotheques with the stalls becoming a carpeted standing area with staggered viewing platforms while the circle remained seated as an alternative. Mile End continued to show some films under the Sundown name. Pop stars such as Slade, Steppenwolf, Uriah Heep and the Kinks were reported as booked to play the venues. But the new idea became a failure within months. Brixton was then used for storing Rank's paper archives until it hit better times as a concert hall in independent hands, renamed the Academy. It was after the Sundown debacle that Mile End was leased out for Asian films, as mentioned earlier.

The Odeon Newton Abbot had done well to survive into 1972, considering that the same small town also had an independent hall, the Alexandra. The Odeon's demise was to the Alexandra's benefit as it continues to this day, now twinned, demonstrating that cinema was still viable in the town in the hands of an independent.

The Odeons at East Dulwich and Kingsbury also closed in 1972. The closure of Kingsbury, together with Burnt Oak, helped the Classic chain with its recent takeover of the former Odeon Colindale from Panton Films because this was no longer barred from the main Rank release, encouraging the addition of a second screen in part of the rear stadium section. East Dulwich

---

★ It returned as a home of pop concerts and endeared itself to a new generation of music lovers as the Rainbow before falling on hard times and, thanks to being listed, surviving many years of disuse before a fine restoration for church use. Films have made at least two further appearances. The Jimi Hendrix picture *Live At Berkeley*, shown in 70mm shortly after the Astoria first re-opened, was dogged by a dim picture and multiple breakdowns – see *Films & Filming*, March 1972 – but the Cinema Theatre Association, publishers of this book, presented *Sunset Boulevard* without a hitch as a special event on 28 February 2004 on a temporary screen even larger than the one on which the film had been shown in 1950.

The Astoria Finsbury Park was renamed Odeon for its final year and is showing an off-circuit revival double-bill. Inside, it retained its full atmospheric scheme including the spiral columns on which lions are sitting to each side of the pros arch – which were omitted from the recent restoration. (CTA Archive. Interior photograph by Kevin S. Wheelan.)

was superfluous now that the nearby Odeon Peckham had been tripled.

The Odeon Byker was the former Black's Regal, a lavishly appointed cinema two miles east of Newcastle city centre. Only in Rank's hands since 1955, it sat disused after closure in 1972, refused a bingo licence in 1975, until converted to supermarket use and later demolished.

By this time, the tripling programme was well underway and it seems to have been decided to close halls near to triples or those whose takings did not encourage an investment in subdivision.

The Odeons at Highgate and Morden closed early in 1973 after the Christmas and New Year holiday break. Highgate was, of course, a postwar opening, not yet twenty years old. It was eclipsed by the larger Holloway Odeon and in later years of split Rank releases tended to be given the weaker fare as though to meet head office booking obligations. This was a rough area and only the circle was used. There was a story that a manager who remonstrated with troublesome patrons was thrown off the first floor landing. The Odeon closed with no immediate use in sight, being bought for replacement by housing later in the year. The Odeon Morden was a wide barn of a place with a gloomy, echoey ambience in its final years. Like Highgate, this tended to play some of the weaker options and was dispensable with the Odeon Wimbledon being close at hand.

Later in the same year Rank vacated Stourbridge and Falkirk, leaving film provision to a single-screen and three-screen ABC respectively.

The Odeon Burnley had remained one of the most attractive Weedon-designed cinemas. This Lancashire industrial town had gained a brand-new twin cinema, Studio 1 & 2, in Market Square in 1970. When this added a third screen in March 1973, Rank seems to have given up on the single-screen Odeon. (There was also the four-screen Unit 4 at Brierfield competing for custom.) Reduced to restricted opening (matinees on Mondays, Wednesdays and Saturdays), the Odeon played the Bond film *Live And Let Die* for a full four weeks (probably a contractual requirement) shortly before closing with a week of soft porn. It was replaced by a Sainsbury's supermarket.

Early in 1974 the Odeon Folkestone closed, leaving the film scene to a Classic which became a twin two months later and then, as the Curzon, a triple. This Odeon was an attractive cinema (its interior and some of its exterior design by Mollo and Egan, reminiscent of their work on the Odeon Surbiton a year earlier). Being centrally located, it should have survived – but a developer seems to have made an irresistible offer and it closed with minimal advance notice.

A compulsory purchase order served by the local council forced the end on the Odeon Brentwood in 1974: this had escaped alteration, apart from its main foyer, and its long auditorium, designed by George Coles, was a joy to behold with all its linear concealed lighting still functioning. The profitable cinema made way for a new shopping centre which included two replacement cinemas not taken by Rank.

Another casualty of 1974 was the Odeon Temple Fortune (recently known as the Odeon Golders Green). This huge and rather unattractive hall was remotely located in the Hampstead Garden Suburb a mile from the centre of Golders Green in north London. Opened in 1930 as the Orpheum with cine-variety, it was more suited to theatrical use with its fully equipped stage (film projection was from an acute angle in the rim of the ceiling dome). Following the closure (for television use) of the Golders Green Hippodrome, the Odeon became the new home of Ralph Reader's celebrated *Gang Shows* featuring Boy Scouts from 1968 – the Queen attended the opening of the fortieth show on Monday 23 October 1972. Seating over 2,300, the cinema had participated in some recent pre-releases (*The Graduate*) and staged pantomimes at several Christmasses. Following a refurbishment, there had been an effort to introduce more live shows in its last three years, including another pantomime at Christmas 1971. Nine months later Rank put forward a scheme to replace it with shops and flats. It was publicly admitted (to the *Hampstead And Highgate Express*, 8 September 1972) that the cinema was not losing money: "We are just about breaking even but of course we are sitting on a very large investment. If we had put the money we have spent on the Odeon into the Post Office, we would have made more money." Although closed in April 1974, the building lingered for eight years before being demolished for flats.

The Odeon Dudley had been passed over for tripling with Rank's Plaza opposite being twinned instead. It struggled on for nearly two years, finally closing in February 1975 and being purchased by Jehovah's Witnesses who were in the process of a major refurbishment when it was made a listed building in 2000. The always sunken entrance has now been enclosed by railings but the faience tilework has been restored (the original green banding mistakenly painted black) while the foyers and auditorium have been expensively and tastefully modernised, introducing high levels of lighting – but unfortunately losing the simplicity and subtle atmosphere of the original design.

The Odeon Surbiton offered a striking exterior as well as a Mollo and Egan auditorium scheme with its concealed lighting in working order at its 1975 closure. The building was lightly converted for many years of retail use before being entirely demolished to make way for a supermarket. As at South Harrow and elsewhere, the attached shops and flats have remained.

The vast Odeon Camberwell (the fourth largest purpose-

Odeon Temple Fortune, Golders Green, in 1968. Note the huge posters for live shows which cover three consecutive weeks: two with its first Gang Show, then one with the London Festival Ballet. Inside, plain redecoration has submerged the decorative plasterwork, especially the frieze just below ceiling level. The Red Army Ensemble and the Hornsey Operatic Society also made use of the stage facilities. (Photographs by John Maltby.)

The Odeon Redhill still had its pylon on the main road in February 1974. The sign above the canopy merely reads "You Can't Beat A Good Film". (Photograph by Allen Eyles.)

built Odeon) had been effectively doomed when Rank tripled the Odeon Peckham just over a mile away. Yet it carried on for eighteen months, still with daily matinees, using only its 986-seat balcony, and often secured quite good films. Its seven neon name signs blazed away to the last night but there was only a minimal display of the current attraction. Here, as at many sites without readographs, the main poster space above the twin entrances merely said YOU CAN'T BEAT A GOOD FILM without revealing what that good film might be. The entrance on Denmark Hill was closed, forcing patrons to walk all around the apex of the site to the matching Coldharbour Lane doors. Here the downstairs foyer was deserted and patrons had to proceed up the staircase to a cash desk set up in the circle lounge. Despite all this, there were healthy attendances on the several occasions I visited during this period but many films advertised as forthcoming in the circle lounge, including *The Four Musketeers* as an August holiday attraction, were never to play there after it closed with little notice in July 1975. The building then held on for nearly twenty years, the auditorium being disfigured by brief use selling discount jeans. Falling into disrepair with no obvious alternative use (the local ABC had taken up the bingo option), it was eventually replaced by flats.

In the autumn of 1975, Rank announced fifteen cinemas as closing besides the six that were sold as going concerns to Brent Walker. (On the positive side, nine additional screens were being created at other cinemas.)

Three of the fifteen (Odeons Bury, Perth and Southport) were reprieved. The twelve that closed included the Odeons Anniesland and Halifax, mentioned previously as converts to bingo, and a Gaumont roadshow house, the Pavilion Newcastle (leaving two other Rank cinemas, the Odeon and Queen's).

Of the remainder, the Odeon Acton in west London retained its original name signs, including the one incorporated into its striking tower feature. In the auditorium, the recessed strips of concealed lighting in the ceiling and side walls still worked. One of George Coles' most accomplished schemes survived both inside and out (and was therefore more complete than his Odeon Woolwich). Like the Odeon Surbiton, it was subsequently little altered as a store before being eventually demolished for a supermarket.

The Odeon Redhill was a little rundown but otherwise barely altered with carpet in the 1930s circuit pattern in some of the aisles. Retained by Rank, it was turned into a nightclub, leaving the balcony largely intact.

At Bootle, the Odeon (ex-Gaumont) had only opened part of the week from 1974 (except during school holidays) and now gave up altogether, just short of its twentieth anniversary.

The Odeon Forest Gate had become particularly seedy and threadbare in places but still retained its circuit-style sofas and ashstands in the balcony lounge. Although opened as an Odeon, it was undistinguished and, apart from being the last cinema in the Stratford area of east London, there was little cause to regret its passing.

However, the Odeon Clacton still exuded a warm welcome and its outstanding exterior and interior had been minimally altered. In fact, Rank re-opened the building for the following summer season. After going dark for the following winter, it was taken over by an independent as noted in the next chapter.

The Odeon Rochdale closed two weeks prematurely after a firework was thrown at the screen, setting it ablaze. ABC had a cinema in the town which it eventually tripled.

At Woking the better sited ABC had scaled down to a balcony cinema with stalls bingo while the Odeon, the rather nondescript building once given the "zing treatment", closed to be replaced by an office block.

The shutting of the Odeon Pennine Derby and the Odeon Hanley underlined the collapse of the roadshow era, leaving each town with a recently tripled Rank cinema. The Odeon Pennine was little more than eight years old. The Odeon Hanley went out after a successful run of *Tommy*. Internally, it had been drastically modernised for roadshow use.

An absence of listings

The Granada Tooting and Rank's New Victoria were the first cinemas to become "listed buildings" in 1972. Rank's two huge "atmospherics", the Astorias at Brixton (closed) and Finsbury Park (pop concert venue), were listed in January 1974 along with the Odeon Shepherd's Bush (the former Gaumont, for its exterior only). But no purpose-built Odeon or other Odeon cinema was honoured with the same statutory protection from change until 1980.

I understand that during the 1970s, in the Greater London Council area, the purpose-built Odeons at Balham, Camberwell, Dalston, Hackney Road, Leicester Square and Muswell Hill were all put forward and rejected for listing, along with the takeover Odeons at Kensington, Richmond, Streatham and Wimbledon, the Leicester Square Theatre, and the Gaumont/Odeon Hammersmith, Dominion Tottenham Court Road and Troxy Stepney. The rejections also extended to the Rialto Coventry Street, London Casino, Piccadilly Theatre (briefly a cinema), Commodore Hammersmith and ABC Forest Hill. They make up a good selection and listing would have been welcomed by most people apart from their proprietors.

Of the other purpose-built Odeons closed or sold around this time, in my view those in the London area at Acton, Erith, South Harrow, South Norwood and Surbiton should have been listed.

And, further afield, the Odeons at Brentwood, Clacton, Crewe and Redhill eminently deserved listed status. Several more Odeons, like Hendon, that were still operating in 1975 also richly warranted consideration, as will be indicated later.

I have been informed that the final arbiters of listing, the custodians of our architectural heritage, regarded cinemas as akin to gaudy fairground design, ephemeral and the work of insignificant architects. By the time this attitude began to change, it was too late for many buildings – and some of those that were eventually listed were no longer showing films, making their preservation as cinemas more difficult or impossible.

Industry changes

Industry-wide changes could not be affected without the support of Rank and ABC. One concerned the start day of runs outside London's West End. This was generally Sunday and became Friday from 1 July 1966 so that films started with the best days of the week, the hope being that favourable word of mouth would boost attendances on the following weekdays, which were traditionally poor. Despite widespread publicity, cinemagoers were confused by the change and sometimes annoyed to find that a film playing earlier during the week had gone on Saturday. (I didn't like it because it reduced the advance notice of what was showing as programmes started on the same day that the local weekly paper appeared.) Rather than persevere until audiences adjusted to the change, the industry panicked and reverted to Sunday openings from 12 February 1967 for the next sixteen years.

By the spring of 1972, pressure was building up from such bodies as the County Councils Association to restrict smoking in public places. In order to demonstrate the industry's concern and in an attempt to head off damaging legislation, Rank initiated experimental non-smoking areas in some of its cinemas. Rank also argued that offering patrons a choice was in an exhibitor's best interest. This must have been well received as by the end of the year it had become standard practice in all Rank's larger auditoria. It involved one side of the central aisle of a balcony or stalls area being designated as a non-smoking area, backed up by on-screen announcements ("your co-operation is appreciated") and by signs at the entrance doors and on the side walls of the auditorium. By the end of 1972, Rank had experimentally banned smoking completely in two of its mini-cinemas where a central block of seating without a middle gangway made a separate no-smoking area impracticable. A majority of the General Council of the Cinema Exhibitors' Association felt this was a dangerous precedent as it might inspire a licensing authority to ban smoking altogether in cinemas (*CEA Newsletter*, no. 134, January 1973). The CEA was particularly concerned that cinemas might be singled out and disadvantaged if other places open to the public did not bring in a ban.

There was a substantial expansion of cinemas licensed for the sale of liquor. By September 1970 Rank offered alcohol at thirty sites, including six in London's West End (but not the Odeon Leicester Square) and others in big cities as well as the Odeons Folkestone, Jersey, Norwich, Portsmouth, Scarborough, Southampton, Stockton and Worthing. A trolley service was tried out in the minis at some triples. ABC had only twelve licensed cinemas, Granada four, Caledonian (Scotland) six, and independents twenty-two. Most of these licences dated from when halls had shown extended runs with separate performances.

Gaumonts become Odeons (continued)

In 1965 and 1966, the Gaumonts at Derby, Walsall and Burton-on-Trent were renamed Odeon, but no further switches occurred until 1968 when the Gaumont Weymouth followed suit.

By 1968, there were twenty-five situations in which an Odeon and Gaumont still competed, ruling out any transfer of name. In several other places – such as Finchley, Hackney, Kilburn, Notting Hill Gate, South Shields and London's Victoria – there were Gaumont cinemas that could have been renamed Odeon but were not. In the cases of the State Kilburn and the New Victoria, this was probably because the existing names were so well established, while at Victoria the Odeon name would have been more applicable to the Metropole as an Odeon theatre historically.

As previously mentioned, the two cinemas re-opened in the subdivision of the Gaumont Bradford in 1969 were called Odeon. Also in 1969, the Gaumont Taunton was renamed, then in 1973 the Gaumont Dundee followed suit.

Overseas

Rank pulled out of Northern Ireland in 1974, accepting an offer of £467,000 from local investors for its remaining circuit of fourteen cinemas after five years of losses, the last straw being the closure of the Odeon Belfast through IRA bomb damage earlier that year.

In the Irish Republic, Rank closed six cinemas in the Dublin suburbs in July 1974 and sold the remainder during the following year, apart from one or two in the centre of Dublin. Rank's solitary cinema in Hamburg, Germany, was sold to 20th Century-Fox during this period. However, Rank acquired full ownership of the 25-strong Rank Tuchinski circuit in Holland in 1973 and added the Corso in Rotterdam at a cost of £1,285,000. Rank also retained its Canadian circuit along with its partnerships in Australia, New Zealand, Malaya and Ceylon.

The Davis touch

Few aspects of the Rank empire's activities escaped John Davis's close scrutiny. Every poster design for a Rank film had to be personally vetted by him – and he would scribble his alterations on the master artwork until the artists learned to protect their work with a layer of acetate. A telling illustration of the Rank boss's far-reaching autocracy comes from this account of the Royal Premiere of *The Charge Of The Light Brigade* in April 1968:

> In order to ensure a perfect première, [director Tony] Richardson introduced his dubbing engineer, Gerry Humphreys, to the team at the Odeon, Leicester Square. Humphreys rehearsed the soundtrack on their equipment, adjusting and fine-tuning the levels to Richardson's direction. On the opening night when the film started rolling it very quickly became evident that the sound was at a much lower level that had been rehearsed. Humphreys rushed off to the projection booth to ask what was happening. The projectionist explained that Sir John Davis, owner of the Rank circuit, was in attendance and he refused to allow the sound beyond a certain level whenever he was in the audience. "But it's Mr. Richardson's film," protested Humphreys. "It may be Mr. Richardson's film," replied the projectionist, "but it's Sir John's theatre." ★

Exit J. Arthur

Lord Rank died on 29 March 1972, aged 83, leaving a gross amount of just under £6 million. He had retained some interest in the world of films, attending *Cromwell*, the Alec Guinness-Richard Harris historical drama, during its run at the Odeon Marble Arch in 1970.

In 1955, Rank had issued a press statement in which he stated that, in preparation for his death, he had rearranged the private companies which controlled his film empire to vest voting power in trustees who would ensure that the group remained in British hands while applying the proceeds of dividends to charitable purposes. He recalled:

> My personal aim throughout my connection with the cinema industry has been to improve the quality and entertainment value of British films, to increase the number of British films produced and to secure the widest possible market for the exhibition of British films throughout the world. I have always believed and still believe that this object is of vital importance in the National interest, not only from financial and economic points of view, but having regard to British cultural and social relations with people throughout the world.

★ Quoted from *The Charge Of The Light Brigade* by Mark Connelly, 2003, published by I. B. Tauris.

Rank's influence was still felt in cinema operation, as former manager James Bettley recalls:

> As late as the 1970s it was still the policy of the Rank Organisation to invite a local Methodist Church minister to speak from the stage of each of the company's theatres on Good Friday. The speech, usually of just a few minutes duration, was on the theme of the Christian Easter Festival and delivered immediately prior to the last showing of the feature film.
>
> I first witnessed such an occasion in the mid-1960s when, before a near capacity audience in York Odeon, the curtains parted and the manager introduced the minister with the words: "Ladies and gentlemen, in common with all Rank Organisation theatres, we are to hear a few words on the meaning of Good Friday from the Reverend —— ——." On that occasion, the film which followed enabled the good man to incorporate its title with his words as he began: "It is indeed a mad, mad, mad, mad world..."
>
> The house note which head office sent to all managers annually reminding them of the policy stressed that the procedure must not be followed at those theatres playing roadshows. During my own time with Rank, I recall introducing ministers to Good Friday audiences in Harrogate and Romford, although I am not aware of when the practice ceased or whether the policy was changed or just "fizzled out".

REACHING THE NADIR (1976-1984)

The Rank Organisation entered a new era with the retirement of John Davis in March 1977. For the next six years, Davis became president, a position with no executive responsibility previously held by Lord Rank. (He died in 1993.)

The company was shrinking. From 1979, Rank took no active part in the Xerox photocopying business but retained a highly lucrative holding. However, the dividends were in decline as other photocopying companies took away much of the market. Southern Television lost its franchise – as one of the partners, Rank found this a "puzzling decision". Rank sold all its dance halls in 1983 except for the one at the Brighton leisure complex. It closed down Rank City Wall and sold that subsidiary's UK property portfolio in October 1984.

By 1980, the unbelievable had happened: Rank was no longer the largest British exhibitor. It had closed so many cinemas that it fell behind ABC in number of sites and screens, even though it had once owned two major circuits compared to ABC's one.

A desperate industry took another look at changing the Sunday start day at local cinemas. It moved to Thursdays from 27 January 1983, a day long favoured in the West End and seaside resorts, then from 11 November 1983 to Fridays where it has remained ever since.

Double bills were being replaced by single features and separate performances which enabled cinemas to potentially double their audiences with two evening showings unless a film was of massive length. Saturday children's shows seemed to be nearly over thanks to competition from TV but Rank was still running twenty-one of them in February 1984.

The showing of crude sexploitation films in Odeons and elsewhere was also on the wane because they were now available on video. Home video generally seemed like it might be the last straw for film exhibition. On the principle of "If you can't beat 'em, join 'em", Rank experimentally opened nine video shops in its cinema foyers, primarily for rental, and added twenty the following year. At the Odeon Barnet, customers were served from one of the two original wood-panelled box-offices that faced each other across the entrance hall. Market research apparently showed that offering videos did no harm as viewers turned out to be the keenest cinemagoers as well – though making it even easier to view at home seemed suspect to this writer.

Adding screens

Some investment in the cinema estate was made in 1976. This involved the subdivision of the better remaining single-screen sites. Plans to replace the Odeon Kensington were dropped and it became a triple. The Odeons at Bromley and Chester received elaborate three-screen conversions (in the manner of York in 1972) with the existing circles being extended forward to create very large main auditoria with stepped seating for 760 and 802 respectively. This did away with the awkward area left vacant in the front stalls at drop wall conversions. But it did, of course, increase the imbalance between the big auditorium and the small ones which seated around 120.

Some drop wall tripling still took place: at the Odeon Uxbridge in 1976, Westbourne Grove in 1978, Streatham in 1979 (where the vast size of the auditorium allowed two mini cinemas seating 267 under the balcony), and Warrington in 1980. Streatham had been an occasional live show venue and made final use of its undivided state with an Ian Dury concert that took place on 20 December 1978. It would have been tripled much earlier but there seems to have been problems with the ground landlord or other interested party.

In 1979/80, the Odeons at Reading, Southampton and Cardiff were twinned by closing off the balcony, enabling the entire stalls to be used as the larger screen. A similar subdivision seems to have taken place at Barnsley.

Further subdivision of already subdivided cinemas was also occurring. In 1976, the lower auditorium at the Odeon Nottingham was carved up into three cinemas creating a still large 681-seater and two holding 141 each, taking the complex to five screens in all.

At Kensington in 1979, just over three years after tripling, the largest auditorium was split into two screens. At two earlier three-screen conversions, at Richmond and Wimbledon, the downstairs minis had proved inadequate to meet demand and were extended forward to increase the number of seats. And at

Romford, one of the minis seems to have more than doubled in size, to seat 358.

At three key theatres in the big cities, an extra screen was added. In 1978-79, old bar areas at the Odeon Leeds twin and the four-screen Odeon Liverpool were turned into an additional cinema as had happened at Nottingham in 1970. At Manchester, a third screen opened in the former mezzanine, where the projection room had been based for the downstairs Odeon Two after twinning. Carl Chesworth recalls:

> When Odeon Three, built on the former mezzanine, was planned, it was decided to update Odeon Two. The fire safety curtain was dropped permanently and a new screen frame built in front of it. This immediately solved the heating problem, stopping heat escaping into the void behind the screen. A new projection room was built in the rear stalls and the mezzanine became the new Odeon Three. This was not the width of the old mezzanine, for ventilation fan rooms were constructed left and right of the auditorium. This ended up having the nicest dimensions of all the three cinemas, with excellent sightlines, lighting, sound and picture. The opportunity was taken to improve the appearance of Odeon Two by installing pleated drapes to the side walls (originally skimmed plaster, painted blue), and concealed trough lighting.

During 1980 an extra screen was fitted onto the stage at the Odeon Newcastle. (In addition, Rank tripled its Metropole Dublin.) The following year saw the tripling of the Odeon Ilford (with larger-than-average cinemas downstairs) and the twinning of the Odeon St. Helier, Jersey.

In 1982, the stadium auditorium of the Odeon Swansea was split into three with two smaller cinemas at the back. The cinema at the front used the original screen but tabs were now added. Also in 1982, the Odeon Edinburgh was tripled (see *Gaumont British Cinemas*, page 174).

Shedding screens

The end of the roadshow era led to a thinning out in the West End. In 1976 Rank dropped the Astoria Charing Cross Road, despite having completely reconstructed the auditorium in 1968. It went over to club use. Similarly, the Metropole Victoria, on the fringe of London's West End, had become redundant. It was leased out for shortlived laser shows, then became a pop concert hall for a while like the New Victoria nearby, which had closed as a cinema two years earlier. (The Dominion Tottenham Court Road hung on, going over to live shows in late 1981.)

In 1977, the Odeon Merrion Centre in Leeds threw in the towel after a run of a little over thirteen years. After roadshows had fizzled out, it had played the quality end of the market with Woody Allen-type films to small audiences. It had become enclosed by later shopping malls and was not permitted signage on the main road to remind people of its existence. It has sat unwanted ever since. The seats were removed on 13 November 1984, seemingly at the end of Rank's 21-year lease. Various uses have been proposed, including re-opening in 2004 as a cut-price cinema aimed at the student community within walking distance – but the cost of meeting current regulations, including the installation of lifts for disabled access (it is above ground floor level), made the idea prohibitively expensive.

In 1978, Wales lost its pre-eminent cinema, the Capitol Cardiff, still seating 2,453. With its plain decor, sticky floors and steaming radiators, the auditorium lacked finesse but still inspired awe for its sheer size. Early in 1977, after the nearby ABC had been tripled, Rank had received planning permission to subdivide the building into two cinemas and a bingo hall but never implemented the scheme. The Welsh National Opera proposed a £3.2 million conversion to an opera house but the idea never really took hold and the closed cinema was eventually demolished for a shopping centre on an enlarged site that included new Odeon cinemas elsewhere. In the meantime, Rank twinned its Odeon in the centre of Cardiff.

Some cinemas were turned over to independents. The Odeon Clacton had been reduced to opening only in the holiday season and it persevered for a further three years from 1977 as the Salon. The Odeon Southsea also became a Salon later that year and the lessee even added a second screen under the balcony in 1981 before closing two years later. The Odeon (former Gaumont) Weymouth was taken over for a combination of films and bingo, but the cinema side was dropped in less than a year.

In 1979, Rank closed six sites: the single-screen Odeons at Camden Town, Hendon, Lowestoft and Southport plus the Gaumont Reading; and the tripled Odeon Dalston.

The cinema at Camden Town was, of course, the one in the former Gaumont balcony and it had lasted eleven years. Bingo continued downstairs and the cinema re-opened as an independent art house a year later. Its return to the Odeon fold is detailed in the next chapter.

At Hendon, the Odeon had survived in a kind of time warp, looking very much as it had when it opened in 1939 with all the distinctive original light fittings in the circle lounge and auditorium intact and working. Visited by the Cinema Theatre Association just prior to closure, it looked tired and faded but eminently deserving of preservation! Rank had been caught hopping here, having sold its more centrally located Gaumont Hendon to Classic in the batch of '67. Classic had astutely seen the potential for reviving its fortunes and lavishly tripled it in 1973, drawing audiences away from the less well-placed Odeon.

In Lowestoft, a developer obtained planning permission to

Odeon Dalston, north London, October 1968, following redecoration. This remained a splendid example of the original Odeon style even after dropwall tripling, and deserved to become a listed building. (Photographs by John Maltby.)

Odeon Sale, seen in summer 1965. The former Pyramid has lost its clock face above the Odeon name sign. (Courtesy of Carl Chesworth.)

redevelop the Odeon's site with a W. H. Smith store in front and Rank set closure for Saturday 28 April 1979. Many thought the Odeon would make a fine civic theatre (a local resident even offered to supply a Wurlitzer organ) but the district council declared the acoustics were unsuitable even though it had put on many live shows in the past. In fact, the Odeon went three days earlier than announced with a double bill of old James Bonds, leaving the town with just the independent Marina (a former ABC house) which entered a very shaky few years including periods of closure. The Odeon Lowestoft had still staged Saturday morning pictures – a "Super Saturday Show" for 15p, doors opening 9.30am.

The Odeon Southport was the former Gaumont, leaving the seaside resort with a two-screen Classic and single-screen ABC.

The loss of the Gaumont Reading followed the twinning of the Odeon there. ABC had two cinemas with four screens so the town was adequately served for the demands of the time.

The closure of the Odeon Dalston reputedly followed the theft of the speakers from behind one of the mini-screens during operating hours. Trading here had been so difficult that the bandit screens over the confectionery counter were never removed. This Odeon was an outstanding example of the circuit style from the 1930s, in tip-top condition, and deserved listing. It sat disused for several years, eventually being replaced by flats.

These departures left Rank with 138 cinemas and 270 screens. There were seventy Top Rank bingo clubs, almost all former cinemas.

The bingo side had continued to nibble away at the cinema circuit. The Odeons at Cosham and Penge became Top Rank bingo clubs in 1976. Cosham remains a bingo club to this day, though in the hands of a smaller circuit. The Odeon Penge was not just faded: it had become one of the dingiest cinemas I have ever visited (to catch that astonishing double bill of *Don't Look Now* and *The Wicker Man*) and still had some of the original design of carpet at the back of the balcony. Perhaps the money spent tarting it up for bingo might have been used to extend its life as a cinema. This quickly passed to another bingo chain and was eventually closed and demolished.

At the Odeon Wrexham, mixed use ended when films were ousted for full-time bingo in May 1976 but the town still had an independent full-time cinema, the Hippodrome. And at the Odeon Shirley, Birmingham, bingo took over full-time in October 1977. Because the Top Rank Club claimed Tuesdays and Wednesdays, the Odeon had only been able to obtain films after the Solihull Cinema and Warwick Acocks Green, and even then didn't improve its position with miniscule local press advertising.

In 1980, the Odeon Perth went to bingo, leaving films to Caledonian Associated Cinemas' three-screen Playhouse, while

bingo took over the entire auditorium of the State Kilburn following closure of the main screen (the 202-seat cinema attached to the subsidiary entrance on Willesden Lane remained open). Bingo did not enter the picture when Rank shut the single-screen Odeons at Guernsey, Plymouth and Walton-on-Thames, the New Oxford Manchester, Carlton Watford, and the Gaumonts at Richmond and Finchley.

Rank had just twinned the Gaumont on Guernsey. In Plymouth, Rank had three screens at the Drake Odeon while there was also an ABC triple in town. Walton closed less than nine years after Rank had become sole operator in the town with the shutdown of the ABC through the Putney deal. Rank declined to lease the basement space reserved for cinema use in the redevelopment of the site and no other operator seemed interested. Then, after a gap of twelve years, the independent The Screens at Walton were opened and have remained open ever since. Even in 1980, it seemed obvious that, if cinema had a future anywhere, it was in such well-heeled areas as this. But Rank apparently thought otherwise.

The New Oxford Manchester, a roadshow house without roadshows, was dropped, leaving Rank with three screens at the Odeon. Similarly in Watford, after the departure of the Carlton, Rank retained its three-screen Odeon. The Gaumont Richmond had survived the tripling of the Odeon for nearly seven years and its eclectic programming had received much praise (and, reportedly, drawn good audiences). Rank had no interest in taking the space allocated for a replacement cinema. At Finchley, Rank were very keen to run two 400-seat cinemas in the upper part of the Gaumont site's redevelopment (and planned to reinstate Newbury Trent's facade frieze about film-making, saved during demolition). But the scheme, to which Rank was still attached as late as 1987, never happened and the whereabouts of the bas-relief are unclear.

A cinema replacement scheme that did proceed closed the Odeon Bristol in 1983 for complete internal reconstruction, leaving Rank without any screens there for more than eighteen months, the Gaumont having been discarded in 1980.

The decimation of '81

Early in 1981 Rank closed the Odeon Lewisham, the former Gaumont which had retained its huge auditorium, latterly seating 2,858 (although the balcony alone was normally used for film shows). Rank had been denied permission on at least two occasions to convert the hall to bingo and some attempt had been made to build it up as a live venue for pop concerts, although it showed films most of the time. It might have become the southwest London equivalent of the Odeon Hammersmith but Rank claimed that groups preferred the larger, more firmly established west London venue and generally wouldn't perform at both places. There was also the competition from the Apollo Victoria (the former New Victoria) but the ending of pop concerts there in favour of a stage production of *The Sound Of Music* seemed to create an opening for Lewisham. Subdivision for continued film use was another option as it had a central location in a heavily populated area (the only other cinema was the ABC Catford) but its wide auditorium would have upped conversion costs and had probably deterred earlier thoughts along those lines. The cinema was closed with no immediate plan for its future use: one idea being mooted was for a developer to turn it into a department store with two smaller cinemas that Rank would lease back. The ABC Catford was twinned as a direct result of the closure. Eventually, the Odeon was demolished for a roundabout.

A closure of a different kind, at the Odeon Southampton, removed Rank's last traditional cinema restaurant on 9 May 1981. The space remained disused until converted to a third cinema in 1988.

Then came the "routine" closing of the Odeon Newport, Gwent, which had somehow escaped a standard tripling. Although reported as closing for bingo, the building was put up for sale instead. This was one of the best purpose-built Odeons, a fact that belatedly dawned on the Welsh listing authorities who gave it protection in 1999 – long after its excellent interior had been wrecked in snooker and nightclub use but in time to encourage restoration of its splendid exterior.

On Friday 19 June 1981, Rank gained damaging national headlines in its familiar manner by announcing the closure of twenty-nine Odeon and Gaumont cinemas (with forty screens), almost a quarter of its 123 sites, with the loss of 650 jobs. The company declared that the cinemas accounted for only 10 per cent of its admissions. The sites were worth £10 million and Rank owned the freehold of twenty-two of them. However, not all the cinemas were losing money. *The Financial Times* (20 June 1981) reported: "Some [...] still made a small profit" but were "not viable in the long term". And Angus Crichton-Miller, the new managing director of Rank Leisure, told *Screen International* (27 June 1981) that "even a few of the sites that may have been making a marginal profit at the moment had to go without the prospect of a more secure future. We took into account both past and future trends before making our decision. Plans are at an early stage, but those plans obviously include outright sales, letting and property development." Among the cinemas believed to have been profitable were the triples at Muswell Hill and Peckham while figures for the Elephant and Castle Odeon indicated a £50,000 operating profit before head office charges of £45,000 were applied. It was suggested that the money received from the disposals would be used to improve some of the surviving ninety-four cinemas (currently with 231 screens), such as tripling its Edinburgh theatre (soon carried out) and adding screens at the Gaumont Birmingham (never done). ABC (with 150 cinemas) pointedly refused to contribute to the gloom: "We have no closure plans – we are optimistic about the future."

In late 1980, Rank had put out advertisements proclaiming "Odeons are full again" and showing a grinning manager holding a "House Full for this Performance" sign, adding "And you can count on Odeon being there all the way, providing the kind of exciting entertainment you enjoy". Yet, only a few months later, you couldn't count on Odeon at all if you lived near any of the doomed sites. As in the 1956 clear-out, the aim seems to have been to reassure institutional shareholders and the City financial community that an effort was being made to improve the poor financial return on the chain (only £1.35 million profit in the preceding financial year).

The cinemas so publicly placed under the axe were: the Odeons at Aldershot; Ashton-under-Lyne; Bury; Canterbury; Chelsea; Chelmsford; Chesterfield; Darlington; Dundee; Ealing (Northfields); East Ham; Eglinton Toll (Glasgow); Elephant and Castle; Lincoln; Muswell Hill; Peckham; Rayners Lane; Rochester; Sale; Shepherd's Bush (Odeon 2); Stafford; Stockton; Twickenham; Well Hall; Westbourne Grove; West Hartlepool; and Woolwich; plus the small screen at the State Kilburn and the Plaza Gabalfa, Cardiff.

Rank's announcement omitted the Odeon (ex-Gaumont) Taunton which in September 1981 was turned over to the bingo division, a move which also ended frequent live show usage. (Films continued at the town's two-screen Classic, the earlier Odeon.)

This time Rank openly indicated its willingness to lease out (or sub-lease) many of the properties and the substantial advance notice allowed time for the cinemas to be taken over without the handicap of a period of closure. By September, Rank announced that, in the London area, it had agreed to lease the Well Hall Odeon and would give "serious consideration" to anyone showing a "serious interest" in taking over the cinemas at Chelsea, East Ham, Elephant and Castle, Muswell Hill, Peckham, Rayners Lane and Westbourne Grove. However, Rank wanted to sell rather than lease out those at Ealing, Kilburn, Shepherd's Bush, Twickenham and Woolwich.

A close relationship with Panton Cinemas (which had taken over the Gaumont Notting Hill in 1977 and restored the building's original name of Coronet) was now extended by that company taking over three of the Odeons in the London area – at Ealing, Elephant and Castle and Well Hall – and renaming each of them Coronet. Well Hall had already been twinned, but the others were single screens. Rank had assessed the Elephant and Castle Odeon for bingo but Ernö Goldfinger's design was so space efficient that there wasn't enough room for the fruit machines that were considered vital to the success of a bingo operation. Regarding the atmospheric-style Odeon Ealing, Rank's Information Services Controller Chris Moore had previously expressed to me the company's irritation at being unable to carry out a drop wall conversion to three screens (announced in March 1980) owing to its listed status and the refusal of the Greater London Council to sanction Rank's scheme which would have interfered with some of the side wall decoration downstairs. In early 2005, Ealing survives as a church and Well Hall is in a state of limbo while the Elephant and Castle and Westbourne Grove properties have been demolished, the former in weekend haste by its new owners to preclude listing (after Panton had pulled out, having taken over the three-screen Cannon immediately opposite).

Also in London, the tripled Odeon Peckham and the single-screen Odeon Rayners Lane went to Ace, a small independent chain which, like Panton, specialised in running ex-circuit halls. (Harrow Council had refused Rank's recent application to turn Rayners Lane into a bingo hall.)

Ace ran Peckham for just over two years. It has since been demolished for flats. Rank had really let Rayners Lane slide: it had recently become a listed building for its outstanding exterior and interior design by architect F. E. Bromige, but had been kept going on a shoestring, closed on Mondays and Tuesdays, and sometimes putting on dire product showing hardly anywhere else in order to placate distributors. Rayners Lane did well in Ace's hands but the company was denied a renewal of its initial five-year lease and the cinema closed in 1986, a few days after a full house celebrating its fiftieth anniversary at 1936 prices. It sat disused for five years and is now owned by a church.

Hutchinson's, which already operated former Odeons at Colwyn Bay, Llandudno and Rhyl, readily took over the Odeon Stafford and quickly tripled it by adding two small cinemas in the circle, reinvigorating it so successfully that it remains open to this day (as part of the Apollo chain).

In the Manchester area, a local operator took over the Odeon Ashton-under-Lyne and nourished it into a considerable success as the Metro. Plans to subdivide had to be abandoned when a multiplex was announced for the immediate area and its subsequent arrival forced closure in 2004. The Odeon Sale continued as the Tatton, operated by the local circuit of that name, but only lasted a couple of years. It subsequently became a listed building for its Egyptian design and, after a long period of disuse, re-opened as a nightclub which has since made way for a fitness centre entered at the back, leaving the foyer area unused.

The Odeon Lincoln was taken over by local operators who built up business and eventually invested in subdivision.

The Odeon Canterbury, the third to open as part of Oscar Deutsch's chain in 1933, survived after a fashion. Although not really large, it had been Canterbury's only venue for major pop concerts and its swansong in that regard was David Essex's appearance on 5 October 1981. Never a building of any distinction, it had become dingy and in need of redecoration while its very shallow balcony overhang made subdivision prohibitively expensive. It was sold and re-opened nearly three years later after extensive alterations as the town's new Marlowe Theatre, the existing one having become very cramped in the former Central cinema. Canterbury was left with a single-screen Cannon, which later added a second cinema and is now the town's Odeon.

The most controversial impending closure on the entire list was that of the Odeon at Muswell Hill, tripled in 1974 by a drop wall conversion. *The Hornsey Journal* (31 July 1981) reported:

It is no secret that the cinema makes money. It regularly displays "House Full" notices and is known to take more money than other local Odeons which, amazingly, are to remain open! No convincing explanation for the proposed closure has been given by Rank. There have been denials by several supermarket giants that they are interested in demolishing the famous 1936 art deco cinema, its adjoining shops and flats, and developing the massive site at the corner of Fortis Green Road and Muswell Hill Road... No one has made any application to Haringey's planning department (as they must, if they wished to change the cinema's use in any way) and it is thought probable that the Planning Committee would not grant permission for a scheme that involved demolition... the Department of the Environment have just told Haringey Council that they are not prepared to include the cinema as Grade II on their list of buildings of architectural interest. But this does not deter planning committee chairman Councillor Gerald Long who says they are to make another approach to the DoE.

Thousands of signatures were collected on petitions. Rank had more than forty years remaining on a lease from Silvert Properties which expressed its willingness to sell the entire site. It was common knowledge that Sainsbury's in particular would have liked to expand onto the Odeon site as its store immediately opposite completely lacked parking facilities.

The Odeon was set to close on 10 October 1981. Rank called a press conference in the circle lounge at 5.15pm on Monday 21 September prior to which the company's press officer, former cinema manager Alex Slatter, would only tell me that I would be pleased. And I was: it had been reprieved. The official explanation was that attendances had shown a big improvement so it was worth carrying on, but there was a widespread belief that Sainsbury's had withdrawn an offer, either fearful of the bad publicity if it demolished the cinema or realising that planning permission would not be forthcoming. (Chairman Sir John Sainsbury confessed to Valerie Grove in *The Sunday Times*, 22 May 1988, that he "had tried to get the Odeon cinema and carpark over the road".)

A group of supporters formed the North London Cinema Society in readiness to oppose any future threat to the Odeon and, with the enthusiastic support of manager Brian Lee, it held numerous film shows and other events at the cinema itself on Sunday mornings and special occasions. In another extraordinary development, the Projected Picture Trust was allowed to store discarded equipment in the disused stalls and put projectors on display in the public areas.

The Odeon Westbourne Grove was the only other cinema to be given a further lease of life by Rank itself. It had been tripled less than three years previously with disappointing results (it was in the wrong part of Bayswater) and Rank persevered with it for another couple of years.

Three of the threatened cinemas did close in 1981 only to reopen at a much later date under new ownership.

The Odeon Chelsea was the 739-seat cinema opened in 1973 in the circle area of the former Gaumont. After a gap of two years, it was leased by art house distributor Artificial Eye and started off on its still continuing career as the Chelsea Cinema, demonstrating that there was another way to run a cinema besides the Rank one.

With 1,840 seats, the Odeon East Ham was vastly oversized yet its location did not encourage tripling – at least, not until 1995 when a new owner finally re-opened the property, having skilfully subdivided it for Bollywood films and rather charmingly called it the Boleyn after the name of the early cinema demolished to make way for the Odeon in the 1930s. In 1981, East Ham cinemagoers still had the Ace Upton Park and the tripled Odeon Barking within fairly easy reach.

After being disused for more than eighteen months, the Odeon Woolwich was belatedly taken over by Panton and added to its group of Coronets. It was subsequently purchased by the company, subdivided with a second screen in the rear stalls, and operated until 1999. The building now survives as a church.

At about the same time, Panton also leased the three-screen Odeon Westbourne Grove but this continued for less than three years before being rapidly demolished to make way for flats.

It was the end of the line for the others on Rank's list. All but the Odeon Rochester were single screens.

The Odeon Aldershot was a large cinema that had missed the boat when the immediately adjacent ABC had been converted to three screens in 1977. It has been sympathetically adapted into a Christian centre.

At Bury, the Classic chain had been quick off the mark to twin its cinema. The Odeon, a striking building designed for the circuit, had survived an earlier closure date – 15 November 1975 – but there was no reprieve on this occasion although subsequent nightclub use preserved many of its features.

The Odeon Chelmsford had been part of the pre-war County circuit, weak externally but with a splendid auditorium featuring a ribbed ceiling and lively splay wall decoration by Mollo and Egan. As the rival Regent had gone over to bingo in 1975, this 1,436-seat hall should have been a prime candidate for tripling with plenty of space for two small cinemas in the rear stalls. Redevelopment plans, along with frequent live show use, probably explain why it had remained single (as at Canterbury, David Essex was the last performer in October 1981). Chelmsford was too large a town to be adequately served only by the one small single-screen independent cinema that remained but the Odeon stood disused until demolition in 1990. Three years after that, Rank returned with a new four-screen cinema (see next chapter).

The Odeon Chesterfield was a cinema of note. David Atwell, in *Cathedrals Of The Movies* (1980), called it:

> a remarkable early example of conservation planning... it was insisted that the new Picture House in Holywell Street, opposite the celebrated Parish Church with its crooked spire, should blend in with its historic surroundings. The result is a unique gabled half-timbered facade that looks as though it has wandered over the border from Cheshire or Herefordshire. The Picture House, which opened on 10 September 1923, later to be taken over in 1936 and become an Odeon, remains virtually untouched. Although only seating 900, it had a large restaurant and ballroom (now a disco-club), and full stage facilities, and even the fly-tower was half-timbered externally!

It has since been converted, fairly sympathetically, into a meeting hall called The Winding Wheel and belatedly became a listed building in 2000.

The Odeon Darlington had been extensively modernised, with metal cladding concealing its original frontage, but ABC had gained the initiative by tripling its cinema in the town in 1977. The Odeon retained 1,223 seats but normally only opened the balcony. The building has been demolished and the site put to retail use.

The Odeon Dundee had a comparatively modern and dull auditorium seating 1,265 and dating from 1961 when it was erected within the shell of the historic King's Theatre. This seemed a surprising closure in a town of Dundee's size although part of the problem was that it could not be easily twinned.

Odeon Chelmsford, seen circa 1970 with queue for Disney's The Aristocats. *Removal of a restaurant sign from the main frontage has left tell-tale marks. (CTA Archive.)*

The Leicester Square Theatre in summer 1983. (CTA Archive.)

Eighteen months later, the building was successfully re-opened for bingo by a regional concern.

The Odeon at Eglinton Toll, Glasgow, was a vast building that still seated over 2,000. It had opened in 1912 as the Cinerama and the emblem of its original owners, the BB circuit ("Bright and Beautiful"), could still be seen in the stonework just above a modern canopy. It had a window with a spectacular sunburst feature on a side wall. With that name it should have installed the Cinerama process but it became the Odeon Eglinton Toll in 1964 to eliminate confusion with ABC's Coliseum Cinerama Theatre nearer the centre of Glasgow. The Odeon had staged live shows and explored full-time use a rock venue: permission was refused while the success of the Apollo on this policy in the heart of Glasgow might have hurt its chances. One hopes that the emblematic stonework and sunburst window were saved during its demolition to make way for a petrol station.

The Plaza at Gabalfa, a suburb of Cardiff, was also included in the list of Rank casualties although it had never been operated by the cinema division or taken the Odeon name. It had fallen into Rank's hands five years earlier along with a bunch of bingo halls.* Dating from 1928, the Plaza by then had a rather lurid orange and blue-green decorative scheme in its 1,228-seat auditorium. It had seemed quite often a dumping ground for first-run programmes that couldn't find playing time in the centre of Cardiff. Although the auditorium was demolished for flats, the cinema entrance was retained – but presumably without the colourful yellow, blue and white neon display that blazed out on my evening visit in 1978.

The Kilburn closure ended films for the time being at the huge State Kilburn. The 202-seat cinema, located in the subsidiary Willesden Lane entrance, had remained open for a year

* Rank spent a reputed £2 million purchasing the Jackson Withers circuit from Welsh financier Sir Julian Hodge to obtain the fourteen highly profitable bingo clubs it operated in former cinemas in south Wales and the southwest of England, all of which became Top Rank Clubs. The deal, which became effective on 1 November 1976, also brought in twelve cinemas (two of them closed: County Rumney, Cardiff, and Capitol Blackwood). The ten then open were the Monico and Plaza in the suburbs of Cardiff, Albert Hall and Carlton Swansea, Windsor Neath, Savoy Penzance, Plaza Truro, Regal Redruth, Camelot Newquay and Palace Bargoed. In Swansea, where Rank had its central Odeon, the Carlton and Albert Hall were closed after a year – the former put up for sale and the latter converted into a Top Rank bingo club. Some cinemas were sold to independents and the only one Rank continued to operate for any length of time was the Plaza at Gabalfa, Cardiff – it was run by the bingo side but occasionally projectionists from the Odeon Cardiff would relieve there and it advertised with the Odeon in the local press. The takeover of the Maxime bingo club at Blackwood, Gwent, brought two small cinemas in the balcony: these retained the Maxime name.

after the vast cinema in the main auditorium closed but was uneconomic on its own. This left Kilburn with the small Classic having a local monopoly of first run films.

Tripled and redecorated in 1974, the Odeon Rochester seemed an unlikely candidate for the chop. I hurried to investigate. Once past its forbidding exterior and plain, draughty, cramped foyer, it proved to have a most attractive main auditorium (Mollo and Egan again). While audiences had been dented a bit by the biggest attractions playing concurrently in the smallest of the three auditoria at the ABC Chatham, this disadvantage had recently been eliminated. It was very busy on the weekday evening I visited it and the manager insisted it was profitable. The local authority was apparently interested in taking it over for community centre and live theatre use but, after being boarded up for several years, it was demolished and replaced by housing.

When Rank shut the Odeon 2 Shepherd's Bush, it still had Odeon 1 a few doors along on the Green in the balcony above a Top Rank bingo club. The closure raised a puzzling question. If it had been worth buying from the rival Classic chain as a recently converted 487-seat luxury cinema in 1973, why was it no longer of any use eight years later? No one else stepped up to take it over (was a restrictive covenant in place?) but, as Rank shut Odeon 1 in 1983, the answer must be that the denizens of Shepherd's Bush had deserted the big screen en masse.

The fall of the Odeon Stockton, only opened in 1968, is charted by former manager James Bettley.

Stockton was a town on the verge of decline. Although once a thriving market town potentially drawing shoppers – and cinemagoers – from nearly Middlesbrough and Billingham, local industries were contracting and business in the town beginning to disappear. With seasons of roadshow product like *Funny Girl*, *Oliver!* and *Hello, Dolly!* the cinema was both popular and successful, but such fare was becoming scarce and, left to share the general Rank releases with the nearby Odeons at Middlesbrough, West Hartlepool and Darlington, the cinema was in financial trouble.

In order that managers could calculate – as near as possible – the profitability of their units and plan to maximise it, they were supplied with detailed costs and charges which had to be offset against income from ticket sales, rent and – increasingly important – ancillary sales. Where theatres had been refurbished, modernised or – as in Stockton's case – rebuilt, such capital expenditure was offset against the theatre's income on a weekly basis over a period of years according to established accounting practice. When Stockton's staple diet of roadshow product ebbed away, the financial burden remained and became a millstone.

It's an ill wind..., as they say, and the desire to turn in a profit was certainly an incentive to try and show something different and special. This led to a successful revival of *The King And I* in 1970 and a remarkably successful one-day presentation of MGM's *King Of Kings* which I had learned was only available in 70mm and consequently denied to the vast majority of cinemas! These desperate flashes of inspiration were impossible to sustain on a regular basis while committed to general releases, and with a large ABC house in the town as well as the independent Hippodrome, the writing was on the wall.

The Odeon Stockton's normal admission price of £2 was considered by cinema historian Geoff Mellor to be "rather steep in an area badly hit by the recession". Classic subsequently took over the Hippodrome and turned it into a three-screen cinema.

With its Egyptian trimmings inside and out, the Odeon Twickenham was a great loss, both from an architectural standpoint and as the last of the town's three major circuit cinemas. Originally called the Luxor, its delightfully composed white-tiled frontage with six columns featuring lotus-bud capitals brought a touch of elegance to a dreary town centre. Although the auditorium had suffered from the removal of its original light fittings, it exuded a faded, creaky charm. The balcony was too shallow to permit a drop-wall tripling but it had been surveyed some time past for splitting into two cinemas. As evidenced by the removal of the Gaumont at nearby Richmond a year before, Rank seemed intent on concentrating attendances on its three-screen Odeon there (with recently enlarged minis) and programming at Twickenham had too often seemed to consist of the leftovers. The Odeon's frontage should certainly have been preserved as part of the redevelopment scheme.

The Odeon West Hartlepool seated 1,278 which made it too large for current needs, although only the circle was normally in use. Rank preferred to close it down rather than subdivide. Evidently Hartlepool wasn't keen on cinema as ABC had already let its hall go to an independent and this became the only screen in town.

To somewhat balance the picture, there were places where the ABC circuit was closing cinemas to Rank's benefit. In 1981, the rival circuit sold its large single-screen cinema in Cheltenham rather than subdivide it to compete with the three-screen Odeon. The following year it closed a single screen in Preston and two screens in Warrington, leaving the field open to a two-screen and three-screen Odeon respectively. And, in 1983, when ABC sold off its two-screen cinema in Harrogate it greatly improved the prospects of the three-screen Odeon.

The closures continue

In the West End of London, the Odeon St. Martin's Lane had become a real problem. Following the termination of the Disney lease in 1980, it had reverted to regular programming. With the right film on an exclusive run, it could still pull in huge audiences as it did with *Being There* – but there were too few of them. Rank made a feeble attempt to relaunch it as an art house, The Lane in St. Martin's Lane (the name modelled on the successful independent hall, The Screen on the Green, at Islington), then let it go in October 1982 to Artificial Eye, the art house distributor and exhibitor which already ran two other former Rank properties as the Chelsea Cinema and Plaza Camden Town and which successfully re-launched the St. Martin's Lane site as the Lumière.

At the 1982 Annual General Meeting, shareholders were informed: "The mainstay of [Rank Leisure Services] remains the Top Rank Clubs and opportunities continue to be sought for strengthening and expanding that operation through cinema conversion and acquisition."

Once important three-screen Odeons at Bolton, Ipswich, Luton, Sunderland, Wolverhampton and Wood Green were transferred to the bingo side of Rank Leisure, de-tripled and re-opened as Top Rank Clubs between 1982 and 1984. In Ipswich, Rank moved its bingo operation out of the Hippodrome Theatre (this Frank Matcham building was subsequently demolished) and retained only the single-screen Gaumont to compete against a tripled ABC. At the other five places, ABC gained a monopoly on film provision (its Turnpike Lane triple covering Wood Green).

In Sunderland, the Top Rank Club transferred from the Theatre Royal and cinemagoers were now served by a two-screen ABC. At Wood Green, cinema admissions had fallen to 2,000 weekly, less than two capacities a week in this huge building. The Top Rank Club in the former Gaumont Finsbury Park was closed down in the hope that its custom would transfer. At Luton, a fire at the Top Rank Club in the former Gaumont prompted the move to the Odeon. Bingo, it seemed, was getting the upper hand.

In 1983, the single-screen Odeon Shepherd's Bush gave its last picture show but bingo continued on the lower level. The two-screen Odeon Bishop Auckland and the three-screen Odeon Oldham went dark without the salvation of bingo. But perhaps the most startling departure was that of the Odeon (former Gaumont) Watford, a well-positioned triple in immaculate decorative order. If Rank couldn't or wouldn't stay open in a thriving place like Watford, then was it really serious about staying in the cinema business at all? The county's largest town was left ridiculously underserved with only a small and unprepossessing twin ABC cinema, seating a total of 567, on the edge of the town centre.*

* EMI, owners of the ABC and Shipman & King circuits, were little better – closing cinemas in the same county at Hertford and Welwyn Garden City rather than investing in them.

Realising property values seemed to be the motive here as well in two further closures. (Rank's gains from selling closed cinemas had become substantial: £7.1 million in 1984, up from £3.5 million the previous year.) The three-screen Odeon Hounslow, the last cinema in town, made way for a supermarket and shops. (Top Rank Bingo carried on in the more central ex-Dominion but there was no chance of bingo being ousted or required to share space with films.) The Odeon Worthing was sold in 1984 to property developers although clearly viable – as it was then leased back for two years until the new owners were ready to proceed.

The Odeon Leicester Square came close to being sold off for its site value in the early 1980s – McDonalds were interested in taking space in the redevelopment and there would have been small cinemas in the basement – but circuit executives successfully argued that the Odeon was vital to the standing of the circuit internationally, being so well known – to Hollywood stars and executives in particular – through its gala premieres.

A devastating fire in 1983 at an EMI bingo hall in Derby triggered off a unique deal between rivals. EMI bought the huge three-screen Odeon (ex-Gaumont) in Derby to re-establish its bingo club in the stalls (removing the minis) and re-opened the balcony as a fourth cinema supplementing its three-screen ABC. Within less than a year, EMI had closed the ABC and Derby was left in the ludicrous situation of having only one mainstream outlet for films.

Against all the slimming down, Rank made a couple of additions in 1983. The Gaumont Ipswich gained a spacious 186-seat second screen in the former restaurant/ballroom, but this was primarily to enable more live use of the main auditorium. In the centre of Birmingham, Rank bolstered its single-screen Odeon Queensway by taking over the closed two-screen Cinecenta next door. This added two small cinemas seating 116 and 113 to the 555 seats of its existing hall and all three were served by a combined entrance and box office. The huge Odeon in New Street remained available for film use between live shows.

Programming

In 1976, Rank's cinema attendances fell by 12.2 per cent, exacerbated by an exceptionally hot summer and the fact that two of the biggest draws, *Jaws* and *Earthquake*, were primarily booked by the rival ABC circuit (both films were Universal releases which, a few years earlier, would have been distributed by Rank, favouring its own cinemas). In America, *Jaws* had been opened simultaneously at as many cinemas as possible, backed by heavy television advertising, to achieve sensational success. The same form of release, simultaneously across the entire country, was repeated here.

However, in 1977, Odeons had the benefit of the latest James

Bond outing, *The Spy Who Loved Me*, which was the year's top box-office draw.

In 1978, cinema admissions recovered from a three-year decline, reaching 127 million compared to 108 million the previous year. Although optimists pointed to the increased choice resulting from twinning and tripling, in fact it was a number of blockbusters that did the trick. Following existing distributor ties, it was predominantly Odeons that benefited from *Star Wars* (the year's top hit), *Close Encounters Of The Third Kind* and the British-made Rank release, *The Wild Geese*, while rival ABC had *Saturday Night Fever* and *Grease*. (Some of the few remaining city centre independents had managed to obtain an allocation of product and occasionally struck lucky: Theatre One Coventry received one film in every five that would normally have gone to the Odeon or ABC and these included *Close Encounters Of The Third Kind* which ran for months to the irritation of the Odeon.)

The Odeon circuit's admissions increased by over 22 per cent in the financial year to the end of October 1978. A look at the figures for the Odeon Gloucester shows that *Star Wars* and *Close Encounters* between them played for twenty weeks in the single-screen cinema and that the ten most successful films occupied forty-six weeks of screen time.

Admissions nationally plunged by 12 per cent in 1979, almost to the levels of 1976 and 1977 (a VAT increase from 8 to 15 per cent was a contributing factor). The latest Bond, *Moonraker*, at Odeons tied for first place at the box office with *Superman*, primarily at ABCs, while Fox's *Alien* made a significant contribution to Rank's coffers.

The next year Rank reaped considerable benefit from the second *Star Wars* picture, *The Empire Strikes Back*. The second biggest draw of the year, Columbia's *Kramer Vs. Kramer*, also played primarily at Odeons but the figures reproduced for Gloucester suggest that it did less than half the admissions of *The Empire Strikes Back*. In fact, Disney's sci-fi *The Black Hole* gained nearly as many patrons in half the time.

The early 1980s were dismal years for film exhibition as video and cable television began to make their presence felt and attendances continued to decline. In 1981, the new Bond, *For Your Eyes Only*, was the top Odeon attraction, taking second place to *Superman II* at ABCs, while the latest reissue of *Snow White And The Seven Dwarfs* proved a substantial hit for Odeons yet again.

E.T. The Extra-Terrestrial took top place at the British box-office in 1983. It was seen predominantly at ABCs but Odeons had first call on the next hottest titles: the third *Star Wars* episode, *Return Of The Jedi*; the latest Bond, *Octopussy*; the biopic *Gandhi*; and the comedy *Tootsie*.

In 1983, Rank had to bend with the times when it lost exclusive premiere runs at its surviving halls in London's West End. The Odeons Leicester Square, Marble Arch and Haymarket, and the Leicester Square Theatre had remained undivided – their seating capacities sufficient, it was hoped, to continue with exclusive premiere runs at a time when openings at several sites were becoming common.

But distributors now felt it was wasteful to promote the opening of a film at only one cinema. Thus the Odeon Haymarket opened *Still Of The Night* on 12 January along with the Odeons at Kensington, Swiss Cottage and Westbourne Grove plus the Classic Chelsea, while cinemas all over London joined the run four days later. Then the Odeon Leicester Square ended its hugely successful run of *Gandhi* to show *Monsignor* on a two-week limited booking which shared the film with cinemas all over London from the first day. The remake of *The Wicked Lady* opened all over London on the same day as it opened at the Leicester Square Theatre. There was still scope for more specialised films to have an exclusive run (such as *Local Hero* at the Odeon Haymarket) but *Tootsie* opened at the Odeon Leicester Square simultaneously with 219 other cinemas in London and across the country. The big question was: would such large cinemas as the Odeon Leicester Square with 1,983 seats and the Leicester Square Theatre with 1,402 seats survive with so much direct competition from other cinemas?

Specialised tastes

With their need to concentrate on films of mass appeal to fill their larger auditoria, it was difficult for the major circuits to cope with the more specialised Hollywood product of what has been called "the psychedelic era". Rank's booking controller from the first day of 1961 (taking over from Richard Hamer, who had held the job since 1942) was George Pinches, who joined Odeon in 1938 and worked in booking ever since completing World War Two service in the RAF. After the tepid response to such films as *Sleeper* and *Love And Death*, it seems that Pinches had written off Woody Allen's films as having negligible appeal. In September 1977 *Annie Hall* opened on two screens at the Cinecenta Panton Street and outlying independent halls plus the Odeon 3 Swiss Cottage, and ran more than a year at the Cinecenta, helped by major Academy Award wins in April 1978. In retrospect, *Annie Hall* should have been ideal material for the Odeon Haymarket but that was a single screen with 600 seats to fill (and may well have had other commitments) whereas the two Cinecenta screens added up to only half that capacity. Of course, miscalculations are part and parcel of film booking and it's easy to be critical with hindsight, but George Pinches seemed to be judging films by his own tastes

ODEON SOUTHAMPTON: TEN MOST POPULAR FILMS
1975-1984

Rank also operated the Gaumont which took many road shows and other releases. Throughout this period opposition came from the twin screen ABC/Cannon (a small third video screen was added in 1981).

The financial year ran from 1 November to 31 October. Each year's total attendances appears in square brackets after the total achieved by the top ten.

1975/6
Jungle Book (5) 36,338
Rollerball (5) 23,771
Bambi (3) 20,227
Return Of The Pink Panther (4) 18,891
The Omen (3) 18,133
Confessions Of A Driving Instructor (3) 13,022
One Flew Over The Cuckoo's Nest (3) 11,859
The Sound Of Music (1) 10,036
The Man Who Fell To Earth (2) 6,782
The Street Fighter (2) 6,469
Total (31 weeks) 165,528 [256,187]

1976/7
A Bridge Too Far (8) 33,512
The Pink Panther Strikes Again (5) 26,472
101 Dalmatians (5) 23,753
Sinbad And The Eye Of The Tiger (2) 19,300
Confessions From A Holiday Camp (3) 8,900
Carquake (2) 8,243
The Shaggy D.A. (1) 7,423
Silver Streak (2) 6,005
Silent Movie (2) 5,896
Rocky (2) 5,738
Total (32 weeks) 145,242 [236,703]

1977/8
Star Wars (11) 108,134
Close Encounters Of The Third Kind (9) 60,044
Revenge Of The Pink Panther (6) 41,851
The Rescuers (6) 31,391
The Wild Geese (5) 22,088
Cinderella (1) 9,624
Midnight Express (3) 9,581
Annie Hall (2) 7,619
Valentino (2) 5,549
Jungle Book (1) 4,548
Total (46 weeks) 300,429 [353,085]

1978/9
(The cinema was closed from 17 February to 14 April 1979 while it was subdivided into two auditoria)
Alien (4) 24,807 [plus three further weeks in 1979/80, total: 30,717]
Pete's Dragon (4) 22,316
The Spaceman And King Arthur (3) 16,648
Lord Of The Rings (5) 16,194
Bedknobs And Broomsticks (3) 16,058
Cat From Outer Space (2) 15,440
Lemon Popsicle (2) 9,750
California Suite (3) 8,764
Bambi (1) 8,717
The China Syndrome (3) 8,353
Total (29 weeks) 147,047 [272,538]

1979/80
The Empire Strikes Back (12) 62,449
Kramer Vs. Kramer (7) 28,070
The Black Hole (4) 23,625
The Aristocats (4) 15,579
The Sea Wolves (6) 14,698
Being There (4) 10,638
Manhattan (3) 9,688
Spiderman - The Dragon's Challenge (1) 8,743
One Flew Over The Cuckoo's Nest (2) 8,213
Silver Dream Racer (3) 7,663
Total (46 weeks) 189,366 [369,774]

1980/1
For Your Eyes Only (14) 56,036
Snow White And The Seven Dwarfs (5) 32,601
Tess (6) 18,382
Close Encounters Special Edition (4) 16,273
Stripes (4) 11,880
The Blue Lagoon (4) 10,940
Popeye (3) 10,421
Chariots Of Fire (5) 9,676
Pinocchio/Spaceman & King Arthur (1) 8,311
Stir Crazy (3) 8149
Total (49 weeks) 182,669 [317,652]

1981/2
The Fox And The Hound (5) 19,395
Annie (6) 17,389
Chariots Of Fire/Gregory's Girl (7) 17,128
The French Lieutenant's Woman (8) 16,405
Porky's (7) 12,789
Who Dares Wins (5) 9,883
Kramer Vs. Kramer/The Jazz Singer (3) 8,142
Bedknobs And Broomsticks (1) 7,985
Death Wish II (3) 6,561
On Golden Pond (4) 6,456
Total (49 weeks) 122,133 [230,500]

1982/3
Octopussy (12) 40,801
Return Of The Jedi (5) 37,116
Gandhi (14) 35,490
Tootsie (6) 16,992
Tron (5) 13,234
War Games (5) 8,032
Raiders Of The Lost Ark (4) 7,150
Blue Thunder (4) 6,890
Porky's II (4) 6,130
Robin Hood (3) 5,783
Total (62 weeks) 177,618 [232,195]

1983/4
The Jungle Book (9) 30,535
Educating Rita (9) 12,480
One Hundred And One Dalmatians (2) 11,866
Splash (6) 6,911
Yentl (4) 6,040
Sword In The Stone (2) 5,886
Gorky Park (5) 5,099
Lady And the Tramp (2) 5,058
The Woman In Red (3) 4,467
Romancing The Stone (3) 3,965
Total (45 weeks) 92,307 [154,651]

Courtesy of James E. Tilmouth, former manager

rather than by their commercial potential when he refused to show the animated version of *The Lord Of The Rings* and the gay farce *La Cage aux Folles*, despite the latter's success in North America.

There were even problems with Odeons showing the product of Rank's revived production arm in the late 1970s (responding to EMI's success with *Murder On The Orient Express*). The prime markets for Rank's film productions had been the UK and the English-speaking Commonwealth countries. By the mid-1970s, these had declined to such an extent that box office income barely covered the cost of the two low-budget series that were still being financed via Rank Film Distributors (RFD) – horror films and *Carry On* comedies. There were two options – pull out of film financing completely or reinvigorate it to take advantage of the burgeoning video market. The second option would help television and video sales of the several hundred films in the Rank library as old pictures could be more easily sold as part of a package headed by new titles. This option was taken.

All Rank's leisure interests were then under divisional chairman Ed Chilton. He re-established a film production unit – Rank Film Productions (RFP), based at Pinewood. Tony Williams, the senior executive placed in charge, recalls:

The unit had its own investment budget but was obliged to release all its films through RFD. As the UK had shrunk to just 4 per cent of the world theatrical market, a key requirement for RFD was the sale of the new films to sub-distributors throughout the world if they were to stand any chance of re-couping their negative cost.
The Rank name still carried enormous recognition and respect in international film circles, but prospective purchasers made no distinction between Rank's various film activities in the UK. They could not understand that RFD and the cinemas had historically traded largely on an arm's length basis, partly due to Rank Organisation group policy and partly as a result of various Office Of Fair Trading/Monopolies And Mergers Commission investigations.
Foreign buyers expected all new Rank titles to be given prominent releases with an opening in Rank's prime West End cinemas. Sadly, Rank's director of cinema booking, George Pinches, was not properly briefed on the situation nor the business strategy underlying it, with the result that he did not support the new production venture.
The first film to come out was the Robert Powell version of *The Thirty-Nine Steps*. It was given a date at the Leicester Square Theatre, a single-screen cinema on a par with the flagship Odeon Leicester Square, with a Royal Charity Premiere attended by HRH Princess Anne. The date, however, was 24 November – the start of the pre-Christmas period during which all cinemas customarily experienced a large admissions dip.

The film received a good press and, in spite of its dating, opened to very good business. It went on to enjoy a very successful UK release. Its appearance in Leicester Square and subsequent good performance attracted interest from American majors and helped RFD achieve satisfactory sales round the world. *The Thirty-Nine Steps* was, however, the first and last RFP film to have a regular opening in Leicester Square.

The only other title that played in the Square was *The Lady Vanishes* – but solely because it had been promised to a charity for a world premiere to be attended by Her Majesty The Queen. RFD was forced to four-wall the Odeon Leicester Square in order to honour its commitment.

RFP was wholly responsible for a total of six films. One of the remaining four, *Silver Dream Racer*, managed to get an opening at Rank's Dominion Tottenham Court Road. The other three were denied an opening in any of Rank's seven central London cinemas and RFD had to book them onto non-Rank screens. The difficulties the films experienced in securing UK exposure were interpreted by distributors around the world as meaning that the films were no good. This made them much harder to sell and the result for RFP was serious recoupment problems.

Two of the films were subject to major critical acclaim – *Eagle's Wing* and Nicolas Roeg's *Bad Timing*. The latter achieved a certain notoriety because Sir John Davis, by then Rank's President, counted the number of times the 'f' word was used. Contrary to some reports, he did not have the film withdrawn nor was this the reason it was denied a Rank opening.

Bad Timing opened in the West End at the Classic Haymarket and Studio Oxford Circus, and further out at the Classic Chelsea, Screen on the Green and the multi-screen Odeons at Kensington, Swiss Cottage and Westbourne Grove. It subsequently played the largest screen at up-market suburban Odeons such as Barnet, Ealing, Richmond and Wimbledon. Rank displayed its own version of bad timing by announcing a withdrawal from further production in June 1980 only three weeks after trumpeting a future spend of nearly £22 million at a lavish party during the Cannes Film Festival. (RFD kept going by investing in outside productions in exchange for distribution rights and also purchasing some completed films.)

George Pinches caused a major furore when he cancelled, at short notice, the opening of *The Raging Bull* at the Odeon Haymarket, pencilled in for 29 January 1981. On seeing Martin Scorsese's black-and-white biopic of boxing champion Jake La Motta, Pinches objected to the violence and bad language which he felt would be a turn-off to cinemagoers (even though it had scored at the box-office in America and received rave reviews). He offered to give it a test run in two smaller Rank theatres.

United Artists, the distributor, was furious and even talked of moving all its product to the ABC circuit. The film (which went on to win several major Academy Awards) opened three weeks later at virtually the same cinemas that had taken *Bad Timing*: the Classic Haymarket and Studio Oxford Street, along with the Classic Chelsea, Gate Notting Hill and Screen on the Hill. It proved to be a big draw and, like *Bad Timing*, subsequently played quite widely at London suburban Odeons. George Pinches brought forward his retirement and was succeeded as chief booker by his assistant, Stan Fishman.

This followed a similar failure to recognise the box-office potential of Roman Polanski's *Tess*. Producer Timothy Burrill recalled (*Sight and Sound*, July 1996, page 59) that the film was rejected by both George Pinches and his equivalent at ABC, Robert Webster. Its 170-minute running time would have been a drawback, plus having at that time a minor distributor lacking the resources to promote it beyond a specialised run. In the end it was picked up by Columbia, for both the USA and UK, and received six Academy Award nominations. After winning three of them, it opened in the spring of 1981 in the main screen at the Empire Leicester Square and proved a huge hit – it became the third most successful booking in the financial year at the Odeon Southampton where it ran for six weeks.

The tripled Odeon Holloway was nearly lost to bingo in the early 1980s when there was a plan to switch the Top Rank Club from Camden Town and sell the site. Cinema executives insisted on retaining Holloway, which could be very profitable (it is still going today). The booking department had a preconceived idea that this "rough" area of north London could only do well with low-brow pictures – and so, despite requests from manager Steve Gaunt to book the more sophisticated *The French Lieutenant's Woman* into the 614-seat main screen in the old balcony, it was slotted into the 216-seat screen 2 downstairs while a Kung Fu film went upstairs. Even though it had already played the nearby Odeon Muswell Hill, *The French Lieutenant's Woman* filled to capacity on the first evening, with many would-be patrons turned away, while only a handful were watching the Kung Fu picture. Steve Gaunt requested the films be switched but the booking department responded that it would be more trouble than it was worth. So Gaunt took matters into his own hands and, as assistant manager James Bettley recalls, transferred the plastic signs identifying the screen numbers so that the big upstairs cinema temporarily became the number 2 screen and the two downstairs cinemas were numbers 1 and 3. Head office must have been baffled to receive admission figures for the no. 2 screen that far exceeded its seating capacity. At no performance were there more than 216 patrons for the displaced Kung Fu film, so its distributor did not lose out.

1984 – the nadir

Rank had a disastrous first half of 1984 and a long hot summer made matters worse. The ABC circuit derived most benefit from the year's top draws, *Indiana Jones And The Temple Of Doom* and rival Bond picture *Never Say Never Again*. Odeons achieved the next best business with a revival of Disney's *The Jungle Book*. ABC had the rest of the year's top ten apart from *Educating Rita* (the slow-burning hit first released by RFD in 1983). Overall, 1984 proved to be the worst year in British exhibition industry with admissions slumping to 54 million, almost half the total of 1980. Odeon clocked up ten million of those attendances.

Thanks to the surviving records of the Odeon Southampton, it is possible to examine in detail the performance of Rank's share of product in 1984, although the town's Gaumont took some of the releases between live shows. The only bookings that produced really high weekly admissions were the reissue of Disney's 1961 animated *One Hundred And One Dalmatians* (8,109 in its first week; 3,757 in its second) and *Ghostbusters* at the end of the year (peaking at 10,987 in its second week just prior to Christmas). Most weeks saw under 2,000 admissions in the larger 756-seat Odeon 2 screen and the worst level of business was reached when there were only 340 patrons during a week of reissues: 88 for three days of *The Great Race*, 78 for a one-day booking of *The Jazz Singer* plus *Kramer Vs. Kramer*, and 174 for three days of *The Ten Commandments*. The preceding week saw the screen's worst performance by a new film, the sex drama *Baby Love* drawing only 547 in seven days. Even Disney was not infallible, as a wild life drama *Never Cry Wolf* brought in a mere 565 patrons in seven days and grossed far less than *Baby Love* through the numerous reduced price child tickets sold. *Educating Rita* became the second most successful film through an extended run: it drew 2,099 in its first week in Odeon 2, then transferred to Odeon 1 (476 seats) where it attracted in successive weeks: 2,090; 2,304; 1,684; 872; and 646. Odeon 1 continued the run of many pictures started in Odeon 2 or at the Gaumont. Its best week was 2,715 admissions for *Return Of The Jedi*, followed by 2,509 for *The Woman In Red* and 2,454 for a post-Christmas return of *One Hundred And One Dalmatians*. Its worst weeks by far witnessed a mere 196 patrons for the British drama *Secret Places* and 247 for the Hollywood remake of the French comedy *The Man Who Loved Women*, but a formerly reliable Bond pairing of *Octopussy* and *For Your Eyes Only* delivered only 373 paying customers.

In a development affecting the circuit as a whole, the time-honoured policy of a supporting programme – even if only a short – was finally abandoned when the Robert Redford film *The Natural* was released in October 1984. As the baseball drama ran

134 minutes, audiences were less likely to feel shortchanged – indeed, given the appalling quality of the cheap travelogues that the now discontinued Eady production levy had encouraged, the absence of a short before *The Natural* must have come as a relief for many cinemagoers.

To sell or not to sell

In 1981 there were widespread rumours that Rank was about to sell its cinema chain, possibly stimulated by the closure of Rank's film production arm and the departure of its leisure division chief, Edmond Chilton. In April 1981, chairman Harry Smith denied that Rank had a £50 million American bid under consideration. In June 1981, a Rank executive told the trade paper *Screen International:* "We have never had an offer for part or whole of the circuit, although it is certainly true that there have been approaches. We have given our opinion of what the circuit might be worth and those approaches have never been followed up with a definite offer."

I am reliably informed that the circuit was almost sold to Lew Grade's Associated Communications Corporation which owned the Classic circuit. Only a disagreement over the price prevented the deal from going through.

In 1983, the Rank Organisation's major shareholders, the City institutions, were unhappy with what they perceived as a lack of direction. They brought about a change in chief executive with Michael Gifford, from Cadbury-Schweppes, taking over on 1 September and dominating Rank for the next thirteen years, during which time profits rose almost seven-fold but Rank's cinemas – and, it was said, its bingo halls and holiday companies as well – lost ground to sharper rivals.

Further listings

In or around 1980, a measure of protection was extended to the remarkable achievements in designing Odeons in the 1930s. Listing notices were served on the Odeon Woolwich (architect: George Coles) and the former Odeon Kingstanding (architect: J. Cecil Clavering in the Harry Weedon practice).

The trademark style of lettering in the Odeon sign was an integral part of that achievement. Woolwich seems to have been listed prior to closure by Rank in October 1981. If so, it still retained some of its original signage. The signs were removed, but should they have been? The auditorium had been ruined by modernisation, so it was the faience-clad exterior that really mattered and it looked too blank without signage in the proper places. When Panton re-opened the building as the Coronet many months later, the name appeared in a small, low-maintenance vertical sign above the entrance where no Odeon sign had ever been. The original signs could have been left unused but in situ.

An explanation for this could have been displayed at the entrance.*

It is an irony that the Odeon with perhaps the most impressive of all the circuit's 1930s exteriors should have been one of the least important contributors to the circuit's profits. This was solely due to location but it had brought about the Odeon Kingstanding's switch to Rank bingo in 1962, eighteen years before listing. Consequently, the dramatically large Odeon sign over the curved entrance had long been replaced by white board with a small flat Top Rank Club sign attached in the centre. The red words CINEMA, mounted on each side of the towering central fins, had been covered over by the words TOP RANK. Otherwise, the exterior survived remarkably well and the straight-forward auditorium had been little touched. Subsequently, the faience tiles were painted over, along with the curved section above the entrance on which the letters of TOP RANK were individually placed. The word BINGO was clamped to the fins, half-revealing the word CINEMA underneath. In recent years, the Top Rank sign has given way to a Mecca one. However, the building still remains a splendid sight.

Other Rank properties listed around this time included two more designed by the George Coles practice – the huge State Kilburn and the Chinese-style Odeon (ex-Gaumont) Southall, then leased out for Asian films** – as well as the Odeons at Edinburgh (ex-New Victoria), Rayners Lane (originally Grosvenor) and York. A former Odeon by George Coles, the Focus Bury St. Edmunds, was listed a few months before closure and then de-listed following substantial local pressure as it blocked a redevelopment scheme. This boasted a strong exterior in the F. E. Bromige style but the narrow auditorium was surprisingly dull.

In 1984, the Odeon (ex-Gaumont) Salisbury became a listed building along with – at last! – the Odeon Muswell Hill.

Overseas

In December 1977, Rank put up for sale its 132-strong Canadian

* Among other examples, the Hoover name has been retained with modifications on the listed Hoover building at Perivale, west London, while Waterstone's bookstore in Piccadilly, London, still displays the distinctive lettering it had as "formerly Simpsons".

** Listing proved most beneficial to this cinema with its extravagant exterior of Chinese dragons and matching interior motifs. It fell into decay as an indoor market when the upper part of the spacious single-level auditorium could be glimpsed between displaced tiles in a low false ceiling. When a fire destroyed the market, a local entrepreneur re-opened it as a three-screen Asian cinema, the Himalaya Palace, following a clean-up of the exterior and faithful restoration of the foyer and front half of the original auditorium (as the largest screen) by English Heritage. This resulted in a surprisingly lurid colour scheme based on the original as revealed by paint scrapings and analysis.

Odeon circuit, citing a rise of nationalist feeling in favour of local ownership (really?) and the need to reduce debt. Rank received nearly £14 million from Mike Zahorchak, the owner of a small family-run circuit of cinemas. After Zahorchak died in 1982, his chain was bought by Cineplex in May 1984 and merged with its cinemas to form Cineplex Odeon.

The foreign empire further shrunk in 1983 when Rank sold its three central Dublin cinemas (with six screens) and its loss-making Dutch circuit (including the landmark Tuchinski in Amsterdam), followed in January 1985 by completion of the sale of its half-interest in Australia's major Greater Union Organisation.

The one cinema in Lisbon, Portugal, seems to have been sold during this period. Rank's remaining foreign holdings included its interest in Kerridge Odeon of New Zealand and its 24 per cent share in the Cathay Organisation of Singapore.

A big question

The most interesting question raised by this ten-year period is why annual cinema attendances declined in this country by more than fifty per cent – from 116.3 million in 1975 to 54 million in 1984 – while in the United States they showed a 11.6 per cent increase despite the rise of home video. This question is not out of place in a history of Odeon cinemas because Rank dominated exhibition and was expected to provide a lead while its co-operation on industry-wide initiatives by anyone else was essential if they were to proceed.

Attendances may have declined in other countries but in Britain they fell far more rapidly. Even before this period, in a *Variety* report (14 November 1973), the trade paper's respected analyst A. D. Murphy referred to "Britain, which continues a disaster area of falling theatre patronage".*

The worst-ever annual total for American cinema admissions was 1973: 864.6 million. In 1974, a figure of 1,010.7 million was reached and attendances have never dipped below 1,000 million since (in fact, they had climbed to nearly 1,500 million by 2001).

The key development in America was the huge investment in multiplex movie theatres in new shopping malls, mostly by small companies like American Multi-Cinema which grew to become the new major circuits. This started in the late 1960s and exploded in the 1970s.

Of course, it was not until similar out-of-town retail develop-

ments took off in this country from the mid-1980s that such multiplexes could be contemplated here. And home video took root in Britain much more rapidly – perhaps encouraged by the uninviting nature of the cinema experience (as well as by cinemas themselves renting videos in the foyers?). We also had owners of cinema chains with divided interests – running television stations and bingo clubs – and increasingly prepared to dispose of cinemas for their site value. But, most inhibiting of all, there was doubt over whether the multiplex concept would work in Britain.

The image I retain of this period is of badly subdivided, poorly maintained cinemas charging excessively high prices. For an insider's view, listen to Ascanio Branca, the head of 20th Century-Fox in Britain, whose films were primarily shown in Rank cinemas. He told *Variety* in 1978: "No country in Europe is so badly served as Britain as to the condition of its theatres. Many of the multi-auditoria put up here are lousy. There are continual complaints about sound and comfort. It is pitiful... [British exhibitors] have no faith in the business."

A night in with a rented video was a far cheaper and more flexible alternative to trekking out to the few cinemas that were left. The outlook for cinemagoing had never looked bleaker. More cinemas closed, even some of those converted to three screens, often to provide a better bingo hall. Local press advertising was cut back. Minute advertisements created a poor impression.

The two largest surviving cinema operators, Rank (Odeon) and EMI (owner of the old ABC and Shipman & King circuits), responded by closing more and more cinemas. The decline in attendances was exacerbated by the reduced number of cinemas available.

Cinemagoing had become unfashionable. Adults were happy with television and video. Young people increasingly gave cinemas a miss.

---

* He placed this country behind Italy, France and West Germany in importance as a foreign market for Hollywood films, whereas for many years it had been by far the leading overseas outlet. Outside North America, Britain ranked behind Japan as well as France, West Germany and Italy in both 1978 and 1985.

THE AGE OF THE MULTIPLEX (1985-2000)

After the disastrous 1984 drop in admissions, the British cinema business seemed either on its way to rapid extinction or bound to make some sort of recovery. In an attempt to ensure the latter, 1985 was named British Film Year for an industry-wide promotional effort that was well rewarded. In a dramatic turn-around, attendances shot up by 18 million – a third higher than 1984 and well ahead of the preceding two years.

In fact, 1984 itself ended brightly with four-week runs of *Ghostbusters* in local Odeons (matched by *Gremlins* at ABCs). 1985 had already turned into a good year for Rank halfway through, with a 40 per cent rise in attendances. After a drop in April and May came the new Bond film *View To A Kill*, a massive summer hit aided by bad weather and the continuing British Film Year promotion.

Both Rank and ABC instituted some price cutting. Rank slashed ticket prices at seventeen cinemas, mainly in depressed areas, to 99p Monday to Thursday (not entirely a good idea, as Odeons had never previously had a cut-price image, but it doubled and even trebled attendances). Further Rank halls reduced prices to £1.99 every day but at some of the best attended Odeons prices were actually increased. Rank ended its financial year in October 1985 with a remarkable increase in admissions – 48 per cent up on the previous year, well ahead of the general rise.

The figures reproduced for the Odeon Southampton indicate the extent to which the top few attractions continued to take the lion's share of the business. In 1984/5 *Ghostbusters* claimed nearly a third of the entire year's admissions. The tenth most successful film, *Cocoon*, drew only 13 per cent of *Ghostbuster*'s numbers. Even the Bond film, *A View To A Kill*, did only half the business of *Ghostbusters*. A similar pattern is evident in other years: in 1988/9 *Who Framed Roger Rabbit* drew twice as many people as the number two, *Rain Man*, while the top ten films as a whole claimed 62.5 per cent of admissions and 71 per cent of the total playing time on the Odeon's two screens.

The year 1985 saw the first American-style multiplex open at the end of November. As it was the only one in the country until December 1986, the amazing million-plus admissions it claimed in its first year could only go part of the way to accounting for the 3.5 million increase in UK total admissions during 1986.

In December 1985, Thorn-EMI put its ABC chain and Elstree Studios up for sale. There were three main bidders: existing management (headed by Gary Dartnall); Cannon (the combination of the former Classic and Star chains); and, according to press reports, Rank. At this point, Rank had 77 halls, Cannon 94 and ABC 105. The idea of either Rank or Cannon acquiring ABC was not popular. "One reason why cinemas in Britain were so depressed when I came back here two-and-a-half years ago was that there was no real competition," Dartnall told Sue Summers in *The Sunday Times* (8 December 1985), adding: "It's been tremendously healthy having three groups of people competing." It was feared that if Rank took over ABC, there would only be one amalgamated chain with many closures where the two circuits competed head-on (as finally happened in 2000), and that Rank, which was no longer in film production itself (only making distribution deals) would stop Thorn-EMI's production plans and sell Elstree while retaining its own Pinewood Studios.

At this point, Thorn-EMI was investing in new ABC multiplexes on greenfield sites while Rank was still closing cinemas (as detailed later). "Rank's desire to buy [Thorn-EMI] is thought to have more to do with keeping Cannon out than a real desire to expand its empire", the article in *The Sunday Times* concluded.

Cannon became the new owner of the ABC chain in the spring of 1986 with 201 cinemas and 485 screens (see *ABC: The First Name In Entertainment*, page 112). This put Odeon into feeble second place with 75 cinemas and 194 screens.

The runaway popularity of the first multiplex failed to stimulate Rank into following its example. The company had its eye elsewhere – spending £67.5 million in June 1986 on the purchase from the Ladbroke Group of forty-two slot machine arcades and thirty-six bingo halls (these included many former Essoldo cinemas) at the time when the new national game was being launched in a successful attempt to revitalise the business. Rank also tried to buy Granada Television and was investing heavily in its Butlin's holiday camps, originally acquired in 1972.

The Odeon circuit saw a further 8 per cent rise in 1986 when the top draws included *Santa Claus – The Movie, Hannah And*

ODEON SOUTHAMPTON: TEN MOST POPULAR FILMS
1984-1993

The periods refer to the Rank financial year which ran to the end of October. Throughout this period the Odeon had two auditoria seating 756 and 478 with a small third screen (127 seats) added in early 1988. Until February 1986 Rank also operated the Gaumont which took many releases as well as hosting live shows. Opposition came from the twin screen ABC/Cannon (where a small third video screen was added 1981-89) until its closure in February 1991. The Odeon itself closed 5 September 1993. From 20 July 1989, the Odeon also competed against the five-screen Cannon multiplex at Ocean Village and may have shown many films in parallel.

Figures are the number of admissions. The number of weeks each film played is shown in brackets after the title. The total number of weeks played by the top ten films is shown in brackets after the word Total. In some weeks, some films played only afternoons or evenings. A + sign after the number of weeks indicates one or two extra days played. Each financial year's total attendance is given in square brackets after the total for the top ten.

1984/5
Ghostbusters (17) 69,795
A View To A Kill (10) 34,656
Return To Oz (7) 17,814
Peter Pan (3) 14,844
Desperately Seeking Susan (5)
  12,212
1984 (5) 8,793
The Never Ending Story (2) 7,140
The Jungle Book (1 + 2 days)
  6,566
Jesus (2) 5,853
Cocoon (3) 5,462
  **Total (55 weeks) 183,135
  [230,073]**

1985/6
Santa Claus (7) 29,388
Rocky IV (6) 23,824
Bambi (3) 15,675
Aliens (6) 14,378
Jewel Of The Nile (6) 13,926
The Karate Kid II (5) 12,343
Mona Lisa (6) 12,014
Cinderella (2) 8,985 (includes
  one week in 1986/7)
Hannah And Her Sisters (5) 8,662
The Black Cauldron (4) 8,240
  **Total (52 weeks) 147,435
  [223,385]**

1986/7
Crocodile Dundee (12) 70,349
The Living Daylights (9) 36,388
Blind Date (8) 17,494
Labyrinth (5) 14,746
Platoon (6) 14,563
The Fly (4) 9,942
The Aristocats (4) 8,480
The Rescuers (1) 8,384
The Color Of Money (5) 8,273
Ruthless People (4) 7,758
  **Total (58 weeks) 196,377
  [281,933]**

1987/8
(Small third screen added early 1988)
Three Men And A Baby (16)
  38,543
Snow White And The Seven Dwarfs
  (8) 21,053
The Jungle Book (7) 19,988
Good Morning Vietnam (6) 17,298
The Last Emperor (8) 15,526
Wish You Were Here (6) 11,428
Robocop (4) 8,403
Predator (4) 7,837
The Fox And the Hound (3) 7,807
Nightmare On Elm Street 3 (4+)
  7,729
  **Total (66 weeks) 155,046
  [256,624]**

1988/9
Who Framed Roger Rabbit (14)
  59,495
The Rain Man (9) 25,388
Cocktail (7) 17,788
Buster (9) 13,986
Licence To Kill (7) 13,777
Big (7) 13,052
Scandal (5) 12,457
Karate Kid III (6) 10,685
Lady And The Tramp (5) 10,366
Working Girl (5) 8,500
  **Total (74 weeks) 185,494
  [296,707]**

1989/90
Look Who's Talking (9) 17,434
Honey, I Shrunk the Kids (6)
  17,404
Pretty Woman (21) 16,700
Wilt (9) 12,386
Ghostbusters II (6) 11,994
Nuns On The Run (9) 11,256
War Of The Roses (8) 11,227
Dead Poet's Society (7) 10,831
When Harry Met Sally (9) 8,653
Total Recall (5) 8,492
  **Total (80 weeks) 126,377
  [210,490]**

1990/1
Robin Hood – Prince of Thieves (10)
  19,233 (includes one week in
  1991/2)
Terminator 2 (8) 17,788
Three Men And A Little Lady (8)
  17,441
Silence Of The Lambs (6) 15,810
Arachnophobia (7) 9,925
Home Alone (7) 9,793
Sleeping With The Enemy (5) 9,062
The Little Mermaid (3) 7,898
Ninja Turtles II (6) 7,172
Look Who's Talking Too (3) 6,197
  **Total (63 weeks) 120,319
  [225,623]**

1991/2
Hook (8) 15,275
Beauty And The Beast (5) 11,528
Lethal Weapon (7) 9,337
Basic Instinct (7) 9,051
The Addams Family (6) 8,733
Batman Returns (6) 8,196
My Girl (5) 8,043
Father Of The Bride (4) 7,071
Cape Fear (4) 6,889
Bill And Ted's Bogus Journey (4)
  6,825
  **Total (56 weeks) 90,948
  [195,148]**

1992/93
(45 weeks only – to closure)
Jurassic Park (8) 30,865
The Bodyguard (9) 12,618
Dracula (6) 10,327
Mr. Nanny (7) 8,438
Jungle Book (7) 7,266
Peter's Friend (5) 7047
A Few Good Men (5) 6299
Honey, I Blew Up The Kid (6)
  4,922
Sister Act (4) 4,678
Bambi (7) 3,964
  **Total (64 weeks) 96,424
  [173,076]**

Courtesy of James E. Tilmouth, former manager.

Her Sisters, *Rocky IV*, *Jewel Of The Nile* and *Aliens*. Attendances in 1987 were 70 per cent above 1984, thanks especially to *Crocodile Dundee* and the Bond film *The Living Daylights*.

Although the Cannon circuit closed many properties and was down to 173 sites and 443 screens by 1987, Odeon, too, continued to reduce in size, to a new low of 73 sites with 189 screens in that year (during which Rank also sold its half interest in New Zealand's Kerridge Odeon circuit to Pacer Pacific).

In 1988, Odeon admissions were "slightly down" when only one film, *Three Men And A Baby*, achieved more than a million admissions at Odeons. But they rose in each subsequent year, except 1992 (blamed on weaker films, new competition and an economic recession) and 1995 when they fell by 7 per cent, attributed to the counter attraction of a particularly hot summer. In 1991, top films at the Odeon tills were *Terminator 2*, *The Silence Of The Lambs* and *3 Men And A Little Lady*. *Jurassic Park* helped fuel an increase of more than 10 per cent in 1993 and *Four Weddings And A Funeral* a rise of over 9 per cent in 1994, while *The Full Monty* elevated profits in 1997.

Under chief executive Michael Gifford, the company turned towards expanding its gaming interests. On 15 August 1990, Rank took over debt-laden Mecca for £500 million, which not only added a further chain of bingo clubs (mostly ex-cinemas) but also other businesses such as the Hard Rock Café chain. The deal increased Rank's debt mountain to £1 billion, bringing the company under pressure to dispose of other assets.

In January 1993, it was reported that a consortium called Premier Media would be making a £400 million bid for Rank's film interests (which, besides Odeon, consisted in the UK of Pinewood Studios, Rank Film Distributors and Rank Laboratories). Michael Gifford, after humorously remarking that he "would sell his grandmother for the right price", subsequently backtracked: "We are approached daily about all kinds of fancy ideas, and we are quite used to showing people the door. We are not in the business of selling our film and TV assets, and there the matter rests – and hopefully dies."

In fact, there was considerable speculation that Rank would expand its cinema interests. Put up for sale in October 1994 by its French owners, Credit Lyonnais, the MGM-Cannon chain was an attractive proposition as it had recently reported a year's profit of £17 million on sales of £110.5 million. Besides running the former ABC and Classic chains, it had built several multiplexes.

Rank was the hot favourite to acquire MGM-Cannon, with Carlton Communications tipped as the other leading contender. Credit Lyonnais, the debt-ridden French bank which had been forced to take over MGM from its previous owner, Giancarlo Parretti, needed a quick sale and a deal with Rank would have been conditional on the approval of the Monopolies and Mergers

Commission because it would then control 45 per cent of the market. Rank would have had to dispose of nineteen cinema in locations where it was in direct competition with MGM, and perhaps shed more to reduce its market share to an acceptable level. David Puttnam fiercely opposed a sale to Rank: "The film industry works at its best when it is highly competitive, with a number of vertically integrated companies with a commitment to production, distribution and exhibition." Nigel Griffiths, Labour's consumer affairs spokesman, expressed the fear that such a takeover would restrict the range of films on offer and threaten independent cinemas.

At the end of June 1995, it was Richard Branson's Virgin company (in partnership with an American investment group) which entered the film exhibition scene by paying £200 million to acquire MGM-Cannon's eighteen multiplexes and 98 traditional cinemas representing 25 per cent of the market. Odeon's managing director at the time, Jim Whittell, recalls that Rank offered £186 million for MGM-Cannon, "the difference of £14 million being our view of the cost of solving asbestos problems".

In April 1996, The Rank Organisation gained a new chief executive, Andrew Teare, formerly head of English China Clays. Four months later he announced a change of name to The Rank Group, an expensive and unhelpful move as "Group" was commonplace and "Organisation" far more distinctive. In Teare's first year, the company bought the Tom Cobleigh pub chain and added sixteen bingo clubs. The entire bingo chain adopted the Mecca name as "Top Rank" was discarded.★

The Rank Group began cutting off its cinema roots. In 1997, Rank Film Distributors was sold to Carlton Television. Film distribution ended almost immediately as the new owners concentrated on exploiting the huge library of old films. The financial press reported that Rank's Odeon cinemas and bingo were performing well in contrast to such activities as Butlin's, the Tom Cobleigh chain of pubs and the London casinos, all of which were described as disappointing. By 1998, speculation that Rank could be broken up and its disparate interests sold off was an encouragement to venture capitalists to look over parts of the company. Cinemas were particularly attractive as they were essentially a cash business with takings on the increase.

Before multiplexing

In many of its 1980s redevelopment schemes, Rank put in only

★ There was at least one problem. After the Mecca name was applied to the Top Rank Club in the former Odeon at Luton, representatives of the town's 20,000 Muslims declared that it was an insult to their religion and the building suffered £3,500 of damage in an attack on Christmas Day 1997. It was sold off, became a listed building while closed, and has re-opened as a church.

two or three screens, the obvious strategy being to concentrate on playing the one or two major draws of the moment and forget about everything else. Most of these schemes took years to happen and this approach, which did have some commercial logic behind it, proved out of step with the market by the time the cinemas opened or shortly afterwards. Audiences had begun to expect choice. In many cases, the expensive remedy was for Rank to start all over again on a bigger site. Similarly, Rank kept adding a further screen or two at traditional sites, then expensively returning to them a few years later to fit in yet another couple of screens rather than maximising the number in one go.

The opening in June 1985 of the new Odeon Bristol made clear Rank's flagging interest in its cinema estate. It had given away the corner to a Mothercare store and switched the cinema entrance to a former exit on one side. The new cinemas seemed secondary to the retail outlet even though a readograph was placed on the corner above the store advertising the film programmes (but without any Odeon name sign).

There were two name signs around the new entrance, in curiously contradictory styles: a vertical one had five separate backlit letters in boxes (like the last main sign before conversion, which had been positioned just above the corner canopy) while a horizontal sign, just beneath a new canopy, had raised letters in red, lit up from within.

The cinemas were in the top of the building (rather than the basement) but it was a long haul to reach them in the absence of escalators. After twenty months of redevelopment, the Odeon offered three screens as before but with a reduced total capacity – although they had a more sensible distribution of seats and were all large, pleasant and comfortable.

To assist the British Film Year promotion, Thorn-EMI declared a moratorium on ABC closures. Rank was almost as obliging but it did let go of the two-screen Odeon in the heart of Croydon. The auditorium was demolished and the space absorbed for retail use by the Whitgift shopping centre at its rear, leaving only a three-screen ABC on the outskirts of town. The Odeon entrance later became a shop. As in the case of Watford in 1983, Rank's withdrawal from such a large and busy city centre without any plans for a replacement cinema suggested it had no interest in maintaining a national circuit.

There was a more positive move in re-opening the small cinema at the State Kilburn which now took the Odeon name. This followed the closure of the Classic Kilburn the previous year. But the difficulties of running a single-screen cinema (even with seating increased to 245) brought about its closure in 1990, since which time it has been left, seats in place, to gather dust. Kilburn, where Rank had operated the largest cinema in England (the State, 4004 seats) and the large Grange (around 2000 seats), now had no cinema at all until the Tricycle came along in 1998.

1986 was the most stable time in Odeon history for more than thirty years in that no major changes – no closures and no openings – took place other than the loss of the tripled Odeon Worthing which had been arranged back in 1984. (This wasn't quite the end of the story as the closed cinema became a Grade II listed building. Had the listing been conferred before its sale to developers, they might have been discouraged from buying it. As it was, they obtained its de-listing by producing unexpected evidence that it was structurally unsound.)

Also in 1986 the decision was taken to put the Odeon name on the three remaining Gaumonts at Bournemouth, Ipswich and – lastly, on 23 January 1987 – Doncaster.

When the new Odeon Sheffield opened in 1987, its two screens seated 824 in place of the former Gaumont's three screens with 2,015 seats. This was a striking building – whether you liked it or not. The exterior displayed a mirrored glass facade and a clear glass canopy within a bright red steel framework. The distorted reflection in the mirrored glass was a little unsettling. A vertical Odeon sign was placed at the corner. The ground floor was given over to retail use and the cinemas were reached through a small entrance area and then by a staircase which divided into two in front of a 31ft.-long mural of Sheffield life featuring a 1930s Harry Weedon-style Odeon with slab tower (rather than the post-war one the town did receive). The two auditoria were nothing special with their mustard-coloured pleated wall drapes, white suspended ceilings, red velvet seats and blue carpets.

No Odeon cinemas were closed in 1987, although as landlords the company brought about the temporary closure of the independently-run Camden Parkway at Camden Town for a proposed redevelopment scheme.

A new look

In the spring of 1985, cheeseparing had reached the point where all four neon signs at the Odeon Barnet – in the original style, dating from 1935 or exact replacements – were discarded for a single name sign in cheap red plastic letters (in trademark style) placed on the lightbox over the entrance at top left with the titles of the films showing crammed in alongside.

In 1986, Jim Whittell, an Odeon veteran who had become managing director two years before, took several important steps to give the circuit a sharper image. He persuaded the Board that Rank Theatres should be renamed Odeon Cinemas. He sought outside designers, such as Marketplace Design Partnership, to bring fresh ideas to the refurbishment of Odeons. "We had most of our design done in-house until recently," he told *Design Week* (6 March 1987), "but we were not sufficiently satisfied.

Marketplace was used successfully to refurbish Exeter Odeon so now it is working on virtually everything."

New slogans of "The Odeon Chain – The First Choice" and (for specific cinemas) "First Choice Odeon" were adopted for the circuit and Whittell insisted on the return of neon signs with their far greater impact, especially after dark. The classic logo was adjusted to a thicker, chunkier version with closer spacing of the five letters in red which, reinforced by neon, were now applied to a dark blue background. In addition, a new style of carpet was introduced – the first special design since the original 1930s style. This repeated a cluster of six letter Os in the revised octagonal shape in white, light blue and red against a dark blue background. The "First Choice" slogan was used in all advertising (replacing the man with the gong) but the new style of signage and predominantly blue decorative schemes were only applied to new builds and refurbishments. They were introduced at the Odeon Brighton in the 1987 re-shaping of the Kingswest Centre which added two further screens plus a new ground floor entrance and foyer to the cinema (with the dancing, banqueting and disco facilities also refurbished and modernised). However, Whittell deliberately avoided using the new look in a refurbishment of the Odeon Muswell Hill, regarding it as the "perfect example" of the circuit's tradition, and had the original colour scheme researched, leading to what he recalls as a predominantly maroon and cream scheme.

The revised name sign unfortunately replaced the original sign on the tower at Weston-super-Mare, even though it had become a listed building. At Wimbledon, the new-style sign went up vertically on one side of the frontage while the earlier five-box sign remained in place horizontally over the entrance – both used until the cinema closed in December 2002.

Under Whittell, the Odeon Leicester Square was refurbished in the first serious attempt to overcome the disaster of its 1967 refit. About £500,000 was allocated for the work, which was carried out from late 1987 without closing the theatre. "Ideally, we would like to restore it to its 1937 original condition," said Whittell, "but that might prove too expensive" – as was the case. At times, the flagship had been struggling, as when it had a month's run of the unintentional disaster movie *Ishtar*, but a decision was taken to retain rather than subdivide the existing auditorium and to add four smaller screens alongside (the number was later increased to five and these opened in 1990).

The flagship's black granite exterior was restored to shine with something like its original brilliance and the low-slung advertising panel was replaced by one which covered up the large recess designed to display the title of the current attraction. The move re-opened a view of Leicester Square from the circle lounge. From outside, the windows of the lounge were now flanked

In November 1987, Odeon reaches out to the cinemagoers that other cinemas neglect.

by five stepped bands of black granite. The edge of the canopy was covered in horizontal bands of blue and red neon while a small new name sign was mounted midway on top. New seating and carpeting appeared in the auditorium while long wavy strips of vertical neon were placed on the splay walls to light up and fade in sequence like giant glow worms or radioactive spaghetti.

In 1987, Rank made a new attempt to completely redevelop the valuable site of its Kensington Odeon. As it was one of the circuit's most lucrative outlets, Rank wanted to retain cinemas along with flats and offices. And as Kensington High Street was such a sensitive area and so many previous planning applications had been refused, Rank mounted an architectural competition, specifying that the scheme should include five cinemas seating 1,500 – one more cinema than it currently had, with 120 extra seats overall. The winners were Bowerbank, Brett and Lacy whose scheme gave the replacement Odeon a central canopied entrance leading immediately underground to the five cinemas, with entrances to the flats and offices at either end of the new frontage. Behind this, a lawn was to be placed on top of the cinemas to form a quadrangle surrounded by flats and offices. Despite an elaborate campaign to gain public support, an application to demolish was rejected in 1989. A further application was submitted in late 1991 based on a new or revised "contingency" scheme to build a five-screen cinema with offices, and seems to have met with another rejection. At any rate, the Odeon remains to this day, its elegant frontage enhancing the streetscape as it has done since 1926.

End of live shows

In March 1987, Rank caused an uproar in Birmingham when the end of thirty years of live shows at the Odeon was announced before a capacity audience for Magnum. Like the Odeon Hammersmith, it had become primarily a pop venue – in fact, the town's main pop venue, used by all performers outside of the very biggest names that played the larger National Exhibition Centre. Although films had been shown, Rank maintained its first-run cinema presence primarily through the three-screen Odeon Queensway at Holloway Circus.

But Rank decided it had to have more screens to compete in the multiplex era. The last performers were Go West on 2 July. Planned appearances by two bands, The Communards and The Housemartins, were cancelled. Rank shut the Odeon Birmingham for five months in 1988 to create six screens with a total of 1,664 seats. The Odeon Queensway was permanently closed once the work had been completed. Three years later, two more screens were added in a former basement and ballroom.

Rank retained a connection with live shows by operating the Odeon Hammersmith for a further three years before selling it

to the Apollo group in 1992. Its other live venue, the Dominion Tottenham Court Road, had been sold to Broadway producer and theatre owner James Nederlander in late 1990 for a price reported to have been over £5 million.

Investment in existing sites

The upswing in attendances encouraged Rank to add extra screens at several locations.

In 1987, the Odeon Ayr underwent the very last tripling based on the drop wall principle. Managing director Jim Whittell recalls:

> The Odeon Ayr tripling was a watershed. I knew exactly the maximum amount of capital I could expend on any conversion to ensure proper returns. Historically, the technical service department of Odeon was never able to deliver a conversion within that capital requirement. By going through the specification item by item, I was able to agree a conversion scenario that met the capital cost criteria. Thereafter, we built an additional thirty-four screens as twin, triple or quad conversions in existing cinemas throughout the country, all of which produced good returns.

At Harlow, new auditoria of slightly differing sizes were created on each side of the rear stepped section of the single floor, leaving a passage down the centre, wide enough to retain a few seats on the steppings, leading to the front section: this formed the largest auditorium, using the existing proscenium arch with the screen size reduced. (The all-stadium Odeon Norwich was similarly tripled in 1991.) Besides the two screens added at the Odeon Brighton, a third screen at the Odeon Bradford utilised the former ballroom; a former restaurant at Cheltenham became a tiny fourth screen; and, in Glasgow, the balcony of Odeon 3 on the old stage was enclosed and turned into a fourth auditorium.

Furthermore, Rank began introducing an extra cinema in the disused front stalls areas of its triples, reducing the size of screen within the old proscenium arch and setting up a new projection box at the back. This also involved enclosing and sound proofing the balcony and putting up a new screen in front of it. The first instance seems to have been at Colchester in 1987 but Sutton Coldfield was in the forefront, as it had been when tripled, and so were Exeter and Leicester. The new auditorium typically seated 250 to 300 people. To provide an access passage, it was often necessary to bring in the side wall of one of the downstairs minis. As a result, a 132-seater was reduced to 118 seats at Sutton Coldfield. At some cinemas (Bromley and, especially, Streatham), the new cinema in the front stalls was absurdly wide and the side seats were presumably only sold as a last resort. The process spread through the circuit and at Ayr a fourth screen was added in 1992, just five years after its belated tripling.

More former café areas became additional mini-screens, usually cramped and with poor sightlines (the tiniest was probably at Salisbury where only half the long disused restaurant space could be used). At Brighton, a sixth screen was shoehorned into a disused kitchen in late 1989, isolated from the other cinemas and awkwardly entered to the side of the screen – but Rank took the precaution of advertising it as a mini-screen and displaying a photograph by the box office.

At most of the early twins, one of the auditoria was carved up into smaller cinemas. At Leeds, the 1,279-seat downstairs Odeon became three cinemas of varying sizes in 1988, seating a total of 815. At Bournemouth, the downstairs auditorium was subdivided into four over three months in 1989. At Manchester, two smaller cinemas appeared at the back of the downstairs auditorium in 1992 plus new cinemas on the stage and in former restaurant space in the basement.

Large balconies were also split into two, as at St. Helier, Jersey (making three screens in total), and Holloway (at the latter, the front stalls area was also converted at the same time to create five screens in all – further expansion into long disused basement queueing areas was put on hold when Rank decided to re-open Camden Town). At St. Helier, Rank again proved overly cautious as three years later the builders were brought back to turn the downstairs screen into two, creating four cinemas in all.

At Holloway, Rank's ingenuity extended to blocking in the disused area behind the tall windows on the first floor above the entrance. This yielded a 78-seat sixth cinema, opened in 1992. A blank wall now appeared alongside the rich plasterwork elsewhere and the mini blocked most of the daylight that had flooded into the grand foyer. In the same year, additional screens were created at Swiss Cottage not only in the front stalls but on the former stage and in the circle foyer.

In fact, the spread of further screens proved so thorough that the few exceptions stood out – the Odeon at Scarborough with a single screen and mere triples like the Odeons at Burton-on-Trent, Doncaster, Muswell Hill and York.

Rank also addressed the problem of its two large auditoria in the West End. Although there was good reason to keep a single auditorium at the Odeon Leicester Square for premieres and opening weeks of blockbusters, there was insufficient justification for retaining all the seats at the Leicester Square Theatre. This closed for three months to be twinned and re-opened as the Odeon West End in 1991. The change of name caused confusion with the flagship just across the Square but at least patrons didn't have far to go if they went to the wrong place.

The Odeon Kensington in 1988. (Photograph by Allen Eyles.)

A new screen for the cinema in the old balcony is placed on its frame at the Odeon Streatham. The old safety curtain can be seen behind. (CTA Archive.)

The twinning created a pleasant 503-seat cinema in the old balcony with a new screen in front (but with a poor view from the ends of the front rows), plus an 838-seat cinema in the former stalls with too slight a rake and a displeasing shape to the ceiling which extended upwards from the front of the circle. There seemed to be an unfortunate side effect with the Odeon West End taking films that might have suited the Odeon Haymarket, making that a problem theatre.

And then there was the Odeon Marble Arch. Rank deserves credit for a bold move here. Investment in cinemas is usually concentrated on the already successful sites rather than on attempting to turn around the failures. The Odeon Marble Arch Odeon had been left high and dry by its location, isolated from other cinemas, and by the end of the exclusive roadshows that forced patrons to seek it out. Its stupendous curved screen had been replaced in 1979 by a smaller, less impressive flatter one (58ft. 6ins. x 28ft.) at the behest of David Lean to avoid distorting the horizontals when his director's cut of *Lawrence Of Arabia* was presented. The Odeon played some dire films that apparently needed a West End run for contractual reasons to help the subsequent video launch.

Steffan Laugharne, who was working there as a projectionist, writes:

> The programming policy from Head Office was pretty miserable with such films as *Nine Months*. Even supposedly big films were not booked, a notable example being The *Hunt For Red October* which would have looked great on the large screen. Instead we were given *Muppet Treasure Island* – on more than one occasion during the run of this film no tickets were sold and all the staff proceeded to the Mason's Arms at the rear of the cinema for a couple of hours. Much of the revenue that the theatre took came from lets on Friday/Saturday/Sunday late nights for Bollywood product. More than once I would be running part one of a Bollywood at Marble Arch and part two would still be running at the Safari cinema, Edgware. We were at the mercy of the traffic to ensure than part two arrived in time to get it on before our theatre licence expired for the night. And, yes, we did miss the deadline on more than one occasion.

In early 1994, Rank had proposed to add an extra floor above the auditorium to take 300 people so that The Talk of the Town cabaret could move out of the New London Theatre. The scheme never proceeded and, at the end of the same year, the subdivision of the Odeon was announced. Steffan Laugharne recalls:

> We were given three or four closure dates which all had stays of execution. Once a final date had been set and contracts for the work signed, the booking policy changed and we were given a run of good product such as *Goldeneye*, *The Rock*,

Mission: Impossible and finally *Independence Day*. These films followed one another and for the final three or four months of opening, we were sold out for the teatime and evening shows. *Independence Day* was followed by two final performances on two separate nights in aid of the Scottish branch of the Cinema Trade Benevolent Fund of *Braveheart* and, finally, *Gandhi* (in 70mm, attended by Lord Attenborough). On both nights, the general manager made a speech at the beginning of the performance on the plans to quin the theatre, which led to much booing from the audience.

There were indeed many who lamented the loss of the giant screen. The Odeon shut in September 1996, re-opening very early the following year. The subdivision involved creating pairs of screens with multiplex-style decoration in the back stalls and circle, leaving the full width of the front stalls for a fifth and largest cinema with a lower false ceiling and smaller-size screen in the old picture area. This auditorium is reached by a long passage down the side of the former rear stalls. The original rough-textured panels remain on the side walls here but have been repainted in a brash colour. In the foyer, the water fountain and fish pond were removed. Total seating was reduced by over 400 to 931. The conversion has proved very successful.

Listing problems

In 1989, Rank put forward plans to further subdivide the tripled Odeon Barnet in a way that would remove or hide all the original decoration. To prevent this, the building was listed by the Department of the Environment. Rank appealed against the refusal of listed building consent for the changes and a public inquiry was held with the Inspector's report supporting Rank.

The alterations that followed in 1992 did preserve most of the decorative features of the original main auditorium. A fourth, completely modern, low-ceilinged auditorium filled the front stalls without touching the upper side wall decoration which could still be viewed from the balcony. A fifth cinema was erected across the stage: to gain enough space, Rank was allowed to replicate the original proscenium arch further forward, in a slightly shallower form, clear of the stage, enabling the old pros arch to be filled in with a new soundproof wall. The new arch and screen faced audiences seated in the old balcony.

At the listed Odeon Weston-super-Mare, Rank were able to enclose the balcony and set up a fourth screen in the front stalls with a low ceiling that rose at the front to reveal the full height of the proscenium arch. The Compton organ remained and is still used for concerts outside of normal operating hours.*

* The Odeons at Edinburgh and Salisbury were also heavily restricted when further subdivision was permitted – see *Gaumont British Cinemas*, pages 174/6.

One protected cinema where Rank was unable to carry out further subdivision was the Odeon Muswell Hill, a drop wall triple when listed. In 1990, Rank wanted to put in two additional screens, removing the proscenium arch, existing screen, orchestra pit, and the detail on the lower part of the auditorium, besides concealing much of the decoration elsewhere. The key decorative lighting strip which crossed the ceiling and descended to the top of the proscenium arch would have been interrupted and damaged. Not only did Haringey Planning Committee refuse permission for the changes but chairman Chris Berry lectured Rank: "The proposed works would have destroyed much of its historical importance and removed the sense of cinema from the audience, who might as well have videos for home viewing. When you have charge of a listed building, you have a duty to act with social responsibility. The Odeon is a marvellous building and must be preserved for future generations."

The more expensive alternative of building new screens over the side passage or rear car park seemingly did not appeal.

Miniplexes

Until 1989 there was a 15ft. wide, slightly squalid passage down the righthand side of the Odeon Leicester Square that provided an escape route from the auditorium and served as a useful shortcut for the general public between the Square and Charing Cross Road. The Odeon's black glass frontage extended over the passage at the Leicester Square end while dressing rooms had been built above it near the other end where a wall with a standard Odeon name sign and advertising for the current attraction faced Charing Cross Road above ground level. (The Odeon site had extended fully to Charing Cross Road but offices were built at that end to defray the cost of the theatre.)

Inspired by the success of the Knightsbridge Minema with its small capacity, Rank spent £1.5 million filling in this passage with five mini-cinemas on three different levels (four seating 60, one seating 50), still leaving enough room at the Charing Cross Road end to provide an exit from the main auditorium next door as well as from the minis. The quintet opened in April 1990 as the Odeon Mezzanine and have carried on runs from larger West End cinemas and the occasional first run of minor films. They had their own separate name sign and readograph with bands of neon above the entrance doors matching those on the front of the main Odeon canopy. The drawback, apart from the generally cramped ambience, is that the screens are placed too high, especially from the front rows, but this was unavoidable as they had to be set above emergency exits and be seen past heads in front on a very slight rake. However, the Odeon Mezzanine has proved to be very successful, the five screens some-times having more patrons in total than the big Odeon next door.

In a similar fashion, Rank built fifth and sixth screens in 1991 over a side passage at the Odeon Colchester.

Rank versus the Multiplex

The idea of purpose-built multi-screen cinemas was not new (there were three-screen examples in Marseilles and St. Petersburg in the 1930s) but it mushroomed in the United States from the mid-1960s to reach Europe in 1969 with the cramped four-screen Cinecenta off Leicester Square in Panton Street (now an Odeon). The number of screens at new American multiplexes grew to ten or twelve. There was no doubt that multiplexes were succeeding in North America but there was widespread scepticism as to whether they would work in Britain. The most enthusiastic exponent of the multiplex was American Multi-Cinema (AMC) which invaded Britain to set up the first multiplex here, with other companies following. This represented a serious challenge to the domination of the market by the Odeon and ABC chains.

Historically, following intense hostility to some provincial expansion by Hollywood film companies in the late 1920s, the Americans had refrained from entering British exhibition outside the West End of London where US distributors controlled the launch of their pictures by having their own premiere houses. Paramount's provincial chain and its takeover of the five London suburban Astorias in 1930 was an exception (and these, of course, had long become part of Odeon).

But American exhibition chains like AMC and National Amusements saw a wide-open market. In setting up multiplexes with ten or more auditoria, they obviously expected to be able to show all the mainstream releases (as they did at home) and they had reached a tacit understanding with the major American distributors that they would be fully supplied before taking the risk of opening here. This is what happened at the first British multiplex, AMC's The Point at Milton Keynes, when it opened in 1985.

The Milton Keynes Development Corporation had originally invited tenders from British operators to run the leisure complex. (Granada put in a bid on 5 January 1979 to operate cinemas and bingo.) It seems that Bass Leisure gained the contract and sought a partner to open a multiplex.

Odeon's head, Jim Whittell, writes: "I was never prepared to seek board approval for any capital investment unless I genuinely saw proper and adequate returns. In the case of Milton Keynes, we did not tender. There was no possible way a profit could be made, never mind adequate returns. Subsequently, I learned that throughout its operation this multiplex never made a profit." And, as former Rank executive Stan Fishman has pointed out to me, it would have been difficult for Odeon to

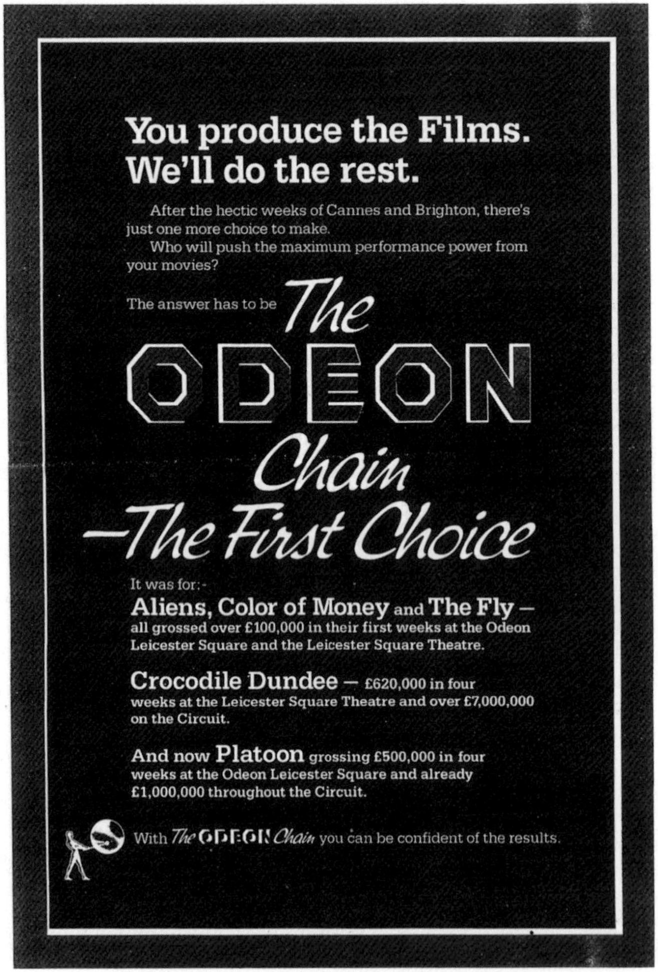
You produce the Films.
We'll do the rest.
After the hectic weeks of Cannes and Brighton, there's just one more choice to make.
Who will push the maximum performance power from your movies?
The answer has to be The
ODEON
Chain
–The First Choice
It was for:-
Aliens, Color of Money and The Fly – all grossed over £100,000 in their first weeks at the Odeon Leicester Square and the Leicester Square Theatre.
Crocodile Dundee – £620,000 in four weeks at the Leicester Square Theatre and over £7,000,000 on the Circuit.
And now Platoon grossing £500,000 in four weeks at the Odeon Leicester Square and already £1,000,000 throughout the Circuit.
With The ODEON Chain you can be confident of the results.

Odeon advertisement in the American trade paper Variety *in June 1987 promoting the chain against the American multiplex invaders.*

have operated a multiplex here without being accused of exercising monopoly powers and trampling competition (The Point forced the closure of at least two cinemas in the vicinity).

One major difference was the high cost of land in Britain, which is why most of the early multiplexes were built away from the southeast of England where land was most expensive. The other British chain, ABC, quickly set about building an eight-screen multiplex at Salford Quays – although owners Thorn EMI then sold all its cinemas and the multiplex opened with the name of its new owner, Cannon.

Another difference was that American operators calculated that multiplexes would raise British cinema attendances to levels at home, which has never happened (in 2003, annual visits were 2.84 per head compared to 5.05 in the USA). Of course, attendances have increased dramatically thanks to the multiplex and when they were a novelty and few on the ground they benefited from greater popularity than traditional cinemas, but this advantage has been dissipated by their proliferation.

Rank had no cinema close to the Milton Keynes development (although the Odeon Aylesbury and others suffered some adverse effect). It did attempt to delay the supply of films to later multiplexes which, it argued, had been built too near to Odeons. AMC claimed that its Gateshead and Crystal Peaks multiplexes were barred by the Odeons at Newcastle and Sheffield. Jim Whittell told *Variety* (13 July 1988): "...we believe that in certain locations like Nottingham and Warrington the new cinemas are too close and that simply dilutes our revenues if product is shared. It is not the case in Newcastle or Sheffield where we regularly have films playing concurrently."

After National Amusements opened its outlying Nottingham and Peterborough Showcases in opposition to city centre Odeons, the American company took umbrage at being denied immediate access to films from Columbia and 20th Century-Fox, both companies with long-standing alliances with the Odeon circuit, and from Orion, which released in the UK through Rank's distribution arm. The Cannon circuit, which also operated cinemas in Nottingham and Peterborough, raised no objection to Showcase showing the product from its regular distributors. In *Variety* (9 November 1988), Stuart Hall, the circuit's chief booker, was quoted as saying: "We have always accepted concurrencies with the multiplexes; they're a fact of life. What we have said to the distributors is that when our multiplexes in cities such as Glasgow and Southampton come on stream, we want exactly the same treatment."

Whittell reckoned a 30 per cent reduction in business had occurred at Nottingham. He was quoted in *Variety* (22 October 1989) as estimating that a multiplex within three miles of an Odeon decreased its take by 30-50 per cent and that within ten miles there was a drop-off of 10 to 25 per cent and no noticeable effect beyond that.

Odeon contracted with Fox for the major new Tom Hanks comedy, *Big*, to play at its Nottingham cinema on an exclusive area run with a standard four-week bar. When National Amusements, which ran its chain from North American headquarters, complained to Fox over there, the British office was instructed to supply *Big* to the Showcase concurrently. Rank responded by refusing to show the film at the Odeon, although the arrangement to play it at seventy-four other Odeons was not affected. National Amusements claimed that it had been promised forthcoming Fox releases as well.

Rank then negotiated lower rental terms in exchange for allowing a film to play concurrently at multiplexes so that it was compensated for the reduction in takings. This enabled Fox's *Die Hard* to play at both the Odeon and Showcase Nottingham. However, Warner Bros. decided to withhold the Tom Cruise hit *Cocktail* from the Odeons at Nottingham and Peterborough rather than agree to reduced terms. Whittell commented (*Variety*, 23 November 1988): "I can understand why Warner have decided to support the US exhibitors. They see their future with them, and they are developing their own multi-screen cinemas in Britain."

Odeon sought to bolster its standing among Hollywood companies by taking several advertisements in the American trade paper *Variety* to assert that it remained "the most attractive, comfortable and appealing network in the UK" and that "investment will go on right into the 1990's to ensure that the Odeon Chain remains Britain's leading cinema exhibitor".

An advertisement in the *Variety* issue dated 3 June 1987 told the American trade that the Odeon chain "will push the maximum performance power from your movies", quoting the high grosses for some recent films that had been achieved in the West End and on the circuit.

A double-page spread in *Variety* (4 November 1987) was headed "We're Spending 5 Times More on the Odeon Chain Than It Cost To Make *Ben Hur*" with a drawing of a chariot race and text that referred to refurbishment of the Odeon Leicester Square with additional screens (the Odeon Mezzanine), its first multiplexes at Stoke-on-Trent and Romford with more new Odeons to follow including Chelmsford, Uxbridge, Finchley, Camden Town and Swiss Cottage, plus many additional auditoria at existing cinemas. The advertisement also mentioned that all Odeons would have Dolby sound systems and that a computerised advance booking facility was being extended across the whole chain. Another whole-page advertisement in *Variety* (27 July 1988) listed fourteen places where screens had been added and sixteen more where they were under construction, including two multiplexes and two miniplexes.

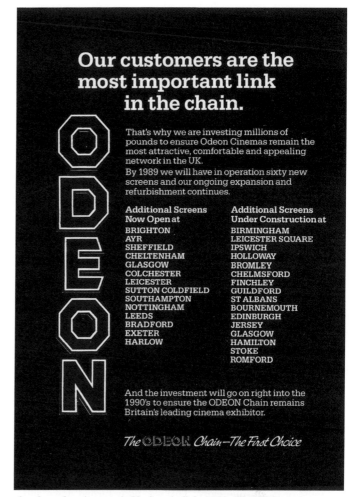

Another advertisement in Variety *in July 1988. This and previous advertisement were originally in two colours, with the Odeon name standing out in red.*

The only concession in film booking that was obtained in the multiplex era was the occasional exclusive opening week of major films at the Odeon Leicester Square before they played everywhere else. This has helped the flagship to register some phenomenal grosses for films like *Titanic* (70mm presentation in late January 1998) and the *Lord Of The Rings* trilogy. (*Dick Tracy* even had a two-week start in 1990.) The Empire and Warner/Vue in Leicester Square have also enjoyed the same one-week lead on some films.

The last intact Odeon

In October 1988 the Odeon Scarborough closed at the same time as extra screens were being added elsewhere on the circuit. Listed a few months earlier, it boasted one of the most celebrated of Odeon's 1930s exteriors (by J. Cecil Clavering and Robert Bullivant) and also had unusually elaborate auditorium decoration by Mollo and Egan. The original signage had been removed (the Odeon name appeared only on the front edge of the curving canopy) and a readograph and new entrance doors had been fitted below the canopy. Otherwise, the cinema had been barely altered over more than fifty years of existence, although much of the balcony café and lounge area had been partitioned off for subletting. Outside, even the art deco pylon advertising the cinema on the roundabout had survived, while in parts of the balcony were to be found strips of Odeon carpet in the classic 1930s design (in a reddish colour rather than the more frequent green). Most significantly, the auditorium had not been subdivided – making it the only one in a 1930s Odeon still in an unaltered state. (The car park, opposite on Northway, had been replaced by shops.)

Jim Whittell recalls:

> The Odeon Scarborough was loss making. I loved the originality of that cinema. I believe the stubbornness of the local authority could have been overcome when I presented them and English Heritage with a very sensitive (and very expensive) tripling scheme which would have maintained the cinema in most of its existing glory. This was flatly turned down and I then "threatened" them that unless we could agree on any compromise scheme they desired, I would have no option but to close the cinema. Over the following nine months they made it clear that they would accept no structural changes of any kind to the building. I called their bluff, closed the cinema, had it boarded up in a very strong and secure fashion and asked them again to change their mind. They refused to do so. Imagine my anger and total frustration that within three years they allowed that beautiful building to be internally destroyed!

The land was owned by Scarborough Borough Council and Rank put the remaining forty-seven years of its lease up for sale.

The town was the home of the celebrated Stephen Joseph Theatre, then based in an old school, which staged theatre-in-the-round and was the nursery of the stream of plays from Alan Ayckbourn. Needing more space, the Stephen Joseph Theatre developed plans to take over the cinema and destroy the interior in order to create two new auditoria: a studio theatre (also to function as a cinema) using the old balcony steppings and another in the round further forward. Judith Strong's case study (in the book *Encore: Strategies For Theatre Renewal*, undated), notes:

> Ayckbourn's plans for the Odeon involved the demolition of much of the auditorium and for this, listed building consent was required. The report prepared for the Historic Buildings Advisory Committee of English Heritage concluded that, despite the unique interior, the building's grade II listed status and its principal interest lay in "its external expression". Having assessed the likelihood of any alternative users making sufficient money to reinstate the exterior, English Heritage came to the reluctant conclusion that there were insufficient grounds for the application made by the Stephen Joseph Theatre to be "called in" for a public inquiry. Consent was granted.

The conversion started in 1994 and was completed at a cost of £5.25 million, much of it from lottery grants, with the building re-opening on 1 May 1996. The exterior, including the pylon, was returned to its 1936 condition with red and green neon on the building and blue neon on the pylon. The word CINEMA was reinstated across the top of the slab tower while lower down the word THEATRE was a modern addition. The same word replaced the Odeon name on the side wall but copied the original Odeon style of lettering. The name Stephen Joseph Theatre with the theatre's logo was mounted on brickwork on the side of the tower. The original style of entrance doors and the stepped bands of lettering just above them were faithfully reintroduced. The foyer and balcony lounge were restored, with the original design and colour of Odeon carpet being replicated although the tables and chairs were in a contemporary style.

So far, so good. In the back of the former balcony, the McCarthy Theatre was created with 165 cinema-style seats in the rear eight rows of the original auditorium (armrests not padded as they had been in 1936) while on the side walls were some of the panels of repetitive design by Mollo and Egan which had occupied the splay walls near the screen. A new stage was erected where the front circle had been. Further forward, nothing of the old interior was retained.

The main performing area, the Round Theatre, was created in the round because that was the passion of Stephen Joseph, founder of the original theatre. However, Stephen Fay noted in an article on Alan Ayckbourn (*Independent On Sunday*, 11 April

1999) that Joseph's "passion did not spread far: only three theatres can house touring productions of Ayckbourn's plays that have originated in that Scarborough theatre. Everywhere else, including London, his work fits snugly behind a proscenium arch." While the Odeon did not have a full stage, nor come with open land at the back on which a deeper stage could have been built, it is highly debatable whether so much of the very last complete Odeon auditorium needed to have been destroyed.*

Early casualties of the multiplex era

In November 1991, the Odeon Peterborough became the first acknowledged Rank victim of multiplex competition. As the Odeon had survived the arrival of the 11-screen out-of-town Showcase for nearly three years (Cannon had closed its three-screen site in November 1989), it is not clear whether the situation was worsening or whether the cinema had been kept open this long out of pride or obstinacy (as its admissions, however few, obviously hurt the multiplex).**

Even before Peterborough, the closure of the two-screen Plaza Dudley in October 1990 cannot have been unrelated to the runaway popularity of the out-of-town Merry Hill Shopping Centre near Brierley Hill with its 10-screen AMC (now UCI) multiplex, opened in October 1988. By early 1989, as a last resort, the Plaza became a discount house with very low prices at all times. Merry Hill blighted the centre of Dudley generally although a new Showcase multiplex has led the fightback, threatening the viability of the UCI.

In Preston, the two-screen Odeon became a lost cause after UCI opened a 10-screen multiplex and Warner Bros. followed with seven screens. The Odeon gave up in September 1992.

Outside Warrington, the AMC (now UCI) opened with 10

---

* Cinema had its revenge when the first attempt to introduce films in the McCarthy Theatre on two nights a week had to be abandoned. Terry Ladlow reported in the *CTA Bulletin* for July/August 1996: "On the first night the projection equipment failed three times and eventually the performance was abandoned. Doubly embarrassing since Alain Resnais, the director of the two French films inaugurating the cinema operation, was there to talk about *Smoking* and *No Smoking*, based on Alan Ayckbourn's *Intimate Exchanges*." It was several weeks at least before film shows started again.

** This was not the end of the story: after nearly ten years of disuse, the building made a dazzling comeback in other hands as the Broadway Theatre for live shows and films following extensive alterations by architect Tim Foster, although the deliberately limited stage facilities have proved a severe handicap. Unlike Scarborough, this was an unlisted building, an inferior Odeon, and it has been skilfully expanded and reinterpreted, retaining the most distinctive design features of the auditorium. (See *Picture House* no. 27, 2002, pages 54-60.)

screens in March 1988 and the town centre Odeon expired on 28 August 1994. Although the UCI had dented attendances, it had survived for more than six years and an attractive offer for the site seems to have been the deciding factor.

Another closure of this period was the Odeon Southampton in September 1993. It had comfortably survived the arrival of a five-screen multiplex in outlying Ocean Village and building contractors had been submitting quotations just the previous year to subdivide the largest auditorium into three, creating five screens. It seems that Rank accepted an irresistible sum from the owners to surrender the lease (which had fifteen years to run) so that the site could be sold for redevelopment. Around this time, Rank held hopes of opening a ten-screen multiplex and other leisure activities at Hedge End, to the east of town.

Rank's first multiplexes – and some miniplexes

Rank's delay in investing in new multiplex cinemas is attributable to Odeon chief Jim Whittell's conviction that multiplexes might be popular but it did not mean they were profitable:

> During my tenure (1985-90), the main board changed from entirely agreeing with my commercial reluctance to spend capital without certainty of return to a situation in the late 1980s when they tried time and again to persuade me to commit to multiplexes and, in every case, I was unable to do so due to the likely return against the capital required. Even today I am satisfied that a large number of new multiplex developments never produce adequate returns – due almost entirely to obscenely high rental and service levels. By 1988 the Rank board forced me to proceed with the construction of multiplexes.

What appealed to the Rank board was the concept of a multi-function leisure centre as was proposed for Romford, combining an eight-screen cinema with bingo hall, disco, bars and restaurant under one roof at a cost of about £7 million, all to be operated by the company. Rank was also keen on a similar proposal for part of a 23.5 acre site at Stoke-on-Trent where the National Garden Exhibition had previously been staged. Here the facilities might extend to a waterworld, bowling and a dry ski run. "The competition only wants to do part of it," chief executive Michael Gifford told *The Times* (27 October 1987). "Rank is the only group which does all these things." The Rank board is said to have decreed that the company would not build stand alone cinemas or any in retail parks. A new Leisure Developments Division was formed to establish these centres.

Ground was broken at Stoke-on-Trent in September 1988 and it overtook the Romford scheme, enabling Rank to open its first multiplex on schedule on 18 October 1989, four years after The Point had opened at Milton Keynes. In fact, the Odeon Stoke-on-Trent was the twenty-third multiplex to appear in this country. The rival Cannon (ex-ABC) circuit had opened three, an independent had opened one at Slough, and American invaders had opened all the rest.★

A half mile downhill from the centre of Hanley with plentiful open-air parking, the Odeon Stoke-on-Trent occupied a large part of a long, low building which also housed a dry ski slope, a Waterworld, ten pin bowling, a snooker club and an amusement arcade. The new cinema had a low-ceilinged foyer with two entrance passages around each side of a bar, and a rather sprawling layout leading to eight auditoria with stepped seating and descending ceilings, fitted out with blue carpet and royal blue side wall drapes. All had Dolby stereo and one was fitted to show 70mm prints as well as 35mm, running *Lawrence Of Arabia* on the first day. There were 1,804 seats in total, ranging from 150 to 521 in the individual screens.

This made redundant the existing three-screen Odeon Hanley, which had been fully redecorated as recently as 1987 (it has since been sold and detripled, reverting to its original name of Regent as a much modernised live theatre). A year after the multiplex opened, Odeon's new chief, Laurie Clarke, commented: "Stoke has come home on budget. It took longer to build business than we first anticipated, but it then grew rapidly." Jim Whittell (who had moved to take charge of Rank's Butlin's holiday operation) today comments: "Stoke and Romford both failed to meet the capital expenditure hurdle rate... Consultants were brought in who massively increased the likely admission levels against my forecast. The particular memory I have is that my projection for Stoke stated a maximum of 550,000 admissions. Third parties stated a minimum of 750,000 admissions. The development proceeded and in the first year Stoke delivered just short of 500,000 admissions. No proper and adequate return for the shareholders here!"

Nevertheless, two more screens were added at Stoke in 1993. As the only mainstream cinema in the towns making up the Potteries, it had a clear run until the opening of the Warner Village multiplex with its later generation stadium-style auditoria in adjacent Newcastle-under-Lyme in 2000.

By seizing on a particular opportunity, Rank opened its second multiplex at Hull in 1990. Hull was one of the largest

towns in England where Rank had never been strongly represented (its one outlying Gaumont hall closed in 1959). The company missed out on the earliest bidding for multiplex sites here but had a second chance after AMC, having opened eight UK multiplexes, sold up in Britain in December 1988, referring to financial pressures in America.

AMC and rival CIC (a partnership of Universal and Paramount) had both planned eight-screen cinemas for Hull at different locations on the same edge of town. After CIC took over AMC and became UCI, it put through its own scheme and dropped AMC's one. This was taken up by Rank which moved with such speed that its Odeon opened in spring 1990, at a reputed cost of £5.9 million including outfitting, more than six months ahead of the UCI. Being only a mile apart in similar retail/leisure parks, these two multiplexes were in direct competition at a time when one was regarded as sufficient and the previous opening of two on opposite sides of Derby almost simultaneously in late 1988 had been openly described as an unfortunate "mistake" by one of the chains involved. Of course, Derby had a smaller population than Hull and perhaps Odeon had hoped its lead would deter UCI from proceeding. In addition, the three-screen traditional MGM cinema in the town centre fought back with budget prices and there was an art house, giving Hull twenty screens in all.

Both the Hull multiplexes started out with similar total seating capacities on their eight screens, although the Odeon's biggest auditorium seated 468 compared to 292 in each of the two largest auditoria at the UCI. Externally, the Odeon looks depressingly unimaginative – a rather grim, low structure clad in shiny panels, its flat, box-like appearance relieved only by an outer foyer with pitched roof extending from a central recess. Two more screens were added in 1995 in an attempt to obtain a competitive edge. Virgin then entered the scene with a third multiplex on the other side of town, opened in 2000 and now called the UGC. This relegated the Odeon to a feeble second place in Hull, becoming the lowest grossing multiplex on the entire chain in 2003. However, the UCI was doing even worse and closed down in July 2004, considerably brightening the Odeon's prospects.

Originally planned for the end of 1989 and opened in July 1990 at a reported cost of around £4.5 million, the Odeon at Romford was situated in a new leisure development, Liberty 2 (as opposed to Liberty 1 across the road), and was not highly visible externally. It occupied an upper level above a Top Rank bingo club, and its foyer and passages, like those at Stoke, seemed to sprawl over a wide area. As at Hanley, Rank closed its more central three-screen Odeon – but there was also an equally central three-screen Cannon. As one Rank manager told me,

★ In late 1989, Rank was reported to be after Gallery, set up by Canada's Cineplex Odeon to build multiplexes here, although Tony Williams, former Rank executive who headed the company, says that no offer was made. (Cineplex Odeon had, of course, been compelled to find a new name to operate in this country.) Gallery had taken over an independent multiplex in Slough and obtained several sites, so this would have given Rank an opportunity to catch up. However, Cannon purchased them to expand its chain.

"The Cannon was supposed to go away but didn't!" A cut-price admission policy kept it going for several years, clipping attendances at the multiplex.

Throughout the multiplex era, Odeon has maintained some differences in auditorium design from its American competitors. In particular, it has avoided overwhelmingly large screens and, until very recently, it has upheld tradition by installing curtains to hide the screen. It has retained masking to provide a sharp edge to the picture and this usually opens out to create a larger screen size for 'scope pictures (in contrast to many chains where the masking often drops in full view of the audience to provide a smaller image). In addition, Odeon multiplexes seem to offer more variety of shape to individual auditoria with suggestions of a proscenium arch and some have descending ceilings rather than the flat ones so prevalent elsewhere.

Rank was not the only late starter in the multiplex race: Warner Bros. came along, spending more on sites (outbidding Odeon on several occasions) and on fitting out its multiplexes than its rivals. Its first multiplex at Bury cost twice the norm (but it did have an adventurous exterior and foyer design and more than 4,000 seats). One Odeon executive told me that he could not figure out how Warner Bros. justified the sums they were expending, which were way beyond what Rank was prepared to pay. "Sometimes, there is a temptation to emulate the level of investment of the US companies," Laurie Clarke told *Moving Pictures International* (17 January 1991), "but we tend to resist that in order to ensure the return will meet the Rank group's criteria. We are hardnosed about investing shareholders' funds, and I don't think we have cause to regret that."

In the same month as Romford, Rank also opened its two-screen Odeon in Uxbridge on part of the site of its three-screen predecessor closed in 1984. At the edge of the town centre, the Odeon was a striking development alongside a roundabout, entered at projection room level (where there were small balconies for wheelchair users). The main foyer and two spacious auditoria were reached by descending stairs. This scheme dated from the time when Rank thought in terms of two screens scooping off the big hits. The long gestation period meant that it was hopelessly inadequate by the time it opened, making it ripe for replacement by a town centre multiplex in 2001.

Ipswich was one of those towns where the cinemagoing habit had died. The ABC and Odeon had both been tripled in the 1970s to lacklustre results and there was a race to convert them to other uses. Less than seven years after its conversion, the Odeon had been turned over to Top Rank Bingo, leaving Rank with the large single-screen Gaumont which concentrated on live shows. In 1983 Rank had opened a small screen in the Gaumont's former ballroom. In 1986, the ABC closed and

Ipswich, with a population of 123,000 and a large hinterland, had only two mainstream screens at best (plus a small two-screen Regional Film Theatre on art house programming). Rank realised this was inadequate and announced in February 1987 that live shows at the Gaumont (or Odeon, as it had just been renamed) would end to allow the main auditorium to be split into four screens, producing a total of five. The threat to this major live venue caused such an uproar that Rank hammered out an agreement with the local authority in November 1989 whereby it gave the building to the town in exchange for the shell of a new five-screen cinema on part of the immediately adjacent car park. The shell was budgeted to cost the local authority £3.7 million. Rank paid for the outfitting and remained in the old site until the new Odeon was ready to open in March 1991.

This is an eye-catching, free-standing building with a streamlined, curved and stepped exterior clad in aluminium sheets, marine in flavour with its portholes (though reminding some of a giant tin can). The three-level foyer spaces are most inviting and bright in daytime thanks to the extensive glazing on the front of the building, but the actual cinemas are – as is so often the case in this period – a dull anticlimax with the usual side drapes and tiles across the ceiling. At least with Rank there were curtains.

In the *CTA Bulletin* (July/August 1992), Jeremy Perkins reported on a visit here:

> The auditorium decoration was pleasantly unobtrusive, but the screen was set with its bottom edge about eight feet above the floor so that everyone was craning upwards – most unappealing! As there were emergency exits set in the screen wall, green exit signs glowed a couple of feet away from the bottom corners of the wide screen. Perhaps worst, the main door was placed centrally in the back wall and each time someone came or went sunlight spread across the screen.

The problem with the high screen was the result of positioning the exit door in the same wall rather than on the side wall. This was a widespread fault in the smaller auditoria of earlier multiplexes.

Although five screens of this size are generally considered enough to qualify as a multiplex, unfortunately for Rank, with the burgeoning of cinema attendances nationally, this low count invited competition – which duly came in 1998, also in the city centre, in the form of an attractive 11-screen Virgin Cinemas multiplex with fully stepped seating, since rebranded UGC. Rank had announced plans to add further screens but this may have been a bluff to deter competition. However, the Odeon has survived even if it was looking dowdy externally and in need of a good clean in 2003. Its metallic exterior certainly lacks the warm glow of the biscuit-yellow faience of 1930s Odeons.

The Capitol Odeon in Cardiff formed part of the Capitol Shopping Centre, an attractive development named after the huge Capitol Cinema closed by Rank in 1978. Although work on the five-screen cinema was stated to be underway in March 1989, it did not open until August 1991. It was on the site formerly occupied by the Cory Hall, a temperance hall later used for concerts, political meetings and many radio broadcasts that was demolished some years after the Capitol (a dingy lane at the back of the Cory Hall had led to the stage door of the Capitol). The entrance to the new cinema through a tall glazed section led to somewhat restricted foyer space. The number of seats in the auditoria ranged from 161 to 435. The complex was called Capitol Odeon to distinguish it from the Odeon in Queen Street which remained open with two larger auditoria. Stephen Dutfield, who worked at the new cinema, writes:

> The five auditoria of this miniplex had shallow stepped floors common at the time. The back of Screen 1 was at ground level – the screen end was about ten feet below pavement level – and went up two floors in height. There was a bar and toilets on the middle floor, and the other four screens were on the top floor, two side by side on each side of the building. Projection rooms were suspended over the back of the auditoria except for number 1 which had its own small box behind the back wall accessed from the bar foyer. Picture and sound quality were good. There were three Dolby SR processors which could be used in any screen required. Later we went digital with Dolby SRD in some screens, including 1. The Capitol Odeon was a huge success when it opened and did well over its budgeted admissions for the first few years. When the UCI opened [with 12 screens in 1997], it initially hit badly but business did claw back as the UCI is well out of the city centre and the Capitol Odeon was well placed for car parks and public transport. Ultimately, Showcase opened north of Cardiff and cut off the rich source of incoming trade from Merthyr and Pontypridd, the Bridgend Odeon opened at the end of 1998 and put paid to the western end of the catchment area, and the writing was on the wall once Virgin/UGC finally started building in the city centre after having the site cleared for many years. The Capitol Odeon also suffered from very poor quality seating that didn't wear well and wasn't strong enough. It could be very uncomfortable during a long film. The standard seating at the Odeon Queen Street (which was the original seating reupholstered) was better than the luxury seating at the Capitol.

The opening of the 15-screen UGC was rapidly followed by the closure of the Odeon Capitol cinemas in August 2001, just a few days short of their tenth anniversary (the Queen Street Odeon had closed the previous year). Further worsening the picture was the construction of a 14-screen Ster Century, which had a delayed opening in 2003. Both the new multiplexes offered spacious stadium-type auditoria and a wider choice with which the Capitol Odeon could not compete. The seats, screens, tabs and projectors are reported to remain in situ at the end of 2004, with only some of the Dolby processors and digital heads having been removed for use at other Odeons.

Announced in June 1990, the Odeon at Bromborough in the south of the Wirral peninsula in Cheshire was part of a £12.5 million investment by Rank in a 93,000 sq. ft. leisure complex under a single roof. The greenfield site, developed by THI, was on the other side of the busy A41 from Bromborough itself. The original total of eight screens had been reduced to seven by the time foundation work started in September 1990. With seating for 1,890, the new Odeon opened on schedule in November 1991 as part of what was called the Wirral Leisure Park which included two discotheques, a bowling alley, amusement centres and bars and restaurants operated by two other divisions of Rank. The leisure facilities formed a separate area beyond a retail park.

CTA member Jeremy Perkins visited the Odeon shortly after opening and noted (*CTA Bulletin*, July/August 1992):

> Inside is an attempt to create a themed New York street with fast food and amusements leading off. Entry to the Odeon foyer is at this level and leads to a large relaxed circulation area with seats, marble-patterned wallpaper and a blue back-lighted Odeon legend at the far end. Entry to each auditorium is through a heavy-duty door reminiscent of Edwardian theatres. So what we have is a bulk-standard box on the outside with an attempt to create an atmosphere within. [...] The auditorium I attended was [...] unobtrusively decorated but with a level view to a screen well-proportioned for the size of the auditorium and with excellent Dolby sound.

"It was slow to begin with when we opened about two years ago but gradually it has picked up and it's still increasing," a manager, Sally Benson, told the *Ellesmere Port Pioneer* newspaper (23 February 1994), adding: "We have people coming to us from places like Wrexham and Connah's Quay, Warrington and Runcorn, as well as the entire scope of the Wirral." Business picked up so well that Rank added four extra screens in 1997. Since then, Odeon itself has opened up in Wrexham, Cineworld now operate a multiplex in Runcorn, Village Roadshow built the Warner Village in Birkenhead and, most damagingly, Warner Village opened a 16-screen multiplex at a much larger and more attractive retail and leisure centre, Cheshire Oaks, about six miles away off the M53. With the benefit of stadium seating, this cinema (now renamed Vue) has become the area's highest grosser. It has also drawn business away from Chester.

The pace quickened in 1992 with new Odeons at five sites,

plus a huge expansion at Sheffield which Rank had in mind the previous year in taking over two small Cannon cinemas, originally opened in 1969 by Cinecenta. It converted the adjacent Fiesta nightclub into five screens and refurbished the two older cinemas to create the Odeon 7 at Arundel Gate, an ad hoc multiplex opened in March 1992. This had a distinctive new entrance featuring a steeply pitched corrugated roof but presented a less attractive rear view perched above a multi-storey car park.

The initial intention was to continue operating the five-year-old Odeon Burgess Street with its two much larger screens, but these were closed in February 1994, just six and a half years after opening, and eventually converted to nightclub use.

Two extra screens were added at Arundel Gate later that year, and a tenth screen in 1997 to better enable it to compete with Sheffield's ten-screen UCI and eleven-screen Warner Village multiplex opened in 1988 and 1993 respectively. The arrival of the 20-screen Virgin (now UGC) multiplex in 1998 made Sheffield seriously overseated. The fallout spared the Odeon as the sole city centre multiplex but forced the closure of the UCI with its lack of stadium seating.

In a generally flattering report on the Rank Organisation, *Variety*'s Terry Ilott reported (6 May 1991) that chief executive Michael Gifford "has steered Rank away from large-scale multiplex investment in the UK because he believes the costs involved are prohibitive... Rank is now thinking small, looking at miniplexes that can cater to smaller populations." Gifford was quoted as saying: "No one knows how to take the cost out of the present system. Building a multiplex is an expensive undertaking and the big multiplexes don't get the returns. Admissions yes, but returns no."

Odeon identified a need for further "miniplexes" like the five making up the successful Odeon Mezzanine in Leicester Square. "There are opportunities to put miniplexes into smaller conurbations that are poorly screened and get a good return," Odeon's managing director Laurie Clarke told *Variety* (15 June 1992). "Odeon is better placed to take advantage of these opportunities than the US exhibitors, which had not shown any interest in four- or five-screen complexes." Chelmsford was to be the next stand-alone example of this line of thinking while the ingenious conversion at Richmond in 1992 of a former snooker hall (recently acquired by Rank in its takeover of Mecca) provided a four-screen supplement to the very profitable three-screen Odeon round the corner. These smaller schemes escaped the requirement that multiplexes be part of broader Rank leisure centres incorporating a multitude of company-operated attractions. Clarke estimated that there were only twenty sites left in Britain where multiplexes would be viable and added that he was negotiating for several of them.

In 1992 Odeon responded to the economic recession of the time by bringing in price reductions and discounts in the worst affected areas, balanced by introducing a number of "superior" seats at the back of most of its 300 auditoria for which an extra 50p to £1 was charged. Eleven per cent of the chain's 94,000 seats were of the superior variety at the beginning of 1993. When tickets were checked in the corridor, patrons were told in which part of the auditorium they should sit but there seemed to be little if any direct supervision, unlike in the days when usherettes ensured you sat in the area you had paid for. No other chain exactly followed Rank's example although some introduced separate higher-priced de luxe auditoria or balconies to new multiplexes with mixed results.

During 1992, new Odeon multiplexes were announced for Blackburn, Hemel Hempstead and Watford. Odeon finally pulled out of its seven-screen Blackburn scheme in 1994, the year it had been scheduled to open. According to a Rank executive, "Council changes caused a review of the deal we had in place. Their view on the land they held and the uses they wanted to make of it changed..." At the out-of-town site in the Garston area of Watford, the developer encouraged a bidding war between Odeon and Warner Bros. "Both parties believed they were about to secure that opportunity. There has to be a point beyond which a price becomes unacceptable... Some of our competitors have invested more in specific schemes that we would have," commented that same Rank executive. Warners went ahead, opening a multiplex in early 1996 with eight screens rather than the seven proposed by Odeon. Also in 1992, Rank seemed to have the edge in Cambridge where three developers were working on rival schemes that included multiplexes. In association with Stock Harvard, Rank were selected by the Council in March to develop a mixed leisure complex on the site of a municipal swimming pool. There was outline planning permission already for a multiplex in the expansion of the more central Grafton Centre retail development but UCI, which had been interested, withdrew because of Rank's lead. "Cambridge is one of those towns where the first past the post scoops the market. It would be foolish for two operators to set up against each other", UCI's managing director told *Leisureweek* (15 May 1992). However, the Grafton Centre won the race with Warner Bros. as tenants, opening eight screens in 1995. In 2004, Cineworld opened a second multiplex on the edge of town.

In 1993, Odeon had 17 per cent of UK screens and a 17.1 per cent share of admissions. Multiplex development generally had slowed down to the point where only four sites opened in 1993, principally because almost all of the most attractive out-of-town locations had been taken.

Rank opened a new six-screen Odeon in Dundee. The company's first plans for a six-screen multiplex dated back to 1990 when it withdrew from one scheme because of concern over the plans for the rest of the leisure centre before settling on another leisure park proposal to the north of the city. "It took about fifteen months from walking through the developer's office to inviting the public through the doors of the Odeon... a clean, quick deal from start to finish. These planning opportunities often don't have a benign planning regime," recalled Dean Morton, Odeon's business development executive, in 1996. Unfortunately, the new choice of location would prove less than satisfactory.

Almost exactly twelve years after the old Odeon Chelmsford had closed, a four-screen replacement with seating for 851 finally opened in the general redevelopment of the same area. The town had been without any cinema for more than a year.

At Taunton, the developers of the out-of-town Riverside Retail Park (formerly Hankeridge Farm) had gained outline planning permission for a multiplex in 1991 and were choosing between two operators in 1992. Odeon was announced as the winner and outfitted a new five-screen cinema which opened to the public on 4 August 1994 at a cost of circa £3 million. Interest was whetted by low price (£1) screenings of recent hits like *Jurassic Park*, *Mrs. Doubtfire* and *Four Weddings And A Funeral* that drew over 14,000 people into the cinema before it officially opened – a common procedure to stir up interest.

Externally, this is a most attractive structure that incorporates many design elements of the 1930s Odeon style in its use of cream panelling above a dark base with rounded corners and an almost free-standing tower feature reminiscent of the pylons at Redhill, Horsham and Scarborough. Canopies were not a common feature in multiplex design but there is a long one here with neon on the front edge, although this is held in place by cables attached to the frontage in the Victorian manner.

This pleasant homage to the traditional Odeon style was not really to the liking of Odeon's bosses. According to Dean Morton, "It was a perception of the local authority of how they viewed a modern cinema might look, which they imposed through the planning regime onto our design – so it wasn't wholly an Odeon-designed concept, it really was in many ways reflecting the desires of the local authority. The image the building portrays isn't as contemporary as we might have liked it to be." Nevertheless, Morton readily conceded that its look hadn't hurt trading at all.

The airy foyer is another plus. The actual auditoria appear from photographs to have been undistinguished but with tabs in differing colours and walls covered in fabric above the horizontally banded dados. Rows of luxury "Pullman" seating were placed at the rear of the three larger screens. Taunton still had its earlier Odeon – now a two-screen independent – in the town centre,

but this closed three weeks later as attendances plummeted.

Once again, Rank underestimated demand. When it first sought permission to add three further screens at Taunton, this was refused by the council in the hope of encouraging another company to open a cinema in the city centre. When no operator expressed interest, Odeon was finally given permission to expand in July 2003 on condition that it improved access by cars and public transport. The company has announced that the existing five screens will be remodelled.

In 1995, Odeon multiplexes were launched at Hemel Hempstead and Lincoln. "We'll spend more than £20 million this year," declared Hugh Corrance, who was the circuit's managing director from 1993 to 1997. "The bulk of it will go on new builds, and a portion on additional screens in existing buildings." Odeon's name was attached to a nine-screen, 2,000-seat cinema in Sunderland to open the following year – but the town had to wait until 2004 to gain a multiplex, part of the Cineworld chain. Rank also expressed hopes of building in Southampton and Crawley, succeeding in the former.

The eight-screen Odeon at Hemel Hempstead was Rank's sixth multi-leisure scheme. A particularly unappealing structure externally, the £22 million Leisure World on the outskirts of the town at Jarman Park (previously Jarman Fields) also included a bowling alley, ice rink, water adventure park, nightclubs, bars and fast food restaurants. The Odeon is at the left end of the long, low Leisure World structure, with its box office to the left inside a general entrance to the complex which provided direct access to Jumpin Jaks on the right and led through to the other attractions. A long foyer leads to the eight cinemas, ranging in size from 120 to 401 seats. Originally six had been planned but the space was reconfigured.

Being near the M1, the M25 and the A41, the Leisure World was targeted at 1.6 million people within a 40-minute drive. There was certainly need to revive interest in cinema locally: since 1974, the existing Odeon in Hemel Hempstead had shared the week with Rank bingo (which had taken over the best night of the week, Saturday, from 1988, reducing films to three days). The Odeon now went to full-time bingo, soon failing. In an attempt to boost audiences for the multiplex, Rank closed its profitable four-screen Odeon at St. Albans, five miles away. This decision was more than unpopular in St. Albans: it unleashed some of the worst criticism Rank has faced, including scathing comment in the national press.

In Lincoln, Rank had disposed of its Odeon to a local independent in the 1981 clear-out. This had reverted to the original name of Ritz and been imaginatively reinvigorated with films and live shows, doing well enough on films to warrant an expensive tripling in 1995 (said to have cost £800,000) and refurbishment which included a return to the three-colour external neon of the 1930s. Six months after the tripling, Rank opened a six-screen ground-floor stand-alone Odeon, modelled in size on Taunton, which put the Ritz out of business. Set in a retail park, Rank's new venture was done on the cheap with second hand seating and equipment (except for a digital sound rack).

The Cityplex

The Warner Village chain coined the word Cityplex when it announced plans in 1997 to build a six-screen cinema in the centre of Worcester, despite the fact that the town's Odeon had just upped its number of screens to seven by dividing the balcony area into three, perhaps hoping to forestall just such competition.

The Cityplex was a multiplex with fewer screens rather than the Rank miniplex where all or most of the auditoria had low seating figures. The interest in city centres was in response to new planning restrictions. After most of the damage had been done, the Government had responded to the fact that new out-of-town shopping centres were killing off old town centres. It issued Policy Planning Guidance papers to local authorities. PPG13 (published March 1994) stated that policies for retail, leisure, tourism, education and health developments should seek to promote the vitality and viability of town centres. A revised version of PPG6: Town Centres and Retail Development (published June 1996) set out to force a whole range of activities back into town centres. It emphasised a sequential approach to selecting sites for redevelopment, favouring in-centre locations, followed by edge-of-centre, and only then out-of-centre sites. In practice, PPG6 made it virtually impossible to develop out-of-town cinemas. Whereas, in May 1996, the Secretary of State allowed the out-of-town 14-screen Showcase Newham to be built despite well-founded objections over its likely impact on the centrally placed Odeon Barking, the new policy did scupper attempts to provide a six- or eight-screen multiplex on the Exeter bypass, first envisaged in 1994, which would have been leased by Odeon, apparently to complement rather than replace its existing city centre cinema. After the developer, Wilson Connolly, was refused permission, an appeal to the Secretary of State was dismissed in March 1997 with a declaration that the proposed cinema would inhibit the possible provision of an additional commercial cinema in the town centre and might threaten the viability of the existing Odeon.

In July 1996, Odeon was named the anchor tenant of a 12-screen multiplex in the £20 million Cleppa Park development outside Newport in Wales but the scheme was called in by the Welsh Office after allegations that it contravened planning policy and its knock-on effect on town centres had not been fully considered. In another demonstration of the musical chairs nature of multiplex development, Warner Village replaced Odeon as the potential operator in summer 1997 but Virgin eventually succeeded in opening an out-of-town multiplex.

In Carlisle, the Secretary of State had called in the front-running out-of-town scheme in January 1997, creating so much uncertainty that it was dropped. Odeon boarded a proposal for the Portland site on the eastern side of Botchergate in the centre of Carlisle in late 1997. Plans for an eight-screen Odeon received approval in September 1998 but the scheme as a whole collapsed two months later and a smaller rival project went ahead the following year on the opposite side of the street through which Village Roadshow opened a seven-screen Cityplex managed by the Warner Village partnership.

At first sight, PPG6 had seemed to offer some measure of support for the remaining older cinemas in city centres. However, it actually encouraged developers to find sites in city centres. Cinemas which might have survived an out-of-town multiplex had no chance against a new complex within walking distance (as was already clear from a few early city centre developments in Slough, Harrow, and elsewhere).

Developers frequently provided a shell for multiplex cinemas at first floor level or higher (rather than ground floor as in most out-of-town schemes) and invited operators to bid for the space. Rents and operating costs at city centre multiplexes were far higher and car parking problems had to be solved. But multiplex operators were encouraged to open in city centres because they felt they could rely on PPG6 to protect them from subsequent edge-of-town and out-of-town competition.

The opportunities appealed to many operators, particularly Odeon with its long experience of city centre markets. After January 1995, when Rank was cash-rich with £625 million obtained by selling part of its Rank Xerox shares holding, Odeon was encouraged by the Rank board of directors to develop as many multiplexes as met the criteria of the cinema chain and the parent company, and they no longer needed to be tied to broader leisure developments.

Thinking bigger

At a time when many multiplex chains were slowing down, Odeon was anxious and ready to catch up. The former operations director of the Top Rank Clubs, Richard Segal, was put in charge of Odeons and there was heady talk of opening sixteen multiplexes in a two-year period with the Tarmac construction group.

In an interview (*Leisureweek*, 25 July 1997), Segal readily acknowledged that Odeon had been a late starter in building multiplexes and that "When Odeon did start... it was too conservative; this resulted in under-screening at the sites it did open and it went back and added screens to these sites". Segal declared:

"...we want to change the way people think and behave. We want them to say 'let's go to an Odeon cinema and decide what film to watch when we get there.' We want the cinema to be the decisive factor as opposed to people making the film the decisive factor." And he added: "We want to accelerate dramatically the acquisition of new sites and to revitalise key city centre sites... Some people feel the company is a bit old-fashioned but I think we'll drive through that fairly quickly." The executive acknowledged the continuing problem of other chains' readiness to pay rents that would make it difficult to earn a profit. Segal's commitment to the company was exemplary: "People ask me what sort of films I like personally – *The English Patient* or *Con Air*? I'm not embarrassed to say I like the films that attract the most people to Odeon Cinemas."

Part of Odeon's efforts were devoted to retaining a presence in places like Guildford, Wimbledon and Newcastle where it had profitable, heavily subdivided traditional cinemas that were doomed by city centre developments incorporating a multiplex. If Odeon had not taken up the opportunity, a rival chain would have done so and its existing cinema would have been forced to close anyway.

In the last four months of 1996, new Odeons opened at Glasgow, Southend and Guildford. With 12 screens and more than 2,500 seats, the Odeon at Springfield Quay was Rank's largest multiplex to date. It formed part of a £20 million leisure park on a 15.5-acre site on the south side of the River Clyde, less than a mile from Glasgow city centre where the existing Odeon remained open. This advertised itself as a "six screen multiplex" and the metal cladding over the corner entrance was removed and vertical sections immediately to each side of a tall readograph painted in colours graduating from yellow through pink to brown, floodlit at night. There was a clear choice for those who enjoyed the city centre ambience and its restaurants and bars and those from out-of-town who wanted easy parking (1,000 spaces), fast food and less hassle. The Quay development benefits enormously in appearance from having separate buildings for its different leisure facilities rather than enclosing them under one roof as at Stoke-on-Trent or Hemel Hempstead. The Odeon is an attractive free-standing building in the modern multiplex idiom whereas the Mecca bingo club on the other side of the site has much more of a traditional cinema look.

Rank's first town-centre multiplex made its debut in Southend during November. The lease was running out on the existing two-screen Odeon a short distance away but, unusually, this remained open for five months after the new £10 million Odeon commenced business (a two-screen ABC also provided competition until January 1998). The newcomer is on one side of a large pedestrianised square, its entrance marked by a tower in dark brick at the end of a crescent-shaped facade incorporating retail space and offices to the left. It has a large foyer at ground level with eight screens stacked high: two on the ground floor, two on the first floor, and four on the top floor, the upper screens reached by staircase with a small lift for the disabled (the use of escalators had not become standard at this time). The architect's drawings showed a readograph covering the window over the entrance but this device had become old-fashioned and never materialised.

In Guildford, the new nine-screen Odeon is much more central than its predecessor with a multi-storey car park adjacent and the railway station a minute or two away. The old Odeon – opened in 1935 on the very edge of town with an awkward layout dictated by a difficult site and little or no parking – had been subdivided into four screens. It closed the evening before its successor opened. Although it could have been taken over by the local authority for arts and cultural purposes, it was demolished six years later (hopefully, the attractive bas reliefs above the entrance were saved).

The architects of the multiplex were required to use high quality brick and stone in this conspicuous location and not exceed the height of the sports centre it replaced. A typical glazed entrance, with an open pitched roof and a modern style of canopy, forms an extension of the brick box which has good detailing on its public sides. In contrast to the bas reliefs on the original Odeon, artist Steve Gelliot, funded by an arts scheme, created wooden and classic sculptures based on such films as *Blade Runner* and *La Belle et La Bête* for part of the wide, nicely landscaped area in front of the entrance. This was an instance of a multiplex being built on schedule and on budget, opening just before Christmas 1996. Thanks in part to a student population, it has proved extremely successful and would probably benefit from additional screens.

In 1997 and 1998 Odeon opened more multiplexes than any of its competitors and they were as large or larger than those of the other chains. In particular, Odeon competed with Warner Village to provide multiplexes in the London suburbs.

In July 1997, Rank opened its new Odeon Leicester. With twelve screens, this is a long, low structure, undistinguished externally, well out of the city centre on the site of the old cattle market at Freemen's Park. It was the second multiplex in the area as a nine-screen Warner Village had opened well out of town by the M1/A46 link. The existing four-screen Odeon, listed for its commanding exterior, closed the previous day. This has eventually become a conference and banqueting centre.

The following month, the £27 million Leisure World at Southampton made its debut. Looking externally like a giant metallic box tied together by blue bands, this adaptation of a former white goods warehouse is more of an eyesore than its predecessor at Hemel Hempstead but it too is outside the town centre, the other side of a retail park, surrounded by warehouses (and its look is softened at night by coloured upward lighting). The 12-acre site provides considerable space for ground level open-air parking.

The thirteen Odeon auditoria are reached through a shared entrance hall (or central mall) where the lofty ceiling suggests an "atmospheric"-style night sky using fibre optics. The cinema takes over the left side of this hall – its box office nearest the entrance doors, followed by a café and the passage to the various screens. Other enterprises were all on the right of the entrance hall: a Jumpin Jaks bar, a Hotshots nightclub, a Stardust amusement machine arcade, and a Frankie and Benny's restaurant.

The external appearance has proved no deterrent to young people – perhaps the opposite, as this Odeon rapidly became the circuit's most popular multiplex, hovering around tenth place in the top grossing sites in the UK. Its success has been at the expense of the older five-screen multiplex at the far more attractive location of Ocean Village, which had claimed a phenomenal 750,000 admissions in 1990.

Investment also continued in some of the older sites. At Cheltenham, the 756-seat cinema in the balcony was split into three in summer 1997, with the front cinema, seating 228, becoming the largest of the seven screens in the building.

And Rank made a return to its former Gaumont/Odeon at Camden Town. The last independent lessee, Peter Walker, had done a magnificent job of sprucing up the foyers and main auditorium as well as creating a luxurious second screen with two sets of curtains out of the old trainee projectionists' area. He made a point of welcoming audiences from the stage at evening shows. It has to be said that Walker's refurbishment did not adhere to the original 1937 look of what had been an exquisite art deco cinema and he readily admitted that the one thousand seats in the main auditorium were never all needed; but he ran the cinemas successfully and refused to quit after developers purchased the cinema in 1992. The local council would not allow the building to be demolished. Considerable uproar followed Peter Walker's eviction in August 1993. (There was further anger when the adjacent well-respected art house Plaza, a former Odeon cinema, was forced to close in September the following year: the auditorium has stood disused ever since.)

Rank, which in 1992 renewed the lease on its bingo club in the former stalls, began negotiations to re-open the cinema area in December 1993 and finally clinched a deal in December 1996 after the council threatened to compulsorily purchase the property. At a cost publicised as £2 million, Rank subdivided the large auditorium into four, retained and refitted Walker's second screen to provide a fifth cinema, and refurbished the lounge and foyer spaces and the entrance, highlighting many of the surviving art deco details (the council had issued a preservation order in 1994 to protect the interior).

When the new Odeon Camden Town was launched in 1997, it also launched a new look intended to revitalise the entire circuit.

The rebranding

A new impetus to market cinemas by name came from Virgin's purchase of the MGM (ex-Cannon) chain in 1995 and the heavy promotional use Richard Branson's company made of its image as a brash and innovative company as well as its bold plans for future expansion. New multiplexes were increasingly in close or direct competition with existing sites and, as they would be showing the same films, they had to compete on image to engender loyalty from audiences (helped in Virgin's case by the introduction of the "Unlimited Movies" subscription pass).

Although the Virgin name and logo were well known in other fields, Odeon had the one name and trademark lettering that was instantly recognised in the cinema field. This had inherent benefits but also the disadvantage of seeming old-fashioned to young audiences.

Since the 1960s had made people more fashion-conscious, it had become modish for big companies to employ designers to create a new brand image and consultants were unlikely to report that an existing design worked perfectly well or that any change might cost more than it would benefit the company in increased turnover and profits. Although Boots and Coca-Cola, for example, have retained their classic logos with minimal "tweaking", change for change's sake seemed to be the norm.

Under Richard Segal's direction, the Odeon circuit's first-ever marketing director, Ron Hanlon, was appointed in January 1997 with a brief to revitalise the brand. Hanlon was quoted (in *Leisureweek*, 7 March 1997) as saying: "We have a strong platform because Odeon is synonymous with cinemas and we have a strong heritage. But we have to engineer the brand to give it modernity to take it forward into the next millennium." Odeon turned to the design consultancy of Wolff Olins.

"The new look covers the Odeon logo, internal signage, retail areas, carpets, decorations, auditoria, cups and cartons, uniforms – basically every aspect of a visit to one of our cinemas," reported Hanlon. "The improvements have enabled us to change a rather tired, old fashioned look into one which is cool, stylish and dynamic."

A new style of Odeon signage was first tried out at the Odeon Camden Town when it re-opened on 11 July 1997. The entrance is located on a busy one-way street and a new vertical name sign in silvery white letters stuck out to face the direction of oncoming

The change in style of local press advertising following rebranding, seen here at the Odeon Brighton.

traffic. As the sign had no backing, the five letters appeared in reverse to anyone approaching on foot from the centre of Camden Town. A large banner or curtain hung in the recess above the entrance which had once advertised the current programme. This was in plain orange, introducing one of the key colours in the new Odeon look.

The five letters of the name were easily recognisable as an elongated variation of the old style. They were no longer red, nor reinforced by a thin outline. The letter E notably lacked the slanted ends at top and bottom right that had corresponded to the corners of the letter O and right corners of the letter D to make the historic logo so distinctive. The new lettering also looked crude in press advertising where the name (along with all the programme information) was reversed out of black. The two letters O resembled razor blades. The detailing that had made the old Odeon lettering a design classic was lost.

A see-through vertical sign in the Camden Town style was placed on the Odeon Haymarket some time after it closed in January 1999 to be refurbished following disruptive building works on the floors above. This sign faced the one-way flow of traffic from the Piccadilly Circus direction but was removed, along with the canopy, in November 2001 after it was decided not to re-open the cinema.★

The outdoor signs then changed. They became much larger and were made of brushed stainless steel, looking white or grey according to the light. They had a white rim which lit up at night and a blue backing plate which was illuminated from within the individual letters to create a blue halo effect – very much like the halo signs on the first Odeons before neon was introduced. (With the introduction of a blue background, the style of lettering resembled that already being used by Blockbuster Video.)

According to one Odeon executive, the new style of name was presented to assembled staff by Wolff Olins as having "all

★ The sign re-appeared on the corner of the Odeon Streatham's frontage where only the few people coming down the side road would encounter it from behind. The same style of sign was applied to the Odeon Salisbury in 2002 (with no illumination at night) where the entrance is in the middle of a busy street and approached from either direction. When the cinema opened as the Gaumont Palace in 1931, its name was displayed in Gothic lettering to match its mock-Tudor facade, historic entrance hall, and Tudor-style auditorium. When it was renamed Odeon in 1964, the five letters appeared in medieval style on separate illuminated boxes mounted vertically. No one has ever suggested that the cinema lost admissions or confused patrons because it did not display a standard logo. Alan Richardson, who led the successful campaign against Rank's earlier attempt to demolish the auditorium, described the latest sign as "an act of cultural vandalism". It is still in place today.

the elements of the old sign while allowing it to breathe". Thereafter, an Odeon manager would sometimes stop a colleague as they approached a cinema to point at the new sign and say, "Look, I can see it breathing."

The rebranding also did away with all the readographs to which lettering had been attached giving film details. Instead, Odeon came up with an ingenious and economical device: white magnetic letters were positioned along faint guide lines to adhere to a dark blue background. This lettering was in the new trademark style, extending its application beyond the name sign.

The boldest and most welcome touch regarding the exteriors was the introduction of blue neon tubes. This is particularly effective at night and often extended the full height of the frontages. Combined with the blue halo signs, it gave a sober and distinguished appearance to the buildings at night.

Inside, the foyers were revamped in a standard style that included walls treated with areas of lime green and orange, and wood flooring in the concessions area, demarcated from the blue carpet elsewhere by a curving line. Signage for the box office, the individual screen numbers, etc. was in the Odeon style, sometimes projected onto plain surfaces rather than mounted in silver letters. The colour theme extended right down to tickets in lime green. The one colour to be almost completely excluded was red – the key colour of the old style.

The auditoria also had a predominantly blue look, with slightly raised panels on the side walls slanting forward, curtains in front of the screens which were attractively lit at intervals in pools of magenta and other colours while "gobos" projected the Odeon name in white around the auditorium in broad sweeps.

After Camden Town, the first public use of the new signs occurred at the new Odeon multiplexes at Wrexham and Kettering, opened in late 1997. As it happened, Rank was flush with funds, part of which it put aside for "refreshing our strong brands", having just sold its remaining holding in Rank Xerox in 1997 for £940 million to its partner, Xerox. In April 1998 Rank announced plans to overhaul Odeon, building new multiplexes and refurbishing its older sites. The full rebranding was applied to the traditional sites at Swiss Cottage, Kensington, Richmond and Holloway between April and July 1998. The relatively new red signs at the earlier multiplexes were replaced to create conformity.

The introduction of blue neon works well on the brickwork at Swiss Cottage even if the halo name signs are not as forceful as the red ones they replaced, especially when viewed obliquely or seen from a distance. At this site, a new box office was established to the right of the entrance, clearing the foyer for the sale of concessions. At Holloway, the chandelier in the foyer was removed because it obstructed the beam of a new style of Odeon clock that was projected onto a side wall. At Richmond (the main Odeon, a listed building), the opportunity to reinstate the "atmospheric" ambience of the main auditorium with a sky ceiling was ignored and the foyer unsympathetically modernised but the detail here wasn't totally swamped, the raised decoration of columns being highlighted in grey on a white background and inner wooden doors surviving unpainted.

A new slogan (or "mission statement"), FANATICAL ABOUT FILM, came into use by May 1998 – possibly inspired by Pret a Manger's PASSIONATE ABOUT FOOD.

On 12 June 1998, Odeon launched the first on-line cinema booking web site in Europe. Designed by Wolff Olins, the site had a web page for each local Odeon showing films and times, with some audio and video clips of current attractions attached.

Richard Segal told *Leisureweek* (5 June 1998), "We're also making a £2.5 million investment in a new call centre to handle bookings. If we become the easiest people to book seats with, that will drive admissions." Odeon had set up a 56-desk national call centre in 1996 at Bromley for telephone bookings. In the autumn of 1998, it launched a 100-desk call centre at Stoke-on-Trent, using voice recognition software to determine which cinema a caller was intent on visiting. This gave all Odeons the same telephone number – 0870 50 50 007 – and patrons the chance to book at any time of the day or night.

By the end of 1998, major rebranding and refurbishment schemes were carried out at seventeen sites, including the Leicester Square flagship. Another third of Odeons were scheduled to be rebranded during 1999.

The rebranding of the Odeon in the centre of Glasgow was accompanied by the subdivision of the 1,142-seat auditorium which dated back to the 1970 twinning. The front half became a 555-seat auditorium, its back wall at the cross aisle. Behind the wall, three cinemas were placed side by side, seating 152, 113 and 173. The middle one was smaller because there was a new projection box behind its screen serving the auditorium in front. Externally, there was the highly welcome removal of the tall readograph and side panels above the corner entrance to allow the reinstatement the original frontage which had survived behind. Vertical neon once again reinforced the front edge of the fins and the tall intervening windows were exposed to view. However, the placement of the new name sign on the canopy weakened the effect, especially with no backing to the open letters (the original Paramount name had been perched on the curving upper edge of the building to be seen from afar).

In fact, mounting excessively large signs on the canopy, presumably to make them more accessible for maintenance, was a weak point with many rebrandings, although not all. The new sign at Richmond (main Odeon) replaced the old one high up and here the words FANATICAL ABOUT FILM were placed on the canopy and lit up with neon.

The Odeon Liverpool went from five to ten screens almost simultaneously with the rise to nine at Glasgow. The upstairs auditorium, dating from the 1968 twinning, was now split into three. The downstairs auditorium from 1968 had already been tripled in 1972 and now the largest of those three auditoria was itself tripled. A former bar had been turned into a screen in 1979. Now unused space on the original stage became a tenth screen. The nine screens (excluding the bar conversion) might be a world record, jointly shared with Glasgow, for the number to be squeezed into a former single auditorium (including stage) – Streatham follows closely with eight.

Renovation of "The Cathedral"

Rank allocated the astonishing amount of £3.5 million to a refurbishment of the Odeon Leicester Square – "The Cathedral", as Odeon now liked to call the flagship – keeping it as a single screen cinema. (This followed the new £15 million multiplex at the Warner West End behind a retained facade.) In a commendable recognition of Odeon's heritage, some of the features so wantonly destroyed in 1967 were reinstated in the "top secret" refurbishment by architects Dry Butlin Bicknell and design consultants Wolff Olins.

Externally, the shrouds came off to reveal a polished black exterior outlined in blue neon. The new style of silver name signage with blue halo was placed on the tower and now looked evenly spaced both horizontally and vertically (the old sign appeared too spread out vertically). The signage looked particularly impressive from the entrance to the Square by the Swiss Centre. Neon outlining had not been used since 1939 and by night the Odeon now looked at least as good as it had back then.

A new box office with a window onto the Square was placed to the right of new glass doors emblazoned with the message EUROPE'S LARGEST CINEMA (since changed to EUROPE'S PREMIERE THEATRE – someone must have recalled the Rex in Paris). The foyer and circle lounge had never been particularly impressive but now they were given a striking if chilly treatment and exposed to view as much as possible from the outside, creating blazes of light in the dark facade. The ceiling of the circle lounge stepped down to the rear and carried concealed lighting that could change colour.

The ground floor foyer was as spacious as possible, with the concessions counter set to the right. Here, as elsewhere, the signs indicating the foyer, circle, etc. were projected onto the walls rather than placed on them. A glass-floored staircase led up to the balcony with the aptly-named Light Café at the back and a glass bridge at the front onto a new glass-sided balcony overlooking the Square (the old canopy had been completely discarded). The balcony was devised with the particular idea that stars at premieres would be photographed (together with the Odeon sign mounted on the front edge) greeting the crowds below in the pedestrianised square.

The Royal Retiring Room in the basement was completely refurbished – hiding or removing the original plaque commemorating the opening – and seemed much smaller in its new guise as the Premiere Suite for VIPs on special occasions.

In the auditorium, the flying ladies on the splay walls were skilfully recreated from photographs by sculptor Neil Simmonds (to some observers, they seem too small but this writer thinks they are the original size). The new (and rather uncomfortable) seats were upholstered in imitation leopard skin again. And, of course, there was still the Duchess, the Compton organ which had survived all the previous changes (as had the safety curtain with elaborate decoration which is never normally seen). The grey ceiling made a rather drab impression but, above the balcony, some modest lighting was introduced to the surviving coves.

The Odeon re-opened with the UK premiere of *Armageddon* on 5 August 1998. Audiences saw new and startlingly different welcoming titles, created by Ridley Scott Associates in a dark and grungy style, that were then used throughout the circuit – the design also provided the background to programme information posters. (The titles were eventually superseded by brightly coloured ones with Caribbean music, again an unexpected touch.)

Since the re-opening, the Odeon has continued to be favoured with the occasional one-week exclusive run of top hits before their general opening nationwide. It has also continued to host many premieres of films (often opening afterwards elsewhere), as well as the BAFTA awards and the opening night of the London Film Festival.

In October 1998, it featured a stage show by the Chinese State Circus of Shandong three times daily for a week to accompany the opening of Walt Disney's Chinese-themed animation feature, *Mulan*. Prices were raised accordingly and reached a new full-price high of £15.00 for the front circle. (This live show followed an earlier one in November 1993 when all performances during the first six weeks of Walt Disney's new animated *Aladdin* were boosted by a ten-minute live stage show featuring costume characters from Euro Disney.★)

On 22 January 2000 the flagship became the first British cinema to host a wedding when two film fans exchanged vows on the stage and had their picture taken on the balcony overlooking the square. A few days later, on 4 February 2000, the

★ The Odeon had also ventured into live concerts with David Essex playing two nights in May 1996 and Bill Cosby two nights in June 1997.

Odeon hosted "Europe's first ever digital presentation" when it premiered the Disney-Pixar *Toy Story 2*. It has subsequently shown a small number of films digitally (initially, at least, backed up by a print running through the projector in case of a breakdown) but the equipment has not been used as much as Odeon had anticipated. (Presentations were promoted as being digital but, as they set out to be only as good as conventional film, cinemagoers expecting anything visibly different were disappointed unless they noticed the rock steady image. In piquant contrast to all the hugely expensive hi-tech equipment, the actual image size reaching the screen was limited top and bottom by black masking tape across the glass window through which the picture was projected.)

Further multiplexes
Some of Rank's hopes for new Odeons were dashed. In 1995, the company was reported to be going into Luton but the multiplex here became a Cineworld. In 1996, the company was linked to a 12-screen cinema in Oldham's South Union Street redevelopment to open late 1998 – but the town has yet to obtain a multiplex. Work on a six-screen Odeon at Hartlepool was expected to start in January 1997 but it was Warner Village that opened seven screens there. In early 1997, Rank wanted to create a leisure complex including a 11-screen Odeon on the site of the former London Rubber factory off the North Circular Road at Chingford (the north London suburb where Oscar Deutsch had built an Odeon in the 1930s). And Rank had 12-screen plans for a leisure park on the Great Cambridge Road, Enfield, but lost out to a 15-screen Virgin scheme nearby which went ahead. In August 1998 Odeon was named as the operator of the 12-screen multiplex in Falkirk, central Scotland on the former Biscon concrete works next to the Central Retail Park and close to the town centre. But Cineworld took over and opened there in April 2001.

Perhaps the biggest disappointment was at Bristol. In December 1998, Odeon signed up with developer Crest Nicholson to operate a split-level, 15-screen, 4000-seat cinema in the £50 million Scene At Bristol leisure complex within the wider £200 million Harbourside project in Bristol. This seems to have been reduced to 12 screens but the scheme was rejected, even after amendments, following fierce objections to the way it would spoil the view of the city's cathedral just behind.

However, every operator experienced setbacks and Odeon was successful in many other places.

Like Hemel Hempstead, Wrexham was a town where Rank had been unable to make a single-screen Odeon work (it had gone to full-time bingo back in 1976), but the company was keen to open a new multiplex. Plans were approved for a six-screen cinema in September 1996 in space previously set to become a pet food store at the out-of-town Plas Coch retail park with 465 spaces for free parking. Work started in February 1997. The owner of the existing cinema, the Hippodrome, warned that it would forced out of business to the detriment of the town centre. Rank reputedly invested £3.5 million in what turned out to be a seven-screen Odeon, opened in December 1997 with a modest total of 1,284 seats. The Hippodrome closed in March 1998.

No doubt because of the late change of intended use, the new Odeon Wrexham was externally a wide characterless shed with a massive amount of pitched grey roof barely relieved by a line of red ridge tiles. A blue canopy of traditional rectangular shape carried the new FANATICAL ABOUT FILM message on its front edge with tall, silver Odeon letters mounted on top.

The new eight-screen Odeon Kettering opened a few days later. This was situated by a Tesco store on the ring road at the junction of the A509 Wellingborough Road with the A14 (the link road to the A1/M1). Work had started in summer 1996 and the end result was a striking exterior featuring a wide, rectangular corner entrance arch with neon-lit fins at each corner and the new style of name sign mounted centrally. Bands of red and blue neon in the ceiling of the foyer could be seen through the tall window above the entrance doors. The largest auditorium offered a suggestion of traditional splay walls at the screen end.

In 1998, Rank overcame its earlier caution at Chelmsford by enlarging the four-screen cinema opened in 1993. This involved extending the foyer and constructing four more screens alongside – one at ground floor level, three more above, neatly adding nearly 600 seats to the previous total of 851. The result looks rather like a towering warehouse. The conspicuous location by the riverside walk required a high finish of brickwork on all sides, relieved by horizontal banding, an impression of rounded arches, and high up – just underneath the eaves – the slightly darker pattern of an octagonal letter O recalling the squatter style of the circuit name sign as seen lower down when the cinema first opened in 1993.

During 1998, Odeon opened no less than five new multiplexes – at Blackpool, Bridgend, Kilmarnock, Maidstone and Switch Island (Liverpool). The internal outfitting followed a design brief to which every Odeon foyer and auditorium conformed, leaving the exterior (its look often dictated by the overall development) as the most variable feature.

The first to open, on 10 July 1998, was on the western side of Scotland at Kilmarnock, with eight screens and 1,914 seats. This is one of the most impressive British multiplexes externally with its pylon sign on the main road, wavy canopy and vertical name sign mounted on a good approximation of a 1930s slab tower –

Odeon Kettering displays the new style of signage.
(July 2000 photograph by David Simpson.)

Odeon Chelmsford, expanded to eight screens with new
style of name sign – but note octagonal O in gable at top left.
(Photograph by Allen Eyles.)

a pity that the five letters weren't properly aligned with the raised horizontal banding.

This was followed by the Odeon at Maidstone, Kent. Back in February 1995, the Borough Council approved plans for a £12.5 million leisure complex on a 9-acre site it owned on the edge of the River Medway, close to the town centre. This was the old cattle market (being put to similar use to the one at Leicester). Warner Bros. was the first operator to enter into detailed discussions with the developer, Leisure England, when the centre was expected to open in autumn 1996 with a nine-screen 2,200-seat multiplex, nightclub, bingo hall and market. Reduced to eight screens with 1,638 seats, the cinema element in the new development, called Lockmeadow, passed to Odeon and opened in September 1998 as part of a Leisure World complex that also featured Rank's Jumpin Jaks theme bar and Hotshots games bar along with a nightclub, health and fitness centre and five restaurants.

Flanked by some of the restaurants, the main entrance consists of three sets of blue doors set in a recess in a tall curving frontage of plain brickwork with a large Odeon sign placed just below the roof line. While the scheme gave a boost to the town centre, it spelled the immediate end of the three-screen ABC cinema, an awkward conversion that could not compete with the Odeon.

In October 1998 came the Odeon at Switch Island, Liverpool. This large cinema (12 screens, 2556 seats) is strategically located in the Switch Island Leisure Park, five or six miles northeast of Liverpool city centre, where motorists switch between the M57, M5 and A59. Its low, wide frontage was more attractively handled than others like Bromborough: a brick base and brick towers to each side of the recessed entrance are let down by the rather crude cross-struts and structure supporting the name sign, mounted on top of what look like two giant blue speakers.

A month after Switch Island came another out-of-town Odeon near Bridgend in South Wales. Built beside the M4 motorway at the McArthur Glen Designer Outlet, this nine-screen venture with 2,100 seats reputedly represented a £4 million investment and was linked internally to the centre's food court.

The last 1998 opening took place at Blackpool in December after Rank beat off multiplex proposals for two or more other sites. This ten-screen £10 million project on a 5.6 acre site just outside the town centre has one of the circuit's best new exteriors with some streamlining reminiscent of the 1930s, especially in the two brick towers to each side of the entrance with their rounded fronts and the use of blue-edged horizontal bands.

Three new Odeons emerged in 1999 – at Coventry, Epsom and Tunbridge Wells.

At Tunbridge Wells, the local council had spent years opposing out-of-town developments before giving permission for a scheme which included the Odeon multiplex in mid-1996. Opened in February 1999, the nine-screen Odeon is close to the A21 with the usual plentiful open-air parking that out-of-town sites provide. Externally, its box-like shape is relieved by a striking entrance in blue and glass, curving forward from a central recess with a projecting glass canopy. The multiplex's location, some three miles out of town near the village of Pembury, enabled the three-screen city-centre ABC to remain in business and its closure by Odeon – soon after taking over ABC, with a restrictive covenant against further film use – drew heavy criticism.

The new Odeon Coventry forms part of a Rank Leisure World scheme, like Hemel Hempstead and Southampton. Within the Skydome retail development in the city centre, it was on the upper level, reached by escalator with plentiful parking alongside. The existing five-screen Odeon (ex-Gaumont) had become part of a quiet backwater and closed just before the new nine-screen Odeon, with 1,943 seats, was ready to open in October.

The new Odeon at Epsom, opened in December, is a very unusual development. Built in the town, at the other end from the previous Odeon (closed in 1971 and long demolished), it occupies the site of a former supermarket and offices as a stand-alone development without any parking facilities (short stay parking for 400 cars, not reserved for cinemagoers, is available at various sites nearby). This is a very attractive building, slightly inconspicuous in a narrow section of Upper High Street (its huge horizontal sign is rather wasted pointed at the shops opposite: a vertical sign visible from a distance would have been better). Despite the pressure on space associated with a central location, it has a spacious foyer and eight auditoria of substantial size and varied shape on two levels with a surprisingly high total of 2,177 seats (more than Coventry). The Odeon development may have hastened the closure of the nearby two-screen ABC Ewell in April 1998.

But further closures

The three-screen Odeon Swansea closed in December 1997, having been refurbished only two years before. According to an informed source, it was doing adequately despite competition from a 10-screen UCI (eight minutes walk away, as checked by an anxious Odeon manager – the closest multiplex competition to any of Odeon's city centre sites when it opened in the early 1990s). Closure occurred when the lease came up for renewal and the landlord demanded an increase in rent while Rank held out for a reduction. After the building stood closed for some time, Rank took out a new lease – but for its Jumpin Jaks nightclub chain.

The Odeon Barking shut down in December 1998 even

Odeon Barnet before and after rebranding.
(Top, CTA Archive. Lower, photograph by Allen Eyles.)

*Odeon Switch Island, Liverpool.
(August 2002 photograph by David Simpson.)*

though it had been subdivided into six screens and had a good location. As previously indicated, it was unable to compete with the 14-screen Showcase Newham (as well as the seven-screen Warner Village Dagenham).

More recently, Odeon has not even waited to gauge the impact of a new multiplex. The tripled Odeon Aylesbury went in October 1999: it had lost significant business to the multiplexes at High Wycombe and Milton Keynes but the final blow was the impending arrival of a six-screen ABC in the new leisure centre in the heart of town, opened in December 1999. (Since the Odeon takeover of ABC, the multiplex has been rebranded an Odeon.) And the three-screen Odeon Reading closed in November 1999 because it was obviously no match for a more centrally placed Warner Village multiplex.

Although the three-screen Odeon Burton-on-Trent initially had a better fate in being taken over by an independent in mid-1996, it closed for good in December 1999 (almost a year before the Cineworld multiplex opened in the centre of town). However, the two-screen Odeon Torquay has not only survived in the hands of an independent since 2000, but it has been converted to four screens.

Odeon Epsom. (Photograph by Allen Eyles.)

ODEONS IN COLOUR

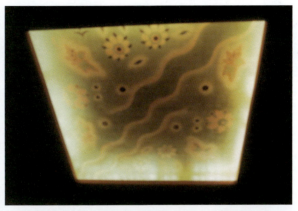

Left, original decoration survived in the ceiling over the balcony at the Odeon Boston even after it became a Classic, to be photographed in 1977 by John Fernee.

Below, the extraordinary cove lighting in the ceiling of the Odeon Hereford, still in full working order when it closed as a Classic in 1984. (Photograph by Allen Eyles.)

Decorative survivals from the 1930s. Above: a rare colour image of the left side of one of the vivid screen tabs that were a feature of 1930s Odeons. It remained, hanging behind the new screen, at Bournemouth in 1973. For the full design, see the Odeon Lancaster in black-and-white in Odeon Cinemas 1, page 85. (Photograph by John Fernee.)

Odeon Manchester. Above left, the queues are out for Goldfinger *in 1964 (CTA Archive and Adam Unger/ photograph by John Squires).*

Above right, a peeling mural discovered under wall covering behind a former kiosk during conversion work in the 1980s. (Courtesy of Carl Chesworth.)

Right, how the auditorium looked prior to the 1975 twinning. The aristocratic figures in the panels on the side wall are just visible. The faded colour may be more due to ageing of the photograph than the state of the decoration. Note the atmospheric sky ceiling. (CTA Archive.)

Four postwar interiors. Above, the main auditorium of the Odeon Worcester in 1976 but little changed since 1950. (Photograph by John Fernee.)

Odeon Sidcup as it looked on re-opening in 1954. Compare with its original appearance on page 64 of Odeon Cinemas 1. (Courtesy of Carl Chesworth.)

The auditorium of the new Odeon Sheffield in 1956. (Courtesy of Carl Chesworth.)

The auditorium of the Odeon Doncaster, the former Ritz, as refurbished by Rank in 1955. (Courtesy of Carl Chesworth.)

Odeon Newport, Gwent, as it looked in autumn 1975. The view of the auditorium makes up for the absence of an interior shot in Odeon Cinemas 1. *(Photographs by John Fernee.)*

Odeon Elephant and Castle, opened in 1966. Exterior in February 1980, auditorium in September 1981. (Photographs by Allen Eyles.)

Threatened in 1981. Odeon Twickenham in February 1981.
All but Twickenham survive in 2005 in non-cinematic uses.
(Photographs by Allen Eyles.)

Odeon Woolwich, seen here with original signage in July 1981.

Odeon Ealing (Northfields) in June 1981.

Odeon Chesterfield in October 1981.

The name sign. Left, an original sign on the side of the slab tower at Sutton Coldfield in May 2001, since replaced by smaller silver version. Centre and right, chunkier 1980s version by day and by night at the second Odeon Uxbridge in April 2001, just prior to its closure in favour of a new multiplex. (Photographs by Allen Eyles.)

The name sign, continued. Above left, the illuminated box style on the second Odeon Wimbledon lasted from 1962 until its closure in 2002, having been replaced by a new multiplex up the road. Above right, the 1980s version with "First Choice" slogan and blue background at the Capitol Odeon Cardiff in October 1998. Below and right, the sign revised at the new Odeon Springfield Quay, Glasgow, seen here in October 1998. (Photographs by Allen Eyles.)

Above, Odeon York with its special original signage of 1937 and the prohibited standard version on the canopy. Right, the balcony extended to form the largest auditorium with the ceiling retaining most of the original decoration but without any cove lighting – compare with original view on page 115 of Odeon Cinemas 1. *(September 1991 photographs by Allen Eyles.)*

Left, a section of carpet in the original 1930s style which survived at the Odeon Scarborough until closure. And, right, the 1980s style of carpet using the octagonal motif of the first letter of the Odeon name, as seen at Muswell Hill in 2002. (Photographs by Allen Eyles.)

Above, the Royal Mail recognised the iconic quality of Odeon design in the 1930s on this stamp which shows the Odeon Harrogate where the classic signage was unceremoniously dumped six years later. The stamp was issued on 16 April 1996 as part of celebrating 100 Years of Going to the Pictures, and was the only one of five to cover cinema architecture. But since when was Odeon second class?

Traditional elements in the design of the Odeon multiplex at Taunton, opened in 1994. The gleam on the neon tubes on the horizontal name sign adds to its impact. (Both courtesy of the architects, Northern Building Design Partnership.) Below right, Taunton rebranded with a new silver sign on tower in August 2002. (Photograph by Allen Eyles.)

The rebranding of the Odeon Leicester Square in 1998 with new entrance and foyer (including projected signs identifying stalls and stairs to circle), the return of the leopard skin pattern to the seats (plus sprinkling of popcorn before the cleaners arrived), and the reinstatement of the flying ladies. For the exterior by night, see back cover. (Photographs by Allen Eyles.)

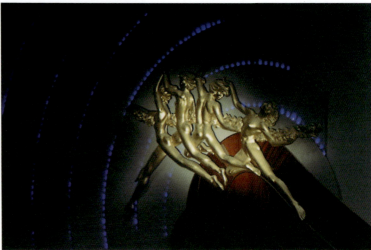

The exterior of the Odeon Ipswich revives 1930s art deco and ocean-liner streamlining. The horizontal banding is reminiscent of many pre-war Odeons. It has been rebranded with new signage in this 2003 view. The spacious three-level foyer has splendid art deco light fittings and other touches. Architects: Northern Building Design Partnership. (Photographs by Allen Eyles.)

Below, CTA member David Daykin was outside the Odeon Harrogate on 8 April 2002 to record the new sign being lowered into position on the front edge of the canopy, well below the original sign which had been good enough to draw patrons for more than sixty-five years. The safety rail around the word "Cinema" on the fin was an unfortunate addition made several years ago. See front cover of Odeon Cinemas 1.

Recent multiplexes. Above, Odeon Kilmarnock, opened in 1998.
(Photograph by David Simpson.)

Odeon Tunbridge Wells, opened in 1999.
(Photograph by David Simpson.)

The foyer of the Odeon Coventry.
(Courtesy of Northern Building Design Associates.)

The second Odeon multiplex in Lincoln, opened in 2001.
(Photograph by David Simpson.)

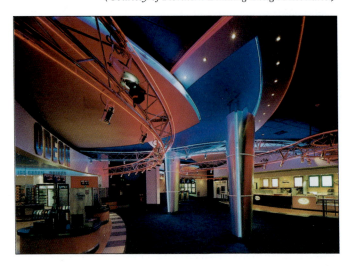

THE SALE AND AFTERWARDS

A new chief executive, Mike Smith, came from Ladbroke's (gambling to hotels) to take charge of The Rank Group from 1 April 1999. Faced with debts of £1.3 billion, Smith instituted cost cuts and disposals. In November 1999, he sold Rank's thirty-five nightclubs, nine Jumpin Jaks and six Hotshots establishments and other related businesses for £150 million. And he had already ordered Odeon Cinemas, with its seventy-five sites, to be auctioned off.

So, after seventy-seven years of single ownership, the business on which the Rank empire had been founded was put up for sale by a chief executive of six months' standing. Of course, there is no room for sentiment in business – and, over the years, many in the film business had prayed that Rank would sell its film interests, wanting to see them in more dynamic hands. But Odeon was not a distress sale. The chain was going great guns – it was reported that Rank had invested over £90 million in the past three years and built up a 26.5 per cent market share.

Odeon was acquired by venture capitalists Cinven for £280 million in a deal completed on 18 February 2000. Rank subsequently reported a profit of £130.4 million from the transaction.

The following month, Pinewood Studios were sold for £62 million to a management team headed by Michael Grade. The Group's half share in Florida's Universal Studios theme park (opened in 1990) also went, along with the holiday business (including Butlin's) and the Tom Cobleigh pubs. Mike Smith told shareholders: "The development of 'New Rank' will centre on our gaming and Hard Rock Café activities."

Rank retains its film processing and video/DVD duplicating plants in early 2005 but the financial press reports that they are about to be sold off or demerged. It has become primarily a gambling and restaurant concern. Of course, it still retains some former cinemas as part of its chain of Mecca bingo halls, but many have been replaced by purpose-built new clubs and most of the survivors have been drastically altered (having usually been on bingo longer than they played films).

The Rank Group has a worldwide chain of over one hundred Hard Rock Cafés, owns Grosvenor Casinos, runs slot machines, has opened the first in a proposed chain of Hard Rock Casinos and purchased the online bookmaker Blue Square as well as launching Hard Rock Casinos online. J. Arthur Rank must be rotating in his grave. It is not a company that he would recognise – or would want to carry his name. It is a pity that when it changed its name it did not become The Mecca Group.

Under new ownership

Under Cinven, the new Odeon company set up its headquarters in Whitcomb Street in London's West End – in the space occupied by the booking department which had originally been the dressing rooms of the Leicester Square Theatre with its stage door entrance. Richard Segal continued as chief executive with the same team of supporting executives. Regarding the purchase price, Segal informed me that "certain third party liabilities within Odeon, which principally related to the construction of new cinemas, resulted in a net cash payment of £272 million. At the time of the deal, contracts for multiplexes had been signed by Odeon for a further ten sites in various stages of development. Of these ten sites, Odeon chose not to proceed with a development in Gloucester."*

The £8 million was taken off the sale price primarily in exchange for relieving Rank of its commitment to completing three multiplexes under construction. Segal identified the nine sites as Dunfermline, Thornbury (also known as Leeds/ Bradford), Dundee, Uxbridge, Lincoln, Colchester, Wimbledon, Kingston and Newcastle. These multiplexes had all opened by the end of

* In October 1998, Rank signed up to become the anchor tenant with a ten-screen, first-floor Odeon in a Crest Nicholson Properties leisure development at Gloucester Docks. The scheme was opposed by the City Council which preferred a rival proposal elsewhere that included a Virgin multiplex to replace its existing six-screen cinema. The scheme with the Odeon gained planning permission on appeal in February 2000 but no new multiplex has appeared here or anywhere else in Gloucester. (Previously, in late 1996, Rank had been interested in an out-of-town 12-screen multiplex at Barnwood, close to the M5, but presumably this had been doomed by the changes in government planning policy described earlier.)

2002 and, having been conceived under Rank, they will be covered here along with the continuation of the rebranding exercise.

Cinven had already spent £68 million backing the acquisition of almost all Virgin's stock of traditional cinemas by a new ABC Cinemas company. These were now amalgamated with the Odeon circuit. This had the unfortunate effect of closing some ABC cinemas in competition with Odeon that might well have remained open otherwise. At Streatham, the ABC closed on the last day of 2000 – but most of the proceeds were applied to upgrading and further subdividing the Odeon to create an eight-screen complex. At the same time, a considerable sum was spent on refurbishing the more useful ABCs (including its handful of multiplexes) and in some cases subdividing them before rebranding them as Odeons.

Nine multiplexes

Originally scheduled to open in 1999, the ten-screen Odeon Dunfermline finally made its debut in July 2000. Located in the Fife Leisure Park outside the town at Halbeath, close to the M90, it obviated the need for cinemagoers to cross the Firth of Forth into Edinburgh. The three-screen independent cinema in the centre of Dunfermline had already closed.

A week after Dunfermline came the new Odeon in a leisure park at Thornbury, two miles east of Bradford city centre. This £5 million development was Odeon's largest multiplex to date, with 13 screens and over 3,000 seats. Odeon signs were placed just above the double entrance doors while a projecting fin higher up carried the name of the leisure park. Glazed projections, V-shaped in plan, extending from the ground to the roof, broke up the walls of the long, low shed containing the cinemas. In this area, there was scope to play Bollywood films on some of the screens. The very conspicuous three-screen Odeon in the centre of Bradford closed a few days before the opening. The new cinema advertised itself as the Odeon Bradford/Leeds. The existing Odeon in the centre of Leeds shut down in October 2001 – this former key theatre was doomed by a new city centre Ster Century multiplex with stadium seating. Bradford has obtained a city centre Cineworld multiplex, leaving the new Odeon most attractive to out-of-town trade.

Three Odeon multiplexes arrived in 2001. First came Uxbridge in March. The town's third Odeon brought the company right into the heart of the town for the first time, to the upper regions of The Chimes shopping centre, with nine screens in place of the two at the preceding Odeon, which closed after a brief life of ten years. The multiplex has two entrances: one from within the shopping centre and the other from the Piazza off the High Street (providing access when the shopping centre is closed).

The original Odeon multiplex in Lincoln was an unprepos-

sessing industrial shed in an out-of-the-way retail park. There was alarm when Virgin came sniffing for a site in the town in 1997. When space was allocated for a multiplex in a central development at Brayford Wharf, Odeon secured it and opened there with nine screens and nearly twice as many seats in October 2001. Built at the upper levels of the development, the new Odeon has a tall glazed entrance on the edge of the water. However, the bulk of the auditoria makes a rather ponderous impression, despite a curving roof treatment echoing the top of the entrance.

Dundee was another town in which the initial Odeon multiplex was replaced. The six-screen Odeon opened in 1993 had found itself in a declining leisure park where more than half the units had closed and it had no hope of standing up to the 11-screen Virgin multiplex which opened in September 1999 with stadium seating. Odeon decided to take up a multiplex opportunity in the new Eclipse Leisure Park at Douglasfield and construction started the month before the Virgin opened. The existing Odeon lingered on until March 2001, past the scheduled opening date of the replacement, but there was still a gap of eight months before the new Odeon opened in November 2001 with ten screens and 2,557 seats.

Almost a year later came the Odeon multiplex at Colchester. Odeon's plans in late 1996 for a multiplex in the town's Cowdrey Avenue had been turned down along with a rival Cineworld scheme in Tollgate. The authorities consistently rejected proposals for out-of-town multiplexes but plans were approved for a town centre scheme in Head Street, just around the corner from the existing Odeon. Warner Village signed up for this, then withdrew at a late stage enabling Odeon to move in after much basic work had been done.

There were eight screens totalling 1,421 seats. This was not much more than the six screens and 1,271 seats in the old Odeon, which had been fully rebranded – but, except for the largest auditorium (in the former balcony), these were way below today's audience expectations in terms of space and sightlines. The existing facade on the new site in Head Street had to be retained, looking nothing like a cinema and comparing unfavourably with the elegant Spanish exterior of its predecessor. Although illuminated signs are not normally permitted above ground floor level in the town centre, Odeon was allowed to put up a huge two-sided vertical name sign on the new building because it had a similar, if smaller, sign on the peak of the old one. This helps overcome the forbidding exterior.

Once inside, the new Odeon Colchester is completely modern. A lofty outer hall features a upper white wall with a rectangular recess providing a screen on which images can be projected. A lower main foyer leads to two cinemas at the back at ground level and an escalator to the other screens spread out above. The upstairs screens have full stadium seating.

Back in 1933, the second Odeon cinema in Oscar Deutsch's fledgling chain had opened in Kingston-upon-Thames. It had gone over to bingo from 1967 to 1987, then been demolished. In October 2002, a day or two after launching Colchester, Odeon returned to Kingston with a vengeance, opening its largest multiplex containing fourteen cinemas (originally announced as sixteen) on a more central site than its earlier hall. The foyer and cinemas were on an upper floor of The Rotunda, a development which also includes shops and restaurants. (The corner entrance was once the site of a small cinema.) The new auditoria have been skilfully incorporated into the former Bentall's Depository, a local landmark and listed building which retains its external appearance. Immediately next door stood the closed ex-Granada, recent home to three cinemas (latterly run by ABC) and a large nightclub.

In Newcastle-on-Tyne, there was some consternation when the existing four-screen Odeon was suddenly made a listed building in October 2000 after a deal had been signed for the company to run a twelve-screen, second floor multiplex as the anchor tenant of a city centre leisure scheme, The Gates. The new Odeon opened in November 2002 with 2,538 seats. The old one (with 1,998 seats) closed two days earlier.

Opened in 1931 by Paramount and elaborately designed in the style of some of its American movie palaces, the former Odeon warranted listing even though it had suffered considerable modifications over the years to its glorious interior (particularly the application of the zing treatment and the subsequent reversible subdivision into four screens). It remains standing in early 2005 and has seen occasional concert use. With a far-sighted local authority and considerable funding, it could be restored to become a remarkable performing arts venue that would revitalise the immediate area and add significantly to the town's already impressive cultural renaissance. One has only to visit the finely restored auditoria of the Paramounts at Aurora, Illinois, and Oakland, California, to see the potential that was crassly ignored when the building was de-listed without proper debate after a mere ten months (thereby making a mockery of the listing process).

When it first appeared as the Regal in 1933, the existing Odeon Wimbledon had been another outstanding example of cinema architecture with an imposing grey stone facade and a vigorous internal decorative scheme by Mollo and Egan. Later called the Gaumont, it took the Odeon name a discreet interval after the original Odeon, in Worple Road, had closed. Converted to five screens, the second Odeon had become uncomfortable and run down, too mutilated to make a convincing case for listing.

Wimbledon's third Odeon, which arrived in December 2002, was more centrally placed than either of its predecessors. The layout is rather unusual with an awkwardly arranged ground floor entrance that contains an escalator to the much more spacious foyer above. Five of the twelve screens are just beyond the foyer while the rest are in the other half of the development, reached by an enclosed bridge over a pedestrian thoroughfare.

It is worth noting how Odeon has become the dominant player in the southwest London area with its new cinemas at Epsom, Kingston and Wimbledon and its older properties at Richmond and Streatham as well as the two former ABCs it has rebranded at Esher and Putney. The competition is provided by four multiplexes: the UCI Sutton, the two Vues (ex-Warner Village) at Croydon, and the Cineworld at Wandsworth.

The completion of rebranding

Various rebrandings had been carried out in the past but this one was different in encompassing every site on the circuit with standardised foyers and full interior redecoration in new house colours (the reduced number of sites did simplify the task). Some rebrandings were accompanied by further subdivision of traditional Odeons.

From early 2001, the faience tiling in the narrow concave frontage at Bromley was floodlit at night and outlined by two strips of blue neon while a curved canopy replaced the old V-shaped readograph, closer in style to the first canopy in 1936. A new name sign across the top of this canopy copies the position of the original one (and perhaps makes the additional vertical signs redundant). The long-lost curving caps to each wing and central flagpole have not been reinstated.★

When the Odeon Streatham was rebranded in 2001, three more screens were added to make a total of eight. The overly wide front stalls cinema was sensibly halved into two smaller auditoria. The huge balcony seated an excessive 1,000 and the side rear sections were enclosed to create two new screens. This left a very awkward, T-shaped cinema seating 451, opening out for a few rows at the balcony front. Total seating capacity was now 1,485 (compared to 2,614 in 1930).

Rebranding became more problematical at the traditional Odeons which had become listed buildings as, in contrast to the

★ Several multiplexes have been proposed for Bromley, and the London Borough commissioned a study of available sites in 1998. No scheme has proceeded so far, although Odeon was tentatively attached to a 12-screen venture in 1997 (*Screen International*, 24 January). A 20-screen UCI Filmworks scheme in the same Borough at Crystal Palace – firmly quashed on 11 May 2001 after a massive protest campaign on environmental grounds – had inhibited investment in existing and proposed cinemas over a wide area (including Streatham) for many years.

approach taken at the unlisted Leicester Square flagship, the company generally sought to bury historic features beneath the new look it regarded as essential to attracting custom in the multiplex era.

At Barnet, improved signage was seen as a large silver Odeon name was mounted on the canopy and a smaller one placed higher up, above the arches. Blue neon strip lighting was introduced on the building's side towers, reminiscent of that installed pre-war. Applying the standard new look to the foyers involved complex negotiations before listing building consent was granted, and certainly the upper foyer gained a brightness and welcoming feel that it had lacked for many years with a much improved light fitting suspended over the central well in place of the tacky plastic one that had taken over from the 1935 art deco original.

Still only a three-screen cinema, the Odeon Muswell Hill had come under pressure from multiplexes in the area, especially two which opened in close proximity at Wood Green. I was informed that, if the Odeon took more than a 15 per cent "hit" from the new competition, it would become loss-making and close. The rebranding in 2002 was a welcome indication that it had survived the new competition. Externally, silver name signs were introduced both at canopy level (where the 1936 Odeon sign had been) and at the top (where the name sign had been resited for the past thirty or more years), while neon – blue, of course – was placed in some (but not all) of the grooves provided for that purpose when it opened. The foyers and balcony lounge received much needed redecoration although this resulted in inappropriate areas of dark blue (easily reversible at some future date but quite a contrast to the more sensitive refurbishment in the 1980s). Work in the balcony included re-stepping the front section to provide greater leg room between rows, putting in some double "love seats", and applying the new house colours everywhere – with dark blue areas again disrupting the decorative effect. Unfortunately, the glass panels in the lighting strip across the ceiling were not cleaned. In a half-hearted nod to the building's historical significance, some spare rolls of old carpet were laid down – not in the classic 1930s design (which is available – the late Museum of the Moving Image ordered some for its Odeon-style foyer) – but of the design introduced in 1985 featuring clusters of the since outmoded octagonal letter O on a dark blue background. A more imaginative approach would have been to restore its 1936 appearance and differentiate it from competing multiplexes with a leaning towards more sophisticated programming (although this would have hurt the nearby Phoenix East Finchley, another listed cinema which has adopted that policy). The rebranding at Muswell Hill overlooked the dilapidated entrance sign to the car park at the rear which continued to display the classic Odeon logo in red.

The Odeon Sutton Coldfield and its twin, the Odeon Harrogate, were listed buildings in which the foyers and auditoria had been drastically altered. Certainly, the exteriors were more significant – they were the quintessence of the circuit style. Although Sutton Coldfield had lost its projecting fin with the word CINEMA on the sides, both Odeons retained a name sign in the original 1930s style on the righthand wall of the recess above the entrance (see back cover). The one at Sutton Coldfield had been remounted on battens but that at Harrogate remained directly attached to the faience behind. (Further name signs on the faience-clad side wall had long been removed – in Sutton Coldfield's case then placed vertically on the back of the projecting slab tower.)

These name signs had survived over sixty years. They were the last ones in the classic trademark style still in their original positions. They were now removed, but listed building consent should never have been granted. However, their significance was at least recognised at Sutton Coldfield as the company was required to store the letters in perspex cases on the premises. As it happened, at both sites the new silver signs were mounted lower down, on the curving edge of the entrance, so the old signs were not in the way and could have been left to make a contrast. If they had to be removed, the new ones should have been placed in the same position to keep as close to the original overall design as possible. They should not have had the standard blue backlighting – it should either have been green to match in with the green bands across the faience or red to correspond with the red neon on the old signs.

The Odeon company was on stronger economic grounds arguing for a new look at Sutton Coldfield. This cinema was harmed by the 30-screen Warner Village at StarCity and had declined into a cut-price local alternative (the modern equivalent of the fleapits that Odeon had always risen above). The neon on the name sign no longer worked and the readograph displayed a miscellany of twee pink letters after the original letters (red with a black edge) were apparently stolen. Here as elsewhere, Odeon seemed happy to let sites become really run down so that the rebranding would make more of an impression. At least when the silver sign has had its run, the original signs will be handy for reinstatement.

No requirement to preserve the original Odeon sign was imposed at Harrogate. Although it was saved from the skip and is being carefully preserved, the authorities in a town as sensitive to its heritage as Harrogate should never have waved through the sign's removal. The cinema was profitable enough to warrant £1 million worth of capital investment. Had the company been required to retain the original sign, either with or without the new version lower down, it is hard to imagine that it would make the slightest difference to the number of people attending the cinema after all the other changes. This was the only cinema in Harrogate and there was no threat of a multiplex.

As at Sutton Coldfield, the tall foyer retained its low false ceiling as it was given the modern make-over. Like Sutton Coldfield, the Odeon already had four screens but re-branding here was accompanied by the splitting of the balcony into two, increasing the number of cinemas to five. The two in the balcony were fitted out with matching walls of forward-sloping panels, modern seating and carpeting, and new screens with curtains. Only the original ceiling with its ventilation grilles and recessed lighting remained visible.

In the 1930s the trademark Odeon sign and use of faience tiles had been considered too brash for cinemas built in the historic cities of Chester and York. With a flexibility lacking in more recent times, circuit founder Oscar Deutsch agreed to put up the Odeon name in more acceptable Trajan lettering and to have entirely brick exteriors.

The Odeons at Chester and York went on to become listed buildings, retaining their alternative signage. They had somehow delivered satisfactory returns for decades despite the stigma of being different in appearance to Odeons elsewhere. Both had been tripled in a more elaborate than usual fashion with the balconies extended forward to the screen. At Chester, the number of screens had been raised to five in 1991 by inserting an extra screen on each side at the back of the balcony. Both Odeons now suffered from out-of-town multiplex competition (and the Odeon at York also had a new three-cinema City Screen complex in the town centre). No one could dispute Odeon's argument that it was essential to refurbish and upgrade these cinemas if they were to stay open.

At Chester, the original name sign was retired after surviving more than sixty years. It had been positioned high up, on the right side of the frontage, to be visible from the town centre along Northgate Street. The silver replacement sign sits lower down, on the right end of the canopy, similarly off centre but not visible for anything like the same distance. However, two vertical blue neon strips rise the full height of the frontage at this end. As elsewhere, the interior has been thoroughly rebranded but the small display of historic artefacts taken from the site before building began is still to be found in the upstairs lounge.

At York, Odeon ran into the only intractable opposition to its rebranding programme. In the refusal of listed building consent for external alterations dated 2 October 2003, the old sign seems to have been the only sticking point. Jonathan Carr, Development Control Officer, informed the Cinema Theatre Association:

"The Council considers that the proposed removal of the existing high level lettering and replacement by new letters in the corporate Odeon style would result in the loss of an important and bespoke architectural feature of the building, to the detriment of its character and appearance."

If only such obduracy had been expressed by Harrogate Borough Council! I haven't nearly so much enthusiasm for retaining a sign that was a compromise in the first place (and where the orange neon no longer worked). However, as it has been a feature of such long standing, an arrangement on the lines of Sutton Coldfield (placing the sign in storage on the premises) – or its donation to a local museum of repute – would, in my opinion, provide a satisfactory solution. As a compromise, the old sign might be left in situ, unlight at night, and a new sign placed at canopy level.

And so the Odeon York remains the one cinema where none of the rebranding has been carried out. Rather ominously, Odeon announced publicly that its viability was under review, although it is still functioning in early 2005. It has been offered to other operators: none were interested but, if they had been, they would have wanted the old name sign removed.*

In the past, as indicated in this book, many Rank properties have been sold as going concerns or to be re-opened by independent operators. When Odeon closed both its cinema and the ABC in Norwich on the same day in October 2000, shortly after the town's second multiplex had opened, it allowed a local chain to re-open the Odeon. Under the new name of Hollywood Cinemas, it seems to be flourishing as the owners have obtained permission to double the number of screens to six.

Further casualties and survivors

As previously mentioned, new signage was erected outside the Odeon Haymarket in London's West End while it was closed during building works in the offices above. By now a little off

---

* Odeon's willingness to let York go to another operator is in contrast to its application of restrictive covenants on many other properties it has sold, preventing anyone else from showing films – usually to assist other cinemas it held or planned to build in the same area. While he was managing director, Richard Segal insisted that it was standard practice, that Odeon itself had been affected by such covenants and that, in any case, the covenants could be lifted for a price. This issue caused most furore at Whiteladies, Bristol, where the ABC, which came under Odeon control when Cinven merged the two circuits, was closed with such a covenant. However, these covenants go back a long way: a few years ago, when City Screen explored the possibility of returning the Blue Hall Annexe at 46 Essex Road, Islington, north London, to cinema use (it closed in 1941), Odeon refused to lift the covenant there, fearing a detrimental affect on attendances at Holloway.

the most heavily beaten track, it had been struggling to find suitable films but offered one of the most spacious and well-proportioned auditoria still left in the West End. The Odeon company advertised it as "closed for refurbishment" in 2000 and then closed due to "essential remedial work" before deciding not to re-open it at all.

The Odeon Nottingham, which had survived the threat of the out-of-town Showcase, succumbed in January 2001 to a new city centre Warner Village (later UGC) multiplex.

The Odeon Middlesbrough shut in June 2001, a few weeks after a 11-screen, 2,800-seat UGC multiplex opened there. It was converted into a Jumpin Jaks nightclub.

At Edinburgh, Manchester and St. Helier, Odeons were rebranded despite impending or existing multiplex competition, but the new look did not save them from closure.

Edinburgh became hugely over-seated with the new 12-screen city-centre Warner Village being the last straw for the Odeon on Clerk Street. This listed building had substantial but fully reversible alterations to its once notable atmospheric auditorium in Greek amphitheatre style (see *Gaumont British Cinemas*, pages 174-5). After the cinema's closure in August 2003, a new four-screen Odeon with specialised programming (in the basement of the redevelopment behind the facade of the former ABC) enabled the chain to resume its presence in the city a few days later. Five of the auditoria in the old Odeon became venues for Edinburgh Festival comedy shows in the summer of 2004, but it seems likely that the frontage will be preserved while the far more important auditorium will be demolished for flats, shops and restaurants, consolidating Scotland's disgraceful record of failing to preserve the best aspects of its few notable cinemas.

In Manchester, the Odeon had been turned into an ad hoc multiplex with seven screens back in 1992 and it seemed sufficiently distant from the more successful Filmworks (with twenty screens) to survive (the closer 12-screen AMC should have damaged it more, but its arrival made little impression). In 1997, Odeon 1 was refurbished with 617 new seats. The stepping was comparable to stadium seating, digital sound was introduced, and the picture size was claimed to be the largest in Manchester. However, the Odeon's viability was being reassessed in summer 2004 and its closure followed at short notice on 2 September. The building was thought to have been sold off for complete redevelopment.

The Odeon St. Helier halved its admission prices to compete with Cineworld's new 10-screen multiplex at the Docks in Jersey but then closed suddenly in October 2004. It was in excellent shape to the end. It has been re-opened as a cinema by an independent.

In Glasgow, the Odeon Renfield Street had kept going after the opening of the circuit's multiplex on the other side of the River Clyde. It seems to have been finally overcome by the city centre 18-screen "killerplex" devised by Virgin and opened by UGC just a short distance away. The Odeon was promptly B-listed by Historic Scotland and its lease was reported to have been offered to eleven other operators who turned it down. The building was sold to a property company which has promised to return the art deco facade to almost its original condition in exchange for redeveloping the interior for retail use. Odeon have found it worth taking a rolling lease to continue operating the cinema on three months' notice while the developer finalises his plans.

Some older sites have fared better. The Odeons at Birmingham and Liverpool are de facto multiplexes in the centre of town. Birmingham still has its low-slung entrance but there are now only hints of its original art deco interior. It suffered from the nearby redevelopment of the Bull Ring but has benefited from the surge of shoppers to the area since the launch of the new shopping complex. Apart from the tiny Electric, it is the only city centre cinema with the UGC and AMC multiplexes in direct competition a mile distant at Five Ways. The Odeon Liverpool also has the city centre to itself apart from the new Picturehouse at FACT, hidden away in Wood Street.

Bournemouth offers the rare sight of an ABC and Odeon in peaceful co-existence. The Odeon company had hoped to replace both with a 12-screen multiplex on the site of the former bus station but, as long as this or any other scheme doesn't proceed, the two should remain open to provide the equivalent of a multiplex with nine screens and a hefty total of 3,221 seats between them, including 757 seats in the still impressive former roadshow auditorium at the Odeon.

The Odeon Doncaster remains an anomaly with just three screens. The largest with 975 seats (the former balcony and front stalls) had hosted some live shows but the licence was dropped in March 1997. It has survived the arrival several years ago of an out-of-town Warner Village multiplex (now Vue).

The three-screen Odeon Harlow has utilised low prices, a central location and astute management to compete against a six-screen UGC (ex Cannon/Virgin) multiplex a good mile away on a retail warehouse estate – ironically, not far from where the town's first cinema, the Regal, had been temporarily established in a warehouse unit. The Odeon's low-price strategy was directly inspired by the tactics successfully adopted by "the enemy", the ABC/Cannon at Romford, to stay in business after the new Odeon multiplex opened there. The Odeon Harlow was refurbished and upgraded to stereo sound in all three screens in 1994 and the more recent rebranding made it a welcoming alternative to the multiplex which has been badly showing its age.

The Odeon Portsmouth has also followed the cut price route to survive the arrival of the six-screen UCI at Port Solent in 1994 and the much greater threat of the 11-screen Warner Village on the Gun Wharf waterfront site in Portsmouth itself, although its condition (especially the landmark tower) gives cause for concern.

Seven screens have been forced into the Odeon at Cheltenham where a scheme for a 10-screen Warner Village multiplex was dropped in early 2001. But, in 2005, the Odeon faces the imminent arrival of a 11-screen Cineworld.

And the threats continue. Apollo Cinemas are intent on running a seven-screen cinema in a new leisure centre on the seafront at Weston-super-Mare, which may be open by the autumn of 2006. This will seriously threaten the viability of the four-screen Odeon, rightly listed for being one of the very best examples of the original 1930s circuit style.

Besides those directly mentioned, rebranding has given new vigour to the pre-multiplex Odeons at Ayr, Barnsley, Brighton, Bristol, Exeter and Worcester.

Postscript

Since changing ownership for the first time in its history in 2000, Odeon has been sold twice. In March 2003, a group headed by the German bank WestLB purchased Odeon from Cinven for £431 million, much more than many observers (and the heads of the chain) thought it was worth. Following the sudden departure of chief executive Richard Segal a few months later and disagreements among the investors, Odeon was put up for auction in June 2004. It was bought by Terra Firma for circa £400 million at the end of August, at which time the same private equity firm also acquired the UCI chain. An agreed divestment of sites to reduce competition in areas such as southwest London to comply with demands from the Office of Fair Trading, could result in the sale of some Odeons. No doubt the UCI name will be replaced by that of Odeon, making the latter much more widespread – if not as omnipresent as it once was under Rank.

When Richard Segal left Odeon, he was able to refer, with obvious pride, to "an estate of cinemas which is unrecognisable from that which existed a few years ago" (*Screen International*, 1 August 2003). I hope that this two-volume history conveys both what Odeon did look like and what it has become. There is much to admire in the forthright way that Odeon has reclaimed a leading place in British film exhibition. It is to be hoped that the company will stay in the forefront with its own clear identity and attract long-term commitment and imaginative refining of its assets.

As true now as when this advertisement appeared (in colour) in The Hollywood Reporter *in 1990.*

THE ODEON RELEASE 1942 - 1979

These are the films that received an Odeon circuit general release, listed in order of appearance in the London suburbs, beginning in the northwest (later north) London area. London West End premiere runs of main features would have normally taken place some weeks earlier and "pre-release" bookings in key cities and holiday areas would have often occurred. (A record of films shown at Odeons from 1938 to 1941 was included in the first volume. A record of films shown at the Odeon Leicester Square from 1937 to 1987 – most of which received an Odeon circuit release – was published in *Picture House* no.11, Winter 1987/88.)

Films listed in brackets were B features or supporting features given minor advertising space compared to the main feature and they were often changed around outside London. Double bills were also sometimes reconfigured. It has not been possible to identify all the shorts and Disney cartoons that were included in programmes. Odeons also played various newsreels (except Pathe News), then the *Look At Life* replacement "interest" series from 1959.

Some Odeons did not play the circuit release because of proximity to other Odeons while some mixed Odeon programmes with other releases.

Abbreviations:
TMA 1 etc. = *short film* This Modern Age No.1 etc.
MOT 1 etc. = *short film* March Of Time No.1 etc.

1942

Birth Of The Blues (+ The Seventh Survivor)
Unfinished Business (+ Private Nurse)
Suspicion [*also Gaumont circuit main feature release*] (+ Jail House Blues)
Sullivan's Travels (+ Penn of Pennsylvania)
Hatter's Castle (+ Henry Aldrich For President)
Hold That Ghost (+ The Great Man's Lady)
Lydia (+ Mexican Spitfire's Baby)

They Met In Bombay (+ Unexpected Uncle)
Kathleen + China Seas *revival*
Great Guns + The Gay Falcon
Belle Starr + Moon Over Her Shoulder
Shadow Of The Thin Man (+Buy Me That Town)
Blood And Sand
Louisiana Purchase (+ Last Of The Duanes)
Lady For A Night + Hearts In Springtime
Paris Calling (+ Radio Revels Of 1942)
Hoppity Goes To Town + Easy Living *revival*
Keep 'Em Flying (+ Man At Large)
The Lady Has Plans (+ Mexican Spitfire At Sea)
Bahama Passage (+ Torpedo Boat)
Babes On Broadway
Confirm Or Deny + Trouble Brewing *revival*
Day Will Dawn (+ Young America)
Reap The Wild Wind (+ Almost Married)
Remember The Day (+ Blue White And Perfect)
They Flew Alone (+ Secret of G.32)
Saboteur (+ Night In New Orleans)
The Spoilers (+ Don't Get Personal)
My Favorite Blonde + Rise And Shine
One Of Our Aircraft Is Missing (+ Henry and Dizzy)
Beyond The Blue Horizon (+ Missing Million)
Let The People Sing (+ The Saint In Palm Springs)
Green Eyed Woman (+Those Kids From Town)
The Gold Rush *revival* (+ True To The Army)
Holiday Inn (+ Lady From Lisbon)
Song Of The Islands (+ Sabotage At Sea)
First Of The Few (+ The Mad Martindales)
The Goose Steps Out (+ Dr. Broadway)
The Palm Beach Story + Salute John Citizen
Secret Mission (+ Timber)
Rings On Her Fingers (+ A Gentleman At Heart)
Miss Annie Rooney (+ I Live On Danger)
The Glass Key (+ Whispering Ghosts)
My Gal Sal (+ About Face)
The Great Mr. Handel + Bluebeard's Eighth Wife *revival*

Coastal Command [*also Gaumont circuit main feature release*] + Are Husbands Necessary?
Who Done It? + The Great Impersonation
The Forest Rangers (+ Thru' Different Eyes)
We'll Smile Again (+ My Heart Belongs To Daddy)
The Magnificent Dope (+ Men Of Destiny)
Road To Morocco (+ Wrecking Crew)
The Pied Piper (+ Henry Aldrich, Editor)

1943

Sherlock Holmes And The Secret Weapon + Moonlight In Havana
The Major And The Minor (+ Hi, Neighbour)
Nightmare + Mrs. Wiggs Of The Cabbage Patch *revival*
Wake Island (+ The Falcon's Brother)
The Navy Comes Through + Asking For Trouble
George Washington Slept Here (+ Little Tokyo USA)
A-Haunting We Will Go + My Son Alone
Happy Go Lucky (+ The Brains Trust)
The Moon And Sixpence + Lady Bodyguard
Footlight Serenade + Natasha
The Silver Fleet + East Side Of Heaven *revival*
Social Enemy No. 1 + Manila Calling
Once Upon A Honeymoon (+ Youth On Parade)
The Immortal Sergeant (+ He's My Guy)
Star Spangled Rhythm (+ Underground Agent)
I Married A Witch (+ Seven Miles From Alcatraz)
The Amazing Mrs. Holliday (+ Everything Happens To Us)
Shadow Of A Doubt (+ Submarine Alert)
No Time For Love + Night Plane From Chungking
Lucky Jordan + The Story Of Stalingrad
The Gentle Sex (+ Keep 'Em Slugging)
Old Mother Riley, Detective + Escape To Happiness *revival*

The Crystal Ball + Algiers *revival*
The Black Swan (+ Taxi, Mister)
Man And His Mate + Salute For Three
We Dive At Dawn + Next Time We Live
China + When We Are Married
Flight For Freedom (+ High Explosive)
This Land Is Mine + Young And Willing
The Life And Death Of Colonel Blimp
Forever And A Day (+ Prairie Chickens)
Undercover + Sing, You Sinners *revival*
Hit The Ice + Aerial Gunner
Five Graves To Cairo (+ Cowboy In Manhattan)
Background To Danger (+ Henry Swings It)
The Flemish Farm + Man About Town *revival*
Striptease Lady + Margin For Error
The Rains Came *revival* + Tonight We Raid
    Calais
Mr. Lucky (+ Fiesta)
Coney Island (+ The Glory of Sebastopol *short*
    + MOT no.2)
White Captive (+ Dixie Dugan)
Escape To Danger (+ The Good Fellows)
Dixie (+ He Hired The Boss)
They Met In The Dark (+ Jacaré)
My Friend Flicka (+ The Falcon Strikes Back)
So Proudly We Hail (+ World Of Plenty *short*)
Stage Door Canteen
Bombardier + The Doctor Takes A Wife *revival*
True To Life (+ Saludos Amigos *short* + MOT
    no.4 *short*)
Bachelor Mother *revival* + Bombers' Moon
The Demi-Paradise (+ Mexican Spitfire's
    Blessed Event)
Let's Face It (+ Alaska Highway)

1944

* *Main film in top twelve most successful films
of the year*

Claudia (+ The Iron Road)
The Sky's The Limit (+ The Volunteer *short*)
The Miracle Of Morgan's Creek + The Cat
    And The Canary *revival*
Wuthering Heights *revival*; *or* Captains
    Courageous *revival* (+ It's In The Bag)
The Night Is Ending (+ Lovely To Look At
    revival)
Behind The Rising Sun + Top Man
And The Angels Sing (+ The Kansan)
*Jane Eyre (+ Cinderella Swings It)
The Nelson Touch + The Golden Hour *revival*
The Girl He Left Behind (+ Ladies' Day)
Hostages + Paris Honeymoon

Johnny Vagabond (+ Get Going)
Phantom Of The Opera (+ The Nazis Strike
    short)
* The Sullivans (+ Lucky Days)
His Butler's Sister (+ There's A Future In It
    short)
Standing Room Only + Tunisian Victory
Lifeboat (+ Good Morning Judge)
The Uninvited (+ Around The World)
Time Flies (+ Spider Woman)
Tender Comrade (+ Tornado)
On Approval + Frontier Bad Man
Melody Inn (+ Timber Queen)
Higher And Higher + The Woman Of The
    Town
The Hour Before The Dawn + The Trail Of
    The Lonesome Pine *revival*
Chip Off The Old Block (+ The Imposter)
The Bridge of San Luis Rey (+ Minesweeper)
Tawny Pipit + Her Jungle Love *revival*
The Way Ahead
Follow The Boys (+ The Falcon And The
    Co-Eds)
Ministry Of Fear + Welcome Mr. Washington
The Great Moment + Gangway For
    To-Morrow
The Eve Of St. Mark + The Singing
    Musketeers
* For Whom The Bell Tolls
Lady In The Dark (+ The Peke Speaks *short*)
It Happened Tomorrow + In Old Chicago
    revival
English Without Tears + The Lamp Still
    Burns *revival*; *or* Millions Like Us *revival*; *or*
    The Man In Grey *revival*
* The Song Of Bernadette [*also Gaumont circuit
    main feature release*]; *or various*
* Going My Way (+ West Of The Sunset
    or various)
* The Story Of Dr. Wassell
Cobra Woman (+ The Navy Way)
Home In Indiana (+ No Greater Love)
Double Indemnity (+ Ladies Of Washington)
Wing And A Prayer (+ You Can't Ration Love)
Till We Meet Again + Thanks For The
    Memory *revival*
Sensations Of 1945 + Medal For The General
Don't Take It To Heart + This Is The Life
The Hitler Gang (+ Take It Big)
Greenwich Village (+ One Body Too Many)
Patrick The Great + Ladies Courageous
Hail The Conquering Hero + The Falcon In
    Mexico

*London-area evening newspaper advertising
for December 1943 and January 1945.*

Step Lively + Our Hearts Were Young And Gay
Rainbow Island (+ Henry – Boy Scout)

1945

Main film in top eighteen box office attractions of the year
Main film in top box office attractions of 1946

Casanova Brown (+ Road To Yesterday *short*)
The Climax (+ My Gal Loves Music)
Laura (+ Reckless Age)
I Love A Soldier (+ Meet Sexton Blake)
Dark Waters + History Is Made At Night *revival*
* Waterloo Road (+ My Pal Wolf)
* Frenchman's Creek (+ Horse Sense *short*)
Sunday Dinner For A Soldier + These Three *revival*
The Man In Half Moon Street + San Diego I Love You
The Woman In The Window (+ National Barn Dance)
Practically Yours + Kipps *revival*
Wilson
And Now Tomorrow (+ I'll Remember April)
Can't Help Singing (+ Spotlight On Dogs *short*)
Guest In The House + She Gets Her Man
None But The Lonely Heart (+ Swing Out Sister)
The Unseen + Souls At Sea *revival*
Something For The Boys (+ Dark Mountain)
* Here Comes The Waves (+ The Battle For New Britain *short*)
Blithe Spirit (+ A Night Of Adventure)
Tin Pan Alley *revival* + Molly And Me
A Place Of One's Own (+ Honeymoon Ahead)
A Medal For Benny + Alibi *revival*
Here Come The Co-Eds (+ Double Exposure)
Czarina + House Of Fear
Tomorrow The World + Murder! He Says
The Suspect + Ghost Catchers
Bring On The Girls (+ High Powered)
* The Way To The Stars (+ Scared Stiff)
The Enchanted Cottage (+ What A Blonde)
Salty O'Rourke (+ Don Chicago)
I'll Be Seeing You (+ Senorita From The West)
* The Princess And The Pirate (+ Solder-Sailor *short*)
Diamond Horseshoe (+ Dangerous Passage)
* The Affairs Of Susan (+ I'll Walk Beside You *revival*)
It's A Pleasure! (+ Within These Walls)
Henry V
Incendiary Blonde (+ After You, Mr. Dickens *short*)

A Bell For Adano + Pan Americana
Out Of This World + The Brighton Strangler
The Strange Affair Of Uncle Harry + That's The Spirit
Captain Eddie + Banjo On My Knee *revival*
You Came Along + Circumstantial Evidence
Johnny Frenchman + Men In Her Diary
Duffy's Tavern (+ Strange Confession)
* The Seventh Veil (+ Follow That Woman)
The Lost Weekend (+ Banana Ridge *revival*)
Where Do We Go From Here? + Journey Together
Along Came Jones (+ The Body Snatcher)
The Southerner + Delightfully Dangerous
I Know Where I'm Going! + George White's Scandals
** Road To Utopia (+ India Strikes *short*)
The Rake's Progress

1946

Main film in top twenty-five box office attractions of the year
Main feature in top nine box-office hits of 1947

That Night With You (+ Pursuit To Algiers)
Love Letters (+ Mama Loves Papa)
Captain Kidd + Two O'Clock Courage
* The House On 92nd Street + Sun Valley Serenade *revival*
Wonder Man (+ Midnight Man Hunt)
The Stork Club + My Learned Friend *revival*
Tomorrow Is Forever (+ Memory For Two)
This Love Of Ours (+ Radio Stars On Parade)
* Kitty (+ Footlight School *short*)
Because Of Him (+ The Spider)
Masquerade In Mexico + The Night Has Eyes *revival*
* The Spiral Staircase (+ People Are Funny)
The Diary Of A Chambermaid (+ The House Across The Bay *revival*)
* Leave Her To Heaven (+ Whose Baby? *short*)
Two Years Before The Mast (+ River Boat Rhythm)
* The Captive Heart (+ Our Hearts Were Growing Up)
The Bride Wasn't Willing (+ When Tomorrow Comes *revival*)
The Well Groomed Bride + The Light That Failed *revival*
Cornered (+ One Way To Love)
Sentimental Journey (+ Sing Your Way Home)
Hold That Blonde + The Lives Of A Bengal Lancer *revival*

The Blue Dahlia + The Gentleman Misbehaves
On The Carpet (+ Smooth As Silk)
The Virginian (+ Tokyo Rose)
Dragonwyck (+ The Skipper Puts To Sea *short*)
Bedelia (+ Johnny Comes Flying Home)
Heartbeat (+ They Made Me A Killer)
Madonna Of The Seven Moons *revival* (+ Talk About A Lady) *(limited)*
Beware Of Pity (+ Welcome Home)
O.S.S. (+ Strange Triangle)
I See A Dark Stranger (+ The Bamboo Blonde)
Cluny Brown (+ Just Before Dawn)
The Strange Love of Martha Ivers (+ Blonde Alibi)
Make Mine Music! (+ It Shouldn't Happen To A Dog)
Caesar And Cleopatra [*also at many Gaumonts*]
To Each His Own (+ The Way We Live)
Mr. Ace + Miss Susie Slagle's
London Town
Night In Paradise (+ She Wrote The Book)
The Searching Wind (+ Hot Cargo)
Smoky (+ The Dark Horse)
Monsieur Beaucaire (+ Mysterious Intruder)
Claudia And David (+ Big Town)
* The Overlanders + The Bride Wore Boots
Angel On My Shoulder (+ Daytime Wife *revival* or Second Honeymoon *revival*)
Without Reservations (+ The Hammond Mystery)
The Magic Bow (+ Danger Woman)
The Perfect Marriage + Swamp Fire
Till The End Of Time (+ Fifth Avenue Girl *revival*)
School For Secrets (+ Crack-Up)
** Blue Skies (+ Her Adventurous Night)
The Dark Mirror (+ The Baxter Millions)

1947

Main feature in top nine box-office attractions of the year
Main feature in top ten box-office attractions of 1948

Mrs. Loring's Secret (+ The Falcon In San Francisco)
My Darling Clementine (+ Inside Job + TMA 4: Fabrics Of The Future)
Sister Kenny (+ Deadline For Murder)
Great Expectations [*Gaumont circuit release main feature*]; or Cross My Heart + The Wicked Lady *revival*

Temptation (+ Mr. Big *revival*)
Calcutta (+ Vacation In Reno)
Meet Me At Dawn + Stanley And Livingstone *revival*
Lover Come Back + If I'm Lucky
Easy Come, Easy Go + Suddenly It's Spring
The Chase + Man Alive (+ TMA 6: Palestine)
* Odd Man Out (+ Roman Holiday *short*)
My Favorite Brunette (+ Strange Journey)
The Razor's Edge
Nicholas Nickleby (+ Beat The Band)
California (+ Criminal Court)
Notorious (+ All The King's Horses *short*)
A Woman Destroyed (+ Riff-Raff)
The Late George Apley (+ The House of Tao Ling)
Welcome Stranger (+ Step By Step)
The Trouble With Women + Hatter's Castle *revival*
Black Narcissus (+ TMA 8: Sudan Dispute)
The Farmer's Daughter (+ Backlash)
The Shocking Miss Pilgrim (+ I Cover Big Town)
The Red House + Ladies' Man
Dear Murderer (+ Idea Girl)
Take My Life (+ Fun On A Weekend)
Wild Harvest (+ The Jewels Of Brandenburg)
The Homestretch (+ Jungle Flight)
Song of Scheherazade (+ Danger Street)
* Frieda (+ Bush Christmas)
Rookies Come Home (+ Black Angel)
Perils of Pauline (+ The Lie Detector + TMA 10: The Rape Of The Earth)
Sinbad The Sailor (+ Seven Keys To Baldpate)
So Well Remembered (+ Beyond Price *short*)
Where There's Life (+ The Falcon's Adventure)
* Jassy (+ Making The Grade *short*)
Time Out Of Mind + Repeat Performance
Moss Rose (+ Wild Beauty)
Master Of Bankdam (+ Second Chance)
Brute Force + A Likely Story
Dear Ruth + Dancing With Crime
Something In The Wind (+ Desperate + TMA 12: Antarctic Whale Hunt)
Ivy (+ Mark Of The Claw)
Fame Is The Spur (+ The Crimson Key)
Bachelor Knight (+ Key Witness)
Desert Fury (+ Dick Tracy Vs. Cueball)
The Woman In The Hall (+ Seven Were Saved *or* The Royal Wedding *short*)
They Won't Believe Me (+ The Royal Wedding *short or* Seven Were Saved)
Golden Earrings (+ Fear In The Night +

TMA 14: Jamaica Problem)
I Wonder Who's Kissing Her Now (+ The Devil Thumbs A Ride)
Variety Girl
** It Always Rains On Sunday (+ Jitterbugs *revival*)

1948

* *Main feature in top ten box-office attractions of the year*

Singapore + Stepchild
Maryland *revival* + While I Live
I Walk Alone + She's My Lovely *revival*
Build My Gallows High + Annabel Takes A Tour *revival* (+ TMA 1: Homes For All)
Great Expectations *revival* (+ Golden Slippers); *or Gaumont circuit release* When The Bough Breaks + Circus Boy
Saigon + Lady Chaser
Fun And Fancy Free + The Navy Steps Out *revival*
When The Bough Breaks *revival* + Circus Boy *revival*; *or Gaumont circuit release* Easy Money + Flight To Nowhere + TMA 15: Land Short Of People)
Vice Versa + Model Wife *revival* (+ TMA 3: Tomorrow By Air)
Daughters Of Darkness (+ Night Work *revival* + TMA 16: The British – Are They Artistic?)
Green For Danger *revival* + The Red Stallion
Blanche Fury (+ The King's Navy *short*)
* Road To Rio
* The Best Years Of Our Lives
Corridor Of Mirrors + Little Accident *revival* (+ TMA 5: Thoroughbreds Of The World)
The Big Clock + Sudden Money *revival*
This Happy Breed *revival* + Carnival *revival* (+ Our King And Queen)
Snowbound + Beauty For The Asking *revival*
The Woman On The Beach + The Way Ahead *revival* (+ TMA 7: Coal Crisis))
A Matter Of Life And Death *revival* + Chip Off The Old Block *revival*
Miranda + Society Smugglers *revival* (+ The Royal Wedding Presents *short*)
Man Within *revival* + Men Of Two Worlds *revival*; *or Gaumont circuit main feature* Broken Journey + *various*
One Night With You + Shadow Of A Doubt *revival*
Good Time Girl + Badlands Of Dakota *revival* (+ TMA 18: The Future Of Scotland)
Hungry Hill *revival* + Hue And Cry *revival*

A Double Life (+ A Song For Tomorrow)
A Woman's Vengeance + The Upturned Glass *revival*; *or Gaumont circuit main feature* The Calendar + *various*
Daybreak (+ Arthur Takes Over + TMA 11: Home And Beauty)
Sitting Pretty (+ Risky Business *revival*)
Fort Apache (+ Penny And The Pownall Case)
So Evil My Love (+ West Point Widow *revival*)
My Brother's Keeper (+ Lady Of Deceit + TMA 20: Fate Of An Empire)
* The Naked City (+ Shaggy + TMA 13: Will Britain Go Hungry?)
I Remember Mama (+ The Invisible Wall)
* Unconquered
The Iron Curtain (+ Everybody's Baby *revival* + TMA 15: A Land Short Of People)
London Belongs To Me (+ Mystery In Mexico)
Holiday Camp + Kiss Of Death; *or Gaumont circuit main feature* XIVth Olympiad – The Glory Of Sport
Mr. Perrin And Mr. Traill + The Spiritualist
Night Has A Thousand Eyes (+ Colonel Bogey)
The Weaker Sex (+ The Challenge)
Out Of The Blue + The Brothers; *or Gaumont circuit main feature* The Blind Goddess
* Oliver Twist (+ TMA 22: Women In Our Time)
The Exile + Trouble In The Air (+ TMA 19: Challenge In Nigeria)
The Miracle Of The Bells (+ Bodyguard)
Woman Hater (+ Fighting Back)
Quartet (+ Linda Be Good)
An Act Of Murder (+ Fly Away Peter + TMA 17: Ceylon The New Dominion)
T-Men + The Noose Hangs High
Up In Central Park + Larceny
Another Shore (+ Raw Deal)
The Foxes Of Harrow + Night Wind

1949

* *Main feature in top ten box-office attractions of the year*

You Gotta Stay Happy (+ To The Public Danger)
Portrait From Life (+ Good Morning Boys *revival*)
* Red River (+ Love In Waiting)
The Walls Of Jericho (+ Half Past Midnight)
Third Time Lucky + Casbah
Warning To Wantons + Mr. Peabody And The Mermaid
Vote For Huggett (+ Diary Of A Bride +

TMA 24: Harvest From The Wilderness)
Green Grass Of Wyoming (+ The Gay
  Intruders + Musical Paint Box series: Wales
  short)
Once Upon A Dream (+ I Know Where I'm
  Going! revival)
* Scott Of The Antarctic (+ The Platypus short)
The Passionate Friends (+ Musical Paint Box
  series: Somerset short)
* The Paleface (+ Disaster)
The Loves Of Carmen (+ Racing Luck)
* The Secret Life Of Walter Mitty (+
  Switzerland Today short)
Apartment For Peggy (+ Bungalow 13)
The Bad Lord Byron + Cover Up (+ TMA 26:
  Europe's Fisheries In Danger?)
All Over The Town + Another Part Of The
  Forest
He Walked By Night + Let's Live A Little
Cardboard Cavalier (Aqua-Show's Sports
  Serenade short)
The Accused (+ Isn't It Romantic)
Fools Rush In + Intrigue
That Wonderful Urge (+ Trouble Preferred
  + Musical Paint Box series: Fantasy On
  Ireland short)
Passport To Pimlico (+ Million Dollar Weekend)
Every Girl Should Be Married (+ Sunset Pass
  + TMA 23: Lancashire's Time For
  Adventure)
The Great Gatsby (+ Mr. Reckless)
Yellow Sky (+ Miss Mink Of 1949)
Adam And Evelyne (+ Rose Of The Yukon)
Melody Time + Station West
The Lady Gambles (+ Here Comes The Sun)
Helter Skelter + Reign of Terror (+ TMA 28:
  Will Europe Unite?)
Tulsa + Murder At The Windmill
Poet's Pub + Impact
Down To The Sea In Ships (+ Daybreak In
  Udi short)
Rope Of Sand (+ Proud Canvas short)
Madness Of The Heart (+ Arctic Manhunt +
  TMA 29: Gambling)
Christopher Columbus (+ Here Comes Trouble)
Obsession (+ Last Of The Wild Horses)
Train Of Events (+ An Old-Fashioned Girl)
Captain From Castile (+ David Hand
  Animaland series: It's A Lovely Day short)
Hamlet
Joan Of Arc (+ Monument To A Pioneer short)
The Snake Pit (+ TMA 30: Fight For A Fuller
  Life)

Top O' The Morning (+ The Argyle Secrets)
The Chiltern Hundreds (+ The Shop At Sly
  Corner)
You Can't Sleep Here (+ Joe Palooka In The
  Big Fight)
Give Us This Day (+ Trouble Makers +
  Cornwall short)
The File On Thelma Jordon (+ Captain China)
The Set-Up (+ Variety Time)
When My Baby Smiles At Me (+ Port Of
  Destiny + Ginger Nutt's Bee-Bother short)
The Spider And The Fly (+ The Life Of Riley)
The Great Lover (+ Post Office Investigator)

1950

* Main feature in top ten box-office attractions
of the year

East Of Java + Calamity Jane And Sam Bass
Everybody Does It + Thieves' Highway
After Midnight (+ Deputy Marshal)
The Velvet Touch + The Big Steal
The Rocking Horse Winner (+ Trapped)
Pinky (+ Streets Of San Francisco)
* Jolson Sings Again (+ Blondie's Hero)
* The Blue Lamp (+ White Cradle Inn revival)
You're My Everything + Undertow
Copper Canyon (+ Chinatown At Midnight)
12 O'Clock High (+ TMA 34: Report On
  Hong Kong + Devon Whey short)
Madeleine (+ Free For All)
The Astonished Heart (+ Treasure Of Monte
  Cristo)
Riding High (+ Dangerous Inheritance)
My Foolish Heart (+ Mary Ryan Detective)
When Willie Comes Marching Home (+
  Outside The Wall)
They Were Not Divided (+ TMA 35: The
  Riddle Of Japan)
The Reluctant Widow (+ I Was A Shoplifter)
She Wore A Yellow Ribbon + Bride For Sale
One Way Street (+ Stop Press Girl + A Day
  With Brumas short)
Dancing In The Dark + Father Was A Fullback
Prelude To Fame + Once More My Darling
No Man Of Her Own (+ Going To Town)
Chance Of A Lifetime (+ Arson Inc.)
In A Lonely Place + Father Is A Bachelor
Cheaper By The Dozen (+ 1950 – British
  Empire Games)
Mrs. Mike + Johnny Holiday
No Sad Songs For Me + A Woman Of
  Distinction
Wabash Avenue (+ Let's Live Again + Queen

Mary's Carpet short)
Ellen + Three Husbands
* Treasure Island (+ Journey For Three short)
Bitter Springs + The Sleeping City
The Furies + My Friend Irma
Panic In The Streets (+ The Golden Gloves
  Story)
Winchester 73 + Peggy
Trio (+ Father Makes Good + TMA 37: The
  True Face Of Japan)
The White Tower (+ Easy Living)
The Gunfighter (+ Customs Agent)
The Black Rose (+ Puzzle Corner No.3 short)
The Milkman + Saddle Tramp
No Way Out (+ The Flying Saucer)
Duchess Of Idaho (+ The Violent Hour)
The Heiress (+ TMA 38: New Zealand – A
  World Power + Three For Breakfast short)
The Woman In Question (+ Panther's Moon
  + Tribute To Greatness short)
Sunset Boulevard (+ Fun At The Zoo short +
  Fowl Hunting short)
The Magnet (+ Captain Boycott revival)
The Jackpot (+ David Harding, Counterspy)
Let's Dance (+ Chain Gang)
Frenchie + Katie Did It (+ TMA 40: The
  Fight In Malaya short)
She Shall Have Murder + The Man On The
  Eiffel Tower
For Heaven's Sake (+ I Killed Geronimo +
  Ginger Nutt's Christmas Circus short)
The Clouded Yellow (+ The Cure revival
  short)

1951

* Main feature in top ten box-office attractions
of the year

September Affair + My Friend Irma Goes West
Highly Dangerous (+ Ma And Pa Kettle Back
  On The Farm)
Crisis (+ Mrs. O'Malley And Mr. Malone)
* All About Eve (+ Yankee Doodle Mouse
  short)
Into The Blue (+ Radar Secret Service)
Harvey + Undercover Girl
Walk Softly, Stranger + The Secret Fury
Blackmailed (+ Under The Gun)
Branded (+ Motor Patrol + TMA 33: When
  You Went Away)
Pandora And The Flying Dutchman (+ Puzzle
  Corner No. 5 short)
Kim (+ Flight Plan short)
The Long Dark Hall (+ Holiday Rhythm)

* Samson And Delilah (+ Get 'Em Young *short*)
Rawhide (+ To Have And To Hold + TMA 25: Struggle For Oil)
Our Very Own + Gambling House
The Browning Version (+ Hey! Hey! USA *revival* + Spirit Of Wine *short*)
Lights Out + Bedtime For Bonzo
The Lemon Drop Kid + The Redhead And The Cowboy
Halls Of Montezuma (+ Gasoline Alley)
Night Without Stars + The Perfect Woman *revival* (+ TMA 27: Education For Living)
Soldiers Three (+ Home Town Story)
Born Yesterday (+ The Flying Missile)
Tom Brown's Schooldays (+ Bandit Queen)
Follow The Sun (+ Assassin For Hire)
Where The Sidewalk Ends (+ Alaska Patrol)
You Belong To My Heart (+ The Painted Hills)
Sirocco + Midnight Episode
My Forbidden Past + Never A Dull Moment
* White Corridors (+ My True Story)
I'd Climb The Highest Mountain + Whirlpool
* On The Riviera (+ Chelsea Story)
Hotel Sahara (+ Armoured Car Robbery)
Here Comes The Groom (+ Never Trust A Gambler)
Alice In Wonderland (+ Beaver Valley *short*)
No Highway (+ Destination Big House)
The Lavender Hill Mob (+ Missing Women)
The Law And The Lady (+ The Tall Target)
The Frogmen (+ Bank Holiday *revival*)
The Golden Horde (+ Francis Goes To The Races)
Valley Of Eagles (+ Reunion In Reno)
People Will Talk (+ Roadblock)
When Worlds Collide + Crosswinds
Flying Leathernecks (+ Hard, Fast And Beautiful!)
Appointment With Venus (+ According To Mrs. Hoyle)
The Lady Pays Off + Mark Of The Renegade
Detective Story (+ Flaming Feather)
Rommel – Desert Fox (+ The Man With My Face)
The Blue Veil (+ Beyond The Heights *short*)
Too Young To Kiss + The Man With A Cloak
Meet Me After The Show + The Sword Of Monte Cristo
Another Man's Poison (+ Curley)
David And Bathsheba (+ Spotlight On Best Sellers *short*)
Encore (+ Street Bandits)

1952

* *Main feature in top ten box-office attractions of the year*

Double Dynamite + Best Of The Badmen
Thunder In The East (+ Noose *revival*)
Mr. Denning Drives North (+ The Rebel)
A Place In The Sun (+ Queer Fish *short*)
Come Fill The Cup (+ Disc Jockey *short* or Norwegian Holiday *short*)
The Treasure Of Lost Canyon + Flame Of Araby
His Excellency (+ Royal Journey *short*)
Elopement + Take Care Of My Little Girl
Secret People + Richer Than The Earth
Sons Of The Musketeers (+ Savage Splendor)
Golden Girl + The Model And The Marriage Broker
The Card (+ Death Of An Angel)
The Big Trees + Inside The Walls Of Folsom Prison
* The Greatest Show On Earth
Where The River Bends (+ Here Come The Nelsons)
Saturday Island + On Dangerous Ground
Viva Zapata! (+ Night Was Our Friend + Britain's Comet *short*)
Tall Headlines + Chicago Calling
Rancho Notorious + The Las Vegas Story
Bronco Buster (+ The Blue Lagoon *revival or* Morning Departure *revival or various*)
Belles On Their Toes + Never Look Back
Curtain Up + The Battle At Apache Pass
High Noon (+ Edward, My Son *revival*)
Emergency Call + Fort Defiance
Deadline (+ Harem Girl)
Just Across The Street + Judgment Deferred
Macao + The Half-Breed
Diplomatic Courier (+ Flight *short*)
Lydia Bailey + Britannia Mews *revival*
Carrie (+ El Dorado *short* + The Olympic Champ *short*)
Something Money Can't Buy + No Room For The Groom
Gift Horse (+ Say Abracadabra)
Penny Princess (+ The Whip Hand)
We're Not Married + Journey Into Light
The Importance Of Being Earnest (+ Ocean Terminus *short* + Honey Harvester *short*)
* Son of Paleface (+ Operation Swallow)
* The World In His Arms (+ Ma And Pa Kettle At The Fair)
Room For One More (+ Cuban Fireball)

Les Miserables (+ As You Were)
Meet Me Tonight (+ Sea Tiger)
Sudden Fear! + Drums In The Deep South
My Wife's Best Friend + The Pride Of St. Louis
Full House (+ Crow Hollow)
Jumping Jacks (+ Silent Dust *revival*)
Hindle Wakes + The Raiders
Because Of You + Horizons West
It Started In Paradise + Bonzo Goes To College
Night Without Sleep + Rose Of Cimarron
The Big Sky (+ Come Back Peter)
The Four Poster + Assignment – Paris!
The Pickwick Papers (+ Tropical Heat Wave)
Bloodhounds Of Broadway + Something For The Birds

1953

* *Main feature in top ten box-office attractions of the year*

The Voice Of Merrill + The Lawless Breed
The Steel Trap + Golden Arrow
Folly To Be Wise (+ The Outlaw And The Lady)
Botany Bay (+ Breakdown)
Limelight
The Snows Of Kilimanjaro
Decameron Nights (+ The Fabulous Senorita *soon replaced by various revivals*)
The Long Memory (+ Gentlemen...The Queen)
My Cousin Rachel (+ Too Many Detectives *short*)
Top Of The Form + The Black Castle
The Star (+ Night And The City *revival*)
Come Back, Little Sheba + Hurricane Smith
The Mississippi Gambler (+ Ma And Pa Kettle At Waikiki)
The Titfield Thunderbolt + San Antone
Treasure Of The Golden Condor (+ The Hasty Heart *revival*)
Desperate Moment (+ North Of The Great Divide)
Destination Gobi + The President's Lady; *or Gaumont main feature release* The Cruel Sea
The Final Test + Sally And Saint Anne
The Lusty Men + Kon-Tiki
The Desert Rats (+ Tangier Incident)
Sea Devils + Every Minute Counts
The Stars Are Singing + My Son John
*A Queen Is Crowned (+ No Escape) [*also Gaumont release*]
Tonight We Sing (+ Deadly Nightshade)
All I Desire + Meet Me At The Fair
The Fake + Raiders Of The Seven Seas

Beautiful But Dangerous + Split Second
Titanic† + House Of Blackmail
Forever Female + Jamaica Run
Trouble Along The Way (+ The Amazing Mr. Canasta *short*)
The Square Ring + It Happens Every Thursday
Innocents In Paris (+ The Broken Horseshoe)
Hans Christian Andersen (+ Storm Over Wyoming)
Way Of A Gaucho + The Glory Brigade
* Malta Story (+ Men Against The Sun)
Salome (+ Winning Of The West)
Let's Do It Again + Ambush At Tomahawk Gap
Call Me Madam (+ The Bosun's Mate *short* + Canterbury *short*)
*The Red Beret (+ Wagon Team)
Roman Holiday (+ Operation Hurricane *short*)
Melba + Treasure Of Kalifa
Return To Paradise + The Secret Four
The Sword And The Rose (+ Water Birds *short*)
Walking My Baby Back Home + The Great Sioux Uprising
The Caddy (+ Mr. Drake's Duck *revival*)
Is Your Honeymoon Really Necessary? + The Man From The Alamo
Inferno + A Blueprint For Murder
Second Chance (+ The Limping Man)
South Sea Woman (+ The City Is Dark)
The Sabre And The Arrow + Serpent Of The Nile
Here Come The Girls (+ Small Town Story)
Personal Affair (+ Spring On Ice)

1954

* *Main feature in top ten box-office attractions of the year*

** *Main feature in top ten box-office attractions of 1955*

† *These three programmes were listed as Gaumont releases in the book* Gaumont British Cinemas. *The actual Gaumont releases were:* Bad For Each Other + The Stranger Wore a Gun, *The On The Waterfront (+ The Green Buddha) and *The Belles Of St. Trinians (+ The End Of The Road)

The Bigamist + Tumbleweed
Rob Roy The Highland Rogue (+ Bear Country *short* + G.I. Jane)
Sangaree + The Girls Of Pleasure Island
* From Here To Eternity† (+ World of Life *or various*)

Gentlemen Prefer Blondes (+ Seven Days To Noon *revival*)
The Million Pound Note (+ Royal Symphony)
The Eddie Cantor Story + Plunder Of The Sun
* The Kidnappers (+ The Stand At Apache River)
* The Glenn Miller Story (+ Star Of My Night)
You Know What Sailors Are (+ Monte Carlo Baby)
It Should Happen To You! + Gun Fury
The Maggie (+ Ride Clear Of Diablo)
O'Rourke Of The Royal Mounted (+ Double Exposure)
The Good Die Young (+ Battles Of Chief Pontiac)
Red Garters + Alaska Seas
West Of Zanzibar (+ Mr. Walkie Talkie)
Witness To Murder + The Diamond
Yankee Pasha + Rails Into Laramie
Devil Girl From Mars + China Venture
Playgirl + Taza, Son Of Cochise
The Wages Of Fear (+ West Country Journey *short* + Bee On Guard *short*)
Forbidden Cargo (+ Ma And Pa Kettle At Home)
* Knock On Wood (+ Johnny On the Spot)
Carnival Story (+ The Queen In Australia)
Trouble in Store *revival; or* The Moon Is Blue; *or* Duel In The Sun *revival; or Gaumont release* Miss Sadie Thompson; *or other revival*
Dangerous Mission (+ The Sea Around Us)
Johnny Guitar (+ Burnt Evidence)
"Take Your Choice": Doctor In The House *revival* (+ Life In The Arctic *revival short* + Two Gun Goofy *short*); *or Gaumont release* The Long Wait + Camels West; *or various*
Father Brown (+ Drive A Crooked Road)
About Mrs. Leslie (+ Jungle Spell)
Tanganyika + Johnny Dark
Malaga (+ Why Men Leave Home)
Dance Little Lady (+ The Master Plan)
Susan Slept Here (+ Below The Sahara)
The Far Country (+ The Embezzler)
The Seekers (+ Delayed Action)
Living It Up (+ The Golden Link)
The Black Knight (+ Devil's Point)
Bengal Rifles (+ Drums Across The River)
* The Caine Mutiny (+ Model Girl *short*)
The Green Scarf (+ Final Appointment)
Suddenly (+ Gog)
Romeo And Juliet [*also at many Gaumonts*] (+ Winter Sports *short*)
A Bullet Is Waiting (+ Massacre Canyon)†

Lease Of Life (+ Hunters Of The Deep)
Rear Window (+ The Link *short*)†
Aunt Clara (+ The Clue Of The Missing Ape)
Passion (+ Silver Lode)
The Happiness Of 3 Women + The Crowded Day
Bud Abbott And Lou Costello Meet The Keystone Kops + Four Guns To The Border
Mad About Men (+ Africa Adventure)
** White Christmas (+ VistaVision Visits Norway *short*)

1955

* *Main feature in top ten box-office attractions of the year*

The Barefoot Contessa (+ Cormorant Fishing *short*)
Sign Of The Pagan (+ Children Galore)
* One Good Turn (+ Armand And Michaela Denis Under The Southern Cross)
So This Is Paris + Destry
The Americano + This Is My Love
The Bridges At Toko-Ri (+ Phantom Caravan)
Simba (+ Fireman, Save My Child)
Women's Prison + Masterson Of Kansas
*The Colditz Story (+ Secret Venture)
Smoke Signal + The Looters
Out Of The Clouds (+ The Man From Bitter Ridge)
Underwater! (+ Quest For The Lost City)
The End Of The Affair (+ The Law Vs. Billy the Kid)
The Long Gray Line (+ Puzzle Corner No.17 *short*)
The Country Girl (+ Peace And Plenty *short*)
Foxfire + A Life In The Balance
Big House U.S.A. + Bud Abbott And Lou Costello Meet The Mummy
The Night My Number Came Up (+ The Great Adventure)
Captain Lightfoot (+ One Jump Ahead)
Passage Home (+ Cult Of The Cobra)
The Prisoner (+ The Black Dakotas)
Run For Cover (+ Tiger By The Tail)
Three For The Show (+ Riot On Pier 6)
The Purple Mask + Ain't Misbehavin'
The Gambler From Natchez (+ Battle Taxi *or* Casimir)
Marty + Stranger On Horseback
One Desire + Kiss Of Fire
Special Delivery + They Rode West
The Vanishing Prairie + The Time Of His Life

'EXCELLENT ... THE BEST HOLLYWOOD HAS TURNED OUT FOR MONTHS' - The Star
'Powerful Drama' - Daily Mail 'Splendid' - Evening News
'A very good film ... Some PICNIC, and very tasty, too' - Daily Mirror
'Hail Columbia' - News Chronicle
'Cheesecake with mustard' - Evening Standard
'The most interesting film I've seen this year' - Daily Herald

Now they were alone,...
the drifter
and the girl ...
and the whole
town knew it!

PICNIC IS HIS STORY! WILLIAM HOLDEN The Drifter...
PICNIC IS HER STORY! KIM NOVAK The Pretty Sister...
PICNIC IS HER STORY! BETTY FIELD The Mother...
PICNIC IS HER STORY! SUSAN STRASBERG The Teen-age Sister...
PICNIC IS HER STORY! CLIFF ROBERTSON Rich Men's Son...
PICNIC IS HER STORY! ROSALIND RUSSELL The Teacher...

COLUMBIA PICTURES presents
WILLIAM HOLDEN in picnic 'A'
with KIM NOVAK
BETTY FIELD · SUSAN STRASBERG · CLIFF ROBERTSON and CO-STARRING
ROSALIND RUSSELL AS ROSEMARY
Colour by TECHNICOLOR CinemaScope

EXTRA ADDED ATTRACTIONS ALL CinemaScope PROGRAMME
'WONDERS of MANHATTAN'
& 'APRIL IN PORTUGAL' both in Colour by TECHNICOLOR

Screen play by DANIEL TARADASH
Based on the play 'Picnic' by WILLIAM INGE
Produced on the stage by THEATRE GUILD Inc & JOSHUA LOGAN
Directed by JOSHUA LOGAN
Produced by FRED KOHLMAR

NOW SHOWING
ODEON THEATRES: BARKING, BETHNAL GREEN, BRENTWOOD, CHINGFORD, CLAPTON, DALSTON, EAST HAM, FOREST GATE, HACKNEY ROAD, HORNCHURCH, HOUNSLOW, ILFORD, ISLEWORTH, KINGSTON, MILE END, RICHMOND, ROMFORD, SHANNON CORNER, SOUTHALL, STEPNEY, SURBITON, TWICKENHAM, UXBRIDGE, WALTON-ON-THAMES, WHALEBONE LANE, GRANGE DAGENHAM, AMBASSADOR HAYES.
EAST SHEEN. (MON. TUE. WED. ONLY) WHITTON. (THU. FRI. SAT. ONLY)
ALSO AT: EMBASSY ESHER RITZ GRAYS, CENTURY LEYTON, CENTURY LEYTONSTONE, PAVILION POPLAR ASTORIA RUISLIP, ASTORIA SEVEN KINGS, SUPER STAMFORD HILL.

"North east" London area suburban first run of an important film in 1956.

Strange Lady In Town (+ Room In The House)
20,000 Leagues Under The Sea (+ Toot, Whistle, Plunk And Boom *short*)
Strategic Air Command (+ Assignment Children *short* + VistaVision Visits Mexico *short*)
* A Kid For Two Farthings (+ Thunder Pass)
Not As A Stranger (+ The Wild Stallion *short*)
* Doctor At Sea (+ Double-Barrel Miracle)
A Man Alone (+ Headline Hunters)
We're No Angels (+ The Flaw)
Value For Money (+ Fury In Paradise)
All That Heaven Allows (+ The Man In The White Suit *revival*)
Cast A Dark Shadow (+ The Reluctant Bride)
The Kentuckian (+ Dial Red O)
My Sister Eileen (+ The Night Holds Terror!)
The Rawhide Years + Timeslip
The Trouble Shooter (+ Stolen Time)
They Can't Hang Me + The Road To Denver
You're Never Too Young (+ Scrooge *revival*)
Joe Macbeth (+ Duel On The Mississippi)
Queen Bee (+ The Gentle Sergeant)
Various revivals in double bills
Flame Of The Islands + A Yank In Ermine
An Alligator Named Daisy (+ Dial 999)
To Catch A Thief (+ The Fighting Chance)

1956

* *Main feature in top ten box-office attractions of the year*
** *Main feature in top fifteen box-office attractions of 1957*
The Ladykillers (+ No Man's Woman)
Never Say Goodbye + French Can-Can
Blood Alley (+ Just For You *short* + VistaVision Visits Hawaii *short*)
* Cockleshell Heroes (+ The Crooked Web)
Glory + The Treasure Of Pancho Villa
All For Mary (+ Red Sundown)
The Desperate Hours (+ Capri *short*)
The Brave And The Beautiful + World In My Corner
The Man With The Golden Arm (+ The Lilt Of The Kilt *short*)
Picnic (+ April In Portugal *short* + Wonders of Manhattan *short*)
Backlash (+ The Gelignite Gang + VistaVision Visits The Suntrails *short*)
Hot Blood + Soho Incident
The Court Jester (+ Sudden Danger)
* A Town Like Alice (+ When Gangland Strikes)

The Conqueror (+ The Alaskan Eskimo *short*)
Richard III; *or* Revenge Of The Creature + The Naked Dawn
Comanche! + The Killer Is Loose
The Feminine Touch (+ Stranger At My Door)
The Harder They Fall (+ Fury At Gunsight Pass)
The Tomahawk And The Cross + The Price Of Fear
The March Hare (+ Ghost Town)
Johnny Concho + A Kiss Before Dying
Nightmare + Patterns... Of Power!
Wicked As They Come + Woman Of The River
The Maverick Queen + Walk Into Paradise
Storm Centre (+ Ten Tall Men *revival or* Uranium Boom)
Slightly Scarlet + Mohawk
The Littlest Outlaw + Huk!
The First Travelling Saleslady (+ Breakaway, *later replaced by various*)
Jacqueline (+ Outside The Law *or various*)
The Man Who Knew Too Much (+ The Big Tip Off)
Odongo (+ Secret Of Treasure Mountain)
The Eddy Duchin Story (+ Sunshine In Soho *short*)
* Trapeze (+ Hot Cars)
* Reach For The Sky (+ We Found A Valley *short*)
The Unguarded Moment + Walk The Proud Land
Pardners (+ The Man Is Armed *or* Breakaway)
The Iron Petticoat (+ And Suddenly You Run *or* Breakaway)
Bandido (+ The Narrowing Circle)
The Solid Gold Cadillac (+ Over-Exposed)
It'a A Wonderful World (+ The Naked Hills *or various*)
The Weapon (+ Home And Away)
The Green Man (+ Every Second Counts)
Written On The Wind (+ Find The Lady)
Attack (+ Five Steps To Danger)
The Mountain (+ A Strange Adventure)
House Of Secrets (+ I've Lived Before)
The Sharkfighters (+ Flight To Hong Kong)
Istanbul (+ Francis In The Haunted House)
The Boss + 7th Cavalry
That Certain Feeling (+ Gun Brothers)
Hollywood Or Bust (+ The Man Between *revival*) / Tiger In The Smoke (+ Fernandel The Dressmaker) /** The Battle Of The River Plate (+ The Red Balloon *short*) [*each programme released in a different London area simultaneously, then switched around*]

1957

* Main feature in top fifteen box-office attractions of the year

Lisbon (+ Accused Of Murder)
Spring Reunion + Crime Of Passion
The Power And The Prize (+ Wiretapper)
Four Girls In Town + Everything But The Truth
Zarak (+ Cha-Cha-Cha Boom!)
Bundle Of Joy (+ No Road Back)
Battle Hymn (+ Suspended Alibi)
The Passionate Stranger (+ Thunder Over Arizona)
* Oklahoma! [also at many Gaumonts]
True As A Turtle (+ Gas-Oil)
Mister Cory + Rock Pretty Baby!
Brothers In Law (+ Duel At Apache Wells)
Davy Crockett And The River Pirates + The African Lion
Fortune Is A Woman (+ Utah Blaine)
High Tide At Noon (+ The Crooked Sky)
The Tattered Dress (+ Showdown At Abilene)
Interpol (+ Murder Reported)
Man Afraid (+ Folies Bergere)
12 Angry Men (+ Night In Havana)
Funny Face (+ Hour Of Decision)
The Steel Bayonet + The Fuzzy Pink Nightgown
Pay The Devil + Joe Butterfly
Gone With The Wind revival
The Unholy Wife + The Young Stranger
Lady And The Tramp revival + The Story of Robin Hood And His Merrie Men revival
The Happy Road + Rumble On The Docks
The Lonely Man + Sabrina Fair revival
* The Admiral Crichton (+ The Phantom Stagecoach)
Interlude (+ The Hypnotist)
Miracle In Soho (+ Joe Dakota)
3.10 To Yuma (+ The Brothers Rico)
Love In The Afternoon (+ The Cruel Tower)
Hell Drivers (+ The Heart Within)
* Gunfight At The OK Corral (+ Pepote)
Saint Joan (+ The Outlaw's Son); or The Monster That Challenged The World + The Vampire; or The Moon Is Blue + various; or Streets Of Sinners + Fort Yuma
Night Passage (+ Man From Tangier)
* The Story Of Esther Costello (+ Hellcats Of The Navy)
Jeanne Eagels (+ The Young Don't Cry)
Campbell's Kingdom (+ The Big Chance)
High Flight (+ The 27th Day)

The Scamp (+ Our Girl Friday revival)
Slaughter On 10th Avenue (+ Above All Things)
Robbery Under Arms (+ Stranger's Meeting, later replaced by The Kidnappers or other revivals)
Omar Khayyam (+ The Violators)
My Man Godfrey (+ Slim Carter)
Men In War + Not Wanted On Voyage
The Joker Is Wild (+ Lost Lagoon or various)
White Christmas revival (+ Conquest Of Space revival or Alaska Seas revival)
It Happened In Rome + The Girl Most Likely (first film dropped after initial week and second retained with various co-features)
Until They Sail (+ Affair In Havana)
The Pride And The Passion (+ Fed Up short) / Just My Luck (+ Summer Love) [programmes released in different London areas simultaneously, then switched around]

1958

* Main feature in top fourteen box-office attractions of the year

Roadshows: Around The World in 80 Days and The Ten Commandments

Dangerous Exile (+ Wetbacks)
The Sad Sack (+ The End Of The Line)
The Naked Truth (+ Simon And Laura revival)
Bitter Victory + Decision At Sundown; or
* The Bridge On The River Kwai (first of two weeks at some Odeons)
* The Bridge On The River Kwai [also at many Gaumonts]
The Truth About Women (+ Fury At Showdown)
Witness For The Prosecution (+ Gun Duel In Durango)
* Pal Joey (+ The Parson And The Outlaw)
* Blue Murder At St. Trinian's (+ Raiders Of Old California)
A Tale Of Two Cities (+ The Diplomatic Corpse)
The Silent Enemy (+ The Lawless Eighties)
* Carve Her Name With Pride (+ Timeless Temiar short)
Paris Holiday (+ The Betrayal)
Orders To Kill (+ The Notorious Mr. Monks)
Gideon's Day (+ Going Steady)
* Peyton Place
Thunder Road (+ A Woman Of Mystery)
Desire Under The Elms (+ Fabulous India short)

Teacher's Pet (+ Hear Me Good)
Stage Struck (+ I Married A Woman)
Touch Of Evil + Kathy O'
Various 20th Century-Fox revival double bills
Cinderella revival + 20,000 Leagues Under The Sea revival or Treasure Island revival
The Big Money (+ Heart Of A Child)
Raw Wind In Eden (+ Last Of The Fast Guns)
This Happy Feeling (+ The Saga Of Hemp Brown)
Hot Spell + Maracaibo
Gunman's Walk (+ The Lineup)
The Key (+ The True Story Of Lynn Stuart)
* The Vikings (+ The Travel Game short)
Intent To Kill (+ My Pal Gus revival)
* A Night To Remember (+ Gaucho Country short) [also at many Gaumonts]
Vertigo (+ Secret Of The Reef)
Nor The Moon By Night (+ Them Nice Americans)
The Man Inside (+ Life Begins At 17)
Kings Go Forth (+ A Woman Possessed)
King Creole (+ Country Music Holiday)
Next To No Time (+ Taming Sutton's Girl)
Twilight For The Gods (+ The Wonderful Years)
The Defiant Ones (+ Moment Of Indiscretion)
Further Up The Creek (+ Naked Gun)
Passionate Summer (+ Dublin Nightmare)
The Naked And The Dead (+ The Bank Raiders)
The Barbarian And The Geisha (+ School For Violence)
Ride A Crooked Trail (+ The Big Story)
Behind The Mask (+ Spy In The Sky!)
Three Men In A Boat revival + Sailor Beware! revival
The Robe revival
The Two-Headed Spy (+ Apache Territory)
Me And The Colonel (+ Antarctic Crossing)
Floods Of Fear (+ Hotel Sahara revival)

1959

* Main feature in top ten box-office attractions of the year

Roadshow: South Pacific

The Remarkable Mr. Pennypacker + Villa!
* The Inn Of The Sixth Happiness (two weeks at some Odeons)
Bachelor Of Hearts (+ The Secret Man)

The Odeon release then ended, cinemas playing the new Rank or National release programme.

THE RANK RELEASE

The following listings are adapted from data kindly supplied by **Michael Fisher**

When the Odeon release ended, most Odeons played the Rank release. Other Odeons played the National release which is listed after each Rank release following the letter *N*, or *A* for alternative release after the name was discontinued. From 1965, *A* refers to an alternative release for the main Rank circuit.

1959 [from 25 January]

* *Main feature among the top twelve box-office attractions of the full year*

Roadshow: Solomon And Sheba

Houseboat (+ Three Crooked Men). *N:* Mardi Gras (+ Diamond Safari)

The Captain's Table (+ Girl In The Woods). *N:* Stranger In My Arms (+ His Butler's Sister *revival*)

The Last Hurrah (+ The Face Of The Cat). *N:* The Geisha Boy (+ The Hot Angel)

Operation Amsterdam. *N:* Anna Lucasta (+ The Great Van Robbery)

The Roots Of Heaven (+ Broken Arrow). *N:* Subway In The Sky + Broth Of A Boy

* The Big Country. *N:* Make Mine A Million (+ Model For A Murder)

The Baited Trap (+ As Young As We Are). *N:* Too Many Crooks (+ Channel Queen short *or* Above Us The Waves *revival*)

The Horse's Mouth (+ Ride Out For Revenge). *N:* Rally 'Round The Flag, Boys! (+ Alaska Passage)

Danger Within (+ The Go-Getter). *N:* Son Of Robin Hood (+ Frontier Gun)

Separate Tables (+ The Child And The Killer). *N:* The Black Orchid (+ When Hell Broke Loose)

Idle On Parade + The Young Land. *N:* Whirlpool (+ Johnny Trouble)

Tiger Bay (+ Badman's Country). *N:* Never Steal Anything Small + No Name On The Bullet

* The 39 Steps (+ No Room For Wild Animals). *N:* These Thousand Hills (+ City Of Fear)

The Man In The Net (+ Riot In A Juvenile Prison). *N:* The Sound And The Fury (+ Law v. Gangster)

Carlton-Browne Of The F.O. (+ The Man Who Died Twice). *N:* The Hound Of The Baskervilles (+ Innocent Meeting)

Imitation Of Life (+ Money Women And Guns).

N: Compulsion (+ Forbidden Island)

Warlock (+ The Littlest Hobo). *N:* The Bandit Of Zhobe (+ Good Day For A Hanging)

It Happened To Jane (+ Gunmen From Laredo). *N:* Al Capone (+ Wolf Larsen)

Sapphire (+ Jacqueline *revival*). *N:* Alias Jesse James (+ Ten Days To Tulara)

The Buccaneer (+ Rivers Of Time *short*). *N:* Beyond This Place (+ Carry On Admiral *revival*)

Pork Chop Hill (+ Crash Drive). *N:* Ten Seconds To Hell + Lonelyhearts

Middle Of The Night (+ Ride Lonesome). *N:* The Hangman + The Matchmaker

Shake Hands With The Devil (+ High Jump). *N:* Parisienne + The Wild And The Innocent

Woman Obsessed (+ Arson For Hire). *N:* Day Of The Outlaw (+ The Green Man *revival*)

The Shaggy Dog (+ Secrets Of Life). *N:* Say One For Me (+ Here Come The Jets)

The Heart Of A Man (+ The Big Arena). *N:* Darby O'Gill And The Little People (+ Tonka)

Some Like It Hot (+ Floating Fortress *short*). *N:* Tarzan's Greatest Adventure (+ Tokyo After Dark)

Ferry To Hong Kong (+ Winter Quarters *short*). *N:* The Mouse That Roared (+ Juke Box Rhythm)

The Diary Of Anne Frank (+ Royal River *short*). *N:* Gunfight At Dodge City (+ Taxi)

Tempest (+ Generator 4 *short*). *N:* Bobbikins (+ The Sad Horse)

The Bridal Path (+ A Woman's Temptation). *N:* Holiday For Lovers (+ The Miracle Of The Hills)

A Hole In The Head (+ This Is Malta *short*). *N:* Don't Give Up The Ship (+ No Safety Ahead)

This Earth Is Mine (+ Life in Danger). *N:* A Private's Affair (+ Machete)

I Want To Live! (+ This Is Burma *short*). *N:* Last Train From Gun Hill (+ Top Floor Girl)

I'm All Right Jack (+ The Legend Of Tom Dooley). *N:* Blind Date (+ Tarawa Beachhead)

Upstairs And Downstairs (+ Ill Met By Moonlight *revival*). *N:* The Man Who Understood Women (+ Two Guns And A Badge)

Blue Jeans (+ Gunfighters Of Abilene). *N:* Gidget (+ The Boy And The Bridge)

My Uncle (+ Two Gun Lady). *N:* The Night We Dropped A Clanger (+ Cry Tough)

Ask Any Girl (+ The Man Who Liked Funerals). *N:* The Blue Angel (+ Speed Crazy)

Classified advertising in London evening newspaper in 1959.

North West Frontier (+ Honeymoon Island *short*). *N:* The Rabbit Trap + Cast A Long Shadow

The Devil's Disciple (+ Pier 5 Havana). *N:* The World, The Flesh And The Devil (+ The Foxiest Girl In Paris)

The Killers Of Kilimanjaro (+ Battle Of The Coral Sea). *N:* The Naked Maja (+ The Beat Generation *or* Lizzie)

S.O.S. Pacific (+ Strictly Confidential). *N:* The Wonderful County (+ Man Accused)

North By Northwest (+ Perthshire Panorama *short*). *N:* Return Of The Fly (+ The Alligator People); *or* The Sheriff of Fractured Jaw *revival* + Family Doctor *revival*

That Kind Of Woman + Thunder In The Sun. *N:* Five Gates To Hell (+ Count Five And Die *revival or* Carmen Jones *revival*)

The House Of The Seven Hawks + Tarzan The Ape Man. *N: various including* Genevieve *revival* + Doctor In The House *revival*

It Started With A Kiss (+ The Big Operator *or* Davy *revival*). *N:* 1001 Arabian Nights + Have Rocket, Will Travel (*later feature later replaced by* The Flying Fontaines)

The Five Pennies (+ The Ama Girls *short*). *N:* Third Man On The Mountain (+ The Nine Lives Of Elfrego Baca)

Follow A Star (+ Devil's Bait). *N:* The Navy Lark (+ The Oregon Trail)

1960

* *Main feature among the top twelve box-office attractions of the year*
Roadshows: Can-Can *and* The Alamo, *plus special presentations of* The Royal Ballet
London suburban waves of The Ten Commandments *and* Around The World In 80 Days

They Came To Cordura (+ Senior Prom). *N:* But Not For Me (+ Web Of Suspicion)

The Horse Soldiers (+ Lifeline *short*). *N:* Babette Goes To War (+ Hey Boy! Hey Girl!)

Libel (+ Mission Of Danger). *N:* The Best Of Everything (+ Murder On Site Three)

Beloved Infidel (+ Switzerland *short*). *N:* Desert Mice (+ Witness In The Dark)

Career (+ The Young Captives). *N:* The Shakedown (+ Destiny Of A Man)

Anatomy Of A Murder. *N:* Pillow Talk (+ The Silent Stranger)

On The Beach (+ How Clever Can You Be *short*). *N:* Journey To The Center Of The Earth (+ Scotland *short*)

Operation Petticoat (+ The Awakening). *N:* Odds Against Tomorrow (+ Fort Bowie)

Never So Few (+ Samoa *short*). *N:* The Jayhawkers (+ Date At Midnight)

A Touch Of Larceny (+ Night Train For Inverness). *N:* The Story On Page One (+ Portugal *short*)

Happy Anniversary (+ Sentenced For Life). *N:* Too Young To Love + Assault In Broad Daylight

Our Man In Havana (+ High Journey). *N:* Jazzboat (+ 12 To The Moon)

The Battle Of The Sexes (+ Born To Be Loved). *N:* Your Money Or Your Wife + Hell Bent For Leather

* Sink The Bismarck! (+ When Comedy Was King). *N:* Hound Dog Man (+ The Rookie)

* Conspiracy Of Hearts (+ New Guinea Patrol *short*). *N:* Heller In Pink Tights (+ Women Are Weak)

* The League Of Gentlemen (+ And Women Shall Weep). *N:* Please Don't Eat The Daisies (+ Operation Cupid)

Once More With Feeling (+ The Crimson Kimono). *N:* A Woman Like Satan (+ Vice Raid)

Summer Of The Seventeenth Doll (+ Inside The Mafia). *N:* Beyond The Curtain (+ Campbell's Kingdom *revival*)

Seven Thieves (+ Blood And Steel). *N:* The Last Angry Man (+ The Enemy General)

Who Was That Lady? (+ Serengeti Shall Not Die). *N:* Wake Me When It's Over (+ Valley Of The Redwoods)

Cone Of Silence (+ Lust To Kill). *N:* The Challenge (+ The House Of Intrigue)

The Day They Robbed The Bank Of England (+ Killer's Cage). *N:* A Terrible Beauty (+ Gun Fever)

The Mountain Road (+ A Death Of Princes). *N:* Visit To A Small Planet (+ The Big Night)

Crack In The Mirror (+ Twelve Hours To Kill). *N:* Confessions Of A Counter Spy + Drum Crazy

Never Let Go (+ Boyd's Shop). *N:* All The Fine Young Cannibals (+ Guns Don't Argue)

Toby Tyler (+ Zorro The Avenger). *N:* Lords Of The Forest + The Third Voice

Wild River (+ The High Powered Rifle). *N:* In The Nick (+ Because They're Young)

The Savage Innocents (+ Dead Lucky). *N:*

Sons And Lovers (+ Thirteen Fighting Men)

The Unforgiven (+ Delta 8-3 *short*). *N:* Five Branded Women (+ The Scamp *revival*)

The Story Of Ruth (+ Code Name Snakes Eyes *short*). *N:* The Bellboy + Tarzan The Magnificent

Make Mine Mink (+ Snowball). *N:* The Last Days Of Pompeii (+ The Great St. Louis Bank Robbery)

Sleeping Beauty (+ Texas John Slaughter). *N:* The Chaplin Revue (+ A Dog's Best Friend)

From The Terrace (+ Jessy *short*). *N:* Kidnapped (+ White Wilderness)

* Doctor In Love (+ Oklahoma Territory). *N:* The Gallant Hours (+ Noose For A Gunman)

* Psycho. *N:* The Lost World (+ The Man Who Never Was *revival*)

Inherit The Wind (+ This Is Alsace *short*). *N:* The Brides Of Dracula (+ Teenage Lovers)

* Suddenly Last Summer (+ The Music Box Kid). *N:* One Foot In Hell (+ Three Came To Kill)

Let's Make Love (+ Hazard *short*). *N:* Piccadilly Third Stop (+ Three Moves To Freedom)

The Apartment (+ Playground Spectacular *short*). *N:* It Started In Naples (+ Walk Like A Dragon)

There Was A Crooked Man (+ Jungle Hell). *N:* Let No Man Write My Epitaph (+ Murder By Contract)

Bells Are Ringing (+ Balloons And Spinifex *short*). *N:* All The Young Men + Anna Of Brooklyn

Strangers When We Meet (+ The Man Who Couldn't Walk). *N:* The Entertainer (+ A Hill In Korea *revival*)

The Fugitive Kind (+ Beyond The Riviera *short*). *N:* The Time Machine (+ Rich, Young And Deadly)

Foxhole In Cairo (+ A Mexican Affair). *N:* The Giant Of Marathon (+ The Smallest Show On Earth *revival*)

Solomon And Sheba. *N:* The Siege Of Sidney Street (+ Hello London)

The Millionairess (+ Squad Car). *N:* Surprise Package (+ The Gentle Trap)

Portrait In Black (+ Chartroose Caboose). *N:* The Spider's Web (+ Cage of Evil)

High Time (+ Walk Tall). *N:* Faces In The Dark (+ The Boatmen)

Various revivals: The Glenn Miller Story + A Town Like Alice; *or* The Wind Cannot Read + To Hell And Back; *or* Man Without A

ALEC GUINNESS ✕ JOHN MILLS

Sets the screen on fire *DAILY EXPRESS*

Wild and brilliant *EVENING NEWS*

A picture to rave about *THE PEOPLE*

TUNES OF GLORY

TECHNICOLOR'

also starring

DENNIS PRICE • KAY WALSH • JOHN FRASER

and introducing Susannah York   Produced by COLIN LESSLIE · Directed by RONALD NEAME

Screenplay by JAMES KENNAWAY ~ A COLIN LESSLIE PRODUCTION

UNITED ARTISTS

THIS WEEK—N. & W. LONDON
SHOWING AT

ACTON Odeon	HENDON Odeon	PARK ROYAL Odeon
BARNET Odeon	HIGHGATE Odeon	SHEPHERDS BUSH Gaumont
BURNT OAK Gaumont	HOLLOWAY Gaumont	SOUTHGATE Odeon
CAMDEN TOWN Gaumont	ISLINGTON Angel	SOUTH HARROW Odeon
CHELSEA Gaumont	ISLINGTON Odeon	STAMFORD HILL Gaumont
EALING Odeon	KENSAL RISE Odeon	ST. ALBANS Odeon
EDGWARE RD. Odeon	KENSINGTON Odeon	SWISS COTTAGE Odeon
EDMONTON Regal	KILBURN State	TEMPLE FORTUNE Odeon
ENFIELD Rialto	KINGSBURY Gaumont	TOTTENHAM Palace
FINCHLEY Gaumont	KINGS CROSS Gaumont	WALTHAM CROSS Embassy
HAMMERSMITH Gaumont	MUSWELL HILL Odeon	WATFORD Odeon
HARLESDEN Odeon	NORTHWOOD Rex	WEMBLEY Odeon
HARROW Granada	PALMERS GREEN Gaumont	WESTBOURNE GROVE Odeor
HAVERSTOCK HILL Odeon		WOOD GREEN Gaumont

NEXT WEEK—N. & E. LONDON • JAN. 22nd—SOUTH LONDON

"STAGGERING TRICK WORK HAS GONE INTO THIS CLASSIC STORY" ERNEST BETTS *THE PEOPLE*

"For the young in heart I recommend 'The 3 Worlds of Gulliver'"
Peter Burnup "News of the World"

COLUMBIA PICTURES PRESENTS

THE 3 WORLDS OF **GULLIVER** in SUPERDYNAMATION and TECHNICOLOR U

starring

KERWIN MATHEWS

JUNE THORBURN · JO MORROW

Screenplay by ARTHUR ROSS and JACK SHER   Based on the JONATHAN SWIFT classic, "GULLIVER'S TRAVELS"   Visual Effects by RAY HARRYHAUSEN

Directed by JACK SHER   Produced by CHARLES H. SCHNEER   A MORNINGSIDE PRODUCTION

SEVEN WAYS FROM SUNDOWN *IN EASTMAN COLOUR*

Audie **MURPHY**   Barry **SULLIVAN**

Co-starring VENETIA STEVENSON · JOHN McINTIRE
Screenplay by Clair Huffaker · Directed by Harry Keller · Produced by Gordon Kay
A Universal-International Picture

NOW SHOWING — national RELEASE THEATRES — NORTH WEST LONDON

ACTON	Granada		HOLLOWAY	Essoldo
BARNET	Regal		ISLINGTON	Gaumont
BURNT OAK	Savoy		KENTON	Odeon
CAMDEN TOWN	Plaza		KILBURN	Grange
EALING	Walpole		NORTHWOOD	Rex
*EAST FINCHLEY	Rex		NOTTING HILL	Gaumont
EDGWARE ROAD	Gaumont		POTTERS BAR	Ritz
EDMONTON	Granada		RAYNERS LANE	Gaumont
ENFIELD	Florida		ST. ALBANS	Gaumont
FINCHLEY	Odeon		TOTTENHAM	Florida
FINSBURY PARK	Astoria		WALHAM GREEN	Gaumont
HAMMERSMITH	Regal		WALTHAM CROSS	Embassy
HARRINGAY	Essoldo		WATFORD	Gaumont
HARROW ROAD	Prince of Wales		WEALDSTONE	Odeon
HAVERSTOCK HILL	Odeon		WEMBLEY	Gaumont
HENDON	Gaumont		WILLESDEN	Granada

*2nd Feature Varies

Numerous Odeons take the Rank release at left but very few are showing this strong holiday National release

Star + The Purple Plain. *N:* Carthage In Flames (+ Danger Tomorrow)

G.I. Blues (+ Identity Unknown). *N:* A Dog In Flanders + Freckles

Song Without End (+ The Golden Fish *short*). *N:* The Three Worlds Of Gulliver + Seven Ways To Sundown

The Bulldog Breed (+ The Final Dream). *N:* Cinderfella (+ Lucky Jim *revival*)

1961

* *Main feature among the top twelve box-office attractions of the year*

Roadshows: Spartacus, The Guns Of Navarone *and* Exodus

London suburban wave of The Guns Of Navarone

* Pollyanna (+ Seven Cities Of Antarctica *short*). *N:* North To Alaska (+ Counterfeit)

Tunes Of Glory (+ A Taste Of Money). *N:* I Aim At The Stars (+ The Walking Target)

Man In The Moon (+ Marriage Of Convenience). *N:* Under Ten Flags (+ Teenage Thunder)

The Pure Hell Of St. Trinian's (+ Ski Troop Attack). *N:* Never On Sunday (+ Feet Of Clay)

Circle Of Deception (+ None But The Brave). *N:* The Great Impostor + Voice In The Mirror

Elmer Gantry (+ A Printer's Tale *short*). *N:* Desire In The Dust + Murder Incorporated

The Wackiest Ship In The Army (+ The Trunk). *N:* Flaming Star (+ The Secret Of The Purple Reef)

The Singer Not The Song (+ Japan *short*). *N:* The Big Fisherman

Esther And The King (+ Young Jesse James). *N:* Doctor Blood's Coffin + Take A Giant Step

Midnight Lace (+ Echo Of Barbara). *N:* A Breath Of Scandal (+ A Blueprint For Robbery)

No Love For Johnnie (+ The Solitary Child). *N:* Five Golden Hours (+ Moment Of Truth)

* Swiss Family Robinson (+ Islands Of The Sea *short*). *N:* The Canadians (+ Sea Wife *revival*)

Mr. Topaze (+ The Long Rope). *N:* The Fiercest Heart + September Storm

The Grass Is Greener (+ The Gambler Wore A Gun). *N:* The Rat Race (+ Triangle On Safari)

The World Of Suzie Wong (+ Rivers Of Life *short*). *N:* Saturday Night And Sunday Morning *revival* + Fasten Your Seat Belts

* The Magnificent Seven (+ The Police Dog Story). *N:* The Right Approach (+ Tess Of The Storm Country)

The Facts Of Life (+ Operation Bottleneck). *N:* Madison Avenue + The Little Shepherd Of Kingdom Come

The Greengage Summer (+ Panama Sal). *N:* The Curse Of The Werewolf + The Shadow Of The Cat

Double Bunk (+ The Wind Of Change). *N:* All Hands On Deck (+ The Emerald Curtain)

Pepe. *N:* Cry For Happy (+ High School Caesar)

The Big Gamble (+ Days Of Thrills And Laughter). *N:* Very Important Person (+ Gunfight)

Nearly A Nasty Accident (+ Home Is The Hero). *N:* Sanctuary (+ Hell Drivers *revival*)

Can-Can. *N:* Macumba Love + So Evil, So Young

The Big Show (+ The Silent Call). *N:* A Raisin In The Sun (+ Out Of The Shadow)

Spare The Rod (+ The Impersonator). *N:* The Secret Ways (+ Posse From Hell)

Return To Peyton Place (+ Shot In The Dark). *N:* There Was A Crooked Man *revival* + Trapeze *revival*

Two Rode Together (+ A Question Of Suspense). *N:* Follow That Man (+ The Boy Who Stole A Million)

Flame In The Streets (+ Partners In Crime). *N:* The Misfits (+ This Is Lebanon *short*)

The Young Savages (+ The Middle Course). *N:* Romanoff And Juliet (+ A Date With Death)

* One Hundred And One Dalmatians (+ Gunfight At Sandoval). *N:* The Wizard Of Baghdad + Battle On The Beach

Wild In The Country (+ Thin Ice). *N:* Greyfriars Bobby + Ten Who Dared

* Whistle Down The Wind (+ The Long Shadow). *N:* The Last Time I Saw Archie (+ You Have To Run Fast)

The Last Sunset (+ Information Received). *N:* The Absent Minded Professor (+ The Horsemasters)

By Love Possessed (+ Transatlantic). *N:* The Hoodlum Priest (+ Compelled)

The Alamo. *N:* Voyage To The Bottom Of The Sea (+ Dossier)

No, My Darling Daughter! (+ Murder In Eden). *N:* A Cold Wind In August + Mary Had A Little

Goodbye Again (+ Girls Girls Girls *short*). *N:* The Trapp Family (+ 20,000 Eyes)

Victim (+ Attempt To Kill). *N:* Marines Let's Go (+ Seven Thieves *revival*)

The Naked Edge (+ Five Guns To Tombstone). *N:* Tammy Tell Me True + Misty

A Taste Of Honey (+ Dangerous Afternoon). *A:* The Wastrel + The Big Bankroll

* The Parent Trap (+ The Horse With The Flying Tail). *A:* Room At The Top *revival* + The Kitchen

Come September (+ The Sergeant Was A Lady). *A:* The Marriage-Go-Round (+ This Other Eden *or* Out Of The Shadows)

The Queen's Guards (+ The Judas Goat)

The Young Doctors (+ The Cow And I). *A:* The Parent Trap *revival* + The Horse With The Flying Tail *revival*

Back Street (+ Man Detained). *A:* Victim *revival* + The League Of Gentlemen *revival*

The Hustler (+ It's All Greek To Me *short*). *A:* The Inn Of The Sixth Happiness *revival*

The Hellions (+ Johnny Nobody). *A:* La Dolce Vita

Town Without Pity (+ Secret Of Deep Harbour). *A:* Warlord Of Crete + Three On A Spree

Francis Of Assisi (+ Temple Of The Swinging Doll). *A:* Paris Blues (+ The Cat Burglar)

The Innocents (+ Anything For Laughs). *A:* Sail A Crooked Ship + Everything Ducky)

Nikki Wild Dog Of The North + Pinocchio *revival*. *A:* Snow White And The Three Clowns (+ Dancing Masters *revival*)

In The Doghouse (+ Wings Of Chance). *A:* Bachelor Flat (+ Sitting Pretty *revival*)

Babes In Toyland (+ The Hound That Thought He Was A Raccoon). *A: various double-bill revivals including* Doctor In Love, The 39 Steps (1959), Carry On Teacher *and* Watch Your Stern

1962

* *Main feature among the top twelve box-office attractions of the year*

** *Main feature among the top twelve box-office attractions of 1963*

Roadshows: El Cid, West Side Story, Barabbas *and* The Longest Day

London suburban wave: South Pacific

The Devil At 4 O'Clock (+ The Pursuers). *A:* On The Waterfront *revival* (+ The Most Dangerous Man Alive)

The Day The Earth Caught Fire (+ Part-Time

Wife). A: Revolt Of The Slaves + Teenage Millionaire

The Best Of Enemies (+ Enter Inspector Duval). A: Purple Noon (+ As The Sea Rages)

★ The Comancheros (+ Womanhunt). A: Twist Around The Clock + Gidget Goes Hawaiian

The Valiant (+ X-15). A: The Second Time Around + Pirates Of Tortuga

Pocketful Of Miracles (+ Transport Command). A: The Outsider + Six Black Horses

All Night Long (+ Never Back Losers). A: The Comancheros revival (+ Womanhunt revival); or Seven Women From Hell (+ Five Fingers revival)

Exodus (+ It's Magic short). A: Tender Is The Night (+ First Left Past Aden short)

Lover Come Back (+ Freedom To Die). A: Stork Talk (+ The One That Got Away revival); or The Naked Truth revival + Sapphire revival

One, Two, Three (+ Incident In An Alley). A: The Young Ones revival + Up Periscope revival or other

The Devil Never Sleeps (+ The Broken Land). A: Only Two Can Play revival (+ Terminus short)

Flower Drum Song (+ Sea Sanctuary short). A: Kapo or various

★ The Road To Hong Kong (+ Boy Who Caught A Crook). A: The Happy Thieves + Vera Cruz revival

★ The Guns Of Navarone. A: Pillow Talk revival + Operation Petticoat revival

H.M.S. Defiant (+ Design For Loving). A: It's Trad, Dad! (+ Battle In Outer Space); or Swiss Family Robinson revival

Sergeants Three (+ She Always Gets Their Man). A: Swiss Family Robinson revival (+ Niok short)

A Pair Of Briefs (+ Taxi To Tobruk). A: The Hands Of Orlac + Expresso Bongo revival

The Prince And The Pauper + Moon Pilot. A: Forever My Love

★ Waltz Of The Toreadors (+ Backfire). A: 13 West Street + Belle Sommers

Lonely Are The Brave (+ Hair Of The Dog). A: The Devil's Daffodil + It's A Great Life

Walk On The Wild Side (+ Two-Letter Alibi). A: Light In The Piazza (+ The Horizontal Lieutenant)

Two And Two Make Six (replaced by A Taste Of Honey revival)(+ Strongroom). A: Village Of Daughters + Guns In The Afternoon

The Four Horsemen Of The Apocalypse. A:

Geronimo (+ What Every Woman Wants)

† State Fair (+ The Desert Rats revival). A: The Road To Hong Kong revival (+ Cast A Long Shadow revival or various)

The Phantom Of The Opera + Captain Clegg. A: various double-bill revivals including Never Let Go and The Brides Of Dracula

Judgment At Nuremberg. A: Jessica (+ Tunes Of Glory revival or various)

The Inspector (+ A Letter To Three Wives revival). A: A Story Of David (+ Happy Is The Bride revival)

Big Red + Dumbo revival. A: Five Finger Exercise (+ Ambush In Leopard Street)

Mr. Hobbs Takes A Vacation (+ Air Patrol). A: Zotz + Don't Knock The Twist

Follow That Dream (+ Saintly Sinners). A: Reprieve (+ Dondi)

★ That Touch Of Mink (+ Emergency). A: The Girl On The Boat (+ The Clown And The Kid)

Bon Voyage! (+ Disneyland After Dark or A Penny For Your Thoughts short)

The Lion + Swingin' Along). A: The Wooden Horse Of Troy (+ She Knows Y'Know)

Tiara Tahiti (+ The Traitors or Gaolbreak). A: Arena Of Fear + The Fast Ones

The Spiral Road (+ Storm Cone short). A: The Cabinet Of Dr. Caligari (+ Pick Up On South Street revival)

The Loudest Whisper (+ Gun Street). A: The Vikings revival (+ Three Spare Wives)

Life For Ruth (+ Band Of Thieves). A: The Truth (+ Cry Double Cross)

The Miracle Worker (+ The Lamp In Assassin Mews). A: Corridors Of Blood + Nights Of Rasputin

Spartacus (+ New World Holiday)

★ Dr. No (+ Deadly Duo). A: Hemingway's Adventures Of A Young Man

Advise And Consent. A: The Boys (+ The Mad Twenties)

Birdman Of Alcatraz (+ Behave Yourself)

The Grip Of Fear (+ Operation Madball revival). A: Spartacus revival or various

The Notorious Landlady (+ 3.10 To Yuma revival)

The Wild And The Willing (+ The Primitives).

† State Fair + Desert Rats opened in south London simultaneously with the preceding programme, Four Horsemen Of The Apocalypse, in north London, then swopped over.

A: The 300 Spartans (+ The Frogmen revival)

The Manchurian Candidate (+ World Of Wax short). A: The Quare Fellow (+ The Battle Of The Sexes revival)

The Amorous Prawn (+ Behind The Great Wall)

Billy Budd (+ Gaolbreak or The Traitors). A: It Happened In Athens (+ Fury At Furnace Creek revival)

If A Man Answers + Island Escape

Kid Galahad (+ Frontier Uprising). A: The Jolson Story revival

Gigot + Three Coins In The Fountain revival

★ On The Beat (+ Tomboy And The Champ). A: Gigot + Three Coins In The Fountain revival [transferred from Rank Release after first week]

1963

★ Main feature among the top fourteen box-office attractions of the year

★★ Main feature among the top fourteen box-office attractions of 1964

Roadshows: Lawrence Of Arabia, 55 Days At Peking and Cleopatra

London suburban waves: South Pacific, The Longest Day, From Russia With Love and West Side Story

★ In Search Of The Castaways (+ Six-Gun Law). A: Harold Lloyd's World Of Comedy + The Wild Westerners

South Pacific. A: Five Weeks In A Balloon (+ The Little Bears)

★ Sodom And Gomorrah

The Bridge On The River Kwai revival. A: Seddok + Frantic

Cape Fear (+ Danger By My Side)

Witness For The Prosecution revival + The Far Country revival. A: Reach For Glory + Woman Of The River revival

Phaedra (+ When The Clock Strikes)

★ The Fast Lady (+ Stranglehold). A: Something Wild (+ The Nun And The Sergeant)

The L-Shaped Room (+ Spike Milligan On Treasure Island W.C.2 short). A: Summer Holiday revival (+ The Clue Of The New Pin revival or Black Gold)

I Could Go On Singing (+ Gang War)

This Sporting Life (+ Sunshine Islands short). A: The L-Shaped Room revival

Nine Hours To Rama (+ Sniper's Ridge). A: Sink The Bismarck! revival (+ The Firebrand)

Barabbas
40 Pounds Of Trouble (+ The Brazen Bell). *A:*
Blood On His Sword + The Courage Of
Black Beauty
Call Me Bwana (+ On The Run *or* The £20,000
Kiss). *A:* On The Beat *revival* (+ The Saw-
dust Ring)
Sammy Going South (+ Crazy Days *short*). *A:*
Madame + The Day That Mars Invaded Earth
Two For The Seesaw (+ The Explosive
Generation). *A:* Just For Fun + The Secret
Mark Of D'Artagnan
The Very Edge (+ Mystery Submarine). *A:*
Sodom And Gomorrah *revival*
The Day Of The Triffids (+ The Legion's Last
Patrol). *A:* Blood Money (+ Pushover *revival*)
Five Miles To Midnight (+ The Gentle Terror).
A: Red River *revival* + The Cool Mikado
Son Of Flubber + Escapade In Florence. *A:*
Woman Of Summer (+ Hand Of Death)
Lancelot And Guinevere (+ The Fur Collar).
A: In Search Of The Castaways *revival*
The List of Adrian Messenger (+ Showdown).
A: Confess, Dr. Corda + Drops Of Blood
The Mouse On The Moon (+ Son Of Thunder).
A: The Yellow Canary (+ The Navy Lark
revival)
The Interns (+ A Guy Called Caesar)
To Kill A Mockingbird (+ The Devil's Children)
The War Lover (+ The Break). *A:* Psycho
revival + The War Of The Worlds *revival*
Diamond Head (+ Take Me Over)
All This And Money Too (+ The Spanish
Sword). *A:* The Mongols + The Three Stooges
Meet Hercules
Savage Sam + The Horse Without A Head.
A: Captain Blood (+ The White Suit)
* Doctor In Distress (+ The £20,000 Kiss *or*
On The Run). *A:* The Three Caballeros
revival + Jungle Cat
Summer Magic + Sammy The Way Out Seal.
A: Marilyn (+ Young Guns Of Texas)
Taras Bulba (+ The Big City *short*). *A:* The
Black Buccaneer (+ Master Spy)
* Jason And The Argonauts + The Siege Of
The Saxons. *A:* Warrior's Rest (+ His Women)
80,000 Suspects (+ The Bay Of Saint Michel).
A: It's All Happening (+ Watch It Sailor *revival*)
* The Great Escape
A Gathering Of Eagles (+ The Bomb In The
High Street)
The Ugly American (+ The Fatal Hour). *A:*
Eve (+ Who Stole The Body?)

* Tom Jones (+ This Is Guernsey *short*)
The Running Man (+ Breath Of Life). *A:* The
Castilian (+ Two Tickets To Paris)
The Birds (+ Incident At Owl Creek *short*,
later replaced)
* The Longest Day. *A:* The Seventh Sword
(+ Flying Deuces *revival*)
* From Russia With Love (+ This Is Jordan
short). *A:* Divorce – Italian Style (+ A Face
In the Rain)
The Flight Of The White Stallions (+ The
Yellowstone Cubs). *A:* The Condemned Of
Altona (+ Thunder Island)
Bitter Harvest (+ Tiger Bay *revival*). *A:* Pressure
Point (+ A Cold Wind In August *revival*)
For Love Or Money (+ Farewell Performance).
A: In The Cool Of The Day (+ Square Of
Violence)
The Informers (+ White Corridors *revival*).
A: Please, Not Now! (+ Police Nurse)
In The French Style + Girl In The Headlines.
A: The Man From The Diners' Club +
Gidget Goes To Rome
Diary Of A Madman + Sword Of The
Conqueror. *A:* Toys In The Attic (+ War
Hunt)
Bye Bye Birdie (+ Cash On Demand). *A:*
Lassie's Great Adventure
** The Sword In The Stone (+ Dr. Syn Alias
The Scarecrow). *A:* Jason And The Argonauts
revival + Siege Of The Saxons *revival*
** A Stitch In Time (+ Live It Up). *A:* Charge
Of The Black Lancers (+ Between Love And
Duty)

1964

* *Main feature among the top fourteen box-office
attractions of the year*
** *Main feature among the top thirteen box-office
attractions of 1965*
Roadshows: It's A Mad, Mad, Mad, Mad World,
The Victors, The Fall Of The Roman Empire,
The Magnificent Showman, Becket *and* The
Cardinal
London suburban waves: The Cardinal *and*
Goldfinger

El Cid. *A:* 30 Years Of Fun (+ The Purple
Hills)
The Thrill Of It All (+ The Silent Raid)
West Side Story. *A:* From Russia With Love
revival

Take Her, She's Mine (+ Harbour Lights). *A:*
The Mysteries Of Paris + The Secrets Of
Buddha
* The Pink Panther (+ The Money Makers *short*)
Father Came Too (+ Impact). *A:* The Terror
(+ The Raiders Of Leyte Gulf)
Ladies Who Do + It's All Over Town
McLintock (+ One Mile Square *short*). *A:* O.S.S.
117 (+ El Hakim)
Under The Yum Yum Tree + Women Of The
World. *A:* Hero's Island + Studs Lonigan
Move Over Darling (+ Surf Party). *A:* King
Kong vs. Godzilla (+ The Raiders)
* The Long Ships (+ Looking In On The
Royal Navy *short*). *A:* Doctor In Love *revival*
+ Dentist In The Chair *revival*
Hot Enough For June! (+ The Switch). *A:* The
Funny Side Of Life + Clash Of Steel
* Charade (+ Strictly For The Birds). *A:* From
The Earth To The Moon + Enchanted Island
Kings Of The Sun (+ Stowaway In The Sky)
Captain Newman (+ Safety Is No Accident
short). *A:* Saturday Night Out + The Spectre
The Ceremony + Lilies Of The Field. *A:* Tom
Jones *revival* (+ *various*)
Dr. Strangelove Or How I Learned To Stop
Worrying And Love The Bomb
Stolen Hours + Johnny Cool
A Jolly Bad Fellow (+ The Quick Gun)
The Incredible Journey + The Waltz King. *A:*
A Tiger Walks + Born To Sing
Woman of Straw (+ Country Of The Vines *short*)
The Chalk Garden (+ *various*)
Girl With Green Eyes (+ The Devil's Agent)
Man's Favorite Sport + Tammy And The Doctor
Man In The Middle + The Sky Above – The
Mud Below
The Finest Hours (+ Boy With A Flute *short*).
A: Gunfight At The O.K. Corral *revival* +
Hell Is For Heroes *revival*
Seance On A Wet Afternoon (+ Following
The Sun). *A: as preceding week*
What A Way To Go! (+ Young Guns Of Texas
or Master Spy *or various*)
The World Of Henry Orient (+ The Road To
Hong Kong *revival*)
The Three Lives Of Thomasina + The
Misadventures Of Merlin Jones
* A Hard Day's Night
The Moonspinners (+ A Penny For Your
Thoughts *short or* Disneyland After Dark *short*)
First Men In The Moon + East Of Sudan
* 633 Squadron (+ Swinging U.K. *short*)

* Marnie (+ Return To The Island *short*)
The Beauty Jungle (+ Blind Corner)
Irma La Douce
55 Days At Peking. *A:* The Girl Hunters + 7
Women From Hell
Bedtime Story (+ Bullet For A Badman). *A: as preceding week*
The 7th Dawn (+ U.K. Swings Again *short*)
The Victors
* Goldfinger (+ Basque In The Sun *short*)
The Pumpkin Eater (+ The Six Sided Triangle *short*)
Guns At Batasi (+ Alone In Moscow)
Behold A Pale Horse (+ Five Against The House *revival*). *A:* Psyche 59 + She Got What She Asked For
Fate Is The Hunter (+ Apache Rifles)
Lord Of The Flies + The Comedy Man. *A:* The Black Torment
Wild And Wonderful (+ The Brass Bottle)
The Third Secret (+ Can-Can *revival*). *A:* The Magnificent Seven *revival* (+ Reels Within Reels *short*)
Flight From Ashiya + The Secret Invasion. *A:* Ferry Cross The Mersey + For Those Who Think Young
** Snow White And The Seven Dwarfs *revival* (+ The Legend Of Lobo)
The Magnificent Showman

1965

* *Main feature among the top thirteen box-office attractions of the year*
Roadshow runs of Lord Jim, The Sound Of Music, Those Magnificent Men In Their Flying Machines *and* The Greatest Story Ever Told
London suburban waves of Mary Poppins, Cleopatra, Genghis Khan *and* What's New Pussycat?

Topkapi (+ Quay To The Tor *short*). *A:* The Wizard Of Oz *revival* + Tom Thumb *revival*
Father Goose (+ The Lively Set)
The New Interns (+ Ride The Wild Surf)
Rio Conchos (+ Lifetime Of Comedy)
* The Train (+ Game Reserve *short*)
Send Me No Flowers (+ I'd Rather Be Rich)
It's A Mad, Mad, Mad, Mad World
The Pleasure Seekers (+ Nightmare In The Sun)
* A Shot In The Dark (+ A Home Of Your Own *short*)
Kiss Me Stupid (+ The Sicilians) [*main feature largely replaced after first week by revivals*]

The High Bright Sun (+ Fargo)
Goodbye Charlie (+ Night Train To Paris). *A:* Zorba The Greek (+ A Great Ship *short* or Island Long Summer *short*)
The Ipcress File (+ Taggart)
The Legend Of Young Dick Turpin + Those Calloways
* Lawrence Of Arabia
* The Intelligence Men (+ Be My Guest)
Masquerade (+ The Mouse On The Moon *revival*)
Good Neighbor Sam + Baby, The Rain Must Fall. *A:* La Ronde (+ The Ringer *or various*)
Hush Hush Sweet Charlotte (+ A Home Of Your Own *revival short*)
Strange Bedfellows (+ The Hanged Man)
A High Wind In Jamaica + Dear Brigitte
The Satan Bug (+ Never Mention Murder). *A:* The Great Escape *revival*
The Truth About Spring (+ Island Of The Blue Dolphins)
Invitation To A Gunfighter + That Man From Rio
Major Dundee (+ The Little Ones)
I'll Take Sweden (+ *various*)
The Knack... And How To Get It (+ Traitor's Gate)
The Art Of Love + That Funny Feeling
Mister Moses (+ Game For Three Losers)
Song Of The South *revival* + The Monkey's Uncle. *A:* John Goldfarb Please Come Home (+ Night Train To Paris); *or* Repulsion + The Black Torment
* Help! (+ Mozambique)
Shenandoah (+ McHale's Navy Joins The Air Force)
* Von Ryan's Express (+ Wild Wings *short*)
* Mary Poppins
Genghis Khan (+ Swing Aboard The Mary *short*)
Cat Ballou + You Must Be Joking!
Lord Jim
How To Murder Your Wife (+ How's Your I.Q. *short*)
The Fall Of The Roman Empire
What's New Pussycat? (+ A Day With Dino *short*)
Cleopatra
The Saboteur Code Name – "Morituri" (+ The Return Of Mr. Moto)
That Darn Cat! (+ Geronimo's Revenge)
Mirage (+ I'd Rather Be Rich *revival or various*). *A:* The Guns Of Navarone *revival*
From Russia With Love *revival* + Dr. No *revival*. *A:* Devils Of Darkness + This Shocking World

Ship Of Fools (+ Way Leggo *short* or Heads I Win *short*). *A:* The Bedford Incident + Love Has Many Faces
The Collector. *A:* A Shot In The Dark *revival* + The Pink Panther *revival*; *or* Devils Of Darkness + This Shocking World
A Study In Terror (+ No Survivors Please)
A Very Special Favor + I Saw What You Did
Peyton Place *revival. A:* The Glory Guys + Billie
Peter Pan *revival* + Emil And The Detectives
The Early Bird (+ The Sword Of Ali Baba *or* Fluffy)

1966

* *Main feature among the top fourteen non-roadshow box-office attractions of the year*
Roadshows: Othello *and* Khartoum
London suburban waves: Thunderball, The Greatest Story Ever Told *and* The Agony And The Ecstasy

* The Heroes Of Telemark (+ European Tapestry *short*)
The Hallelujah Trail (+ Pink Phink *or* Pickled Pink *shorts*)
Do Not Disturb + Up From The Beach
King Rat (+ Heads I Win *or* Way Leggo *shorts*)
The War Lord (+ The World Of Abbott And Costello)
Sky West And Crooked (+ Mission For A Killer)
Return From The Ashes + A Rage To Live
* Thunderball
Bunny Lake Is Missing (+ Arizona Raiders)
Blindfold (+ Bus Riley's Back In Town)
The Flight Of The Phoenix (+ Land Of The Red Dragon *short*)
* Our Man Flint (+ March Of The Movies)
Life At The Top (+ The Vanishing Busker *or* Sports A Go Go *shorts*)
* Doctor In Clover (+ Dateline Diamonds)
* That Riviera Touch (+ Incident At Phantom Hill)
The Ugly Dachsund (+ Winnie The Pooh And The Honey Tree *short* + The Tenderfoot)
The Silencers (+ Broken Sabre)
Frankie And Johnny + The Swingin' Set
Ride Beyond Vengeance + That Man In Istanbul
Stagecoach (+ The Murder Game)
Moment To Moment (+ The Ghost And Mr. Chicken). *A:* A Man Could Get Killed (+ Gunpoint)
Modesty Blaise (+ Round The Bend *short*)
The Trouble With Angels + Kimberley Jim

Tom Jones *revival* + Never On Sunday *revival*
Weekend At Dunkirk + The Horror Of It All.
  A: The Agony And The Ecstasy
Viva Maria! (+ Shotgun Wedding)
The Wrong Box (+ The Runaway)
Lost Command (+ New Faces Of Taiwan *or*
  Taiwan Today *shorts*)
Duel At Diablo + Boy Did I Get A Wrong
  Number!
Lt. Robin Crusoe U.S.N. (+ Run, Appaloosa,
  Run!)
* Those Magnificent Men In Their Flying
  Machines
Walk, Don't Run (+ The Tattooed Police Horse)
* Born Free (+ Hey There It's Yogi Bear)
How To Steal A Million (+ *various shorts*)
The Rare Breed (+ Fluffy *or* The Sword Of Ali
  Baba)
Cast A Giant Shadow (+ The Mighty
  Dolomites *short*)
Arabesque (+ Love And Kisses)
The Russians Are Coming, The Russians Are
  Coming (+ The Invisible Dr. Mabuse)
The Trap (+ The Pad And How To Use It)
Torn Curtain (+ All In A Flying *short*)
The Chase (+ Let's Laugh)
Fantastic Voyage (+ Guns For The Dictator)
The Fighting Prince Of Donegal (+ Stampede
  At Bitter Creek)
After The Fox (+ City Of Fear)
The Sandwich Man + They're A Weird Mob
What Did You Do In The War, Daddy? (+
  The Boy Cried Murder)
Beau Geste + Madame X
Alvarez Kelly (+ Winter A-Go-Go). *A:* Three
  On A Couch (+ The Texican)
Southwest To Sonora (+ The Young Warriors)
Georgy Girl + Rage
Batman (+ The Man Called Flintstone). *A:*
  Lady And The Tramp *revival* (+ Ballerina)
Thunderbirds Are Go (+ Namu The Killer
  Whale)
** Press For Time (+ And Now Miguel *or*
  Munster Go Home!)

1967

* *Main feature among the top fourteen non-
roadshow box-office attractions of the year*
Roadshows: The Taming Of The Shrew,
A Man For All Seasons, The Bible In The
Beginning, Doctor Dolittle *and* Custer Of
The West

London suburban waves: The Professionals *and*
You Only Live Twice

Finders Keepers (+ Greta: The Misfit Grey-
  hound *short*)
The Quiller Memorandum (+ Palaces Of A
  Queen *short*)
* The Blue Max
Gambit (+ The Plainsman)
Return Of The Seven (+ Ambush Bay)
Deadlier Than The Male (+ Gunfight In
  Abilene)
Murderers' Row (+ The Crooked Road)
Accident (+ Just Like A Woman). *A:* Psycho
  revival + War Of The Worlds *revival*
The Night Of The Generals
A Countess From Hong Kong (+ Agent For
  H.A.R.M.)
Follow Me, Boys! (+ Wind In The Willows *short*)
Don't Lose Your Head (+ The Reluctant
  Astronaut)
Hawaii
The Deadly Affair (+ Kiss The Girls And Make
  Them Die)
Maroc 7 + Let's Kill Uncle
Tobruk (+ The Ride To Hangman's Tree)
* Casino Royale (+ Take It From The Top
  short)(*two weeks*)
A Funny Thing Happened On The Way To
  The Forum (+ My Wife's Husband)
Hombre (+ The Naked Brigade)
Monkeys Go Home (+ Mosby's Marauders,
  later replaced by Bambi *revival as top feature*)
Caprice (+ Spaceflight IC-1). *A:* Meet
  Whiplash Willie (+ Caribbean Carousel *short*)
A Fistful Of Dollars (+ Lord Love A Duck)
How To Succeed In Business Without Really
  Trying (+ The Hills Run Red). *A:* The Great
  Escape *revival* + 633 Squadron *revival*
The Sand Pebbles. *A:* The Honey Pot
Stranger In The House (+ The Trygon Factor)
The Jokers + Texas Across The River
The Way West (+ Frozen Alive)
The Gnome-Mobile (+ The Million Dollar
  Collar)
In Like Flint (+ The Road To St. Tropez *short*)
* The Magnificent Two (+ Munster Go Home!
  or And Now Miguel)
Khartoum (+ Cirrhosis Of The Louvre *short*)
* The Professionals (+ Driving Force *or* Miss
  MacTaggart Won't Lie Down *shorts*)
The Long Duel (+ The Plank)
A Guide For The Married Man (+ Rapture)
Divorce American Style (+ Seven Guns For

The MacGregors)
* You Only Live Twice (+ How To Live With
  A Neurotic Dog *short*)
A Man And A Woman + The Sailor From
  Gibraltar. *A:* The Whisperers (+ Terror In
  Tokyo)
Fathom + Way...Way Out
In The Heat Of The Night (+ The Soldier)
Two For The Road (+ Sudden Summer *short*).
  A: The Alamo *revival*
For A Few Dollars More (+ Winter Wonder-
  land *short*)
To Sir With Love (+ Who's Minding The Mint?)
Rough Night In Jericho (+ Banning). *A:* Two
  Weeks In September + Some May Live
Pretty Polly (+ I Like Birds). *A:* How I Won
  The War + Baby Face Nelson *revival*
The St. Valentine's Day Massacre + One Born
  Every Minute
Berserk + The Torture Garden. *A:* The
  Happening (+ *various*)
Dead Heat On A Merry-Go-Round (+ The
  Big Mouth)
Night Of The Big Heat + The 10th Victim
Danger Route + Hour Of The Gun
** The Jungle Book + The Adventures Of
  Bullwhip Griffin
** The War Wagon (+ The Perils Of Pauline)

1968

* *Main feature among the top sixteen non-
roadshow box-office attractions of the year*
Roadshows: Thoroughly Modern Millie,
Doctor Faustus, The Charge Of The Light
Brigade, Star!, Oliver! *and* Chitty Chitty Bang
Bang

London suburban waves: A Man For All
Seasons *and* The Graduate

Follow That Camel (+ Sullivan's Empire)
Billion Dollar Brain (+ The Second Sin)
Tony Rome (+ Young Dillinger)
The Ambushers (+ 40 Guns To Apache Pass)
I'll Never Forget What's 'is Name (+ The
  Champagne Murders)
Valley Of The Dolls (+ The Tortoise And The
  Hare *short*)
Assignment K + The Tiger Makes Out
Here We Go Round The Mulberry Bush (+
  All The Way To Paris)
The Secret War Of Harry Frigg (+ Deadly
  Roulette)
The Bible...In The Beginning
The Scalphunters (+ Kill A Dragon)

* Guess Who's Coming To Dinner (+ Miss MacTaggart Won't Lie Down or Driving Force shorts)
Madigan (+ Games, replaced outside London by The Trap revival)
Blackbeard's Ghost (+ Old Yeller revival)
* Carry On Doctor (+ The Doomsday Flight)
* Planet Of The Apes (+ Promenade short)
A Dandy In Aspic (+ The Wild One revival)
Operation Kid Brother + Beach Red
The Ballad Of Josie + Rosie. A: Bedazzled (+ Track Of Thunder)
New Face In Hell (+ Nobody's Perfect)
Custer Of The West (+ Glasgow Belongs To Me short)
Don't Look Now We're Being Shot At! + The Shakiest Gun In The West
Clambake + Eight On The Run. A: The Man Outside + Amsterdam Affair
Woman Times Seven (+ The Further Perils Of Laurel And Hardy). A: Sex From A Stranger + Dead Run
Yours Mine And Ours + "Fitzwilly" Strikes Back
How To Save A Marriage... And Ruin Your Life + The Game Is Over. A: Luv + The Long Ride Home; or Vivre Pour Vivre (+ Targa Florio 500)
A Lovely Way To Go + What's So Bad About Feeling Good?
The Charge Of The Light Brigade
Never A Dull Moment (+ The Parent Trap revival)
Goldfinger revival + Thunderball revival with afternoon shows of Thunderbird 6 + Pink Panther cartoons
Yellow Submarine (+ Attack On The Iron Coast)
Bandolero! (+ A Little Of What You Fancy)
For The Love Of Ivy (+ Crocodile Safari)
The Happiest Millionaire
* The Devil's Brigade (+ 300 Sunny Days short)
* The Good, The Bad And The Ugly (+ King Of Blades or Autostrada shorts)
The Battle For Anzio (+ Don't Raise The Bridge, Lower The River)
* Prudence And The Pill (+ A Degree Of Murder)
Nobody Runs Forever (+ They Came From Beyond Space)
The Detective (+ The Changing Forest short)
Decline And Fall Of A Birdwatcher (+ The Algarve short)
The Graduate (+ Skater Dater short)

Duffy + Hammerhead
Hang 'Em High (+ Water Water Everywhere short)
Interlude (+ 30 Is A Dangerous Age, Cynthia. A: The Magnificent Seven revival + Return Of The Seven revival
Deadfall (+ Next Stop Scotland short)
House Of Cards (+ Journey To Shiloh)
The Sweet Ride (+ various). A: A Flea In Her Ear (+ The Cape Town Affair)
Corruption + Dead Or Alive. A: Where Angels Go...Trouble Follows (+ Young Americans)
Charly (+ The Million Dollar Man). A: Inspector Clouseau (+ A Twist Of Sand)
Cinderella revival + The Horse In The Gray Flannel Suit
Doctor Dolittle (+ The King's Breakfast short)

1969
* *Main feature among the top fourteen box-office attractions of the year*
Roadshows: Funny Girl, The Battle Of Britain *and* The Lion In Winter
London suburban waves: The Sound Of Music, Mackenna's Gold, Chitty Chitty Bang Bang *and* Midnight Cowboy

* Carry On Up The Khyber (+ King Kong Escapes!)
Lady In Cement (+ The Secret Life Of An American Wife)
Thoroughly Modern Millie
Play Dirty (+ Prospect Of Iceland short)
Some Girls Do (+ The Road To Corinth)
The Thomas Crown Affair (+ Submarine X-1)
The Wrecking Crew (+ The Big Gundown)
Coogan's Bluff + The Night Of The Following Day
Hellfighters (+ The King's Pirate)
The Sound Of Music [London only]. A: The Sweet Ride (+ various)
Joanna + Pretty Poison
Buona Sera Mrs. Campbell + Death Rides A Horse. A: You Only Live Twice revival +/or From Russia With Love revival +/or Dr. No revival
Hannibal Brooks + The Party
Those Magnificent Men In Their Flying Machines revival
* Candy (+ The Window Cleaner short)
Baby Love (+ An Eye For An Eye or Hellbenders)

Sweet Charity
Pendulum (+ The Desperados)
If He Hollers Let Him Go! + Today It's Me – Tomorrow You. A: Hell in the Pacific + various
Sinful Davey + The Night They Raided Minsky's
The Southern Star + You Must Be Joking! revival
100 Rifles (+ Panic In The City or The Money Jungle)
Before Winter Comes + Otley
The Boston Strangler (+ Naked Evil)
The File On The Golden Goose + Sam Whiskey. A: Support Your Local Sheriff + Salt and Pepper
Seven Brides For Seven Brothers revival (+ A Prince For Wales short; or various)
Guns Of The Magnificent Seven (+ A Prince For Wales short or various)
The Most Dangerous Man In The World (+ Gendarme In New York or The Gendarme Of St. Tropez)
Mackenna's Gold (+ A Place To Stand short)
* The Love Bug (+ Guns In The Heather)
Run Wild Run Free + First Men In The Moon revival
One Hundred And One Dalmatians revival (+ Ride A Northbound Horse). A: Cinderella – Italian Style + Mrs. Brown, You've Got A Lovely Daughter
Ring Of Bright Water + various
The Longest Day revival
* Carry On Camping (+ Did You Hear The One About The Traveling Saleslady or Hell Is Empty)
The Bridge At Remagen (+ Young Billy Young)
*3 Into 2 Won't Go (+ Eye Of The Cat)
The Pride of Miss Jean Brodie (+ World Of Fashion short)
Justine (+ shorts)
Whatever Happened To Aunt Alice? (+ Gappa – The Triphibian Monster)
The Undefeated (+ The Talking Mood short)
20,000 Leagues Under The Sea revival (+ Winnie The Pooh And The Blustery Day short)
Doppelganger + Death Of A Gunfighter
* The Virgin Soldiers (+ Thunder At The Border or various)
Che! (+ The Gendarme Of St. Tropez or Gendarme In New York)
Hard Contract + The Touchables
You Don't Need Pajamas At Rosie's + Where

It's At. *A:* A Nice Girl Like Me + The Tiger
And The Pussycat
Emma Hamilton (+ Kill Them All And Come
Back Alone)
The Mad Room + Land Raiders. *A:* Age of
Consent + Michael Kohlhaas
Crossplot + A Professional Gun. *A:* A Run
On Gold + How To Commit Marriage
Alice In Wonderland *revival* (+ Rascal)
Chitty Chitty Bang Bang (+ Animated Animals
short)

1970
* *Main feature among the top seven box-office
attractions of the year*
** *Main feature among the top ten non-roadshow
box-office attractions of 1971*
Roadshows: Hello Dolly, Anne Of The
Thousand Days, The Virgin And The Gypsy,
Patton: Lust For Glory *and* Cromwell
London suburban waves: The Sicilian Clan, The
Battle Of Britain *and* The Lion In Winter

David Copperfield (+ Last Of The Sixties *short*)
Carry On Again, Doctor (+ Hell Is Empty *or*
Did You Hear The One About The Travel-
ling Saleslady)
Topaz (+ Story Of A Woman). *A:* 9 Ages Of
Nakedness + The Babysitter
Funny Girl
* Midnight Cowboy (+ Carved Out Of Eden
short or various)
The Looking Glass War (+ Rampage At
Apache Wells *or* Thunder At The Border)
Twinky (+ Diamond Rush). *A:* For A Few
Dollars More *revival* + A Fistful Of Dollars
revival
The Reckoning (+ Model Shop)
* On Her Majesty's Secret Service (+ Schooners
Of The Caribbean *short*)
West Wide Story *revival*
John And Mary (+ The Last Shot You Hear)
Krakatoa – East Of Java (+ The Festival Game
short)
The Computer Wore Tennis Shoes (+ My Dog
The Thief)
* Butch Cassidy And The Sundance Kid (+
Happening In White)
Marooned (+ *shorts*)
The Lost Man (+ Better A Widow)
Tell Them Willie Boy Is Here (+ The Love God)
The Last Grenade (+ No Time To Die)

Chicago Chicago (+ Popi)
In Search Of The Castaways *revival* (+ King
Of The Grizzlies)
Winning (+ The Pipeliners *short*)
The Only Game In Town (+ The Pale Faced
Girl *short*)
The Happy Ending (+ Matchless)
Stiletto (+ Generation)
Beneath The Planet Of The Apes (+ The
Money Jungle *or* Panic In The City)
Let It Be + The Yellow Submarine *revival*. *A:*
Barquero + Hostile Witness
Cactus Flower (+ Machine Gun McCain). *A:*
The Kremlin Letter (+ *various*)
* M-A-S-H (+ Flight Of Fancy *short*)
Ned Kelly (+ Massacre Harbor). *A:* Born Free
revival (+ *various*)
The Boatniks (+ Hang Your Hat On The Wind
+ It's Tough To Be A Bird *shorts*)
The Secret Of Santa Vittoria (+ Down At The
Heel *short*)
The Games (+ Joaquin Murieta)
Airport (+ Portrait Of A People *short*)
* Carry On Up The Jungle (+ Mister Jericho)
Goodbye Gemini + Mumsy, Nanny, Sonny
And Girly
Toomorrow (+ The Last Adventure *or* Don't
Just Stand There)
The Executioner (+ A Man Called Sledge)
Doctor In Trouble (+ OSS 117 Murder For Sale)
The Sicilian Clan (+ BaJor)
They Shoot Horses, Don't They? (+ The Pale
Faced Girl *short*)
** Too Late The Hero (+ The Borders *short*)
The Battle Of Britain (+ Am I My Brother's
Keeper *short*)
The Butterfly Chain (+ A Walk)
Fragment Of Fear + Loving
The Man Who Had Power Over Women +
Picture Mommy Dead
Master Of The Islands (+ Hellboats)
Hello Goodbye (+ Prudence And The Pill
revival). *A:* Sunflower
The Mind Of Mr. Soames + The Liberation
Of L. B. Jones
I Start Counting + Mosquito Squadron. *A:*
Suppose They Gave A War And Nobody
Came? + Take The Money And Run
The Adventures Of Gerard (+ One More
Time). *A:* The King And I *revival*
** The Aristocats (+ Charlie, The Lonesome
Cougar)

1971
* *Main feature among the top ten non-roadshow
box-office attractions of the year*
Roadshows: Tora! Tora! Tora!, Song Of
Norway, Scrooge, The Last Valley, Waterloo
and The Music Lovers
London suburban waves: Cromwell, Oliver!,
Waterloo *and* Anne Of The Thousand Days

Carry On Loving (+ Under The Table You
Must Go *or* Mister Jericho)
Patton: Lust For Glory
The Private Life Of Sherlock Holmes (+ Under-
ground *or* Mosquito Squadron)
Hello, Dolly!
Take A Girl Like You + Getting Straight. *A:*
You Can't Win 'Em All + Hook, Line And
Sinker
They Call Me Mister Tibbs! + Hornet's Nest
Countess Dracula + Hell's Belles
The House That Dripped Blood (+ The
Honeymoon Killers). *A:* Say Hello To
Yesterday (+ To Commit A Murder)
Myra Breckinridge + Beyond The Valley Of
The Dolls
Assault (+ Subterfuge)
Games That Lovers Play (+ One On Top Of
The Other). *A:* One Brief Summer (+ Fathom
revival)
10 Rillington Place (+ For Singles Only)
Murphy's War (+ The Crazy World Of
Laurel And Hardy)
Dad's Army (+ *various*)
The Wild Country + The Barefoot Executive
Perfect Friday (+ The Girl Who Couldn't Say
No)
When Eight Bells Toll (+ White Comanche *or*
Kona Coast)
Lawman (+ Last Escape *or* If It's Tuesday It
Must Be Belgium)
You Can't Win 'Em All + I Walk The Line. *A:*
A Severed Head
The McKenzie Break (+ Sabata)
The Statue (+ Change Of Mind) *A:* The Great
White Hope
Black Beauty (+ *various*)
* Soldier Blue (+ *various*)
The Landlord + Cotton Comes To Harlem
A: You Only Live Twice *revival* + A Fistful
Of Dollars *revival*
The People Next Door + C.C. And Company.
A: Macho Callahan + Rider On The Rain
A Town Called Bastard (+ The Samurai)

I Love My Wife (+ Violent City). *A:* One Of Those Things + Explosion

Valdez Is Coming (+ Man of Violence *or* Walk A Crooked Path)

All The Right Noises + B.S. I Love You. *A:* The Mephisto Waltz + One Brief Summer; *or* Lawrence Of Arabia

The Aristocats *revival* (+ *various*)

Flight Of The Doves (+ Taffy And The Jungle Hunter *or* The Terronauts)

Million Dollar Duck (+ The Living Desert *revival*)

Tora! Tora! Tora!

Escape From The Planet Of The Apes (+ *various*)

Carry On Henry (+ The Firechasers)

The Owl And The Pussycat (+ *various*)

Vanishing Point (+ The Soldier Who Declared Peace)

Revenge (+ Beyond The Law). *A:* Quest For Love (+ Company Of Killers); *or* Goldfinger *revival* + For A Few Dollars More *revival*

Sunday, Bloody Sunday (+ 500 Islands *or* It's Strictly For The Birds *shorts*)

Captain Apache (+ The Last Adventure *or* Don't Just Stand There)

* The Last Valley (+ The Sword And The Geisha *or* Aphrousa *shorts*)

Twins Of Evil + Hands Of The Ripper

Scandalous John (+ Robin Hood *revival*)

The Hunting Party (+ *various*)

The Horsemen (+ *various*). *A:* Blind Terror + Doctors' Wives

Walkabout (+ *various*). *A:* Hannie Caulder (+ *various*)

Outback + What's The Matter With Helen? *A:* The Awful Story Of The Nun Of Monza (+ *various*)

Willard (+ *various*). *A:* Five Easy Pieces + The Lady In The Car With Glasses And A Gun

The Grissom Gang (+ *various*) *A:* Doc + The Red Baron

The Marriage Of A Young Stockbroker (+ Making It). *A:* Red Sky At Morning + One More Train To Rob

The Mickey Mouse Anniversary Show (+ The Mooncussers). *A:* Where's Poppa? + Bananas (*matinees*: Chitty Chitty Bang Bang)

Sleeping Beauty *revival* + Treasure Island *revival*

1972

* *Main feature among the top ten non-roadshow box-office attractions of the year*

** *Main feature among the top ten box-office attractions of 1973*

Roadshows: * Nicholas And Alexandra, * Bedknobs And Broomsticks, * Fiddler On The Roof, * Cabaret, Young Winston *and* Alice's Adventures In Wonderland

London suburban waves: * Cabaret, * Diamond Are Forever, * The French Connection, Song Of Norway, Pancho Villa, The Music Lovers, * Bedknobs And Broomsticks *and* Nicholas And Alexandra

Scrooge (+ The Tall Ships *short*)

Please Sir! (+ Company Of Killers *or* Beyond The Law)

Carry On At Your Convenience (+ White Comanche *or* Kona Coast)

Carnal Knowledge (+ Hellbenders *or* An Eye For An Eye)

Straw Dogs (+ *shorts*)

And Now For Something Completely Different + The Last Warrior

Bloomfield + The Undefeated *revival*

The Anderson Tapes (+ Brother John *or* Summertree)

Catch Me A Spy (+ Conquista)

Dynamite Man From Glory Jail + The Love Machine

Burke And Hare + More Dead Than Alive

Bad Man's River (+ Quackser Fortune Has A Cousin In The Bronx)

* Diamonds Are Forever (*two weeks*)

* The French Connection (+ Gift Of The Sea *short*)

The Organisation + Cannon For Cordoba

Zee And Co (+ Welcome To The Club *or* Cisco Pike)

Vampire Circus (+ The Side Hackers *or* Angels Who Burn Their Wings)

Thunderball *revival* + Dr. No *revival*. *A:* Anne Of The Thousand Days

Buck And The Preacher (+ *shorts*)

Madame Sin (+ *various*)

Kidnapped (+ *various*)

Danny Jones + My Old Man's Place. *A:* The Touch + Lovers And Other Strangers; *or* Kotch + How Do I Love Thee?

Made For Each Other (+ *various*). *A:* Cat Ballou *revival* + Red Circle

Zero Population Growth (+ *various*)

Hospital (+ The Honkers)

Chato's Land (+ Here We Go Round The Mulberry Bush *revival*)

Catlow + The Jerusalem File. *A:* The Culpepper Cattle Company + The Seven Minutes

The Red Sun (+ The Executioner *revival*) *various revivals* (matinees: Lucky Luke + Kes *revival*)

Now You See Him, Now You Don't (+ Menace On The Mountain)

Living Free (+ *various*)

Dumbo *revival* + Napoleon And Samantha

How To Steal A Diamond In Four Uneasy Lessons (+ The Darwin Adventure)

Carry On Matron (+ Top Gear)

Junior Bonner (+ The Moon And The Sledge-hammer)

The Possession Of Joel Delaney (+ Crucible Of Terror)

Pulp (+ Pussycat, Pussycat, I Love You)

Conquest Of The Planet Of The Apes (+ What Became Of Jack And Jill?)

A Fistful Of Dynamite (+ York *short*)

The Burglars (+ *various*)

The Heist (+ Summertree *or* Brother John)

* Bedknobs And Broomsticks. *A:* Endless Night + Dead Men Ride

The Nightcomers (+ Road To Salina). *A:* The Strange Adventure Of Rosalie + To Kill A Clown

Tales From The Crypt + The Fiend

Butterflies Are Free + And Now For Something Completely Different *revival*. *A:* The Glasshouse + Pancho Villa

Fuzz + Hickey And Boggs

Blood River (+ Bury Them Deep) *A:* Night Hair Child + Death Line

The Magnificent Seven Ride (+ Winged Devils). *A:* When The Legends Die (+ *various*)

The Last Picture Show (+ Five Easy Pieces *revival*). *A:* To Find A Man; *or* Ben + The Baby Maker

The Pied Piper (+ Baffled!)

** Snow White And The Seven Dwarfs *revival* + Pablo And The Dancing Chihuahua

Carry On Abroad (+ East Side, West Side *short*)

1973

* *Main feature among the top ten box-office attractions of the year*
** *Main feature among the top ten box-office attractions of 1974*

Roadshows: Man Of La Mancha *and* Lost Horizon

Provincial release: ★ Last Tango In Paris

London suburban waves: The Ruling Class, Man Of La Mancha *and* The Great Waltz

The Mechanic (+ Impasse)
Nothing But The Night (+ All Coppers Are... *or* The Falling Man)
Ooh...You Are Awful (+ Some Kind Of Hero)
Innocent Bystanders (+ Captain Apache *or various*)
Precinct 45 Los Angeles Police (+ A Reflection Of Fear)
Elvis On Tour (+ Earth II)
Adolf Hitler, My Part In His Downfall (+ The Bounty Hunters)
The Ragman's Daughter + The Salzburg Connection
★ The Poseidon Adventure (+ Are You Ready Go *short*)
The Offence + Support Your Local Gunfighter
Soldier Blue *revival* + Carnal Knowledge *revival*. A: When Eight Bells Toll *revival* + Puppet On A Chain *revival*
Travels With My Aunt + Never Mind The Quality Feel The Width
Psychomania + The Baby. A: The Asphyx (+ Zero Population Growth *revival or* The Possession Of Joel Delaney *revival*)
Fiddler On The Roof
Snowball Express (+ Saludos Amigos *revival or* The Magic Of Walt Disney World *shorts*)
Alice's Adventures In Wonderland (+ The Duna Bull *short*)
Shamus + Black Gunn. A: The National Health + The Deadly Trap
Everything You Always Wanted To Know About Sex (+ *various*)
The Love Ban (+ Two Minds For Murder). A: A Man To Respect (+ The Law Enforcers)
Heat (+ *various*)(*limited*)
Father Dear Feather (+ Nickel Queen *or* Go For A Take)
Across 110th Street + Jennifer On My Mind
Something To Hide + Confessions Of A Police Captain
Hitler: The Last Ten Days (+ *various*)
Theatre Of Blood + Hammer
Avanti! (+ Magic Carpet *short*)
The Bridge On The River Kwai *revival*. A: A Warm December + The Only Way Out Is Dead
Penny Gold (+ Baffled! *or various*)
Bless This House (+ The Gamblers *or* The Five Crazy Boys)

The Sword In The Stone *revival* + The Incredible Journey *revival*
Battle For The Planet Of The Apes + The Neptune Factor
Tom Sawyer + Gawain And The Green Knight
The World's Greatest Athlete (+ Diamonds On Wheels)
No Sex Please – We're British (+ The Hungarians *short*)
Young Winston
★ Live And Let Die (+ Time Was The Beginning *short*)(*two weeks*)
A Touch Of Class (+ They Call Me Trinity)
Emperor Of The North (+ Trouble Man). A: The Hireling + Love, Pain And The Whole Damn Thing
Scorpio (+ Crossplot *revival*)
The Lovers! (+ Birds Of Prey)
Lost Horizon. A: Let The Good Times Roll
The Man Called Noon + The Winners
Night Watch (+ Thumb Tripping). A: Fist Of Fury (+ Jesse And Lester)
White Lightning + Harry In Your Pocket
The Legend Of Hell House (+ Vault Of Horror)
Oklahoma Crude. A: To Find A Man + Stand Up And Be Counted
The Adventures Of Barry McKenzie (+ Assassin). A: The Long Goodbye (+ Return Of Sabata)
The Last American Hero (+ Honor Thy Father)
Diamonds Are Forever *revival* + From Russia With Love *revival*. A: Man Of The East (+ *various*)
Charlotte's Web. A: The Pied Piper
★★ Mary Poppins *revival*

1974

★ *Main feature among the top ten box-office attractions of the year*
★★ *Main feature among the top ten box-office attractions of 1973*

London suburban waves: The Last Detail (+ The Pursuit Of Happiness), Robin Hood (+ Wild Geese Calling)

The Belstone Fox (+ The Plank *revival or* They're A Weird Mob *revival*)
Carry On Girls (+ Go For A Take *or* Nickel Queen)
Blindman + Gordon's War

Sleuth (+ *shorts*). A: The Canterbury Tales (+ *shorts*); or The Big Boss (+ *various*)
Don't Look Now (+ The Wicker Man)
The Day Of The Dolphin (+ Trinity Is Still My Name)
Godspell (+ *shorts*). A: My Fair Lady
Executive Action. A: Penny Gold
Soft Beds, Hard Battles (+ The Last Chapter *short*). A: Hap-Ki-Do (+ *shorts*)
Electra Glide In Blue (+ *various*). A: You Only Live Twice *revival* + Thunderball *revival*
★ The Way We Were (+ The Orient *short*)
The Stone Killer (+ Santee)
The Seven-Ups + Lady Ice
The Golden Voyage Of Sinbad + Lost In The Desert
★ Herbie Rides Again (+ Run, Cougar, Run)
Digby – The Biggest Dog In The World (+ Northwest Frontier *revival*)
Cops And Robbers (+ The Outside Man)
Billy Two Hats (+ Three). A: House Of Whipcord + Hotel Of Free Love
Frankenstein And The Monster From Hell + The Fists Of Vengeance. A: Kung Fu – The Headcrusher + The Hit Man
The Beast Must Die + Blood Sisters. A: The Affair + The Winners
The Optimists Of Nine Elms (+ *various*)
Sleeper (+ Visit To A Chief's Son)
Busting + I Escaped From Devil's Island. A: Dr. No *revival* + Goldfinger *revival*
The Way Of The Dragon (+ Back Alley Princess *or* Deaf And Mute Heroine)
Investigation Of A Murder + Payday. A: The Heartbreak Kid
Zardoz (+ Cross Country Go *short*)
★ Papillon
Horror Express + The Godfather Of Harlem. A: Superchick + Knuckle-Men; *or* The Guns Of Navarone *revival*
Mr. Majestyk + The Spikes Gang
Song Of The South *revival* + One Little Indian
Carry On Dick (+ That's Your Funeral)
Huckleberry Finn (+ Hercules Against Kung-Fu)
Superdad (+ That Darn Cat! *revival*)
★ The Three Musketeers (+ The Buried Island *short*)
For Pete's Sake (+ Dirty Money)
★★ Last Tango In Paris (+ The Fiend *or* Nobody Ordered Love)
Caravan To Vaccares (+ A Murder Is A Murder...Is A Murder *or* Son Of Blob)
The Tamarind Seed (+ Thunder Of Silence

short or The Hunter short). A: The Internecine
Project (+ Joe)

Confessions Of A Window Cleaner (+ The
Take)

Ash Wednesday (+ The Mad Bomber). A:
Don't Just Lie There, Say Something (+
Carry On Camping revival)

11 Harrowhouse + Butch Cassidy And The
Sundance Kid revival. A: The Nine Lives Of
Fritz The Cat (+ Weekend With The Baby-
sitter)

Live And Let Die revival + On Her Majesty's
Secret Service revival. A: Herbie Rides Again
revival (+ Run, Cougar, Run revival)

* Robin Hood (+ Wild Geese Calling)

Lightning Sword Of Death (+ Crazy Joe). A:
Vampira (+ The Gravy Train)

Thunderbolt And Lightfoot (+ A Pride Of
Islands short)

Escape From The Planet Of The Apes revival
+ Planet Of The Apes revival. A: Cabaret
revival (+ shorts)

Bank Shot + Dead Cert. A: A Reason To Live,
A Reason To Die (+ The Clones)

And Now The Screaming Starts + Doctor
Death. A: Persecution (+ The Anderson
Tapes revival)

Chosen Survivors + The Mutations. A: One-
Armed Boxer + The Sky Hawk

no release

Oliver! revival. A: The Island At The Top Of
The World (+ Winnie The Pooh And Tigger
Too short)

Peter Pan revival + Charley And The Angel

1975

* Main feature among the top ten box-office
attractions of the year

** Main feature among the top ten box-office
attractions of 1976

London suburban waves: A Man For All
Seasons, The Night Porter and The French
Connection Number 2

The Mad Adventures Of Rabbi Jacob (+ That
Riviera Touch revival or The Magnificent
Two revival)

Gold (+ A Sport Of Kings short)

Juggernaut (+ Reserved For Animals short)

Cinderella Liberty + Call Harry Crown

The Apprenticeship Of Duddy Kravitz (+
Ruthless or Manhunt In Milan)

Open Season + Thomasine And Bushrod

Advertisement in a national newspaper, much reduced in size, for all the Odeons in the southern half of England at Christmas 1974.

Flame (+ Radio Wonderful *short revival*)
Dirty Mary, Crazy Larry (+ Hex). A: When Taekwondo Strikes + Kung Fu Girl
Ransom (+ Vive Le Sport *short revival*)
The Taking Of Pelham One Two Three (+ Don't Gape *short*)
Frightmare (+ The Living Dead At The Manchester Morgue). A: My Pleasure Is My Business + To Kill Or To Die
Escape To Witch Mountain (+ The Castaway Cowboy)
* The Man With The Golden Gun (+ Woes Of Golf *short*)(*two weeks*). A: (*first week*) Buster And Billie (+ *various*)
The Odessa File (+ Listen To The Sunrise *short*). A: California Split (+ *various*)
Bring Me The Head Of Alfredo Garcia (+ *shorts*)
What Changed Charley Farthing? (+ The Doberman Gang *or* The Gamblers)
Breakout (+ The Lords Of Flatbush)
Capone + Deadly Strangers
Rosebud (+ *shorts*). A: Arabian Nights (+ *various*)
The Land That Time Forgot (+ The Tender Warrior)
Young Frankenstein (+ The King's Revolution *short*)
I Don't Want To Be Born + The Ghoul
no release
Three For All (+ *various*)
Funny Lady (+ Thames And Tower *short*) (*limited*)
Claudine (+ *various*). A: Panic In Needle Park (+ *various*)
Brannigan (+ Clydescope *short*)
Lady And The Tramp *revival* (+ The Bears And I)
Paper Tiger (+ Superargo *or* The Fast Lady *revival*)
* The Island At The Top Of The World (+ Winnie The Pooh And Tigger Too *short*)
The Seventh Voyage Of Sinbad *revival* (+ Watch Out, We're Mad)
The Apple Dumpling Gang + The Donald Duck Story
The Four Musketeeers: The Revenge Of Milady (+ The Magic Dream *short*)
The Wilby Conspiracy (+ Mixed Company)
The Klansman (+ The Triple Echo *revival*)
Shampoo (+ Falling Angels *short*)
Confessions Of A Pop Performer (+ Police Story)

French Connection Number 2 (+ Sun And Games In Paradise *short*). A: The Wild Party + The Twelve Chairs
That Lucky Touch (+ The Execution *or* The Con Man)
The Happy Hooker (+ *various*). A: The Fortune (+ The National Health *revival*)
Operation Undercover (+ Pieces Of Dreams). A: The Rocky Horror Picture Show
The Wind And The Lion (+ Two Man-Made Wonders *short*)
Race With The Devil (+ The Blue Knight)
Bite The Bullet (+ Taming The Tide *short*)
White Line Fever + Night Caller
The Reincarnation Of Peter Proud + Arnold
Legend Of The Werewolf + Vampire Circus *revival*. A: Take A Hard Ride (+ Blue Water, White Death *revival*)
The Man With The Golden Gun *revival* + Live And Let Die *revival*. A: Killers Of Killers *revival* + Chato's Land *revival*
Sharks' Treasure + Moonrunners
** The Jungle Book *revival* + Return Of The Big Cat (*two weeks*)

1976

Main feature among the top ten box-office attractions of the year

London suburban waves: Tommy (+ Dawn-breakers *short*), The Duchess And The Dirt-water Fox (+ Wurzelfield *short*) and Taxi Driver

Royal Flash + W. W. And The Dixie Dancekings
Carry On Behind (+ Fraud)
The Streetfighter (+ And Now For Something Completely Different *revival*)
The Adventure Of Sherlock Holmes' Smarter Brother + White Fang
The Man From Hong Kong (+ The Killer Is On The Phone)
The Romantic Englishwoman (+ Thunder Of Light *short*) A: Love And Death (+ Smile)
The Best Of Walt Disney's True-Life Adventures + The Absent Minded Professor *revival*
Breakheart Pass (+ Jeremy)
* The Return Of The Pink Panther (+ Where The Americas Meet *short*)
* Rollerball (+ Skater Dater *revival short*)
Lucky Lady (+ The Banger Boys *short*)
The Killer Elite (+ *various shorts*)
Farewell, My Lovely (+ Jory)
Great Expectations (+ *shorts*)

One Of Our Dinosaurs Is Missing (+ Man, Monsters And Mysteries *short* + *cartoons*)
The Man Who Would Be King (+ Guns At The Wood *short*)
* One Flew Over The Cuckoo's Nest (+ It's A Dog's Life *short*)
Diamonds + Russian Roulette
The Black Bird + The Fortune
The Man Who Fell To Death (+ Kama Sutra Rides Again *revival short*)
Blackbeard's Ghost *revival* (+ Nikki, Wild Dog Of The North *revival*)
The Count Of Monte Cristo (+ Spot)
Sky Riders (+ Peeper)
Papillon *revival* + The Way We Were *revival*. A: Last Tango In Paris *revival* + Everything You Always Wanted To Know About Sex *revival*
Gator (+ Freelance)
Vigilante Force (+ The Devil Within Her). A: The "Human" Factor (+ The Swordsman); *or* Lenny (+ *shorts*)
The Diamond Mercenaries (+ ...All The Way Boys)
The Last Hard Men (+ Fighting Mad)
The Rocky Horror Picture Show (+ *various*). A: Phantom Of The Paradise (+ *various*); *or* The Antichrist (+ *various*)
The Sound Of Music *revival*
Escape From The Dark (+ Winnie The Pooh And The Honey Tree *revival short*)
Robin And Marian (+ For Pete's Sake *revival*)
Bambi *revival* + The Strongest Man In The World
At The Earth's Core + The Red Pony
Shout At The Devil
The Missouri Breaks (+ The Boat *short*)
Confessions Of A Driving Instructor (+ Baby Blue Marine)
The Duchess And The Dirtwater Fox (+ Wurzelfield *short*). A: The Devil's Rain + Vampyres
* The Omen (+ Bizarre And The Beautiful *short*)(*two weeks*)
Murder By Death (+ Flight Without Feathers *short*)
From Noon Till Three + Stay Hungry
No Deposit, No Return (+ Dr. Syn Alias The Scarecrow *revival*)
Carry On England (+ The Stoolie *or* The Wrestler)
Diamonds Are Forever *revival* + Gold *revival*
* The Omen *repeat* (+ Bizarre And The

Beautiful *revival short*). *A:* Tommy (+ Dawn-breakers *short*)
The Sailor Who Fell From Grace With The Sea (+ W)
Obsession (+ The Streetfighter *revival*)
Trackdown + Rancho Deluxe
no release
One Hundred And One Dalmatians *revival* + Ride A Wild Pony (*two weeks*)

1977

* *Main feature among the top ten box-office attractions of the year*
** *Main feature among the top ten box-office attractions of 1978*

Bugsy Malone (+ John And The Magic Music Man *short*). *A:* Raid On Entebbe
The Return Of A Man Called Horse (+ A Town Called Ayr *short*)
Grizzly + Drive-In
Taxi Driver (+ Concorde *short*)
Mother, Jugs And Speed + Breaking Point
I Will, I Will For Now (+ *various*). *A:* (*London only*) Texas Chainsaw Massacre (+ Escape To Entebbe *short*)
Silent Movie (+ 7 Days In Summer *short* or Asian Variations *short*)
Carrie (+ *various*)
Blue Belle + Death Dealers
Helter Skelter + Abduction. *A:* The Front + Harry And Walter Go To New York
The Little Girl Who Lives Down The Lane + Nothing But The Night *revival*
C.A.S.H. + Hang Up
Next Stop Greenwich Village + Alex And The Gypsy
The Pink Panther Strikes Again (+ Free As A Bird *short*) (*two weeks*). *A:* Jabberwocky
The Treasure Of Matecumbe (+ Wind In The Willows *revival short*)
Silver Streak (+ Wild Life USA *short*)
Network (+ *shorts*)
Jabberwocky (+ Midnight Spider *short*)
Joseph Andrews + Jackson County Jail
Carquake + The Giant Spider Invasion
Tentacles + Mr. Billion
Freaky Friday (+ Run, Appaloosa, Run! *revival*)
Burnt Offerings (+ *various*)
Inserts (+ Arabian Nights *revival*) (*limited*)
Rocky (+ Mountain Rescue *short*)
Bound For Glory (*limited*)

The Cassandra Crossing (+ Asian Variations or Seven Days In Summer *short*)
The Jungle Book *revival* + One Of Our Dinosaurs Is Missing *revival*
The Shaggy Dog (+ Niok The Orphan Elephant *short*)
Donald Duck Goes West + Blackbeard's Ghost *revival*
* Sinbad And The Eye Of The Tiger (+ Lost In The Wild)
Cinderella *revival* + Texas John Slaughter *revival*
The Prince And The Pauper (+ The Angelos Incident *short*)
* The Spy Who Loved Me (+ Dangerous Game *short*)(*two weeks*)
Fun With Dick And Jane + Murder By Death *revival*
no release
Confessions From A Holiday Camp (+ Shadow Of The Hawk or Anger In His Eyes)
* A Bridge Too Far (*two weeks*)
March Or Die (+ The Man Who Would Be King *revival*)
Swiss Family Robinson *revival* (+ Minado The Wolverine *short*)
Communion + Tintorera
Black Joy (+ Carquake *revival*)
Rollerball *revival* + Juggernaut *revival*
The House Of Exorcism (+ Innocent Bystanders *revival*)(*limited*)
Twilight's Last Gleaming (+ Woodlands Harvest *short*)
no release (*two weeks*)
** The Rescuers (+ Born To Run) (*three weeks*) *A:* (*second week*) Annie Hall (+ The Waiting Room *short*)

1978

* *Main feature among the top ten box-office attractions of the year*
** *Main feature among the top ten box-office attractions of 1979*

* The Rescuers (*third week*)
New York, New York (+ The End Of The Road *short*)
Valentino (+ The Speed Sailors *short*)
The Other Side Of Midnight
* The Deep (+ Good Olde England *short*) (*two weeks*). *A:* (*second week*) * Star Wars (+ Fast Company *short*)
The Pink Panther Strikes Again *revival* + The

Return Of The Pink Panther *revival*
Goodbye Emmanuelle + Rosie Dixon – Night Nurse
Audrey Rose (+ *various*) *A:* Fellini's Casanova
Golden Rendezvous + That's Carry On. *A:* * Star Wars
Yellow Emmanuelle + The French Governess (*limited*)
Spiderman + You Light Up My Life
Candleshoe + Alice In Wonderland *revival*
* Star Wars
Tomorrow Never Comes (+ The Uncanny or Persecution *revival* or The "Human" Factor *revival*)
Live And Let Die *revival* + The Man With The Golden Gun *revival*. *A:* Holocaust 2000 + Tigers Don't Cry
The Savage Bees + The Incredible Melting Man. *A:* Julia (+ R.H. & D.R. *short*)
The Four Feathers (+ *shorts*). *A:* * Close Encounters Of The Third Kind
Rocky *revival* + Network *revival*
Madame Claude (+ *various*)(*limited*)
The Stick Up (+ Jeremy *revival*)
no release
The Four Musketeers *revival* + The Three Musketeers *revival*. *A:* Salon Kitty (+ *various shorts*)
Assault On Precinct 13 (+ Interruptions *short*) (*limited*)
no release
The Betsy (+ *shorts*)
Equus (+ *various shorts*). *A:* Go Tell The Spartans (+ *various*)
The Turning Point (+ Hobbs Choice)
Thank God It's Friday (+ Let The Good Times Roll *revival*)
Pinocchio *revival* + The Hound That Thought He Was A Racoon *revival*
The Last Waltz (+ *shorts*)(*limited*)
* Close Encounters Of The Third Kind (*two weeks*) *A:* (*second week*) An Unmarried Woman (+ Pride Of Penguins *short*)
* Herbie Goes To Monte Carlo (+ Mysteries Of The Deep *short*)
* The Revenge Of The Pink Panther (+ London Skateboards *short*)(*two weeks*). *A:* (*second week*) Midnight Express (+ Sea World *short*)
Julia (+ R.H. & D.R. *short*)
The Wild Geese (+ The Great Pram Race *short*) (*two weeks*)
The Legacy (+ The Lords Of Flatbush *revival*)
The Odd Job (+ The Red Pony *revival*)

The Cheap Detective (+ *various*). A: Coming Home (+ *shorts*)

The Cat From Outer Space (+ Yellowstone Cubs *revival*). A: The World's Greatest Lover + Fire Sale

An Unmarried Woman (+ Pride Of Penguins *short*)

F.I.S.T. (+ *various shorts*). A: The Hound Of The Baskervilles + The Giant Spider Invasion *revival*

Confessions Of A Window Cleaner *revival* + Confessions Of A Driving Instructor *revival*

High Anxiety (+ Captain Scott Goes East *short*)

Piranha (+ Carrie *revival*)

Carry On Emmanuelle (+ Speedtrap)

The Silent Flute (+ *various*)

Bugsy Malone *revival* + Digby – The Biggest Dog In The World *revival*

** Pete's Dragon (+ Arizona Sheepdog *short*) (*two weeks*). A: (*second week*) A Wedding (+ Diamonds *short*)

1979

* *Main feature among the top ten box-office attractions of the year*

Force Ten From Navarone (+ Guards On Parade *short*)

The Fury (+ Crystal Venom *short*)

Damnation Alley + Thunder And Lightning

Midnight Express (+ Sea World *short*)

The First Great Train Robbery (+ A Fantasy For Real *short*)

The Thirty Nine Steps (+ *shorts*)

20,000 Leagues Under The Sea *revival* (+ Nature's Strangest Creatures *short*). A: Just A Gigolo

Eyes Of Laura Mars (+ Anger In His Eyes *or* Shadow Of The Hawk). A: Interiors (+ *various*); *or* The Chant Of Jimmie Blacksmith (+ *shorts*)

Damien – Omen II (+ Red *short*)

Somebody Killed Her Husband (+ *various*). A: Lemon Popsicle + Shark's Cave

Magic (+ Columbus Link *short*)

Invasion Of The Body Snatchers (+ Blow Out *short*)

Ashanti (+ *various*) A: Dog Soldiers (+ *various*)

The Thief Of Baghdad + Spider Man Strikes Back

Return From Witch Mountain (+ Chico The Misunderstood Coyote *revival*)

California Suite (+ Time On Your Hands *short*)

The Passage (+ Chameleon Soho *short*)

Halloween (+ *shorts*). A: Comes A Horseman (+ *shorts*)

The Manitou (+ *various*)

Firepower (+ Migrate To Survive *short or* Lifespan *short*)

The Humanoid (+ Jason And The Argonauts *revival or* Mysterious Island *revival*)

The Lady Vanishes (+ Mad Dog And Cricketers *short*)

Seven + Dominique

The Buddy Holly Story (+ Rags To Riches *short*). A: The Riddle Of The Sands (+ *shorts*)

Tilt (+ *various*) A: Young Frankenstein *revival* + Silent Movie *revival*

That Summer + Billion Dollar Threat

Nocturna + Island Of Mutations. A: The Hardcore Life (+ *various*)

The Muppet Movie + Grayeagle

Bedknobs And Broomsticks *revival* (+ Winnie The Pooh And The Blustery Day *short*). A: Nosferatu – The Vampyre (+ *various*)

Avalanche Express (+ Sky Riders *revival or* Tentacles *revival*)

Star Wars (+ Rock Faces *short*) A: Lord Of The Rings (+ A Little Piece Of London *short*)

The Spaceman And King Arthur + Dumbo *revival*

The Shape Of Things To Come + King Solomon's Treasure *revival*. A: Norma Rae (+ Summer Sunshine *short*)

* Moonraker (+ Flare A Ski Trip *short*) (*two weeks*)

The China Syndrome (+ Three Men On A Boat *short*) (*two weeks*). A: (*second week*) Hanover Street (+ *various*)

Butch And Sundance – The Early Days (+ Love Tapes *short*)

* Alien (+ Steppin Out *short*) (*two weeks*)

Lost And Found (+ Ice Castles *or* Casey's Shadow)

Hill's Angels (+ The Ugly Dachshund *revival*)

Love At First Bite + East Of Elephant Rock. A: Hair (+ Freshwater Dye *short*)

Sybil (*limited*)

Game For Vultures (+ Confessions Of A Pop Performer *revival*)

Eagle's Wing (+ *cartoon*) (*limited*)

Revenge Of The Pink Panther *revival* + Return Of The Pink Panther *revival* (*limited*)

no release (*four weeks*)

The Aristocats *revival* + The London Connection (*two weeks*). A: (*first week*) Manhattan (+ The Night Shift *short*)

The above runs of two weeks were minimum. Alternative programmes in later years were often aimed at smaller screens.

For various reasons – the increasing complexity of the release schedule, limitations on space, a desire to parallel the period covered in the listing of ABC circuit releases in the companion volume *ABC: The First Name In Entertainment* – these listings extend this far but no further.

However, Michael Fisher, whose documentation of the circuit releases has proved invaluable, declares that *Trainspotting* in March 1996 was the first major film to omit a circuit release and to pick up the best bookings available. The two-release system only completely finished with the May 1996 sale by Virgin of much of the ex-ABC/Cannon-MGM circuit which split it into two groups.

AN A TO Z OF ODEON CINEMAS

Odeon Cinemas 1: Oscar Deutsch Entertains Our Nation listed all the Odeon cinemas and others associated with Oscar Deutsch in order of opening or takeover up until the end of 1941 when Deutsch died. This section includes all those cinemas except for a few purchased in the 1930s solely to make way for new Odeons and operated only briefly if at all (the previous volume also recorded the cost of each new cinema according to company records).

The following list adds all the others taken over or opened after 1941 in Great Britain by the British Odeon company or associated with it by the management company, CMA. It is arranged alphabetically by town or suburb to conform with the lists of ABCs, Gaumonts and Granadas in my previously published histories of those circuits. Gaumonts are also included here if they underwent a change of name to Odeon. Entries extend beyond the date when Rank sold the circuit in 2000 to include nine Odeon multiplexes initiated by Rank.

Also included, to provide a complete listing of Rank's UK cinemas, are certain cinemas purchased by CMA or Rank which do not seem to have been specifically attached to either the Gaumont or Odeon circuits, namely the Astor Springburn, Astoria Possil, Avon Possilpark, Carlton Townhead, Roxy and Seamore at Maryhill and Standard Partick; and the Palace Crewe and King's Stourbridge. For a full picture of Rank's involvement in particular towns, combine the listings in this book with those in *Gaumont British Cinemas*.

Excluded are the cinemas operated by Rank's quite separate companies in Northern Ireland, the Irish Republic, and elsewhere overseas, plus those in Rank's holiday camps at Bognor Regis, Minehead, Pwllheli and Skegness which were given the Odeon name and managed by Odeon. Further excluded are the Top Rank Cinemas at bingo clubs at Blackwood, Gwent, and Felixstowe, Suffolk, which were owned by Rank's bingo division.

The first name shown for each cinema taken over is the name it had at that time. Information in round brackets usually relates to periods when buildings were not owned or operated by Odeon and concludes with the current use of the building or site if it has been demolished.

With multiplexes opened by Rank, the official opening date and the first day of public shows were sometimes different, resulting in two dates being shown. In addition, there may have been earlier previews or public test screenings which are not always noted. Current seating figures, kindly supplied by Odeon Cinemas (Ann Merryman), do not include wheelchair spaces which are provided in all screens at purpose-built multiplexes and at some screens in older sites. Because of the design restrictions imposed by developers and circuit branding, architects and designers have not been identified for multiplexes.

Following the sale of Odeon, it was merged with the ABC circuit and the following ABCs were renamed Odeon: Allerton, Aylesbury, Banbury, Beckenham, Bury St. Edmunds, Canterbury, Darlington, Dumfries, Esher, Gerrards Cross, Grimsby, Hastings, Hereford, London West End (Panton, Street, Shaftesbury Avenue, Swiss Centre, Tottenham Court Road), Nuneaton, Oxford (two), Putney, Quinton, Rochdale, Wester Hailes and Woodford. Being outside the period covered by this book, they are not included here.

The listings have been brought as up to date as possible. Having asked for current information on certain sites in the *CTA Bulletin*, I am grateful to the following Cinema Theatre Association members for responding: Gordon Barr, David Bennett, Paul Bland, Fabian Breckels, Norman G. Buxton, Carl Chesworth, Janice Clark, P. D. Clark, Robin Dakin, Paul Daniczek, John Duffin, Tony Duggan, Stephen Dutfield, David A. Ellis, David Eve, Andy Garner, Geoffrey Gill, Peter Good, Mervyn Gould, John Griffiths, Keith Hanman, Roy E. Heaven, Hector Hill, Oliver Horsbrugh, Ian Johnson, Richard Lacey, Reg Larkman, Steff Laugharne, J. M. Lewis, Bryan Lindop, Geoffrey Lord, Mike Luck, Colin Lund, Frank Manders, Tim McCullen, Sally McGrath, John J. McKillop, Ian Nash, Peter Nash, J. A. Newey, James Nielsen, Alan North, Gary Painter, Tony Parkinson, John Platford, Bob Preedy, John M. Pritchard, Michael Pugh, Stephen Pugh, Eddy Rhead, Harry Rigby, D. Rimell, Andrew Roberts, Norman Robins, Chris Roe, Tom Ruben, Michael Ryder David Sharp, David Simpson, John Skinner, Bernard Snowball, Martin Tapsell, N. Walley, Wally White, Jim Whittell, John S. Wilkinson, Ian Williams, Jon Williams, Tony Williams, Michael Wood and John Yallop.

ABERDEEN Grampian

PALACE, Bridge Place. (Opened 8.4.29 by Poole's circuit, former live theatre with some film use, 1714 seats. Closed 7.3.31 for internal reconstruction and extension, architect: C. T. Marshall of Marshall & Tweedy. Reopened 28.11.31, seating 2000. Taken over 6.36 by County.) Taken over 9.39, part of County circuit. Licensed in 1947 for 1778 seats: 1120 stalls + 658 balcony. Closed 14.11.59. (Altered, architect: Lennox D. Paterson, and stalls floor and stage reopened 24.3.60 by Rank as New Palace Ballroom. Nightclub. Renamed Fusion. Renamed Ritzy's Discotheque. Renamed Bonkers. Renamed The Palace. Open in 2004.)

REGENT, Justice Mill Lane. (Opened 27.2.32 by Poole's circuit, architect: T. Scott Sutherland. Taken over 6.36 by County. 2000 seats.) Taken over 9.39, part of County circuit. Renamed ODEON 29.7.40. Licensed in 1947 for 1865 seats: 1433 stalls + 432 balcony. 1420 seats. Triple from 8.4.74, seating 793 balcony/front stalls + 123 & 123 rear stalls. Front stalls converted to two further cinemas in 1991: 219 & 219 seats. Category C listed building. Refurbished 1994/5. 1111 seats in 1.01: 415 + 123 + 123 + 225 + 225. Closed 13.6.01. (Health & fitness club from 8.02.)

ACCRINGTON Lancashire

REGAL, Broadway & Cornhill. (Opened 12.4.37, architects: Drury & Gomersall, 1266 seats.) Taken over 28.2.44. Renamed ODEON 9.4.45. 1026 seats. (Taken over 10.12.67 by Classic, renamed Classic. Triple from 11.10.73: 338 + 189 + 128 seats. Taken over circa 1982 by Hutchinson's, renamed Unit Four. Taken over by Apollo. 315 + 195 + 100 seats. Closed 25.3.90. Demolished. Retail use, including Boots and Specsavers in 2004.)

ACTON West London

ODEON, King Street. Opened 8.11.37, architect: George Coles, 1870 seats: 1230 stalls + 640 balcony. 1840 seats. Closed 18.10.75. (B&Q DIY store. Closed 1.88. Demolished. Safeway supermarket.)

AIRDRIE Strathclyde

PAVILION, Graham Street. (Opened pre-1914. Taken over pre-1920 by Singleton.) Taken over 8.8.37, part of Singleton circuit. 1092 seats in 1939: 838 stalls + 254 balcony. 995 seats. (Taken over 17.12.67 by Classic, renamed Classic. Closed 27.9.70. Demolished. Airdrie Sheriff Courthouse.)

ALDERSHOT Hampshire

ALEXANDRA, Alexandra Road. (Taken over 11.27 by County. Rebuilt 1928, architect: Henry G. Baker, with balcony added). Taken over 9.39, part of County circuit. 710 seats in 1939: 493 stalls + 217 balcony. Closed 25.3.67. (Star bingo. Demolished 1986. Office block: Communications House.)

MANOR PARK PAVILION, High Street. (Taken over 1.28 by County.) Taken over 9.39, part of County circuit. 836 seats in 1939. 932 seats in 1947: 698 stalls + 234 balcony. Closed 29.9.56. (Demolished. Office block: Campbell House.)

EMPIRE, High Street. (Opened 1.8.30, architect: Harold S. Scott, 1599 seats. Taken over circa 1931 by County.) Taken over 9.39, part of County circuit. 1462 seats in 1947: 976 stalls + 486 balcony. Renamed odeon 18.1.64.

Closed 17.10.81. (Christian centre: The King's Centre, open in 2004.)

ALFRETON Derbyshire

ROYAL, High Street. Opened 16.4.31 by Oscar Deutsch & associates, architect: Harry Clayton. Taken into the Odeon circuit 17.7.35. 1450 seats: 1103 stalls + 347 balcony. Renamed ODEON circa 1936. 1000 seats circa 1956. Closed 30.5.64. (Demolished 4.65. Boots store on part of site.)

ALLERTON Liverpool

PLAZA, Allerton Road. (Opened 31.3.28 by GTC, architect: A. Ernest Shennan, 1432 seats. Taken over 5.28 by Gaumont, part of GTC circuit. Renamed GAUMONT 11.9.50.) Renamed ODEON 25.11.62. 1384 seats by 1963. (Taken over 10.12.67 by Classic, renamed Classic. Closed 19.4.71. Demolished. New Classic opened 28.7.73, 493 seats, above supermarket in redevelopment. Renamed Cannon 4.86. Taken over 7.95 by Virgin. Taken over 2.5.96 by ABC. Renamed ABC Cinemas. Taken over 2000 by Odeon. Renamed Odeon. Open in 2.05, 459 seats.)

ALLOA Central Scotland

GAUMONT, Mill Street (site of La Scala). (Opened 29.4.39 by Gaumont/PCT, architect: W. E. Trent, 1000 seats, stadium. 923 seats circa 1956: 611 front + 312 rear.) Renamed ODEON 19.10.64. (Taken over 17.12.67 by Classic, renamed Classic. Taken over by independent, renamed De Luxe, with part-week bingo. Closed 30.7.71, except for children's shows to 13.6.75. Full-time De Luxe bingo, open in 2004.)

ANDOVER Hampshire

PALACE, Junction Road. (Opened circa 1926, architect: F. Henshaw.) Taken over 6.11.35. Renamed ODEON circa 1937. 867 seats: 611 stalls + 256 balcony. 760 seats in 1967. (Taken over 3.12.67 by Classic, renamed Classic. Bingo club from 19.1.68. Split for bingo and films, 114 seats. Films ended 29.9.73, bingo continuing as Mecca Club in 2004.)

ANNIESLAND Glasgow

GAUMONT, 1544 Great Western Road and Ascot Avenue. (Opened 6.12.39 as Ascot, associated with Alexander B. King, architects:

Charles J. McNair and Elder, 1963 seats. Taken over 31.5.43 by Gaumont/PCT. Renamed Gaumont 6.2.50. 1894 seats by 1956.) Renamed ODEON 23.3.64. Closed 25.10.75. (Bingo. Category B listed building. Auditorium demolished, facade retained with new housing behind.)

ASHFORD Kent

ODEON, High Street. Opened 31.8.36, architect: Andrew Mather, 1570 seats: 1102 stalls + 534 balcony. 1466 seats circa 1960. Closed 30.8.75. (Re-opened early 1976 as Top Rank Club for bingo. Renamed Mecca. Open in 2004.)

ASHTON-UNDER-LYNE Greater Manchester
see also Guide Bridge

GAUMONT, Old Street and Delamere Street. (Opened 22.4.20 as Majestic by PCT, architect: Arnold England, 1233 seats.) Taken over 2.29 as part of PCT circuit. Renamed Gaumont circa 1946.) Renamed ODEON 11.11.62. 1007 seats. (Taken over 1.11.81 by independent, renamed Metro. 945 seats. Closed 9.03. Disused in 12.04.)

AYLESBURY Buckinghamshire

ODEON, Cambridge Street. Opened 21.6.37, architect: Andrew Mather, 1451 seats: 954 balcony + 497 stalls. 1304 seats. Triple from 26.8.73, seating 497 balcony + 99 & 108 rear stalls. Refurbished 1984. New screen in front of upstairs cinema from 1985. Closed 30.10.99, seating 450 + 108 + 113. (Disused in 12.04.)[Current Odeon is former ABC multiplex elsewhere.]

AYR Ayrshire

ODEON, Burns Statue Square. Opened 30.7.38, architect: Andrew Mather, 1732 seats: 1303 stalls + 429 balcony. 1468 seats in 1985. Triple from 10.7.87, seating 433 balcony + 138 & 138 rear stalls. Fourth cinema added 1992 in front stalls with new screen in front of upstairs cinema and one rear stalls cinema reduced to 135 seats. Open in 2.05, 4 screens, 1128 seats: 386 + 164 + 129 + 449.

BALHAM South London

ODEON, Balham Hill at corner of Malwood Road. Opened 16.4.38, architect: George Coles, 1822 seats: 1216 stalls + 606 balcony. 1780 seats by 1964. Closed 9.9.72. (Re-opened 13.12.74 as Asian cinema, renamed Liberty. Closed 1979. Auditorium gutted 3-4.83 for indoor market. Auditorium demolished circa 5.85. Foyers gutted for Majestic wine warehouse with frontage retained. Flats built on site of auditorium. Flats introduced above wine warehouse: Foyer Apartments.)

BARKING Northeast London

RIO, Longbridge Road. (Opened 17.8.35 by Kay Bros. [Kessex], architect: George Coles, 2200 seats. Taken over 1936 by GCF, later Eastern Cinemas [GCF].) Taken over 28.2.43, part of GCF. Renamed ODEON 31.12.45. 2160 seats circa 1955. 1892 seats. Triple from 26.12.74, seating 846 balcony + 149 & 144 rear stalls. Refurbished 1988. Subdivided into six screens from 13.4.90, seating 1444: 806 + 83 + 131 + 130 + 132 + 162. Closed 10.12.98. (Demolished 3.01. Flats.)

BARNET Hertfordshire

ODEON, Underhill, Western Parade, Great North Road. Opened 15.5.35, architect: Edgar Simmons, 1553 seats: 1010 stalls + 543 balcony. 1543 seats. Triple from 10.3.74, seating 543 balcony + 130 & 130 rear stalls. Grade II listed building from 13.10.89. Fourth cinema in former front stalls opened 18.12.92, seating 217. Fifth cinema on former stage opened 28.12.92, seating 158. Open in 2.05, 5 screens, 1238 seats: 532 + 182 + 182 + 187 + 155.

BARNET CINEMA, 122 High Street, High Barnet. (Opened 26.12.12 as Cinema Palace, one floor. Balcony added 9.10.26, renamed Cinema. Redecorated 7.33.) Taken over circa 12.36. 1038 seats in 1939. Renamed GAUMONT 10.1.55. Closed 8.8.59, 1035 seats. (Demolished 1961. Waitrose supermarket. Iceland store in 2002.)

BARNSLEY South Yorkshire

ALHAMBRA, Doncaster Road. (Opened 1.10.15 as live theatre.) Taken over 5.6.38. 2100 seats in 1939: 826 + 325 + 449. 1562 seats circa 1957. 1111 seats circa 1959 with upper balcony closed. Closed 26.11.60. (Re-opened 13 June 1968 as Top Rank Club for bingo, capacity of 1400. Closed 1976. Re-opened as Vale Bingo. Closed. Demolished 1982. Part of Alhambra Shopping Centre, at Sheffield Road rear entrance.)

GAUMONT, 62-68 Eldon Street (site of Empire). (Opened 27.2.56, architect: T. P. Bennett & Son, 1283 seats: 706 stalls & 532 balcony.) Renamed ODEON 9.9.62. Closed 1.80 for twinning. Re-opened 26.4.80, 419 & 636 seats. Open in 2.05, 841 seats: 403 + 438.

BARNSTAPLE Devon

GAUMONT, Boutport Street (site of Theatre Royal). (Opened 3.8.31 as Gaumont Palace by Gaumont/Albany Ward-PCT, architect: W. H. Watkins [Percy Bartlett], 1124 seats: 702 stalls & 422 balcony. Renamed Gaumont.) Renamed ODEON 21.10.62. (Taken over 10.12.67 by Classic, renamed Classic. Part-week bingo. Twinned for films balcony and bingo in stalls. Taken over circa 1982 by independent, renamed Astor. Grade II listed building from 31.8.88. 360 seats in cinema. Taken over late 2000 by Scott Cinemas, renamed Central. Bingo area converted to three cinemas. All four open in 2005, seating: 360 + 80 + 80 + 130.)

BARROW-IN-FURNESS Cumbria

ROXY, Cavendish Street. (Reconstruction of Royalty Theatre, opened 9.8.37, architects: Drury & Gomersall, 1200 seats.) Taken over 21.7.43. Renamed ODEON 5.11.45. 948 seats circa 1956. 804 seats. (Taken over 17.12.67 by Classic, renamed Classic. Closed 15.5.76. Champers nightclub to 1984. Disused to 1991. Manhattan's nightclub. Paolo Gianni's restaurant on side, auditorium disused in 2004.)

BATH Avon

REGAL, 16 Southgate Street. (Opened pre-1914 as Picturedrome. Enlarged 1930, renamed Regal. Taken over by Union.) Taken over 31.7.35. Renamed ODEON 2.12.35. 863 seats in 1939: 714 stalls + 149 balcony. 789 seats circa 1960. Closed 13.12.69. (Taken over 25.12.69 by City of London Real Property. Demolished for part of Southgate shopping centre. Boots store in 2002.)

BECKENHAM Southeast London
see Elmers End

BECONTREE Northeast London

REGENT, Green Lane, corner of Waldegrave Road. (Opened 3.29, architect: Lewis Solomon & Son, 1500 seats. Taken over by Kay Bros./Kessex. Taken over 1936 by GCF, later Eastern Cinemas [GCF].) Taken over

28.2.43, part of GCF. Renamed ODEON 29.7.46. 1447 seats. Closed 4.4.70. (Bingo from 14.4.70. Coral Club. Gala Club, closed 9.4.97. Elim Pentecostal Church.)

BEDMINSTER Bristol

AMBASSADOR, Winterstoke Road. (Opened 7.12.36 by London & Southern, completion of stalled scheme, new architect: F. J. Mitchell.) Taken over circa 7.37, part of London & Southern circuit. 1249 seats, stadium: 808 front + 441 rear. Renamed ODEON 27.1.47. Closed 22.7.61. (Top Rank Club for bingo. Closed 1995. Winterstoke Tyre & Exhaust Centre + Alphabet Zoo Play Centre & Party Venue.)

BELSIZE PARK Northwest London
see Haverstock Hill

BETHNAL GREEN Northeast London

FORESTERS, 93 Cambridge Heath Road. (Opened circa 9.26, former music hall reconstructed, architect: George Coles.) Taken over 10.5.37. 1057 seats in 1939: 674 stalls + 383 balcony. Closed 3.5.47 to war damage. Re-opened 10.10.49. Advertised as part of Gaumont circuit. 986 seats circa 1956. Closed 20.8.60. (Demolished circa 1964. Block of flats: Sovereign House.)

MUSEUM, 172 Cambridge Road. (Opened 1913, 500 seats. Taken over by D. J. James. Closed 6.31 for internal reconstruction & enlargement, architect: Leslie H. Kemp. Re-opened 12.10.31, 1000 seats, one floor. Taken over 1936 by Eastern Cinemas [GCF].) Taken over 28.2.43, part of GCF. Renamed ODEON 20.3.50. 809 seats circa 1956. Closed 1.12.56. (Demolished. Mayfield House block of flats.)

BILSTON Wolverhampton

PALACE, Lichfield Street. (Opened 17.11.21 as Wood's New Picture Palace, architect: Hurley Robinson, interior design: Val Prince, 1400 seats. Renamed Palace.) Taken over 2.9.36. Renamed ODEON 30.7.37. 1251 seats in 1939: 965 stalls + 286 balcony. 1170 seats circa 1959. Closed 22.2.64. (Re-opened 5.3.64 as Top Rank Club for bingo. Sold 2.9.71 to Hutchinsons, renamed Surewin. Sold and renamed Cascade. Closed. Asian venue. Multi-purpose hall from 7.11.99.)

BIRMINGHAM West Midlands
see also Kingstanding, Perry Barr and Shirley

PARAMOUNT, 139 New Street. (Opened 4.9.37 by Paramount, architects: Verity & Beverley, 2424 or 2439 [1517 + 922] seats.) Taken over 25.8.42. Renamed ODEON 29.11.42. Modernised & re-opened 24.6.65. Much live show usage. Closed 26.5.88 for subdivision. Re-opened 10.88, 6 screens, 1664 seats: 330 + 387 + 308 + 239 + 210 + 190. Two further screens opened 1991 in former basement bar & half of former ballroom/bar, seating 126 + 80. Refurbished summer 1998. Open in 2.05, 8 screens, 1732 seats: 231 + 390 + 298 + 229 + 194 + 180 + 130 + 80.

SCALA SUPERAMA, 30 Holloway Circus, Smallbrook Ringway. (Opened 23.11.64 by Compton, architect: James A. Roberts, 604 seats, stadium.) Taken over 22.2.70, renamed ODEON RINGWAY. Renamed ODEON QUEENSWAY 6.72. Refurbished 1983, 555 seats. Closed 18.9.88. (Disused in 2004.)

CINECENTA, Holloway Circus. (Opened 21.8.77 by Cinecenta. Second screen opened 10.6.79. Taken over 12.79 by Star. 114 + 113 seats. Club cinema. Public cinema from circa 1980. Closed 26.3.83.) Taken over, refurbished and re-opened 18.12.83 as addition to ODEON QUEENSWAY, 116 + 113 seats. Closed 18.9.88. (Disused in 2004.)

BISHOP AUCKLAND Co. Durham

MAJESTIC, Tenters Street. (Opened 21.11.38, architect: Joshua Clayton, 1380 seats.) Taken over 12.3.44 (Sunday), operated from 13.3.44. Renamed ODEON 2.4.45. 1385 seats circa 1960. Twin from 13.5.73, 552 + 123 seats. Closed 15.10.83. (Demolished 4.95. Aldi superstore in 2004.)

BLACKBURN Lancashire

RIALTO SUPER, Penny Street. (Opened 21.12.31, architects: S. Butterworth & Duncan, 1883 seats. Taken over 28.7.57 by Gaumont, 1878 seats.) Renamed ODEON 16.3.59. 1481 seats. Closed 23.3.74. (Demolished. NCP carpark.)

BLACKFEN Southeast London

PLAZA, Westwood Lane. (Opened 26.7.37, architect: Robert Cromie, 1280 seats.) Taken over 21.6.43. Renamed ODEON 6.5.46. 1250 seats circa 1955. Closed 27.10.56. (Demolished. Supermarket.)

BLACKHEATH West Midlands

ODEON, Long Lane. Also known as Odeon Quinton and Blackheath. Opened 20.10.34, architect: Stanley A. Griffiths, 1228 seats, stadium: 796 front + 432 rear. Closed 19.11.60. (Bingo club from 10.2.67. Ballroom. B&Q DIY store by 1980. Demolished 1984. Lowsure Outdoor Superstore.)

BLACKPOOL Lancashire

ODEON, Dickson Road, between Lord Street and Springfield Road. Opened 6.5.39, architects: Harry Weedon & W. Calder Robson, 3088 seats: 1684 stalls + 1404 balcony. 3070 seats circa 1955. Modernised from 12.64 to 2.65, closing for four days, seating reduced to 2744. Triple from 16 October 1975, seating 1404 balcony + 190 & 190 rear stalls. Grade II listed building from Spring 1994. Main cinema reduced to 1375 seats. All closed 5.12.98. (Funny Girls gay venue in stalls area from 19.4.02. Balcony lounge into gay pub, The Flying Handbag.)

ODEON, Rigby Road. Opened 11.12.98, 10 screens, 2749 seats: 422 + 139 + 346 + 153 + 200 + 397 + 159 + 351 + 381 + 201. Open in 1.05. Open in 2.05, 2710 seats: 417 + 137 + 342 + 151 + 198 + 393 + 157 + 340 + 376 + 199.

BLETCHLEY Buckinghamshire

COUNTY, High Street. (Opened 1911, former Methodist chapel. Taken over circa 1.28 by County. Enlarged and renamed King George's Cinema. Renamed County in 1932. 460 seats.) 400 seats in 1939. 447 seats circa 1955. Closed 29.6.57. (Demolished circa 1972. Durrans Court – housing in courtyard on enlarged site.)

BLOOMSBURY Central London

SUPER, Theobalds Road. (Opened 3.9.21 as Victory, architects: Ernest A. Mann & Victor Peel, 1346 seats: 894 stalls + 452 balcony. Renamed Bloomsbury Cinema mid-1920s. Taken over 11.29 by London & Southern, renamed Super.) Taken over circa 7.37, part of London & Southern circuit. 1373 seats in 1939: 918 stalls + 455 balcony. Closed 9.11.40 by war-time conditions. (Severely damaged by bombing early 1941. Demolished. Office block.)

BLOXWICH Walsall

GROSVENOR, High Street. (Opened 11.12.22

on site of Electric, architects: Hickton & Farmer. Taken over 11.31 by Oscar Deutsch & associates.) Taken into Odeon circuit 17.7.35. Renamed ODEON. 939 seats. 892 seats circa 1955. Closed 2.5.59. (Flix nightclub. Youth club in 2001.)

BOGNOR REGIS West Sussex

ODEON, 64 London Road. Opened 14.7.34, architects: Whinney, Son & Austen Hall, 920 seats, stadium: 592 front + 328 rear. (Leased to independent from 23.1.71, renamed Regal. Closed 16.11.74. Regal bingo club. Renamed Crown bingo club 12.87, open 2004.) [Subsequent Odeon was part of Southcoast World holiday centre elsewhere.]

BOLTON Greater Manchester

ODEON, Ash Burner Street, corner of Black Horse Street. Opened 21.8.37, architect: Harry Weedon [assistant: W. Calder Robson], 2534 seats: 1598 stalls + 936 balcony. Modernised circa 1960. 2354 seats. Triple from 20.8.72, seating 879 balcony + 148 & 148 rear stalls. Closed 8.1.83. (Re-opened late 3.83 as Top Rank Club for bingo. Renamed Mecca. Closed circa 11.04.)

BOOTLE Merseyside
see also Switch Island

GAUMONT, Stanley Road (site of Broadway). (Opened 23.1.56 by Rank, architects: T. P. Bennett & Son, 1312 seats, one floor.) Renamed ODEON 28.4.64. Open part-week only from 7.74 except during school holidays. Closed 1.11.75. (Skateboard centre. Snooker centre.)

BORDON Hampshire

EMPIRE, Bordon Camp. (Opened 29.10.38 by W. J. May/County, reconstruction of existing premises, architect: David E. Nye.) Taken over 9.39, part of County circuit. 475 seats in 1939. (Taken over circa 1968 by independent. Closed 8.73.)

BOSTON Lincolnshire

ODEON, South Square, off Market Place. Opened 18.8.37, architect: Harry Weedon [assistant: Budge Reid], 1592 seats: 1067 stalls + 525 balcony. 1430 seats in 1967. (Taken over 3.12.67 by Classic, renamed Classic. Split-week films and bingo 31.1.68. Taken over 2.12.81 by independent for films & live shows, renamed Haven. Part-week bingo.

Closed 27.5.87 by fire. Demolished 1-2.99. Medical practice with car park behind.)

BOURNEMOUTH Dorset

ODEON, Christchurch Road, Lansdowne. Opened 7.8.37, architect: George Coles, 1978 seats: 1336 stalls + 642 balcony. 1662 seats circa 1960. Closed 16.1.74. (Top Rank Club for bingo. Closed 1976. Re-opened. Gala Club for bingo in 12.04.)

GAUMONT, Westover Road. (Opened 13.5.29 as Regent by Gaumont/PCT, architects: W. E. Trent and Seal & Hardy, 2267 seats. Renamed Gaumont 22.8.49. Closed 16.11.68 for twinning, architects: Dry, Halasz & Associates. Re-opened 15.7.69 as Gaumont 1 & 2, seating 758 extended balcony & 1182 below.) Renamed ODEON 30.10.86. Lower cinema closed 6.3.89 for subdivision. Re-opened 6.89 as ODEON 2, 3, 4 & 5, seating 359 & 267 & 119 & 121. ODEON 6 opened 24.2.95 in balcony bar, 140 seats. Open in 2.05, 6 screens, 1761 seats: 757 + 146 + 266 + 119 + 119 + 354.

BRADFORD West Yorkshire

ODEON, Manchester Road, corner of Town Hall Square. Opened 17.12.38, architect: Harry Weedon [assistant: Robert Bullivant], 2713 seats: 1750 stalls + 963 balcony. Closed 31.8.40 by bomb damage. Re-opened 11.11.40. Closed 28.1.61 for modernisation. Re-opened 27.2.61, 2447 seats: 1484 stalls + 963 balcony. Closed 22.3.69. (Sold to Bradford Corporation for redevelopment scheme. Demolished. West Yorkshire Police building.)

GAUMONT, Brewery Street [now Prince's Way], Thornton Road and Quebec Street. Opened 22.9.30 as New Victoria by Gaumont/PCT, architect: William Illingworth, 3318 seats. Renamed Gaumont 25.9.50. Redecorated early 1954. 3282 seats. 2551 seats after upper balcony closed 24.7.60. Closed 30.11.68 for twinning plus bingo in stalls, architects: Gavin Patterson & Son, interior designers: Trevor & Mavis Stone.) Re-opened 21.8.69 as ODEON 1 & 2, 467 & 1207 seats. ODEON 3 opened 6.87 in ball-room, 244 seats. Closed 2.7.00. (Disused in 12.04.)

ODEON, Gallagher Leisure Park, Thornbury. Advertised as Odeon Leeds/Bradford. Opened 7.7.00, 13 screens Open in 2.05, 3086 seats:

126 + 228 + 150 + 233 + 382 + 442 + 442 + 211 + 257 + 157 + 170 + 140 + 148.

BRENTWOOD Essex

ODEON, High Street. Opened 18.5.38, architect: George Coles, 1350 seats: 920 stalls + 430 balcony. 1347 seats circa 1955. Closed 20.4.74. (Taken over 1.5.74 by Brentwood Council under compulsory purchase order. Demolished for part of Chapel High Shopping Centre which included Focus 1 & 2 cinemas.)

BRIDGEND Mid Glamorgan

ODEON, McArthur Glen Designer Outlet Village, The Pines, Pen-y-Cae Lane. Opened 10.11.98, 9 screens, 2070 seats: 428 + 324 + 252 + 245 + 219 + 176 + 154 + 162 + 110. Open in 2.05.

BRIDGWATER Somerset

ODEON, Penel Orlieu (now at corner of Mount Street). Opened 13.7.36, architect: T. Cecil Howitt, 1525 seats, stadium: 931 front + 594 rear. 1441 seats in 1967. (Taken over 10.12.67 by Classic, renamed Classic. Sub-divided for bingo in front section + cinemas in rear, Classic 1 & 2, opened 22.1.73, seating 250 + 250. One Classic briefly renamed Tatler in 1973 for "adult" films. Closed 3.83. Re-opened 9.12.83 by independent, renamed Film Centre. Open in 2005.)

BRIERLEY HILL West Midlands

PICTURE HOUSE, High Street. (Opened 1.10.28 by Oscar Deutsch & associates, architect: Stanley A. Griffiths.) Taken into the Odeon circuit 17.7.35. Renamed ODEON 1.36. 944 seats in 1939: 680 stalls + 264 balcony. 778 seats circa 1955. Closed 25.7.59. (Demolished. Fine Fare supermarket. Part of Higgs offices + Firkin's bakery on front in 1.05.)

BRIGHTON Sussex
see also Hove and Kemp Town

PALLADIUM, 85 King's Road. (Opened 6.4.12 as Palladium cinema, live theatre. 1000 seats.) Taken over 15.4.35. Modernised, architect: Andrew Mather. Renamed ODEON 8.6.35. Renamed PALLADIUM 28.11.37. Closed 26.10.40. (Taken over circa 1942 by independent. Closed 26.5.56 by compulsory purchase order. Demolished 1963. Part of site for Brighton Centre.)

ODEON, West Street at corner of Little Russell Street. Opened 18.12.37, architect: Andrew Mather, 1920 seats: 1236 stalls + 684 balcony. 1874 seats circa 1955. 1708 seats circa 1960. Modernised 1969. Closed 17.4.73. (Demolished 4.90. Family Assurance House block of offices from 1992.)

ODEON, Kingswest, West Street. Opened 19.4.73, conversion of skating rink and conference hall in Kingswest Centre, 1779 seats, three screens: 390 + 885 + 504 seats. Refurbished (designers: Marketplace Design Partnership) with new entrance and two additional screens opened 21.5.87 in basement, seating 275 + 242. Sixth screen opened 8.89 in disused kitchen space, seating 103. Largest auditorium subdivided into three & re-opened 14.12.01. All open in 2.05, seating 2217: 389 + 220 + 238 + 238 + 514 + 286 + 232 + 100.

BRISTOL Avon
see also Bedminster and Kingswood

ODEON, Union Street and Broadmead. Opened 16.7.38, architect: T. Cecil Howitt, 1945 seats: 1051 stalls + 894 balcony. Closed 3.12.40 by bomb damage. Re-opened 17.12.40. 1693 seats by 1965. Modernised 1967. Triple from 27.5.74, seating 844 balcony + 108 & 103 rear stalls. Closed 15.10.83 for redevelopment of interior, architects: Dowton & Hurst (Donald Armstrong). New three-screen Odeon opened 13.6.85 with new side entrance on Union Street, seating 840: 400 + 225 + 215. Open in 2.05, seating 858: 399 + 224 + 215.

EMPIRE, Old Market Street. (Opened 13.4.31, former variety theatre with some film use. Taken over circa 10.32 by ABC. 1437 seats.) Taken over 25.6.39, 1452 seats: 1132 stalls + 320 balcony. Closed 9.12.39. (Re-opened 26.12.39 as live theatre. Closed 1954. BBC Studios from mid-1950s to 1962. Demolished 1963. Pedestrian underpass.)

BRIXTON South London

ASTORIA, 211 Stockwell Road. (Opened 19.8.29, architects: E. A. Stone & T. R. Somerford, interior decoration: Marc Henri, 2982 seats. Taken over 12.30 by Paramount.) Taken over 27.11.39, part of Paramount circuit. 2976 seats. 2709 seats by 1964. Closed 29.7.72. (Sundown discotheque. Closed. Grade II listed building from 16.1.74. Listing upgraded 26.3.90 to Grade II★. Academy live music venue. Open in 2005.)

BROADSTAIRS Kent

ROYALTY, York Street. (Opened 15.10.34, architect: P. V. Levett, 788 seats, stadium.) Taken over 27.5.35. (Taken over 8.4.38 by independent, H. Godwin Longthorn. Subleased to Sax Cinemas in 1.39. Closed by bomb damage 1.11.40.) Taken back, repaired & re-opened 3.8.50 as ODEON. 794 seats. Closed 29.9.56. (Disco. Demolished. Serene Court block of flats + one shop.)

BROMBOROUGH Merseyside

ODEON, Wirral Leisure Park, Welton Road. Opened 14.11.91, 1890 seats, 7 screens: 465 + 360 + 211 + 206 + 310 + 169 + 169. Four screens added circa 5.97, 2360 seats: 465 + 356 + 248 + 203 + 338 + 168 + 168 + 86 + 135 + 71 + 122. Open in 2.05, 11 screens, 2319 seats: 458 + 356 + 238 + 197 + 327 + 162 + 162 + 90 + 133 + 76 + 120.

BROMLEY Southeast London

ODEON, 242 High Street (also known as The Mart). Opened 21.9.36, architect: George Coles, 1492 seats: 1018 stalls + 474 seats. Modernised 1961: 1266 seats. Closed for tripling. Re-opened 12.4.76, seating 760 balcony extended over front stalls + 125 & 116 rear stalls. Cinema in balcony and one in rear stalls closed 9.10.88 to add additional cinema on former stage & front stalls. Closed cinemas re-opened 16.12.88, seating 402 (with new screen) & 98. New cinema opened 3.2.89, seating 273. All refurbished early 2001. All open in 2.05, seating 392 + 124 + 105 + 277.

BURNAGE Greater Manchester

LIDO, Kingsway & Green End Road. (Opened 28.12.29, architect: Robert Cromie, 1560 seats. Taken over 24.2.36 by Union. Taken over circa 1938 by John Buckley.) Taken over 5.12.42. Renamed ODEON 30.7.45. 1146 seats. (Taken over 10.12.67 by Classic, renamed Classic. Closed. Kwiksave supermarket in stalls + balcony opened 1.7.71 by independent as Concorde cinema, 400 seats. Second screen opened 22.6.73 in former café, 103 seats. Both closed 12.84. Re-opened 18.2.87. Closed 26.4.91. Auditorium destroyed by fire in 1990s. Front demolished summer 2004. Lidl supermarket under construction in 12.04.)

BURNLEY Lancashire

ODEON, Gunsmith Lane. Opened 28.8.37, architect: Harry Weedon [assistant: Robert Bullivant], 2136 seats: 1404 stalls + 732 balcony. 1878 seats by 1965. Closed 17.11.73. (Demolished. J. Sainsbury supermarket on enlarged site. Staples Office Superstore in 2005 on ex-cinema area.)

BURNT OAK Edgware

REGENT, The Broadway, High Road. (Opened 25.2.29, architect: George Coles, 900 seats. Balcony added and frontage rebuilt in 1932, architect: George Coles.) Taken over 16.7.36. Renamed ODEON 30.7.37. 1476 seats in 1947: 980 stalls + 496 balcony. Renamed GAUMONT 13.3.50. Renamed ODEON 16.12.62. 1189 seats. Closed 12.2.72. (Demolished. Shops and flats.)

BURTON-ON-TRENT Staffordshire

PICTUREDROME, Curzon Street (site of earlier Picturedrome). (Opened 26.12.31 as New Picturedrome, architects: John Fairweather & Thomas Jenkins, 1800 seats. Renamed Picturedrome.) Taken over 5.9.55, 1599 seats. Renamed ODEON 16.7.56. 1296 seats. Closed 5.6.65. (Top Rank Club for bingo. Renamed Mecca. Closed circa 12.03.)

GAUMONT, Guild Street, corner of George Street (site of Opera House, retaining facade as rear wall). (Opened 11.3.35 as Ritz, architects: Thomas Jenkins & John Fairweather, 1600 seats. Taken over by PCT 5.9.55. 1471 seats. Renamed Gaumont 25.2.57. 1355 seats.) Renamed ODEON 14.11.66. Triple from 14.4.74. 502 + 110 & 110 seats. (Taken over 1.7.96 by Robins, renamed Robins. Closed 2.12.99. Disused in 2004.)

BURY Greater Manchester

ODEON, Rochdale Road at corner of Clerke Street. Opened 16.11.36, architect: Harry Weedon [assistant: P. J. Price], 1487 seats: 1027 stalls + 460 balcony. 1463 seats by 1965. Closed 24.10.81. (Club use: Arena in 1988, Sol Viva nightclub in 2.05.)

BURY ST. EDMUNDS Suffolk

ODEON, Brentgovel Street and Well Street. Opened 5.7.37, architect: George Coles, 1289 seats: 867 balcony + 422 stalls. 1252 seats by 1965. (Taken over 4.10.75 by Brent Walker, renamed Focus. Grade II listed building from 1.5.81. De-listed 11.8.81. Closed 30.10.82. Demolished 1983. Shopping arcade.)

BYKER Newcastle

BLACK'S REGAL, Shields Road. (Opened 3.9.34 by George Black, architect: Edwin M. Lawson, 1838 seats.) Taken over 4.7.55. 1836 seats. Renamed ODEON 14.11.55. 1455 seats by 1965. Closed 11.11.72. (Byker Superstore from late 1982. Closed. Demolished early 1987. Petrol station.)

CAMBERLEY Surrey

ARCADE, London Road. (Opened 22.1.23. Taken over circa 1936 by County.) 682 seats in 1939. Closed 29.9.56.

REGAL, 303 London Road. (Opened 27.8.32 by County, architect: Harold S. Scott.) 1,210 seats in 1939. Renamed ODEON 21.1.46. 1,017 seats in 1967. (Taken over 3.12.67 by Classic, renamed Classic. Tripled with bingo from 1.10.75, cinemas seating 444 + 155 + 129. Renamed Cannon 1985. Taken over 18.2.94 by Robins, renamed Robins Cinemas. Taken over by independent. Closed 17.7.03. Snooker in stalls, cinema area disused in 1.05.)

CAMBERWELL Southeast London

ODEON, Corner of Denmark Hill and Coldharbour Lane (partly on site of New Empire cinema). Opened 20.3.39, architect: Andrew Mather [assistant: Keith P. Roberts], 2470 seats: 1484 stalls + 986 balcony. 2118 seats by 1963. Only balcony used in final years. Closed 5.7.75. (Dickie Dirts jeans emporium from 24.10.81. Demolished Spring 1993. Sold to London & Quadrant Housing Trust. Flats: The Foyer.)

CAMDEN TOWN North London

BEDFORD, 93/95 Camden High Street. (Former live theatre. Taken over 1933 by ABC. 1259 seats.) Taken over 25.6.39, 1115 seats: 471 + 224 + 420 (gallery). Closed 11.12.39. (Re-opened as variety theatre. Closed 1959. Demolished 1969. Curry's, Job Centre and other shops in front in 2002, flats on auditorium.)

PLAZA, 211 High Street. (Opened 1909 as Electric Theatre, conversion of bakery, 500 seats. Renamed Theatre De Luxe circa 1914. Renamed Britannia 1919. Improved, architect: Cecil Masey, & re-opened 12.9.37 as Plaza, 731 seats, one floor. Taken over circa 1938 by Town Theatres circuit.) Taken over 26.1.42, part of Town Theatres circuit. 699 seats by 1956. 620 seats by 1963. (Taken over by Panton

Films circa 1969. Taken over by Artificial Eye, improved & re-opened 9.6.77 as Camden Plaza, 340 seats. Closed 29.9.94. Aquarius shop in foyer in 3.05. Auditorium disused.)

GAUMONT, 14 Parkway. (Opened 25.1.37 as Gaumont Palace by Gaumont/PCT, architects: W. E. Trent, W. Sydney Trent & Daniel Mackay, 2742 seats. Renamed Gaumont circa 1937. 2410 seats by 1963.) Renamed ODEON 30.5.64. Closed 4.11.67 for Top Rank Club bingo in stalls + new Odeon in balcony, opened 26.2.68, 1198 seats. Cinema closed 29.9.79, bingo continued. (Cinema re-opened 9.10.80 as Gate 3, 424 seats. Closed 19.7.82. Re-opened 15.12.83 as Camden Parkway, 1000 seats. Former projectionists' training school area converted to Regency cinema, 90 seats, main auditorium known as King's. Both closed 2.3.87. King's re-opened 15.12.89. Regency re-opened 9.2.90. Both closed 30.8.93.) Cinema area subdivided & re-opened 11.7.97 as ODEON, 5 screens. Open in 2.05, 926 seats: 403 + 92 + 238 + 90 + 103.

CANNING TOWN Northeast London

ODEON, Barking Road, between Star Lane and Alexandra Street, backed by Edward Street. Opened 25.5.39, architect: Andrew Mather [assistant: Keith P. Roberts], 2240 seats: 1418 stalls + 822 balcony. Closed 2.10.40 by bomb damage. Re-opened 3.3.41. Closed 11.5.41 by bomb damage. (Sold 15.12.70 to East London Housing Association and site cleared for block of flats: Odeon Court.)

CANTERBURY Kent

FRIARS, The Friars. Opened 5.8.33 by Odeon, architects: Alfred & Vincent Burr, 1291 seats: 878 stalls + 413 balcony. Renamed ODEON 4.4.38. Renamed FRIARS in 1938. Renamed ODEON 19.12.55. 1128 seats by 1964. Closed 17.10.81. (Re-opened 8.7.84 after extensive alterations as Marlowe live theatre, seating 993. Open.) [Town's present Odeon is former ABC.]

CARDIFF South Glamorgan
see also Gabalfa

NEW IMPERIAL, 55 Queen Street. Taken over circa 11.35. Closed for conversion. Re-opened 14.9.36 as ODEON, architect: William S. Wort, 1663 seats: 1135 stalls + 528 balcony. 1597 seats by 1956. 1284 seats by 1964. Closed 12.1.80 for subdivision. Re-opened as twin, seating 643 stalls + 448 seats

balcony. Closed 16.3.00. (Demolished circa 1.03. Two stores including HMV.)

CAPITOL, 116/8 Queen Street. (Opened 24.12.21, architects: J. H. Phillips & Wride, 2800 seats. Leased circa 1931 by Paramount.) Leased 3.8.41. 2596 seats in 1956. Bought 4.64. 2492 seats by 1964. 2453 seats in 1977: 1445 stalls + 1008 balcony. Closed 21.1.78. (Demolished circa 2.83. Part of Capitol shopping centre, including Capitol Odeon cinemas elsewhere.)

CAPITOL ODEON, Capitol Shopping Centre, Station Terrace, at corner of North Edward Street. Opened 22.8.91, 5 screens, 1266 seats: 435 + 261 + 223 + 186 + 161. Closed 12.8.01. (Disused in 2004.)

CARLISLE Cumbria

GAUMONT, 37 Botchergate. (Opened 8.15 as Picture House, architect: George Gunn. 1006 seats. Taken over 5.9.55 by Rank. Renamed Gaumont 18.6.56.) Renamed ODEON 13.1.64. 954 seats by 1964. Closed 17.5.69. (Auditorium demolished. Liptons supermarket, later Presto. Demolished.)

CHADWELL HEATH Northeast London
see also Becontree and Whalebone Lane

GAUMONT, High Road. (Opened 17.5.34 as Embassy, architect: Harry Weston, 1812 seats: 1232 stalls & 580 balcony. Taken over Gaumont/PCT 19.10.34, renamed Gaumont Palace. Renamed Gaumont circa 1937. 1780 seats circa 1955.) Renamed ODEON 24.2.64. 1738 seats. Closed 28.7.66. (Top Rank Club for bingo from 18.8.66. Renamed Mecca, open in 2004.)

CHEETHAM HILL Manchester

RIVIERA, Cheetham Hill Road. (Opened 14.5.31. architects: J. & H. Patterson, decorative artist: A. Sherwood Edwards, 2117 seats.) Taken over 6.38. 2117 seats in 1939: 1625 stalls + 492 balcony. Renamed ODEON 2.10.44. 2099 seats circa 1955. 1974 seats. Closed 4.3.61. (Reconstructed internally for Top Rank Bowl, opened 21.8.61. Closed. Sold 9.7.71 to Rayburn Trading. Demolished. Space between Comet Electric and Rayburn Trading retail warehouse units.)

CHELMSFORD Essex

RITZ, Baddow Road. (Opened 8.11.35 by County, architect: Robert Cromie, interior

decoration: Mollo & Egan, 1748 seats.) Taken over 9.39, part of County circuit. 1750 seats in 1939. Renamed ODEON 6.5.46. 1439 seats by 1963. Closed 17.10.81. (Demolished 3-4.90. Meadows multi-storey car park.)

ODEON, Kings Head Walk. Opened 14 & 15.10.93, 4 screens, 851 seats: 337 + 108 + 172 + 234. Extension with four screens opened 4.98, seating 148 + 152 + 127 + 136. Open in 2.05, 8 screens, 1413 seats: 339 + 108 + 158 + 235 + 171 + 143 + 128 + 131.

CHELSEA West London

GAUMONT, 206/222 King's Road, corner of Upper Manor Street (site of William Friese-Green's studio & laboratory). (Opened 8.12.34 by Gaumont/PCT as Gaumont Palace, architects: W. E. Trent & Ernest F. Tulley, 2502 seats. Renamed Gaumont circa 1937. Modernised circa 1960. 2107 seats by 1963.) Renamed ODEON 6.1.63. Closed 11.3.72. (Converted to Habitat store, offices, flats in old flytower, plus smaller cinema.) New ODEON in former balcony with new entrance [former exit, 206 King's Road] opened 9.9.73, 739 seats. Closed 21.11.81. (Re-opened 15.9.83 as Chelsea Cinema by Artificial Eye. Closed 10.04 for repairs. Re-opened 16.12.04. Open in 2.05.)

CHELTENHAM Gloucestershire

GAUMONT, Winchcombe Street. Opened 6.3.33 as Gaumont Palace by Gaumont/Albany Ward-PCT, architect: W. E. Trent, 1774 seats. Renamed Gaumont circa 1937. 1789 seats by 1955.) Renamed ODEON 16.12.62. 1440 seats by 1964. Triple from 1.1.73, seating 756 balcony + 110 & 110 rear stalls. Odeon 2 (downstairs) enlarged to 129, Odeon 3 (downstairs) reduced to 104. Fourth screen opened late 1987 in former café/ballroom, 90 seats. Fifth screen opened 6.10.89 in former front stalls & stage area, 204 seats. Odeon 1 (old balcony) tripled and re-opened 31.7.97 seating 228 front + 180 & 180 rear. All open in 2.05, 7 screens, 1120 seats: 261 + 184 + 183 + 82 + 129 + 104 + 177.

CHESTER Cheshire

ODEON, Hunter Street at corner of Northgate Street. Opened 3.10.36, architect: Harry Weedon [assistant: Robert Bullivant], 1628 seats: 1080 stalls + 548 balcony. Triple from 11.4.76, seating 802 in balcony extended over front stalls + 122 & 122 rear stalls. Two cinemas opened 22.3.91 in rear of balcony, seating 151 & 151, reducing existing cinema to 406 seats. All open in 2.05, seating 406 + 148 + 148 + 122 + 122.

CHESTERFIELD Derbyshire

PICTURE HOUSE, Holywell Street. (Opened 10.9.23.) Taken over 9.11.36. Renamed ODEON circa 1937. 1559 seats in 1939: 991 stalls + 568 balcony. 1335 seats by 1956. 1087 seats by 1964. Closed 17.10.81. (The Winding Wheel - meeting hall. Grade II listed building from 10.00. Open in 2004.)

CHICHESTER West Sussex

PLAZA, South Street. (Opened 18.12.36 by County, total reconstruction of Picturedrome, architect: Andrew Mather, 1063 seats.) Taken over 9.39, part of County circuit. Renamed ODEON 14.5.45. 1067 seats circa 1955. Closed 6.2.60. (Fine Fare supermarket, opened 1961. Iceland store in 2004.)

CHINGFORD Northeast London

ODEON, 6-8 Cherrydown Avenue, Chingford Mount. Opened 9.9.35, architect: Andrew Mather, 1400 seats (approximately). 1142 seats in 1967. (Taken over 10.12.67 by Classic, renamed Classic. Closed 3.6.72. Demolished. Wallis supermarket, later Gateway, £stretcher in 2004 + offices.)

CHIPPENHAM Wiltshire

GAUMONT, Timber Street. (Opened 14.11.36 as Gaumont Palace by Gaumont/Albany Ward-PCT, architects: W. E. Trent & W. Sydney Trent, 1084 seats. Renamed Gaumont circa 1937.) Renamed ODEON 21.10.62. (Taken over 10.12.67 by Classic, renamed Classic. Closed 27.4.74. Store. Nightclub, closed circa 2000.)

CHORLEY Lancashire

ODEON, Market Street. Opened 21.2.38, architect: Harry Weedon [assistant: P. J. Price], 1526 seats: 1092 stalls + 434 balcony. Closed 6.2.71. (Sold 9.8.73 to Tudor Bingo for bingo club. Taken over by Gala, renamed Gala. Open in 2004.)

CLACTON-ON-SEA Essex

ODEON, West Avenue, corner of Jackson Road. Opened 30.5.36, architect: T. Cecil Howitt, 1214 seats: 746 stalls + 468 balcony.

Closed 8.11.75. Re-opened 4.4.76 for summer season. Closed autumn 1976. (Taken over 3.6.77 by independent, renamed Salon. Closed 30.11.80. Demolished 1984. Shops.)

CLAPTON Northeast London

KENNING HALL, 229 Lower Clapton Road. (Opened pre-1915, former function room of adjacent White Hart public house.) Taken over 25.4.38 (through London & Southern?), 641 seats, one floor. New foyer and frontage added. 612 seats circa 1955. (Taken over 2.3.58 by D. Mistlin. Closed 6.79. Nightclub from 1983: Dougies Dine and Dance in 2000.)

CLEVELEYS, Lancashire

ODEON, Crescent West & Runnymede Avenue. Opened 24.11.34, architect: George Tonge, 1156 seats: 900 stalls + 256 balcony. Closed 7.1.61. (Live theatre from 1961 with dressing rooms added. Orion bingo from 1965, open in 2004.)

COATBRIDGE Strathclyde

EMPIRE, Main Street. (Opened pre-1921, former live theatre. 1200 seats.) Taken over 8.3.37, part of Singleton circuit. Renamed ODEON circa 1938. 1140 seats in 1939: 844 stalls + 296 balcony. 1027 seats by 1957. 1018 seats by 1965. Closed 8.5.71. (Sold to Burgh 19.10.71. Shops.)

COLCHESTER Essex

HEADGATE, St. John's Street. (Opened 31.11.10, former Liberal Club and Assembly Rooms. Taken over 24.3.35 by County. 320 seats on one floor.) Taken over 9.39, part of County circuit. Closed 22.6.52 on expiry of lease. (Taken over by independent, renamed Cameo. 319 seats. Taken over 1972 by Star. Closed 12.76. Taken over by independent. Closed. Interior demolished. Planet Ace/Headgate House.)

REGAL, Crouch Street. (Opened 23.2.31, architect: Cecil Masey, 1446 seats. Taken over 24.3.35 by County.) Taken over 9.39, part of County circuit. 1450 seats in 1939. Closed 1944 by fire for three months. Renamed ODEON 18.9.61. Refurbished circa 3.64. 1200 seats. Triple from 4.74, seating 482 balcony + 110 & 110 rear stalls. Refurbished 1984. Small cinemas enlarged circa 1986, seating 150 & 150. Fourth cinema added 1987 in former front stalls. Two further cinemas

opened in 1991 in new side extension. All six cinemas closed 12.10.02, seating 480 + 237 + 118 + 133 + 126 + 177. (Disused in 2004, nightclub use anticipated.)

ODEON, 29-33 Head Street. Opened 16.10.02 (previews from 14.10.02), 8 screens, 1421 seats: 120 + 168 + 206 + 119 + 166 + 305 + 130 + 207. Open in 2.05.

COLINDALE Northwest London

ODEON, Wakemans Hill Parade, 287 Edgware Road (with attached shops, 279/295 Edgware Road). Opened 28.1.35, architect: A. P. Starkey [assistant: Frederick Adkins], 1005 seats, semi-stadium: 726 front + 279 rear. Closed 24.9.60. (Re-opened by Panton Films late 1967, renamed Curzon. Taken over 2.1.72 by Classic, renamed Classic. Classic 2 opened 27.1.73 in one half of rear section. Classic 2 renamed Tatler Film Club from 27.1.74. Tatler reverted to Classic 2 from 2.4.78. Both closed 4.7.81. Colindale Snooker Club from circa 1986, open in 2001.)

COLWYN BAY Clwyd

ODEON, Conway Road, corner of Marine Road. Opened 25.4.36, architect: Harry W. Weedon [assistant: J. Cecil Clavering], 1706 seats: 1128 stalls + 578 balcony. Closed 5.1.57. (Taken over by Hutchinson's, split for stalls bingo and balcony cinema as Astra Entertainment Centre. Cinema re-opened 10.6.67, seating 578. Bingo opened 29.5.67. Bingo closed 9.3.86. Cinema closed 16.10.86. Demolished circa 1987. Block of flats: Swn Y Mor.)

CORBY Northamptonshire

ODEON, Stephensons Way. Opened 16.3.36, architect: Laurence M. Gotch, 1042 seats: 770 stalls + 272 balcony. 895 seats by 1965. (Re-opened 19.1.69 by local independent as Rutland Cinema. Closed late 1969. Rutland Bingo Club. Furniture store from 1996. Chicago Rock Café from 5.11.97.)

COSHAM Portsmouth

AMBASSADOR, High Street. (Opened 8.3.37 by London & Southern, architect: F. C. Mitchell, 1645 seats: 1124 stalls + 521 balcony.) Taken over circa 7.37, part of London & Southern. Renamed ODEON 30.4.45. 1462 seats by 1965. Closed 3.7.76. (Top Rank Club for bingo. Crown bingo in 2005.)

COVENTRY West Midlands
see also Earlsdon
CROWN, Far Gosford Street. (Opened circa 9.12, architect: J. H. Gilbert, 850 seats.) Taken over 1.6.25 by Oscar Deutsch. (Sold as going concern early 1928. Temporarily closed 10.40 by air raid damage. Closed 10.57 for modernisation. Re-opened 1.3.58, renamed Paris. Closed 1.78. Re-opened 1978. Closed 25.3.80. Re-opened 26.10.80. Closed 21.11.81. Riley's American Pool and Snooker Club in 2001.)

GLOBE, Primrose Hill Street. (Opened 9.14, architect: J. H. Gilbert.) Taken over 1.6.25 by Oscar Deutsch. (Leased from 2.4.34 to Charles Orr. 1004 seats.) Taken back 5.40, part of Orr circuit. Closed 1.12.56. (Majestic Ballroom, opened 4.10.57 by Rank. Closed 14.1.61. Taken over by Mecca 6 or 7.61. Mecca Club for bingo. Walkers bingo club from 1987. Closed 1989. TicToc entertainment venue from 1990.)

REGAL, Foleshill Road, Great Heath. (Opened 1911 as Grand. Taken over 1934 by Charles Orr.) Taken over 5.40, part of Orr circuit, 1016 seats: 712 stalls + 304 balcony. 944 seats by 1956. Closed 26.11.60. (Sketchley's dry cleaners by 1976. Front rebuilt.)

RIALTO, Moseley Avenue. (Opened 1928 by Charles Orr.) Taken over 5.40, part of Orr circuit, 1261 seats: 911 stalls + 350 balcony. Closed 15.11.40 by enemy action. (Frontage demolished circa 1958.)

SCALA, Far Gosford Street. (Opened 2.10.35 by Charles Orr on site of old Scala. 1559 seats.) Taken over 5.40, part of Orr circuit, 1557 seats: 1079 stalls + 478 balcony. Renamed ODEON 13.3.50. 1531 seats by 1962. Closed 2.2.63. (Top Rank Club for bingo. Closed 1970 by fire. Demolished circa 1973. Car park.)

GAUMONT, Jordan Well. (Opened 5.10.31 as Gaumont Palace by Gaumont, architect: W. H. Watkins [Percy Bartlett], 2517 seats.) Renamed Gaumont 10.1.37. Closed 14.11.40 by bomb damage. Re-opened 23.12.40. Restored and redecorated 1949 without closing, architect: Harry Weedon. Modernised 1960: 2146 seats.) Modernised & re-opened 31.7.67 as ODEON. Triple from 16.11.75, seating 716 balcony + 170 & 172 rear stalls. ODEON 4 and 5 opened 8.2.90, seating 390, former front stalls, & 121, former café. Closed 10.99. (Taken over by Coventry University, converted to Ellen Terry Building from 12.12.00 with some performance spaces.)

ODEON, SkyDome, Croft Road. Opened 22.10.99 by Odeon, 9 screens, 1943 seats: 228 + 415 + 180 + 359 + 174 + 137 + 115 + 163 + 172. Open in 2.05.

CREWE Cheshire
ODEON, Delamere Street. Opened 26.7.37, architect: Harry Weedon [assistant: Budge Reid], 1129 seats, stadium: 855 front + 274 rear. 995 seats by 1964. (Taken over 25.10.75 by Brent Walker, renamed Focus. Closed 25.5.83. Demolished. McDonalds and other shops.)

PALACE, Edleston Road. (Opened 16.5.10. 850 seats.) Taken over 12.12.55 by CMA. Closed 29.9.56. (MFI store. Subdivided horizontally, carpet shop downstairs & snooker club upstairs, in 2004.)

CROSBY Merseyside
PLAZA, Crosby Road North, Waterloo. (Opened 2.9.39, architect: Lionel A. G. Pritchard, 1450 seats: 1000 stalls + 450 balcony.) Taken over 29.3.43. Renamed ODEON 18.6.45. 1390 seats by 1956. (Taken over 10.12.67 by Classic, renamed Classic. Triple from 6.8.76, seating 670 balcony + 103 & 103 rear stalls. Taken over by Cannon. Renamed Cannon 4.86. Taken over by Apollo, renamed Apollo. Closed 8.11.96. Re-opened 18.7.97 by independent as Plaza, seating 600 + 92 + 74. Open in 2004.)

CROYDON South London
PICTURE HOUSE, 108 North End. (Opened 21.4.28, architects: Clayton & Black, 1280 seats.) Taken over circa 12.36. Renamed ODEON 11.9.36. 1220 seats: 744 stalls + 476 balcony. Modernised 1956: 1115 seats. 1109 seats by 1964. Closed 3.6.72 for twinning. Re-opened 11.9.72, seating 454 downstairs + 430 upstairs. Closed 31.10.85. (Auditorium demolished summer 1986 for shops. Entrance hall converted to shop – Couture menswear in 12.04.)

HIPPODROME, Crown Hill. (Opened Spring 1918, former music hall. 1250 seats. Taken over 2.2.31 by ABC. Subleased to Regent from 5.33 to circa 1935. Closed 18.4.42.) Taken over & re-opened 4.5.42. 830 seats by 1956. Closed 3.11.56. (Demolished. British Home Stores. Converted to Classic 1, 2 & 3 cinemas.

Taken over by Brent Walker, renamed Oscar 1, 2 & 3, later Focus 1, 2 & 3. Closed 14.8.82. Fitness centre & snooker club. Walkabout pub & Loop Poolbar in 12.04.)

DAGENHAM Northeast London
GRANGE, London Road, corner of Goresbrook Road. (Opened circa 12.28, 1200 seats, one floor. Taken over by Kessex. Taken over 1936 by GCF, later Eastern Cinemas [GCF].) Taken over 28.2.43, part of GCF. 980 seats by 1956. Closed 24.8.63. (Demolished. Comfort House, retail units with offices above, in 2004.)

HEATHWAY, Heathway. (Opened 29.7.36 by Kay Bros.[Kessex], architect: George Coles, 2198 seats. Taken over 1936 by GCF, later Eastern Cinemas [GCF].) Taken over 28.2.43, part of GCF. Renamed GAUMONT 14.11.49. 2154 seats by 1956. Renamed ODEON 30.5.64. Closed 20.2.71. (B&Q DIY store. Shopping centre. Destroyed by fire night of 21/22.7.83. The Link Centre, retail units, in 2004.)

DALSTON North London
ODEON, Stamford Road, off Kingsland Road. Opened 1.5.39, architect: Andrew Mather, 2064 seats: 1319 stalls + 745 balcony. 2038 seats by 1956. 1760 seats by 1963. Triple from 10.12.72 seating 745 balcony + 120 & 120 rear stalls. Closed 31.3.79. (Demolished 1984. Block of flats: De Beauvoir Place.)

EMPIRE, 103 Kingsland High Street, corner John Campbell Street. (Opened 29.4.15, architects: [Percy H.] Adams & [George] Coles. Taken over by Classic, closed 11.7.37 for complete reconstruction, architect: F. E. Bromige. Re-opened 10.37 as Classic, 562 seats.) Shown as "Kingsland Empire (Let)" on Odeon Associated Theatres Group property list circa 1950. Never operated by Odeon. Date of sale not known. (Tatler Club for "adult" films from 3.5.70. Classic [partweek public] 26.9.71. Tatler Club 1.9.72. Classic 2.8.75. Taken over by independent, renamed Rio 1.4.76. Open in 2.05. 405 seats.)

DARLINGTON Co. Durham
EMPIRE, Quebec Street, off Crown Street. (Opened 6.11. 890 seats.) Taken over 7.2.44. Licensed for 970 maximum capacity in 1947: 765 (later 777) stalls + 205 balcony. 720 seats by 1957. Closed 5.11.60. (Demolished. Wilkinson's store.)

MAJESTIC, 78/80 Bondgate. (Opened 26.12.32, architect: Joshua Clayton, 1580 seats: 1039 stalls + 541 balconies. Taken over 12.35 by Union. Taken back circa 1937.) Taken over 16.7.43. Renamed ODEON 9.4.45. 1402 seats in 11.58. 1223 seats in 1980. Closed 24.10.81. (Riley's snooker club in 2004.) [Present Odeon is former ABC.]

DEAL Kent

ODEON, Queen Street. Opened 25.7.36, architect: Andrew Mather, 932 seats, stadium: 602 front + 330 rear. 894 seats by 1964. (Taken over 10.12.67 by Classic, renamed Classic. Twin from 30.6.72, seating 284 & 284. Closed 31.1.85. Snooker hall. One cinema re-opened 11.9.86 by independent, named Flicks, seating 173. Second cinema opened 27.11.97 in former bar area, seating 99. Both open in 2004.)

DEPTFORD Southeast London

ODEON, 23/27 Deptford Broadway at corner with Deptford Church Street [site including former Palladium cinema]. Opened 3.10.38, architect: George Coles, 1729 seats: 1200 stalls + 529 balcony. Closed 16.6.44 by bomb damage. Restored, architect: George Coles, and re-opened 17.12.51. 1722 seats in 1956. 1592 seats by 1963. Closed 16.5.70. (Sold 16.1.73 to Marshamheath. Demolished autumn 1988. Shops and flats on enlarged redevelopment site.)

DERBY Derbyshire
see also Normanton

WHITE HALL, St. Peters Street. (Opened 14.12.14, 870 seats. Taken over circa 1.29 by ABC.) Taken over 22.4.35, 913 seats. Closed 29.6.35 for modernisation. Re-opened 3.8.35, renamed ODEON. 783 seats by 1958. Closed 1.5.65. (Demolished. British Home Stores, open in 2004.)

HIPPODROME, Green Lane. (Opened 15.9.30, former live theatre. Taken over circa 6.36 by County. Modernised and re-opened 30.7.38.) Taken over 9.39, part of County circuit. 1901 seats in 1939. Transferred directly to Odeon 3.43. Closed 28.10.50. (Sold to Stoll Theatres for live theatre use. Closed 1959. Bingo club from 1962. Grade II listed building from 1996.)

GAUMONT, London Road. (Opened 17.9.34 as Gaumont Palace by Gaumont/PCT, architects: W. E. Trent & W. Sydney Trent, 2175 seats. Renamed Gaumont circa 1937. Modernised 1962. 2076 seats by 1963.) Renamed ODEON 8.10.65. Triple from 29.12.74, seating 800 balcony & 138 + 138 rear stalls. Closed 4.5.83. (Taken over by EMI, re-opened 26.8.83 as New Trocadero Entertainments Centre with stalls converted to bingo, cinema with 559 seats in former balcony area. Cinema closed 19.12.88 after part of ceiling collapsed. Zanzibar nightclub from 11.99, open in 2004.)

SUPERAMA, Pennine Hotel [Heritage Hotel in 2004], Colyear Street. (Opened 9.2.67 by Compton, architect: John Ambrose [Julian Keable & Partners], 649 seats, stadium.) Taken over 22.2.70, renamed ODEON PENNINE. Closed 31.10.75. (Sadie's Discotheque. Molly Magoos. Brannigan's. Destiny And Elite, closed in 11.04. Heroes wine bar in entrance foyer in 11.04.)

DEVONPORT Devon

HIPPODROME, Prince's Street. (Opened 12.29, former live theatre gutted and enlarged, architects: Marshall & Tweedy.) Taken over 9.39, part of County circuit. 2000 seats in 1939. Closed 24.4.41 by bomb damage. Transferred directly to Odeon 3.43. (Site cleared. Salvation Army offices: Red Shield House.)

DONCASTER South Yorkshire

RITZ, Hallgate. (Opened 26.11.34, architect: William A. Kellett, 2470 seats.) Taken over 2.4.55. Closed for alterations. Re-opened 24.5.55 renamed ODEON, 1993 seats. 1877 seats by 1964. Modernised 1969. Closed 7.7.73. (Demolished. Car park.)

GAUMONT, Hallgate, corner of Thorne Road (enlarged site of old Majestic). (Opened 3.9.34 as Gaumont Palace by Gaumont/PCT, architects: W.E. Trent & W. Sydney Trent, 2020 seats. Renamed Gaumont. 1719 seats by 1964. Modernised summer 1968. Triple from 8.4.73, seating 1003 balcony/front stalls + 144 & 144 rear stalls.) Renamed ODEON 22.1.87. Open in 2.05, seating 975 + 159 + 161.

DOVER Kent

KING'S HALL, 49 Biggin Street. (Opened 21.10.11, architect: A. H. Steele, 800 seats. Variety theatre from circa 1913 to 6.4.31. Closed 29.12.37 by fire. Rebuilding started 8.39, architects: Verity and Beverley. Naval training establishment during World War Two.) Taken over 19.7.43. Re-opened 14.7.47, 1050 seats. Renamed GAUMONT 15.1.51. Closed 26.11.60. (Top Rank Club for bingo from 19.3.61. Zetters bingo in 1982. Gala bingo in 2004.)

REGENT, London Road, Buckland (site of old Regent). (Opened 27.3.37, architects: Percy A. Kelly & Kenneth M. Winch of Elgood & Hastie, 1850 seats.) Taken over 19.7.43. Renamed ODEON 18.1.46. 1761 seats by 1956. 1711 seats by 1964. Closed 2.10.71. (Sold 10.1.74 to Territorial Association. Demolished. Territorial Army training headquarters.)

DUDLEY West Midlands

ODEON, Castle Hill. Opened 28.7.37, architect: Harry Weedon [assistant: Budge Reid], 1876 seats: 1234 stalls + 642 balcony. 1780 seats by 1965. Closed 22.2.75. (Sold 9.3.76 to International Bible Students Association. Re-opened 1977 as church. Grade II listed building from 10.00, during major refurbishment. Open in 2005 as Assembly Hall of Jehovah's Witnesses.)

PLAZA, Castle Hill (site of old Plaza, ex-Scala). (Opened 28.5.36, architect: Hurley Robinson, 1600 seats.) Taken over by CMA/Rank 19.9.55, 1374 seats. 1143 seats by 1964. Twinned from 29.4.73, seating 551 balcony + 199 rear stalls. (Closed 27.10.90. Laser games centre. Demolished 1997. Krushh nightclub in 12.04.)

DUNDEE Tayside

EMPIRE, Rosebank Street, Hilltown. (Opened pre-1914, former live theatre. Taken over 3.1.27 by Singleton.) Taken over 8.3.37, part of Singleton circuit. 1092 seats in 1947: 898 stalls + 194 balcony. 953 seats by 1957. Closed 30.10.57 by fire. (Sold 17.2.67. Demolished. Housing.)

VOGUE, 146 Strathmartine Road. (Opened 21.9.36 by Singleton, architect: James McKissack & Son. 1534 seats, stadium: 1011 front + 523 rear.) Taken over 8.3.37, part of Singleton circuit. Renamed ODEON 6.38. 1493 seats by 1964. Closed 24.2.73. (Demolished 1973. Safeway supermarket, open in 2004.)

GAUMONT, 27 Cowgate, corner of St. Andrews Street. (Opened 24.9.28 as King's by PCT, former King's Theatre, 1458 seats.

Taken over 2.29, part of PCT circuit. Renamed Gaumont 8.5.50. Interior completely rebuilt 1961, 1265 seats.) Renamed ODEON 2.9.73. Closed 24.10.81. (Bingo from 5.83, open in 1994. Nightclub in 2004.)

ODEON, Stack Leisure Park, Harefield Road. Opened 25.6.93, 1646 seats, 6 screens: 574 + 210 + 216 + 233 + 192 + 221. Closed 4.3.01. (Retail outlet.)

ODEON, Douglasfield, Douglas Road. Opened 10.11.01, 2557 seats, 10 screens: 411 + 234 + 317 + 182 + 102 + 481 + 256 + 294 + 161 + 119. Temporarily closed late 1.05 due to structural problems.

DUNFERMLINE Fife

ODEON, 1 Whimbrel Place, Fife Leisure Park. Opened 7.7.00, 2564 seats, 10 screens: 265 + 333 + 265 + 207 + 137 + 415 + 265 + 333 + 207 + 137. Open in 2.05.

DUNSTALL Wolverhampton

PICTURE HOUSE, Stafford Road, Bushbury. (Opened 19.11.34, architect: Hurley Robinson.) Taken over 15.11.37: Renamed ODEON circa 1938. 1338 seats in 1939: 990 stalls + 348 balcony. 1345 seats by 1960. Closed 5.11.60. (Top Rank Club for bingo from 16.2.62. Sold to Hutchinsons 2.9.71, renamed Surewin Bingo. Closed 23.9.81. Demolished 11-12.81. Retirement flats.)

DURSLEY Gloucestershire

VICTORIA, Silver Street. (Opened circa 1918, adaptation of Victoria Coffee Rooms, architect: O. Wainwright.) Taken over 29.7.35, part of Hinckley and Dursley Theatres circuit. 333 seats in 1939: 231 stalls + 102 balcony. Closed by severe fire damage in early hours of 25.1.47. Re-opened 2.8.48, renamed ODEON. Closed 30.10.54. (Indoor market.)

EALING West London

AVENUE, Northfield Avenue, Northfields. (Opened 5.9.32, architect: Cecil Masey, 1538 seats.) Taken over 18.2.36. Renamed ODEON circa 1937. 1530 seats in 1939: 1054 stalls + 476 balcony. 1510 seats in 1956. 1254 seats by 1964. (Taken over 15.11.81 by Panton Films, renamed Coronet. Closed 1.85. Sold 9.3.87 to Cadant. Grade II listed building. Top Hat nightclub from 5.88. Listing raised to Grade II*. Taken over 1995 by Ealing Elim

Pentecostal Church, re-opened as Ealing Christian Centre, open in 2004.)

WALPOLE, Bond Street. (Opened 29.7.12, 1200 seats, one floor. Converted to roller skating rink circa 1919. Converted, architect: J. Stanley Beard, to cinema, re-opened 16.11.25.) Taken over 18.2.36. 1432 seats in 1939: 1233 front + 199 rear. 1319 seats in 1947: 1116 front + 203 rear. 1280 seats in 1956. 1115 seats by 1964. Closed 28.10.72. (Carpet showroom. Music rehearsal studio. Demolished. Offices: Walpole House. Frontage saved and displayed in Mattock Lane nearby.)

EARLSDON Coventry

ASTORIA, Albany Road. (Opened 3.11.22 as Broadway. Taken over 1.34 by Charles Orr, renamed Astoria.) Taken over 5.40, part of Orr circuit, 791 seats: 547 stalls + 244 balcony. (Leased from 2.1.55 by F. W. Allwood Theatres. Closed 5.59. Wades furniture warehouse. Factory for burglar alarms in 2001.)

EAST DULWICH Southeast London

PAVILION, 72 Grove Vale, Goose Green. (Opened 30.7.36 on site of old Pavilion, architect: A. H. Jones.) Taken over 8.37. 1288 seats in 1939: 792 stalls + 496 balcony. Renamed ODEON circa 1939. 1275 seats in 1956. 1221 seats by 1963. Closed 21.10.72. (Sold 7.6.73 to Divine Light Mission. Palace of Peace, Indian temple. Taken over 1978 for warehouse use, renamed London House. Part demolished spring 2001. Completely demolished by 1.03. Flats.)

EAST HAM Northeast London

ODEON, 9 Barking Road (on site including former Boleyn cinema). Opened 18.7.38, architect: Andrew Mather [assistant: Keith P. Roberts], 2212 seats: 1418 stalls + 794 balcony. 2178 seats by 1956. Modernised in 1960s. 1840 seats by 1964. Closed 31.10.81. (Taken over by independent, tripled and re-opened late 1995 for Asian films as Boleyn Cinema, seating 1334: 794 balcony + 270 & 270 rear stalls. Open in 2004.)

EAST MOLESEY Surrey

COURT, Bridge Road. (Opened as Picture Palace. Rebuilt 1932, architect: F. Bolton Trim, renamed Court. 472 seats. Taken over by Town Theatres.) Taken over 26.1.42, part

of Town Theatres circuit. (Taken over 3.12.51 by independent, John A. Ferris. Closed 8.11.58. Warehouse. Printers. Demolished circa 1999. Housing.)

EAST SHEEN Southwest London

EMPIRE, Sheen Lane, corner of Larches Avenue (site of Picturedrome). (Opened 22.12.30 as The Sheen by Joseph Mears Theatres, architects: Leathart & Granger, facade sculpture: Eric Aumonier, 1448 seats: 956 stalls + 492 balcony. Renamed Empire 7.40.) Taken over 3.1.44. Renamed ODEON 17.6.45. 1477 seats by 1956. 1455 seats by 1961. Closed 3.6.61. (Demolished 7.61. Parkway House office block with shops.)

EDGWARE North London
see Burnt Oak

EDGWARE ROAD Northwest London

ODEON, 319 Edgware Road. Opened 9.11.37, architect: George Coles, 2370 seats: 1528 stalls + 842 balcony. 2065 seats by 1963. Closed for subdivision. Re-opened 20.2.68 with smaller Odeon, seating 1116, extending balcony with new screen + Top Rank Club for bingo in stalls. Cinema closed 7.6.75. (Cinema re-opened 24.3.79 for Asian films, renamed Liberty. Closed. Bingo closed 1983. Market in stalls area. Auditorium demolished 7.90. Frontage demolished 11.94. Part of Church Street open-air car park.)

EDINBURGH Lothian

NEW VICTORIA, 7 Clerk Street. (Opened 25.8.30 by Gaumont/PCT, architects: W. E. Trent and J. W. Jordan, 2058 seats: 1226 stalls + 772 balcony + 60 in boxes. 1999 seats by 1956. Modernised 1960 with proscenium arch modified.) Renamed ODEON 6.4.64. 1718 seats. Listed building. Triple from 3.4.82, seating 695 balcony + 293 & 201 rear stalls. Two further screens opened 12.89, seating 259 former front stalls + 182 former stage. All closed 30.8.03. (Temporarily re-opened as performing venue in Edinburgh Festival.) [Present Odeon is new building elsewhere.]

EGLINTON TOLL Glasgow

NEW CINERAMA, 201 Victoria Road, corner of Butterbiggins Road. (Opened 7.8.22 as B. B. Cinerama by J. J. Bennell circuit, architect: McInnes Gardner. 2004 seats. Taken over 12.28 by Gaumont. Auditorium extended at screen end, architect: James L. Ross, and re-opened 1931, 2662 seats. Renamed New Cinerama circa 1940. 2365 seats by 1957.) Modernised, renamed ODEON 24.2.64. 2342 seats by 1965. 2003 seats. Many live shows. Balcony only for film shows. Closed 17.10.81. (Demolished late 1986. Petrol station in 1994.)

ELEPHANT AND CASTLE South London

ODEON, New Kent Road (on part of Trocadero site). Opened 22 & 23.12.66, architect: Erno Goldfinger, 1040 seats, stadium. (Taken over 1.11.81 by Panton Films, renamed Coronet. Closed 28.7.88. Demolished 8.88. Car park.)

ELMERS END Beckenham

ODEON, 46 Croydon Road at Elmers End Green. Opened 26.8.39, architect: Andrew Mather [assistant: Keith P. Roberts], 1518 seats: 1028 stalls + 490 balcony. 1496 seats by 1956. Closed 5.1.57. (Sold to Muirhead's. Office use of balcony foyer. Demolished. Office tower, originally Muirhead's, Maunsell House in 2003.)

ELTHAM HILL Southeast London

ODEON, Eltham Hill, at corner of Kingsground. Opened 14.4.38, architect: Andrew Mather, 1711 seats, semi-stadium: 883 front + 828 rear. Renamed GAUMONT 28.11.49. Closed 16.9.67. (Top Rank Club for bingo. Renamed Mecca. Open in 12.04.)

EPSOM Surrey

ODEON, High Street. Opened 19.4.37, architect: Whinney, Son & Austen Hall, 1434 seats: 1016 stalls + 418 balcony. 1372 seats by 1964. Closed 19.6.71. (Sold to Four Millbank Nominees [Star West] 12.7.71. Demolished. J. Sainsbury supermarket.)

ODEON, 14B-18 Upper High Street. Opened 10.12.99, 8 screens, 2151 seats: 320 + 210 + 271 + 246 + 172 + 298 + 242 + 392. Open in 2.05.

ERITH Southeast London

ODEON, High Street and Avenue Road. Opened 26.2.38, architect: George Coles, 1246 seats: 826 stalls + 420 balcony. 1226 seats in 1967. (Taken over 10.12.67 by Classic, renamed Classic. Subdivided for stalls bingo plus new balcony cinema, opened 16.9.73.

Both taken over by Mecca, cinema renamed Mecca 3.1.74. Cinema closed 25.9.76. Balcony re-opened as part of bingo hall. Taken over 1995 by Jasmine, renamed Jasmine. Closed 4.2.96. Demolished end 2002. Retail units + flats or offices under construction in 2.05.)

EXETER Devon

ODEON, Sidwell Street. Opened 30.8.37, architect: Harry Weedon [assistant: Robert Bullivant], 1920 seats: 1176 stalls + 744 balcony. Temporarily closed 4.5.42 by bomb damage. Re-opened 1.6.42. Closed 23.3.54 for urgent repairs to roof etc., architects: Harry Weedon and Partners. Re-opened 1.6.54. 1916 seats by 1956. Refurbished late 1960s: 1630 seats. Triple from 6.8.72, seating 742 balcony + 119 & 118 rear stalls. Refurbished 1986. Fourth cinema added early 8.88 in former front stalls, seating 344, with new screen in front of upstairs cinema and second small cinema reduced to 105 seats. All open in 2.05, seating 684 + 120 + 105 + 324.

FALKIRK Central Scotland

CINEMA, Melville Street. (Opened circa 1917 as New Cinema House, 580 seats. Taken over circa 1925 by Singleton. Renamed Cinema circa 1926.) Taken over 8.3.37, part of Singleton circuit. 574 seats by 1956. Closed 22-23.5.56 by fire. (Demolished.)

GAUMONT, Newmarket Street. (Opened 8.14 as Pavilion, 950 seats. Taken over by Thomas Ormiston circuit. Taken over 3.28 by Denman/Gaumont. Enlarged by 6.33, 1337 seats. Renamed Gaumont 3.4.50. 1141 seats by 1956. Closed 30.9.57 by fire damage. Re-opened 28.10.57.) Renamed ODEON 16.12.62. 1027 seats circa 1965. Closed 22.9.73. (Demolished. Shops and offices.)

FALMOUTH Cornwall

ODEON, Killigrew Street. Opened 17.12.36, architect: Harry Weedon [assistant: P. J. Price], 1148 seats, semi-stadium: 707 front + 441 rear. 929 seats in 1967. (Taken over 17.12.67 by Classic, renamed Classic. Closed 3.5.70. Demolished. Tesco supermarket, open in 2001.)

FARNBOROUGH Hampshire

REX, London Road. (Opened 25.9.37 by County, architect: David E. Nye, 1208 seats.) Taken over 9.39, part of County circuit. 1218 seats in 1947: 828 stalls + 390 balcony. Fully

acquired 13.6.48. 1122 seats in 1967. (Taken over 3.12.67 by Classic, renamed Classic. Closed 16.6.73, except for "adult" films briefly continued. Bingo club. Concert use. Demolished mid-1970s. Kingsmead House and Shopping Centre.)

SCALA, Camp Road, North Camp. (Opened 14.11.27, architect: R. A. Briggs, 716 seats. Taken over circa 1936 by County.) Taken over 9.39, part of County circuit. 727 seats in 1939: 537 stalls + 190 balcony. Fully acquired 13.6.48. 700 seats by 1956. Closed 27.10.56. (Bingo club. Laser games centre. Church: Kingdom Hall of Jehovah's Witnesses.)

FARNCOMBE Godalming

COUNTY, Meadrow, corner of King's Road. (Opened 1921 as King George's. Taken over late 7.27 by County. Renamed County 10.36.) Taken over 9.39, part of County circuit. 583 seats in 1939. Renamed ODEON 7.5.45. Closed 28.1.56. (Sausage pie factory. Deep freeze centre. Vickers supermarket. Demolished 2000. Flats: Surrey Cloisters.)

FARNHAM Surrey

COUNTY, 8 East Street. (Opened as Palace cinema. Taken over circa 1936 by County. Reconstructed, architect: Harold S. Scott, with balcony removed, and re-opened 26.12.36, renamed County. 500 seats.) Taken over 9.39, part of County circuit. 483 seats by 1956. Closed 27.10.56. (Auditorium demolished for shopping centre including J. Sainsbury supermarket. Frontage retained as Cambridge House.)

REGAL, East Street. (Opened 31.3.33 by County, architect: Harold S. Scott.) Taken over 9.39, part of County circuit. 1280 seats in 1939. 1238 seats by 1956. Renamed ODEON 21.10.62. (Taken over 23.8.71 by Star, renamed Cinema. Re-opened 1971, split for Studio 1 & 2 cinemas seating 114 & 114 + bingo. Taken over by Classic. Closed 13.9.85. Demolished 1987. Vacant site in 2004.)

FARNHAM ROYAL Slough

AMBASSADOR, Farnham Road, corner of Essex Avenue. (Opened 17.2.36 by London & Southern, architect: Sydney R. Croker in association with F. C. Mitchell.) Taken over circa 7.37, part of L&S circuit. 1315 seats in 1939: 928 stalls + 387 balcony. 1183 seats by 1964. Closed 10.2.68. (Sold to Star Cinemas.

Demolished. MFI store. GFE lighting specialists store in 2002.)

FAVERSHAM Kent

ODEON, Market Place. Opened 9.3.36, architect: Andrew Mather, 729 seats, stadium: 444 front + 288 rear. 674 seats in 1967. (Taken over 3.12.67 by Classic, renamed Classic. Taken over by Coral for films + bingo. Bingo only from 1.5.74. Films part-week until 8.6.85. Full-time bingo. Closed. Grade II listed building from 22.3.88. Some film use from 8.90. Re-opened 11.2.94 as New Royal cinema, 448 seats. Open in 2.05.)

FINCHLEY North London

ODEON, 894 High Road, from corner of Mayfield Avenue to corner of Friern Watch Avenue, North Finchley. Opened 14.10.35, architect: A. P. Starkey [assistant: Frederick Adkins]. 1296 seats, semi-stadium: 878 front + 418 rear. 1248 seats by 1964. Closed 26.12.64. (Garage & showrooms for Halls [Finchley] Ltd. Frontage largely rebuilt. Furnitureland.)

FINSBURY PARK North London

ASTORIA, 232/6 Seven Sisters Road, corner of Ilsedon Street. (Opened 29.9.30, architect: E.A. Stone, interior decoration: Marc Henri & Laverdet, 3040 seats. Taken over 12.30 by Paramount.) Taken over 27.11.39. 3018 seats in 1939. 3012 seats by 1956. Renamed ODEON 17.11.70. Closed 25.9.71. (Rainbow concert hall. Grade II* listed building from 16.1.74. Closed 24.12.81. Taken over 1995 by Universal Church of the Kingdom of God. Auditorium restored 1999. Foyer restored 2001.)

FLEET Hampshire

COUNTY. (Opened 20.11.37 by County as reconstruction of old County, architect: David E. Nye.) Taken over 9.39, part of County circuit. 774 seats in 1939: 610 stalls + 164 balcony. Renamed ODEON 29.4.46. Closed 12.10.57. (Demolished. Shops, including Co-Operative Funeral Directors.)

FOLKESTONE Kent

ASTORIA, 24 Sandgate Road and Oxford Terrace. (Opened 20.4.35, architects: E. A. Stone & Ewen Barr, interior decoration: Mollo & Egan, 1670 seats: 1120 stalls + 550 balcony. Taken over 12.35 by County.) Taken over

9.39, part of County circuit. Renamed ODEON 2.6.40. 1657 seats by 1956. Modernised 4.60. Closed 26.1.74. (Demolished. Albion House offices with Boots store on ground floor in 2001.)

FOREST GATE Northeast London

ODEON, Romford Road. Opened 1.3.37, architect: Andrew Mather, 1806 seats: 1110 stalls + 696 balcony. Closed 21.4.41 by bomb damage. Re-opened 4.8.41. 1647 seats by 1965. Closed 31.10.75. (Snooker hall. Pot Black snooker in 1984, using former exit as entrance. Closed by 1994. Muslim centre in 2001: Minhaj-ul-Quran Mosque and Cultural Centre.)

FOREST HILL Southeast London

CAPITOL, 11/15 London Road. (Opened 11.2.29, architect: J. Stanley Beard. 1691 seats. Taken over 4.29 by London & Southern. Leased out from 8.32. Leased or subleased by ABC from 7.33.) Taken over circa 7.37, part of London & Southern circuit, still leased out and never operated by Odeon. 1687 seats. Sold 6.12.65 by Rank. (Renamed ABC 22.12.68. Closed 13.10.73 by ABC. Mecca bingo club, taken over by Jasmine & renamed circa 1991. Grade II listed building from 14.9.93. Closed 9.96. Capitol pub from 8.5.01, open in 2004.)

FULHAM West London – see Putney

GABALFA Cardiff

PLAZA, North Road. (Opened 12.3.28, architect: Howard Williams, 1500 seats. Part of Jackson Withers circuit.) Taken over 1.11.76 by Rank. Some association with Odeon. Closed 17.10.81. (Auditorium demolished. Meridian Court flats retaining cinema entrance.)

GANTS HILL – see Ilford

GATESHEAD Tyne & Wear

BLACK'S REGAL, 308 High Street. (Opened 15.2.37 by George & Alfred Black, architect: E. M. Lawson, 2272 seats: 1582 stalls + 690 balcony.) Taken over 1.1.44. Renamed ODEON 4.45. 2380 seats by 1957. Closed 18.1.75. (Top Rank Club for bingo from 14.4.78. Closed 1995. Demolished late 2003.)

GILLINGHAM Kent

EMBASSY, Gardiner Street. (Opened 3.10.36, architect: Robert Cromie, 1762 seats.) 1744 seats in 1938: 1276 stalls + 468 balcony. Renamed ODEON 17.6.46. 1634 seats in 1967. (Taken over 3.12.67 by Classic, renamed Classic. Taken over by independent 13.6.77, renamed Embassy. Closed 17.9.77. Bingo club, Gala by 7.01.)

GLASGOW Strathclyde

see also Anniesland, Dennistoun, Eglinton Toll, Gorbals, Maryhill, Paisley Road Toll, Partick, Possil, Possilpark, Rutherglen, Scotstoun, Shettleston, Springburn and Townhead

PARAMOUNT, 56 Renfield Street & Regent Street. (Opened 31.12.34 by Paramount, architects: Verity & Beverley, 2784 seats: 1760 stalls + 1024 balcony.) Taken over 25.8.42. Renamed ODEON 4.11.46. 2792 seats by 1956. Closed circa 9.69 for modernisation & tripling, architects: Gavin Patterson & Son, interior design: Dry Halasz & Associates. Re-opened 2.10.70, seating 1138 + 1243 + 558 [Odeon 3 in former backstage area with balcony and separate West Regent Street entrance]. Odeon 3 split and re-opened 11.87, seating 288 + 222. Odeon 2 tripled circa 1991: 208 + 227 + 240. Odeon 1 subdivided & re-opened circa 6.99: 555 + 153 + 173 + 113 seats. Category B listed building 29.5.03. Sold for redevelopment and leased back, open in 2.05 seating: 555 + 152 + 113 + 173 + 188 + 231 + 239 + 249 + 222.

ODEON, The Quay, Paisley Road. Opened 20.9.96, 12 screens, 2553 seats: 428 + 128 + 89 + 201 + 200 + 277 + 321 + 128 + 89 + 194 + 242 + 256. Open in 2.05, 2576 seats: 431 + 131 + 91 + 200 + 202 + 280 + 324 + 131 + 90 + 194 + 244 + 258.

GLOUCESTER Gloucestershire

THEATRE DE LUXE, Northgate Street. (Opened 17.4.22, architect: William Leah, 1062 seats.) Taken over 11.10.37. 1014 seats in 1938: 668 stalls + 346 balcony. Closed by fire on night of 29/30.1.39. (Sold and site cleared 1959. Lloyds Bank, shops & offices.)

PLAZA, Barton Street. (Opened 25.11.35, architect: E. C. M. Wilmott, 1832 seats.) Taken over 11.1.56. Modernised & renamed ODEON 28.1.57. 1602 seats by 1963. 1317 seats by 1973. Closed 30.8.75. (Top Rank Club for bingo from circa 11.75.)

GODALMING Surrey

see also Farncombe

REGAL, Ockford Road. (Opened 2.8.35 by County, architect: Robert Cromie, interior decoration: Mollo & Egan, 1210 seats.) Taken over 9.39, part of County circuit. Renamed ODEON 7.5.45. 1132 seats in 1967. (Taken over 3.12.67 by Classic, renamed Classic. Bingo club from 18.1.68. Balcony opened as Classic cinema in 1971. Taken over by Mecca, cinema renamed Mecca. Closed 13.12.75. Balcony re-opened as part of main auditorium for bingo. Closed. Demolished 2-3.96. Housing.)

GOLDERS GREEN Northwest London

see also Temple Fortune

REGAL, 765 Finchley Road. (Opened 19.9.32 by County, conversion of ice rink, architect: Robert Cromie. 2200 seats on one floor.) Taken over 9.39, part of County circuit. 2218 seats in 1939. 2040 seats in 1947. Closed 1.12.56. (Top Rank Bowl, opened 3.60. Closed. Sold 25.10.71 to Bruno Newton. Demolished 2-3.96. Offices: Smiths Ltd.)

GORBALS Glasgow

PARAGON, 403 Cumberland Street. (Opened 1912. 1300 seats. Taken over 11.12 by Singleton. Reconstructed 1927, architects: A. V. Gardner & W. R. Glen.) Taken over 8.3.37, part of Singleton circuit. 1319 seats in 1938: 950 stalls + 369 balcony. Closed 11.11.51 for ceiling repairs. Re-opened 19.11.51. 1236 seats by 1956. Closed 5.1.57. (Demolished. Housing.)

GREENOCK Strathclyde

KING'S THEATRE, 138 West Blackhall Street. (Opened 1928, former Alexandra live theatre, 1500 seats.) Taken over 3.10.55. Modernised, architect: Lennox Paterson, & re-opened 16.1.56 as ODEON, 1183 seats. Closed 10.69 by compulsory purchase order for road straightening. (Demolished spring 1973.)

GREENWICH Southeast London

TRAFALGAR, 82 Trafalgar Road, corner of Maze Hill. (Opened 26.12.12, architects: Ward & Ward, 815 seats. Taken over 9.34 by D. J. James. Largely rebuilt, architects: Kemp & Tasker, with balcony added & re-opened 16.9.35, 1400 seats. Taken over 4.37 by Eastern Cinemas [GCF.]) Taken over 28.2.43,

part of GCF. Renamed ODEON 30.7.45. 1346 seats by 1956. Closed 30.4.60. (Frontage demolished as part of Penfold's Car Mart from 2.69. Leslie's Frozen Food Centre. Furniture store briefly from 6.95. Demolished circa 1998. Office block on frontage, flats behind, in 2004.)

GRIMSBY Humberside

GAUMONT, Victoria Street. (Opened 1920 as Savoy. Taken over 3.27 by Gaumont. 1430 seats. Renamed Gaumont 10.4.50.) Renamed ODEON 21.10.62. 1241 seats. (Taken over by Brent Walker 5.10.75, renamed Focus. Closed 24.12.77. Shops from circa 1983.)

GUERNSEY Channel Islands

see St. Peter Port

GUIDE BRIDGE Ashton-Under-Lyne

ODEON, Stockport Road. Opened 29.6.36 [built as Verona cinema and acquired shortly before opening], architects: Drury and Gomersall. 1164 seats: 834 stalls + 330 balcony. 1146 seats by 1957. Closed 11.3.61. (Roman Catholic church.)

GUILDFORD Surrey

ODEON, Upper High Street, Epsom Road and Jenner Road. Opened 13.5.35, architects: Andrew Mather & J. Raworth Hill. 1623 seats: 1145 stalls + 478 balcony. 1436 seats by 1956. Triple from 19.8.73, seating 452 balcony + 121 & 121 rear stalls. Fourth cinema in front stalls from 2.89, seating 320. All closed 8.12.96. (Demolished late 2002. Trinity Gate block of flats with shops under construction in 1.05.)

PLAYHOUSE, High Street. (Opened circa 1922. Taken over 1929 by County.) Taken over 9.39, part of County circuit. 925 seats in 1939. 930 seats in 1947: 705 stalls + 225 balcony. 927 seats by 1956. Closed 12.6.65. (Demolished. Tunsgate Square shopping arcade.)

PLAZA, Onslow Street. (Taken over 1930 as Central Hall by County. Renamed Plaza.) Taken over 9.39, part of County circuit. 511 seats in 1939. 492 seats by 1956. Closed 29.9.56. (Bingo club. The Drink nightclub in 2001.)

ODEON, Bedford Road. Opened 12 & 13.12.96, 9 screens, 2224 seats: 430 + 361 + 343 + 273 + 297 + 148 + 112 + 130 + 130.

Open in 2.05, 2110 seats: 422 + 353 + 269 + 269 + 293 + 144 + 108 + 126 + 126.

HACKNEY ROAD Northeast London

ODEON, 211 Hackney Road between Thurtle Road (now Dawson Street) and Scawfell Street. Opened 27.7.38, architect: Andrew Mather, 1926 seats: 1260 stalls + 666 balcony. 1884 seats by 1956. Closed 20.5.61. (Top Rank Club for bingo, opened 21.5.61. Renamed Mecca. Open in 2004.)

HALIFAX West Yorkshire

ODEON, Broad Street, corner of Orange Street (also onto Great Albion Street). Opened 27.6.38, architect: George Coles, 2058 seats: 1344 stalls + 714 balcony. 1818 seats by 1964. Closed 18.10.75. (Top Rank Club for bingo. Renamed Mecca. Open in 2004.)

HAMILTON Strathclyde

ODEON, Townhead Street. Opened 14.11.38, architect: Andrew Mather, 1819 seats: 1353 stalls + 466 balcony. 1534 seats by 1966. Closed 1.3.80 for tripling. Re-opened 5.4.80, seating 466 balcony with new screen + 224 & 310 stalls. Closed 26.8.99. (Demolished 1999. Car park.)

HAMMERSMITH West London

GAUMONT, Queen Caroline Street. (Opened 28.3.32 as Gaumont Palace by Gaumont, architect: Robert Cromie, 3487 seats. Renamed Gaumont circa 1937.) Renamed ODEON 25.11.62. 3485 seats by 7.73. Concert venue with very occasional films by early 1980s. Grade II listed building from 26.3.90. (Taken over 6.92 by Apollo, renamed Apollo. Concert and show venue only, open in 2005.)

HAMPSTEAD Northwest London

see Haverstock Hill

HANLEY Staffordshire

see also Stoke-on-Trent

ODEON, Trinity Street at corner of Foundry Street (site of Grand Theatre). Opened 13.2.37, architect: Harry Weedon [assistant: Arthur J. Price], 1580 seats: 1036 stalls + 544 balcony. Modernised circa 1960: 1401 seats. Closed 15.11.75. (The Foyer pub in foyer space by 1999, Chicago Rock Café in auditorium area by 2003.)

GAUMONT, Piccadilly. (Opened 11.2.29 as Regent by Gaumont/PCT, architect: W. E. Trent, 2151 seats. Renamed Gaumont 25.9.50. 2152 seats by 1963. Triple from 12.5.74, seating 1137 former balcony & front stalls + 159 & 159 rear stalls.) Renamed ODEON 6.6.76. Closed 12.10.89. (Grade II listed building from 30.11.89. Listing raised 18.1.94 to Grade II*. Stage end rebuilt & enlarged, foyers modernised, re-opened 1999 as Regent Theatre for live use. Open in 2005.)

HARLESDEN Northwest London

ODEON, Craven Park Road and St. Albans Road. Opened 12.7.37, architects: Whinney, Son & Austen Hall, 1719 seats: 1224 stalls + 495 balcony. 1519 seats by 1964. Closed 15.4.72. (Re-opened as Asian cinema, renamed Liberty. Concert/dance hall. Tara nightclub. Closed. Demolished 8-9.89. Odeon Court block of flats by 2.94.)

HARLOW Essex

REGAL, Unit 50, Road No. 1, Templefields Industrial Estate. (Opened 18.8.52, 690 seats, one floor.) Taken over 28.2.55. Closed 30.1.60. (Expanded offices of Regal House in 2003.)

ODEON, The High, now West Square. Opened 1.2.60, T. P. Bennett & Son, 1244 seats, one floor. Closed 7.6.87 for tripling. Odeon 1 opened 17.7.87, 450 seats, front. Odeon 2 opened 28.8.87, 243 seats, rear. Odeon 3 opened 11.9.87, 201 seats, rear. All open in 2.05, seating 399 + 217 + 179.

HARROGATE North Yorkshire

ODEON, East Parade, at corner of Station Avenue. Opened 28.9.36, architect: Harry Weedon [assistant: W. Calder Robson] [based on Odeon Sutton Coldfield: architect: Harry Weedon, assistant: J. Cecil Clavering], 1647 seats: 1049 stalls + 598 balcony. 1446 seats by 1964. Triple from 14.8.72, seating 532 balcony + 108 & 108 rear stalls. Refurbished 1984. Fourth cinema added 12.89, seating 259 in former front stalls with new screen in front of upstairs cinema and one downstairs cinema reduced to 75 seats. Grade II listed building. Modernised and balcony subdivided into two screens, opened 19.4.02. All open in 2.05, seating: 298 + 242 + 101 + 76 + 329.

HARTLEPOOL Cleveland
see West Hartlepool

HATFIELD Hertfordshire

REGENT, 46 The Common, Hatfield Road. (Opened 7.10.35, architect: E. B. Parkinson, 800 seats. Taken over 4.37 by Eastern Cinemas [GCF].) Taken over 28.2.43, part of GCF. Renamed ODEON 30.9.46. 780 seats by 1956. (Taken over 17.12.67 by Classic, renamed Classic. Taken over 2.69 by independent, renamed Curzon. Closed 2.6.73. Bingo. Closed Re-opened 1998 for bingo.)

HAVERSTOCK HILL Northwest London

ODEON, 201 Haverstock Hill. [Also known as Odeon Belsize Park and Odeon Hampstead.] Opened 29.9.34, architects: T. P. Bennett & Son, 1544 seats, stadium: 652 front + 892 rear. Closed 10.41 by bomb damage. Restored, architects: T. P. Bennett & Son, and re-opened 13.12.54, seating 1466. 1396 seats by 1963. Closed 23.9.72. (Demolished. Budgens supermarket with Screen on the Hill opened 9.11.77 in adjacent space through former shop, open in 2005.)

HAWICK Borders

KING'S, Exchange Buildings. (Opened circa 1922, former live theatre. Taken over circa 1929 by Singleton.) Taken over 8.3.37, part of Singleton circuit. 1288 seats in 1939: 1055 stalls + 233 balcony. Renamed ODEON 12.8.46. 1024 seats by 1957. (Taken over 17.12.67 by Classic, renamed Classic. Partweek bingo from 14.1.68. Taken over 1.1.71 by independent, renamed Marina. Partweek bingo by 1980. 750 seats. Closed. Nightclub. Closed by fire circa 1994. Demolished. Car park.)

HAYES West London

AMBASSADOR, East Avenue. Opened 19.12.38 by London & Southern, controlled by Odeon, architect: F.C. Mitchell, 1517 seats, semi-stadium: 989 front + 528 rear. Closed 10.6.61. (Demolished. GPO Centre telephone exchange, later British Telecommunications Centre.)

HAYES Southeast London

REX, Station Approach. (Opened 6.8.36 by General Cinema Theatres, architect: Cecil Masey, 1000 seats. Taken over by Town Theatres.) Taken over 26.1.42, part of Town Theatres circuit. Renamed ODEON 30.7.45. 1081 seats by 1956. Closed 27.10.56. (Demolished. Supermarket.)

HAYMARKET London
see London West End

HEMEL HEMPSTEAD Hertfordshire

ODEON, Marlowes, corner of Coombe Street. Opened 29.8.60, architect: Robert Bullivant of Harry Weedon & Partners, 1148 seats, one floor. 1100 seats by 1964. Part-week bingo from 27.3.74, 785 seats. Closed 22.8.95. (Taken over by Jasmine for full-time bingo. Closed. The Full House pub from 21.7.98.)

ODEON, Leisure World, Jarman Park. Opened 25.8.95, 8 screens, 1651 seats: 120 + 170 + 170 + 276 + 210 + 401 + 152 + 152. Open in 2.05, 1832 seats: 130 + 183 + 183 + 317 + 261 + 431 + 166 + 161.

HENDON Northwest London

ODEON, corner of Church Road and Parson Street. Opened 28.8.39, architects: Harry Weedon & Robert Bullivant, 1362 seats: 868 stalls + 494 balcony. 1376 seats in 1948: 872 stalls + 504 balcony. 1242 seats by 1964. Closed 13.1.79. (Demolished 12.81. Ferrydale Lodge, block of flats.)

HENLEY-ON-THAMES Oxfordshire

REGAL, Bell Street. (Opened 14.5.37 by County, complete reconstruction of Picture House, architect: Arthur F. Hunt.) Taken over 9.39, part of County circuit. 941 seats in 1939. Renamed ODEON 14.5.45. Closed 21.3.59. (Re-opened 1960 by Theatre Administration, renamed Regal. Closed 29.5.86. Demolished. Waitrose supermarket and access road.) [Current Regal cinema is on nearby site.]

HEREFORD Hereford & Worcester

ODEON, 6 Commercial Street, High Town. Opened 17.4.37, architect: Roland Satchwell, 1133 seats: 788 stalls + 345 balcony. 958 seats by 1956. 1132 seats by 1965. (Taken over 26.10.75 by Brent Walker, renamed Focus. Taken over 3.6.83 by Classic, renamed Classic. Closed 1.3.84. Demolished. Frontage into retail units: Early Learning Centre & Bay Trading in 2.05. Auditorium now retail units along Gomand Street.) [Current Odeon is former ABC.]

HERNE BAY Kent

ODEON, 4 Avenue Road. Opened 2.11.36, architect: Andrew Mather, 974 seats, stadium: 518 front + 456 rear. 814 seats in 1967.

(Taken over 3.12.67, renamed Classic. Renamed Cannon. Closed 8.10.87. Demolished 1988. Flats.)

HIGHGATE North London

ODEON, Junction Road, corner of Bickerton Road. Opened 19.12.55, architects: T. P. Bennett & Son (revised completion of pre-war scheme), 1734 seats: 998 stalls + 736 balcony. Closed 6.1.73. (Sold 17.8.73 to Utopian Housing Society. Demolished 1974. Flats: Ash Court.)

HIGH WYCOMBE Buckinghamshire

MAJESTIC, Castle Street. (Opened 27.1.30, architect: S. B. Pritlove, interior decorator: W. E. Greenwood, 1480 seats. Taken over circa 1932 by County.) Taken over 9.39, part of County circuit. Renamed ODEON 7.8.44. 1447 seats in 1956. 1340 seats by 1965. Closed 25.1.69. (Demolished 2.69. Woolworth's.)

HINCKLEY Leicestershire

NEW BORO', The Borough. (Opened 4 or 11.4.35, incorporating Old Boro' cinema as foyer.) Taken over 29.7.35, part of Hinckley and Dursley Theatres circuit. 967 seats: 658 stalls + 309 balcony. Renamed ODEON 1.1.36. Closed 3.6.61. (Front demolished for offices. Auditorium into nightclub, open in 2003.)

REGENT, Rugby Road and Lancaster Road. (Opened 11.3.29, architect: Horace G. Bradley. Designed for theatre and cinema use, opened with live show.) Taken over 29.7.35, part of Hinckley and Dursley Theatres circuit. 970 seats: 670 stalls + 300 balcony. Renamed GAUMONT 18.4.55. 1002 seats by 1957. 897 seats in 1967. (Taken over 3.12.67 by Classic, renamed Classic. Closed 30.6.68. Bingo - Flutters in 8.02.)

HOLLOWAY North London

MARLBOROUGH THEATRE, 383 Holloway Road. (Opened 28.5.18, former live theatre with some films shown earlier. Taken over 1925 by PCT, 2612 seats. Taken over 2.29 by Gaumont as part of PCT circuit. 1685 seats. Closed 9.40.) Taken over 2.42. Re-opened 9.3.42, 1500 seats. 1189 seats by 1956. Closed 31.8.57. (Demolished 1962. Marlborough House office block.)

GAUMONT, 419-427 Holloway Road. (Opened 5.9.38 by Gaumont/GTC, architect:

C. Howard Crane, alterations: W. E. Trent, 3006 seats. Closed 11.8.44 by wartime bomb damage. Auditorium reconstructed, architects: T. P. Bennett & Son, & re-opened 21.7.58, 1987 seats.) Renamed ODEON 25.11.62. Triple from 6.5.73, seating 614 balcony + 216 & 216 rear stalls. Balcony closed 4.9.88 for subdivision into two cinemas plus new cinema in former front stalls, all opened 16.12.88. Sixth cinema opened 5.6.92 over main foyer, 78 seats. Two further screens added. Grade II listed building from 10.00. All open in 2.05, 1575 seats: 330 + 315 + 72 + 231 + 183 + 249 + 92 + 103.

HORNCHURCH London

TOWERS, 31 High Street. (Opened 3.8.35, architects: Kemp and Tasker, 2000 seats. (Taken over 4.37 by Eastern Cinemas [GCF].) Taken over 28.2.43, part of GCF. Renamed ODEON 26.6.50. 1865 seats by 1956. 1781 seats by 1963. Closed 6.10.73. (Top Rank Club for bingo. Renamed Mecca, open in 2005.)

HORSHAM West Sussex

ODEON, North Street. Opened 7.10.36, architect: George Coles, 1258 seats: 766 stalls + 492 balcony. 1240 seats in 1967. (Taken over 10.12.67 by Classic, renamed Classic. Split for Mecca bingo in stalls + two Classic cinemas opened 26.5.72, seating 310 balcony & 110 in former restaurant. Cinemas taken over by Mecca, renamed Mecca. Cinemas closed 10.1.76. Bingo closed. Demolished by 11.81. Office block.)

HOUNSLOW West London

DOMINION, London Road at corner of North Drive. (Opened 28.12.31, architect: F. E. Bromige.) Taken over by Odeon circa 7.37. 2022 seats in 1939: 1460 stalls + 562 balcony. Advertised as a Gaumont theatre in 1950s. 1990 seats in 1953: 1428 stalls + 562 balcony. 1908 seats in 1961. Closed 30.12.61. (Top Rank Club for bingo from 3.62. Renamed Mecca 14.4.97. Open in 2005.)

AMBASSADOR, Bath Road, Hounslow West. (Opened 7.9.36 by London & Southern, architect: W. J. King.) Taken over circa 7.37, part of London & Southern circuit. 1876 seats in 1939: 1332 stalls + 544 balcony. Renamed ODEON 16.4.45. 1872 seats in 1953: 1328 stalls + 544 balcony. Triple from 16.6.74, seating 490 balcony + 114 & 114 rear stalls.

Closed 7.1.84. (Demolished 1.84. Shops & restaurant with Gateway supermarket - Somerfield in 2004.)

HOVE Brighton

LIDO, Denmark Villas. (Opened 6.5.32 by County, conversion of ice rink, architect: Robert Cromie, 2137 seats on one floor.) Renamed ODEON 31.7.44. 2081 seats by 1957. Closed 18.2.61. (Top Rank Bowl from 1961. Closed. Sold 30.4.69 to Food Securities [Properties]. Demolished 1970. New Marina Car Sales.)

HULL Humberside

ODEON, Kingston Park, Kingston Street. Opened 5 & 6.4.90, 1568 seats, 8 screens: 170 + 170 + 150 + 172 + 418 + 206 + 132 + 150. Two screens added 21.7.95, 1882 seats: 170 + 170 + 150 + 172 + 466 + 273 + 132 + 150 + 110 + 89. Open in 2.05, 10 screens, 1862 seats: 169 + 169 + 148 + 170 + 458 + 272 + 132 + 148 + 108 + 88.

ILFORD Northeast London

SAVOY, Eastern Avenue, corner of Perth Road. (Opened 3.9.34 by Kay Bros. [Kessex], architect: George Coles, 2190 seats. Taken over 1936 by GCF, later Eastern Cinemas [GCF].) Taken over 28.2.43, part of GCF. Renamed ODEON 28.11.49. 2158 seats by 1956. 1910 seats by 1963. Closed 1.7.67 for modernisation. Re-opened 15.7.67. Closed 15.11.80 for tripling. Re-opened 22.2.81, seating 768 balcony + 255 & 316 rear stalls. Front stalls converted to fourth screen from 16.3.90, seating 290, with one screen reduced to 190 seats for access corridor. Former café converted 1991 to fifth screen seating 62. 1565 seats in 6.01: 768 + 255 + 290 + 190 + 62. All closed 2.4.02. (Demolished 2002. Flats and supermarket proposed.)

IPSWICH Suffolk

ODEON, Lloyds Avenue. Opened 7.9.36, architect: George Coles, 1764 seats: 1141 stalls + 623 balcony. Modernised 1959/1960: 1523 seats. Triple from 9.11.75, seating 609 balcony + 109 & 109 rear stalls. Closed 3.7.82. (Top Rank Club for bingo. Renamed Mecca. Open in 6.02.)

GAUMONT, Major's Corner/8 St. Helens Street. (Opened 4.11.29 as Regent by Gaumont/PCT, architect: W. E. Trent, 1800 seats, stadium plan: 1070 stalls & 660 raised rear section & 70 from 14 boxes of 5 seats. Renamed Gaumont 24.4.50. 1780 seats in 1955. 1742 seats by 1963. 1666 seats. Seating increased to 1813 in 1985, mostly live show use. GAUMONT 2 opened 22.8.83 in former restaurant/ballroom area, 186 seats.) Both renamed ODEON 9.1.87. Both closed 20.3.91. (Main auditorium re-opened late 21.9.91 as live theatre, renamed Regent. Grade II listed building from 10.00. Open in 2005.)

ODEON, 10 St. Margaret's Street. Opened 20 & 21.3.91, architects: Renton Howard Wood Levin Partnership, 1550 seats, 5 screens: 506 + 318 + 290 + 218 + 218. Open in 2.05, seating 510 + 313 + 281 + 210 + 210.

ISLEWORTH West London

ODEON, 484 London Road, corner of Harvard Road. Opened 20.3.35, architect: George Coles, 1408 seats: 994 stalls + 414 balcony. Closed 5.1.57. (Isleworth Studios. Auditorium completely transformed. Auditorium area demolished for flats, opened 2003. Entrance block refurbished.)

ISLINGTON North London

LIDO, 276 Upper Street, corner of Florence Street. (Opened 27.9.28, conversion of vestry hall, architects: Gray and Webb.) Taken over 3.12.35: Renamed ODEON circa 1936. 1138 seats in 1939: 642 stalls + 496 balcony. 1136 seats by 1960. Closed 21.1.61. (Demolished. Petrol station.)

ANGEL, 7 High Street (stalls entrance in White Lion Street). (Opened 31.12.12 by Davis circuit, architect: H. Courtenay Constantine, 1463 seats. Taken over by APPH 8.26. Taken over 2.29, part of PCT/APPH circuit, 1403 seats.) Advertised as an Odeon theatre in 1950s. 1450 seats by 1955. 1299 seats by 1963. Renamed ODEON 21.8.63. Closed 18.3.72. (Auditorium demolished 1974 for offices. Tower frontage Grade II listed building from 31.1.91. Entrance: Coffee Republic in 8.02.)

JERSEY Channel Islands – see St. Helier

KEMP TOWN Brighton

ODEON, 38 St. George's Road, corner of Paston Place. Opened 1.2.34, architect: Andrew Mather (adaptation of an existing structure), 958 seats, semi-stadium: 556 front

+ 402 rear. Closed 14.9.40 by bomb damage. Restored and re-opened Boxing Day 1940. 956 seats by 1956. Closed 5.11.60. (Re-opened 12.1.62 as Top Rank Club for bingo. Sold 4.9.72 to Boswell Concessions — Kemptown Bingo and Social Club. Religious centre: 'The City'. Demolished 1.86. Cavendish Court block of flats.)

KENSAL RISE Northwest London

PAVILION, Chamberlayne Road at corner of Bannister Road. (Opened 19.11.14, architect: Cecil Masey, 1500 seats.) Taken over 1.7.37. 1455 seats in 1939: 994 stalls + 461 balcony. Renamed ODEON circa 1940. 1261 seats by 1964. Closed 2.5.70. (Sold 30.12.70 to Toupata Management. Demolished. Garage.)

KENSINGTON West London

MAJESTIC, 263 High Street. (Opened 3.1.26 as The Kensington by Joseph Mears Theatres, architects: J. R. Leathart and W. R. Granger, 2370 seats. Renamed Majestic 7.40. Taken over by Government for war-time storage.) Taken over 3.1.44. Re-opened 9.10.44, renamed ODEON, 2075 seats. Modernised circa 1960. 1819 seats. Closed 24.4.65 for further modernisation. Re-opened 5.7.65. Triple from 22.4.76, seating 665 + 301 + 193. ODEON 1 closed 24.6.79. ODEON 1 re-opened 16.8.79. Fourth screen opened 27.9.79, seating 234. Two further screens opened 26.7.91, seating 73 + 110. Refurbishment, completed by 7.98. Open in 2.05, seating 520 + 66 + 91 + 266 + 172 + 204.

KENTISH TOWN North London

GAISFORD, 1a Gaisford Street. (Opened 23.12.10 as The Kentish Town Cinema. 502 seats. Renamed Gaisford 1933. Taken over by Town Theatres.) Taken over 26.1.42, part of Town Theatres circuit. 481 seats by 1956. 469 seats. Closed 25.6.60. (Warehouse. Demolished. Northumberland House.)

KENTON Northwest London

ODEON, 202 Kenton Road. Opened 11.3.35, architect: George Coles, 1396 seats: 979 stalls + 417 balcony. Closed 25.3.61. Demolished. (Waitrose supermarket & Brent House office block in 1993. Pick & Save supermarket in 2001.)

KETTERING Northamptonshire

ODEON, Gold Street. Opened 19.9.36 (re-

construction of Victoria Picture House), architect: Harry Weedon, interior decoration: Mollo & Egan, 1090 seats: 740 stalls + 350 balcony. Closed 29.10.60. (Top Rank Club for bingo. Closed, sold to Borough of Kettering. Demolished 1974. Shops.)

ODEON, Pegasus Court, off Wellingborough Road. Opened 11 & 12.12.97, 8 screens, 1464 seats: 173 + 123 + 229 + 345 + 103 + 81 + 103 + 307. Open in 2.05.

KILBURN North London

GAUMONT STATE, 195/9 High Road and Willesden Lane. (Opened 20.12.37 by Gaumont Super Cinemas, architect: George Coles, 4004 seats: 2648 stalls + 1356 balcony. Closed mid-10.40 by wartime conditions. Re-opened 2.11.40, initially weekends only. Fully taken over 28.2.44. 3996 seats in late 1951. 3990 seats in 1959. Closed 16.1.60 for conversion of stalls area beneath balcony into ballroom opened 25.5.60, capacity 1000, later bingo club. Re-opened 2.60, 1300 seats [balcony + 742 in front stalls if needed, later reduced by expansion of bingo hall]. Second cinema opened 23.11.75 in former restaurant/ dance studio, 202 seats. Main cinema closed 18.9.80. Grade II listed building from 10.10.80. Second cinema closed 10.10.81. Dividing wall removed and whole of main auditorium used for bingo.) Second cinema re-opened 12.85 as ODEON with entrance on Willesden Lane, 245 seats. Closed 14.6.90. (Disused. Entire building listed Grade II* from 10.00. Bingo open as Mecca Club in 2005.)

KILMARNOCK Strathclyde

ODEON, Queens Drive. Opened 10.7.98, 8 screens, 1891 seats: 304 + 304 + 143 + 183 + 432 + 183 + 143 + 199. Open in 2.05.

KING'S CROSS North London

GAUMONT, 279 Pentonville Road, corner of King's Cross Road. (Opened 26.4.20 as King's Cross Cinema, architect: H. Courtenay Constantine, 1800 seats. Taken over by Davis circuit. Taken over 21.12.26 by APPH. Taken over 2.29, part of PCT/APPH circuit. Closed 8.5.49 to repair wartime damage. Re-opened 17.3.52 as Gaumont. 1302 seats by 1955. 1275 seats by 1962.) Renamed ODEON 25.11.62. Closed 22.8.70. (Taken over by independent, re-opened 22.2.71 as King's Cross Cinema. Closed 29.3.75. Re-opened as the Primatarium. Stalls floor to snooker.

Balcony re-opened circa 6.81 with new screen as Scala, 350 seats. Closed 6.93. Church. Scala nightclub.)

KINGSBURY Northwest London

ODEON, 632/8 Kingsbury Road. Opened 30.5.34, architect: A. P. Starkey, 1003 seats: 724 stalls + 279 balcony. Renamed GAUMONT 20.3.50. 860 seats by 1964. Renamed ODEON 30.5.64. Closed 9.9.72. (Demolished except for wings. J. Sainsbury supermarket - Aldi in 2001 with flats and Fitness First health club above.)

KINGSTANDING West Midlands

ODEON, Junction of Kings Road and Kettlehouse Road. Opened 22.7.35, architect: Harry W. Weedon [assistant: J. Cecil Clavering], 1292 seats: 968 stalls + 324 balcony. 1261 seats by circa 1960. Closed 2.12.62. (Re-opened 6.12.62 as Top Rank Club for bingo. Grade II listed building from 10.10.80. Renamed Mecca. Open in 2005.)

KINGSTON-UPON-THAMES Southwest London

ODEON, 24/28 High Street. Opened 3.7.33, architects: Col. James E. Adamson, Marshall & Tweedy. 1516 seats: 990 stalls + 526 balcony. Closed 15.7.67. (Re-opened 10.8.67 as Top Rank Club for bingo. Closed 9.8.87. Demolished circa 1989. Rose Theatre.)

ODEON, The Rotunda, Clarence Street. Opened 18.10.02 (previews 17.10.02), 14 screens, 3016 seats: 199 + 431 + 112 + 186 + 178 + 146 + 308 + 118 + 161 + 182 + 256 + 183 + 339 + 217. Open in 2.05.

KINGSWOOD Bristol

AMBASSADOR, Regent Street. Opened 26.3.38 by London & Southern, controlled by Odeon, architect: F. C. Mitchell. 1794 seats in 1939: 1314 stalls + 480 balcony. Closed by war-time damage. Re-opened late 3.41. Renamed ODEON 6.11.44. Closed 11.3.61. (Reconstructed internally for Top Rank Bowl. Sold 3.69 to Safeway. Demolished. Safeway supermarket.)

KIRKCALDY Fife

GAUMONT, 204 High Street. (Opened 2.24 as Rialto. Part of Thomas Ormiston circuit. Taken over 3.28 by Denman/Gaumont. 1212 seats. Renamed Gaumont 1.5.50. 1185 seats

by 1956.) Renamed ODEON 16.12.62. 1081 seats by 1964. Destroyed by fire morning of 26.12.74. (Demolished. Sold 28.8.75. House of Fraser store.)

LANCASTER Lancashire

ODEON, King Street and Spring Garden Street. Opened 7.11.36, architect: Harry Weedon [assistant: W. Calder Robson], 1592 seats: 950 stalls + 642 balcony. (Taken over 3.1.71 by Star, split for stalls bingo and Studio 1 & 2 cinemas in balcony, opened 12.8.71 seating 260 & 260. Cinemas taken over by Cannon, renamed Cannon. Taken over 7.95 by Virgin. Taken over 2.5.96 by ABC. Renamed ABC Cinemas. Taken over 2000 by Odeon. Closed 1.9.02. Taken over by Northern Morris Associated, re-opened 17.1.03 as Regal. Cinemas and stalls bingo continue in 2.05.)

LANCING West Sussex

ODEON, 45/49 Penhill Road. Opened 31.10.33, architect: unknown ("arranged by builder"), 691 seats, one floor. Renamed REGAL 2.3.36. (Taken over 7.3.39 by B. E. Fortescue. Closed 23.3.40. Taken over by Mrs. Merriman Langdon & re-opened 16.10.41.) Taken back 30.8.42. Renamed ODEON 25.3.45. Closed 20.1.52. (Taken over by Shipman & King and put up for sale without re-opening. Chromium plating works. Welding and engineering workshop. Regal House in 1996: auditorium area used by Ingleside Garage with new roof and entrance, plumbers' merchants Leamey's of Lancing in foyer area and former shop, offices on first floor and elsewhere.)

LEEDS West Yorkshire
see als\o Bradford

PARAMOUNT, corner of The Headrow & Briggate. (Opened 22.2.32 by Paramount, architects: Frank T. Verity & Samuel Beverley, exterior design: Sir Reginald Blomfield, 2556 seats.) Taken over 27.11.39, part of Paramount circuit. Renamed ODEON 15.4.40. 2564 seats by 1956. 2532 seats by 1964. Closed 9.68 for twinning, architects: Gavin Patterson & Son, interior design: Anthony Sharp. Re-opened 15.5.69, seating 978 balcony extended + 1297 seats in stalls. Third cinema opened 23.7.78, seating 126 in former bar area. Downstairs cinema closed for triping. Re-opened 1.4.88, seating 441 + 200 + 174.

Grade II listed building (for exterior) from 15.10.93. Closed 28.10.01, seating 982 + 441 + 200 + 174 + 126.

ODEON, Merrion Centre. Opened 17.8.64, 892 seats, one floor. Closed 17.5.69 for Cinerama installation. Re-opened 8.69. Closed 1.10.77. (Disused.)

LEICESTER Leicestershire

ODEON, Queen Street and Rutland Street. Opened 28.7.38, architect: Harry Weedon [assistant: Robert Bullivant], 2182 seats: 1307 stalls + 875 balcony. Modernised in 1960. 1914 seats. Triple from 3.2.74, seating 1237 in balcony & front stalls + 123 & 111 rear stalls. Fourth cinema added circa 1988 in front stalls, seating 401, with upstairs cinema seating 872 with new screen. All closed 16.7.97. (Grade II listed building from 1998. Athena conference and banqueting centre in 2005.)

ODEON, Market Place. Opened 12.10.64, redevelopment of The City/Gaumont site within original walls, 822 seats, stadium, above shopping arcade. Closed 31.5.75. (Liberty cinema for Asian films. Bingo.)

ODEON, Freemens Park, 90 Aylestone Road. Opened 17 & 18.7.97, 12 screens, 2574 seats: 128 + 164 + 154 + 239 + 210 + 362 + 332 + 212 + 329 + 154 + 164 + 126. Open in 2.05, 2526 seats: 129 + 165 + 154 + 239 + 230 + 362 + 332 + 230 + 239 + 154 + 165 + 127.

LEICESTER SQUARE London
see London West End

LEIGH Greater Manchester

HIPPODROME, Leigh Road. (Opened circa 1922, former live theatre. Reconstructed, architects: Gray, Evans & Crossley, & re-opened 5.8.39, 1350 seats.) Taken over circa 12.55, improved & re-opened 23.1.56, renamed ODEON, 1219 seats. 840 seats after balcony closed. 734 seats by circa 1956. (Taken over 17.12.67 by Classic, renamed Classic. 694 seats. Twin from 17.6.79, seating 392 & 228. Taken over by Cannon. Renamed Cannon. Closed 10.89. Laser Quest centre. The Hippdrome nightclub, later renamed The Cube, closed in 2004.)

LEWES East Sussex

ODEON, Cliffe High Street. Opened 2.6.34, architect: Andrew Mather, 986 seats, semi-stadium: 518 front + 468 rear. 944 seats by

1957. Closed 2.10.71. (Sold 20.4.72 to A. L. Hawton. Demolished 1982. Shops and housing.)

LEWISHAM Southeast London

GAUMONT, 1-5 Loampit Vale. (Opened 12.12.32 as Gaumont Palace by Gaumont, architect: W. E. Trent [assistant: James Morrison], 3050 seats: 1819 stalls + 1232 balcony. Renamed Gaumont circa 1937. Modernised circa 1960. 2896 seats. Closed 27.2.62 by fire.) Re-opened 29.7.62, renamed ODEON, 2860 seats: 1628 stalls + 1232 balcony. Closed 14.2.81. (Disused. Demolished 1991 for round-about.)

LEYTON North London

GAUMONT, Lea Bridge Road and Church Road. (Opened 26.12.28 as Savoy, architect: George Coles, 1797 seats. Part of United Pictures Theatres circuit from 1.30. Under Gaumont management from 7.30 as part of UPT circuit. Renamed Gaumont 20.2.50. 1649 seats by 1956. 1647 seats by 1963.) Renamed ODEON 2.3.64. (Taken over by independent circa 1968, renamed Curzon. Closed circa 1971. Bingo. Taken over by Classic, balcony opened 26.1.73 as separate Classic cinema, 435 seats, with Vogue bingo in stalls. Cinema closed 10.3.79. Gala bingo in 2004.)

LICHFIELD Staffordshire

REGAL, Tamworth Street. (Opened 18.7.32, architect: Harold S. Scott. Operated for local owners by County from 11.32.) Taken over 9.39, part of County circuit. 1235 seats in 1939. (Reverted to local owners' control circa 1941. Taken over by Mayfair circuit. Taken over 30.8.43 by ABC. Taken over 1.7.69 by Star. Part-week bingo. Closed 10.7.74, bingo continuing. Bingo closed circa 1979. Supermarket, Kwiksave in 2001.)

LINCOLN Lincolnshire

ASTORIA, Cornhill, Market Square. (Opened 28.5.10 as Cinematograph Hall, 1750 seats on one floor. Known as Corn Exchange Cinema. Part of Gale & Repard circuit. Taken over 3.28 by Denman/Gaumont. Taken over 1931 by independent. Renamed Exchange. Refurbished, re-opened 8.2.54, renamed Astoria, 1008 seats.) Taken over 2.1.56. 828 seats. Closed 23.6.56. (Roller skating rink from 2.57. Bingo from 1972. Closed. McDonalds

restaurant in entrance from 1982. Auditorium in retail use in 2.05.)

RITZ, 147 High Street, corner of Firth Road. (Opened 22.2.37, architect: Leslie C. Norton, 1750 seats.) Taken over 2.1.56, 1478 seats. Renamed ODEON 20.8.56. 1447 seats by 1965. (Taken over late 1981 by independent, renamed Ritz. Tripled: balcony re-opened 28.3.95, 485 seats; two screens in stalls opened 7.4.95, seating 300 + 300. All closed 8.97. Ritz, Wetherspoon's pub in foyer and part of rear stalls.)

ODEON, Valentine Road. Opened 24.11.95, 6 screens, 1034 seats: 279 + 164 + 181 + 138 + 134 + 138. Closed 7.10.01. (Superbowl in 2.05.)

ODEON, Brayford Wharf North. Opened 19.10.01, 9 screens. Open in 2.05, 2011 seats: 169 + 163 + 410 + 160 + 169 + 213 + 265 + 360 + 102.

LITTLEHAMPTON West Sussex

ODEON, High Street. Opened 23.5.36, architect: Andrew Mather, 970 seats: 438 stalls + 532 balcony. 918 seats in 1967. (Taken over 17.12.67 by Classic, renamed Classic. Part-week bingo. Closed as cinema 31.5.74 or 1.6.74. Taken over by independent for full-time bingo, renamed Regal Bingo Club. Closed. Demolished 1984. Shops.)

LIVERPOOL

see also Allerton, Crosby, Switch Island

PARAMOUNT, London Road, corner of Pudsey Street. (Opened 15.10.34 by Paramount, architects: Verity & Beverley, 2670 seats: 1972 stalls + 698 balcony.) Taken over 25.8.42. Renamed ODEON 6.2.44. 2667 seats by 1956. 2595 seats by 1964. Closed 29.6.68 for twinning, architects: Dry Halasz & Associates. Re-opened 20.3.69, 983 + 1405 seats. ODEON 2 closed 1.9.73 for tripling, re-opened 23.12.73, seating 595 + 166 + 166. ODEON 5 opened 4.11.79 in former bar, 148 seats. Five more screens opened 8.99 by tripling two largest screens and adding cinema on stage. Open in 2.05, 10 screens, 1859 seats: 482 + 154 + 157 + 149 + 211 + 128 + 132 + 123 + 191 + 132.

LLANDUDNO Gwynedd

WINTER GARDENS, Gloddaeth Street. (Opened 25.3.35 as live theatre & cinema. Taken over 12.36 by Brooklyn Trust.) Taken

over 12.36. 1883 seats in 1939: 1074 stalls + 809 balcony. Renamed ODEON circa 1943. 1845 seats by 1965. (Sold to Hutchinson circuit 13.10.69, renamed Astra. Open summers only. Closed circa 10.86. Demolished. Residential homes: Ormside Grange.)

LLANELLI Dyfed

ODEON, Station Road, Lloyd Street and Minor Street. Opened 18.6.38, architect: Harry Weedon [assistant: P. J. Price], 1450 seats: 900 stalls + 550 balcony. 1364 seats in 1967. (Taken over 10.12.67 by Classic, renamed Classic. Triple from 1.10.71, seating 516 balcony extended forward + 273 & 122 rear stalls. Taken over 30.5.76 by Borough Council, renamed Llanelli Entertainment Centre. Modernised: upstairs auditorium equipped for live shows plus films, renamed Theatr Elli in 1984, seating 500, with downstairs cinemas renamed Theatre Two and Three, seating 310 & 122. All open in 2.05.)

LONDON West End

see also Victoria

for suburbs, see Acton, Balham, Barking, Becontree, Bethnal Green, Blackfen, Bloomsbury, Brixton, Bromley, Burnt Oak, Camberwell, Camden Town, Canning Town, Chadwell Heath, Chelsea, Chingford, Clapton, Colindale, Croydon, Dagenham, Dalston, Deptford, Ealing, East Dulwich, East Ham, Edgware Road, Elephant and Castle, Eltham Hill, Erith, Finchley, Finsbury Park, Forest Gate, Forest Hill, Golders Green, Greenwich, Hackney Road, Hammersmith, Harlesden, Haverstock Hill, Hayes (2), Hendon, Highgate, Holloway, Hornchurch, Hounslow, Ilford, Isleworth, Islington, Kensal Rise, Kensington, Kentish Town, Kenton, Kilburn, King's Cross, Kingsbury, Kingston-on-Thames, Lewisham, Leyton, Mile End, Morden, Muswell Hill, Northwood Hills, Old Kent Road, Park Royal, Peckham, Penge, Putney, Richmond, Romford, Shannon Corner, Shepherd's Bush, Sidcup, South Hackney, South Harrow, South Norwood, Southall, Southgate, Stamford Hill, Stepney, Streatham, Sudbury Town, Surbiton, Swiss Cottage, Temple Fortune, Tolworth, Twickenham, Upminster, Uxbridge, Wallington, Walton-on-Thames, Wealdstone, Well Hall, Welling, Wembley, West Wickham, Westbourne Grove, Whalebone Lane, Whitton, Wimbledon, Wood Green, Woolwich and Worcester Park

ODEON, Leicester Square (on site of Alhambra Theatre). Opened 2.11.37, architects: Harry Weedon, Andrew Mather. 2116 seats: 1140 stalls + 976 balcony. Closed 15.10.40 by bomb damage overnight. Re-opened 18.11.40. Closed 14.11.48 for war damage repairs. Re-opened 30.12.48. Closed 13.5.53 for wide screen installation. 2068 seats. Closed 19.9.67 for modernisation, designer: Anthony Sharp. Re-opened 27.12.67, seating 1994. Modernised, architects: Dry Butlin Bicknell, 12.87 to 1.88. Closed 13.4.98 for modernisation. Re-opened 5.8.98, seating 1943. Open in 2.05.

PARAMOUNT, Tottenham Court Road, corner of Grafton Street. (Opened 10.2.36 by Paramount, architects: Verity & Beverley, 2568 seats: 1676 stalls + 892 balcony.) Taken over 25.8.42. Renamed ODEON 11.11.46. Closed for Cinemiracle installation & re-opened 15.5.58, 1862 seats. Closed 1.11.58 for de-installation. Re-opened 9.11.58. 2570 seats. Closed 5.3.60. (Demolished. "Temporary" car park.)

REGAL, Marble Arch & Edgware Road. (Opened 29.11.28 by Hyde Park Cinemas, architect: Clifford Aish, interior decorator: Charles Muggeridge, 2400 seats. Taken over 28.9.29 by ABC. Closed 3.1.45.) Taken over & refurbished, architect: Leonard Allen, re-opening 9.9.45, renamed ODEON. (Taken over 8.4.54 by 20th Century-Fox.) Taken back at end 3.55. 2124 seats circa 1956. Closed 22.3.64. (Demolished. Office block, shops, new Odeon on enlarged site.)

LEICESTER SQUARE THEATRE, 40 Leicester Square, corner of St. Martin's Street. (Opened 19.12.30, architect: Andrew Mather, designed for dual theatre/cinema use, 1760 seats, three levels. Taken over 3.31 by RKO Radio. Renamed Olympic 21.3.32 with re-designed entrance, architect: Alister MacDonald. Returned 8.32. Taken over by United Artists, re-opened 27.9.33 as Leicester Square Theatre. Taken over circa 1938 by General Film Distributors. Closed 17.10.40 by wartime bomb damage. Re-opened 9.7.41.) Taken over 10.7.46. Closed 23.7.50 for war damage repairs. Re-opened 2.8.50. Closed 26.5.55 for further war damage repairs. Re-opened 27.7.55, 1672 seats. 1738 seats by 1963. Closed 3.4.68 for complete interior reconstruction, architects: Arnold Dick Associates, interior designers: Cassidy, Farrington and Dennys. Re-opened 12.12.68, 1402 seats, minus gallery: 900 stalls + 507 balcony.

Renamed ODEON WEST END 22.7.88. Closed 11.7.91 for twinning. Re-opened 11.10.91 upstairs, seating 503, and 1.11.91 downstairs, seating 848. Open in 2.05.

WINTER GARDEN THEATRE, Drury Lane. Taken over circa 10.45. Cinematograph licence held by 29.11.46, then continuously until 30.11.56, but no known cinema use. Sold 30.4.60. (Demolished. New London Theatre in redevelopment.)

ODEON Haymarket, corner of St. James's Market (site of Gaumont). Opened 4.6.62, architect: Leslie C. Norton, 600 seats, one floor, in basement of original building. 566 seats. Closed 14.1.99. (Disused.)

ODEON, 10 Edgware Road, Marble Arch (site of old Odeon). Opened 2.2.67, architects: T. P. Bennett & Son, 1360 seats. Closed 10.9.94. Re-opened. Closed 7.9.96 for subdivision. Re-opened 3.1.97 with five screens, 1022 seats: 254 + 126 + 174 + 229 + 239. Open in 2.05, seating 254 + 117 + 171 + 229 + 239.

ODEON, 42-49 St. Martin's Lane. Opened 12.10.67, architects: Casson, Condor & Partners, 737 seats underground. Renamed ODEON DISNEY 20.7.75 with Disneyland decor. Renamed THE LANE 5.11.81. (Taken over 3.10.82 by Artificial Eye. Re-opened 7.10.82, renamed Lumière. Closed 7.6.97 by water damage. Attached to adjacent hotel for occasional varied use.)

ODEON MEZZANINE, 24-26 Leicester Square. Opened 20.4.90, five screens, 290 seats: 60 + 50 + 60 + 60 + 60. Open in 2.05.

LOUGHBOROUGH Leicestershire

ODEON, Baxtergate. Opened 21.11.36, architect: Harry Weedon [assistant: Arthur J. Price], 1625 seats: 1029 stalls + 596 balcony. 1452 seats in 1967. (Taken over 3.12.67 by Classic, renamed Classic. Closed 12.1.74. Bingo. Open in 6.01.)

LOWESTOFT Suffolk

ODEON, London Road North. Opened 23.1.37, architect: Andrew Mather, 1868 seats: 1262 stalls + 606 balcony. 1867 seats in 1956. Closed 25.4.79. (Demolished 1981. W. H. Smith store.)

LUTON Bedfordshire

ODEON, 127 Dunstable Road, Bury Park.

Opened 12.10.38, architect: Andrew Mather [assistant: Keith P. Roberts], 1958 seats: 1332 stalls + 626 balcony. 1874 seats by 1963. Triple from 24.11.74, seating 800 balcony/front stalls + 115 & 110 rear stalls. Closed 4.6.83. (Detripled, re-opened 7.83 as Top Rank Club for bingo. Renamed Mecca. Closed late 1.99. Grade II listed building from Spring 1999. Re-opened 9.2.01 as Calvary Church of God in Christ, open in 3.05.)

MAIDSTONE Kent

ODEON, Lock Meadow, Barker Road. Opened 18.9.98, 8 screens, 1638 seats: 86 + 89 + 127 + 111 + 240 + 240 + 398 + 347. Open in 2.05.

MANCHESTER

see also Ashton-under-Lyme, Bolton, Burnage, Bury, Cheetham Hill, Guide Bridge, Leigh, Prestwich, Radcliffe, Rochdale and Whalley Range

PARAMOUNT, Oxford Street between George Street and St. James Street. (Opened 6.10.30 by Paramount, architects: Frank T. Verity and Samuel Beverley, 2920 seats.) Taken over 27.11.39. Renamed ODEON 8.4.40. 2916 seats by 1957. 2737 seats by 1966. Closed 21.7.73 for twinning. Re-opened 25.1.74, seating 629 balcony + 1030 stalls. Third cinema opened 10.6.79 in former mezzanine, seating 211. Odeon Two (former stalls) closed 1992 for tripling, seating 326 + 145 & 142, plus new cinemas on stage, 97 seats, and in former restaurant space in basement, 97 seats. All closed 2.9.04. (Sold. Disused in 2.05.)

OXFORD PICTURE HOUSE, Oxford Street. (Opened 12.11 as Oxford Picture House by PCT. Taken over 2.29 by Gaumont, part of PCT circuit. Taken over by independent 8.31. 1150 seats.) Taken over 11.6.60 by Rank [Group Theatres Ltd.], renamed NEW OXFORD, 1079 seats. 971 seats by 1966. 854 seats. Closed 25.10.80. (McDonalds fast food outlet.)

MARBLE ARCH London

see London West End

MARGATE Kent

REGAL, Cecil Square. (Opened 21.12.34 by County, architect: Robert Cromie, 1795 seats: 1315 stalls + 480 balcony) Taken over 9.39, part of County circuit. Closed by bomb damage on night of 7.12.41. (Site cleared.

Entrance to magistrates' court + shopping centre.)

MARLOW Buckinghamshire

COUNTY, Spital Street. (Opened circa 1914 as Palace. Modernised 1926 and renamed King George's. Taken over 7.27 by County. Renamed County early 1937. Closed 1.38 on opening of new County.) Used as Odeon circuit offices during World War Two. Sold 1952. (Light industrial use.)

COUNTY, Station Road. (Opened 14.1.38 by County, architect: David E. Nye, 748 seats.) Taken over 9.39, part of County. Renamed ODEON 4.2.41. 742 seats by 1959. (Taken over 22.3.59 by Theatre Administration, renamed Regal. 622 seats. Closed 24.3.85. Demolished 1985. Offices.)

MARYHILL Glasgow

ROXY, 1397 Maryhill Road. (Opened 15.9.30, architects: Lennox and McMath, 2270 seats. Taken over 2.5.55 by CMA, 2276 seats. Closed 15.10.60. (Demolished 1962 for shopping development.)

SEAMORE, 220 Maryhill Road. (Opened 21.12.14, architects: Boswell and Thomas, 1942 seats. Rebuilt 1926, architect: H. Barnes. Enlarged 1932.) Taken over 2.5.55 by CMA, 1672 seats. 1579 seats. Closed 5.3.66. (Demolished 1968.)

MERTON Southwest London
see Shannon Corner

MIDDLESBROUGH Cleveland

ODEON, Corporation Road. Opened 25.2.39, architect: Harry Weedon [assistant: W. Calder Robson and/or Basil Herring], 1761 seats: 1034 stalls + 727 balcony. 1531 seats by 1965. Triple from 29.9.74, seating 720 balcony + 110 & 110 rear stalls. Fourth cinema added late 1989 in front stalls area, seating 254, with new screen for upstairs cinema, seating 611, and minis enlarged: 129 & 148 seats. Refurbished circa 1999. Closed 24.6.01. (Jumpin' Jaks nightclub.)

MILE END Northeast London

ODEON, 401 Mile End Road, corner of Frederick Place. Opened 17.10.38, architect: Andrew Mather [assistant: Keith P. Roberts], 2304 seats: 1528 stalls + 776 balcony. 2284 seats by 1956. 1882 seats by 1964. Closed 10.68 for modernisation, re-opened 27.12.68.

Closed 17.6.72. Re-opened 8.9.72 as Sundown for pop concerts and some films. Closed 1.73. (Leased by independent for Asian films, re-opened 3.75, renamed Liberty. Closed 1978. Demolished 5.84. Bosso House block of flats.)

MILLFIELD Peterborough

PRINCESS, Lincoln Road, corner of Northfields Road. (Opened 22.7.29, 942 seats, one floor.) Taken over 22.3.36. (Leased 9.11.36 by Emery circuit. Closed 21.3.58. Kennings' garage. Frontage demolished for larger forecourt. Former auditorium: Machine Mart tools showroom in 2002.)

MORDEN Southwest London

MORDEN CINEMA, London Road and Aberconway Road. (Opened 8.12.32, architects: J. Stanley Beard & Clare.) Taken over 28.10.35. Renamed 30.7.37. 1638 seats in 1939: 1110 stalls + 528 balcony. 1605 seats by 1956. Closed 13.1.73. (B&Q do-it-yourself centre. Demolished. Lady St. Helier pub and other shops.)

MORECAMBE Lancashire

ODEON, Thornton Road and Euston Road. Opened 2.9.37, architect: Harry Weedon [assistant: W. Calder Robson], 1560 seats: 1084 stalls + 476 balcony. 1274 seats in 1967. (Taken over 17.12.67 by Classic, renamed Classic. Closed 28.2.76. One Stop DIY store, using stalls & foyer only, open in 2004.)

MOTHERWELL Strathclyde

ODEON, Brandon Street. Opened 3.12.38, architect: Andrew Mather, 1752 seats: 1242 stalls + 510 balcony. 1520 seats by 1964. Closed 25.10.75. (County Bingo. Closed 11.95. Demolished 1996. Centre Point: Mega Bar and Hype Club plus offices and parking in 1.05.)

MUSWELL HILL North London

ODEON, Fortis Green Road. Opened 9.9.36, architect: George Coles, 1827 seats: 1217 stalls + 610 balcony. 1546 seats by 1964. Triple from 26.5.74, seating 610 balcony + 134 & 129 rear stalls. Grade II listed building from 6.3.84. Refurbished 2002. Open in 2.05, seats: 436 + 165 & 166.

NETHERTON Merseyside
see Switch Island

NEWCASTLE-ON-TYNE Tyne & Wear
see also Byker

PARAMOUNT, Pilgrim Street. (Opened 7.9.31 by Paramount, architects: Verity & Beverley, 2604 seats.) Taken over 27.11.39. 2602 seats in 1939. Renamed ODEON 22.4.40. 2453 seats by 1964. Closed 25.1.75 for tripling. Re-opened 9.3.75, seating 1228 balcony extended forward + 158 & 250 rear stalls. Fourth cinema on former stage opened 1.2.80, seating 361. Grade II listed building from 10.00. De-listed 8.01. Closed 26.11.02. (Disused. Temporary live show use in 11.03.)

ODEON, The Gate, Newgate Street. Opened 28.11.02, 12 screens. Open in 2.05, 2538 seats: 436 + 102 + 273 + 346 + 130 + 160 + 199 + 67 + 120 + 318 + 157 + 230.

NEW MALDEN Southwest London
see Shannon Corner

NEWPORT Gwent

ODEON, Clarence Place, corner of East Usk Road (site including former Palladium/Regal cinema). Opened 12.3.38, architect: Harry Weedon [assistant: Arthur J. Price], 1546 seats: 1054 stalls + 492 balcony. 1430 seats by 1964. Closed 30.5.81. (Snooker hall circa 1986. Closed circa 1991. Capones American Bar nightclub. Listed building from 12.3.99. Closed. Newport City Live Arena in 2004.)

TREDEGAR HALL, 12/22 Stow Hill. (Opened 10.22, former public hall. Taken over circa 1929 by London & Southern.) Taken over circa 7.37, part of London & Southern. 1019 seats in 1939: 600 stalls + 419 balcony. Closed 20.12.45 for floor repairs. Re-opened 7.4.46. 924 seats by 1956. Closed 29.3.58. (Majestic Ballroom. Returned 16.9.65 to Odeon division of Rank. Taken over by Star. Jesper Bar & Nightclub in 2001.)

NEWPORT Isle of Wight

ODEON, Pyle Street and Town Lane. Opened 17.10.36, architect: Andrew Mather, 1228 seats: 742 stalls + 486 balcony. 1234 seats by 1957. (Taken over 2.1.61 by Isle of Wight Theatres, renamed Savoy. Taken over 1969 by Star. Closed 18.12.82. Demolished summer 1984. Savoy Court flats above Daybell's Furnishings shop in 2000.)

NEWTON ABBOT Devon

ODEON, Wolborough Street. Opened 17.2.36,

architect: Howard Williams, 958 seats: 708 stalls + 250 balcony. 929 seats by 1965. Closed 1.7.72. (Car showroom. Demolished 8-10.83 for relief road.)

NORMANTON Derby

CAVENDISH, Stenson Road & Derby Lane (site of Pavilion). (Opened 28 & 29.12.37, architects: J. Browning & W. S. Hayes, 1650 seats.) Taken over 30.8.43. 1613 seats by 1956. Closed 19.11.60. (Demolished. Fine Fare supermarket.)

NORTH FINCHLEY North London
see Finchley

NORTH SHIELDS Tyne and Wear

GAUMONT, Russell Street. (Opened 7.10.29 as Prince's Theatre, architects: Dixon & Bell, 1750 seats.) Taken over 6.31 by Gaumont/PCT. Renamed Prince's. Closed circa 11.49 for war damage repairs. Re-opened 16.10.50, renamed Gaumont. 1454 seats by 1956. 1446 seats by 1964.) Renamed ODEON 4.8.68. (Taken over 5.7.70 by independent, renamed Prince's. Taken over 2.1.72 by Classic, renamed Classic. Closed 18.9.76. Bingo. Old balcony opened 1.6.77 by independent as two cinemas, Crown 1 & 2. Cinemas closed 7.82. Bingo open in 2004.)

NORTH WATFORD Hertfordshire

ODEON, St. Albans Road. Opened 27.11.37, architects: J. Owen Bond & Son, interior decoration: Mollo & Egan, 1394 seats: 942 stalls + 452 balcony. Closed 30.5.59. (Waitrose supermarket from 1961. Closed 10.87. Demolished 1.89. Flats: Gladesmere Court.)

NORTHAM Southampton

PLAZA, 201 Northam Road. (Opened 11.10.32, architect: Robert Cromie, interior decoration: Mollo & Egan, 2015 seats. Taken over 5.34 by County.) Taken over 9.39, part of County circuit. 2170 seats in 1939. 2134 seats by 1957. Closed 30.11.57. (Taken over 6.1.58 by Southern Television. Converted to television studios & offices. Demolished. Office block.)

NORTHAMPTON Northamptonshire

GAUMONT, 4 The Parade, Market Square. (Opened 2.8.20 as Exchange, former Corn Exchange used as part-week cinema. Taken over circa 1924 by PCT. Taken over 2.29 by Gaumont, part of PCT circuit. 1916 seats. Renamed Gaumont 10.4.50. Modernised 1951. 1732 seats by 1964.) Renamed ODEON 16.3.64. Closed 7.9.74. (Top Rank Bingo. Sold as going concern 1977. Open in 1995.)

NORTHWOOD HILLS Northwest London

ODEON, Pinner Road. Completed & sold mid-11.36 before opening, architect: A. D. Clare, circa 1000 seats. (Opened 28.12.36 by Shipman and King circuit, renamed Rex. Closed 22.9.73. Demolished. Somerfield supermarket.)

NORWICH Norfolk

ODEON, Botolph Street. Opened 7.2.38, architect: Harry Weedon [assistant: Basil Herring], 2054 seats: 1246 stalls + 808 balcony. 1842 seats by 1964. Closed 26.6.71. (Sold 10.7.71 to Sovereign Securities. Demolished.)

CARLTON, All Saints Green. (Opened 1.2.32 by Victor Harrison, architect: J. Owen Bond. Taken over 8.36 by County.) 1920 seats in 1939. Taken over 9.39, part of County. 1906 seats by 1956. Modernised and re-opened 11.1.60, renamed Gaumont, 1515 seats. Closed 6.1.73. (Top Rank Club for bingo. Renamed Mecca, open in 6.01.)

ODEON, Anglia Square, Magdalen Street. Opened 8.7.71, architect: Alan Cooke, 1016 seats, stadium. Closed 17.7.91 for tripling: 442 + 197 + 195 seats. Closed 29.10.00. (Re-opened circa 1 & 2.2.01 by independent, renamed Hollywood. Open in 2.05.)

NOTTINGHAM Nottinghamshire

RITZ, Angel Row. (Opened 4.12.33 by County, architects: Verity & Beverley with A. J. Thraves, 2426 seats: 1754 stalls + 672 balcony.) Taken over 9.39, part of County. Renamed ODEON circa 1944. 2110 seats by 1964. Closed 16.11.64 for conversion to twins. Re-opened 12.7.65, seating 1446 stalls + 924 balcony extended. Third cinema from 11.6.70 in former restaurant area, 101 seats. Former stalls cinema tripled from 1.2.76, seating 581 + 141 + 141. Sixth cinema added 7.3.88 in former restaurant space, seating 98. 903 + 557 + 150 + 150 + 113 + 100 seats in 2000. Closed 28.1.01. (Disused in 2004.)

OLDHAM Lancashire

ODEON, Union Street. Opened 19.8.36, architect: Harry Weedon (interior reconstruction of Palace Theatre of Varieties, former live theatre), 1707 seats: 1122 stalls + 585 balcony. 1415 seats by 1964. Triple from 14.7.74, seating 585 balcony + 110 & 110 rear stalls. Closed 29.10.83. (Disused. Demolished 1992. The Link, Council Social Services building from 2000.)

OLD KENT ROAD Southeast London

ASTORIA, 593/613 Old Kent Road, corner of Sandgate Street. (Opened 10.2.30, architect: Edward A. Stone, 2899 seats. Taken over 12.30 by Paramount.) Taken over 27.11.39, part of Paramount circuit. 2894 seats by 1956. 2623 seats by 1963. Closed 29.6.68. (Mad Dog Bowl from 5.78. Astoria Sports Centre for skateboarding, squash, gyms, sauna. Demolished 10.84. DIY store.)

PAIGNTON Devon

PALLADIUM Torquay Road, Preston. (Opened 7.1.33, architects: William E. Wolff & Joseph E. Walter, 1060 seats. Closed early in World War Two. Re-opened 7.40 by Lou Morris.) Taken over 23.8.43. Renamed ODEON 1.6.47. Closed 7.12.57. Re-opened for summer seasons. 976 seats. Closed 30.9.61. (Top Rank Club for bingo from 1.62. Palladium bingo by 3.86. Some films shown summer 1986. Closed 9.87. Demolished 1989. Flats.)

PARK ROYAL Northwest London

RITZ, Ritz Parade, Western Avenue. (Opened 9.4.38 by London & District, architect: W. J. King, 1868 seats: circa 1300 stalls + 550 balcony. Taken over 1939 by local company.) Taken over 27.3.44 from W. J. King. Renamed ODEON 22.4.46. 1768 seats by 1964. (Taken over 17.12.67 by Classic, renamed Classic. Part-week Vogue bingo from 12.12.68. Films weekends only by 1.69. Tatler Club for "adult films" from 1.7.72. Taken over 5.2.74 by independent for Asian films, renamed Paradise. Closed 1980. Demolished 7-8.83, leaving rest of Ritz Parade. Part of Orbis House office block.)

PARTICK Glasgow

STANDARD, 95 Dumbarton Road. (Opened 10.13, architect: Albert V. Gardner, 1153 seats. Re-opened 11.22. 1132 seats in 1949.)

Taken over 2.5.55 by CMA, 1100 seats. Closed 29.9.56. (Disused. Demolished circa 1967.)

PECKHAM Southeast London

ODEON, 24/26 High Street (site including former Queen's Hall Picture Theatre). Opened 1.6.38, architect: Andrew Mather, 2110 seats: 1442 stalls + 668 balcony. Columns on frontage removed in 1960s. 1877 seats by 1963. Triple from 27.1.74, seating 668 balcony + 118 & 118 rear stalls. (Taken over 1.11.81 by independent, renamed Ace. Closed 1.12.83. Demolished circa 1985. Job Centre + offices.)

PENGE Southeast London

ODEON, 162 High Street. Opened 31.7.37, architect: Andrew Mather, 1582 seats: 1096 stalls + 486 balcony. 1420 seats by 1964. Closed 4.9.76. (Bingo club from 16.9.76. Coral Bingo from 1978. Closed 12.3.90. Demolished 1994. Wetherspoon's pub: The Moon and Stars.)

PERRY BARR Birmingham

ODEON, 271 Birchfield Road, between Canterbury Road and Thornbury Road. Opened 8.4.30 by Oscar Deutsch & associates, architects: Stanley A. Griffiths & Horace G. Bradley, 1638 seats: 1160 stalls + 478 balcony. Taken into the Odeon circuit 17.7.35. Façade completely rebuilt circa 1958. 1494 seats in 1961. Closed 3.5.69. (Re-opened 14.8.69 as Top Rank Club for bingo. Closed 19.2.83. Taken over by Dale Leisure and re-opened 27.10.83 as Perry Social Club for bingo. Taken over 1985 for bingo by Granada, renamed Granada. Taken over 5.91 for bingo by Gala, renamed Gala. Closed 5.4.97. Re-opened by 8.02 as Royale Suite for banquets and receptions. Open in 2.05.)

PERTH Tayside

GAUMONT, 32/36 Kinnoull Street. (Opened 1924 as Alhambra, former live theatre. Part of Thomas Ormiston circuit. Taken over 3.28 by Denman/Gaumont. 1009 seats by 1955. Closed by fire at screen end. Modernised and re-opened 9.1.56 as Gaumont, 1288 seats. 1148 seats by 1964.) Renamed ODEON 16.12.62. Closed 1.11.80, 1012 seats. (Bingo. Leisureland nightclub. Destroyed by arson late summer 1993. Site cleared. Housing.)

PETERBOROUGH, Northamptonshire

ODEON, 46 The Broadway. Opened 2.9.37, architect: Harry Weedon [revision of Roland Satchwell scheme], 1752 seats: 1208 stalls + 544 balcony. Modernised circa 1960: 1512 seats. Triple from 25.2.73, seating 544 balcony + 110 & 110 rear stalls. Closed 23.11.91. (Taken over by Peter Boizot, adapted [architect: Tim Foster] and re-opened 30.5.01 as Broadway, seating 1200 in stalls and balcony, for cinema, theatre, conference and concert use, with new Gildenburgh Art Gallery and Gaston Restaurant adjacent.)

PLYMOUTH Devon
see also Devonport

REGENT, Frankfort Street/New George Street/Cambridge Street. (Opened 21.11.31, architect: W. Watson of Chadwick, Watson. Taken over 6.36 by County.) Taken over 9.39, part of County. 3254 seats in 1939. Taken over directly 17.6.40, renamed ODEON. 2816 seats by 1962. Closed 8.9.62. (Demolished. Littlewood's store.)

DRAKE, Derry's Cross & Union Street. (Opened 5.6.58 by 20th Century-Fox, architect: Leonard Allen, 1639 seats.) Taken over 26.3.61, renamed DRAKE ODEON, 1641 seats. Triple from 27.3.75, seating 946 stalls + 168 & 168 balcony. Closed 10.99. (Demolished 2002. Grosvenor Casino in 2003, open in 1.05.)

GAUMONT, Union Street (site of Andrews Picture House and adjacent property). (Opened 16.11.31 as Gaumont Palace by Gaumont/PCT, architect: W. H. Watkins [Percy Bartlett], 2252 seats: 1462 stalls & 790 balcony. Renamed Gaumont circa 1937. Closed 2.12.61 for subdivision into ground floor ballroom and upstairs cinema extending old balcony.) Cinema opened 10.9.62 as ODEON, 1043 seats. Closed 9.4.80. (Roller disco from 12.80. Nightclub/rock venue from 1987.)

PORT TALBOT West Glamorgan
see also Taibach

MAJESTIC, Bethany Square. (Opened 1.38, architect: Thomas Gibb, 1500 seats.) Taken over 13.12.43. Renamed ODEON 21.4.47. 1370 seats by 1956. 1316 seats by 1964. Closed 27.3.71. (Sold 16.9.71 to Wyndham Lewis. Bingo. Closed 6.9.80. Demolished 7.95. Shops.)

PORTSMOUTH Hampshire
see also Cosham

ODEON, London Road, North End. Opened 14.12.36, architect: Andrew Mather, 1824 seats: 1224 stalls + 600 balcony. Closed 10.9.60 for modernisation. Re-opened 25.9.60. 1852 seats. Triple from 26.8.73, seating 567 balcony + 132 & 132 rear stalls. Lower cinemas enlarged to 228 & 228 seats. Fourth cinema added 1990 in former front stalls, seating 250, with new screen upstairs and one rear stalls cinema reduced for access to front cinema. Refurbished 12.98. Open in 2.05, seating 1292: 631 + 227 + 175 + 259.

PORTSLADE East Sussex

ROTHBURY, Franklin Road. Opened 27.3.34, architect: George Coles (adaptation of building planned and partly built as an assembly hall), 548 seats, one floor. Associated with Odeon at opening but locally run from start. (Taken over by Langdon Enterprises. Taken over by Robert Gordon Cinemas. Closed 19.1.64. Bingo hall. Radio House from 1983, extensively converted. Home of Southern FM by 1993, continuing in 2003.)

POSSIL Glasgow

ASTORIA, 67 Possil Road, Round Toll. (Opened 2.2.31, architect: A. V. Gardner, 3002 seats.) Taken over 2.5.55 by CMA, 2969 seats. 2233 seats by 1962. Closed 19.11.62. (Top Rank Club for bingo. Sold 1977 as going concern. Renamed County. Closed 3.95. Demolished.)

POSSILPARK Glasgow

AVON, 281 Saracen Street. (Opened 1920 as Possilpark Picture House, architect: Albert V. Gardner, 1282 seats.) Taken over 2.5.55 by CMA, 1222 seats. 1404 seats. Closed 24.9.60. (Sold 28.1.72 to Reo Stakis. Demolished. Public house.)

PRESTON Lancashire

GAUMONT, Church Street. (Opened 17.9.28 as New Victoria by PCT, architect: W. E. Trent, 2100 seats. Taken over 2.29 by Gaumont as part of PCT circuit. Renamed Gaumont 22.9.52. 2111 seats by 1956. Modernised circa 1959. 1972 seats. Closed 16.6.62 for subdivision into ground floor ballroom/disco and upstairs cinema extending old balcony.) Cinema opened 28.1.63 as

ODEON, 1229 seats. ODEON 2 opened 4.70 in former restaurant, 105 seats. Both closed 10.9.92. (Entire building disused in 2004.)

PRESTWICH Greater Manchester

ASTORIA, Bury New Road, Sedgeley Park. (Opened 3.9.31 by Emery circuit, architect: Charles Swain.) Taken over 18.9.37. Renamed ODEON 20.9.37. 1699 seats in 1939: 1108 stalls + 591 balcony. 1704 seats by 1957. Closed 12.8.61. (Lancastrian Bingo Club. Demolished. Lidl supermarket.)

PUTNEY Southwest London

HIPPODROME, Felsham Road. (Opened 14.4.24, former live theatre with films. Taken over 1.28 by United Picture Theatres. Under Gaumont management from 7.30 as part of UPT circuit. Taken over 7.35 by ABC. Taken over circa 1938 by independent. 1420 seats. Closed by war conditions.) Re-opened [by Odeon?] 17.2.41. Odeon-operated by 5.41. 865 seats [balcony disused] by 1956. Closed 14.1.61. (Demolished 1973. Flats.)

PUTNEY BRIDGE KINEMA, Putney Bridge Approach, south corner of Gonville Street, Fulham. (Opened 23.5.11 as Putney Bridge Cinematic Theatre, architect: Francis J. Barrett. Renamed Putney Bridge Kinema 1915. 700 seats. Taken over by Town Theatres. Closed 1.40 for major alterations not carried out.) Taken over [closed] 26.1.42 as part of Town Theatres circuit. Not re-opened. (Demolished 1957/8. Premier Travel Inn.)

GAUMONT, 23 High Street. (Opened 1911 as Electric Pavilion by Israel Davis, architect: H. Harrington. Taken over circa 1918 by independent. Renamed Blue Hall in 1920. Reconstructed and enlarged, architect: J. Stanley Beard, and re-opened 10.26 as Palace, 1430 seats. Taken over 3.12.28 by United Picture Theatres. Under Gaumont management from 7.30 as part of UPT circuit. Closed during World War Two. Re-opened 22.3.42. Closed, then re-opened 28.1.45. Renamed Gaumont 22.8.55. 1332 seats.) Renamed ODEON 25.11.62. Closed 11.12.71. (Sold to EMI. Demolished for part of redevelopment including new ABC cinemas, now Odeon.)

QUINTON West Midlands
see Blackheath

RADCLIFFE Greater Manchester

ODEON, corner of Foundry Street and Egerton Street. Opened 14.8.37, architect: Harry Weedon (assistant: W. Calder Robson), 1138 seats: 822 stalls + 316 balcony. Closed 27.4.57. (Liquorsave Discount Wines & Spirits. Kwik Save supermarket, closed 26.3.04. Disused.)

RAMSGATE Kent

ODEON, King Street at corner of Broad Street. Opened 22.8.36, architect: Andrew Mather, 1568 seats: 1034 stalls + 534 balcony. 1466 seats in 1967. (Taken over 3.12.67 by Classic, renamed Classic. Split for stalls bingo and balcony cinema seating 534. Second cinema replaced bingo from 30.6.83, seating 256 in part of stalls. Both closed 17.10.85. (Demolished 1988, leaving attached parade of shops and flats. Iceland store & car park.)

RAYNERS LANE Harrow

GROSVENOR, 440 Alexandra Avenue. (Opened 12.10.36, architect: F. E. Bromige.) Taken over 5.5.37. 1235 seats in 1939: 830 stalls + 405 balcony. Renamed ODEON circa 1941. Renamed GAUMONT 23.10.50. Renamed ODEON 27.4.64. 1185 seats by 1964. 1020 seats. Grade II listed building from 13.3.81. (Taken over 1.11.81 by independent, renamed Ace. Closed 16.10.86. Listing raised 6.10.88 to Grade II★. Grosvenor Cine/Bar Experience with foyer as Ace Bar and auditorium as Studio Warehouse nightclub, both from 1991. Closed. Taken over circa 2000 by Zoroastrian Centre for Europe, church use.)

READING Berkshire

ODEON, Cheapside. Opened 8.3.37, architect: A. P. Starkey [assistant: Frederick Adkins], 1704 seats: 1210 stalls + 494 balcony. 1562 seats by 1965. 1413 seats by 1979. Twin from 14.4.79, seating 410 balcony + 640 stalls. Car park sold for redevelopment. Lower cinema subdivided in 1989 into two cinemas, seating 221 & 221. All closed 25.11.99. (Demolished 1.02. Flats: The Picture House.)

VAUDEVILLE, 47 Broad Street, corner of Union Street. (Opened 9.21, enlarged reconstruction of earlier cinema, architects: Emden, Egan, 1500 seats. Taken over 9.29 by County.) Taken over 9.39, part of County circuit. 1457 seats in 1939. Renamed GAUMONT 23.2.53. 1454 seats. Closed 30.11.57. (Largely demolished. Timothy White's store, later Boots, open in 1995.)

PAVILION, 143/5 Oxford Road, corner of Russell Street. (Opened 21.9.29, architect: Harold S. Scott, 1361 seats. Taken over 1930 by County.) Taken over 9.39, part of County circuit. 1357 seats in 1939. Improved and renamed GAUMONT 20.1.58. Closed 21.4.79. (Bingo club. Snooker hall, using only stalls.)

REDHILL Surrey

ODEON, Station Road. Opened 23.5.38, architect: Andrew Mather [assistant: Keith P. Roberts], 1474 seats: 1000 stalls + 474 balcony. 1442 seats by 1964. Closed 18.10.75. (Nightclub, called British Embassy Rock Bar in 2004.)

RHYL Flintshire

ODEON, Brighton Road and High Street. Opened 30.10.37, architect: Harry Weedon [assistant: Robert Bullivant], 1408 seats: 862 stalls + 546 balcony. 1354 seats by 1964. (Taken over 13.10.69 by Hutchinson, renamed Astra. Triple from 24.4.72, seating 750 stalls + 250 & 225 balcony. Stalls converted to bingo. Grade II listed building from 4.1.89. Taken over by Apollo, renamed Apollo. Cinemas closed 10.95. Building reverted to single auditorium for bingo, open as Apollo Bingo Club in 2002.)

RICHMOND Southwest London

PREMIER, 72 Hill Street. (Opened 21.4.30 as The Richmond by Joseph Mears Theatres, architects: Leathart & Granger, 1533 seats. Renamed Premier 29.6.40.) Taken over 3.1.44. Renamed ODEON 5.44. 1561 seats by 1956. 1340 seats by 1964. Triple from 30.12.73, seating 516 balcony + 118 & 118 rear stalls. Odeon 2 & 3 closed 13.1.79 for enlargement – re-opened 8.4.79, seating 201 & 201. Grade II listed building from 26.3.90. Refurbished, completed 18.7.98. Open in 2.05, seating 406 + 177 + 177.

ROYALTY, 5 Hill Street. (Opened 24.12.14 as New Royalty, architect: Sidney J. Davis, incorporating 18th century Georgian house for foyer, 1020 seats. Renamed Royalty 10.6.29. Taken over by Joseph Mears Theatres. Closed 26.10.40 by war conditions. Re-opened 25.5.42.) Taken over 3.1.44. Renamed GAUMONT 28.11.49. 1112 seats by 1956. 1136 seats by 1964. Closed 25.10.80. (Auditorium demolished 1983 for offices and Richmond Filmhouse cinema, open in 2.05; foyer into offices, dental surgery in 2.05.)

ODEON STUDIO, 6 Red Lion Street, corner of Lewis Road. (Opened 12.3.92, former Mecca billiard hall, 329 seats, 4 screens: 81 + 78 + 78 + 92. Open in 2.05, seating 79 + 76 + 78 + 91.

RICKMANSWORTH Hertfordshire

ODEON, High Street. Opened 29.1.36, architect: Andrew Mather, 920 seats, stadium: 574 front + 346 rear. Closed 5.1.57. (Taken over by Urban District Council. Demolished 1965. Offices: Union Carbide House, with car park behind.)

ROCHDALE Greater Manchester

RIALTO, Drake Street & Milnrow Road. (Opened 25.8.28, architects: Butterworth & Duncan, 1848 seats.) Taken over 27.7.57 by Gaumont. 1724 seats.) Renamed ODEON 17.8.59. 1426 seats by 1964. Closed 1.11.75. (Demolished mid-1980s. MFI store.) [Present Odeon is former ABC multiplex.]

ROCHESTER Kent

GAUMONT, High Street, Star Hill. (Opened 15.4.35 as Majestic by Gaumont-associated company, architects: Harry Weston & Arthur W. Kenyon, interior decoration: Mollo & Egan, 2012 seats. Renamed Gaumont 3.4.50.) Renamed ODEON 21.10.62. Triple from 9.3.74, seating 730 balcony + 120 & 120 rear stalls. Closed 31.10.81. (Demolished 1987. Homes.)

ROMFORD Northeast London

HAVANA, 108 South Street, corner of Havana Row. (Opened 29.1.36 by D. J. James and others, architects: Kemp & Tasker in association with W. Evans, 2351 seats. Taken over 4.37 by Eastern Cinemas [GCF].) Taken over 28.2.43, part of GCF. Renamed ODEON 28.11.49. 1995 seats by 1963. Triple from 24.3.74, seating 758 balcony + 127 & 127 rear stalls. Odeon 3 closed 22.9.79 for enlargement, re-opened 28.10.79: 358 seats. All closed 8.7.90. (Laserquest briefly. Nightclub in 2004.)

PLAZA, South Street. (Opened 20.1.30, architect: W. Evans of Harrington & Evans, 1620 seats. Taken over by D. J. James. Taken over 4.37 by GCF, later Eastern Cinemas [GCF].) Taken over 28.2.43, part of GCF. Renamed GAUMONT 29.8.49. 1522 seats by 1956. Closed 8.9.62. (Demolished for shopping centre.)

ODEON, Liberty 2 Shopping Centre, Mercury Gardens. Opened 18.7.90, 8 screens, 1915 seats: 410 + 255 + 150 + 181 + 181 + 150 + 335 + 253. Closed 12.4.01.

ROTHERHAM South Yorkshire

REGAL, Corporation Street. (Opened 22.12.34 by Lou Morris, architects: Blackmore, Sykes, 1850 seats. Taken over 1.4.35 by London & Southern.) Taken over circa 7.37, part of London & Southern. 1825 seats in 1939: 1097 stalls + 728 balcony. Renamed ODEON 21.10.46. 1502 seats by 1964. Closed 29.11.75. (Taken over by independent and re-opened 7.12.75, renamed Scala. Seating reduced 1981 to 728 seats, balcony only. Closed 21.9.83. Entertainment centre. Ritz bingo club from 25.5.89. Mecca bingo in 6.04.)

RUTHERGLEN Glasgow

VOGUE, 58/60 Main Street. (Opened 29.1.36 by Singleton, architect: James McKissack, 1741 seats.) Taken over 8.3.37, part of Singleton circuit. 1741 seats in 1939: 1184 stalls + 557 balcony. Renamed ODEON 24.6.38. 1752 seats by 1957. 1702 seats by 1965. Closed 12.10.74. (Top Rank Club for bingo. Renamed Mecca. Open in 6.01.)

ST. ALBANS Hertfordshire

CAPITOL, 166 London Road (site of Regent). (Opened 3.12.31 by Lou Morris, architect: Martin Hatfield, decorations: Robert Cromie, 1500 seats. Taken over circa 1932 by D. J. James. Enlarged, architects: Kemp & Tasker, & re-opened 1934, 1728 seats. Taken over circa 4.37 by Eastern Cinemas [GCF].) Taken over 28.2.43, part of GCF. Renamed ODEON 18.6.45. 1620 seats by 1956. Triple from 21.1.73, seating 452 balcony + 115 & 128 rear stalls. Fourth screen opened late 1988 in former front stalls, seating 145. All closed 20.8.95. (Disused.)

GRAND PALACE, Stanhope Street. (Opened 8.6.22, architects: Mence & Finn [Harry R. Finn], 1400 seats. Part of D. J. James circuit. Taken over 4.37 by Eastern Cinemas [GCF].) Taken over 28.2.43, part of GCF. Renamed GAUMONT 20.2.50. 1336 seats by 1956. Closed 27.10.73. (Sold May 1974. Bingo. Demolished circa 1987. Flats — Chatsworth Court.)

ST. AUSTELL Cornwall

ODEON, Chandos Place. Opened 11.7.36, architect: Harry Weedon [assistant: P. J. Price], 1274 seats: 806 stalls + 468 balcony. (Taken over 3.12.67 by Classic, renamed Classic. Taken over 8.1.78 by independent, renamed Film Centre. Triple from 16.4.81, seating 605 stalls + 125 & 135 balcony. Rear stalls converted to two further cinemas opened 24.5.91, seating 70 & 70. Open in 2.05.)

ST. HELIER Jersey (Channel Islands)

OPERA HOUSE, Gloucester Street. (Taken over by 1914 by Albany Ward. Closed 1921 by fire and rebuilt. Part of PCT circuit. Taken over 2.29 by Gaumont, part of PCT circuit. Mainly live theatre. Under enemy occupation during part of World War Two.) Taken over by Odeon (Jersey) Ltd. 684 seats. 705 seats by 1958. Closed (sold) 20.12.58. (Live theatre in 2005.)

ODEON, Bath Street. Opened 2.6.52, architects: T. P. Bennett & Son, 1360 seats. 1373 seats by 1956. Closed 27.9.80 for twinning. Re-opened 22.2.81, seating 719 stalls + 592 balcony. Upstairs screen subdivided 1989, seating 231 & 171. Downstairs screen subdivided circa 1992, seating 409 + 244. Listed 2001 as site of Special Scientific Interest. Closed 7.10.04.

FORUM, La Chasse. Taken over in 1970s. 1229 seats. Closed 17.1.81. (Demolished. Offices.)

ST. PETER PORT Guernsey (Channel Islands)

REGAL, Upland Road. (Opened 31.5.37 by Lou Morris, architect: Henry Cooper, 1098 seats. Taken over by enemy during World War Two.) Taken over circa 1948. Renamed ODEON 30.1.50. 1134 seats by 1956. Closed 31.5.80. (Demolished. Car park in 2004.)

SALE Cheshire

PYRAMID, 22 Washway Road and Ashton Lane. (Opened 24 & 26.2.34, architects: Drury & Gomersall, 1908 seats.) Taken over 21.12.42. Renamed ODEON 18.6.45. 1909 seats by 1956. 1852 seats by 1964. (Taken over by Tatton, renamed Tatton. Closed 1984. Grade II listed building from 13.11.87. JFK's nightclub. LA Fitness in auditorium with entrance at rear in 2.05, foyer disused after bar and restaurant closed.)

SALISBURY Wiltshire

PICTURE HOUSE, Fisherton Street. (Opened 27.9.37 as New Picture House by Gaumont/Albany Ward, architects: W. E. Trent, W. S. Trent & R. C. H. Golding, 1313 seats, stadium. Renamed Picture House.) Renamed ODEON 27.2.50. 1341 seats. Closed 30.12.61. (City Hall concert venue. Major refurbishment in 1985. Open.)

GAUMONT, 15 New Canal. (Opened 7.9.31 as Gaumont Palace by Gaumont/Albany Ward incorporating Ye Halle of John Halle as vestibule, architect: W. E. Trent, 1675 seats: 1125 stalls & 550 balcony. Renamed Gaumont circa 1937. 1693 seats by 1955.) Renamed ODEON 10.8.64. Triple from 26.11.72, seating 471 balcony + 120 & 120 rear stalls. Listed building: foyer already grade I, remainder grade II from 1984. Fourth cinemas, 70 seats, opened circa 1993 in former restaurant. Front stalls converted to fifth cinema, 278 seats, opened 6.4.95. Open in 2.05, seating 471 + 276 + 127 + 111 + 70.

SCARBOROUGH North Yorkshire

ODEON, Westborough. Opened 28.3.36, architect: Harry W. Weedon [assistants: J. Cecil Clavering, Robert Bullivant], interior decoration: Mollo & Egan, 1711 seats: 946 stalls + 765 balcony. Grade II listed building from 1.88. Closed 21.10.88. (Taken over 1989 by Alan Ayckbourn and partners. Auditorium gutted, exterior refurbished, architects: Osbourne Christmas, and re-opened 1.5.96 as Stephen Joseph Theatre with two auditoria seating 413 + 165. Open in 2.05.)

SCOTSTOUN Glasgow

COMMODORE, 1297 Dumbarton Road. (Opened 26.12.32 by Singleton, architect: James McKissack, 1919 seats: 1236 stalls + 683 balcony.) Taken over 8.3.37, part of Singleton circuit. Renamed ODEON 24.6.38. 1845 seats by 1964. Closed 25.11.67. (Bingo. Disused. Destroyed by fire 19.8.76. Demolished. Flats.)

SEVENOAKS Kent

MAJESTIC, London Road. (Opened 22.8.36, architect: George Coles, 1600 seats.) Taken over 23.8.43. Renamed ODEON 2.7.45. 1442 seats by 1956. 1367 seats by 1965. Triple from 24.12.72, seating 457 balcony + 102 & 106 rear stalls. (Taken over 26.10.75 by Brent

Walker, renamed Focus 1, 2 & 3. Taken over 31.10.82 by independent, renamed Ace 1, 2 & 3. Taken over, renamed Stag Theatre, large cinema used mostly, then exclusively, for live shows, small cinemas continuing. Open in 2.05.)

SHANNON CORNER Southwest London

ODEON, Kingston By-Pass and Burlington Road, Shannon Corner, New Malden. [Also known as Odeon New Malden and Odeon Merton]. Opened 7.11.38, architect: George Coles, 1611 seats: 961 stalls + 650 balcony. Closed 2.1.60. (Offices for Decca Navigation. Closed circa 1979. Demolished 2.85. Car park.)

SHEFFIELD South Yorkshire

ODEON, Flat Street and Norfolk Street [now Esperanto Place]. Opened 16.7.56, architects: Harry Weedon & Robert Bullivant, 2319 seats: 1505 stalls + 814 balcony. Closed 5.6.71. (Top Rank Club for bingo from 9.71. Renamed Mecca. Open in 2.05.)

ODEON, Burgess Street (site of Gaumont). Opened 20.8.87, architect: Barry Wheat (Hadfield, Cawkwell & Partners), 2 screens, 824 seats: 500 + 324. Closed 20.2.94. (Nightclubs.)

CANNON 1 & 2, 60 Flat Street. (Opened 30.1.69 as Cinecenta 1 & 2 by Cinecenta, 189 + 141 seats. Cinecenta 2 renamed Cine-Club 24 circa 4.69. Cine-Club 24 renamed Penthouse Club 22.11.71. Both taken over 12.79 by Star. Both taken over 1985 by Cannon. Renamed Cannon 1 & 2 Flat Street 5.86.) Taken over 8.89, renamed Fiesta. Closed 29.9.91 for inclusion in Odeon 7.

ODEON 7, Arundel Gate. Opened 5.3.92, adaptation of former Fiesta nightclub plus Cannon 1 & 2 cinemas, 1316 seats, 7 screens: 254 + 254 + 251 + 117 + 115 + 186 + 139. Two screens added 26.12.94, complex renamed ODEON. Tenth screen added 20.12.97, 123 seats. Open in 2.05, 1673 seats: 252 + 229 + 248 + 113 + 113 + 129 + 171 + 148 + 150 + 120.

SHEPHERD'S BUSH West London

GAUMONT, Shepherd's Bush Green. (Opened 16.8.23 as Pavilion by Davis circuit, architect: Frank T. Verity, 2776 seats. Part of original Gaumont circuit in 3.27. Closed 7.44 by World War Two bomb damage. Interior

entirely rebuilt, architect: Sam Beverley, and re-opened 25.7.55, 2036 seats.) Renamed ODEON 25.11.62. Closed 31.5.69 for subdivision into ground floor bingo club and smaller Odeon in extended balcony, opened 7.3.70, 815 seats. Renamed 1.4.73 ODEON 1. Grade II listed building from 16.1.74. Cinema closed 17.9.83. (Bingo continued as Top Rank Club, cinema disused. Bingo renamed Mecca, closed 2001. Entire building disused in 2004.)

CLASSIC, 57 & 57a Shepherd's Bush Green/Rockwood Place. (Opened 3.3.10 as Shepherd's Bush Cinematograph Theatre by Pyke circuit, 763 seats, one floor. Taken over by ACT. Renamed Palladium circa 1915. Modernised 1923, architect: J. Stanley Beard. Taken over 1945 by Southan Morris [SM Super Cinemas]. Taken over 26.8.54 by Essoldo. Renamed Essoldo circa 6.55. Closed 24.6.68 for internal reconstruction. Re-opened 12.6.69, 487 seats. Taken over 2.4.72 by Classic, renamed Classic.) Taken over 1.4.73, renamed ODEON 2. Closed 17.10.81. (Walkabout theme pub in 2004.)

SHETTLESTON Glasgow

BROADWAY, 19 Amulree Street. (Opened 5.6.30 by Singleton, architect: James McKissack, 1640 seats: 1102 stalls + 538 balcony.) Taken over 8.3.37, part of Singleton circuit. Renamed ODEON 24.6.38. Closed 25.1.67. (Top Rank Club for bingo. Closed circa 1991. Demolished 8.95. Housing.)

SHIRLEY Southampton

RIALTO, 325 Shirley Road, Shirley (auditorium along Janson Road). (Opened 9.1.22. Booked circa 1932/33 by Oscar Deutsch's Cinema Service.) Taken over through London & Southern subsidiary on 6.2.39. 945 seats in 1939: 737 stalls + 208 balcony. 928 seats. Closed 5.11.60. (Top Rank Club for bingo. Closed 6.62. Blundell's furniture store. Disused in 1994. Town and Country Pine furniture store in 2001. Demolished 2004.)

SHIRLEY West Midlands

ODEON, Corner of Stratford Road and Solihull Road, Solihull. Opened 15.4.35, architect: Satchwell & Roberts [Roland Satchwell], 1156 seats: 768 stalls + 388 balcony. Part-week bingo. Closed 29.10.77. (Full-time bingo from 10.3.78. Closed. Demolished 9-10.85. Safeway supermarket, renamed Morrisons by 1.05.)

SIDCUP Southeast London

ODEON, Station Road. Opened 21.10.35, architect: A. P. Starkey [assistant: Frederick Adkins], 1371 seats, semi-stadium: 1029 front + 342 rear. Closed 16.10.44 by war-time bomb damage to auditorium. Reconstructed, architect: Leonard Allen, and re-opened 2.8.54, seating 1268. Closed 14.1.61. (Reconstructed internally for Lamorbey baths from 1967, open in 2004.)

SITTINGBOURNE Kent

ODEON, High Street. Opened 4.1.37, architect: F. C. Mitchell, 1593 seats: 1077 stalls + 516 balcony. 1551 seats in 1967. (Taken over 3.12.67 by Classic, renamed Vogue. Closed 13.1.68. Bingo club from 24.1.68. Classic Cinema opened 9.8.71 in former café, seating 111. Second Classic cinema opened in former balcony, seating 330. Renamed Cannon 1 & 2. Cinemas taken over 7.1.97 by Picturedrome, renamed Picturedrome. Cinemas taken over in 2000 by Reeltime, renamed New Century. Open in 2.05 with Mecca bingo club on ground floor.)

SKETTY Swansea

MAXIME, Sketty Cross. (Opened 3.12.38 by Max Corne, 1600 seats.) Taken over 13.12.43. Renamed ODEON 21.7.47. 1562 seats. Closed 17.2.62. (Top Rank Club for bingo from 23.2.62. Renamed Mecca. Closed 10.95. Auditorium demolished circa 2000 for flats: Maxime Court. Frontage vacant retail space in 2.05.)

SKIPTON North Yorkshire

REGAL, Keighley Road. (Opened 1929 as Morriseum. Renamed Regal 1932.) Taken over 26.8.36. 927 seats in 1939: 618 stalls + 309 balcony. Renamed ODEON 19.6.50. 872 seats in 1967. (Taken over 17.12.67 by Classic, renamed Classic. Taken over 29.1.71 by Hutchinson circuit, renamed Regal. Split for stalls bingo + twin cinemas in old balcony, latter opened 18.6.71, seating 150 & 150. Closed 10.9.87. Bliss and The Vestry night-club from 12.99.)

SLOUGH Buckinghamshire
see Farnham Royal

SMETHWICK West Midlands

BEACON, Brasshouse Lane. (Opened 30.9.29, architect: Harold S. Scott. Associated with County from 11.32.) Taken over 9.39, part of County circuit, 962 seats. (Taken over circa 1942 by Mayfair circuit. Taken over 30.8.43 by ABC. Closed 15.2.58. Asian cinema. Clothing factory.)

SOUTH DAGENHAM Northeast London
see Whalebone Lane

SOUTH HACKNEY Northeast London

PICTURE HOUSE, 133/7 Well Street. (Opened circa 1913 as Picture Palace, 1500 seats, one floor. Enlarged, front rebuilt, architect: George Coles, and re-opened 8.33, renamed Picture House.) Taken over 10.5.37. 1201 seats in 1939. Closed 17.4.41 by bomb damage. (Furniture store until 1946. Derelict. Demolished 1959. Extension to Frampton Park Housing Estate.)

SOUTH HARROW Northwest London

ODEON, 337 Northolt Road, between Scarsdale Road and Wyvenhoe Road. Opened 4.9.33, architect: A. Percival Starkey, 997 seats, semi-stadium: 718 front + 279 rear. 970 seats by 1964. Closed 12.2.72. (Auditorium and foyer area demolished & replaced by Duncan House block of flats. Shops and flats remain at corners.)

SOUTH NORWOOD South London

ODEON, Station Road. Opened 26.7.37, architect: Andrew Mather, 1572 seats: 1020 stalls + 552 balcony. 1568 seats by 1956. Closed 20.2.71. (Demolished. Safeway super-market + Paladin House.)

SOUTH SHIELDS Tyne & Wear

REGAL, King Street. (Opened 4.11.35 by Black's, conversion of Empire Theatre, architect: E. M. Lawson, 1412 seats.) Taken over circa 1943. Renamed ODEON 18.6.45. 1427 seats. Closed 30.6.62. (Top Rank Club for bingo.)

SOUTHALL West London

ODEON, High Street. Opened 17.8.36, architect: George Coles, 1580 seats: 1122 stalls + 458 balcony. Closed 25.2.61. (Reconstructed internally and re-opened 14.8.61 as Top Rank Bowl. Closed. Sold 9.7.70 to MFI, converted to store. Queenstyle Carpet Centre in 1996.)

GAUMONT, 14 South Road. (Opened 11.29 as Palace on enlarged site of former Palace by United Picture Theatres, architect: George Coles, 2000 seats, one floor. Under Gaumont management from 7.30 as part of UPT circuit. Renamed Gaumont 13.3.50. 1562 seats.) Renamed ODEON 10.12.61. 1253 seats. (Taken over 27.6.71 by independent, renamed Godeon. Asian cinema from 31.1.72, renamed Liberty. Grade II listed building from 18.9.80. Closed 1982. Indoor market. Closed 7.98 by fire. Re-opened 14.9.01 as Himalaya Palace cinema, seating 450 front + 150 & 150 rear.)

SOUTHAMPTON Hampshire
see also Northam and Shirley

REGAL, Above Bar. (Opened 22.6.34 by County, partly on site of Alexandra Picture House, architects: Verity & Beverley, 1756 seats: 1078 stalls + 678 balcony.) Taken over 9.39, part of County circuit. 1736 seats in 1939. Renamed ODEON 15.4.45. 1778 seats by 1957. Closed 10.2.62 for modernisation. Re-opened 7.5.62. 1578 seats. Closed 17.2.79 for twinning. Re-opened 14.4.79, seating 756 downstairs, and 26.5.79, seating 476 upstairs. Third cinema added early 1988, seating 98 in former restaurant space. All closed 5.9.93. (Demolished late 1993. Virgin megastore/Waterstone's bookshop, etc. on site in 2004.)

ODEON, Leisure World, West Quay Road. Opened 21 & 22.8.97, 13 screens. Open in 2.05, 3102 seats: 540 + 495 + 169 + 111 + 99 + 139 + 270 + 318 + 331 + 288 + 102 + 102 + 138.

SOUTHEND-ON-SEA Essex

ASTORIA, 127 High Street. (Opened 15.7.35, architects: E. A. Stone & T. R. Somerford, interior decoration: Mollo & Egan, 2750 seats. Taken over 6.36 by County.) Taken over 9.39, part of County circuit. 2745 seats in 1939. Renamed ODEON 9.6.40. Modernised 1960: 2287 seats. Closed 7.1.70 for subdivision into ground floor supermarket with new cinemas above, opened 4.11.70 with 455 seats in former café/dance studio + 1235 seats in extended balcony, with new entrance on Elmer Approach. Closed 5.4.97. (Disused. Entire building demolished 7.04 to 1.05. University of Essex central campus building scheduled for site.)

RITZ, Church Road. (Opened 14.2.35 by County, architect: Robert Cromie, interior decoration: Mollo & Egan, 2250 seats.) Taken over 9.39, part of County circuit. 2231 seats by 1956. Modernised 1956: 1891 seats. Closed 29.7.72. (Top Rank Club for bingo. Closed 1976. Demolished 1981. Part of Royals Shopping Centre.)

ODEON, Victoria Circus, The Broadway, London Road. Opened 22.11.96, 8 screens. Open in 2.05, 1935 seats: 200 + 264 + 145 + 221 + 388 + 260 + 260 + 197.

SOUTHGATE North London

ODEON, Corner of The Bourne and Tudor Way, Old Southgate. Opened 16.10.35, architect: Bertie Crewe, 1438 seats: 810 stalls + 628 balcony. 1288 seats by 1964. Closed 7.9.72. (Taken over by independent & re-opened 27.12.75 as Capitol, stalls only. Balcony partly re-opened 1979. Closed 2.1.81. Demolished 1982. Hobart House office block.)

SOUTHPORT Merseyside

GAUMONT, Lord Street. (Opened 1.10.30 as New Palladium by Gaumont/GTC, retaining front of old Palladium, architects: W. E. Trent & Ernest Tulley, 2126 seats. Renamed Palladium. Renamed Gaumont 24.7.50. 2120 seats by 1956.) Renamed ODEON 21.10.62. Closed 28.11.79. (Demolished. Supermarket.)

SOUTHSEA Hampshire

ODEON, Highland Road and Festing Road. Opened 4.12.37, architect: Andrew Mather, 1688 seats: 1152 stalls + 536 balcony. 1542 seats by 1965. (Taken over 20.11.77 by independent, renamed Salon. Second cinema opened circa 2.81, seating 400 in rear stalls. Both closed 9.83. Demolished 1985. Sportsfield of Craneswater Junior School.)

SPALDING Lincolnshire

ODEON, London Road, corner of Haverhill Road. Opened 28.2.38, architect: Harry Weedon [assistant: Basil Herring], 1208 seats, stadium: 886 front + 322 rear. 1142 seats by 1964. 1090 seats in 1967. (Taken over 10.12.67 by Classic, renamed Classic. Partwide bingo from 8.1.68. Twin from 7.5.71, seating 768 + 248. Taken over 6.10.74 by independent, renamed Regent 1 & 2. Renamed Gemini. Closed 7.83. Demolished 10.87. Retirement flats from 7.01: Georgian Court.)

SPRINGBURN Glasgow

ASTOR, Wellfield Street. (Opened 1920 as Springburn Picture House, architect: Albert V. Gardner, 1535 seats. Renamed Astor 11.47.) Taken over 2.5.55 by CMA, 1375 seats. Closed 26.11.60. (Demolished.)

SPRINGFIELD QUAY Glasgow
see Glasgow

STAFFORD Staffordshire

ODEON, Newport Road. Opened 5.10.36, architect: Roland Satchwell, 956 seats: 535 stalls + 421 balcony. Temporarily closed during 2.46 by flooding. 955 seats in 1964. (Taken over 26.7.81 by Hutchinsons, renamed Astra. Triple from 27.12.81, seating 435 stalls + 170 & 168 balcony. Taken over 1988 by Apollo. Cinemas renamed Apollo. Downstairs cinema closed for bingo, then re-opened 1990. All open in 2004, seating 305 + 170 + 164.)

STAINES Surrey

MAJESTIC, High Street. (Opened 11.12.29, architect: S. B. Pritlove, interior decoration: W. E. Greenwood, 1558 seats: 1038 stalls + 520 balcony. Taken over circa 1932 by County.) Taken over 9.39, part of County circuit. 1507 seats in 1939: 1035 stalls + 472 balcony. 1502 seats by 1960. Closed 27.5.61. (Demolished. Shops and offices.)

STAMFORD HILL North London

GAUMONT, 1a Amhurst Park, corner of Stamford Hill. (Opened 18.2.29 as Regent by Gaumont/PCT, architect: W. Sydney Trent, 2172 seats. Renamed Gaumont 24.1.60.) Renamed ODEON 21.10.62. Closed 16.9.72. (Top Rank Club for bingo. Closed. Demolished 4.81. Supermarket.)

STEPNEY Northeast London

MAYFAIR, Brick Lane (site of Palace Theatre). (Opened 29.1.36 by D. J. James, architects: Kemp & Tasker, 1500 seats. Taken over 4.37 by Eastern Cinemas [GCF].) Taken over 28.2.43, part of GCF. Renamed ODEON 20.2.50. 1491 seats in 1956. Closed 22.7.67. (Sold 31.7.67, Asian cinema, renamed Naz. Store. Demolished. Car park by 1994. Café Naz at front, Odeon Court block of flats at rear in 2004.)

STOCKTON-ON-TEES Cleveland

REGAL, High Street. (Opened 22.4.35, architect: Joshua Clayton, 2080 seats.) Taken over 7.2.44. Renamed ODEON 12.3.45. Closed circa 20.3.45 by effects of earlier bomb damage. Repaired and re-opened 22.7.46. 2082 seats. Closed 3.9.66. (Demolished for new Odeon.)

ODEON, 89-91 High Street (site of old Odeon). Opened 25.4.68, interior design: Anthony Sharp, 1225 seats, stadium. Closed 24.10.81. (The Mall disco from 1987. Zanzibar nightclub from 2000, open in 2004.)

STOKE NEWINGTON North London

AMBASSADOR, 117 Stoke Newington Road. (Opened 1913 as Apollo. Taken over by London & Southern. Modernised & re-opened 7.8.33 as Ambassador. 1160 seats. Taken over circa 1936 by Watford Amusements.) Taken over (leased out) circa 7.37, part of London & Southern. Shown as "Let" on Odeon Associated Theatres Group property list circa 1950. Seemingly never operated by Odeon. Closed 16.2.61? (Closed 7.12.63. Taken over by Star for bingo by 1965. Closed. Re-opened 8.9.74 as Astra cinema. Cinema club showing uncensored martial arts films. Closed 7.83. Aziziye Mosque & Community Centre.)

STOKE-ON-TRENT Staffordshire

ODEON, Etruria Road, Etruria. Opened 18.10.89, 1804 seats, 8 screens: 177 + 177 + 309 + 150 + 160 + 160 + 521 + 150. Ninth & tenth screens added 7.93, 2206 seats: 201 + 216 + 368 + 162 + 169 + 185 + 564 + 162 + 104 + 75. Open in 2.05, 2170 seats: 197 + 212 + 364 + 158 + 165 + 181 + 560 + 158 + 101 + 74.

STOURBRIDGE West Midlands

CENTRAL, 63/5 High Street. (Opened 16.5.29, architects: Webb & Gray, 1500 seats.) Taken over 22.11.37. Renamed ODEON 1938. 1378 seats in 1939: 797 stalls + 581 balcony. 1383 seats by 1956. Closed 16.6.73. (Sold 24.6.73 to Maple Macowards [Jessel Securities]. Shop and other commercial use. Closed 1990. Demolished. Wilkinsons store by 2000.)

KING'S HALL, New Road. (Opened circa 1912, 1300 seats. Enlarged circa 1939, 1800 seats. Part of Poole's Theatres circuit. Also known as King's Super Cinema.) Taken over 1.10.56 by CMA. Closed 22.6.57. (MFI Furniture Centre.)

STREATHAM South London

ASTORIA, 47-49 High Road. (Opened 30.6.30, architect: Edward A. Stone, interior decoration: Marc Henri & Laverdet, 2614 seats. Taken over 12.30 by Paramount.) Taken over 27.11.39, part of Paramount circuit. 2576 seats in 1939. Closed 2.9.61 for completion of modernisation. Re-opened 18.9.61, renamed ODEON. 2128 seats. Triple from 16.12.79, seating 1095 balcony + 267 & 267 rear stalls. New screen installed in front of balcony circa 1990. Fourth cinema in front stalls & fifth cinema on former stage area opened 27.9.91, seating 240 + 196, with one rear cinema reduced to 168 for entry passage. Refurbished early to mid-2001 with two new cinemas from circa 5.01 in rear balcony and front stalls cinema divided in two later in 2001. Open in 2.05, 1485 seats: 451 + 110 + 110 + 103 + 237 + 209 + 93 + 172.

STROUD Gloucestershire

GAUMONT, Russell Street. (Opened 31.8.35 as Gaumont Palace by Gaumont/Albany Ward-PCT, architects: W. E. Trent & W. Sydney Trent, 994 seats, semi-stadium plan. Renamed Gaumont.) Renamed ODEON 11.11.62. 887 seats by 1964. (Taken over 10.12.67 by Classic, renamed Classic. Split for bingo on stalls floor and new cinema in former raised rear section, opened 2.3.72, 184 seats. Cinema closed 3.9.72. Taken over by Mecca 11.1.74. Cinema re-opened as Mecca. Cinema closed by 31.12.76. Bingo only. Closed 22.7.95 as Cascades bingo club.)

SUDBURY London

ODEON, Odeon Parade, Allendale Road, Sudbury Heights, Greenford. Originally known as Odeon Sudbury Town. Opened 16.9.35, architect: A. P. Starkey [assistant: Frederick Adkins], 1009 seats, semi-stadium: 730 front + 279 rear. Closed 27.10.56. (Frontage rebuilt, foyer and auditorium rebuilt within old walls and occupied by Starlite Bingo and Social Club. Sudbury Town Nursery School on ground floor and Starlite Snooker Club above in 2001 with Sudbury House offices at rear on Sudbury Heights Avenue within part of old auditorium.)

SUNDERLAND Tyne & Wear

BLACK'S REGAL, Holmeside. (Opened 28.3.32 by George & Alfred Black, architects: Gray & Evans, 2522 seats.) Taken over 4.7.55,

2538 seats. Renamed ODEON 28.11.55. 2156 seats by 1965. Closed 8.2.75 for tripling. Re-opened 9.3.75, seating 1200 balcony/front stalls + 150 & 150 rear stalls. Closed 26.6.82. (Re-opened as Top Rank Club for bingo. Renamed Mecca. Open in 2004.)

BLACK'S THEATRE ROYAL, Bedford Street. (Former live theatre with some early films. Closed 1933. Boxing stadium. Taken over 8.36 by Black's. Closed late 1939 for complete interior reconstruction, architect: Edwin M. Lawson, and re-opened 11.11.40, 950 seats.) Taken over 5.10.59. 924 seats. Closed 19.9.64. (Top Rank Club for bingo from 1964. Closed circa 1983 on transfer of Club to former Odeon. Blue Monkey nightclub. Closed 1994 by fire. Demolished 1997. Petrol station. Demolished. Part of site for new leisure centre including Cineworld multiplex opened 27.11.04.)

SURBITON Southwest London

ODEON, Claremont Road. Opened 14.4.34, architect: Joseph Hill, interior designers: Mollo & Egan, 1502 seats: 974 stalls + 528 balcony. 1358 seats by 1964. Closed 8.2.75. (Sapphire Carpet & Furniture Centre. Closed 1977. B&Q store. Closed. Demolished 3.99. Waitrose supermarket.)

SUTTON COLDFIELD West Midlands

ODEON, Birmingham Road at Maney Corner and Holland Road, Maney. Opened 18.4.36, architect: Harry Weedon [assistant: J. Cecil Clavering], 1600 seats: 1028 stalls + 572 balcony. 1618 seats by 1957. Triple from 9.4.72: 591 seats balcony + 132 & 132 rear stalls. Refurbished 1984. Fourth cinema added 1987 in former front stalls, seating 330, with one mini-cinema reduced to 110 seats and new screen erected in front of balcony. Grade II listed building from 18.11.98. Open in 2.05, seating 582 + 134 + 109 + 327.

SWANSEA West Glamorgan
see also Sketty

ODEON, The Kingsway (site of Plaza). Opened 17.5.67, architects: Cassidy, Farring-ton & Dennys, 1378 seats, stadium. Triple from 17.5.82, seating 708 front + 242 + 172 rear. Refurbished 1995. Closed 14.12.97. (Jumpin Jaks bar & nightclub, open in 2004.)

SWINDON Wiltshire

GAUMONT, Regent Circus. (Opened 16.9.29

as Regent by Gaumont/Albany Ward-PCT, architect: W. Sydney Trent, 1322 seats, one floor. Frontage completed circa 11.31, architects: W.E. Trent & Ernest F. Tulley. Renamed Gaumont 9.2.53.) Renamed ODEON 2.6.63. Closed 24.8.74. (Top Rank Club for bingo, renamed Mecca, open in 12.04.)

SWISS COTTAGE Northwest London

ODEON, 96 Finchley Road (backing onto Upper Avenue Road). Opened 4.9.37, architect: Harry Weedon [assistant: Basil Herring], 2115 seats: 1281 stalls + 834 balcony. 2075 seats by 1956. Modernised circa 1960. 1873 seats. Triple from 25.2.73, seating 742 balcony + 105 & 109 rear stalls. Latter cinemas enlarged to 152 & 155 seats. Three further cinemas opened 19.6.92 in former front stalls, stage and upstairs foyer, seating 250 + 200 + 112. Refurbished & re-opened 26.6.98 with new box-office. Open in 2.05, seating 715 + 111 + 220 + 120 + 154 + 156.

SWITCH ISLAND Liverpool

ODEON, Switch Island Leisure Park, Dunnings Bridge Road, Bootle. Opened 16.10.97, 12 screens. Open in 2.05, 2519 seats: 369 + 228 + 130 + 149 + 243 + 156 + 338 + 228 + 130 + 149 + 243 + 156.

TAIBACH Port Talbot

REGENT, High Street. (Opened 26.10.36.) Taken over 13.12.43. 887 seats. Closed 27.10.56. (Co-Op store. Closed 1980. Body Shape health studio and gym by 1994.)

TAUNTON Somerset

LYCEUM, Station Road. (Opened circa 8.13, architects: Stone and Lloyd. Altered, architect: F. C. Mitchell, and re-opened 4.1.32.) Taken over 24.9.35. Renamed ODEON circa 1936. Improved in late 1930s, architect: Andrew Mather, 681 seats: 432 stalls + 249 balcony. 673 seats in 1967. (Taken over 3.12.67 by Classic, renamed Classic. Classic 2 added 4.70, seating 71. Renamed Cannon in 1985. Both closed 10.10.90. Taken over by independent and re-opened 11.12.92, renamed Plaza. Closed 25 8.94. Demolished 12.98. Laverock Court block of flats.)

GAUMONT, Corporation Street, Castle Way and Tower Street. (Opened 11.7.32 as Gaumont Palace by Gaumont/Albany Ward-

PCT, architect: William T. Benslyn, 1476 seats: 982 stalls & 494 balcony [or 1487 seats: 989 stalls & 498 balcony]. Renamed Gaumont circa 1937.) Renamed ODEON 1.4.68. 1272 seats. Closed 5.9.81. (Top Rank Club for bingo from 11.81. Renamed Mecca. Open in 2004.)

ODEON, Heron Gate, Riverside, off Junction 25 of M5. Opened 4.8.94, 998 seats, 5 screens: 106 + 316 + 218 + 252 + 106. Extension adding three screens opened 3.05, new total 1592 seats: 124 + 304 + 258 + 330 + 212 + 153 + 86 + 125.

TEMPLE FORTUNE Northwest London

ORPHEUM, Finchley Road. (Opened 11.10.30, architects: Yates, Cook & Darbyshire, 2800 seats. Taken over circa 1932 by ABC. Taken over 3.34 by County.) Much live show use. Renamed ODEON circa 1945. Redecorated 1966 and 1971. Renamed Odeon Golders Green. 2343 seats in 1971. Closed 27.4.74. (Demolished circa 5.82. Flats.)

THORNBURY Bradford
see Bradford

TOLWORTH Southwest London

ODEON, Hook Rise, Kingston By-Pass Road. Opened 9.1.34, architects: Yates, Cook and Darbyshire, 891 seats: 439 stalls + 452 balcony. 889 seats by 1959. Closed 10.10.59. (Demolished 3.61. Tolworth Tower – Marks & Spencer food store with office block above.)

TORQUAY Devon

ROYAL, 29 Abbey Road. (Opened 27.3.33, former Theatre Royal.) Taken over 29.7.35. Renamed ODEON 12.4.37. 883 seats in 1939: 571 stalls + 312 balcony. 765 seats by 1965. Closed 27.10.73 for twinning. Re-opened 24.3.74, seating 360 downstairs + 309 upstairs. Closed 11.99, seating 333 + 304. (Taken over by Merlin Cinemas, re-opened 11.2.00 as Central, seating 333 + 308. Downstairs cinema tripled in 2001, seating 122 + 78 + 42. All open in 2.05.)

TOTTENHAM COURT ROAD London
see London West End

TOWNHEAD Glasgow

CARLTON, 144 Castle Street. (Opened 4.1.26, architects: Duff & Cairns, 1619 seats.)

Taken over 2.5.55 by CMA, 1597 seats. 1516 seats by 1966. Closed 5.3.66. (Demolished for new road.)

TROWBRIDGE Wiltshire

GAUMONT, 27 Fore Street (partly on site of Palace cinema). (Opened 29.11.37 by Gaumont/Albany Ward-PCT, architects: W. E. Trent & W. S. Trent, 1220 seats: 860 stalls & 360 balcony. 1246 seats by 1956.) Renamed ODEON 11.11.62. 1228 seats by 1964. Closed 20.3.71. (Demolished. Knees store by 4.95.)

TUNBRIDGE WELLS Kent

ODEON, Knights Park, Knights Way. Opened 5.2.99, 9 screens, 2219 seats: 439 + 272 + 258 + 221 + 139 + 272 + 258 + 221 + 139. Open in 2.05, 2212 seats: 437 + 271 + 257 + 221 + 138 + 271 + 257 + 221 + 139.

TWICKENHAM Southwest London

QUEENS, Richmond Road, corner of Oak Lane. (Opened 15.10.28 as The Twickenham Cinema by Joseph Mears, architects: Leathart & Granger, 1141 seats. Renamed Queens 29.6.40. Requisitioned & closed 26.10.40.) Taken over (closed) 3.1.44. Re-opened 24.12.45. 1,077 seats: 736 stalls + 341 balcony. Renamed GAUMONT 8.5.50. Closed 1.12.56. (Demolished. Shell petrol station in 2004.)

LUXOR, Cross Deep & Heath Road. Opened 18.11.29 by Walter Bentley, architect: J. Stanley Beard of Beard & Clare, 1709 seats. Taken over circa 1931 by Joseph Mears. Taken over 3.1.44. Renamed ODEON 21.1.46. 1703 seats in 1947: 1117 stalls + 586 balcony. 1462 seats by 1964. Closed 10.10.81. (Demolished 1986. Sports Club and Bar, etc.)

TYSELEY Birmingham

TYSELEY CINEMA, Warwick Road. (Opened circa 1921, architect: Hurley Robinson. Balcony added in 1930. Associated with County from 11.32.) Taken over 9.39, part of County circuit. 960 seats in 1939. Closed 12.40 by Second World War bomb damage. (Re-opened 1941 by independent. Taken over circa 1954 by Essoldo. Closed 1958. Shops.)

UPMINSTER Northeast London

CAPITOL, St. Mary's Lane, corner of Tudor Gardens. (Opened 10.10.29 by Lou Morris,

architect: James Martin Hatfield, 1158 seats. Taken over by D. J. James. Taken over 4.37 by Eastern Cinemas [GCF].) Taken over 28.2.43, part of GCF. Renamed ODEON 19.8.46. Renamed GAUMONT 29.8.49. 1204 seats in 1956. 1186 seats by 1960. Closed 15.7.61. (Top Rank Club for bingo. Closed 1973. Demolished 1974. Wallis supermarket, renamed Somerfield in 1.05.)

UXBRIDGE London

ODEON, High Street. Opened 20.6.38, architect: Andrew Mather [assistant: Keith P. Roberts], 1837 seats: 1215 stalls + 622 balcony. 1847 seats circa 1947: 1217 + 630. 1556 seats by 1964. Triple from 25.4.76, seating 630 balcony + 140 & 140 rear stalls. Closed 5.6.82. (Demolished 1984. New two screen Odeon on part of enlarged redevelopment site.)

ODEON, Harefield Road. Opened 12 & 13.7.90, two screens seating 439 + 230. Closed 4.3.01. (Fitness First health & fitness club.)

ODEON, The Chimes Shopping Centre, 320 High Street. Opened 8 & 9.3.01, 2175 seats, 9 screens. Open in 2.05, 2258 seats: 310 + 414 + 254 + 251 + 153 + 193 + 241 + 189 + 253.

VICTORIA South London

METROPOLE, 160 Victoria Street. (Opened 27.12.29 by Hyams brothers, architect: George Coles, 2000 seats.) Taken over 3.10.43. Modernised circa 1960. 1394 seats. Closed 11.6.77. (Re-opened 21.6.77 for laser shows as Laser Metropole Theatre. Closed 26.9.77. Concert hall: The Venue. Demolished except for entrance, converted to restaurant, named Ask in 2004. Office block behind.)

WALLINGTON Southeast London

ODEON, Corner of Woodcote Road and Ross Parade. Opened 26.5.34, architects: Yates, Cook & Darbyshire, 925 seats, stadium: 574 front + 351 rear. Closed 27.4.57. (Auditorium demolished for Wallis supermarket. Whispering Moon public house from 1993, adapting original corner entrance.)

WALSALL West Midlands
see also Bloxwich

GAUMONT, The Bridge, Bridge Street. (Opened 29.7.20 as Picture House by APPH, architects: Percy L. Browne & Glover, 1500 seats. Restored 1923 after serious fire damage. Taken over 2.29 by Gaumont, part of PCT/APPH, 1615 seats. Renamed Gaumont circa 1948. 1619 seats by 1956.) Renamed ODEON 22.10.65. Modernised and re-opened 26.7.67, 1291 seats. Closed 2.3.71 by major fire. (Demolished. Tesco supermarket in 1995.)

WALTON-ON-THAMES Surrey
CAPITOL, High Street. (Opened 23 & 26.12.27 by Lou Morris, architect: J. Stanley Beard. Taken over circa 1934 by London & Southern.) Taken over circa 7.37, part of London & Southern. 1015 seats in 1939: 725 stalls + 290 balcony. Renamed ODEON 18.3.46. 997 seats by 1956. Closed 29.11.80. (Demolished. The Screens at Walton in redevelopment, opened 25.9.92. Open in 2.05.)

WARLEY West Midlands
THE WARLEY, Hagley Road West and Wolverhampton New Road, West Warley. Opened 22.12.34 by Odeon, architects: [exterior] T. Cecil Howitt, [interior] Harry Weedon [assistant: J. Cecil Clavering], Roland Satchwell, 1530 seats: 1066 stalls + 464 balcony. Renamed WARLEY ODEON circa 1935, then ODEON. 1506 seats in 1960. Closed 25.11.61. (Auditorium demolished. Warley Bowl opened 3.9.62 by Rank. Closed 29.4.70. All demolished early 1973. Office block.)

WARRINGTON Cheshire
ODEON, Buttermarket Street. Opened 11.1.37, architects: Drury & Gomersall, 1635 seats: 1059 stalls + 576 balcony. Closed early 1968 by fire. Re-opened circa 5.68. Triple from 14.9.80, seating 576 balcony + 291 & 196 rear stalls. Closed 28.8.94. (Demolished 1.95. Yates Wine Lodge.)

WATFORD Hertfordshire
PLAZA, 125-7 The Parade, High Street, at corner of Albert Road. (Opened 29.4.29, architects: Emden, Egan, 2060 seats.) Taken over 28.9.36. Renamed ODEON 12.10.36. 1989 seats in 1939: 1253 stalls + 736 balcony. 1952 seats by 1956. Closed 30.11.63. (Sold 15.6.64 to Ravenseft Properties with leaseback of ballroom in redevelopment. Demolished. Cater's supermarket with Top Rank Suite above, latter sold to Bailey Organisation 14.6.74. Multiyork store and Kudos nightclub in 2001.)

CARLTON, 24 Clarendon Road. (Opened 21.2.21 as Super, conversion of roller skating rink, architect: F. Edward Jones, 1228 seats. Renamed Carlton circa 9.30.) Taken over 14.7.50 by Group Theatres, Rank subsidiary, but not directly operated until 30.4.62. 966 seats, Closed 20.7.63 for major alterations. Re-opened 23.9.63, 778 seats. Closed 12.7.80. (Demolished 1982. Arliss Court office block + Green Room Bar and Café.)

GAUMONT, 65 The Parade, High Street. (Opened 3.5.37 by Gaumont Super Cinemas, architect: J. Owen Bond, 2000 seats: 1398 stalls + 602 balcony. Taken over fully 28.2.44. 1994 seats by 1955.) Renamed ODEON 20.9.64. 1948 seats. Triple from 2.6.74, seating 612 balcony + 120 & 120 rear stalls. Closed 15.10.83. (Demolished 1985. New shops on front, access road and part of supermarket in former auditorium area.)

WEALDSTONE Northwest London
ODEON, corner of High Road and Bruce Road. Opened 15.10.34, architect: A. P. Starkey [assistant: Frederick Adkins], 1222 seats: 880 stalls + 342 balcony. Closed 4.3.61. (Demolished in early 1970s. Marlborough House office block.)

WEDNESBURY West Midlands
GAUMONT, 115 Walsall Street (site of Picture House). (Opened 10.10.38 by Gaumont/APPH, architects: W. E. Trent, W. Sydney Trent & H. L. Cherry, 1594 seats.) Renamed ODEON 9.3.64. 1572 seats. (Taken over by independent 30.1.72, renamed Silver. Closed 19.4.74. Bingo.)

WELL HALL Southeast London
ODEON, Well Hall Road at Rochester Way. Opened 20.5.36, architect: Andrew Mather [assistant: Horace Ward], 1480 seats: 1028 stalls + 452 balcony. Closed by 1963. Twin from 7.1.73, seating 450 balcony + 130 rear stalls. (Taken over 1.11.81 by Panton Films, renamed Coronet. Grade II listed building. Closed 13.1.00. Disused in 2.05.)

WELLING Southeast London
ODEON, Upper Wickham Lane. Opened 22.10.34, architect: George Coles, 1374 seats: 928 stalls + 450 balcony. 1364 seats by 1956. Closed 22.10.60. (Top Rank Club for bingo. Refurbished 1994, entrance heavily altered. Open in 1.05, renamed Mecca.)

WEMBLEY Northwest London
MAJESTIC, 47 High Road. (Opened 11.1.29, architects: Field & Stewart, interior decoration: W. E. Greenwood. Taken over circa 1935 by County.) Taken over 9.39, part of County circuit. 1906 seats in 1939. 1810 seats in 1947: 1322 stalls + 488 balcony. Renamed ODEON 25.3.56. Closed 27.5.61. (Demolished. C&A store, closed.)

GAUMONT, High Road. (Opened 1914 as Wembley Hall Cinema. Extensively reconstructed and enlarged, re-opened 12.35, 1050 seats.) Taken over 23.5.55 by Rank. 981 seats. Renamed Gaumont 25.3.56.) Renamed ODEON 17.12.61. 843 seats by 1964. Closed 18.1.75. (Re-opened as Asian cinema, renamed Liberty. Closed 1981. Demolished. Office block.)

WEST HARTLEPOOL Cleveland
MAJESTIC, 81/9 Raby Road & York Road. (Opened 27.7.36, architects: William & T. R. Milburn, 1588 seats.) Taken over 22.11.43. Renamed ODEON 2.4.45. 1570 seats by 1956. 1547 seats by 1964. Closed 24.10.81. (Grade II listed building from 1992. Caesars Palace & Joe Pools bars from late 1990s. Closed circa 2002. Disused in 2004.)

WEST WICKHAM Southeast London
PLAZA, 88 Station Road. (Opened 4.9.33, architects: J. Stanley Beard & Clare.) Taken over 1.7.37. 886 seats in 1939: 616 stalls + 270 balcony. Renamed ODEON 15.5.38. Renamed GAUMONT 19.3.51. Closed 5.1.57. (Demolished 6.61. Rosemallow House with Finefare supermarket, Boots etc. from 1971.)

WESTBOURNE GROVE
Northwest London
ODEON, 114/120 Westbourne Grove, corner of Chepstow Road. Opened 29.8.55, architect: Leonard Allen (redesigned from uncompleted pre-war scheme by Andrew Mather practice), 1726 seats. Closed 9.12.78 for tripling. Re-opened 21.12.78, seating 698 balcony + 200 & 200 rear stalls. (Taken over 24.9.83 by Panton, renamed Coronet. Closed 6.86. Demolished late 1986. Flats + shops including Rico's Cafe Bar & Westbourne Estate Agents in 2004.)

WESTON-SUPER-MARE Avon
ODEON, The Centre, at Locking Road and Walliscote Road (partly on site of Electric/

Premier cinema). Opened 25.5.35, architect: T. Cecil Howitt, 1807 seats: 1174 stalls + 633 balcony. Triple from 23.12.73, seating 632 balcony + 110 & 133 rear stalls. Grade II listed building from 21.8.86. Fourth cinema opened circa 6.91 in front stalls, seating 268. Open in 2.05, seating 581 + 104 + 120 + 273.

WEYBRIDGE Surrey

ODEON, Queens Road, corner of York Road. Opened 9.4.34, architect: A. P. Starkey, 912 seats: 656 stalls + 256 balcony. Closed 31.12.60. (Roman Catholic Church of St. Martin de Porres.)

COUNTY, Church Street. (Opened 24.6.20 as Kinema. Taken over circa 1927 by County, renamed King George's. Renamed County late 1936.) Taken over 9.39, part of County circuit. 443 seats. Closed 29.9.56. (Public hall: Weybridge Hall.)

WEYMOUTH Dorset

ODEON, Gloucester Street. Opened 2.6.33, architect: Harry Clayton (conversion of bus garage), decorative scheme: Allied Guilds [John Jackson], 541 seats, one floor. 540 seats in 1956. (Taken over 10.12.67 by Classic, renamed Classic. Renamed Cannon. Taken over 14.1.94 by Picturedrome Theatres, renamed Picturedrome. 418 seats. Closed 31.10.99. Children's play zone. Demolished, retaining south-facing wall, by 3.05 for flats.)

GAUMONT, St. Thomas Street. (Opened 1909 as Royal Victoria Jubilee Hall and Picture Palace, former public hall. Taken over by Albany Ward. Taken over by PCT. Reconstructed retaining Jubilee Hall, architect: W. E. Trent, and re-opened 2.8.26 as Regent, 1234 seats. Taken over 2.29, part of PCT. Renamed Gaumont 26.2.51. 1138 seats by 1964.) Renamed ODEON 22.9.68. (Taken over 8.2.76 by independent for cine-bingo, renamed New Invicta. Closed 29.1.77. Bingo only from 7.4.77. Closed. Demolished 1989 except for original Jubilee Hall, dismantled and removed. Car park. Debenham's store and other retail outlets in development of wider area by 2004.)

WHALEBONE LANE Northeast London

MAYFAIR, Whalebone Lane, South Dagenham/Chadwell Heath. (Opened 9.12.33 by D. J. James, architects: Kemp & Tasker, 1764 seats. Taken over 4.36 by Eastern Cinemas

[GCF].) Taken over 28.2.43, part of GCF. Renamed ODEON 31.12.45. 1872 seats by 1956. 1786 seats by 1963. Closed 12.2.72. (Top Rank Club for bingo. Demolished. Supermarket.)

WHALLEY RANGE Manchester

WEST END, Withington Road and Dudley Road. (Opened 8.12.30, architect: John Knight, 2032 seats.) Taken over 13.9.37. Renamed ODEON. 2031 seats in 1939: 1507 stalls + 524 balcony. 1987 seats by 1957. Closed 23.12.61. (Top Rank Club for bingo from 1962. Sold 15.4.67 to Star Cinemas for Star Bingo. Taken over by EMI. Closed circa 1980. Demolished 1986. Flats: Crystal House in 10.01.)

WHITTON Northwest London

RITZ, High Street. (Opened 27.3.37 by London & District, architect: W. J. King, 1774 seats: 1234 stalls + 540 balcony. Taken over 1939 by local company.) Taken over 27.3.44. Renamed ODEON 21.5.45. 1728 seats by 1961. Closed 30.12.61. (Demolished 1972. Offices of Fourways House plus shops including Ladbroke's in 1.05.)

WIMBLEDON Southwest London

ODEON, 19 Worple Road (partly on site of Queen's/Savoy cinema). Opened 20.4.36, architects: Yates, Cook and Darbyshire, 1501 seats: 924 stalls + 577 balcony. Closed 26.11.60. (Demolished. Lidl store with office block.)

REGAL, The Broadway. (Opened 20.11.33 by County, architect: Robert Cromie, interior decoration: Mollo & Egan, 2000 seats.) Taken over 9.39 by Odeon, part of County circuit. Renamed GAUMONT 28.11.49. 1861 seats by 1956. Renamed ODEON 9.9.62. 1524 seats by 1964. Triple from 5.11.72, seating 705 seats balcony + 128 & 107 rear stalls. Mini-cinemas closed 6.1.79 for enlargement. Re-opened 8.4.79: 218 & 190 seats. New screen installed in front of old balcony in 1985. Fourth & fifth cinema opened 29.3.91, seating 175 front stalls + 90 in former café. Closed 1.12.02, seating 702 + 90 + 190 + 175 + 218. (Demolished 2003. Offices of Chartered Institute Of Personnel & Development.)

ODEON, The Crescent, The Broadway. Opened 6.12.02, 12 screens, 2823 seats: 203 + 197 + 217 + 383 + 205 + 173 + 378 + 188 + 261 + 172 + 232 + 214. Open in 2.05.

WINCHESTER Hampshire

REGAL, North Walls. (Opened 1933, architect: Robert Cromie.) Taken over 6.11.35. Renamed ODEON 29.12.35. 1132 seats in 1939: 816 stalls + 316 balcony. 1114 seats by 1957. 1094 seats by 1965. (Taken over 3.1.71 by Star, renamed Cinema. Sold 23.8.71 to Star. Split for bingo in stalls and Studio 1, 2 and 3 cinemas, opened 16.3.72, seating 140 in former storage area + 107 & 112 balcony. Taken over by Cannon, renamed Cannon. Taken over 1988 by independent, renamed Cinema. Closed 26.1.89. Entire building demolished 2-3.89. Flats.)

PICTURE HOUSE, 56 High Street. (Opened circa 4.14. 450 seats. Closed 14.6.26 for enlargement. Re-opened 9.26.) Taken over 6.11.35. Closed 28.3.36. (Superdrug store in 1985.)

ROYAL, Jewry Street. (Opened 1920, former Theatre Royal, live theatre. Full-time cinema by 1926. Taken over 11.34 by County. 514 seats.) Taken over 9.39 part of County circuit. 551 seats in 1939. 548 seats in 1947: 377 stalls + 171 balcony. (Leased 18.4.54 by independent. Sold by Rank 28.5.71 to Star. Closed 29.6.74. Live theatre. Some cinema use from 24.8.89. Closed circa 1996 for restoration. Live theatre.)

WOKING Surrey

ASTORIAL, Duke Street. (Opened 5.12.32 by London & Southern on site of Palace Theatre, architect: F. C. Mitchell.) Taken over circa 7.37, part of London & Southern. 1172 seats in 1939: 880 stalls + 292 balcony. Renamed ODEON 28.5.45. Closed 28.10.61 for modernisation. Re-opened 13.11.61, 852 seats. Closed 19.4.75. (Demolished. Office block.)

PLAZA, Chertsey Road. (Opened 1913 as Central. 780 seats. Enlarged, front rebuilt, architects: Wilfred Travers & Frank C. Spiller, and re-opened circa 9.26, 1046 seats. Taken over circa 1929 by London & Southern, renamed Plaza.) Taken over circa 7.37, part of London & Southern. 914 seats in 1939: 563 stalls + 351 balcony. Renamed GAUMONT 29.5.50. 806 seats by 1956. Closed 13.6.59. (Demolished. Supermarket.)

WOLVERHAMPTON West Midlands
see also Dunstall

ODEON, Skinner Street. Opened 11.9.37, architect: Harry Weedon [assistant: P. J.

Price], 1940 seats: 1272 stalls + 668 balcony. Triple from 7.10.73, seating 622 balcony + 96 & 111 rear stalls. Closed 4.6.83. (Top Rank Club for bingo. Renamed Mecca. Grade II listed building from 10.00. Open in 2.05.)

WOOD GREEN North London

GAUMONT, 9 The Broadway, High Road. (Opened 26.3.34 as Gaumont Palace by Gaumont/APPH, architects: W. E. Trent & Ernest F. Tulley, 2556 seats. Renamed Gaumont circa 1937.) Renamed ODEON 9.9.62. 2164 seats by 1964. Triple from 30.12.73, seating 814 balcony (+ 450 front stalls) + 149 & 150 rear stalls. Closed 7.1.84. (Top Rank Club for bingo from 4.9.84. Grade II listed building from 26.3.90. "Gaumont Palace" name reinstated on frontage in 1993. Closed 10.7.96. Listing raised 10.00 to Grade II★. Oval club/bar in former café opened 2002. Main foyer, balcony lounge and enclosed rear of stalls re-opened 29.5.04 as church, Dominion Centre.)

WOOLWICH Southeast London

ODEON, Parsons Hill, now John Wilson Street. Opened 25.10.37, architect: George Coles, 1828 seats: 1178 stalls + 650 balcony. 1852 seats by 1956. Modernised internally circa 5.64: 1111 seats. Grade II listed building. Closed 17.10.81. (Taken over by Panton Films, re-opened 14.7.83 renamed Coronet. Twin from 6.7.90, seating 678 balcony + 360 rear stalls. Closed 9.6.99. Re-opened 2001 as church by New Wine Church.)

WORCESTER Hereford & Worcester

SILVER, Foregate Street. (Opened 1919.) Taken over circa 1.29 by Oscar Deutsch & associates. Taken into the Odeon circuit 17.7.35. 741 seats. Closed 3.39. (Demolished 3.39 as part of enlarged site for new Odeon.)

ST. JOHN'S, Malvern Road. (Opened circa 9.14, 600 seats.) Taken over 6.41. (Taken over 29.9.52 by independent. Closed 8.53. Bingo. Offices and meeting halls. Nightclub. Disused in 2004.)

ODEON, Foregate Street (partly on site of Silver cinema). Opened 2.1.50, architect: Robert Bullivant of Harry Weedon & Partners [revised completion of pre-war scheme], 1674 seats. 1639 seats by 1964. Triple from 3.3.74, seating 720 balcony + 103 & 103 rear stalls. Front stalls (and stage?) converted circa 1990

to two additional screens seating 205 + 66. Upstairs cinema reduced to fit sixth & seventh screens in rear balcony, opened 16.7.97. Refurbished 1999. Open in 2.05, seating 273 + 175 + 172 + 67 + 128 + 95 + 202.

WORCESTER PARK Southwest London

ODEON, Central Road, corner of Windsor Road. Opened 8.1.34, architects: Yates, Cook and Darbyshire, 894 seats: 543 stalls + 351 balcony. Closed 29.9.56. (Supermarket, initially Macmarket, later International and Somerfield. Closed. Demolished 1998. Public library.)

WORTHING West Sussex

ODEON, Liverpool Road. Opened 24.3.34, architects: Whinney, Son & Austen Hall, 1531 seats: 1076 stalls + 455 balcony. 1369 seats by 1964. Triple from 6.6.74, seating 450 balcony + 120 & 120 rear stalls. Closed 27.9.86. (Grade II listed building from Spring 1987. De-listed. Demolished late 1987. Part of shopping mall and offices.)

PLAZA, Rowlands Road, corner of Eriswell Road. (Opened 14.12.33 by Lou Morris, architect: Harry Weston, interior designers: Mollo & Egan, 2270 seats.) Taken over 1935, may never have been directly operated. (Leased to ABC from 5.2.36. Closed 11.12.68. Bingo club from 1.69. Open as Gala Club in 2005.)

WREXHAM Clwyd

ODEON, Brook Street. Opened 13.3.37, architect: Harry Weedon (assistant: Budge Reid), 1246 seats: 958 stalls + 288 balcony. 1104 seats by 1964. Split-week films and bingo from 1972. Closed 15.5.76. (Top Rank Club for full-time bingo. Renamed Mecca. Closed 5.99. Chicago Rock Café in former front stalls and Liquid nightclub to rear, both opened 6.4.02.)

ODEON, Plas Coch Retail Park, Plas Coch Road. Opened 4.12.97, 7 screens, 1283 seats: 354 + 191 + 148 + 254 + 112 + 112 + 112. Open in 2.05, 1274 seats: 342 + 190 + 145 + 251 + 113 + 115 + 118.

YEOVIL Somerset

ODEON, Court Ash Terrace. Opened 10.5.37, architect: Harry Weedon (assistant: Budge Reid), auditorium decoration: Mollo & Egan, 1580 seats: 978 stalls + 602 balcony.

1576 seats by 1957. (Taken over 1972 by Classic, renamed Classic. Triple from 2.11.72, seating 600 balcony + 400 & 400 stalls. Renamed Cannon. Renamed MGM. Taken over July 1995 by Virgin. Taken over 2 May 1996 by ABC. Renamed ABC Cinemas. 575 + 239 + 247 seats in 2001. Closed 31.3.02. Bed centre from 3.1.04.)

YORK North Yorkshire

ODEON, Blossom Street. Opened 1.2.37, architect: Harry Weedon (assistant: Robert Bullivant), 1484 seats: 934 stalls + 550 balcony. Triple from 20.8.72, seating 820 balcony extended over front stalls + 111 & 111 rear stalls. Grade II listed building from 23.4.81. Open in 2.05, 799 + 111 & 111 seats.

BIBLIOGRAPHY

Books and booklets

All Pals Together – The Story Of Children's Cinema. By Terry Staples. (Edinburgh University Press, 1997.)

The Big Five – Lewisham's Super Cinemas. By Ken George. (London SE6, Ken George, 1997). Re Odeon Deptford, pages 62-74. Also Odeon (ex-Gaumont Palace) Lewisham.

Cathedrals Of The Movies – A History Of British Cinemas And Their Audiences. By David Atwell. (The Architectural Press, London, 1980.)

Cinemas In Britain – One Hundred Years Of Cinema Architecture. By Richard Gray. (Lund Humphries/Cinema Theatre Association, London, 1996.)

Gaumont British Cinemas. By Allen Eyles. (Cinema Theatre Association/BFI Publishing, London, 1996. ISBN 0-85170-519-7 £19.99.) Companion volume to this Odeon history.

The Granada Theatres. By Allen Eyles. (Cinema Theatre Association/BFI Publishing, London, 1998. ISBN 0-85170-680-0 £19.99.) Companion volume to this Odeon history.

J. Arthur Rank And The British Film Industry. (Routledge, 1993).

J. Arthur Rank: The Man Behind the Gong. By Michael Wakelin. (Lion Books, 1996).

Mr. Rank – A Study Of J. Arthur Rank And British Films. By Alan Wood. (Hodder and Stoughton, London, 1952.)

The Picture House in East Anglia. By Stephen Peart. (Terence Dalton, Lavenham, Suffolk, 1980).

United Artists – The Company Built By The Stars. By Tino Balio. (The University Of Wisconsin Press, 1976.)

Articles

"Dinner Suit After Six." By Roger Bennett. About CMA's management training centre in the early 1950s. (*The Veteran*, issue 99, summer 2003, pages 5-6.)

"The Flying Ladies Of Leicester Square." By Richard Gray. (*The Theatres Trust Newsletter* no.50, December 1998. pages 6-9.) (Abridged as "The New-Look Odeon Leicester Square", *CTA Bulletin*, July/August 1998.) The design of the Odeon Leicester Square in the context of its 1998 refurbishment.

"Four Years Of War In Heart Of London's West End." By William H. Thornton, manager of the Odeon Leicester Square. (*Kinematograph Weekly*, 13 January 1944.) Reprinted under title "The Odeon At War" in *Picture House* no. 11, Winter 1987/8, page 29.

"The Odeon at 50." By Allen Eyles (*Picture House* no.11, Winter 1987/8.) This history of the Odeon Leicester Square includes a list of every feature film shown. Plus note on the organ by Tony Moss.

"The Odeon Lewes." By John Fernee. (*Picture House* no.2, Autumn 1982, pages 12-17.)

"An Odeon Miscellany: Frontages of 1949". Sixty-six photographs from a circuit survey with commentary by Allen Eyles. (*Picture House* no.24, Autumn 1999, pages 33-49)

"Odeon Muswell Hill – The Case For Preservation." (*Picture House* no.3, Spring 1983, pages 3-9, back cover.) With twenty-one photographs.

"Odeon Salisbury." Extracts from the Inspector's report that supported the Save The Odeon Group and rejected Rank's case for demolishing the listed cinema. (*Picture House* no.9, Winter 1986, pages 3-7.)

"The Ontario Odeons Of Jay I. English" by Paul S. Moore. (*Marquee*, Vol. 34 no.3, Third Quarter 2002, pages 4-13.) Includes many illustrations and also lists Odeons opened in British Columbia and Montreal.

"Oscar And The Odeons – 'A Romance Of Finance'." By Allen Eyles. (*Focus on Film* no. 22, Autumn 1975.) Listed for the record, this was the original history of the circuit by the author of this book. It is totally superseded by the present volume and its predecessor, *Odeon Cinemas 1: Oscar Deutsch Entertains Our Nation*. Readers' comments in the "For the Record" section of issues 23 and 24 and the "Feedback" section of issue 25 have also been re-used where appropriate.

INDEX TO ILLUSTRATIONS

PREVIOUSLY PUBLISHED

in this series of major British cinema circuit histories by Allen Eyles

ODEON CINEMAS
1: Oscar Deutsch Entertains Our Nation

This book examines the creation of the circuit by the remarkable Oscar Deutsch and his colleagues, the evolution of the now celebrated house style in the hands of key architects, the takeover of other cinemas, the start of the Odeon circuit release and the impact of World War Two. It concludes with Deutsch's early death in 1941. Lavishly illustrated with exterior and interior photographs of virtually every purpose-built Odeon as it looked in the 1930s, the book also draws on company records and reminiscences from Deutsch's closest associates, and includes a chronology of every cinema that was part of Odeon in Deutsch's lifetime.

Published 2002. 256 pages. 385 illustrations.
ISBN: 0 85170 813 7. Price £19.99

THE GRANADA THEATRES

The Granada circuit was notable for its distinctive interior decoration by Theodore Komisarjevsky and the aggressive independent spirit of its founder, Sidney Bernstein. Granadas favoured live shows and organ interludes along with films, and the Tooting "cathedral" was the first Grade I listed cinema. Other listed Granadas were at Woolwich, Clapham Junction, Harrow, Kingston, Shrewsbury and Walthamstow. None survive as cinemas but many are in other uses. This book draws on Sidney Bernstein's business papers for rare illustrations and insights, and includes interviews with many managers, plus a special chapter on Granada organists by the late Tony Moss.

Published 1998. 256 pages. 379 illustrations (12 in full colour).
ISBN: 0 85170 680 0. Price £19.99

GAUMONT BRITISH CINEMAS

This book provides the complete history of the national circuit which was the rival of Odeon and ABC and operated six of the largest ten cinemas in this country, including the Gaumont State Kilburn, Gaumont Hammersmith and the Elephant and Castle Trocadero. All its opulent Gaumont Palaces of the 1930s are described and illustrated, there is a detailed list of the 400 Gaumont cinemas with key information, plus a record of all the films given the Gaumont circuit release from 1932 to its demise in 1959, and an account of the circuit's slow loss of identity as it was absorbed into Odeon. With many examples of press advertising and publicity.

Published 1996. 224 pages. 280 illustrations.
ISBN: 0 85170 519 7. Price £19.99

ABC
The First Name In Entertainment

This history of the circuit created by Scotsman John Maxwell describes its creation, the cinemas which were purpose-built to the design of staff architect W. R. Glen, the acquisition of other cinemas, the booking policy (favouring the films of its production arm Associated British, and Warner Bros. and MGM), the live shows and organ interludes, the response to 3-D and CinemaScope, the subdivision of cinemas, and the first steps into the multiplex era. With a detailed listing of nearly 600 cinemas which were part of the circuit, a list of the main films given the ABC circuit release from 1937 to 1979, rare illustrations of cinemas and company advertising.

Published 1993. 160 pages. 127 illustrations (11 in full colour).
Out of print in spring 2005

ALL PAPERBACK 200 x 214mm

PUBLISHED BY THE CINEMA THEATRE ASSOCIATION · DISTRIBUTED BY BFI PUBLISHING